Many Americas

Reading and Writing
Across the Cultural Divides

Gilbert H. Muller

The City University of New York

LaGuardia

D0099372

Houghton Mifflin Company
BOSTON NEW YORK

Publisher: Patricia Coryell
Editor in Chief: Suzanne Phelps Weir
Senior Development Editor: Meg Botteon
Assistant Editor: Jane Acheson
Editorial Associate: John McHugh
Project Editor: Kerry Doyle
Senior Marketing Manager: Cindy Graff Cohen
Marketing Associate: Wendy Thayer
Manufacturing Coordinator: Chuck Dutton

Cover images:
New Citizens Say the Pledge of Allegiance © S. Meltzer/Photolink
Amish Farmer © Corbis, Royalty-Free.
Man with Flag © The Olympian, Olympia, Washington
Antiques Roadshow © Jeffrey Dunn for WGBH

Credits appear on pages 749–756, which is an extension of the copyright page.

Printed in the U.S.A.

Library of Congress Control Number: 2005926850

ISBN: 0-618-60828-1

1 2 3 4 5 6 7 8 9-MP-09 08 07 06 05

Brief Contents

Contents

1 | Critical Thinking, Reading, and Writing Across the Cultural Divides   1

2 | Red or Blue? Values, Culture, and Community   *39*

3 | Voting and Values: Are We Indivisible?   *93*

The ostensible message is eat no fat; the cynical, maybe unconscious, one is eat.

11 | Safe and Secure: What Are We Afraid Of?   625

12 | From Outside In: America in the World   *698*

Rhetorical Contents

Illustration

Comparison and Contrast

Definition

Classification

Process Analysis

Causal Analysis

Argument and Persuasion

Satire and humor

Preface

Many Americas: Reading and Writing Across the Cultural Divides presents provocative essays, first-person accounts, clever satire, and rigorous argument about the many fractures and fault lines of contemporary American society. Whether imagined or documented, feared or mocked, these divisions were brought to the forefront of America's national conscience by the 2004 presidential election. That said, this is emphatically *not* a book about politics. Nor does it join the long shelf of composition readers exclusively about multiculturalism. What *Many Americas* documents is a series of events and perspectives, deliberately contradictory but often surprisingly coincident, that challenge readers to reconsider and reflect on the relationship between American cultural ideals, American political rhetoric, and American hopes and fears.

Although you and your students will recognize many of the authors whose works appear here, what you might *not* expect is to see some of these writers sharing the same rhetorical table. Each thematic chapter of *Many Americas* includes perspectives, experiences, arguments, and ideologies from across the American political and cultural spectrum. You'll find Barbara Ehrenreich's first-person account of trying to maintain her dignity while holding several service jobs in Florida; you'll also find Steven Malanga, a financial journalist and member of the conservative think tank Manhattan Institute, who questions Ehrenreich's methodology and conclusions. Pundit David Brooks, well known for his brand-name quips about upper-middle-class consumerism, gets taken to task by agricultural journalist Blake Hurst. Gay parents, lesbian couples, Italian-American grandsons, and missionaries who minister to porn addicts all have their say in a conversation about "family values." And, unlike most anthologies about American culture, *Many Americas* includes writers who explore their faith and who reflect on the increasingly conflicted intersection of personal spirituality and civic action.

Many Americas invites students from across the cultural divides to think critically about their own values, experiences, and beliefs, while learning to consider and respect the opinions and experiences of different or opposing points of view. Although you'll find both deeply moving personal accounts and snarky hits of political satire included in this book, each chapter is centered around a core of well-researched, thoughtful, beautifully written, and ethically challenging arguments. Suggested writing assignments after each reading include many opportunities for analysis and argument, with a particular emphasis on finding and exploring unexpected correlations between authors and viewpoints. A rich assortment of images, including two four-color inserts of photographs, invite exploration of the way in which visual media influence political and cultural discussion. These readings and images also invite students to become at once more candid and more careful in the expression of their own political, moral, and cultural viewpoints—especially if their viewpoints are not the most popular in your campus culture. After an election season that would have scandalized George Orwell with its use of grand but empty rhetoric, repeated over and over at high volume (see Mark Danner, "How Bush Really Won," on p. 93), it is critical that we not simply mock what seems ridiculous, but find both the creativity and the coherence to articulate our *own* views with compassion and clarity. We would be remiss, however, if we didn't, at the same time, willingly and with open minds read thoughtful arguments and insightful first-person accounts from across the "cultural divides."

The writers in *Many Americas: Reading and Writing Across the Cultural Divides* range from the Chinese American, Ph.D.-pursuing, hip-hop DJ and cultural critic Hua Hsu ("Vote or Lie," p. 160) to proud new dad and outrageously explicit sex columnist Dan Savage ("Grieving Our Infertility," p. 177). Activist journalist Maggie Jones ("Migrants No More" p. 235) and Upton Sinclair-style muckraker Eric Schlosser ("Adam and Eve" p. 450) combine first-person reporting and a strong commitment to social justice with serious background research and well-constructed argumentation. The very young reporter Tamara Odisho ("A Night in the Emergency Room" p. 438) reports on the stark and sparse comforts of an inner-city hospital, and the late Edward Said ("Terror in America" p. 720) reports for an English newspaper about the haunting atmosphere in New York immediately after the 9/11 attacks. Garry Wills ("The Day the Enlightenment Went Out," p. 113) and Wendy Kaminer ("The Real Danger Behind the Christian Right," p. 137) simmer about the incursion of religion or "values" into presidential politics, while Andrea Elliott ("The Political Conversion of New York's Evangelicals," p. 116) discovers lost opportunities for both Democrats and Republicans in the black, Hispanic, and immigrant evangelical storefront churches of New York City, and Alan Wolfe ("Scholars Infuse Religion with Cultural Light," p. 145) offers a calm, reasoned rebuke to academia for "having missed the boat" on the increasing influence of religion on politics. With headnotes that offer information about individual authors and the publications where these articles first appeared, creative and provocative discussion and writing prompts after each essay, challenging research ideas at the end of each chapter, an appendix on conducting research across the cultural divides, and a dynamic web site, *Many Americas: Reading and Writing Across the Cultural Divides* is an unparalleled core text for contemporary composition courses.

Features

Provocative, Challenging, and Surprising Selections in Chapters That Go Far Beyond "Pro-Con"

Many Americas: Reading and Writing Across the Cultural Divides presents more than 100 readings in twelve interrelated chapters. The first chapter introduces students to the challenges of thinking, reading, and writing about their place in a culturally divided America. Eleven subsequent chapters include readings that range from brief opinion pieces to the complex researched essay, with examples throughout of investigative journalism, first-person narrative, political satire, moral reflection, and arguments for many different audiences and purposes. Finally, most chapters include clusters of essays that offer different perspectives on the same issue (such as obesity in Chapter 8 and airplane security in Chapter 11), challenging students to practice critical thinking across the cultural divides.

Chapter 1. Critical Thinking, Reading, and Writing Across the Cultural Divides. This concise introductory chapter offers guidelines for students as they think, read, and write about key issues in a culturally divided contemporary America. Clear thinking about "cultural divides" involves a knowledge of both what has gone before and what may lie ahead, as well as mastery of the analytical and cognitive skills at the heart of the reading and writing processes. Three analytical essays, four visual texts, and one argument permit students to practice their critical thinking, reading, and writing skills. Conservative education writer and commentator William J. Bennett offers a surprising view on immigration and what it means to be "American." Andrew Sullivan, a British-born conservative gay American, writes passionately about this critical point in gay politics and culture. Thomas Frank, in an excerpt from his much-discussed book *What's the Matter with Kansas?*, offers a compelling and provocative thesis about why some "red states" vote with their morals rather than with their pocketbooks. Political scientist Morris P. Fiorina, whose most recent work challenges the idea of an American "cultural divide," offers statistical research to support his thesis. And Barbara Ehrenreich, an activist-journalist best known for her field reporting on America's struggling working class, challenges the Democratic Party's response to the 2004 elections.

Chapter 2. Red or Blue? Values, Culture, and Community. Writers in this chapter take to the roads of America, traveling and comparing different communities in an effort to move beyond the abstractions of "red" and "blue." Rebecca Skloot, Bill McKibben, and Jedediah Purdy explore the many ways in which smaller communities and neighborhoods allow for diversity, and they challenge the simplistic red/blue split. (The *Many Americas* web site at www.hmco.com/English features an interview with Rebecca Skloot, "Reporting the Cultural Divides," in which she discusses the community's reaction to her article, as well as excerpts from earlier drafts of the introduction to her essay.) David Brooks contributes his usual drive-by sociology and is brought up short by Blake Hurst's patient, compassionate, and thoughtful view of what it means to hold "red state" or "blue state" values. Advertising critic Leslie Savan considers the broader concept of "community," and how the word is being emptied of any real meaning through its overuse by politicians, entertainers, and pundits.

Chapter 3. Voting and Values: Are We Indivisible? Presenting essays from across the ideological spectrum, this chapter explores the particularly American intersection of the pew and the polling place. Mark Danner, a political science professor and *New Yorker* staff writer, contributes an observant combination of analytical essay and ethnographic report on how issues of "values" and faith rumbled through the 2004 electorate, largely undetected by the mainstream media. Journalists Andrea Elliott and Deborah Caldwell discover that, while some politicians successfully exploit the faiths of voters, others in the political sphere let entire communities escape genuine outreach. Garry Wills and Wendy Kaminer deplore the larger trend toward faith-based politicking, while scholars Alan Wolfe and Jon Meacham suggest that both sides need to work toward mutual understanding. *Economist* journalists John Micklethwait and Adrian Wooldridge provide historical context for the 2004 election and its repercussions. Finally, Hua Hsu pointedly observes that, given the opportunity to feel important, American consumers will vote for practically anything.

Chapter 4. The Home Front: Who Is the American Family? Perhaps the most intimate of the stages for cultural division, conflicting ideals about "family values" roil not only in electoral politics but in movie theaters, town halls, and around the dinner table. Unexpected voices and perspectives shape this chapter about what really constitutes the value of a family—from gay activist Dan Savage's compassion for infertile couples in his adoption support group, to Ted Rall's bitter reflections on growing up with a part-time father. Joe Miceli takes the occasion of his grandmother's death—and the responses of inmates and guards alike in the federal prison where he is serving a long sentence for an unnamed crime—to reflect on how his grandmother preserved Miceli's Brooklyn family traditions even as other relatives were lost to crime. Social scientist Elijah Anderson's study of the importance of the grandmother to black urban communities is full of compassion as well as anger, while fellow sociologist Stephanie Coontz offers historical and statistical evidence that there never was an ideal *Leave It to Beaver*-type American family in the first place.

Chapter 5. Getting and Spending: Shopping, Working, and Values. From issues of social class and social justice, to the uniquely American ability to equate shopping with patriotism, this chapter includes essays on topics from the emptying-out of rural communities to the enormous efforts made by the "working poor" to enjoy the most basic American consumer comforts. Naomi Klein and Omri Elisha describe how marketing gurus attempt to package and sell abstractions from "Christian" to "cool," and Ronald Bishop offers insights into why the Americans lining up for *Antiques Roadshow* are so eager to have a "value" placed on their family heirlooms.

Chapter 6. Faith and Reason: What Do We Believe? The writers in this chapter explore the ways in which faith, credulity, and reason manifest themselves in—or subtly underscore—all aspects of American life. This is *not* a chapter about religion. Indeed, if there's anything that writers Natalie Angier, Eric S. Cohen, and Jill Neimark agree on, it's the propensity of Americans to believe in angels, unicorns, life after death, creationism, and UFOs—sometimes simultaneously. *The Economist* chimes in with a brief, witty, and rather spooky take on why, for some Americans, Armageddon and political destiny are one and the same. Rachel Watson's haunting first-person narrative describes a terrible moment when her "faith," such as it was, met its ultimate challenge. Novelist and environmental activist David James Duncan writes passionately about the "divorce between spirituality and science" and the devastating effects of this schism on the environment, and physicist Mano Singham explores the inconsistencies in the ways both science and faith are discussed in culture. Finally, the *Wall Street Journal*'s Carrie Dolan reports on efforts to translate the Bible into Klingon—a mingling of faith, scholarship, and pop culture that could happen only in America.

Chapter 7. America the Beautiful: Wilderness or Resource? Although environmental issues might not be at the forefront of America's political agenda in a time of war, the writers in this chapter report on the schisms between those who believe America's natural resources should be exploited and those who feel that they should be conserved. What's remarkable about this chapter—and, indeed, what's true of every chapter in this book—are the unexpected perspectives and unusual alliances presented. A personal essay on the almost mystical call to hunt comes from the pen of environmentalist and western regional writer Rick Bass. *Sierra*, the magazine of green activist group the Sierra Club, notes the ways in which the National Rifle Association supports the work of environmental preservation groups. Susan Orlean, a *New Yorker* staff writer with a matchless eye for the peculiar in American culture, documents a taxidermy convention. Finally, a cluster of essays about the vast, pristine Alaskan wilderness and the American craving for fossil fuels captures this American dilemma at its most fundamental: Can anyone really "own" the wilderness? And who pays the ultimate price for either its maintained purity or its eventual exploitation?

Chapter 8. The Body Politic: Public Health. Although health care issues have been at the forefront of the electoral agenda for a decade, writers in this chapter explore subtle ways in which American anxieties are inscribed on the American body. Are we too fat? Not pretty enough? Inadequately insured, having safe sex, and keeping our children chaste? Reports from different perspectives on the health of the average American make this chapter especially provocative. Compare a night spent in an inner-city hospital emergency room, on which local residents rely for even the most basic care, with the posh and private facilities enjoyed by their elected representatives to Congress. Eric Schlosser offers a historical narrative on the progression of the condom from whispered embarrassment to fashionable accessory. Journalist Lynn Harris reports on one school district's battles over an "abstinence-only" school health curriculum. Virginia Postrel speculates about the easy availability of cosmetic technology—and the increasing pressures on men and women alike to have "a little work done." A cluster of essays and reports on America's obsession with its collective waistline offers, if you'll pardon the irresistibly bad pun, plenty of food for thought.

Chapter 9. Johnny Can't Read: The Value of an Education. From the repercussions of Columbine to the emphasis on self-esteem, the desperate, unmet needs of urban and poor rural schools to the energy expended on how or whether evolution should be part of the curriculum, there is perhaps no public arena where the "culture wars" are so blatantly played out as in the nation's schoolrooms. Ongoing fault lines in American education explored in this chapter include "zero tolerance" safety policies meant to prevent another school shooting and the overprotection and risk-avoidance of middle-class American parenting; the supposed preponderance of old-school left-wing bias among American college faculty (in the liberal arts, especially, of course); the uneasy accord between popular culture and faith-based commitments on the campuses of religious schools; and the need for American academics to acknowledge both the religious and the pop-culture influences students bring to the classroom.

Chapter 10. What's the Frequency? Values, Media, and Entertainment. Taking cultural critic James Poniewozik's prescient essay about the loss of a "mainstream" American popular culture and the corresponding fracture of American political culture as a starting point, this chapter explores the ways in which popular culture reflects and deflects both mainstream and fringe "values." Douglas Rushkoff and Harry Stein explore the deeper moral agendas of "trash" and reality television; M. Graham Spann and Selena Roberts compare the audiences for NASCAR racing and other sporting events; and a cluster of essays on rap and hip-hop culture offers a surprisingly knowledgeable and compassionate understanding of how this music transcends its racial, economic, and social context.

Chapter 11. Safe and Secure: What Are We Afraid Of? In the years since the terrorist attacks of September 11, 2001, American political and popular culture has revisited a host of intermittent panics and long-term anxieties. This chapter examines the impact of the USA PATRIOT ACT on civil liberties and privacy, the new anxieties and frequent scares about biological warfare and disease, suspicions about Muslim and Islamic Americans, and the free-floating existential paranoia as described in the fictional *Matrix* film series. A cluster of essays examines a specific and exceedingly well-publicized case of airplane hysteria.

Chapter 12. From Outside In: America in the World. *Many Americas* concludes with a tentative look outward. Different political and cultural Americas hold different, and often conflicting, views about the ways in which the idea of "America" is presented and perceived abroad. Naomi Klein and Lynn Hirschberg analyze the ways in which American popular culture tends to represent "America" as a political concept on an international stage. Edward Said offers a sobering internationalist viewpoint from inside America's borders, and literature professor Michael Gorra writes a haunting, elegiac essay on America's fraught cultural relationship with Europe.

A Concise Research Appendix

Appendix: Researching Across the Cultural Divides. This unit provides students with cutting-edge, practical information on the kinds of research skills they are expected to acquire during their college careers. The appendix stresses the new world of information technology that increasingly guides research and offers extensive guidelines on locating and evaluating print and online sources. The appendix includes a concise review of the most recent MLA citation guidelines, with particular attention paid to citing electronic sources.

Rhetorical Table of Contents

This rhetorical table of contents adds flexibility for teachers who prefer to organize their syllabi around such traditional forms as narration and description, comparison and contrast, process and causal analysis, and argumentation and persuasion.

Consistent Editorial Apparatus with a Sequence Approach to Exercises

Many Americas includes, with each reading, a headnote that gives equal emphasis to authority, audience, and purpose. Most headnotes, supplemented by the *Many Americas* companion website, provide links to author websites as well as websites for publications and sponsoring institutions. Following each reading, two sets of detailed, sequential questions provide students with the opportunity to discuss issues in class as well as elaborate on their responses in journals and on course web pages. Further prompts encourage traditional analytical and argumentative essay responses as well as the creation of multimedia web pages, in-class presentations, and blogs. Each chapter concludes with exercises that demand critical thinking within chapters and across the text.

- **Thinking Critically.** The first set of questions after each reading builds on the student's ability to comprehend how the writer's ideas develop through essential rhetorical and stylistic techniques.
- **Writing Critically.** Two or three writing and research activities reflect and expand on the questions in the first section, offering opportunities for students to write personal, analytical, and argumentative responses to the text, as well as create websites that draw on available archival and multimedia resources.
- **Arguing the Cultural Divides.** These writing prompts, at the end of each chapter, ask students to consider issues across a variety of ideologies, perspectives, and experiences. Correspondences among readings in different chapters offer further challenges to student writers.

Exciting Visual Materials

Students today need to read and analyze visual as well as written texts, and understand the relationships between the two. *Many Americas* integrates photographs, cartoons, graphs, and charts into the chapters, and features two four-color inserts that reflect thematic perspectives on the "cultural divides." These illustrations add a visual dimension to aid students' comprehension of the issues raised by written texts, and they offer a further opportunity to practice the critical understanding of visual texts discussed in Chapter 1.

Interactive Website

Houghton Mifflin offers dynamic student and instructor websites for this book. The website for *Many Americas* includes chapter links for additional information and exploration, a list of films and videos on the book's key themes and issues, links to periodicals and journals across the political and ideological spectrum, interactive guidelines for grammar and writing, and exercises in visual thinking. A special feature on Rebecca Skloot's article "Two Americas, Two Restaurants, One Town" reproduces the text of the article along with an interview with Rebecca Skloot, in which she candidly and generously discusses the reaction of her subjects to the published article, and selections of earlier drafts of her article that clearly show how professional writers seek feedback and constantly revise both approach and content. Go to *http://college.hmco.com/English*.

Instructor's Resource Manual

The Instructor's Resource Manual for *Many Americas: Reading and Writing Across the Cultural Divides* provides new as well as experienced teachers with suggested reading sequences, additional assignments, resources (both print and online) for further information and research, and possible responses for all activities in the student textbook. In addition, the IRM (which is available through the instructor's website) discusses classroom management issues unique to the teaching and discussion of challenging, controversial material in the composition classroom.

Acknowledgements

This book would not exist if not for the inspired work of Meg Botteon, senior development editor for English composition at Houghton Mifflin. Meg had the idea for this timely text, convinced management of the urgent need for the book, conceived and with fierce energy generated its materials, and then invited me along for the ride. Wise and witty, efficient beyond belief, Meg was more than a full partner in this project and deserves major credit for bringing *Many Americas* to life.

Suzanne Phelps Weir, the executive editor for English, was enthusiastic about this project from the outset, and with the keen insight and experience I have come to expect of her, succeeded in placing *Many Americas* on a dizzyingly fast track. Suzanne supports authors and demonstrates grace in dealing with them.

It was a pleasure to work hand-in-hand with other members of the Houghton Mifflin team. Publisher Patricia Coryell approved a complex project and endorsed some of its more novel and challenging features. Development Manager Sarah Helyar Smith brought wisdom and excitement to the project, and Editorial Assistants John McHugh and Jane Acheson skillfully juggled its many pieces. Permissions editor Mary Dalton-Hoffman cut to the chase immediately and worked overtime to obtain approval for reprinting the exciting materials in this book. Production services manager Charline Lake and senior project editor Kerry Doyle moved mountains to bring *Many Americas* from concept to reality. Working with Houghton Mifflin, production coordinator Merrill Peterson saw the manuscript swiftly and safely through production despite an incredibly accelerated schedule. Photo researcher Susan Holtz has a quick, keen sense of how visuals both complement and subvert a story, and was great fun to work with. Copyeditor Pat Herbst was superb to the last detail, smoothing out a complex manuscript with that subtlety particular to the best practitioners of her art.

I am indebted to John Wright, friend and agent, who worked magic to make this project feasible.

Several reviewers advised us on the development of *Many Americas*; many thanks to the following:

Lisa Buranen, California State University, Los Angeles
Linda Cullum, Kutztown University of Pennsylvania
Michael Morris, Eastfield College
Annette J. Saddik, New York College of Technology
Dana Vazquez, Rio Hondo College

Gilbert Muller

Critical Thinking, Reading, and Writing Across the Cultural Divides

According to American news and entertainment media, contemporary American public **discourse** involves individuals and ideas colliding across a vast cultural divide. Media talking heads and molders of public taste tell us that there are several Americas—red, blue, purple—rather than one united nation. Of course, cultural ideas in the United States have always clashed. For example, during the nation's early history, Calvinist minister Jonathan Edwards terrified his parishioners with horrifying visions of hell—yet those same Puritans consumed more alcohol and, on average, produced more babies out of wedlock than Americans today. Issues involving faith, family, and community are not new. In fact, arguments over culture have been vital to the American sense of destiny.

Nevertheless, it is hard to ignore what seems to be a growing cultural divide in America today. We see and hear of numerous cultural controversies, some long-standing and others more recent: same-sex marriage, stem-cell research, prayer in public places, global warming, Web censorship, immigration reform, corporate thievery—an expanding universe of divisive issues. These competing ideas about American culture, as you will see, do not necessarily exist in strict opposition. Often arguments over complex cultural issues have several sides.

Although American popular and political culture has always been marked by disagreement and divisiveness, the current controversy over America's "culture wars" may have its origins in the 1992 Republican National Convention, when maverick presidential candidate Patrick Buchanan brought supporters to their feet with a ringing declaration of a battle over values that Buchanan said was unfolding. "There is a religious war going on in this country," he claimed, "a cultural war as critical to the kind of nation we shall be as the Cold War itself, for this is a war for the soul of America." Today, as a writer and television commentator, Buchanan continues to elaborate on the idea that a cultural divide exists in America; and a chorus of loud, competing voices have joined him in declaring that this cultural crisis is persistent and inevitable.

But is a clash of cultures (which mirrors in interesting ways current arguments over the global clash of civilizations) inevitable? Are Americans fated as a people to be divided into right-wingers and left-wingers, lowbrows and highbrows, coffee guzzlers and latte sippers, heartlanders and urbanites, boobs and snobs—to list a few of the many labels concocted to validate a cultural divide? Are we estranged 50–50 (or 51–49) as a nation? Now more than ever, we must think critically about the shifting and complex contours of American culture. And even though it might be uncomfortable to admit, not all ideas about culture are created equal. Ideas about American culture must be tested and held to reasonable account. Especially as college students, you have to be willing to subject your own ethical, religious, and moral values to scrutiny, and refine or even change them under the weight of alternative ideas, if you are to understand and respect opposing ideas and find common ground.

Thinking Critically About the Cultural Divide

Core debates about American culture are as diverse as the nation itself. And the issues underlying these debates—for example, about immigration or marriage—raise complex assumptions about human behavior and the type of society Americans want to create. Consequently you need to think critically (that is, to use forms of academic discourse based on careful analysis and logical argument) in order to understand the ideas, values, and assumptions of the writers whose essays appear in this book. Equally important, you must employ, as Aristotle was the first to suggest, "all the available means of persuasion" to stake out your own claims concerning America's many cultures.

Most writing in college, as well as in civic contexts, tends to be analytical and argumentative rather than personal, descriptive, or creative. When you write critically, you analyze problems and argue positions in a systematic way. To read and write critically, you must possess a repertoire of critical thinking skills—for instance, the ability to compare, classify, define, analyze processes and causes and effects, argue and persuade—that you can bring to bear on a subject. Critical thinking about a subject allows you to make sense of culture and translate that understanding to others. As the late novelist and essayist Susan Sontag (a great critic of, and skeptic about, American culture and politics) once observed, "In my view, the only intelligence is critical, dialectical, skeptical, desimplifying." What Sontag meant is that to be critically intelligent, you cannot simplify or blindly accept ideas, beliefs, and values; instead, you must interrogate them, analyze competing assertions, and work to achieve a synthesis of ideas that might lead to more inclusive or universal truths.

Critical thinking about American culture (or any culture) requires you to

- Understand relationships among cultural ideas and ideological positions
- Test claims or assertions about culture and examine evidence
- Seek consistency in viewpoints
- Avoid logical fallacies—errors based on incorrect reasoning from assumptions or faulty use of evidence
- Consider alternative viewpoints
- Solve problems and predict outcomes

Later in this chapter, more is said about these critical thinking skills. For now, just be aware that you should engage a subject or issue with an inquiring attitude—and without too many of the preconceptions and misconceptions that close you off from new knowledge and reasonable debate.

Consider the following selection by William J. Bennett, a "public intellectual" who variously provokes respect or hostility in many arenas (especially among college teachers). Bennett, a spokesperson for the American conservative movement, served in the administrations of Ronald Reagan and George H. W. Bush, as director of the National Endowment for the Arts, secretary of education, and "drug czar." The author of the best-selling *Book of Virtues: A Treasury of Great Moral Stories* (1993), Bennett in this passage from a somewhat longer essay advocates a policy whereby immigrants would be acculturated into American values and society.

Making Americans: Immigration and Tolerance

WILLIAM J. BENNETT

The immigration issue evokes the strongest passions in the cultural, and not   1
the economic, arena. Indeed, immigration cannot be fully understood outside a larger cultural context. There is an alarming reluctance in our schools and universities to affirm, advance and transmit our common American culture. And while it has profound implications for immigration, I believe contemporary American society's most serious problems are more fundamental than, and different from, immigration. Our problem does not have to do with legal immigration but with assimilation—and assimilation not just for people born in foreign lands but for the people born in this nation.

Cultural anthropologist David Murray has referred to new-born chil-   2
dren as the "ultimate undocumented aliens." By that he means that children are not born with any culture or society; they must be helped to
become citizens every bit as urgently as, say, refugees from Southeast Asia.
If we fail the American-born children, they will be the aliens who overwhelm us. And this is precisely what we are seeing happen today.

Because of American diffidence and neglect, many children are not being   3
acculturated and socialized. The repayment for that neglect is now being played
out on our urban streets, in hospital emergency rooms, in our courts and our
classrooms. In too many places, republican virtues are not being inculcated.

The advocates for ending immigration argue that immigrants pose a   4
cultural threat to America and that our society is no longer capable of as-
similating them. But pinning the blame on immigrants for America's social
decay is a dodge and a distraction. And it happens to be exactly wrong.
One can make a strong argument that many new immigrants have been
corrupted by those same degraded aspects of American culture that trouble so many American parents.

It's time we get on with the real work that needs to be done: Revivify   5
our character-forming institutions and put an end to misguided govern-
ment-sponsored politics that foster social fragmentation, resegregation and
racial tension. The argument for dismantling the current welfare state and
stopping its corrupting dependency has received an extensive public hearing. But there are three other areas that bear on this issue.

- *Bilingualism:* Mastery of English is a key to individual opportunity in
America. Teaching English to those whose native language is not English is a continuation of the struggle to provide for all Americans the
opportunity to participate fully in our political, economic and social
life. Having a common language is an essential condition of a unified
nation. We should not be bashful about proclaiming fluency in this language as a critical education goal, and we should not be timid in reforming our policies so as to secure it.

- *Multiculturalism:* One of the arguments that the anti-immigration advocates rely on is that immigrants promote ethnic separatism and their
foreign culture will contaminate our culture. In fact, radical multiculturalism has its origins in America and finds its intellectual home in
America's elite universities. Francis Fukuyama has pointed out that
"the ideological assault on traditional family values . . . was not the creation of recently arrived Chicano agricultural workers or Haitian boat
people, much less of Chinese or Korean immigrants." Rather, he says,
it "originated right in the heart of America's well-established white, Anglo Saxon community."

- *Counting by Race:* Quotas, race norming, racial gerrymandering and set-asides undercut the rounding American principle of equality under the law. These policies judge individuals on the color of their skin, not on the "content of their character," and they have the effect of prying Americans apart. We need to reestablish a principle that many of us thought we settled three decades ago: the moral case for putting a *de jure* end to racial discrimination and preferences. A good place to advance the cause is in California, where right now a group is undertaking an effort to place a civil rights initiative on the primary election ballot in 1996. Called the California Civil Rights Initiative, it is a constitutional amendment prohibiting the state and its "subdivisions" (colleges, agencies, or local governments) from "us[ing] race, color, ethnicity, national origin, sex or religion as a criterion for either discriminating against, or granting preferential treatment to, any individual group in the operation of the state's system of public employment, public education or public contracting."

"The first step in liquidating a people is to erase its memory," the historian Milan Hubl says in Milan Kundera's *The Book of Laughter and Forgetting*. "Destroy its books, its culture, its history. Then have somebody write new books, manufacture a new culture, invent a new history. Before long the nation will begin to forget what it is and what it was." 6

Our collective cultural task is to remember what we were and what we still are. If we once again get that right, then immigrants will fit in and flourish, as they always have. If we keep getting it wrong, then it won't really matter where the people come from. For whatever their place of origin, they will be citizens without a culture, and they will bear children without a future. 7

Bennett covers much ideological ground here, and you might very well want to **annotate** the text, making notes in the margins, underlining and commenting on main points so that the architecture of ideas becomes clearer as you read. Bennett's vision of the values American culture should reflect challenges the ideas of both conservatives and liberals, and he asks us to look at salient issues raised by immigration—for example, welfare, bilingualism, multiculturalism, and affirmative action quotas— with an open mind. (Demonstrating his own openness to ideas, Bennett angered conservatives and surprised liberals when he opposed California's Proposition 187, which would have denied social services to undocumented aliens.)

Admittedly, Bennett's vision of American culture is a traditional one, rooted in conservative ideas about democracy. Especially provocative is his conclusion that new immigrants might become "citizens without a culture" who "bear children without a future." Bennett's essay provides a model for debates on cultural issues because it addresses these issues in a reasonable way (although many would argue against his viewpoints). As an example of critical thinking about American culture, the piece is a welcome relief from the diatribes that often attempt to pass for debate in the public forum, in particular in the media and among opportunistic politicians. To this end, the selection serves a useful function in demonstrating that you can debate issues about American culture without becoming embroiled in strident opinion or excess emotion.

Of course, it is often impossible to strip emotion from debates over culture. But it is important when you are thinking critically about a cultural issue to dispense with prejudiced or stereotyped views. Essential to critical thinking is the ability to consider the author's argument with an impartial mind, neither ignoring your emotional responses nor allowing them to overwhelm your ability to listen and consider. As you read the next essay, by Andrew Sullivan, try to monitor your response so your biases do not enter into your evaluation of the author's ideas.

A Call to Arms

ANDREW SULLIVAN

There's a strange lull in gay America right now. Strange because it presages   1
one of the most wrenching political struggles gay Americans have ever fought. While we revel in greater cultural acceptance, in a realignment of attitudes among the younger generations, as we see openly gay men and women reach unprecedented levels of visibility and respect, 51 words should give us pause. These words could change the direction of gay rights in this country forever: "Marriage in the United States shall consist only of the union of a man and a woman. Neither this Constitution or the constitution of any state, nor state or federal law, shall be construed to require that marital status or the legal incidents thereof be conferred upon unmarried couples or groups."

These are the words of the Federal Marriage Amendment. Right now it   2
is the main focus of activists in the religious right, who are making it their first priority in the coming months. Backed by social conservatives in the Republican Party, they hope to amend the U.S. Constitution to ban gay equality in marriage forever.

But read more closely. The amendment wouldn't simply ban equality in   3
civil marriage, a right that is now guaranteed to murderers, child abusers, deadbeat dads, multiple divorcees, and foreigners. It would also make it unconstitutional for a state or federal law to give any benefits whatsoever to

gay couples. Where do I glean that? From the words "or the legal incidents thereof." Even the weakest forms of domestic partnerships contain benefits, i.e., "legal incidents," that are also part of marriage. This amendment would make every such benefit subject to abolition through the courts.

You think civil unions are a good idea? If this amendment passes, there 4 will be no civil unions. Vermont and California will have to repeal their laws. You think such an amendment will be overcome by changing attitudes in time? An amendment is not a law that can be easily repealed. It becomes part of the Constitution itself, the very meaning of America. Yes, it's very hard to pass one. You need two-thirds majorities in the House and Senate as well as three quarters of the state legislatures. But crazy amendments have passed in the past—remember Prohibition? It's no exaggeration to say this is the biggest assault on gay rights in U.S. history. It would write discrimination into the Constitution; it would effectively state that gay people are not fully citizens, that our loves are anathema to the meaning of America, that we do not fully belong here and can live here only as second-class citizens.

So what are they waiting for? They are waiting for a state court—probably 5 Massachusetts's—to come to the inexorable conclusion that excluding gay couples from civil marriage is the denial of a basic civil right. When you look at the Constitution, it is indeed hard to come to any other conclusion. The freedom to marry, according to the U.S. Supreme Court, "has long been recognized as one of the vital personal rights essential to the orderly pursuit of happiness by free men." Once you recognize that gay people are free people, that their loves are as good as straight loves, and that we do not have a meaningful right to marry when that right is restricted to members of the opposite sex, then the importance of this is hard to miss. Everything in the Constitution points toward our equality. Everything in the meaning of America demands our equal treatment under the law. That's why the hard right has to change the Constitution itself to keep us enslaved forever.

We must resist—and you have to take a stand. Talk to your coworkers 6 and straight friends about your relationships; explain why this matters; write your congressman or senator; give money to the Freedom to Marry coalition. This is something that can and should transcend any of our internal debates and divisions—right, left, Democrat, Republican, gay, lesbian, white, black, transgendered, bisexual. Future gay generations will look back and see this moment as the most critical one yet for our dignity, equality, and safety. And they will ask: What did you do in this climactic cultural war? Let us be able to answer with pride: We won it.

Sullivan, who graduated from Harvard and has written for magazines on both the left and the right of the political spectrum, is openly gay.

Consequently it is understandable that he opposes a Federal Marriage Amendment. You probably approach his topic as well as his sexual orientation with your own opinions and emotional reactions. To be sure, same-sex marriage is such a politicized issue that you may already have developed attitudes toward it. But Sullivan, who usually promotes conservative causes, asks readers to think objectively about gay marriage—and to consider the gay rights movement as akin to the civil rights movement. He advocates a position that might antagonize conservative allies and prompt liberal detractors to accuse him of hypocrisy. However, Sullivan essentially is thinking outside the box of ideological labels and across the *cultural divides* in an effort to convince us about his viewpoint and persuade us to act.

Both Bennett and Sullivan demonstrate a capacity to think critically about the state of American culture. Their writing reflects personal principles and standards for reasoning. Both present the "truth" of their positions or claims, offering reasons and evidence to support their viewpoints. Each writer introduces us to the fluid reality of American cultural values as the nation enters the twenty-first century—and each writer hopes to prompt his audience to move beyond ideological labels and hardened positions in order to pursue knowledge about core culture values with an open mind.

Thinking Critically

1. Using Google or another search engine, conduct a search using the keywords "American culture" or "American values." After visiting at least three websites, write an essay that defines *culture*. Provide your readers with a basic understanding of the reasons why this word causes so much misunderstanding and disagreement among people today.

2. Keep a log for a week of all the debates about contemporary American culture that you encounter in the media—radio, television, newspapers, blogs, and elsewhere. With other class members, construct a complete list of all these conflicts, controversies, and debates, and discuss their cumulative impact on your understanding of the state of culture today.

3. Working with three or four class members, go online and find out more about William Bennett and Andrew Sullivan. Retrieve this information, and then use it as the basis for a definition of what it means to be a conservative or a liberal on cultural issues. Share your findings during class discussion.

Analyzing Texts

Writers who consider American culture usually present analyses of or arguments about the nation's values, beliefs, and ideological foundations. They focus on issues of family, community, and faith. Such texts reflect a core principle: the right of people in a democratic nation to disagree with each other and even dissent from established ideas and laws. Americans are protected by the Constitution—its Bill of Rights and other amendments—in the expression of ideas and opinions that others find offensive or might reject. As citizens in a democracy, Americans can disagree both privately and publicly with politicians and officials, newspapers and neighbors, radio shock jocks and television pundits. Disagreement is at the heart of American democracy.

Studying texts about American culture, especially those designed to elicit agreement with an author's claim, can help you become a better reader and writer by requiring you to refine your critical thinking skills. Such texts invite you to think critically about such matters as the authority of the author, the writer's purpose or intent, the composition of the audience, the ethical and emotional subtexts underlying the writer's opinions, and the clarity of the writer's claims and support. Texts rooted in cultural disagreements encourage you to accept the writers' viewpoints. Therefore, you must take a stand—agree or disagree or perhaps offer alternative arguments or divergent explanations—in an effort to produce a richer explanation or greater appreciation of the common values and beliefs underlying American civilization.

Critical reading requires you both to understand and to evaluate a text and relationships among competing texts. There is no set formula for this process, but the following guidelines will help you to develop a critical perspective as you study the selections in this book:

- **Who is the author?** Before you read a text critically, it is helpful to know something about the author. (Often basic information about the author's identity appears in a book's front matter, in headnotes preceding essays in an anthology, on a book's dust jacket, or on the contributors' page of a magazine. A simple Web search on the author's name is likely to turn up reviews, interviews, and other useful background information.) Here are some questions to consider: What is the writer's age, gender, and racial and ethnic background, and how might these factors influence his or her thinking? What is the writer's level of education, and what specialized knowledge does he or she possess? What is the writer's political, religious, or ideological orientation? What level of authority or reputation for accuracy and honesty does the writer possess? A Web search at a specialized site such as GaleNet will provide you with biographical and publication information about many authors.

- **What is the author's purpose and main point?** In general terms, a writer's purpose is to inform, persuade, or entertain. Regardless of purpose, a writer sets forth a main idea called a *thesis* or, if there is an argument, a *claim*. Carefully designed around a limited topic, the thesis controls all other elements in a paper. If a writer's basic purpose is to inform, he or she might explain the process of stem-cell cloning. But if the writer's primary purpose is to persuade readers to accept his or her viewpoint, that stem-cell research should be supported by the federal government, the writer's main idea becomes a claim, or proposition that can be debated. Sometimes, a writer's primary purpose is to entertain (as when a writer speculates about comic consequences of stem-cell research), although if the writer employs satire, irony, or sarcasm his or her final purpose may be to persuade. Many of the essays in this book reveal overlapping purposes. For instance, in "Making Americans," William Bennett both *informs* you about the consequences of immigration and *argues* a point of view on the subject.

- **What is the writer's tone?** Tone is the writer's attitude toward her or his subject, topic, or material. It is the "voice" that a writer gives to an essay. A writer's tone may be objective, subjective, ironic, satiric, critical, argumentative, or nostalgic, or it may be a reflection of other emotional and intellectual attitudes. Sometimes a uniform tone permeates an essay; at other times, the writer varies or mixes tones to create a desired effect.

- **Who is the writer's audience?** Quite often writers tailor their texts or messages to a specific audience—for instance, to readers of *The Nation* (a weekly magazine on the left of the political spectrum) or to readers of the *National Review* (a conservative weekly). Writers for either of these magazines expect their intended audience to be well educated and sympathetic to certain points of view. However, a writer composing an article for a broader audience that might not understand complex cultural issues or share certain *assumptions* (what students of rhetoric refer to as warrants) may craft the substance of the essay in more general or less opinionated ways. Writers also can direct their texts to both *primary* and *secondary* audiences. Someone writing an op-ed piece for the *New York Times* on the battle over teaching evolution and creationism in the nation's public schools has *Times* readers primarily in mind but knows also that the media, local and national politicians, theologians and scientists, and Web surfers and bloggers might constitute secondary audiences. Finally, a writer has to think about the various cultural attitudes and possible responses of an intended audience—especially whether an audience is likely to be receptive to a claim, hostile to it, or wavering in its response.

- **What is your response to the author's ideas, conclusions, and recommendations?** Perhaps the content of the essay and the author's perspective on the subject are consistent with your own ideas and opinions. The subject matter might parallel your own experience, or you might identify with the issue or problem the writer presents. As you read critically, try to monitor and record your personal reactions to the text, while considering other ways—psychological, cultural, historical, feminist, political—to respond to a text. Remember that there is nothing wrong with a personal response to an essay, even as you search for answers to any objective questions you might have about the substance or logic of the piece.

- **How does the writer substantiate or prove his or her case?** Most writers attempt to persuade you to see things in a certain way. They argue a point, applying formal strategies for convincing an audience. It is not enough to merely assert an idea—for example, that evolution is not a scientifically proven fact. What is required is an effort, through the application of varieties of evidence—details, facts, reasons, and logic—to substantiate any given idea. If writers do not substantiate their claims, and if the support is not accurate, credible, and relevant, these claims (and the entire essay) in all likelihood are weak or invalid.

Read this analysis of America's cultural divide from the introduction to Thomas Frank's book, *What's the Matter with Kansas?* (2004); then turn to the "Thinking Critically" items that follow.

What's the Matter with America?

THOMAS FRANK

The poorest county in America isn't in Appalachia or the Deep South. It   1
is on the Great Plains, a region of struggling ranchers and dying farm towns, and in the election of 2000 the Republican candidate for president, George W. Bush, carried it by a majority of greater than 80 percent.

This puzzled me when I first read about it, as it puzzles many of the peo-   2
ple I know. For us it is the Democrats that are the party of workers, of the poor, of the weak and the victimized. Understanding this, we think, is basic; it is part of the ABCs of adulthood. When I told a friend of mine about that impoverished High Plains country so enamored of President Bush, she was perplexed. "How can anyone who has ever worked for someone else vote Republican?" she asked. How could so many people get it so wrong?

Her question is apt; it is, in many ways, the preeminent question of our   3
times. People getting their fundamental interests wrong is what American political life is all about. This species of derangement is the bedrock of our civic order; it is the foundation on which all else rests. This derangement has put the Republicans in charge of all three branches of government; it has elected presidents, senators, governors; it shifts the Democrats to the right and then impeaches Bill Clinton just for fun.

If you earn over $300,000 a year, you owe a great deal to this derange-   4
ment. Raise a glass sometime to those indigent High Plains Republicans as you contemplate your good fortune: It is thanks to their self-denying votes that you are no longer burdened by the estate tax, or troublesome labor unions, or meddling banking regulators. Thanks to the allegiance of these

sons and daughters of toil, you have escaped what your affluent forebears used to call "confiscatory" income tax levels. It is thanks to them that you were able to buy two Rolexes this year instead of one and get that Segway with the special gold trim.

Or perhaps you are one of those many, many millions of average-income 5 Americans who see nothing deranged about this at all. For you this picture of hard-times conservatism makes perfect sense, and it is the opposite phenomenon—working-class people who insist on voting for liberals— that strikes you as an indecipherable puzzlement. Maybe you see it the way the bumper sticker I spotted at a Kansas City gun show puts it: "A working person that *supports* Democrats is like a chicken that *supports* Col. Sanders!"

Maybe you were one of those who stood up for America way back in 6 1968, sick of hearing those rich kids in beads bad-mouth the country every night on TV. Maybe you knew exactly what Richard Nixon meant when he talked about the "silent majority," the people whose hard work was rewarded with constant insults from the network news, the Hollywood movies, and the know-it-all college professors, none of them interested in anything you had to say. Or maybe it was the liberal judges who got you mad as hell, casually rewriting the laws of your state according to some daft idea they had picked up at a cocktail party, or ordering your town to shoulder some billion-dollar desegregation scheme that they had dreamed up on their own, or turning criminals loose to prey on the hardworking and the industrious. Or perhaps it was the drive for gun control, which was obviously directed toward the same end of disarming and ultimately disempowering people like you.

Maybe Ronald Reagan pulled you into the conservative swirl, the way 7 he talked about that sunshiny, Glenn Miller America you remembered from the time before the world went to hell. Or maybe Rush Limbaugh won you over, with his daily beatdown of the arrogant and the self-important. Or maybe you were pushed; maybe Bill Clinton made a Republican out of you with his patently phony "compassion" and his obvious contempt for average, non-Ivy Americans, the ones he had the nerve to order into combat even though he himself took the coward's way out when his turn came.

Nearly everyone has a conversion story they can tell: how their dad had 8 been a union steelworker and a stalwart Democrat, but how all their brothers and sisters started voting Republican; or how their cousin gave up on Methodism and started going to the Pentecostal church out on the edge of town; or how they themselves just got so sick of being scolded for eating meat or for wearing clothes emblazoned with the State U's Indian mascot that one day Fox News started to seem "fair and balanced" to them after all.

Take the family of a friend of mine, a guy who came from one of those   9
midwestern cities that sociologists used to descend upon periodically because it was supposed to be so "typical." It was a middling-sized industrial
burg where they made machine tools, auto parts, and so forth. When Reagan took office in 1981, more than half the working population of the city
was employed in factories, and most of them were union members. The
ethos of the place was working-class, and the city was prosperous, tidy, and
liberal, in the old sense of the world.

My friend's dad was a teacher in the local public schools, a loyal mem-   10
ber of the teachers' union, and a more dedicated liberal than most: not only
had he been a staunch supporter of George McGovern, but in the 1980 Democratic primary he had voted for Barbara Jordan, the black U.S. Representative from Texas. My friend, meanwhile, was in those days a high school
Republican, a Reagan youth who fancied Adam Smith ties and savored the
writing of William F. Buckley. The dad would listen to the son spout off
about Milton Friedman and the godliness of free-market capitalism, and he
would just shake his head. *Someday, kid, you'll know what a jerk you are.*

It was the dad, though, who was eventually converted. These days he   11
votes for the farthest-right Republicans he can find on the ballot. The particular issue that brought him over was abortion. A devout Catholic, my
friend's dad was persuaded in the early nineties that the sanctity of the fetus
outweighed all of his other concerns, and from there he gradually accepted
the whole pantheon of conservative devil-figures: the elite media and the
American Civil Liberties Union, contemptuous of our values; the la-di-da
feminists; the idea that Christians are vilely persecuted—right here in the
U.S. of A. It doesn't even bother him, really, when his new hero Bill O'Reilly
blasts the teachers' union as a group that "does not love America."

His superaverage midwestern town, meanwhile, has followed the same   12
trajectory. Even as Republican economic policy laid waste to the city's industries, unions, and neighborhoods, the townsfolk responded by lashing
out on cultural issues, eventually winding up with a hard-right Republican
congressman, a born-again Christian who campaigned largely on an anti-
abortion platform. Today the city looks like a miniature Detroit. And with
every bit of economic bad news it seems to get more bitter, more cynical,
and more conservative still.

Thinking Critically

1. With another member of your class, conduct an electronic search for biographical information on Thomas Frank. Explain how this information informs your understanding of the text.

2. Highlight (by underlining, using a felt-tip marker, or making marginal notations) aspects of the text that reveal Frank's intended audience or audiences.

3. Is Frank's purpose to inform, persuade, or entertain? Point to specific passages to support your response.

4. Summarize Frank's ideas in approximately 50 words. State the central idea of the passage in your first sentence, and write three or four additional sentences that capture the basic stages in Frank's thought process. Revise your summary to make certain that you have captured the most important concepts in Frank's text.

5. With four or five class members, discuss the themes and key ideas that Frank presents in this excerpt. Are his ideas consistent with your own experience or that of other group members? Where do you agree or disagree with Frank's perspective on American culture? Select one member of your group to summarize your discussion to the whole class.

Analyzing Visual Texts

In your reading for most of your college courses, you will find visual texts—reproductions of art, photographs, cartoons, advertisements, tables and graphs, and so forth—designed to support and inform a written text. Such visual representations highlight or provide examples or summaries of specific content, offering graphic evidence that is as compelling or convincing as the written word. In this age of information technology, we have to think critically about the cultural images that surround us.

Tables, charts, and graphs often appear in articles and books about American culture. When you encounter these visual materials, examine them critically to determine their relationship to the verbal text. For example, consider the table in the next excerpt and the written text surrounding it.

Culture War? The Myth of a Polarized America

MORRIS P. FIORINA

If the gender gap is not caused by abortion, then from what issues does it   1
arise? Research finds that men's and women's views differ on two clusters of issues, a sampling of which appears in Table 1.[1] The first consists of

1. Robert Shapiro and Harpreet Mahajan, "Gender Differences in Policy Preferences: A Summary of Trends from the 1960s to the 1980s," *Public Opinion Quarterly* 50 (1986): 42–61.

Table 1   Women's and Men's Attitudes Differ

	Women	*Men*
Role of Government		
Consider self conservative	29%	43%
Government should provide fewer services	30	45
Poverty and homelessness are among the country's most important problems	63	44
Favor affirmative action programs for blacks and other minority groups	69	58
Force/Violence		
American bombers should attack all military targets in Iraq, including those in heavily populated areas	37	61
Handguns should be illegal except for use by police and other authorized persons	48	28
Favor death penalty	76	82
Approve of caning the teenager in Singapore who committed acts of vandalism	39	61
Approve of the way the Justice Department took Elian Gonzalez from his Miami relatives	35	52

Source: The Public Perspective, August/September 1996: 10–27; *The Public Perspective,* July/August 1994: 96. Gallup Tuesday Briefing, May 2, 2000.

issues of violence, the use of force, and peace and war. For example, women are less likely to support the death penalty, more likely to favor gun control, and less likely to favor going to war. A particularly striking example of this sort of gender gap emerged in 1994, when an American teenager living in Singapore who had vandalized property, was sentenced to a traditional Singaporean punishment of caning. A majority of the mothers and sisters of America considered the sentence barbaric, while a majority of the fathers and brothers viewed it as appropriate—the item produced a twenty-two-point gender gap.

The second cluster of issues on which men and women differ has to do with 2
protecting the vulnerable—the aged, the sick, the poor, and other "at risk" categories. Women are more compassionate, registering higher levels of support for government programs to help the disadvantaged and greater willingness to support government spending for the disadvantaged.[2] Thus, women favor a

2. See, for example, Ann Beutal and Margaret Marini, "Gender and Values," *American Sociological Review* 60 (1995): 436–48.

more activist government than men, and are slightly more likely to label themselves liberals and less likely to label themselves conservatives.

The table provides data on the "gender gap" over issues in American culture and supports the author's contention that men's and women's differing attitudes are politically significant. Fiorina, a research scholar at the Hoover Institution at Stanford University, does not think that America is polarized over such issues as abortion, but he does acknowledge that men and women, for several reasons, have different attitudes toward such issues as the role of government in protecting the less fortunate members of society or the use of force in society. His table—one of many in his book—reveals some of these polarities.

When you study a table, chart, or graph, ask yourself the following questions:

- What is the context for the graphic? How does the visual support, inform, or reinforce the verbal text surrounding it?
- What is the purpose of the visual text? What thesis or point of view does it advance? What information or data contribute to this central idea?
- How current is the data? Is the data accurate and verifiable? Does the information support the larger thesis of the article, chapter, or book?
- Is the design or structure of the visual clear, concise, and comprehensible?

Remember to subject a visual text to the same degree of critical inquiry that you bring to a verbal text. Take nothing for granted: carefully sift through the information in a table, graph, or chart, using a critical eye to understand and evaluate the writer's sources of information as well as the writer's purpose or aim.

Visual texts such as paintings, photographs, and advertisements also make compelling statements about American cultural experience. Whether standing alone or embedded in verbal texts, they present the same critical challenges as tables, charts, and graphs. Often they have a persuasive purpose and complement a written argument. Images also can enhance narrative and descriptive essays as well as various forms of expository writing—for example, essays offering analysis, definition, comparison and contrast, and classification.

The photograph on page 17 of a soldier voting appeared in a 2004 issue of *Newsweek*. It complemented an essay in which writer and media commentator Fareed Zakaria evaluated the agenda of the Bush administration's second term in office. The photograph reinforced the writer's assertion that the Iraq war both dominated the 2004 presidential campaign and would determine the contours of George W. Bush's second term. It was centered on the page of Zakaria's essay, pulling all of the text into its visual field.

When you study and analyze a painting, photograph, or advertisement, ask yourself these questions:

- What is the image's primary purpose, and does the image achieve this aim?
- How do color, light, and shadow operate to produce a unified effect?
- What details—the arrangement of people and objects—stand out, and what is the relationship among them?
- What foreground and background elements are highlighted within the frame?
- What ideas, inferences, and values does the image convey?

Throughout this book you will find visuals intended to complement written texts. Exercises will invite you to look critically at a visual—a photograph, cartoon, or advertisement—and interpret its purpose, design, and meaning. These visuals, in context, bring together diverse materials on American culture and illuminate some core cultural issues.

Thinking Critically

Analyze the elements, composition, and symbolism of the Statue of Liberty photograph on page 18. What is its message, and how persuasive is the statement the photograph makes? How do you think people from other cultures would respond to this image?

Analyzing Arguments

A majority of the writers in this book develop arguments about various issues in American culture. At the outset, think of the arguments that they advance as written or visual texts presenting a debatable point of view. Writers use argumentation to convince you about their viewpoints; they typically engage also in persuasion, trying to move you to adopt a desired course or position. Writers skilled in argumentation and persuasion make carefully organized appeals on potentially explosive issues, such as same-sex marriage or the treatment of evolution in high school textbooks, that are designed to elicit agreement with their viewpoints and produce desired responses.

The contemporary American "establishment" is in a state of agitation over the nation's cultural beliefs and values. Writers, media pundits, religious authorities, politicians, pollsters, and public relations gurus assume you are a red-stater or a blue-stater, a gun aficionado or a gun hater, a woman's rights activist or a right-to-life supporter, a believer or a pagan. In reality, you might prefer to negotiate such cultural divides, picking and choosing carefully reasoned (and reasonable) viewpoints as you move from issue to issue. Or you might reject these oppositional categories entirely, preferring to seek negotiation, consensus, or middle ground. Admittedly it is challenging to stake out consistent positions and beliefs on so many potentially explosive cultural issues.

Analyzing and evaluating argumentative texts about America requires you to acknowledge the diversity or plurality of national experience. When reading the essays in this book, you should accept as a fundamental truth the idea that writers offer divergent viewpoints and perspectives even as they advance a core belief: the vitalness of free speech, open inquiry, and debate to the health of civil society. Writers treat you as a member of an audience who is prepared to explore a given topic or issue, think or act in a given way, make decisions, and possibly seek consensus. To read an argumentative text and arrive at a personal position or decision about consequential cultural issues—for example, the role of religion in public schools and public life—is a powerful act of both self-discovery and citizenship.

Just as you need tools to build a house, you need critical strategies to understand and evaluate a writer's viewpoint. As a college student, you have to be willing to reinterpret and reargue core American issues, seeking the deep roots of the national experience that will survive current controversies. By understanding the basic strategies of argumentation and persuasion, you can decode a writer's claim or message and, in response, communicate your own viewpoints.

When you read an argumentative or persuasive text, use these core questions, along with those appearing in the earlier "Analyzing Texts" section, as tools for understanding:

- **What is the writer's claim?** A claim is a statement that needs to be justified or proved. It is a statement of belief or truth expressing a viewpoint that others find to be debatable or controversial. A claim is like a thesis or main idea, but it is a form of thesis that can be argued. (Some writing experts say that "Everything is an argument," that all texts advance a claim, position, belief, or conclusion. Do you agree?) Claims are also called major propositions.

- **What are the grounds offered to support the claim?** *Grounds* are minor propositions or key reasons, along with evidence and support, used to bolster or "prove" the claim.

- **What types of evidence does the writer provide?** Evidence can consist of facts, examples, data, statistics, results of scientific and laboratory experiments, field research, case studies, accepted opinions, interviews, expert testimony, and even representative personal experience. Evidence should be valid—in other words, precise and accurate—and preferably current and authoritative.

- **What are the warrants assumed by the writer?** A warrant is the connection, often assumed or unstated, between the claim and the supporting reasons. It is the underlying or transcendent belief, rule, or universal principle (God, salvation, martyrdom, patriotism) governing certain claims or statements. It is the assumption that makes a claim appear to be valid or acceptable.

- **What is the nature of the writer's appeals?** Aristotle's *Rhetoric* suggests that the best arguments combine appeals to reason, to beliefs and values, and to emotion—to *logos, ethos,* and *pathos,* respectively. These appeals work together to change opinions and prompt action. Aristotle identifies two basic types of appeals to reason—inductive and deductive. A writer who uses induction to develop an argument argues from evidence. A writer who uses deduction argues from general principles. Ethical appeals, according to Aristotle, reveal "the personal character of the speaker [or writer]," conveying the values and beliefs that the speaker (or writer) and the audience have in common. Emotional appeals establish an empathetic bond between the writer and his or her audience while reinforcing the logical and ethical dimensions of the argument.

- **Does the writer acknowledge and deal effectively with opposing viewpoints?** No argument is completely effective unless the writer acknowledges that there is more than one way to look at a controversy and attempts to weaken, rebut, or invalidate opposing claims or viewpoints. This strategy of dealing with the opposition is called refutation. A carefully constructed argument blends refutation into the fabric of the essay.

An argumentative essay creates a "court of standards" in which the rules of reasoning and evidence just outlined apply. Read this argumentative essay by Barbara Ehrenreich, and reflect on the questions that follow it. (A second essay by Ehrenreich and information about her appears on pages 275–84.)

The Faith Factor

BARBARA EHRENREICH

Of all the loathsome spectacles we've endured since November 2—the vampire-like gloating of CNN commentator Robert Novak, Bush embracing his "mandate"—none are more repulsive than that of Democrats conceding the "moral values" edge to the party that brought us Abu Ghraib. The cries for Democrats to overcome their "out-of-touch-ness" and embrace the predominant faith all dodge the full horror of the situation: A criminal has been enabled to continue his bloody work with the help, in no small part, of self-identified Christians.

With their craven, breast-beating response to Bush's electoral triumph, leading Democrats only demonstrate how out of touch they really are with the religious transformation of America. Where secular-type liberals and centrists go wrong is in categorizing religion as a form of "irrationality," akin to spirituality, sports mania and emotion generally. They fail to see that the current "Christianization" of red-state America bears no resemblance to the Great Revival of the early nineteenth century, an ecstatic movement that filled the fields of Virginia with the rolling, shrieking and jerking bodies of the revived. In contrast, today's right-leaning Christian churches represent a coldly Calvinist tradition in which even speaking in tongues, if it occurs at all, has been increasingly routinized and restricted to the pastor. What these churches have to offer, in addition to intangibles like eternal salvation, is concrete, material assistance. They have become an alternative welfare state, whose support rests not only on "faith" but also on the loyalty of the grateful recipients.

Drive out from Washington to the Virginia suburbs, for example, and you'll find the McLean Bible Church, spiritual home of Senator James Inhofe and other prominent right-wingers, still hopping on a weekday night. Dozens of families and teenagers enjoy a low-priced dinner in the cafeteria; a hundred unemployed people meet for prayer and job tips at the "Career Ministry"; divorced and abused women gather in support groups. Among its many services, MBC distributes free clothing to 10,000 poor people a year, helped start an inner-city ministry for at-risk youth in DC and operates a "special needs" ministry for disabled children.

MBC is a mega-church with a parking garage that could serve a medium-sized airport, but many smaller evangelical churches offer a similar array of services—childcare, after-school programs, ESL lessons, help in finding a job, not to mention the occasional cash handout. A woman I met in Minneapolis gave me her strategy for surviving bouts of destitution: "First, you find a church." A trailer-park dweller in Grand Rapids told me that he often turned to his church for help with the rent. Got a drinking problem, a vicious spouse, a wayward child, a bill due? Find a church. The closest analogy to American's bureaucratized evangelical movement is Hamas, which draws in poverty-stricken Palestinians through its own miniature welfare state.

Nor is the local business elite neglected by the evangelicals. Throughout the red states—and increasingly the blue ones too—evangelical churches are vital centers of "networking," where the carwash owner can schmooze with the bank's loan officer. Some churches offer regular Christian businessmen's "fellowship lunches," where religious testimonies are given and business cards traded, along with jokes aimed at Democrats and gays.

Mainstream, even liberal, churches also provide a range of services, from soup kitchens to support groups. What makes the typical evangelicals' social welfare efforts sinister is their implicit—and sometimes not so implicit—linkage to a program for the destruction of public and secular services. This year the connecting code words were "abortion" and "gay marriage": To vote for the candidate who opposed these supposed moral atrocities, as the Christian Coalition and so many churches strongly advised, was to vote against public housing subsidies, childcare and expanded public forms of health insurance. While Hamas operates in a nonexistent welfare state, the Christian right advances by attacking the existing one.   6

Of course, Bush's faith-based social welfare strategy only accelerates the downward spiral toward theocracy. Not only do the right-leaning evangelical churches offer their own, shamelessly proselytizing social services; not only do they attack candidates who favor expanded public services—but they stand to gain public money by doing so. It is this dangerous positive feedback loop, and not any new spiritual or moral dimension of American life, that the Democrats have failed to comprehend: The evangelical church-based welfare system is being fed by the deliberate destruction of the secular welfare state.   7

In the aftermath of election '04, centrist Democrats should not be flirting with faith but re-examining their affinity for candidates too mumble-mouthed and compromised to articulate poverty and war as the urgent moral issues they are. Jesus is on our side here, and secular liberals should not be afraid to invoke him. Policies of pre-emptive war and the upward redistribution of wealth are inversions of the Judeo-Christian ethic, which is for the most part silent, or mysteriously cryptic, on gays and abortion. At the very least, we need a firm commitment to public forms of childcare, healthcare, housing and education—for people of all faiths and no faith at all. Secondly, progressives should perhaps rethink their own disdain for service-based outreach programs. Once it was the left that provided "alternative services" in the form of free clinics, women's health centers, food co-ops and inner-city multi-service storefronts. Enterprises like these are not substitutes for an adequate public welfare state, but they can become the springboards from which to demand one.   8

One last lesson from the Christians—the ancient, original ones, that is. Theirs is the story of how a steadfast and heroic moral minority undermined the world's greatest empire and eventually came to power. Faced with relentless and spectacular forms of repression, they kept on meeting over their potluck dinners (the origins of later communion rituals), proselytizing and bearing witness wherever they could. For the next four years and well beyond,   9 liberals and progressives will need to emulate these original Christians, who stood against imperial Rome with their bodies, their hearts and their souls.

Thinking Critically

1. With three class members, conduct electronic research on Barbara Ehrenreich. How does biographical information aid in understanding her beliefs, her audience, and her probable approach to any topic dealing with American culture?

2. What is the writer's central claim? What sentence best expresses it?

3. What is Ehrenreich's implied warrant in this essay?

4. What grounds and types of evidence does the writer provide? Identify sentences and passages to support your answer.

5. Where do appeals to reason, ethics, and emotion appear? Refer to specific parts of the essay to justify your answer. How do these appeals affect the writer's tone?

6. How does the writer respond to the arguments of the opposition?

Analyzing Visual Arguments

Although America is still a print-oriented society, the present information age is fueled by an electronic revolution that frequently elevates visual texts (and aural ones as well) to the same level of importance as verbal texts. Whether you encounter posters, streaming Internet advertisements, commercials on television, cartoons in newspapers, illustrations in books, photo essays, Web-based magazines, or multimedia presentations of research, you need to identify the ways in which visual texts mold your response to verbal information. It is especially important to develop a critical awareness of the methods used by those designers of visual texts whose purpose is not only to present information about a topic but also to advance an argument.

Visual arguments are often designed to make you buy a certain product, embrace or fear a person, party, or idea, or sanction a course of action. In each instance, someone or some agency organizes and manipulates images to achieve a collective response, establish a common will, or martial group energies. When, for example, the nation's two major political parties spend tens of millions of dollars every presidential election cycle on negative media advertising that relies heavily on scary images, they succeed (as a wealth of research validates) in demonizing the opposition's candidate. To accomplish argumentative aims in the political or cultural arena—for example, to convince people that the administration is concerned about the environment because it publicizes in both print and visual imagery a "clear skies" and "healthy forests" agenda—you need to get people thinking not only that the government's aims are right but that opposing viewpoints are wrong.

Visual arguments are a form of discourse containing certain components that you can isolate and identify to see how the artist gets an audience to think or act in a certain way. Especially when they focus on cultural issues, visual arguments depend in good part on manipulating the emotions, attitudes, and responses of a targeted audience—for example, single women, white males, Hispanics, evangelicals, or middle-class voters. Visual texts can project powerful cultural messages and arguments for specific or general audiences.

When you encounter visual texts containing overt or covert arguments, you need to analyze and evaluate the ways in which the artist or designer "massages" the message (to echo the late Marshall McLuhan) to produce the desired audience response. When, for instance, a 30-second advertisement on television sponsored by an environmental group shows a logged swath of forest in a national preserve, combined with an admonitory voice-over, you know that the organization paying for this commercial desires your political allegiance and ideological faith. Or when a pop-up on your computer screen reveals a link to a faith-based charity that incorporates a graphic showing an impoverished rural family, you know that the power of the image can move some viewers to action. Visual arguments often reveal the workings of American culture, promoting people, products, ideas, and ideologies.

We are smart enough to know that visual arguments contain political or cultural goals or ends. At the same time, we have to discriminate among the various claims and assumptions such images project, and ask how they appeal to our emotional and intellectual lives. Visual arguments by their very definition are graphic forms of representation that have to be dissected for their cultural assumptions and ideological intricacies. To look at visual arguments and think about them critically, consider these questions:

- **Who is the intended audience, and who is the author or sponsor?** Is the author an individual, government or commercial organization, or some other institution or authority? What level of influence or credibility does the author possess, and how do you know? If the author has a website, how credible is this site, who sponsors it, and how often is it updated? What cultural and ethical assumptions does the author make about the audience?

- **What is the argumentative aim of the visual?** What is the claim or message? Does the author provide support for the claim? Can this evidence be verified independently from other sources?

- **What design elements contribute to the effectiveness of the argument?** What images or details stand out? What is the effect of color or black-and-white? From what perspective or angle (for example, left to right, top to bottom, foreground to background) do we "read" the visual text? How do these elements create a dominant impression or unified effect? Do you respond positively or negatively to the dominant impression, and why?

- **What logical, emotional, and ethical appeals appear in the visual text?** Are these appeals reasonable or excessive? Are they directed to one specific culture or cultural group, or might they be directed to multiple cultures?

When we turn our eyes to visual texts, we often encounter clear and potent images of the cultural skirmishes in contemporary America. Such visual texts offer vivid portraits of the many ongoing debates over cultural values, and they provide us with the opportunity to decode the assumptions and claims implicit in them. Cultural arguments embedded in images do not necessarily tell us the "truth" about any cultural reality. It is up to us as critical viewers to see if any visual argument gets to the heart of the country.

Thinking Critically

Collaborate with two class members in an analysis of the Benetton advertisement. What is the purpose of this advertisement? Who is the targeted audience?

What argument and persuasive appeal does it make? In what ways does it try to influence the audience's emotions and values? What details in the composition stand out? Do you find the advertisement effective? Why or why not? Report your conclusions to the class.

The Composing Process

Very few informed, carefully reasoned essays about American culture arrive full-blown from a writer's keyboard or pen. As the distinguished novelist, essayist, and poet John Updike admits, "Writing and rewriting are a constant search for what one's saying." By stressing a process of writing *and* rewriting, Updike demolishes the notion or myth of the author as some divinely inspired creature from whom well-wrought prose erupts spontaneously. This rapid process might work for a small percentage of professional writers (especially those having to work under strict deadlines in media jobs), but most writers plan, write, rewrite, and edit before submitting any text for consideration by an audience.

Rather than thinking of an essay for a college course as a one-shot effort, adopt the more professional (and more rewarding) attitude that writing is a composing process involving prewriting, drafting, and revising. Admittedly this process is not strictly a three-step procedure; rather it is recursive, flowing back and forth, and subject to personal composing styles. And it is fair to say that every writer has a unique composing process: some individuals prefer to engage in only a few prewriting activities, others jump immediately into drafting activities, and still others find little need for revision. However, within this variety of personal writing preferences, the prewriting, drafting, and revision stages offer a useful framework for composition.

Prewriting is the first stage in the composing process. At this stage you generate ideas for an essay *before* you actually begin to write the first draft. In this particular course, prewriting begins with your reading of an assigned essay from this book, your evolving response to the text, and the deepening of your thoughts through class discussion. If you underline key passages in the text or use the margins to annotate it with questions or statements of your own, you will want to review these markings early in the prewriting stage. You might also want to write a summary of the essay, capturing as many of the writer's main ideas as briefly as possible, or keep a journal in which you write entries on the theme or topic of a given essay. Some bloggers post their ideas, reactions to texts, and working drafts in their blog to solicit input from other readers.

The next step in the prewriting process is to consider your purpose and your audience. Ask yourself what you want to accomplish in your essay. Your answer will signal your purpose. In all likelihood, you also will ask these related questions: What do I want to say about the topic? How do I plan to accomplish this goal? Perhaps you have read several of the essays on red and blue states, and you have decided that your purpose is to claim that this division dangerously oversimplifies the reality of voter opinion in the United States. Your primary purpose, then, would be to argue a position, but you also have already established your claim and, quite possibly, determined that such strategies as definition, illustration, and comparison and contrast will assist you in supporting the claim and organizing the essay.

Complementing your consideration of purpose is your audience analysis. Focus on your intended or implied reader. Such attributes as age, ethnicity, gender, education, and interests might factor into your analysis of this audience. Clearly your professor will be the primary audience, but your peers and even readers outside the classroom might constitute secondary audiences. Most teachers welcome writing that goes beyond a classroom audience to imagine a readership in the world at large. With e-mail and the Web at your fingertips, you might very well find that your instructor, in applauding your essay, will suggest that you post it for your peers in the college community or even transmit it to a much wider audience.

During prewriting, you can try out various composing strategies. At the outset, you might want to write one sentence expressing the thesis or claim underlying your paper. Or you might want to develop a sketch outline. Some students brainstorm, listing ideas down the side of a sheet of paper or a computer screen. Others like to freewrite for a certain amount of time without monitoring sentence correctness or the logic of their ideas. Others keep a notebook of ideas and projects. Some like to visualize the project by centering the topic on a sheet of paper and then creating maps or trees, using lines to connect various subtopics and related ideas to the main topic. You might want to try the journalist's tried-and-true strategy of posing and answering key questions: *who, what, where, when, why?* Select the prewriting strategies that you find most congenial and practical. Use them not only to limber up your thinking or escape writer's block but also to plan the entire essay.

Identifying and limiting your thesis is your most important task at the prewriting stage. It might seem liberating to simply dive into the drafting of an essay, but if you want to avoid hidden dangers, take time to write down your controlling idea or claim, and to narrow it in accordance with the demands of the project or assignment. If you must write a 1,000-word paper on the topic of red and blue states, you might have a thesis—that this cultural division is artificial and simplistic—but you also need to limit your claim significantly. One way to control the boundaries of this assignment would be to reformulate the thesis so that it applies only to the state in which you live. Another strategy would be to focus on one issue—such as gun ownership across the red and blue divide—to reveal another more focused and nuanced approach to the topic. Writers have a much easier time in writing essays when they limit the topic and thesis in advance.

Your next step during prewriting is to gather and organize **evidence.** A thesis without evidence is like a bird without feathers. You might have to conduct research at the library or online to obtain this evidence. Keep in mind that evidence that you quote or paraphrase, is the intellectual property of others. You must acknowledge the sources of your evidence in order to avoid plagiarism or the theft of other writers' ideas (see "A Note on Documenting Outside Sources," page 30). You will need various types of evidence to support the central idea of your essay. This evidence underpins the grounds—the main supporting points. For a paper of 1,000 words, you will want from three to five major points of evidence to support your thesis. These major points in turn will determine the sequence of paragraphs when you draft the essay. Remember that evidence can consist of everything from representative personal experiences to key reasons to quotations from authorities.

After assembling the raw material, you must decide how to organize it. To begin the organizing process, you can assemble related information under subheadings, refine your scratch outline, connect similar ideas with lines or arrows, circle major points, add items, or use any other strategy that helps shape preliminary ideas. Moreover, as you prepare to move from the prewriting to the drafting stage, you can begin to think about the many rhetorical strategies—for example, analysis or argumentation—that you can employ to structure your essay.

After completing your prewriting activities, you are ready to begin drafting. The first draft of the essay might flow smoothly from the well-crafted prewriting materials you have assembled, or it might be a rough, hesitant affair. Think of creating the first draft as a process of discovery. Try to work rapidly. Do not worry about grammar and sentence structure, which you can improve in later drafts. You might want to follow this pattern:

1. Write the title. Make it short and catchy.
2. Write the introductory paragraph, placing your thesis at the beginning or end of it.
3. Write the supporting paragraphs. Place a topic sentence (the main idea in the paragraph) at the beginning of each one.
4. Connect ideas within and between the supporting paragraphs.
5. Write a concluding paragraph.

This is a minimal prescription for a first draft. Do not expect your first draft to be perfect, even if you are a natural-born writer or are adept at self-editing. In fact, editing at this stage can be counterproductive, for you can get bogged down and waste time and creative energy.

After composing the first draft, you can begin the third stage of the composing process: revision, or rewriting. During this stage, you might decide that you have to refine your thesis, locate more evidence, add a new paragraph, address your audience in a more reasonable tone, delete weak or irrelevant material, or integrate new patterns of development such as definition or comparison and contrast. A carefully planned revision reshapes your paper, producing a text that is clear, coherent, and correct in large elements like well-organized paragraphs and smallest details such as correct spelling and punctuation. Revision should not be a hasty or slapdash effort. As the word itself suggests, when you revise you "re-vision" or see the text in a sharper, more focused light.

There is no single best way to revise your text prior to submission. However, you are likely to find these guidelines useful:

- Complete your revised draft before the submission date. If possible, set aside this draft for a few days to gain perspective and a degree of objectivity about it. Then return to the draft with fresh critical eyes.

- Keep this draft—and earlier drafts—in a separate file in your computer. It is much easier to attend to the entire writing process when you have texts readily available on a computer screen. Remember to retain a backup for all this material. Instructors will not accept excuses that your computer ate your document.

- Respond to your instructor's feedback. Quite probably your instructor reviewed an earlier draft of your paper and offered suggestions for improvement. Perhaps the instructor also discussed the essay with you in conference. Honor the instructor's evaluation by systematically incorporating these recommended changes into your final draft.

- Reread your draft several times, at least once out loud, until you have a deep sense of its strengths and weaknesses. As you reread, try to implement a step-by-step review of the document, starting with its largest features (paragraphs), working through the details (evidence), and then down to the level of words, phrases, and sentences (style).

- Engage in peer review—in class, in the dorm, or online. By sharing your paper with another class member or with a small collaborative group, you become part of a learning community devoted to the production of quality work. Remember that both you and your partner or partners in this activity must approach peer review with seriousness and professionalism. You don't want to say that a paper is great when you know it is not. At the same time, you don't want to be unnecessarily critical just because you don't agree with the writer's claim or the grounds supporting it. Admittedly it takes practice and guidelines (in most instances provided by your instructor) to become a skilled peer reviewer.

The "Checklist for Revision and Peer Review," page 30, should aid you in polishing a final draft and serve also as a framework for peer review.

In the final analysis, commitment to the composing process prevents you from being too hasty or idiosyncratic in the papers that you present to a targeted audience. Especially when instructor response and peer review are built into this process, or when you produce and submit collaborative work,

Checklist for Revision and Peer Review

1. Does the title reflect the topic and capture the reader's interest?

2. Does the opening paragraph hook the reader? Does it establish and limit the topic? Is the thesis or claim clear, limited, and interesting or provocative?

3. Do all body paragraphs support the thesis? Is there a single topic and topic sentence for each paragraph? Is there sufficient evidence for each paragraph? Is each paragraph unified, coherent, and complete?

4. Are there clear and effective transitions linking ideas within and between paragraphs?

5. Have the best strategies for essay and paragraph development—whether narrative, descriptive, expository, argumentative, or a combination of these—been selected?

6. Is the tone appropriate for the subject and thesis?

7. Has the audience been identified and its expectations addressed properly?

8. Are all assertions clearly stated, defined, and supported? Is the sequence of ideas or logic sound?

9. Does the end paragraph conclude or wrap up the essay effectively?

10. Are grammar, sentence structure, and mechanics correct?

11. Does the manuscript conform to acceptable guidelines for submitting written work?

A Note on Documenting Outside Sources

Evidence that you use from other sources needs to be documented according to MLA (Modern Language Association) or APA (American Psychological Association) guidelines. These materials require documentation:

1. Direct quotations

2. Paraphrased material

3. Summarized material

4. A key idea or opinion derived from another writer

5. Specific data

6. Disputed facts

Failure to cite or document your sources will lead to charges of plagiarism.

you become part of a community of writers wishing to communicate clearly with each other. The composing process prepares you for the challenging work of dissecting, analyzing, and arguing about the contours of American culture.

Thinking Critically

Write an essay in which you reflect on differences of opinion about a specific cultural controversy of your own choosing. First, employ the prewriting strategies that you find most useful to generate ideas and content. Next, write a rough draft of 500 to 750 words. Exchange this draft with a class member for peer review. Compose a final draft for submission. Keep all these materials—and all essays you write this term—in a folder or electronic portfolio.

Writing Analytical Essays

By now, you have learned the importance of asking questions about texts—the *who, what, when, where,* and *why* queries that are the foundation of critical inquiry. When you ask such questions, you actually are analyzing texts and preparing to write analyses of your own. We all think about the relationships governing our world and our culture. Why is the sky blue or the sunset red? Why have certain states been called "red" and others "blue"? How did this cultural polarity come about? When did the debate over red and blue states begin, and who are the principals in the debate? What are the consequences? Analysis or critical investigation answers questions about relationships, processes, causes, and effects. It seeks to understand these relationships and make connections among them. An essay discussing the impact of acid rain on forests in the Northeast, a report linking obesity to a growing national health crisis, an editorial providing an explanation of American involvement in Iraq—all are rooted in types of analysis.

Professional writers compose paragraphs and complete essays within an analytical framework, often blending analysis with other patterns of development. Consider this paragraph from an essay by Jedediah Purdy entitled "The New Culture of Rural America" that appears in Chapter 2 (see pp. 68–78):

> The change in farming contributes to its decline as a cultural icon. Americans understand that their farmers are not rough-handed husbandmen, but investors, managers, and heavy-equipment operators who, when not planting or harvesting their one or two crops, have a lot of time on their hands. Giant hog barns and Roundup Ready soybeans resist romanticizing. Also, as the number of farmers has plummeted, so has the number of people with childhood memories of a father's or grandfather's farm or even a cousin still on the land. Finally, in a culture

impatient with its crises, the eruption of concern, sympathetic films, and fundraising concerts that accompanied the farm crisis of the 1980s is unlikely to repeat itself; Americans, especially media programmers, are not attracted to two-time losers.

The paragraph reflects the writer's broader purpose in the essay as a whole: to analyze the causes and effects of the decline of American farming as a way of life. Purdy offers evidence to support the intricate pattern of causality that he traces in this paragraph and the essay. His tone is both hardnosed and elegiac, suggesting a persuasive purpose in the larger essay, as he laments the passing of a lifestyle and argues the need for readers to understand the consequences.

Analysis (along with argument, with which it often blends) is the primary type of writing that you will need to use in a broad range of college courses. Many assignments and exams require analytical responses. Consequently you must learn to handle analysis well, to view it as perhaps the core expository talent that you need to perfect. Writing about causes, effects, and processes, and explaining the connections among discrete phenomena and bits of information, enable you to make sense of complex cultural issues and events.

Quite often you will receive a course assignment that calls for analysis. Especially when reading and responding to essays about culture that you read in this book, you will have to identify the type of analysis needed to satisfy the requirements of the assignment. Even when an assignment does not call explicitly for causal analysis (the analysis of causes and effects) or for process analysis, the need for analysis will be signaled by other key expository terms such as "contrast," "define," "explain," "classify," or "evaluate." In all these instances, analysis is either central to the execution of your essay or a vital supplement to the main expository strategy.

Assume, for example, that your instructor asks you to write an essay in which you explain the word *community,* basing your explanation on your reading of Leslie Savan's "Did Somebody Say 'Community'?" (see pp. 80–83). You could develop this essay by mixing patterns—perhaps definition and comparison—but you will also have to analyze the reasons why controversies over community seem so prevalent today (especially if the assignment calls for references to Savan's essay). Similarly, even if the assignment calls for an argumentative response—for example, arguing that the lack of safe public spaces is causing an erosion of the sense of community— you probably would have to spend some time developing specific examples and tracing the causes and effects underlying this situation.

Although there is no set formula for writing an analytical essay, here are several basic strategies that can serve as valuable guidelines:

- **Decide at the outset on the purpose of your analysis.** Do you want to inform or convey factual information to your audience, describe or trace a natural or historical process, argue a position, consider or compare relationships, predict outcomes, classify ideas, people, or events? You could have more than one purpose in mind. For example, in a paper exploring the reasons why so few young people vote in national elections, you might want to inform *and* argue a viewpoint. Nevertheless, you must be clear at the outset about the overall purpose underpinning your paper.

- **Identify your readers and adjust your tone to them.** Remember that the aim of audience analysis is to adapt content and tone to what you think will be your audience's expectations. If, for example, an essay you are planning on the failure of young people to vote will be addressed to your peers, you might want to offer personal (even emotional) experience and evidence while exhorting them to understand the reasons why they do not vote and to change their ways. But if you are writing for a general audience, you could establish a more formal or objective tone while presenting facts and statistics that help you to explain a chain of causality that produces young, apathetic nonvoters.

- **Establish a thesis and create a plan of analysis.** A thesis for an analytical essay keeps the entire paper on track. In addition to stating the main idea, such a thesis should suggest the type of analysis you plan to undertake. For example, will you concentrate on causes, effects, or both, or will you analyze a process? Answering this basic question will also help you to identify the specific writing strategies you will employ: causal analysis, process analysis, illustration, comparison and contrast, argument, and so forth. Will organizing material chronologically or emphatically (from the least to most important) be best? Keep in mind that analysis helps us understand cultural, social, and political change: What caused the conservative revolution of the 1990s? Why does America seem to be divided equally between those on the right and those on the left? Will the No Child Left Behind initiative improve school standards? Intellectual curiosity—the desire to answer questions and get to the bottom of an issue, to uncover deep knowledge about processes, causes, and effects—is at the heart of analysis.

- **Identify the kinds of processes, causes, and effects that are relevant to your topic.** When selecting a cultural topic for analysis, you have to determine both the *immediate* and the *ultimate* causes (also termed *less important* and *most important* causes, or *contributory* and *main* causes) giving rise to a social situation or political reality. For example, if you think about the events of September 11, 2001, you might decide that the immediate cause was a careful plot by a small group of terrorists linked to Osama bin Laden; and you could investigate their motives and even trace the process whereby they planned the attacks. However, there are deeper, ultimate causes that you would want to explore and perhaps speculate about: Why is the United States perceived so negatively in the Islamic world? What caused this seeming "clash of civilizations"? Often you have to consider numerous causes and, depending on the length of the essay, rank them, selecting the most important for development. One practical strategy is to make a list of major causes and provide at least one piece of evidence to support each cause.

- **Avoid oversimplification.** Analysis is only as good as the careful chain of reasoning that you establish in an essay. One difficulty in working with analysis is the need to establish clear links between and among complex processes and causalities. Analysis is a demanding form of exposition precisely because it must "expose" these complicated functions or events. Whether you plan to analyze all the essential steps in a process or sort out the relationships between the causes and effects underlying an event, you have to think deeply and critically about the subject. When thinking about complex causes, you also have to avoid weak reasoning, especially the form of faulty logic known by the Latin phrase *post hoc, ergo propter hoc,* meaning "after this, therefore because of this." Just because one event follows another doesn't mean that the first event caused the second.

Do not write an analytical paper based on faulty reasoning or loose generalizations. And try not to be dogmatic, for the analysis of connections and relationships is rarely absolute and is often open to interpretation. To avoid rigid, uncompromising analysis, especially of causal connections, hedge your bets by using such qualifiers as "perhaps," "most likely," and "probably." Above all, be prepared to dig into a subject, conducting research if necessary, to analyze your topic reasonably and effectively.

Thinking Critically

The term *pluralism* refers to a perspective on culture and society that values differences among people of various ethnic origins, religious beliefs, sexual preferences, and economic classes. Drawing on your own experience, reading, and research, analyze the ways in which a pluralistic vision helps a nation overcome cultural divisions and promotes civil society.

Writing Arguments

Argumentation in writing is not the rabid knock-down battle to the finish that you often encounter on shock radio and television but rather is an attempt to convince readers of the validity of your position on a controversial issue. Argumentation is an appeal to reason. When it combines an appeal to reason (*logos*) with appeals to beliefs and values (*ethos*) and to emotion (*pathos*), argument takes on a persuasive purpose, attempting to get readers or an audience to adopt a belief or engage in a specific course of action.

Assume that you are writing a paper investigating the growing number of people in the United States who are living in poverty. To substantiate your argument, you might present reasons for this rise, provide evidence, and analyze objectively the causes that have led to an increase in poverty among Americans. If you also decide that your purpose is to recommend changes in government policy and perhaps even urge readers to act on this social problem, you will combine argumentation with persuasion. In fact, because readers typically respond to controversial issues in both rational and emotional (as well as ethical) ways, argumentation usually blends with persuasion in an essay.

Writing an argumentation-persuasion essay requires you to select the rhetorical strategies that best promote your purpose. Virtually every type of writing—a description of a toxic waste site, a narrative about a child suffering from AIDS, an analysis of sexism in rap lyrics, a comparison of fuel-efficient hybrid cars and gas-guzzling SUVs—contains an explicit or implicit point of view. Such viewpoints suggest that, instead of setting forth a thesis or a main idea, many essays essentially project claims to be substantiated or positions to be defended. However, pure argumentation-persuasion involves more than presenting your own viewpoint. A sound argumentative essay also requires you to acknowledge and understand the viewpoints of others with whom you might disagree—in truth, to consider the idea that there are often many conflicting viewpoints on a controversial issue.

As you will see in the selections in this book, argumentation is a reasoned way of staking out a claim or position on various issues raised by America's "cultural divides." Some writers take a pro-con approach to certain divisions they see in the American cultural landscape, constructing their essays in the form of a debate. Others reject the notion that an argument necessarily has to have a winner and loser, preferring to offer reasons that might reduce conflict about such volatile issues as religion, bioethics, or sexual orientation. (Rogerian theory, named after the psychologist Carl Rogers, promotes the idea that argument should not heighten hostility but rather ameliorate it by seeking common ground.) Several writers look objectively at certain cultural divisions or assumptions without necessarily taking sides. Many writers argue that we must move beyond cultural misconceptions and biases in order to understand the wellsprings of national identity. Andrea Elliott, for example, in her essay "The Political Conversion of New York's Evangelicals" (see pp. 118–22) challenges weak cultural assumptions and stereotypes:

> While Hispanics and African Americans in New York City have traditionally voted Democratic, those who attend evangelical churches may feel a different pull. José Casanova, a professor of sociology who specializes in religion and politics at New School University and has studied evangelicals around the world, said that even if they are poor, they tend to vote for conservative candidates.
>
> "They do not so much identify with their economic position right now, but with the one they ought to have with the help of God," he said. "They are very conservative and pro-market and do not expect the government to help them."

A sound argument about American culture seeks out the truth (supported by evidence, in this case a quotation from an authority) that often can be obscured by untested assumptions and unyielding impressions.

To write your own argumentative essay, follow these guidelines:

1. **Select a topic and take a stand.** Any topic might lend itself to argument, but you should choose a topic that you have some intellectual or emotional stake in. At times generating this degree of interest or commitment might be difficult, especially if the topic is assigned. Nevertheless, you normally can find a perspective on an issue or controversy that interests you, that you are informed about, or that you think you can handle effectively. Once you have selected this topic, take a stand by stating your position or claim (akin to a thesis statement) on the topic. Write this claim in a single sentence that will serve as the focal point of your essay.

2. **Analyze your audience.** You cannot write an effective paper without first targeting your audience. In argumentation, it is especially important to anticipate the characteristics and values of readers. You can anticipate their opinions (including those of your instructor) and have a pretty good sense of whether readers will be friendly, hostile, or neutral to your claim. It is easy to convince a reader who already agrees with you. But remember that you also have to engage in the hard task of persuading a reader whose ideas, opinions, values, and experience might not coincide with yours.

3. **Support your claim.** To convince a broad range of readers about the merits of your thesis or claim, you must provide evidence that is specific, accurate, plausible, sufficient, and representative. A good research or reference librarian can help you uncover solid evidence. If you prefer to rely on the World Wide Web, it is best to adopt the skeptical temperament recommended by Susan Sontag as one measure of true intelligence. Although you can find texts and entire books chock-full of supporting evidence, remember that misinformation abounds on the Web: unreliable sources, wild claims, and faulty data pop up all over, and the "information" swamping blogs and chat rooms is not the sort of evidence you want to incorporate into your paper. Appropriate electronic sources provide evidence that is credible and complete.

4. **Organize your argument.** Once again, remember that there is not one best way to plan an argument. Recall that the grounds of your argument—the supporting reasons and evidence you develop—establish the validity of your claim. As you gather this information, keep in mind the way your supporting material can be used to develop minor propositions. For instance, you might want to introduce your claim, state the first minor proposition and supporting information, followed by second and third minor propositions and supporting evidence, before moving to refutation and the conclusion of the essay. But any of the ways and combinations mentioned in this chapter—description, narrative, comparison

and contrast, causal analysis, definition, and so on—can serve as an organizing principle. In the final analysis, your evidence should be presented in the most emphatic and compelling way; to achieve dramatic effect or to close your case, you might want to save your strongest minor proposition and evidence for last.

5. **Check your warrants.** Recall that a warrant is a broad idea or principle that serves as the essential underpinning for your assertion or claim. It functions like an absolute value justifying not only your claim but also the supporting information. However, if readers are likely to question or reject your warrant, you will have to defend it. Because warrants often reflect core values and beliefs, they are debatable. For example, if the warrant in your paper opposing abortion is that all life from conception is sacred, you need to anticipate that some readers will question this faith-based value.

6. **Combine logical, ethical, and emotional appeals.** Above all else, an argumentative essay must be a carefully reasoned document. It must be free of broad or hasty generalizations, either-or reasoning, unproven conclusions that essentially beg the question, and a host of other logical fallacies. Strong written arguments reflect logical thinking. Moreover, the logical appeal of your paper can be enhanced by carefully crafted emotional appeals to basic human emotions such as sympathy or love, physical needs and desires, and higher "truths" such as patriotism and belief in God. The appeal to emotion, which should not be excessive, can be a powerful complement to the logical claims and evidence appearing in your essay. Likewise, when your voice or tone seems honest, reasonable, and well intentioned—when it conveys a strong sense of right and wrong—you create a sense of credibility and goodwill that is essential to good argument.

7. **Acknowledge and deal with the opposition.** Because of the very nature of argumentation, you know that there will be opposing viewpoints. Many readers will simply disagree with your claim and question your warrants, reasons, and evidence. Consequently you have to deal with the opposition effectively and fairly. As noted already, you have options. You can tackle your opponents head-on, pointing out weaknesses or logical inconsistencies in the opposition's warrants, claims, and evidence. Or, applying Rogerian strategy, you can offer an unbiased summary of opposing viewpoints, acknowledge their possible validity and concede minor points, and even indicate areas of common agreement before demonstrating that your position is stronger. One way to establish a tone of goodwill in an argumentative paper is to treat the opposition with respect.

When you tackle a controversial cultural issue in an essay, you have to present both yourself and your position in the strongest possible light. You will want to proceed in a logical, carefully reasoned manner while appealing to readers' emotions and values. As with all writing, but especially with argumentation, you will have to rework and revise your draft to tighten the internal logic, strengthen and document the evidence, and eliminate weak spots in refutation. Only then will your argument be convincing.

Thinking Critically

With four or five class members, review the table of contents for *Many Americas*. Using the blurbs as a guideline, compose a list of all the cultural controversies that you see reflected in this table of contents. Using the blurbs, identify three essays that interest the group members and that seem likely to contain strong arguments. Quickly skim these essays to confirm initial impressions. Present your findings in class discussion.

Red or Blue? Values, Culture, and Community

Two Americas, Two Restaurants, One Town

REBECCA SKLOOT

This article was the cover story of the *New York Times Magazine* for October 17, 2004. In the months leading up to that year's presidential election, the media explored (and, some would say, overexploited and oversimplified) the idea of an American "cultural divide." New York City–based freelance journalist Rebecca Skloot has taught nonfiction writing at the University of Pittsburgh and is a faculty member of the annual Mid-Atlantic Summer Creative Nonfiction Writer's Conference. Skloot is a contributing writer for *Popular Science* magazine, and her journalism has also appeared in the *Wilson Quarterly* and the *Chicago Tribune* as well as on National Public Radio. As her biography on the National Association of Science Writers website puts it, "She financed her undergraduate and graduate degrees in biomedical sciences and nonfiction writing by working in emergency rooms, neurology labs, veterinary morgues and martini bars." Skloot participates in many writing workshops as a teacher and guest lecturer around the country, including workshops for high school students.

Patrons at a Bob Evans restaurant in New Martinsville, West Virginia. There are 576 Bob Evanses in the United States. "We want to make sure the experience someone has in New Martinsville is the same as the one they'd have in Orlando, St. Louis or Baltimore," says Tammy Roberts Myers, the public relations director for Bob Evans.

To call Baristas a restaurant would be a serious understatement. It is a   1
restaurant, but it's also a barbershop. And a coffeehouse. And, of course,
a massage parlor. Naturally, it's run by the same guy who turned the funeral home around the corner into a gym, with cardio machines in the
viewing room and free weights in the old embalming chamber.

Baristas occupies a huge turn-of-the-century white house in New Mar-   2
tinsville, W.Va., with steep fire-engine-red steps, a porch full of rainbow-
colored tables and pillars painted to look like cloudy skies and candy canes.
You walk inside to high ceilings, oak floors, purple walls and one of the
owners, Jill Shade, making her famous mocha crushes or hopping around
singing an old Cher song she has had stuck in her head for weeks. When I
first walked in, Shade pointed to a huge wooden board behind her.
"Menu's up there," she told me, "but if you're craving something you don't
see, just holler and I'll try to make it."

Baristas' menu is not exactly an exercise in overwhelming choice—a cou-   3
ple of homemade soups, a salad, some appetizers, sandwiches and one dinner
special on Friday nights. But ambience is another story. You can eat in the

basement pub, with its low oak ceiling and stone walls. You can eat on the patio overlooking the Ohio River, in the garden next to the hibiscus plants or in the cafe surrounded by walls of local art. You can get a haircut or a bona fide Swedish massage while you wait, then sit at a table covered in quotes from Camus or Malcolm X. It's exactly the kind of place I love, and exactly the kind of place I would never expect to find in New Martinsville, where I live part of each year. It's a town of about 5,000 people and 36 churches, a town full of all-you-can-eat buffets, Confederate flags, "No Trespassing" signs and folks who still feel the need to point out the local lesbian couple. But then again, I never expected to find Jeff Shade in New Martinsville either.

Shade is a local boy, a 38-year-old former high-school football star who   4
left West Virginia with dreams of becoming a minister. But he lost God somewhere in Texas and got kicked out of seminary, he says, for "asking too many questions." He studied philosophy and theology at Princeton, then went to massage school in Manhattan while serving as the pastor for a New Jersey church where he preached from *The New York Times* instead of the Bible. A few years later, he headed back to New Martinsville with his wife, Jill, their 2-year-old son, Soren Aabye Shade (as in Soren Aabye Kierkegaard), and degrees in Greek, theology, philosophy and massage. With all that education, he and Jill decided they wanted to expand the minds of the folks back home. The tool they chose was the burger.

The Barista burger is the creation of Tammy Wilson, a compact, pony-   5
tailed whirlwind with tie-dyed flip-flops and a T-shirt that says "Save the drama for your mama." Wilson is Baristas' main cook, and she works in a kitchen that looks more like a home than a restaurant. Teenage girls run in and out asking her questions about prom dates and haircuts, Jill appears from the garden with a bag of peppers for roasting and Jeff wanders around tasting soups and sauces while cracking jokes about politicians or saying things about Foucault that nobody understands. Wilson spends hours each week pressing fresh garlic and adding it to vats of ground beef for burgers; when she's done, she rolls up her sleeves and plunges her hands into the meat. "I learned to cook from my hillbilly grandma, and I'm proud of it," she told me. "And if there's one thing I know, it's that burgers only taste right when you mix the spices by hand."

Clearly, she's onto something. People drive 60 miles up and down the   6
Ohio River for her burger: a juicy half-pound of ground beef with hints of ginger and garlic and soy, some spices, a touch of West Virginia honey and enough sweet smokiness from the grill to make you think she cooked it over fresh mesquite. Mix that with a salad fresh from the garden and hand-cut fries, and you've got a room full of people who simply can't believe any-one wouldn't want to eat at Baristas.

But in fact, a lot of locals can't imagine even walking into Baristas, let   7
alone eating there. The truth is, most of them would rather go to Bob Evans.

The first time I drove up to the New Martinsville Bob Evans, Billy Joel's   8
"Just the Way You Are" was echoing through the parking lot from the
speakers above the doors. Everything about the place said "national chain."
I walked past a red-white-and-blue banner into a world lined with plaid curtains and Old Fashioned things, like copper teakettles and washboards that
looked so new they might as well have still had price tags on them. The
eggnog- and pecan-pie-scented candles by the cash register overwhelmed
any smells from the kitchen. A short woman in black polyester slacks and a
white button-up shirt with a Bob Evans logo stitched on it smiled at me,
menu in hand, and said: "Hi, welcome to Bob Evans. One for dinner?"

Baristas and Bob Evans are less than a mile apart, but they might as well   9
be in different cities. Baristas sits on Main, a quiet tree-lined street with
wide sidewalks and a historic courthouse. You're guaranteed to miss it if
you don't know to turn toward the river at the BP station. But you can't
miss Bob Evans. It has the tallest sign on this strip of Route 2, a highway
lined with a Wal-Mart, a McDonald's, a Dairy Queen and a Pizza Hut that
could be anywhere in the country.

There is only one Baristas, but there are 576 Bob Evanses, in 21 states;   10
in 2004, the company rang up $1.2 billion in sales. Bob Evans is part of a
giant and fast-growing retail category known as "full-service family-style
dining" (you know the kind: Cracker Barrel, Denny's, Friendly's); it's a sit-
down restaurant that leans more toward down home than fast food, with
a serious emphasis on all-day breakfast. Like most Bob Evanses, the one in
New Martinsville is in a red-and-white "farmhouse" with a sprawling
parking lot and a few benches out front.

The goal at every Bob Evans restaurant is to be the same as every other   11
Bob Evans restaurant. "We want to make sure the experience someone has
in New Martinsville is the same as the one they'd have in Orlando,
St. Louis or Baltimore," said Tammy Roberts Myers, the P.R. director at
the Bob Evans headquarters in Columbus, Ohio. The company's guiding
principle is simple: consistency, in everything from ambience to the distance between tables to the arrangement of food on your plate.

"Going out to eat is risky," said Steve Govey, the Bob Evans regional   12
manager for the Ohio Valley. "You never know what you're going to get.
But at Bob Evans, that's not true. Our strategy is being completely predictable, something people know they can count on."

Bob Evans was packed when I arrived. It was full of customers of all ages   13
and sizes, with lots of khakis, denim shorts and camouflage hats with pictures of guns or slogans like "National Wild Turkey Federation." There were

three women at three different tables wearing identical neon orange T-shirts. I'd just come from Baristas, where people danced at the counter to Ray Charles and talked across the room about how so-and-so woke up with a weird rash yesterday and what John Kerry said at the rally in Wheeling about helping millworkers. At Bob Evans, I sat alone at the counter. The people around me stared at their plates and ate in silence; behind me, people spoke so quietly I could barely hear their murmurs over the clanking silverware.

I ate a raspberry grilled-chicken salad with exactly four slices of straw- 14 berries, four chunks of pineapple and a tough sliced chicken breast with raspberry vinaigrette. I followed that with a classic turkey dinner. The stuffing was great, but the rest was just barely edible—a little dry, too salty, with oily biscuits and mashed potatoes that tasted like fake movie-popcorn butter. Honestly, I didn't get it.

But I went back to Bob Evans the next day, and I kept going back and 15 kept trying things on the menu. I was determined to understand why so many people in town chose this place over Baristas. (The prices at the two restaurants, by the way, are about the same.) I ate a southwestern omelet smothered in jack cheese, and a pork chop dinner that took four people to make. None of the chefs spoke while they cooked; they just threw still-frozen vegetables and meat straight onto the griddle. (They let me watch.) They measured lettuce and arranged the food on my plate so it would look exactly like the instructional diagram hanging on the kitchen wall: pork chop over here, frozen vegetables over there, one sprig of parsley right there.

After a waitress put the whole package down in front of me, I took a 16 bite and thought, They're right, it is just like grandma used to make. Thing is, my grandmothers couldn't cook. From my New York grandmother, I got burned matzo brei and gefilte fish from a jar. From my southern Illinois grandmother, I got food that tasted just like Bob Evans's: soggy vegetables, rubbery bread and meat so overcooked it crumbled when you bit it.

I'd gone meat shopping a couple of days earlier with Tammy Wilson from 17 Baristas, and I watched her hand-pick every pound of meat from the butcher's counter as he leaned through the window and told her it had just come in fresh. "He gets most of his meats local," she told me. I wanted to find out the same sort of thing about the Bob Evans pork chop, so I called the folks in Columbus. Tammy Roberts Myers said she would be happy to trace my dinner for me, all the way from the animal to the table. But a couple of weeks later, she called to say that someone at headquarters had a change of heart. "Sorry," she said. "We can't tell you that, because it's proprietary information. What I can tell you is, it was on a farm somewhere at some point."

I didn't start to understand the appeal of Bob Evans (for other people, 18 anyway) until I met Daisy and Wally Kendall. They eat at Bob Evans nearly

At Baristas restaurant in New Martinsville, West Virginia, patrons can get a haircut or a massage while they wait for their fresh, homemade food, most of it made with locally-sourced ingredients. "I learned cook from my hillbilly grandma, and I'm proud of it" says head cook Tammy Wilson. "And if there's one thing I know, it's that burgers only taste right when you mix the spices by hand."

every day, sometimes more than once. They sit in a maroon vinyl booth giggling and finishing each other's sentences. When I asked why they eat at Bob Evans all the time, Daisy said: "It's clean, and there are no surprises. I know what I'm going to get."

Wally shrugged and said: "People say, 'Why do you only go to Myrtle   19 Beach for vacation every year? Don't you want to see somewhere else?' We never know what to say—we tried it, we know we like it, why risk spoiling our vacation somewhere new we might not like?"

When I asked other people why they chose Bob Evans over Baristas, most   20 folks just smiled and shook their heads. One young woman told me her father doesn't like her eating at Baristas because "it's like feeding your money to Satan." One regular said he didn't know why he ate at Bob Evans, but he thought it might have something to do with it being so consistent. "I'm not big on change," he told me. "That's why I'm voting for George W. It's just too dangerous to change stride now. It's best to leave well enough alone."

One woman lowered her voice and whispered: "Baristas' problem is, 21 they try to make fancy food. We're simple people here. We don't like a lot of spices and stuff. A little salt and pepper is good enough for us. You have to develop a taste for that fancy stuff, and we don't really want to."

Another woman pointed to my pork chop dinner and said: "You've got 22 to remember, this is what we were raised on. If people want to go into Baristas for a bean-sprout sandwich, that's fine, but around here, we don't do that sort of thing."

In fact, Baristas' menu is full of traditional New Martinsville food (ham- 23 burgers, grilled-cheese sandwiches, steaks, fried green tomatoes), and there isn't a bean-sprout sandwich in sight. But there are a few things on the menu that give some locals the creeps: hummus, pesto, eggplant, feta. The way they see it, Jeff's a local boy, and New Martinsville loves him, but that doesn't mean they're about to eat weird food in a restaurant that sounds as if it might as well be a brothel, what with all the drinking and massaging going on there.

Daisy and Wally have known Jeff Shade since he was a kid. When I 24 asked them why they'd never gone to Baristas, they looked at each other as if it had never occurred to them. "We love Jeff," Daisy said. "The only reason we haven't gone there is really just negligence.

"We were going to go there once," Daisy went on, "but a deer ran into 25 the car." Then she paused. "We really should go sometime," she told Wally.

How about now, I asked. I'll go with you. 26

"Oh, no," they said in unison, then giggled. "We're expecting a call 27 from Wally's doctor later."

Daisy and Wally have always been Bob Evans people, but they didn't start 28 going daily until they came down with severe health problems—lymphoma for Wally and serious respiratory problems for Daisy—which they attribute to years of breathing in toxins while working at a local chemical plant. They got sick and weak, they couldn't cook and Bob Evans became their life. Daisy looked at me and whispered: "You know, the food here is wonderful. We've never had a bad meal. But really, we don't come for the food. We come for the people." She gestured around the restaurant. "This is our social life."

When I walked back into Baristas after a few days of nothing but Bob 29 Evans, I literally felt as if I had come home. The walls were the exact shade of purple that I painted my bedroom when I was a teenager, and these days my kitchen is maroon, just like Baristas' back dining area. One of my favorite Jayhawks songs was playing, and I sat down at the bar next to Gary, a former airplane-engine specialist who lives in an octagonal penthouse he built on top of an old hog barn.

I told him what I'd been doing, and he looked at me as if I were crazy. 30 "I can't imagine hanging out at Bob Evans every day," he said. "I just find that place so . . . so . . . the same." I knew what he meant. I loved talking to Daisy and Wally and a few other regulars at Bob Evans, but I couldn't handle going in there every day. I'm a Baristas person to the bone—just as Daisy and Wally are pure Bob Evans. The question is: Why? What makes them Bob Evans people and me a Baristas person?

Some of it is simple aesthetics: I think fresh food tastes a lot better than   31
frozen, and I want herbs instead of salt. Local art on colorful walls makes me happy, and fake old-fashioned teakettles make me sad. Mostly I love Baristas because of the buzz, the energy I feel when I'm in the midst of people who thrive on resisting predictability, like the Catholics who come to Baristas to hear Buddhist monks speak about reincarnation, or the Republicans who came in to meet the Kerry people who stopped by one night to stump.

Maybe I had an idea that I could convert people—that I could per-   32
suade some Bob Evans folks that they should be open to change, that the food really was better at Baristas; and maybe persuade some Baristas people that the Bob Evans people are interesting and funny and friendly, too. But in all my time shuttling back and forth between the two restaurants, I didn't change a single person's mind. At some point, it hit me: it's not just New Martinsville. Bob Evans people and Baristas people live together all over the United States. They often go to the same stores and send their kids to the same schools, but try as they might, they simply can't understand why anyone in his right mind wouldn't eat the way they do, think the way they do and vote the way they do. Unfortunately, I'm not sure a burger can change that, not even a really, really good one.

Thinking Critically

1. This is a particularly effective example of a comparative essay; Skloot's observational skills and flair for description give "Two Americas, Two Restaurants, One Town" an especially vivid feel. How does Skloot use her observational skills to support her thesis? (Before you answer that, first determine what her thesis is.) How can you tell, as a writer, if you are providing too much detail or not enough detail in your own work?

2. Skloot writes in the first person. How much of her self—her lifestyle, her age, her background—does she actually reveal? What would you guess about her, based on this essay?

3. Perhaps because she is writing in the first person, this essay is as much about how Skloot challenged and changed her own perceptions as it is about "two Americas." How does Skloot's awareness of "two Americas, one town" change over the course of the article?

Writing Critically

1. Rebecca Skloot takes a large, abstract, and contentious idea—that there is a "cultural divide" in American society—and sets about finding that divide by choosing a very specific example of a division. Read the section on conducting field research in the Appendix, "Researching Across the Cultural Divides," and plan an essay on some aspect of the "cultural divides" that you can demonstrate by visiting and observing someplace unexpected.

2. What are the specific qualities, in Rebecca Skloot's argument, that make someone a "Bob Evans person" or a "Baristas" person? Does she suggest that there are other factors involved? Given these qualities, do you consider yourself a "Bob Evans person" or a "Baristas person"? What might you learn from getting to know someone from the opposing restaurant?

3. Does Skloot make or imply value judgments about either "Bob Evans people" or "Baristas people"? Write a letter to the editor of the *New York Times Magazine* in which you challenge Skloot's assumptions about the character and behavior of either or both groups of people.

One Nation, Slightly Divisible

DAVID BROOKS

Cultural critic and *New York Times* columnist David Brooks is best known for his skewering of American consumer culture, especially "aspirational" or upper-middle-class "blue-state" consumers, in books such as *On Paradise Drive* and *Bobos in Paradise: The New Upper Class and How They Got There.* He has worked as a reporter for the *Wall Street Journal* and as senior editor at the conservative magazine the *Weekly Standard,* and he is a contributing editor at *Newsweek* and the *Atlantic Monthly.* Brooks also frequently appears on the PBS program *The NewsHour with Jim Lehrer* and contributes to National Public Radio. On the op-ed pages of the famously liberal *New York Times,* Brooks plays the role of conservative commentator. To be sure, such a prominent position means that he is held up to extraordinary scrutiny; the website <http://www.mediatransparency.org/people/dbrooks.htm> keeps a particularly close watch on what Brooks says and writes. In "One Nation, Slightly Divisible," which appeared in the *Atlantic Monthly* in December 2001, Brooks used the now-familiar red and blue electoral map of the 2000 presidential election as the starting point for an inquiry into just how "divided" the nation was.

Sixty-five miles from where I am writing this sentence is a place with no Star-   1
bucks, no Pottery Barn, no Borders or Barnes & Noble. No blue *New York Times* delivery bags dot the driveways on Sunday mornings. In this place people don't complain that Woody Allen isn't as funny as he used to be, because they never thought he was funny. In this place you can go to a year's worth of dinner parties without hearing anyone quote an aperçu he first heard on Charlie Rose. The people here don't buy those little rear-window stickers when they go to a summer vacation spot so that they can drive around with "MV" decals the rest of the year, for the most part they don't even go to Martha's Vineyard.

The place I'm talking about goes by different names. Some call it Amer-   2
ica. Others call it Middle America. It has also come to be known as Red America, in reference to the maps that were produced on the night of the 2000 presidential election. People in Blue America, which is my part of America, tend to live around big cities on the coasts. People in Red America tend to live on farms or in small towns or small cities far away from the coasts. Things are different there.

Everything that people in my neighborhood do without motors, the   3
people in Red America do with motors. We sail; they powerboat. We cross-country ski; they snowmobile. We hike; they drive ATVs. We have vineyard tours; they have tractor pulls. When it comes to yard work, they have rider mowers; we have illegal aliens.

Different sorts of institutions dominate life in these two places. In Red   4
America churches are everywhere. In Blue America Thai restaurants are everywhere. In Red America they have QVC, the Pro Bowlers Tour, and hunting. In Blue America we have NPR, Doris Kearns Goodwin, and socially conscious investing. In Red America the Wal-Marts are massive, with parking lots the size of state parks. In Blue America the stores are small but the markups are big. You'll rarely see a Christmas store in Blue America, but in Red America, even in July, you'll come upon stores selling fake Christmas trees, wreath-decorated napkins, Rudolph the Red-Nosed Reindeer collectible thimbles and spoons, and little snow-covered villages.

We in the coastal metro Blue areas read more books and attend more   5
plays than the people in the Red heartland. We're more sophisticated and cosmopolitan—just ask us about our alumni trips to China or Provence, or our interest in Buddhism. But don't ask us, please, what life in Red America is like. We don't know. We don't know who Tim LaHaye and Jerry B. Jenkins are, even though the novels they have co-written have sold about 40 million copies over the past few years. We don't know what James Dobson says on his radio program, which is listened to by millions. We don't know about Reba or Travis. We don't know what happens in mega-churches on Wednesday evenings, and some of us couldn't tell you

the difference between a fundamentalist and an evangelical, let alone describe what it means to be a Pentecostal. Very few of us know what goes on in Branson, Missouri, even though it has seven million visitors a year, or could name even five NASCAR drivers, although stock-car races are the best-attended sporting events in the country. We don't know how to shoot or clean a rifle. We can't tell a military officer's rank by looking at his insignia. We don't know what soy beans look like when they're growing in a field.

All we know, or all we think we know, about Red America is that millions and millions of its people live quietly underneath flight patterns, many of them are racist and homophobic, and when you see them at highway rest stops, they're often really fat and their clothes are too tight. 6

And apparently we don't want to know any more than that. One can 7
barely find any books at Amazon.com about what it is like to live in smalltown America—or, at least, any books written by normal people who grew up in small towns, liked them, and stayed there. The few books that do exist were written either by people who left the heartland because they hated it (Bill Bryson's *The Lost Continent,* for example) or by urbanites who moved to Red America as part of some life-simplification plan (*Moving to a Small Town: A Guidebook for Moving from Urban to Rural America; National Geographic's Guide to Small Town Escapes*). Apparently no publishers or members of the Blue book-buying public are curious about Red America as seen through Red America's eyes.

Crossing the Meatloaf Line

Over the past several months, my interest piqued by those stark blocks of 8
color on the election-night maps, I have every now and then left my home in Montgomery County, Maryland, and driven sixty-five miles northwest to Franklin County, in south-central Pennsylvania. Montgomery County is one of the steaming-hot centers of the great espresso machine that is Blue America. It is just over the border from northwestern Washington, D.C., and it is full of upper-middle-class towns inhabited by lawyers, doctors, stockbrokers, and establishment journalists like me—towns like Chevy Chase, Potomac, and Bethesda (where I live). Its central artery is a burgeoning high-tech corridor with a multitude of sparkling new office parks housing technology companies such as United Information Systems and Sybase, and pioneering biotech firms such as Celera Genomics and Human Genome Sciences. When I drive to Franklin County, I take Route 270. After about forty-five minutes I pass a Cracker Barrel—Red America condensed into chain-restaurant form. I've crossed the Meatloaf Line; from here on there will be a lot fewer sun-dried-tomato concoctions on restaurant menus and a lot more meatloaf platters.

Franklin County is Red America. It's a rural county, about twenty-five   9
miles west of Gettysburg, and it includes the towns of Waynesboro, Chambersburg, and Mercersburg. It was originally settled by the Scotch-Irish, and has plenty of Brethren and Mennonites along with a fast-growing population of evangelicals. The joke that Pennsylvanians tell about their state is that it has Philadelphia on one end, Pittsburgh on the other, and Alabama in the middle. Franklin County is in the Alabama part. It strikes me as I drive there that even though I am going north across the Mason-Dixon line, I feel as if I were going south. The local culture owes more to Nashville, Houston, and Daytona than to Washington, Philadelphia, or New York.

I shuttled back and forth between Franklin and Montgomery Counties   10
because the cultural differences between the two places are great, though the geographic distance is small. The two places are not perfect microcosms of Red and Blue America. The part of Montgomery County I am here describing is largely the Caucasian part. Moreover, Franklin County is in a Red part of a Blue state: overall, Pennsylvania went for Gore. And I went to Franklin County aware that there are tremendous differences within Red America, just as there are within Blue. Franklin County is quite different from, say, Scottsdale, Arizona, just as Bethesda is quite different from Oakland, California.

Nonetheless, the contrasts between the two counties leap out, and they   11
are broadly suggestive of the sorts of contrasts that can be seen nationwide. When Blue America talks about social changes that convulsed society, it tends to mean the 1960s rise of the counterculture and feminism. When Red America talks about changes that convulsed society, it tends to mean World War II, which shook up old town establishments and led to a great surge of industry. . . .

From Cracks to a Chasm?

These differences are so many and so stark that they lead to some pretty   12
troubling questions: Are Americans any longer a common people? Do we have one national conversation and one national culture? Are we loyal to the same institutions and the same values? How do people on one side of the divide regard those on the other?

I went to Franklin County because I wanted to get a sense of how deep   13
the divide really is, to see how people there live, and to gauge how different their lives are from those in my part of America. I spoke with ministers, journalists, teachers, community leaders, and pretty much anyone I ran across. I consulted with pollsters, demographers, and market-research firms. Toward the end of my project the World Trade Center and the Pen-

tagon were attacked. This put a new slant on my little investigation. In the days immediately following September 11 the evidence seemed clear that despite our differences, we are still a united people. American flags flew everywhere in Franklin County and in Montgomery County. Patriotism surged. Pollsters started to measure Americans' reactions to the events. Whatever questions they asked, the replies were near unanimous. Do you support a military response against terror? More than four fifths of Americans said yes. Do you support a military response even if it means thousands of U.S. casualties? More than three fifths said yes. There were no significant variations across geographic or demographic lines.

A sweeping feeling of solidarity was noticeable in every neighborhood,   14
school, and workplace. Headlines blared, "A NATION UNITED" and "UNITED STATE." An attack had been made on the very epicenter of Blue America—downtown Manhattan. And in a flash all the jokes about and seeming hostility toward New Yorkers vanished, to be replaced by an outpouring of respect, support, and love. The old hostility came to seem merely a sort of sibling rivalry, which means nothing when the family itself is under threat.

But very soon there were hints that the solidarity was fraying. A few   15
stray notes of dissent were sounded in the organs of Blue America. Susan Sontag wrote a sour piece in *The New Yorker* about how depressing it was to see what she considered to be a simplistically pro-American reaction to the attacks. At rallies on college campuses across the country speakers pointed out that America had been bombing other countries for years, and turnabout was fair play. On one NPR talk show I heard numerous callers express unease about what they saw as a crude us-versus-them mentality behind President Bush's rhetoric. Katha Pollitt wrote in *The Nation* that she would not permit her daughter to hang the American flag from the living-room window, because, she felt, it "stands for jingoism and vengeance and war." And there was evidence that among those with less strident voices, too, differences were beginning to show. Polls revealed that people without a college education were far more confident than people with a college education that the military could defeat the terrorists. People in the South were far more eager than people in the rest of the country for an American counterattack to begin.

It started to seem likely that these cracks would widen once the American   16
response got under way, when the focus would be not on firemen and rescue workers but on the Marines, the CIA, and the special-operations forces. If the war was protracted, the cracks could widen into a chasm, as they did during Vietnam. Red America, the home of patriotism and military service (there's a big military-recruitment center in downtown Chambersburg), would

undoubtedly support the war effort, but would Blue America (there's a big gourmet dog bakery in downtown Bethesda) decide that a crude military response would only deepen animosities and make things worse?

So toward the end of my project I investigated Franklin County with a   17 heightened sense of gravity and with much more urgency. If America was not firmly united in the early days of the conflict, we would certainly not be united later, when the going got tough.

"The People Versus the Powerful"

There are a couple of long-standing theories about why America is divided.   18 One of the main ones holds that the division is along class lines, between the haves and the have-nots. This theory is popular chiefly on the left and can be found in the pages of *The American Prospect* and other liberal magazines; in news reports by liberal journalists such as Donald L. Barlett and James B. Steele, of *Time,* and in books such as *Middle Class Dreams* (1995), by the Clinton and Gore pollster Stanley Greenberg, and *America's Forgotten Majority: Why the White Working Class Still Matters* (2000), by the demographer Ruy Teixeira and the social scientist Joel Rogers.

According to this theory, during most of the twentieth century gaps in in-   19 come between the rich and the poor in America gradually shrank. Then came the information age. The rich started getting spectacularly richer, the poor started getting poorer, and wages for the middle class stagnated, at best. Over the previous decade, these writers emphasized, remuneration for top-level executives had skyrocketed: now the average CEO made 116 times as much as the average rank-and-file worker. Assembly-line workers found themselves competing for jobs against Third World workers who earned less than a dollar an hour. Those who had once labored at well-paying blue-collar jobs were forced to settle for poorly paying service-economy jobs without benefits.

People with graduate degrees have done well over the past couple of   20 decades: their real hourly wages climbed by 13 percent from 1979 to 1997, according to Teixeira and Rogers. But those with only some college education saw their wages fall by nine percent, while those with only high school diplomas saw their wages fall by 12 percent, and high school dropouts saw a stunning 26 percent decline in their pay.

Such trends have created a new working class, these writers argue—not   21 a traditional factory-and-mill working class but a suburban and small-town working class, made up largely of service workers and low-level white-collar employees. Teixeira and Rogers estimate that the average household income for this group, which accounts for about 55 percent of American adults, is roughly $42,000. "It is not hard to imagine how [recent economic trends] must have felt to the forgotten majority," they write.

As at least part of America was becoming ever more affluent, an afflu- 22
ence that was well covered on television and in the evening news, he did
not seem to be making much progress. What could he be doing wrong to
be faring so poorly? Why couldn't he afford what others could? And why
were they moving ahead while he was standing still? Stanley Greenberg tailored Al Gore's presidential campaign to appeal to such voters. Gore's most
significant slogan was "The People Versus the Powerful," which was meant
to rally members of the middle class who felt threatened by "powerful
forces" beyond their control, such as HMOs, tobacco companies, big corporations, and globalization, and to channel their resentment against the
upper class. Gore dressed down throughout his campaign in the hope that
these middle-class workers would identify with him.

Driving from Bethesda to Franklin County, one can see that the theory 23
of a divide between the classes has a certain plausibility. In Montgomery
County we have Saks Fifth Avenue, Carrier, Anthropologie, Brooks Brothers. In Franklin County they have Dollar General and Value City, along
with a plethora of secondhand stores. It's as if Franklin County has only
forty-five coffee tables, which are sold again and again.

When the locals are asked about their economy, they tell a story very 24
similar to the one that Greenberg, Teixeira, Rogers, and the rest of the
wage-stagnation liberals recount. There used to be plenty of good factory
jobs in Franklin County, and people could work at those factories for life.
But some of the businesses, including the textile company J. Schoeneman,
once Franklin County's largest manufacturer, have closed. Others have
moved offshore. The remaining manufacturers, such as Grove Worldwide
and JLG Industries, which both make cranes and aerial platforms, have
laid off workers. The local Army depot, Letterkenny, has radically shrunk
its work force. The new jobs are in distribution centers or nursing homes.
People tend to repeat the same phrase: "We've taken some hits."

And yet when they are asked about the broader theory, whether there 25
is class conflict between the educated affluents and the stagnant middles,
they stare blankly as if suddenly the interview were being conducted in
Aramaic. I kept asking, Do you feel that the highly educated people
around, say, New York and Washington are getting all the goodies? Do you
think there is resentment toward all the latte sippers who shop at Neiman
Marcus? Do you see a gulf between high-income people in the big cities and
middle-income people here? I got only polite, fumbling answers as people
tried to figure out what the hell I was talking about.

When I rephrased the question in more-general terms, as Do you believe 26
the country is divided between the haves and the have-nots?, everyone responded decisively: yes. But as the conversation continued, it became clear

that the people saying yes did not consider themselves to be among the have-nots. Even people with incomes well below the median thought of themselves as haves. . . .

Hanging around Franklin County, one begins to understand some of 27
the reasons that people there don't spend much time worrying about economic class lines. The first and most obvious one is that although the incomes in Franklin County are lower than those in Montgomery County, living expenses are also lower—very much so. Driving from Montgomery County to Franklin County is like driving through an invisible deflation machine. Gas is thirty, forty, or even fifty cents a gallon cheaper in Franklin County. I parked at meters that accepted only pennies and nickels. When I got a parking ticket in Chambersburg, the fine was $3.00. At the department store in Greencastle there were racks and racks of blouses for $9.99.

The biggest difference is in real-estate prices. In Franklin County one 28
can buy a nice four-bedroom split-level house with about 2,200 square feet of living space for $150,000 to $180,000. In Bethesda that same house would cost about $450,000. (According to the Coldwell Banker Real Estate Corporation, that house would sell for $784,000 in Greenwich, Connecticut; for $812,000 in Manhattan Beach, California; and for about $1.23 million in Palo Alto, California.)

Some of the people I met in Franklin County were just getting by. Some 29
were in debt and couldn't afford to buy their kids the Christmas presents they wanted to. But I didn't find many who assessed their own place in society according to their income. Rather, the people I met commonly told me that although those in affluent places like Manhattan and Bethesda might make more money and have more-exciting jobs, they are the unlucky ones, because they don't get to live in Franklin County. They don't get to enjoy the beautiful green hillsides, the friendly people, the wonderful church groups and volunteer organizations. They may be nice people and all, but they are certainly not as happy as we are.

Another thing I found is that most people don't think sociologically. 30
They don't compare themselves with faraway millionaires who appear on their TV screens. They compare themselves with their neighbors. "One of the challenges we face is that it is hard to get people to look beyond the fourstate region," Lynne Woehrle, a sociologist at Wilson College, in Chambersburg, told me, referring to the cultural zone composed of the nearby rural areas in Pennsylvania, West Virginia, Maryland, and Virginia. Many of the people in Franklin County view the lifestyles of the upper class in California or Seattle much the way we in Blue America might view the lifestyle of someone in Eritrea or Mongolia—or, for that matter, Butte,

Montana. Such ways of life are distant and basically irrelevant, except as a source of academic interest or titillation. One man in Mercersburg, Pennsylvania, told me about a friend who had recently bought a car. "He paid twenty-five thousand dollars for that car!" he exclaimed, his eyes wide with amazement. "He got it fully loaded." I didn't tell him that in Bethesda almost no one but a college kid pays as little as $25,000 for a car.

Franklin County is a world in which there is little obvious inequality, 31 and the standard of living is reasonably comfortable. Youth-soccer teams are able to raise money for a summer trip to England; the Lowe's hardware superstore carries Laura Ashley carpets; many people have pools, although they are almost always above ground; the planning commission has to cope with an increasing number of cars in the county every year, even though the population is growing only gradually. But the sort of high-end experiences that are everywhere in Montgomery County are entirely missing here.

On my journeys to Franklin County, I set a goal: I was going to spend 32 $20 on a restaurant meal. But although I ordered the most expensive thing on the menu—steak au jus, "slippery beef pot pie" or whatever—I always failed. I began asking people to direct me to the most-expensive places in town. They would send me to Red Lobster or Applebee's. I'd go into a restaurant that looked from the outside as if it had some pretensions— maybe a "Les Desserts" glass cooler for the key-lime pie and the tapioca pudding. I'd scan the menu and realize that I'd been beaten once again. I went through great vats of chipped beef and "seafood delight" trying to drop twenty dollars. I waded through enough surf-and-turfs and enough creamed corn to last a lifetime. I could not do it.

No wonder people in Franklin County have no class resentment or class 33 consciousness; where they live, they can afford just about anything that is for sale. (In Montgomery County, however—and this is one of the most striking contrasts between the two counties—almost nobody can say that. In Blue America, unless you are very, very rich, there is always, all around you, stuff for sale that you cannot afford.) And if they sought to improve their situation, they would look only to themselves. If a person wants to make more money, the feeling goes, he or she had better work hard and think like an entrepreneur.

I could barely get fifteen minutes into an interview before the local 34 work ethic came up. Karen Jewell, who helps to oversee the continuing-education program for the local Penn State branch campus, told me, "People are very vested in what they do. There's an awareness of where they fit in the organization. They feel empowered to be agents of change." People do work extremely hard in Franklin County, even people in supposedly dead-end jobs. You can see it in little things, such as drugstore shelves. The drugstores in Bethesda look the way Rome must have looked after a visit from the Visigoths. But in Franklin County the boxes are in perfect little rows. Shelves are fully stocked, and cans are evenly spaced. The floors are less dusty than those in a microchip-processing plant. The nail clippers on a rack by the cash register are arranged with a precision that would put the Swiss to shame. . . .

A Cafeteria Nation

These differences in sensibility don't in themselves mean that America has 35 become a fundamentally divided nation. As the sociologist Seymour Martin Lipset pointed out in *The First New Nation* (1963), achievement and equality are the two rival themes running throughout American history. Most people, most places, and most epochs have tried to intertwine them in some way.

Moreover, after bouncing between Montgomery and Franklin Counties, I became convinced that a lot of our fear that America is split into rival camps arises from mistaken notions of how society is shaped. Some of us still carry the old Marxist categories in our heads. We think that society is like a layer cake, with the upper class on top. And, like Marx, we tend to assume that wherever there is class division there is conflict. Or else we have a sort of *Crossfire* model in our heads: where would people we meet sit if they were guests on that show?

But traveling back and forth between the two counties was not like 37 crossing from one rival camp to another. It was like crossing a high school cafeteria. Remember high school? There were nerds, jocks, punks, bikers, techies, druggies, God Squadders, drama geeks, poets, and Dungeons & Dragons weirdoes. All these cliques were part of the same school: they had different sensibilities; sometimes they knew very little about the people in the other cliques; but the jocks knew there would always be nerds, and the nerds knew there would always be jocks. That's just the way life is.

And that's the way America is. We are not a divided nation. We are a 38 cafeteria nation. We form cliques (call them communities, or market segments, or whatever), and when they get too big, we form subcliques. Some people even get together in churches that are "nondenominational" or in political groups that are "independent." These are cliques built around the supposed rejection of cliques.

We live our lives by migrating through the many different cliques asso- 39 ciated with the activities we enjoy and the goals we have set for ourselves. Our freedom comes in the interstices; we can choose which set of standards to live by, and when.

We should remember that there is generally some distance between 40 cliques—a buffer zone that separates one set of aspirations from another.

People who are happy within their cliques feel no great compulsion to go out and reform other cliques. The jocks don't try to change the nerds.

What unites the two Americas, then, is our mutual commitment to this way 41
of life—to the idea that a person is not bound by his class, or by the religion of his fathers, but is free to build a plurality of connections for himself. We are participants in the same striving process, the same experimental journey.

Never has this been more apparent than in the weeks following the Sep- 42
tember 11 attacks. Before then Montgomery County people and Franklin County people gave little thought to one another: an attitude of benign neg-lect toward other parts of the country generally prevailed. But the events of that day generated what one of my lunch mates in Franklin County called a primal response. Our homeland was under attack. Suddenly there was a positive sense that we Americans are all bound together—a sense that, de-spite some little fissures here and there, has endured.

On September 11 people in Franklin County flocked to the institutions 43
that are so strong there—the churches and the American Legion and the VFW posts. Houses of worship held spontaneous prayer services and large ecumenical services. In the weeks since, firemen, veterans, and Scouts have held rallies. There have been blood drives. Just about every service organ-ization in the county—and there are apparently thousands—has mobilized to raise funds or ship teddy bears. The rescue squad and the Salvation Army branch went to New York to help. . . .

If the September 11 attacks rallied people in both Red and Blue America, 44
they also neutralized the political and cultural leaders who tend to exploit the differences between the two. Americans are in no mood for a class struggle or a culture war. The aftermath of the attacks has been a bit like a national Sab-bath, taking us out of our usual pleasures and distractions and reminding us what is really important. Over time the shock will dissipate. But in important ways the psychological effects will linger, just as the effects of John F. Kennedy's assassination have lingered. The early evidence still holds: although there are some real differences between Red and Blue America, there is no fundamental conflict. There may be cracks, but there is no chasm. Rather, there is a com-mon love for this nation—one nation in the end.

Thinking Critically

1. David Brooks's writing style is immediately recognizable to anyone who has read his criticism of consumer culture. How would you describe his style, and how do you react to it? For whom—and about whom—do you think Brooks is writing?

2. What are the characteristics of red and blue America, as defined by Brooks? What are the most important indicators of being either red or blue?

3. How did the events of September 11, 2001, change Brooks's purpose in writing this article? Do you think those events changed the way Brooks approached and interpreted the evidence he was gathering?

Writing Critically

1. Rebecca Skloot and David Brooks use similar organizational strategies and gather similar kinds of information to support their claims about a divided American culture. In an essay, compare "Two Americas, Two Restaurants, One Town" and "One Nation, Slightly Divisible." Which essay makes a stronger, more coherent argument, and why?

2. In an essay, discuss the two Americas Brooks finds with the two hypothetical communities described in Scott Russell Sanders's "Common Wealth" (see pp. 292–99). According to Brooks's criteria, which of the two communities that Sanders imagines would be red, and which would be blue?

3. In 2004, journalist Sasha Issenberg decided to follow Brooks's travels in "One Nation, Slightly Divisible." In an article published in the April 2004 issue of *Philadelphia* magazine—available online at <http://www.phillymag.com/ArticleDisplay.php?id=350>—Issenberg systematically challenged and refuted many of Brooks's observations, including his attempt to spend more than $20 on a restaurant meal in Franklin County. Issenberg interviewed Brooks and asked him to explain some of the inconsistencies his research had turned up. In reply, Brooks said that Issenberg was taking the article "too literally." Issenberg also asked Brooks how a reader was supposed to distinguish between comedy and sociology. "Generally, I rely on intelligent readers to know—and I think that at the *Atlantic Monthly,* every intelligent reader can tell what the difference is," Brooks replied. (Later in Issenberg's account, Brooks becomes considerably less patient and polite with the young reporter's inquiries.) In an essay, consider Issenberg's charges and their impact on Brooks's credibility. To what extent is it acceptable, even expected, for a writer to adjust the evidence to suit his claim?

The Plains vs. the Atlantic: Is Middle America a Backwater, or a Reservoir?

BLAKE HURST

As noted in the "Writing Critically" questions following David Brooks's article "One Nation, Slightly Divisible," writers across the political spectrum challenged Brooks's approach and observations. One of the most thoughtful responses came from Blake Hurst, a contributing writer at the conservative and, in its own words, "fiercely independent" *American Enterprise* magazine. Hurst, a farmer and greenhouse grower who lives in the small town of Tarkio, Missouri, also writes for the *Kansas City Star* and on agricultural topics for numerous other publications. He has long been active in regional agriculture and community groups, serving as chairman of the Missouri State Farm Bureau's Young Farmers and Ranchers Committee and serving on the American Farm Bureau's Young Farmers and Ranchers National Committee.

L ike an anthropologist touring deepest, darkest Africa, the writer David   1
Brooks has courageously trekked to Middle America, studied the natives there, and reported back to readers of *The Atlantic Monthly,* one of the nation's toniest opinion magazines. He reports that out here in Red America (as the last election maps dubbed George Bush country) we're dumber, poorer, fatter, and less well dressed than those in Blue America (the parts of the country that voted for Al Gore). At least, his data shows, our wives have more orgasms.

Brooks didn't do his investigating in actual fly-over country—not as far   2
as I'm concerned anyway. His model for Red America was Franklin County, Pennsylvania (population 121,000). Brooks says Pennsylvanians joke that their state has "Philadelphia on one end, Pittsburgh on the other, and Alabama in the middle." Well, maybe, but any state that calls Arlen Specter a Republican isn't truly Red America.

According to Brooks, "We in the coastal Blue areas read more books   3
and attend more plays than the people in the Red heartland. We're more sophisticated and cosmopolitan—just ask about our alumni trips to China or Provence, or our interest in Buddhism. But don't ask us, please, what life in Red America is like. We don't know." Brooks goes on at great length to fill in readers about the results of his Pennsylvania trip. But he misses a few things. In fact, it's quite easy to imagine that many of the observations Brooks records as Red America gospel were actually examples of the deer hunters and truck drivers of Franklin County having a little fun with the Ivy Leaguer from inside the Beltway.

Brooks is exactly right, though, when he talks about how Middle Amer-   4
icans view their station on the economic ladder. He's surprised at the lack of class-consciousness, and Red Americans' willingness to consider themselves among the "haves," even when they're being paid at levels that wouldn't convince yuppie teenagers in Blue America to leave the house.

Charles Murray has pointed out that true wealth in America is limited to the few entrepreneurs and inheritors of wealth who make up the Forbes 400 . . . plus the upper income folks living in small-town America.

The combination of progressive taxation and urban real-estate prices   5 ensures that almost nobody on the coasts has more spendable income than the highest paid people in Franklin County or the rest of rural Red America. People here in Missouri's small towns can buy a beautiful older home for less than $100,000. Brooks makes much of the fact that he literally could not spend more than $20 for a meal in Franklin County. The fare in Red America is a bit limited. You can't buy one of those meals with a dime-sized entree in the middle of a huge plate, with some sort of sauce artfully squirted about. But you can buy a pound of prime rib for ten bucks. Class-consciousness isn't a problem in Red America, because most people can afford to buy everything that's for sale.

Brooks touches on the non-pretentious nature of Red Americans. The   6 guy in threadbare overalls just behind you at the parts counter may well be a multimillionaire. And Brooks is on target when he talks about the reaction Franklin County residents would have to a Lexus. A foreign-made car on Main Street of my small town is a sure indicator of a visitor, and it will be the only car in the whole town with its doors locked. The status vehicle here, of course, is a large SUV.

The lack of pretension extends to the way we dress. Our jeans are dirty   7 not because they're rarely washed, but because we work with grease, dirt, or steel. That ground-in grime is a badge of a day's work well done. And no, Mr. Brooks, those are not pocket-knives connected to those strings and chains you noticed extending from Red America's pockets, but wallets big enough to hold all the information in your Palm Pilot, plus the receipts from last week's business.

We are, for sure, fatter than the rest of America. But there's a certain   8 freedom in a paunch, as it says to all that the work we do can be measured in bushels, pounds, shingles nailed, and bricks laid, rather than the fussy judgments that make up office employee reviews. And a little extra weight helps when you have to "grab aholt" of heavy things and make them move.

Contentment with one's lot may well be the greatest difference between   9 Red and Blue America. People living in the great middle are perfectly happy to be slightly overweight, a little underpaid, and dressed in fashions that cause comment when we interact with our betters. We aren't overly impressed with formal credentials, often commenting that so and so is "educated beyond his level of competence." My congressman happens to be from our small town, and when he's home on the weekends, he's shingling his house. His constituents are proud of the fact that their representative can run a nail gun, and is still humble enough to get his hands dirty. Just the same, the project has taken over a year, and we all think it's time he finished.

We respect formal learning, but we value practicality over more esoteric 10 fields of knowledge, and treasure self-sufficiency above all. "Settle down and go to work. Keep your mind on your own business. Think about what you're doing. Buckle down." All of these sayings, repeated ad nauseam in the workplace, on sporting fields, and at schools across Red America, are exhortations to seriousness, concentration, and the unfrivolous business of getting jobs done in the safest and most efficient manner.

Brooks details the religious differences between Red and Blue America, 11 recognizes that we Red Americans have different religious beliefs than Blue Americans, and includes the familiar statistic that church attendance is a better predictor of voting patterns than is income (or most any other factor). But he finds no indication that Red America is about to man the ramparts in a culture war.

Blue America should really relax about this whole subject and quit wor- 12 rying about people with bad haircuts showing up at their front doors talking about Jesus. Small-town Americans have to balance what we say and do with the necessity of getting along with the people we live with: people who have kids in the same schools, who do business with us, are on the school board with us, and may well go to the same church. As Brooks points out, living in a small town often leads to a greater level of tolerance, because we interact with everyone around us on so many levels. There are no anonymous store clerks or people in line at the checkout counter. Not only do we know the person ahead of us, but we can probably tell you the color of his pickup and may even remember the time he scored the winning touchdown in 1973.

And our religious beliefs do inform the way we vote and how we regard 13 our public officials. We seldom debate politics or culture openly here, because we already know what our neighbors think. Our beliefs are not monolithic, but everyone knows his neighbors so well that he can predict how they'll react to most political questions. And by and large, all of us are pretty disgusted with the culture of Blue America.

Most interesting about Brooks' article is that it is impossible to imag- 14 ine a piece written from the opposite perspective. Would *The Atlantic* pay my way to go prowling around Chevy Chase, or the Hamptons, or Marin County, contrasting the culture there with the one I'm familiar with? Not likely. It's not that subscriptions to *The Atlantic* aren't sold in my part of the world. We Red America residents are much better informed about Blue America than the reverse.

A certain arrogance explains the lack of reciprocal interest. It seems 15 that Blue Americans just can't imagine that the rest of the country isn't downright envious of the way they think, or dress, or spend their days. The differences between the two parts of the country can no longer be assigned to the provincialism of Middle Americans. The deregulation of airlines and communications, the Interstate system, and mail order have guaranteed that our exposure to coastal life is easy and cheap. Red America is peppered with satellite dishes, Internet connections, and book club memberships. In fact, these links may well be responsible for accentuating the nation's cultural divide. From the Playboy Channel to Johnnie Cochran to non-stop news about Monica, we get a bellyful of Blue America whether we want to or not.

Brooks recognizes that "one can barely find any books at Amazon.com   16
about . . . small-town America—or at least, any books written by normal people who grew up in small towns, liked them, and stayed there." He describes how any books about my part of the country are "either by people who left the heartland because they hated it (Bill Bryson's *The Lost Continent,* for example), or by urbanites who moved to Red America as a part of some life-simplification plan." Brooks concludes: "Apparently no publishers or members of the Blue book-buying public are curious about Red America as seen through Red America's eyes."

The real reason for the lack of books about America's heartland by the   17
people who actually live here is the assumption that small-town residents can't possibly live rich and interesting lives without Starbucks, modern art, and expensive universities. Brooks himself confides that he wouldn't want to live in Red America, because he finds our way of life "too unchanging." If one is happy, though, change isn't eagerly anticipated.

Most Red Americans can't deconstruct post-modern literature, give   18
proper orders to a nanny, pick out a cabernet with aftertones of licorice, or quote prices from the Abercrombie and Fitch catalog. But we can raise great children, wire our own houses, make beautiful and delicious creations with our two hands, talk casually and comfortably about God, repair a small engine, recognize a good maple sugar tree, tell you the histories of our towns and the hopes of our neighbors, shoot a gun and run a chainsaw without fear, calculate the bearing load of a roof, grow our own asparagus, live in peace without car alarms, security guards, or therapists—even find the same wife a lifetime source of interest and joy.

Brooks is concerned that the differences between Red and Blue Amer-   19
ica will lead to a divided country, where the modes of living will be so different, and at such logger-heads, that common ground could be difficult to find. In truth, these divisions have always existed in our country, they're just now becoming emphasized. Sinclair Lewis wrote with love and hatred of Red America 80 years ago. I think most of the Snopeses worked on our

farm for a while when I was a kid. And reading Faulkner just reintroduced me to my grandfather's neighbors. Davy Crockett was outsmarting city slickers from under his coon skin cap nearly two centuries ago, and *Mr. Smith Goes to Washington* had a similar theme, contrasting rural values to the decadence of the nation's capital. The exceptional qualities of non-urban Americans are only an issue to the movers and shakers along the coasts when we surprise them by winning an election and the country doesn't go to hell in a handbasket after all.

One of the most interesting statistics that Brooks uses to contrast the 20 two Americas is the fact that only 53 percent of conservatives consider themselves intellectuals, while 75 percent of self-identified liberals do. In the Red America I know, humility is a cardinal virtue, and most of us wouldn't be caught dead calling ourselves intellectuals, though we do often identify ourselves as conservative.

We're used to subtle condescension about our smarts. Brooks quotes 21 SAT scores that show a marked difference between Waynesboro High in Franklin County and Walt Whitman High School in the D.C. suburb of Bethesda. It's not surprising that one of the richest suburbs in the country would have higher scoring students than Franklin County. The real estate prices in the Bethesda area limit the students there to the progeny of people able to shop for the best schools, while Waynesboro no doubt matriculates students from all strata of Franklin County society. Brooks doubts that the products of Franklin County schools can compete in college with urban students. But it has been my observation that students from smaller, less challenging schools catch up with urban students in about two semesters, as psychological stability and hard work compensate for any inadequacies in high-school education.

After his sortie into the minefield of SAT scores, Brooks pretty well leaves 22 the whole question of a Red-Blue intellectual gap alone, but it is certainly a subtext to his piece. While it's true that many of the best and brightest leave rural America at some point for college and city jobs, they often try to get back as soon as they can. Is it really so dumb to choose to live in a place where life is affordable, the roads aren't crowded, and you don't have to put up with obnoxious megalomaniacs and self-important snobs? Red America is full of smart people, as many employers are learning. It's just that intellect, like wealth, isn't flaunted here.

Veiled disdain for the intellectual wattage of the people of Middle 23 America helps explain the media's shock when individuals like John Ashcroft perform well—as he did at his Senate hearing and in his conduct since confirmation as attorney general. Critics of Ashcroft are quick to remind us of his small-town upbringing, and his unabashed faith, and his father (who was a preacher in a conservative church), using those facts as a sort of shorthand for narrow-mindedness, indicators that a person is probably not up to life in the fast lane. Those of us who have known John Ashcroft for a long time aren't the slightest bit surprised at his aplomb in facing his critics, and his job performance since. Anybody paying attention and not blinded by the fact that he comes from Red America, where priorities are merely different, not lower, could see that Ashcroft's background was excellent preparation for the demands of his current responsibilities.

Residents of the "less sophisticated" part of the nation see examples of intellectually and professionally inspiring natives all around us. My father-in-law, after a successful career as an electrical engineer conducting research in the nuclear field, returned to central Missouri and started an apple orchard. He listens to opera in German, the news in Spanish, and recently had an article about stress testing printed in a peer-reviewed journal after conducting his experiment with tools he had in his farm shop, along with a few items from his kitchen. My high-school class of 65 includes engineers, a dentist, and a lawyer who recently won a case before the Supreme Court. My long-time hired hand has a son who is an engineer for Microsoft. Examples like this aren't hard to find in most any part of Red America.

Aside from religion, one of the most marked differences between the two parts of our country is the way we think about the military. Red Americans and Blue Americans volunteer for military service at radically divergent rates, and we honor those who have served in the armed forces differently. It is a staple of post-Vietnam liberalism that black Americans bore an unfair burden during that war. That is not accurate—the black casualty rate in Vietnam tracked fairly closely with the minority population. It is, however, most certainly true that rural Americans, southerners in particular, bore a disproportionate part of our national fighting, then and in all engagements since. According to historian Victor Davis Hanson:

> The vast majority of those who fought in Vietnam as frontline combat troops—two thirds of whom were not drafted but volunteered—were disproportionately lower-income whites from southern and rural states. These were young men of a vastly different socioeconomic cosmos from the largely middle- and upper-class journalists who misrepresented them, the antiwar activists and academics who castigated them, and the generals of the military high command who led them so poorly.

The prayer list at my small Southern Baptist church is currently full of families with loved ones deployed to the Middle East or Central Asia. I wonder how many churches in Bethesda are similarly occupied. Every small town I travel through in my region has a monument in the city square, or a plaque at the city park, listing those who were lost in each of America's wars. The rosters run on and on. Red America may be deficient in producing poets and advertising men, but the guy who used to sell me gas was a paratrooper on D-Day, and I spent an interesting hour at my wedding reception with two close relatives, on different sides of the family, discussing their tours of duty in Korea. Red America is never redder than on our bloodiest battlefields. We may be thought of as hick cousins, we will always be caricatured for our faith in God, our children's accomplishments will probably be discounted by the most prestigious colleges, and Hollywood and Manhattan will always draw their rubes and villains in our clothes. But patriotism in Red America didn't have to be relearned after September 11. Selfless sacrifice is still an honored tradition in our communities, whether it takes place on the nation's battlefields or at home in the nursery.

Brooks ends his article wondering whether Americans will stay the   27
course in the war against terrorism. After ten pages of patronizing my neighbors and me it's interesting that he's not worried a bit about Red America's response to the terrorist threat. Instead, he frets over the ability of his Blue neighbors to find the sturdiness required to win the war. So on the most important question to face our nation in decades, the gut instincts of middle America are, despite our SAT scores, the right ones.

Farmers like me spend a lot of time worrying about the state of our   28
"subsoil moisture." In our part of the world, we almost never receive enough rain during the growing season to raise a successful crop, so we depend on the moisture stored in the deeper soil profile from late fall rains, winter snowstorms, and early spring downpours.

I often think that Red America serves as that same sort of reservoir   29
for the rest of the country, supplying the moral perception and practical instincts, the life-giving moisture of good citizenship, that are necessary to the long-run survival of our nation. The deep soil profile is never as impressive as good black topsoil, and there is much less organic activity down there. The top layer of soil is where most of the life is located. But a good charge of moisture in those deeper, more stable regions saves us time and again during the scorching days of July and August.

Our nation is enduring a fierce heat wave right now. And in its midst I,   30
for one, am very glad to have a group of men and women drawn primarily from the "less sophisticated" and "unchanging" midlands of our country leading us to our destiny.

Thinking Critically

1. What are the values that Hurst ascribes to people in blue states and people in red states? How are those values different from what Brooks describes?

2. Does Hurst use humor in his essay? Point out observations or uses of language in the essay that seem humorous, and explain what makes them funny.

Writing Critically

1. Hurst notes, dryly, that "it is impossible to imagine a piece written from the opposite perspective" of David Brooks's "One America, Slightly Divisible," and he remarks that the *Atlantic Monthly* probably wouldn't be interested in paying Hurst himself to conduct similar "research" in wealthy blue state communities. Take Hurst up on the challenge, and write an essay that follows the structure and adopts the strategies and tone of "One America, Slightly Divisible," but from what Hurst would consider a "Red American" perspective.

2. Hurst makes a compelling argument for the ways in which the explosion of media outlets and easy, inexpensive access to travel have contributed to "accentuating the nation's cultural divide." Write an essay in which you agree or disagree with Hurst's claim. Be sure to cite specific examples from the mass media (both news and entertainment) to support your argument.

3. Do you agree with Hurst that "If one is happy . . . change isn't eagerly anticipated"? Remember that, according to the Declaration of Independence, "life, liberty, and the pursuit of happiness" are "unalienable rights." How does Hurst understand this fundamental right to "happiness"? In an analytical essay and using extended definition, explain how different views of "happiness" have divided American culture.

The New Culture of Rural America

JEDEDIAH PURDY

Duke University assistant professor of law Jedediah Purdy published his first book, *For Common Things: Irony, Trust, and Commitment in America Today* (1999), when he was just twenty-four years old. If any publicity is better than no publicity, then Purdy certainly received his fair share of attention. The book's reviews ranged from the warmly welcoming ("Beautifully written, erudite, unpretentious and, most of all, earnest" wrote a reviewer in *Newsday*) to the chillingly condescending (the liberal online magazine *Salon.com* called *For Common Things* "a book of intellectual-fogy porn"). Purdy's thesis in that book was that the trend toward irony in late-twentieth-century popular culture revealed a great malaise and lack of faith and trust in American society. Home-schooled until age fourteen at his parents' West Virginia farm, Purdy went on to public high school and [30] then to Harvard University (where he majored in social studies) and to Yale Law School. Since writing his first book, Purdy has continued to contribute essays about American culture to periodicals such as the *Atlantic Monthly* and the *American Prospect* (where this essay appeared in December 1999). He has also published articles in legal journals on ethics and international law. Purdy's most recent book, *Being America: Liberty, Commerce, and Violence in an American World*, was published in 2003.

D uring the Roaring Twenties, President Calvin Coolidge had himself [1] photographed in a Vermont hayfield, a fresh pair of overalls covering his dress shirt, his black shoes still gleaming from their morning shine. Despite the incongruity, no one laughed. In 1994, after the Republican takeover of Congress, Bill Clinton's pollsters devised the model American vacation for a president on the defensive: a hiking and horseback-riding expedition to the high country of Wyoming. A few years later, when candidate Al Gore recalled pitching manure during summers on his father's Tennessee farm, the political press hooted as delightedly as if the vice president had claimed as his birthplace a log cabin on K Street.

These incidents are minor landmarks in a cultural shift more than 100 [2] years in the making. Although the idea was as much conceit as reality, America long thought of itself as essentially connected with farming and farm communities. According to this idea, landholding produced self-reliant, free-thinking citizens, unlike the immigrants of the cities who were dependent on their priests and party bosses. In a tradition famously identified with Jefferson, the man who worked the land was upright, reliable, uniquely able to serve his local village and defend his country.

That tradition was already in decline when Coolidge hurried through [3] his sham photograph, and since then, it has steadily lost plausibility. It has given way to the ideal that President Clinton enacted uncomfortably against the backdrop of Wyoming's mountains. In this ideal, nature is not a site of hard and fruitful work, but a source of recreational challenge, aesthetic inspiration, and spiritual solace; America is the country of pristine nature and rugged outdoors enthusiasts, home to the North Face, Patagonia, ubiquitous hiking boots, and the Nature Store, with its upscale bestiary of wild things. This is John Muir's America, in search of the places where, as Muir wrote of his beloved Sierra Nevada, there is "[nothing] truly dead or dull, or any trace of what in manufactories is called rubbish or waste; everything is perfectly clean and pure and full of divine lessons."

The transformation does not stop at photo opportunities or buying pat-   4
terns. It shows itself in economics, politics, and demographics, and the concert of changes is reworking the American countryside. If the pattern holds, farming as a way of life will mainly disappear within the next 50 years, large swaths of the country will be virtually depopulated, and the two coasts will be balanced by a third cultural and economic center in the valleys and peaks of the mountain West.

Trouble in the Heartland

Halfway out the flat and arid Oklahoma panhandle, Texas County used to   5
raise wheat, hay, cattle, and some—not many—hogs. In 1995 Seaboard Farms moved in to set up a giant pork slaughterhouse with more than $60 million in direct subsidies and tax breaks. To supply the plant, Seaboard set up hundreds of giant metal barns, each containing nearly 1,000 hogs. Texas County now raises more than a million hogs annually.

Seaboard produces as much sewage as the city of Philadelphia, and it   6
sits in open-air lagoons, some as large as 14 acres and as deep as 25 feet. Neighbors complain of intolerable stench, and everybody worries about water pollution. Because processing plants and, to a lesser extent, giant barns employ mainly immigrant labor, Texas County has absorbed more than 2,000 Mexican-American workers and their families. Many live in company-owned trailer parks with rent and utilities deducted from their paychecks, and thanks to wages that start at $6.25 an hour and an annual turnover rate of 120 percent, many draw food stamps. Since 1995 crimi-nal violence and property crime in the county have increased by more than half, while crime rates in surrounding counties have gone down.

Eight hundred miles north, in Lemmon, South Dakota, every other win-   7
dow on Main Street holds a sign announcing "America's Rural Crisis." Ex-cept for a few Jehovah's Witnesses in the area for a conference, everybody knows which crisis. For three years, wheat and cattle have sold below break-even levels; so have hogs and soybeans in the state's eastern half. Al-most all the local farmers and ranchers are in deep debt and are going deeper after each harvest. Farm families urge their children to find other work. Business has dropped by as much as a third in downtown shops, even though the regional Wal-Mart is still two hours away. Local social workers say that depression, domestic violence, and suicide are up markedly, and they expect more trouble if, in a year, the cautious local

banks begin foreclosing again. This downturn follows decades of steady population loss across a band of the High Plains running from Texas through Montana, which has put the population density of many counties below two people per square mile and has left large regions barely able to support a single town for shopping and social gatherings.

Sixty years ago, the typical midwestern farm ran between 80 and 300   8 acres—half of today's average size—and produced several kinds of grain, livestock, and hay, and a garden's worth of vegetables. Until tractors replaced them between 1920 and 1950, draft horses provided heavy labor, entire families worked the farm, and there was work to do in every season. Contrary to myth, farming west of Pennsylvania was never an old or especially settled existence. Pedigrees reached back at most a century, and for every family that remained, more had moved on, forced out by hard times or bought out by an expanding neighbor.

So it was the latest of many changes when, after the Second World War, a   9 farm economy that had been static since the beginning of the Depression opened up to big tractors, large amounts of chemical fertilizer, and herbicides and pesticides. Yields went up, competition stiffened, and vast numbers of farms disappeared during the 1950s. Within 20 years, almost every farm in the Midwest was on a two-crop rotation: corn and soybeans, the giant commodities of the heartland. In the early 1970s, a boom in grain exports brought a rush of wealth, farmers purchased a new generation of giant harvesting machinery, and ambitious operators again expanded their land. That bubble burst in the farm crisis of the 1980s, but when the upheaval shook out, the shape of agriculture was largely the same, minus several hundred thousand farmers.

In the past 10 years, however, farming has entered a dramatic new re-   10 structuring. The farmer is an anomalous link in a food-production chain that, on both sides of him, involves some of the world's most powerful and concentrated industries. It is as if auto production began with the manufacture of parts in great factories and ended with Ford and General Motors marketing cars and SUVs, but, in the middle, the parts were shipped out to several million small craftsmen who assembled them in their garages as best they could, then drove or shipped them to Detroit for painting, finishing, and quality checks. This odd arrangement has persisted partly because farmers have the land, partly because farming combines low returns with high risk—drought, flood, freeze, heat, or disease can wipe out a year's work in a day or a week—and corporate strategists have been content to leave the risk with farmers and let a sympathetic Congress provide bailouts when disaster strikes.

Now this is changing. The change began in poultry farming, long a part   11 of family farm operations. In the 1960s, meat-processing companies began contracting with farmers to raise chickens in large metal barns, becoming an integrated step in a single production chain. The chickens were delivered to the farmer as chicks and were retrieved as broilers; they never left the company's ownership. By 1980, except for a few specialty products, there was no place for independent chicken farmers to sell their birds. The poultry industry has become notorious for the low pay and dangerous work conditions of the employees who manhandle the birds, and for stream-killing pollution.

In the early 1990s, new technology made the same kind of confinement   12 possible for hogs. With antibiotic injections and climate control, raising animals suddenly required none of the skill and attention farmers had always maintained. As in poultry, tending pigs could become a low-wage job. Some meat-processing companies began contracting out hogs on the model of chickens, while others built their own massive barns. The pressure on small operators was intense. Between 1993 and 1998, more than 104,000 farmers raising 500 hogs or fewer gave up pigs or left farming altogether— a 55-percent reduction in six years. Meanwhile, the number raising more than 2,000 hogs increased by more than 2,300, or 53 percent, and the number with more than 5,000 hogs nearly doubled to just under 2,000. By 1998 the five largest pork companies raised about 19 million hogs, nearly a third of the number produced that year.

Market structure drives the new agriculture nearly as much as technol-   13 ogy. The top six pork processors slaughter three-quarters of the country's hogs, up from one-third in 1989, and they want a steady supply of cheap pigs whose quality they can control. The top four beef processors control 80 percent of their industry. Between 1993 and 1998, the number of farmers and ranchers raising fewer than 100 cattle dropped by 89,000, while the number with more than 500 head grew by more than 1,500, both movements of about 10 percent. Small operators face low prices on the cash market partly because processors prefer to arrange purchases well in advance with large ranchers or else raise their own cattle, leaving small operators to fill in last-minute gaps.

Similar market concentration is half the reason that grain farming may   14 be in for a reworking as well. In processing corn and soybeans and milling flour, the top four companies control between 57 and 80 percent of operations. Two companies, Archer Daniels Midland (ADM) and Cargill, are among the top four in all three areas and have been buying up smaller competitors for 20 years. (Cargill is also among the largest beef and pork packers and is the fifth-largest owner of feedlots, the stage of cattle raising between the ranch and the slaughterhouse.) The other half of the reason grain is ripe for a rehaul is biotechnology. Genetic engineering is just finding its feet in seed production, and already two-fifths of the nation's soybean crop is genetically modified and millions of acres of corn carry a gene that poisons the most common insect pest. These seeds carry patents, which mean 21-year monopolies on the best seed varieties, renewable with each new modification. Seeing the potential for profits, biotech companies have purchased seed companies and, seeking to ensure markets for their plant lines, have allied themselves with grain-processing companies.

Cargill, one of the largest seed firms in the world, sold its seed division 15 to the chemical and biotech company Monsanto in 1998. The two then announced a joint venture, including acquiring control of the "terminator gene," which sterilizes second-generation seeds and so ensures that farmers must buy new seeds from the manufacturer each year. Although the terminator gene was shelved in the face of political pressure and scientific uncertainty about its ecological consequences, technological ways of ensuring that farmers buy more from the chemical and biotech industries develop apace. Monsanto also owns the predominant transgenic soybean "Roundup Ready," which is designed to survive applications of Monsanto's popular and deadly Roundup herbicide. ADM has developed several joint ventures with Novartis, a Swiss biotech firm that has been expanding rapidly. As in pork and poultry, farmers face increasingly concentrated and coordinated markets at both ends of their operations.

And so a long-running trend is reinforced: As agriculture becomes more ex- 16 pensive and more productive, its natural scale is less and less that of the small farm. This is true partly because of the sheer advantage of size, partly because of the shape of agricultural markets, and partly because as technology becomes more powerful, the individual farmer's knowledge of his animals and his land becomes more superfluous. In 1900 farmers received 21 cents out of every dollar spent on agriculture; today they get a nickel, with the difference going to fertilizer, seed, chemical, equipment, and processing companies. Farmers' portion has fallen 13 percent since 1979 alone. Sixty percent of the income that remains goes to the 6 percent of American farms that are genuinely large.

All of this came home with a vengeance after 1996, when Congress 17 ended the price supports that had kept many small farmers on the right side of a tight margin. As technology makes size important and skill dispensable, the hog barns of Texas County look more like the future. It is becoming conventional wisdom in much of the Midwest and Great Plains that in the future a few large farmer-managers will grow grain on contract for seed-and-processing conglomerates, completing the same cycle that governs poultry and is reshaping pork farming. Where farming is the only economy, which it is in much of the already depopulating region east of the Rockies, the landscape would become little more than an empty plantation. It is a plausible prediction.

High Country Boom

The change in farming contributes to its decline as a cultural icon. Ameri-   18
cans understand that their farmers are not rough-handed husbandmen, but
investors, managers, and heavy-equipment operators who, when not planting or harvesting their one or two crops, have a lot of time on their hands.
Giant hog barns and Roundup Ready soybeans resist romanticizing. Also,
as the number of farmers has plummeted, so has the number of people with
childhood memories of a father's or grandfather's farm or even a cousin
still on the land. Finally, in a culture impatient with its crises, the eruption
of concern, sympathetic films, and fundraising concerts that accompanied
the farm crisis of the 1980s is unlikely to repeat itself; Americans, especially
media programmers, are not attracted to two-time losers.

Instead, the defining American encounter with nature now expresses a   19
delight in rugged scenery and equally rugged activity that, since its origin
with aristocrats such as Teddy Roosevelt and popular adventurers like
John Muir, has become a staple of middle-class taste. Visits to national
parks have increased dramatically; the growth has been even greater in
sales of outdoor gear, which announces a spirit of ruggedness even in the
absence of opportunities to practice it. And more Americans are finding
ways to live in the settings they have come to love.

Except for a few counties in Colorado and New Mexico, the mountain   20
West grew little in the 1980s. Then, in the first six years of the 1990s, a
thick band of the West, including much of Colorado, mountain New Mexico, western Montana, Idaho, northern Nevada, and parts of Utah grew
more than 15 percent. Census estimates extending to 2005 project growth
over 20 percent for only five states nationwide, all in the region, and over
15 percent for Wyoming, Montana, and Colorado. (These states are divided between the declining Great Plains and the booming Rockies, and
growth in the mountains is as great as in the five super-boom states.) Both
population and economic growth have clustered around striking landscapes, especially federal lands: the Yellowstone region of Montana and
Wyoming, where a condominium in one of many fast-growing developments costs at least $300,000; Jackson Hole, Wyoming, which recently
tried to stem middle-income flight from high housing prices by offering
subsidies to families with annual incomes near $80,000; and Boulder, Col-
orado, where a new tract house costs close to $200,000 and larger, well-
situated homes press quickly into the millions.

Population figures do not reflect the full influx into the region. Tourism   21
has also increased rapidly, and expensive second homes dot lake shores and
mountain valleys in the most desired regions. All these shifts come because
the nation's love of the outdoors has grown at the same time as enormous

wealth on both coasts. That and growth in telecommuting have been enough to convince many that if they can have mountains in their backyards, they almost certainly should.

The new western economy has another side. Montana, whose moun- 22 tain regions have grown quickly and have attracted the likes of Harrison Ford and Ted Turner, has seen its average wage fall to 49th in the nation as hotel and restaurant jobs have expanded to take in most of its low-skill work force. While the state's mining and timber industries—now devastated by mechanization and a much deserved two-thirds reduction in timbering on federal lands—were heavily unionized and paid high wages, organizers from the Hotel Employees and Restaurant Employees International Union estimate that less than 5 percent of workers in their industry hold a union card. Wages run near the federal minimum. Organizing is all the harder because local employees are leavened with a population of transient, young outdoors enthusiasts from affluent homes, who have come for the gorgeous landscape and have no interest in union politics. In regions with longer-standing tourism wealth, such as Vail, Colorado, trailer parks in valleys command views of the ridgetop homes whose owners the trailer residents serve.

An even more basic paradox haunts monied newcomers to the moun- 23 tains. They come for open spaces, uncrowded hiking trails, uncluttered vistas, and, in many cases, intact communities of manageable size. Yet as they pour in, they threaten to undo the same qualities that have drawn them. Land is scarcer than maps suggest, with huge pieces of the Rockies in federal ownership and many slopes too steep for building. Views are many miles long, and a population density that could be invisible in the folded, forested East makes for a crowded western landscape. East of the continental divide, the region is arid, and pressure on water systems mounts rapidly. In some valleys, temperature inversions turn exhaust fumes and wood smoke into severe air pollution.

Unsurprisingly, then, some of the most adamant opponents of further 24 growth are recent arrivals. Many come in an echo of Daniel Boone's apocryphal remark that he felt crowded enough to move westward when the first neighbor came into view. That attitude depends on the availability of open space, and it is threatened by the approaching close of the development frontier, a century after Frederick Jackson Turner famously declared the closing of the first. There is a slightly alarmed quality in Montana's billing itself "the last best place." Moreover, many new residents not only chose the mountains but also rejected the cities they left, sometimes because of distaste for racial diversity and urban—usually Democratic—politics. A monied, edgy libertarianism affects western politics and has contributed to the election of far-right senators and representatives in a region once known for its progressive politicians.

After the Frontier

American farming and American real-estate development share a debt to the   25
frontier. Just as we are building up the West as if the valleys and vistas would
not end, so we have never farmed in the manner of a people who expect to
live in a place for a long time and have thought about what staying will require. Under Texas County, Oklahoma, and much of the Plains, the Ogalalla
Aquifer is estimated to have perhaps 50 years of water left at current irrigation rates. When it is gone, a good deal of the region's farming will end as
well. Already, spring-fed rivers have dried up as the water table has dropped.
Throughout the country, we have turned an activity that is at once productive, nonpolluting, and self-renewing into one that is only productive. We do
this by isolating the elements of agriculture: concentrating livestock so that
manure turns from a fertilizer to a pollutant; sapping soil of its nutrients each
year and rebuilding it with chemical fertilizer mined abroad (phosphorous)
or blasted out of compressed, super-heated air (nitrogen) and which creates
large pollution problems of its own; controlling weeds and pests with poisons whose effect on human health is often poorly documented; and permitting topsoil erosion at many times the natural rate of replenishment.

It seems to be the tendency of a frontier economy that has run out of   26
room to create sacrifice zones, areas used badly or ruinously to support the
comfort of neighboring regions. Our massive diversion of Western water
to the irrigated fields of California's Central Valley fits this idea, as do the
draining of the Ogalalla, the willing loss of topsoil, and the transformation
of regions like Texas County into hard-luck rural industrial sites.

There are better ways of governing both farming and growth, but they   27
require clarity about what we are doing and why we are doing it. Better
planning of growth faces considerable cultural resistance in the West, but
it will be necessary if the region's attractions are to be preserved, and that
fact may move self-interest to impose restraints alien to both locals' and
newcomers' sensibilities. There are more innovative approaches to preserving open space as well. Several private land-trust organizations in
Montana have put more than half a million acres under permanent conservation easements. They buy or receive as gifts the development rights on
both wild land and ranches, which they then permanently retire. On the
latter, ranching continues, but subdivision will never come. There are similar organizations throughout the West. Farther afield, speculative policy
thinkers have proposed taxing each new acre of development enough to
buy and retire development rights on another acre of land. The proportion

could be greater or smaller, but the central idea is exactly right: We will run out of open space, and we need to decide how much we want to preserve forever and set about doing so at a pace to match its disappearance.

Preserving open land always involves the question of who is to benefit   28 from the land, and this issue is highlighted in the land politics of the West. It is a familiar and often deserved charge that growth controls benefit those whose houses are already built. More striking is that a great deal of the money behind Montana's land-conservation easements comes from the New York financial community, whose leaders have long enjoyed hunting and fishing in the state and would like to keep their favorite regions open— and free of lower-income interlopers. A system of tax-financed conservation easements would require deciding whether to create limited public access for preserved land, so that anyone could tramp through otherwise private woods or cut through a field while hiking. An economy based on sacrifice zones inspires compensation in beauty zones, the national parks being an especially noble example, and who shares in those is a question of first importance.

In farming, any improvement would mean first ending our politics'   29 false piety toward the family farm. The elaborate and expensive price controls that ended in 1996 were never intended to stop the trend toward consolidation. Today the country's basic policy is to step aside as the market passes by. This year's frantic debate over a bailout package was a bit of costly backwash in a river running the other way.

A more serious approach to agricultural policy would begin with the   30 environmental effects of today's agriculture. Although farming has long been one of the country's most regulated areas by virtue of its complex subsidies, it has substantially escaped environmental regulation. Farmers impose environmental harm on everyone else through the fertilizer runoff that chokes rivers and fouls groundwater, through haphazardly governed pesticides, and through topsoil erosion. Large-scale, consolidated agriculture often does more harm than the smaller sort: Huge fields lack brakes against erosion, standardized fertilizer and pesticide application often means applying too much to many sites, and large operations are less able than smaller ones to replace chemical inputs with on-farm substitutes like crop rotation and manure. North Carolina got an object lesson in the hazards of size this fall when Hurricane Floyd burst manure lagoons and left thousands of drowned pigs strewn across the state's river bottoms. When the rest of the country absorbs these costs, the result is a very large subsidy to farmers, one that is too large in proportion to each farmer's (or corporation's) environmental irresponsibility. If stricter rules required agriculture to pay its own way by preventing erosion and controlling pollution, the

industry would be both less destructive and somewhat less inclined to corporate concentration.

It is possible to reward good environmental behavior as well as dis-   31
courage harms. Already the federal government conditions some of its farm
payments on farmers' protecting their wetlands and pays landowners to retire millions of acres of marginal land through the Conservation Reserve
Program. Both programs have problems with enforcement, and the Conservation Reserve Program has attracted many opportunistic participants,
but the model directs federal money more productively than traditional
price supports. Denmark, an admittedly extreme case, now devotes a quarter of its national agriculture budget to converting farms from conventional
to organic techniques. While that model is politically infeasible and perhaps economically inappropriate in this country, directing technical and financial support to farmers of moderate size who adopt environmentally
sound techniques is a possibility. Some of these ideas might emerge from a
courageous and environmentally minded White House. That would at least
be a beginning.

Rural places have always had a double significance in American culture.   32
While politicians and editorialists long praised their virtues and pleasures,
those qualities have few literary expositors. Serious writers such as Flannery
O'Connor, William Faulkner, and Robert Frost have concentrated instead
on a persistent darkness in country life: poverty, solitude, hidden violence,
endless labor, and nature's arbitrary, indifferent thwarting of human ends.
Yet the places they document are not blights on the landscape, not mistakes—or, at any rate, not reversible errors. They have a hold on those who
inhabit them, and their satisfactions—community, labor and its temporary
respites, sheer survival, and the nearness of living things—are real as well.
Good farming has long been a demanding craft whose reward is knowing
the meaning of a changing wind, the requirements of a calf's health, or the
potential of a piece of land.

The current economy threatens to sever the burdens of the country   33
from its satisfactions and to divide working landscapes geographically and
economically from regions of beautiful playgrounds. This change would
foster an often ignorant delight in Muir's nature, where God is everywhere
and all welcoming, and it would sanction the disappearance of Frost's,
which challenges the land's inhabitants to decide whether God is absent or
only indifferent. It would also turn economic division yet again into geographic division, multiplying a new industrial poverty in the countryside
that we have decided is not beautiful and settling a new affluence in the
landscapes that we have found we love. We shall have to decide whether
that is for the best. It is surely what is coming.

Thinking Critically

1. To what does Purdy attribute the economic and cultural crisis affecting rural America? What solutions does he propose, and to whom does he ascribe responsibility for addressing these problems?

2. Purdy suggests that there are two ways, both with deep historical roots, in which Americans have perceived and used "nature." What are those two distinct traditions? What are their values, and where do they most sharply disagree?

3. Prepare a brief presentation for your class, with visuals, about one of the following figures named by Purdy: John Muir, Daniel Boone, Frederick Jackson Turner, or Teddy Roosevelt. Find an image, a film clip, a letter or song, or some other piece of evidence that contributes to your understanding of this person's role in Purdy's argument.

Writing Critically

1. Create a website that uses visual images, sound files, and anything else you like that depicts one of the romanticized versions of "nature" that Purdy describes (such as the family farm, the idealized midwestern small town, the unspoiled American West). Write an accompanying narrative that explains the significance of each visual or aural artifact and shows how each contributes to a kind of fantasy about rural America.

2. Read Sarah Anderson's "Wal-Mart's War on Main Street" (see pp. 259–65). In what ways do Anderson's and Purdy's essays share a common argument? How can evidence from one essay be used to support the thesis of the other? In an analytical essay, discuss what these writers have observed about a specific problem facing rural America. If rural America continues to decline, what, according to Anderson and Purdy, would be lost?

3. Using the kinds of values ascribed to blue-state or red-state residents by other writers in this book, determine how such a division could be applied to the communities and conflicts that Purdy describes.

Did Somebody Say "Community"?

LESLIE SAVAN | Leslie Savan's witty, sharp-eyed criticism of advertising was a feature of the New York alternative weekly newspaper the *Village Voice* between 1976 and the mid-1990s, earning her two nominations for a Pulitzer Prize in criticism. Savan's book *The Sponsored Life: Ads, TV, and American Culture* (1994) also received accolades; the *New York Times Book Review* described Savan as having "an unerring moral compass that enables her to score hits on the corporate

> fictions that increasingly structure our world view."
> Savan's perspective on advertising extends, as in "Did
> Somebody Say 'Community'?" to larger shifts and
> reflections in American culture. She has been a frequent
> contributor to *Stay Free!* magazine, where this article
> originally appeared in 1998. Based in Brooklyn, New
> York, *Stay Free!* is a nonprofit print and online
> magazine about American life and culture.

"In the polling community," Republican pollster Tony Fabrizio said dur-   1
ing the '96 elections. "We have a saying: The trend is your friend." And
the friendliest trend rolling through speech patterns today is the discovery of
"communities" where previously there were only interests or professions.
Places like Fabrizio's imaginary Pollstertown now dot the map of America,
as any group of more than two individuals consecrates itself as a community.

"It's time to get UFO investigations out of the UFO community," a true   2
believer asserted on a Fox TV show about (Twentieth Century Fox's) *Independence Day.* According to the *Dallas Morning News,* "the stock-car
racing community wrapped its arms around car owner Rick Hendrick" at
NASCAR's annual awards banquet (he was recently indicted on federal
charges). An Emmy Award winner thanked "all of you in the television
community out there." One member of that community, Peter Jennings,
described Christopher Reeve at the Democratic National Convention as an
icon of "the paralyzed community."

Real communities in the traditional sense may be struggling to survive,   3
but *community,* the word, is booming, cheerfully riding any modifier that
waddles its way, as in these recent sightings: "the eco-design community,"
"the S&M community," "the creative community," "the transplant community," "the hockey community," "the legal community," "the criminal
community," and, from the nonplace where this kind of thinking seems to
be the default drive, "the online community," "the networked community," and "the virtual community."

Clearly, the Internet has popularized the idea of nonphysical communities,   4
pushing cup-of-sugar-borrowing, town-meeting-decision-making neighborhoods to the definition. And our president's it-takes-a-village touchy-feeliness
has raised expectations of group coziness so much that it takes a community
to have a conversation. But there's a more fundamental emotional shift in the
meaning of the word as well, away from describing an inclusive, indiscrimi-
nate mix of people (the sort of community served by the United Way) to something more about personal choice. As a Sausalito interior designer told the
design monthly *Metropolis* (which devoted its November issue to answering
"What is community?"): "The communities that have some importance to me

are communities of intellect or spirit. They are the design community, the artistic community, the psychologically aware community, the health-conscious community, the nonviolent community, the ecologically sound community."

If this busy guy ever gets to New York, he's got to check out a new 5 Chelsea restaurant—it's called Community.

Almost everybody who isn't a member of the misanthropic community 6 seems to be oversold on the sweets of togetherness. But most of the world's users tend to fall into three, uh, categories: First, minorities, like gays, blacks, and Jews, who may or may not have a cohesive group identity but who, by virtue of their contrast to the majority, have the most natural claim to being at least a community in name. Second, people who share an interest or occupation ("the advertising community," "the cultural community") who aren't a community by the usual standards but apparently feel girded by the label. And finally, anyone who wants to invoke some form of social consensus, no matter how imaginary. (As Elaine does in a *Seinfeld* episode: Worried what people will think if they discover she dumped a man after he had a stroke, she frets, "I'll be ostracized by the community!" Jerry: "Community? There's a community? All this time, I've been living in a community. I had no idea.")

Identity politics has surely contributed to *community*'s rise, and the 7 word, with its emphasis on collective rather than individual virtue, does serve as a righteous liberal retort to the right's *family values*. But *community* isn't limited to a specific p.c. left. "When *Firing Line* began," William F. Buckley, Jr., said on radio last week, "conservatives were a very isolated community." And of course, *community* is unfettered capitalism's favorite humanizing device: the business community, the investment community, and the financial community are among the worst abusers.

Like so many values, *community* is on everyone's lips just as it seems to be 8 disappearing. The enormous social upheavals of the past few generations—globalization, suburbanization, television technologies that collapse time and space—have all forced the notion of community to shift from one grounded in a physical closeness that fostered mutual concerns and responsibilities to . . . what?

"My definition of community has two components," says Amitai Etzioni, the "guru" of communitarianism, the movement that focuses on balancing rights and responsibilities among individuals and groups, which President Clinton made famous during his 1992 campaign. (Etzioni acknowledges *community*'s overuse: "We've not only noticed it, but we're the culprits.") "The first element," he says, "is a bonding, not one on one, but a group of people to each other. The second is a shared set of values and culture—it's much more than interests."

He doesn't find all self-named communities spurious: "Bankers may 10
not be a strong community, but they are more than an interest group—they
often know each other personally, they hang around the same country club.
But people who have only a narrowly defined group interest—people who
sell office equipment and lobby Congress, for example, when they share no
bond, just shared greed—they're not community."

Robert Putnam, the Harvard government professor who wrote "Bowl- 11
ing Alone," an essay on the decline of civic participation in America, says
he's "ambivalent to the word *community.* The word has become so vague
and banal and meaningless, I try to use another term—*social capital,* which
means social networks of connectedness, of reciprocity and trust. But if I
say 'social capital' before a group of Rotarians, their eyes glaze over." The
old community cornerstones, "the PTA, bowling leagues, Sunday schools,"
Putnam says, "no longer fit the way we live . . . but as a people, we don't
seem to want to give up this word for something we long for—a sense of
warm, cuddly connectedness to people with whom we share things in
common."

And as boomers face their mortality, "we're going to hear a lot more 12
about community," he adds. "In a certain sense, there's a market out there
for people who have ideas on how to connect." The success of the Saturn
car company, for instance, is due largely to its decision to market community, complete with "reunions" for Saturn owners—who, of course, have
never previously met.

But why can't the damn word at least be slowed down, maybe by sub- 13
stituting other nouns that used to work well enough and that, depending
on the context, can actually be more descriptive: network, industry, circle,
field, movement, association, public, constituency? In fact, why not go for
broke and state the entity—investors, artists, scientists—without any appendage? Obviously, *community* softens and bestows respect on racial and
ethnic words that, standing alone, could too easily be turned into slurs. On
the other hand, *community* makes it awfully easy to feign a respect that isn't
there (an exercise common on TV and radio talk shows).

The reason everyone wants to be a part of a community, rather than an 14
association or a movement, goes beyond respect: The bright and rounded
word lends an instant halo effect. Anything it touches seems valiant; whatever the endeavor, it is noble.

Whether community is vanishing or merely evolving, fear of its loss is 15
what keeps us chanting the word. The word provides comfort—it's a
prayer or wishful thinking, as if we could yak it into being.

Community's quasireligious overtones may reflect an authentic 16
yearning, but too often we're reaching less for spiritual kin than self-

amplification: we want to see our individual selves turned into a multitude—a thousand other people who cherish *The X-Files,* do eco-design, or make a killing in online investments. We're not alone; our identity is validated.

But since community is generally a good thing, why niggle over how the word is used? Sometimes magical thinking really works. Writer Robert Atkins recently edited an issue on community for the online journal *Talk-Back!* He began by zinging those who "prattle about virtual community as if sex-chat rooms . . . constitute community." But looking back on the project, he now says he "can see the value of adhering to some ideas even if we don't quite believe in them, like Santa. Maybe the fact we say 'community' all the time is an important wake-up call that it's an endangered phenomenon." 17

Maybe. But if past habits are any clue, we're far more likely to continue to choose a verbal hologram over the real thing. Who wants to *do* anything if you can merely say it? You don't have to join local organizations, do volunteer work, or even vote because you're already part of the creative community, the Channel 13 community, or—who knows?—the polling community. 18

You've done your duty by pronouncing the word.

19

Thinking Critically

1. This essay is an example of extended definition. What is Savan's thesis, and how do the many possible definitions of *community* that she cites support her thesis?

2. Visit the website of *Stay Free!* magazine at <http://www.stayfreemagazine.org/>. How would you describe the magazine's demographics (that is, its target audience)? Why would Savan's writing style and the content of her argument appeal to *Stay Free!*'s audience?

Writing Critically

1. Can a word or concept become so overused that it loses all meaning? Choose another abstract word or phrase that is everywhere in American popular and political culture, and write an essay that uses Savan's structure and rhetorical strategies to demonstrate how the word or phrase you've chosen either has lost all relevance or can still be redeemed.

2. Savan writes of *community:* "The bright and rounded word lends an instant halo effect. Anything it touches seems valiant; whatever the endeavor, it is noble." In an essay, discuss how a group's specific invocation of the word *community* illustrates Savan's point. As you draft your essay, be sure to consider the connotations of Savan's word choices: "endeavor," "valiant," "halo," and "noble."

3. Like Savan's longtime employer the *Village Voice, Stay Free!* magazine is considered part of the alternative press in America. Is an alternative voice available to your community? Perhaps there is a free weekly newspaper or a member-supported local radio station. Write a comparative, analytical essay in which you evaluate differences in coverage between a mainstream and an alternative local media source. You might wish to include numerical information, such as the number of ad pages compared to the number of editorial pages, or the number of paragraphs given to lead stories. For an alternative radio station, keep a log in which you record the topics of a news broadcast compared to the news on a mainstream radio network. How important is an alternative media presence to your community?

Small World: Why One Town Stays Unplugged

BILL MCKIBBEN

Writer Bill McKibben is known for his passionate, often spiritual analyses of the human impact on global ecosystems. Frequently he brings moral and religious ideas to bear on the ways in which human behavior—from consumerism to industrial shortsightedness—degrades the natural world. McKibben says that with respect to nature and Earth's ecosystem, he tries to "counter despair." In books such as *The End of Nature* (1989), *Hope, Human and Wild: True Stories of Living Lightly on the Earth* (1995), and *Enough: Staying Human in an Engineered Age* (2003), McKibben balances a sense of alarm about our profligate waste of natural resources with a tempered optimism that we can revere and preserve fragile natural resources. The moral impact of caring for the land, McKibben often argues, is reflected in the way we live with each other—in building diverse, sustainable communities and focusing on the quality of our lives, rather than on the quantity of stuff we accumulate. "What I have learned so far," McKibben observes, "is that what is sound and elegant and civilized and respectful of community is also environmentally benign." This essay by McKibben appeared in *Harper's Magazine* in December 2003. Published continuously since 1850, *Harper's* presents thoughtful writing on politics, culture, and the arts, as well as literary fiction and poetry. The magazine's political stance is liberal, and editor Lewis Lapham's monthly "Notebook" column is often a passionate defense of liberal or left-leaning ideals.

When you think about Vermont, Barre is not the town you're imagining.   1
Main Street has seen better days. There are few covered bridges and
fewer rusticators in J. Crew sweaters. There is a heroin problem. The town's
peculiar local geology—it is the self-proclaimed "granite capital of the
world"—has given rise to a peculiar local economy. For nearly a century, Rock
of Ages Corporation has been one of the town's biggest employers, providing
tombstones for a nation. Barre is—literally and figuratively—a gritty town.

Thunder Road, "the nation's site of excitement," sits just down the hill   2
from the quarry, and on summer Thursday nights (because quarrymen used
to get paid on Thursday afternoons) it vibrates with noise—cars doppler-
ing around the half-mile track, the whine rising and falling as they flash by
the grandstand straight. It's glorious fun—the booth selling homemade
videos of last year's best crashes, the "battle flags" of last year's champion
cars flapping over the infield. Those grandstands hold ten thousand people
on a big night, and most nights are big. Ten thousand—one Vermonter in
sixty—is more people than gather anyplace else in the state.

"After the war, that's when all this started," said Ken Squier, who built   3
Thunder Road. Car racing may be big time now, but it began as a local
sport, and not just down South. "The soldiers came back from Okinawa,
from Iwo Jima, from the Bulge. They were not going to play a children's
game like baseball. This was their thing. It was always the people's sport.
Always the sport for the unshined shoes."

I could listen to Ken Squier most of the night. He's a talker, and he   4
comes by it honestly, having spent the better part of six decades in front of
the microphone at the radio station his father helped build—"WDEV, Radio Vermont . . . the friendly pioneer . . . Ninety-six-point-one on your FM
dial." Naturally he broadcasts races from his Thunder Road, at least on
those Thursdays when the Red Sox aren't playing at the same time. And of
course he discusses the races in loving detail on his morning sports wrap.
He even has a weekly auto-racing hour hosted by one of his sidekicks, Dave
Moody. Any businessman would do the same—when Disney and ABC or
AOL and Time Warner do it they call it "synergy."

But here's the odd part. When Dave wraps up the auto-racing show on   5
Monday evening, the next thing you hear is Dinner Jazz—two hours of
Cannonball Adderley and Miles and Coltrane and Dave Brubeck, brought
to you by the same advertisers (Lenny's Shoes and Apparel, Shore Acres
restaurant) that bring you, at various times during the week, the bird-watch-
ing hour, *Music to Go to the Dump By*, and the station's own bluegrass
band ("We don't want to be strangers . . . We're the Radio Rangers . . . from
WDEV"). Some nights in the winter they'll carry two different girls' high
school basketball games back-to-back or hockey from Norwich College.

There's some gospel preaching on Sunday morning, and *Dairyline* with the latest hundredweight prices in the five o'clock hour so you can hear it during morning milking. There's a conservative talk show for an hour in the morning, of course—but oddly, in the afternoon, there's an hour of left-wing talk, hosted by socialist congressman Bernie Sanders and by Anthony Pollina, of the state's Progressive Party.

In other words, this is a very strange radio station. Forget the red states   6 and the blue states. WDEV exists in a kind of purple state. Many parts of its schedule sound like things you can hear elsewhere. If you've got the new satellite radios, you can get bluegrass twenty-four hours a day and nineteen flavors of jazz. Modern radio stations aim for a particular niche—say, thirty-five-year-old males who want sports around the clock. But it's a rare place in our society where Thelonious Monk and stock-car racing coexist. It's radio that actually reflects the reality of local life, and it seems very strange because it's all but disappeared everywhere else.

A couple of miles downhill from Thunder Road, on the slightly tired   7 main street of Barre, Tod Murphy opened up a diner about a year ago, right next to the hardware store. Ham and eggs, breakfast all day, bottomless cup of coffee. A local joint. But the Farmer's Diner is maybe the most local joint in the whole United States—something like 80 percent of the food it serves was raised within sixty miles of the kitchen. In a country where the average forkful of dinner travels 1,500 miles to reach your lips, this makes Murphy's diner perhaps the most interesting restaurant in America. Sure, other chefs work with local food—Alice Waters has been doing it for years, to great and deserved acclaim. But not at $5.50 for the hamburger platter. Diner food comes frozen in great plastic sacks on the backs of trucks.

Great local food in a diner is as odd as jazz and stock-car racing sharing a   8 radio frequency. America has been Clear Channeled and Olive Gardened with enormous success, but it's possible that success has begun to breed a reaction. Politicians were bowled over last summer when hundreds of thousands of Americans from across the political spectrum wrote in to decry new FCC deregulation that would have let media giants own even more stations than they do now. And people are flocking in the hundreds, anyhow, to line the counter at Murphy's new eatery. Some are old hippies, and some are on their way to Thunder Road. But there are enough of them that Murphy has begun to think big— begun to imagine Farmer's Diners all across America, serving food grown from whatever region they happen to be in. " 'Local' is the new 'organic,' " he said. "Everywhere that there's an Applebee's, there could be a Farmer's Diner."

In fact, the longer I spent around Squier and Murphy, the more I began   9 to wonder if maybe "local" really is what comes next—whether as the globalized world begins to fray, socially and environmentally and even economically, people might start wanting to shorten their supply lines. Energy that comes from a windmill on the ridge instead of an oil tanker from the Gulf, say. We're not going to build computer chips in local workshops, but does every chicken need to come from some enormous Tyson shed in the Southeast? A resurgence of the local would be counterintuitive. The momentum in the direction of globalization seems too powerful to buck, the economic logic unmatchable. But in a region where jobs are draining away, and where an ethic of self-reliance remains a dim, vestigial, but honored memory, it seems at least an outside possibility. And inside the Farmer's Diner, with cops and housewives and truck drivers hunched over chili from local steers and local beans, it seems awfully appealing.

The train of thought that led to this Barre lunch counter began, oddly 10 enough, in the 1990s, when Tod Murphy was working in a cool new coffee place in Seattle called Starbucks, soon to be the poster child for the destruction of local commercial culture. "I was a damned good Starbucks counter guy," Murphy said. "That's where I got my chops. I found out that I really liked customers. It fits in with my Aquarian personality—you don't have to make a long-term commitment to them, but you get to converse." He learned plenty of other things, too, watching Starbucks owner Howard Schultz. "He was always able to see the possibilities. He knew about the 'half hour vacation,' and how people wanted a new public space, and all of that. He understood what was happening in the culture."

In the mid-nineties, Murphy and his girlfriend, a Starbucks manager, 11 moved east to Atlanta to launch their own start-up—"Coffee Station," they called it. The plan was to make as much money as quickly as possible. "The whole idea was to flip it, to turn it—all those late nineties words." Murphy ended up in New York as operations director. "In three years in Manhattan, I saw Patrick Stewart in a Shakespeare play and that was pretty much my tourist life. We were full-out." Coffee Station didn't turn into Starbucks—in fact it went out of business—but Murphy and his partners had sold out near the top of the boom, clearing a small bundle. "It made having a farm possible."

Ah, a farm. Murphy grew up suburban, but his grandparents were still 12 farming in rural Connecticut (just down the road from what's since turned into Mohegan Sun, the gaudiest of the Indian casinos). He knew what he wanted to do: "I would get the Sears and Roebuck farm catalogue and price out what a laying flock would cost me," he said. So when he sold off his stake in overpriced Manhattan latte, he drove north to Vermont and started looking.

He found a place—a beautiful, scraggly hill farm ten miles south of Barre, 13 where he started raising veal calves. "Great organic veal calves, nursing off old dairy cows. They were out on pasture too, so they actually had some flavor from grass. I went to start selling them because shortly they were not going to be veal anymore, they were going to be young beef. The first chef I talked to said, 'Great, I'll take three cases of top round.' Well, Christ, the entire herd didn't have three cases of top round. And no one wanted the front legs."

Murphy had discovered the essential fact of modern agriculture: veal   14 calf, ear of corn, gallon of milk, what you've grown is a commodity. You either sell it into the huge industrial food stream, at a price set by the lowest-cost, highest-volume grower in some distant market, or you can begin the laborious task of figuring out how to market your product for a higher price: at a farmer's market, or through an organic co-op, or maybe marinated in some special sauce and Fed-Exed from your website. (You could also do what most small farmers in Vermont or elsewhere in America have in fact done: sell your farm to someone else, who will either try one of the above strategies or turn it into ski condos.) In this case, Murphy sold his veal calves to the New England Culinary Institute for use in their meat-cutting class. But that was clearly a limited market. And anyway, he was cursed with the brain of an entrepreneur.

"I started to ask myself, how do you create a company that will take   15 food off the farmer's hands in the easiest way for a farmer, and set it in front of the customers in the easiest way for them, and do it at a price point everyone could live with? And a diner was the answer I came up with. People know what to expect from it. It's a ground-beef business. Nothing fancy."

In fact, though, a diner was not so intuitively obvious. Virtually all the other   16 restaurateurs who want to use high-quality local produce have gone high-end, for the obvious reason that a $50 check covers a multitude of sins. You can afford to pay the higher price of hand-raised organic veal, and the high price of having a chef take the time to hack it apart, and the higher price of going down to the farmer's market to shop for it, and the high price of the fresh flowers on the table to make your customer feel as if $50 was money well spent. If you're going to try to use the same ingredients to compete with, say, Denny's, you're going to have to think a lot harder. And if you're going to try it in Vermont, where winter lasts awhile, you're going to have to think harder still.

Local sounds good, but most of American history has been spent trans-   17 forming local into national and now global. The result is the society we inhabit. Considering only just these two categories, food and communications, it's easy enough to see what's happened. Whereas once most people grew their own food, and perhaps a small surplus to sell, farmers now make up 1 or 2 percent of the population. The rest of us have moved on, making the economy vastly larger by doing other things. We now can get fresh food from around the planet, flown or shipped in at every season, and it's all incredibly cheap—once upon a time an orange was a rare treat in the bottom of a Christmas stocking for most Americans, and now orange juice is a staple of our lives, available in low-acid and high-calcium and everything in between. It's kind of a miracle that consumer capitalism can deliver you an apple from South Africa for forty cents. Similarly, communication was once largely confined to the people in your immediate vicinity, unless you were willing to write a letter. Now we are entertained virtually nonstop by hundreds of channels of television and radio and Internet radio and legally and illegally downloaded tunes and you name it. There is no vaguely musical sound emitted by anyone on the planet that is not available, again for a vanishingly low price, to any of the rest of us at any time. Vermont alone has seventy-eight radio transmitters—the dial is pretty crowded even in this small state.

Or, of course, you could say it another way. We now grow our food 18 with so few farmers that lots of rural communities have simply shriveled up and disappeared, and many of the rest are impoverished and hopeless. Farmers working thousands of acres apiece can't take good care of the land—soil erodes, pesticides and herbicides go on by the ton. Animals grown in vast factory farms are, by definition, animals abused. Flying and trucking food from one end of the world to the other spews carbon into the atmosphere. By the time the apple from New Zealand reaches your supermarket it tastes like nothing special. Vast quantities of cheap food have, in the last couple of decades, helped to make us, well, vast.

When a train car overturned in Minot, North Dakota, last year, a large 19 quantity of ammonia spilled out, sending up a cloud of poison gas. Local officials quickly tried to contact the town's seven radio stations to send out the alarm—only to find that there was no one actually working in six of them. They were simply relaying a satellite feed from Clear Channel headquarters in Texas—there was plenty of country music and golden oldies and Top 40 and right-wing chat, but no one to warn about the toxic cloud drifting overhead. It's true that you can hear anything from anywhere at any time, but, oddly, it's gotten a lot harder to hear much about your immediate vicinity. All fall, talk radio covered the fine points of the California recall in obsessive detail—did Arnold grope all those women? But try spinning the dial to find out about say, the extent of domestic abuse in your own county. That's one reason people rose up last summer to fight the FCC when it moved to make the world even safer for the Clear Channels. It was supposed to be a quiet backroom deal, but pretty soon activists of every stripe were fighting the regulation: When Bernie Sanders held a hearing in Vermont, for instance, there weren't enough seats for all the people who wanted to testify; Congress got so many emails that the Senate actually tried to reject the new regulations. Michael Powell, the shocked and peeved chairman of the FCC, whined to the *New York Times* in September that "there was a concerted grassroots effort to attack" the new regulation. "I've never seen that," he added.

Here's another way of saying it. A couple of clicks up the dial from   20
WDEV, you come to a Clear Channel Vermont station, one of a half-dozen
area signals controlled by the $8 billion corporation. It styles itself The
Zone, and it carries Rush. After Rush, it carries the Don and Mike show.
A few days ago, I listened to Don and Mike for an hour. They tried to fry
an egg on the sidewalk because it was so incredibly hot (in Washington,
D.C., where they're located; in Vermont it was raining). They also had a
big discussion about a porno film they'd recently watched on a cable channel and whether or not it was gross that the male actor had an uncircum-
cised penis. This turned disputatious, and either Don or Mike told either
Mike or Don to kiss his ass. "Kiss the inside of my ass. Kiss the eye. Kiss
the eye!" Then a woman came into the studio who had tanned the words
"Don" and "Mike" onto her breasts in order to win a hundred dollars.
There was more dispute, this time about whether or not she'd tanned them
low enough, "across the round part, the aureole."

An economist would argue that we've chosen this world, that if we   21
didn't want the Sysco track unloading frozen dinners into the back door
of the family-casual chain dining house, we wouldn't go there. That if we
wanted to listen to local radio, local radio would ipso facto exist. And
there's plenty of truth in all that—by and large we have picked (with the
assistance of immense quantities of advertising) the cheapest, the easiest,
the saltiest, the greasiest. Something in dirty talk appeals to many of us,
and community has often seemed like more work than it's worth. Our
choices have in some ways built our world. On the other hand, it's hard
to test whether these are the choices we really, or still, want to make. If
most every radio station in your town is owned by some big broadcaster,
you need many millions of dollars to buy a frequency, if indeed one is even
open. If your choice of restaurants is confined to twenty places with a
loading ramp at the back for the tractor trailer, then it's harder to make a
statement of your desires.

In other words, if you wanted to find out whether, in the early twenty-   22
first century, local "works," or whether it's simply a romantic fantasy,
you'd need to have some test cases, some examples to look at. A few places
that exist slightly outside the conventional economy. Like the Farmer's
Diner, or like WDEV. . . .

If you took a poll and asked people if they wanted more "community"   23
in their lives, a huge majority would say yes. Left, right, and center, it's a
lack we profess to feel. But it's not at all clear that we mean it in anything
other than a wistful, sentimental way—that, given the choice, we have any
real interest in community, or in the institutions (like WDEV or the
Farmer's Diner) that might build it.

That's because a local community is in some ways an exercise in ineffi- 24
ciency. Take the modern radio industry as an example. It's the furthest
thing from local, but it's incredibly focused on you. It's entirely set up
around the idea that you are a part of a predictable demographic whose
tastes can be reliably commodified. If you walk into the headquarters of,
say, Kansas City's Entercom Broadcasting, a Clear Channel wanna-be, it
looks like you're in a food court. In the center, ad salesmen work from a
line of cubicles. Around them, a ring of small sound booths house each of
the company's stations—there's a country, a classical, a smooth jazz, a
news, a rock, a classic rock, an alternative rock, and a continuous soft rock
(KUDL) geared toward women. If that kind of segmentation isn't enough
for you, you can sign up for satellite radio—on XM's 101 channels, rock
and roll comes in an endless variety of flavors, including "stadium rock"
and "hair bands." And of course the whole premise of talk radio is that you
can go all day long without hearing an opinion you disagree with—Limbaugh's
fans, after all, call themselves "dittoheads."

Whereas on WDEV, if you listen regularly, you hear Ann Coulter de- 25
crying the treason of the American left, but you also hear the American left,
or at least the Vermont version of it, decrying plant closings and failing
dairy farms, demanding national health insurance and dissing the president. You hear jazz in the evening, and you hear stock-car racing. You hear,
in other words, things that other people are interested in. Which is pretty
much the definition of community. If you're a senior citizen you find out
what's going on in the schools, and if you're a jazz fan you hear some bluegrass, and everyone gets the Norwich ice-hockey scores. Television, of
course, is so expensive it has to chase the largest possible audience, and the
Internet, by virtue of its design, splits people off into narrow avenues of interest. Radio is the ideal community vehicle, its signal confined by the hills
and mountains to a narrow area—or was, until big money figured out how
to buy up those local stations and turn them into ghost repeaters.

Now there are just survivor stations like WDEV hanging on, for who 26
knows how long. I was in the studio one morning when Squier was interviewing his grandchildren about the new Harry Potter book. Their mother, Squier's
daughter Ashley Jane, squeezed into the booth too, and when she started talking it was with the practiced air of a radio pro. She'd grown up in the studio,
hosting the *Green Mountain Ballroom*, a dance program for kids. But she took
up religion instead—she's an Episcopal priest in Chicago, and her brother's the
soundman for the California band the Smokin' Armadillos. Monthly, Squier
said, one or another of the big outfits makes an offer for the station. "The value
probably went up another forty percent when the FCC passed the last deregulation." It's a little hard to see how the station will outlast him.

The barriers to entry in the restaurant business are a lot lower than they   27
are in broadcasting—the most important license comes from the local
health department. Still, the Farmer's Diner is another difficult example of
embracing a certain kind of inefficiency. Since it's always summer somewhere and we know how to fly tomatoes around the planet for next to
nothing, why bother seeking out blemished local hydroponic tomatoes to
top your burgers in mid-winter? Lettuce is a commodity item, and it comes
at $18 a box; why bother paying $21 a box simply because the local farmers say that's what they need to make a profit? Murphy took me to Thistle
Hill Farm in Pomfret, where they make a stunning Tarentaise cheese; it
costs $10 a pound wholesale, however, and it would be a lot easier not to
use it in your version of a Ploughman's Lunch. Why bother with ice cream
from the small organic herd in nearby Stratford when you know, based on
experience, that they're going to run out a few times in the course of the
summer and your whole menu is going to be screwed up? It's so much easier just to take it all out of the back of the tractor trailer and serve it up.

All you get in return for the effort is a story, the story that the food   28
comes from your neighbors, that by eating it you're helping local agriculture. It's possible that the story is worth a buck—people might pay Murphy $6 for a hamburger lunch even though Denny's would serve them the
same number of calories for $5 (especially since Murphy's hamburger, from
beef raised on the western side of the Green Mountains in Starksboro, is
really, really good). It's possible that by cutting out the middleman and using prefab diner buildings and finding investors who think it's a good idea
as well as a good scheme, Murphy can make it work.

Look—we live in a world where Wal-Mart and McDonald's, with their   29
unbelievable efficiency, have managed to erode away most of what were
once local economies—"Low Prices Always" might as well replace "In
God We Trust." So it's a stretch to imagine that a really good hot turkey
sandwich might matter—that the pendulum might be poised to swing back
the other way. But it's sweet to imagine it too.

Thinking Critically

1. What, in McKibben's view, makes radio station WDEV a kind of "purple state"?

2. McKibben's argument about a trend toward the "local" in culture and politics
   is complex. How does McKibben define *local* for the purposes of his argument? What are the benefits of going "local," and what are the challenges?

3. Both Leslie Savan (page 77) and Bill McKibben explore the concept
   of "community." In what ways do they agree or disagree about what
   "community" represents?

Writing Critically

1. Compare McKibben's exploration of Barre, Vermont, with Rebecca Skloot's explorations and descriptions of New Martinsville, West Virginia (page 39). How do these authors approach their selected towns, and what are their attitudes toward the inhabitants and institutions of each town? How much time does each writer spend in each town, and how many people do they talk to? Do Skloot and McKibben share any preconceived ideas (perhaps based on a working thesis) that changes as they get to know each town? In an essay, use both Rebecca Skloot's version of New Martinsville and Bill McKibben's account of Barre to write an analysis about a potentially divisive issue in American culture or politics.

2. McKibben offers a brief history of the consolidation of the food and communications industries in American life. Keep a log (or a blog) for a week in which you record the origins of everything you eat, or the names of the news and entertainment outlets you read, watch, or listen to. Then, in an essay that uses description and process analysis, trace the food (or the media) that you consume from its point of origin. Do you know, for example, who picked the tomatoes on the salad you had for lunch at the student union? Should you care if the daily newspaper you read is part of a media empire that owns and operates newspapers across the country?

Arguing the Cultural Divides

1. Several essays in this chapter discuss the impact of consumer choice and behavior on local communities. Drawing upon at least three of these selections (you might also consult the readings in Chapter 5, "Getting and Spending: Shopping, Working, and Values"), write an autobiography based on what you own, what you aspire to own, and how your behavior as a consumer reflects your values. (You could and should, of course, feel free to disagree with the basic premise of this prompt. If you believe that what and how you consume has *nothing whatsoever* to do with your values, then write the essay from that point of view.)

2. Bill McKibben (page 82) and Jedediah Purdy (page 66) both explore the economic and political reasons for the marked decline in the standard of living for many rural communities. Select a region of the country (the Midwest, Appalachia, the Great Plains), and conduct an Internet and database search using the keywords "rural depopulation" or "rural population migration" along with the name of the region you're describing. Look for first-person narratives, photographs or other images, and other archival resources that describe both how life used to be in a rural community and what it has now become. Create a webpage that describes the plight of a rural community from the point of view of people who live (or lived) there. Your webpage should draw on the objective, statistical, and historical information offered

by McKibben and Purdy; but the purpose of your webpage is to give voice and form to the individuals directly affected by these policies.

3. Read Lynn Hirschberg's essay "What Is an American Movie Now?" (see pp. 712–19). How does the image of America seen in mainstream, block-buster movies compare with the individual communities described through-out Chapter 2? According to Hirschberg's argument, why would movies about the lives and issues of rural communities probably not be made by commercial studios or distributed overseas? What was the last film you saw that portrayed an aspect of rural, or "average," American life? How accu-rately did that movie reflect what you know about an American community?

Voting and Values: Are We Indivisible?

How Bush Really Won

MARK DANNER

Journalist Mark Danner is a staff writer for *The New Yorker,* specializing in foreign affairs. His investigative and often revelatory reporting has also appeared in *Harper's,* where he was a senior editor, and in the *New York Times Magazine,* where he was the foreign affairs editor. For his fearless reporting of post–Cold War failings of U.S. diplomacy in El Salvador, Haiti, Bosnia, and elsewhere he won numerous awards and in 1999 was named a MacArthur Fellow. Since the terrorist attacks of 9/11, Danner has reported exhaustively on America's sudden shifts in foreign policy and especially on the buildup to the war with Iraq. It was Danner, in the pages of the *New York Review of Books,* who brought to national and international attention the abuses of Iraqi prisoners being held by American forces at Abu Ghraib prison. His reports, collected along with government documents, were published in the 2004 book *Torture and Truth: America, Abu Ghraib, and the War on Terror,* which the *Los Angeles Times* called "essential reading for Americans who want to know how the United States has careened into chaos—moral, political and organizational—over its methods of interrogating detainees around the world." Mark Danner is a professor of journalism at the University of California at Berkeley and is the Henry R. Luce Professor of Human Rights, Democracy and Journalism at Bard College. For more information about his books, and for links to other articles and essays he has published, go to <http://www.markdanner.com>. This essay appeared in the *New York Review of Books* in January 2005.

1.

I have won what I call political capital and now I intend to spend it.
— George W. Bush, November 3, 2004

Driving north from Tampa on Florida's Route 75 on November 1, as the   1
battle over who would hold political power in America was reaching a climax but the struggle over what that battle meant had yet to begin, I put down the top of my rented green convertible, turned the talk radio voices up to blaring, and commenced reading the roadside. Beside me billboards flew past, one hard upon another, as if some errant giant had cut a great deck of cards and fanned them out along each shoulder. Hour by hour, as the booming salesman's voice of proud Floridian Rush Limbaugh rumbled from the radio, warning gravely of the dangers of "voting for bin Laden" ("Haven't you noticed that bin Laden is using *Democratic talking points?*"), and other ominous voices reminded listeners of the "hundreds of votes" Senator Kerry cast "against our national defense" ("In a time of terror, when our enemies are gathering . . . *can we afford to take that risk?*"), I watched rush by, interspersed with the blaring offers of "Florida Citrus! One Bag $1!" and "Need Help With Sinkholes?," a series of perhaps fifty garish signs announcing an approaching "Adult Toy Café!" and "Adult Toy Extravaganza!" and then "We Bare All!" and finally, the capper, "All Nude—Good Food—Truckers Welcome!"

It wasn't long before this billboard parade had acquired its stark spiri-   2
tual counterpoint—"Jesus Is Still the Answer!"—and by the time I reached the promised "extravaganza"—a sad and windowless two-room shack just off the highway, smaller than most of the signs advertising it—I found, standing just down the road from the pathetic little house of sin, a resplendent white church more than twice its size. In the world of American hucksterism, the sin may be the draw but the payoff's always in redemption.

This was perhaps thirty-six hours before an army of self-interested   3
commentators, self-appointed spiritual leaders, and television pundits hot for a simple storyline had seized on the answers to a clumsily posed exit

poll question—more than one respondent in five, offered seven choices, had selected "moral values" as their "most important issue"—and used those answers to transform the results of the 2004 election into a rousing statement of Americans' disgust with abortion, promiscuity, R-rated movies, gay marriage, late-night television, and other "Hollywood-type" moral laxity. Some, like the Reverend Bob Jones III, president of Bob Jones University, wrote the President with admirable directness to remind him what the election meant, and what he now owed:

> In your re-election, God has graciously granted America—though she doesn't deserve it—a reprieve from the agenda of paganism. You have been given a mandate. . . . Don't equivocate. Put your agenda on the front burner and let it boil. You owe the liberals nothing. They despise you because they despise your Christ. . . .
>
> Undoubtedly, you will have opportunity to appoint many conservative judges and exercise forceful leadership with the Congress in passing legislation that is defined by biblical norm regarding the family, sexuality, sanctity of life, religious freedom, freedom of speech, and limited government. You have four years—a brief time only—to leave an imprint for righteousness upon this nation that brings with it the blessings of Almighty God. . . .
>
> If you have weaklings around you who do not share your biblical values, shed yourself of them.

And yet the voters of Union County, Florida's smallest, whom I found   4
crowding the election supervisor's office in tiny Lake Butler, seemed unaware that they had been impelled to vote by a newfound quest for redemption. In Lake Butler, turnout was higher than anyone could remember; in Union County, voter registration had risen by 25 percent over 2000, when I had last visited.[1] But none of the voters who spoke to me there volunteered a word about "moral values." Their answers tended to be much more concrete. "It's because of 9/11—you know, because of the terrorism," said Babs Montpetit—a.k.a. Miss Babs, election supervisor of Union County since 1985. "Because of the terrorism people are afraid *not* to vote." Through the window behind her I could see Lake Butler's main street, with its scattering of stores and bars—a tiny, isolated place, with barely seven thousand registered voters, far from any major city. Why should its citizens worry about terrorism? "Why, who could have expected that would happen, that business in New York?" Miss Babs asked me in return, leaning forward and lowering her voice. "You just *don't know.*"

Back in the car, I turned on the radio to find the Florida news feed,   5
which led with this story:

> A suspicious package that seemed to be vibrating forced the closing of the State Board of Elections today. The parcel, it turned out, was an

> ordinary package that happened to have been placed next to an air
> conditioner, the breeze from which accounted for the apparent vi-
> brating action. . . .

This embarrassing incident, which in other times might have been   6
treated as a humorous item about the haplessness of government officials,
was reported in dead seriousness: a dark dispatch from the front lines. As
I left Lake Butler, stepping on the accelerator, I turned the radio up and the
air around me filled again with the booming voice of Rush Limbaugh, in
full and impressive rant:

> Osama bin Laden cannot launch an attack on the United States of Amer-
> ica. Osama bin Laden can only deliver a tape, and on that tape, bin Laden
> appeals to the very appeasers in this country who would allow him to
> gain strength by agreeing with what he says and voting for the man who
> is being quoted by bin Laden. John Kerry, as much as Michael Moore,
> was quoted by Osama bin Laden in that video that we all saw. . . .
> Michael Moore is not on the ballot; John Kerry is. Osama bin Laden par-
> roting John Kerry in his tape on Friday. We have a unique responsibility
> to lead the world in confronting and defeating this evil threat. . . .
>   Returning to the days of appeasement, trying to meet a "global
> test" of world opinion, ignoring threats from hostile nations and
> groups is a deadly mistake we simply can't afford to make. . . . The
> Democrat Party in this country is eager to point to the things bin
> Laden said and suggest that he is right—a man who happily murdered
> three thousand Americans and is eager to do so over and over and
> over again! You say, "Rush, I haven't heard the Democrats say that."
> Oh, you can find it on their Web sites. You can find people who are
> going to vote for John Kerry who have said this. You can find people
> on various Democrat Web sites who are excited bin Laden said what
> he said. They're hoping for an Osama smackdown of Bush, if I may
> quote one of the things I saw.

Interspersed with Limbaugh's extraordinarily fluid and persuasively de-   7
ceptive tirade—heard, according to his home station in Sacramento, by
"nearly 20 million people over 600 stations"—came the political advertisements, one after another, which turned skillfully around a concentrated version of the same plotline: First, the threat America faces today is as great as
any in the country's history. Second, that threat makes this election "the
most important in history," because if Americans make "the wrong choice"
they could make themselves and their families more vulnerable. Third,
therefore, Americans must vote, and must make "the right choice." Fear is
joined skillfully to risk: a risk that is personal and looming, and—most important—that could very well increase if the election goes the wrong way.

The script of the famous "Wolves" television ad, with its simple image   8
of a pack of ravenous, circling carnivores readying for the attack, embod-
ied this plotline in perhaps its purest form:

> In an increasingly dangerous world. . . . Even after the first terrorist
> attack on America . . . John Kerry and the liberals in Congress voted
> to slash America's intelligence operations. By six billion dollars. . . .
> Cuts so deep they would have weakened America's defenses. And
> weakness attracts those who are waiting to do America harm.

A vote for Bush is a vote to stave off that weakness. More important, a 9
failure to vote could make way for that "weakening of America's de-
fenses." As I headed to Jacksonville, grave voices from the radio warned
again and again of what was at stake:

> John Kerry. The most liberal man in the Senate. The most liberal per-
> son to ever run for president. He voted to cut our military. . . . To se-
> verely cut our intelligence agencies. . . . He voted for higher taxes 350
> times. . . . And now he wants to be our President. . . . We live in a
> dangerous world that requires strong and steady leadership. John
> Kerry is a risky choice for America . . . a risk we cannot take.

This rhetoric of risk carries forward a narrative that Republicans began 10
shaping soon after the attacks of September 11, 2001, and that came boldly
to the fore as a political strategy the following May, when Vice President
Cheney declared that the statements of several Democratic senators, who
had rather timidly questioned some of the decisions made in conducting the
war in Afghanistan, were "unworthy of national leaders in a time of war."
Though this bold shot across the bow essentially put an end to any overt
Democratic criticism of the administration on the conduct of the war on
terror, Republicans clearly realized that when it came to terrorism and national security, as Karl Rove observed during a speech to the Republican
National Committee in January 2002, they could "go to the country on
this issue, because [Americans] trust the Republican Party to do a better job
of protecting and strengthening America's military might and thereby protecting America."

That autumn Republicans triumphed in the midterm elections, largely 11
because they effectively exploited Americans' apparent willingness to believe that the Republicans could better protect the country. This strategy
was displayed most dramatically in Saxby Chambliss's victory over the incumbent Max Cleland in the Senate race in Georgia, in which the challenger
portrayed Cleland, a highly decorated veteran who had lost three limbs in
Vietnam, as an ally of bin Laden. Though the claims were obviously
trumped up—they rested on the fact that Cleland had not instantly voted
for the creation of the Department of Homeland Security—the images of
Cleland's and bin Laden's faces side by side in effect doomed the incumbent.

The attacks of September 11 restored to Republicans their traditional po- 12
litical advantage in matters of "national security" and "national defense"—

an advantage the party had lost with the end of the cold war—and Republicans capitalized on that advantage, not only by running President Bush as "a war president," as he repeatedly identified himself, but by presenting a vote for John Kerry—whom the Republicans succeeded in defining (with a good deal of help from the Swift Boat Veterans, and from Kerry himself) as indecisive, opportunistic, and untrustworthy—as a vote that was inherently, dangerously risky. The emphasis placed on Bush's much-promoted personal strengths—decisiveness, determination, reliability, transparency—served to base his candidacy at once on "moral values" and on "national security," in effect making possession of the first essential to protect the second. Bush's decisiveness was put forward as the flip side of Kerry's dangerous vacillation, the answer to the threat of weakness Kerry was alleged to pose. This equation was dramatized, perfected, and repeated, with much discipline and persistence, in thousands of advertisements, speeches, and "talking heads" discussion programs on conservative networks, especially Fox. (In Lake Butler, Miss Babs's husband, she told me, "watches only Fox News. He believes all the other channels are propaganda.") Despite all the talk about "moral values," the 2004 election turned on a fulcrum of fear.

2.

Famously, as I have mentioned, more than one in five Americans—22 percent— 13
who spoke to pollsters as they left the voting places said, when presented with seven choices, that their "most important issue" had been "moral values," and of these four out of five cast their votes for George Bush. On the other hand, 19 percent selected "terrorism" and another 15 percent chose "Iraq," meaning that more than one in three voters said the war—the Iraq war or the "war on terror"—was their most important issue. In fact, the most striking single result of the exit polls was Bush's much stronger appeal to women—many of them, apparently, the much-discussed "security moms," who were thought to be especially concerned about protecting their families. All of these numbers and conclusions, needless to say, bear further scrutiny.

Using an exit poll to draw precise conclusions from a national election 14
is like using a very blurry magnifying glass to analyze the brushstrokes in a huge and complicated pointillist painting. Our tools for judging what elections "mean" are quite crude, depending as they do on the willingness of voters to speak to pollsters, on their ability to speak honestly about the choices they made, and on their particular talents for understanding and expressing their own motives. As we saw this year—when faulty exit polls that suggested an overwhelming Kerry victory significantly distorted election-day press coverage—they can often produce downright wrong

Margins of Victory: Republican Presidents Reelected During the Last Hundred Years

	President	Popular Vote	Electoral Vote
1904	Theodore Roosevelt	17%	196
1956	Dwight D. Eisenhower	16%	384
1972	Richard M. Nixon	23%	503
1984	Ronald Reagan	18%	512
2004	George Bush	2%	34

conclusions. Despite the "scientific" feel that numbers lend to any analysis, there is more art to it than science and, despite the impression that election and analysis are starkly separate, much analysis, as the Reverend Jones's letter to President Bush suggests, simply carries forward beyond the election a self-interested political narrative that preceded it.

If one stands back a bit and lets the drifting smoke of the pundits and the preachers and the exit poll analysts begin to clear, three interesting facts about the 2004 election stand out. The first is that the election was very close—historically close, in fact. The table on this page shows the margins of victory, in percentage of the popular vote and in electoral votes, of sitting Republican presidents who have won reelection during the last hundred years.

As these numbers show, incumbency is a huge advantage; nonetheless, Bush's reelection was a squeaker, the closest for a Republican in more than a century.[2] Four years after the historically close election of 2000, and after a hard-fought eight-month campaign in which the candidates, the parties, and so-called "independent" groups spent more than a billion dollars to woo voters, the electoral map hardly changed. Only three small states switched sides: the Democrats picked up New Hampshire (four electoral votes) and the Republicans very narrowly won Iowa (eight) and New Mexico (five). Bush had a net gain of only nine electoral votes, which, added to the seven that the Republicans gained through reapportionment, gave him his narrow margin of victory.[3]

Had fewer than 60,000 Ohio voters decided to cast their ballots for the Democrat rather than the Republican (and according to the exit polls one voter in twenty decided whom to vote for on election day), John Kerry would have won Ohio's twenty electoral votes and with them the presidency—and would have entered the White House in January 2005, as George W. Bush had done in January 2001, having won the votes of fewer Americans than the man he defeated. About 2,991,437 fewer, which, as I write, is George W. Bush's margin of victory, out of 122,124,783 votes cast for president.

Which leads to the second interesting fact about the 2004 election: a 18
great many more people turned out to vote, nearly seventeen million more,
than turned out four years ago. Nearly 60 percent of those Americans eligible cast ballots in 2004, an increase in turnout of almost 6 percent.[4] In
the so-called battleground states, where vast sums were spent on advertising and one could not escape the barrage of political messages blaring from
television and radio and pouring out of the telephone and the mailbox, the
increase in turnout was even greater. A million and a half more Floridians
cast ballots than had four years before: in 2000—itself an intensely fought
election in which turnout substantially increased—fewer than 56 percent
of eligible Floridians voted; in 2004 more than 65 percent did.

This leads, finally, to the third interesting fact about the election, which 19
is that in the days leading up to it many of the "indicators" which political
professionals have traditionally taken to suggest whether or not an incumbent will win were running distinctly against President Bush. Most notably,
more Americans (55 percent) said they thought the country was "headed in
the wrong direction" than those who said it was headed in the right one,
and fewer than half of Americans polled (49 percent) said that they approved of the President's performance in office. More disapproved than approved of the President's handling of foreign policy (49 percent to 45
percent) and of the economy (51 percent to 43 percent). Finally more Americans disapproved than approved of the President's handling of Iraq (50 percent to 45 percent), his most important foreign policy, and, perhaps most
strikingly, more than two Americans in three told pollsters that Mr. Bush's
tax cuts—his signal domestic accomplishment—had either been bad for the
economy (17 percent) or had not made much difference (51 percent).[5]

The President went into the election, then, with Americans mildly pes- 20
simistic about the direction of the country and broadly disapproving of his performance and his policies. Most polls showed the race "too close to call," and
many of the major indicators, "historically" speaking, suggested the incumbent would lose. Small wonder that so many experts, including apparently the
President's own political team, were willing to believe the election-day exit
polls that into the early evening showed their man losing by a considerable
margin. (The widely circulated numbers from the respected polling firm Zogby
International, for example, showed Mr. Kerry winning 311 electoral votes.)
The fact was that though President Bush was personally popular, many of his
major policies were not. The problem for the Bush campaign was how to turn
attention away from policies voters didn't like—particularly the President's decisions on Iraq and his conduct of the war there—toward policies they approved of—particularly his conduct of "the war on terror" (into which Iraq
would be "folded")—and toward his personal qualities.

3.

> If your babies were left all alone in the dead of night, who would you rather have setting there on the porch—John Kerry and his snowboard or George W. with his shotgun?
>
> —Sean Michaels, professional wrestler, warming up the crowd,
> Tinker Field, October 30, 2004

On a beautiful October evening three days before the election, Orlando's 21 Tinker Field had become an enormous bowl filled with 17,000 screaming, chanting Bush partisans floating in a sea of red, white, and blue. On the stadium wall hung a great fifty-foot high sign proclaiming that George W. Bush was "MOVING AMERICA FORWARD!" Inside, flanking the stage in letters that dwarfed it, and echoed by smaller signs bobbing up and down everywhere in the crowd, was the terse slogan "AMERICA: SAFER STRONGER BETTER!" And then, precisely placed around the stadium in enormous letters, were the words on which the campaign was built: "STRENGTH! LEADERSHIP! CHARACTER! INTEGRITY!" Disciplined, organized, relentless, the Bush campaign would never be accused of subtlety.

"Well . . ., I'm just so proud of the way he handled 9/11—I mean, that 22 was . . . *amazing!*" Dot Richardson-Pinto told me as we sat together near the podium. When I'd asked why she supported the President, she had had to search a moment for an answer, and not entirely because she couldn't understand how it could be that anyone wouldn't. She'd had to think for a moment, I came to realize, because her ardor had so much more to do with who he was than with what he did. And who he was could be summarized by those four giant words looming over the stage.

"It doesn't matter if the man can talk," Ms. Richardson-Pinto told me. 23 "Sometimes, when someone's real articulate you can't trust what he says, you know?" As the security helicopters circled overhead, and the crowd launched into yet one more chant of "*Kerry is scary!*" I was struck again by how precisely the campaign had managed to define Bush's strengths in perfect contradistinction to what they had defined as Kerry's weaknesses, and then to devote all its resources to emphasizing both. Every repetition of what Bush was—and the repetitions were unending, and intricately varied—was crafted to be a perfect reminder of what his opponent was not. Practically every word emitted by the campaign, whether through the thousands and thousands of television and radio commercials, or the words of the campaign spokesmen, or the speeches of the candidate himself, moved in gorgeously disciplined lockstep to drive home to voters not only who George W. Bush was but who his opponent was not. As Bush became more and more Bush ("*STRENGTH! LEADERSHIP! CHARACTER! INTEGRITY!*"), Kerry, little-known, chilly, distant, was turned into the anti-Bush, a weak,

All over but the shouting Supporters of presidential contenders John Kerry and George W. Bush near th▸ Supervisor of Elections office in Jacksonville, Fla., Tuesday, Nov. 2, 2004.

shallow, flipflopping, shillyshallyer whose every word was an attempt to deceive Americans about who he really was.

In blue shirt and black slacks the President strode into the stadium, 24 flanked by his wife and brother Jeb, and raised his hands to the rock-star reception. When the thunderous chants—"*Viva Bush! Viva Bush!*"—had finally dropped off to a scattering of shouts, he launched into a speech whose terms I knew well but whose effectiveness, with Ms. Richardson-Pinto sitting beside me, I only now understood. George W. Bush seemed to be speaking directly to her, to be bringing her into his family:

> Sometimes I'm a little too blunt—I get that from my mother. [*Huge cheers*] Sometimes I mangle the English language—I get that from my dad. [*Laughter and cheers*]
>
> But you always know where I stand. You can't say that for my opponent. . . .
>
> The fact is that *all* progress on other issues depends on the safety of our citizens. The most solemn duty of the American president is to protect the American people. [*Loud cheers. Chants of "Four More Years! Four More Years! Four More Years!"*]
>
> The president must make tough decisions and stand behind them. Especially in time of war mixed signals only confuse our friends and embolden our enemies.

> If America shows uncertainty or weakness in these troubling times
> the world will drift toward tragedy—*and this will not happen on my*
> *watch!*

In a few blunt lines Bush had subsumed everything else beneath the pre-   25
eminent shining banner of the war on terror, and subsumed that war beneath his own reputation for forthrightness, decisiveness, and strength.
And he had identified uncertainty, hesitation, vacillation—even the sort of
nit-picking that would seek to separate the war in Iraq from the war on terror—as not simply mistaken or foolish but dangerous. "Relentless" . . .
"Steadfast" . . . "Determined": these words came fast and strong, again
and again. And then the climactic line: "*We will fight the terrorists across*
the globe so we do not have to fight them here at home!" It drew a huge
response and after the applause and chanting had finally died down he followed up with his most important words about the current shooting war:

> I will use every asset at our disposal to protect the American people
> and one of the best assets we have is *freedom!* Freedom is *powerful!*
>   Freedom is not America's gift to the world, it is the Almighty's gift
> to everyone. . . . Iraq is still dangerous but Iraq will have free elec-
> tions in January—think how far that country has come!
>   On good days and bad days, whether the polls are up or the polls
> are down, I am determined to protect the American people!

The Iraq war was not only irrevocably part of the war on terror—who   26
could think, gazing at the car bombs and beheadings every night on television, that they were any different?—it had become a leading part of the ideological response to the threat of terror: a first step in the expansion of the
holy cause of freedom. As Reagan had dared to go beyond staunch anti-
communism and imagine a world after communism's collapse, so Bush
looked beyond the present chaotic world of terror to see a blessed land of
freedom.[6] ("In this election, my opponent has spent a lot of time talking
about a day that is gone. I'm talking about the day that is coming.") It was
a striking vision, clear and absolutely simple to understand. And it linked,
firmly and directly, the so-called "moral values" of justice, fairness, and the
Almighty to the cause of national security, and specifically to the war on
terror that the Bush people kept relentlessly at the campaign's heart. "Terror," "Iraq," and "moral values," supposedly separate "important issues,"
had been seamlessly joined.

Of course whatever its virtues as a campaign theme, the picture the Pres-   27
ident offered was not especially "fact-dependent." Many well-known facts—
on which Kerry, in his campaign, had laid such stress—were either irrelevant
to it (the missing weapons of mass destruction, which went unmentioned) or
directly contradicted by it (the failure to demonstrate connections between

Iraq and the attacks of September 11). But the facts did not matter—not necessarily because those in the stadium were ignorant of them, though some certainly were, but because the President was offering in their place a worldview that was whole, complete, comprehensible, and thus impermeable to statements of fact that clearly contradicted it. The thousands cheering around me in that Orlando stadium, and the many others who would come to support Bush on election day, faced a stark choice: either discard the facts, or give up the clear and comforting worldview that they contradicted. They chose to disregard the facts.

Two weeks before the election, after the Senate Intelligence Committee   28 report on Iraqi weapons of mass destruction and the Duelfer Report, and after intensive news coverage of the administration's failure to find such weapons in Iraq, nearly three Bush supporters in four told pollsters they believed Iraq had either had weapons of mass destruction (47 percent) or had had a "major program" to develop them (26 percent). Nearly three in five said they believed that the widely publicized Duelfer Report, which directly contradicted this, had in fact confirmed it. Three in four believed that Iraq had either been directly involved in the September 11 attacks (20 percent) or had given al-Qaeda "substantial support" (55 percent), and nearly three in ten wrongly believed that the 9/11 Commission had confirmed that they had. Similar majorities believed that the President and his administration still publicly supported these positions.

Many of the Bush supporters I spoke to were educated, well-informed   29 people. They watched the news and took pleasure in debating politics. And yet they clung to views about important matters of fact that were demonstrably wrong. Steven Kull, the public opinion expert at the University of Maryland who authored the study from which these numbers are drawn, acknowledges that although one reason they "cling so tightly to beliefs that have been so visibly refuted . . . is that they continue to hear the Bush administration confirming these beliefs," the prevalence, and persistence, of these misperceptions is "probably not due to a simple failure to pay attention to the news." Rather, Kull writes, "Bush supporters cling to these beliefs because they are necessary for their support for the decision to go to war with Iraq":

> Asked whether the US should have gone to war with Iraq if US intelligence had concluded that Iraq was not making WMD or providing support to al Qaeda, 58 percent of Bush supporters said the US should not have, and 61 percent assume that in this case the president would not have. To support the president and to accept that he took the US to war based on mistaken assumptions is difficult to bear, especially in light of the continuing costs in terms of lives and money. Apparently, to avoid this cognitive dissonance, Bush supporters suppress awareness of unsettling information.[7]

This analysis suggests the difficulties Kerry faced in pressing home his 30 highly "fact-dependent" argument that the Iraq war was separate from the war on terror and thus a mistaken distraction from it. Not only did accepting the point require a good deal of sophistication and knowledge, not only did it seem to contradict the evidence on Americans' television screens each night, which often showed vivid depictions of terrorism in Iraq; it also seemed to imply to some voters that they should take what must have seemed an unpatriotic position. For if they accepted the false pretenses on which the war had been based, how could they go on supporting it, as Kerry, somewhat illogically and even dishonestly, seemed to be asking them to do?

Those running the Bush campaign clearly counted on the talent and in- 31 fluence of impressive propagandists like Limbaugh, and the help they received from an often acquiescent mainstream press. More, they counted on the President's reputation for forthrightness, together with the political folk wisdom that many people, particularly "during wartime," believe "the man, not the fact." When Bush, in full rhetorical flower in Tinker Field, declared to his delirious audience that "Americans need a president who doesn't think terrorism is 'a nuisance,'" my neighbor Ms. Richardson-Pinto nudged me with her elbow and shouted over the laughter and cheers, "Do you *believe* Kerry said that?" Actually, I shouted into her ear, Kerry hadn't said that, and then I paraphrased for her the actual quotation:

> We have to get back to the place we were, where terrorists are not the focus of our lives, but they're a nuisance. As a former law enforcement person, I know we're never going to end prostitution . . . [and] illegal gambling. But we're going to reduce it, organized crime, to a level where . . . it's something that you continue to fight, but it's not threatening the fabric of your life.[8]

Hardly exceptional; indeed, Bush himself had only weeks before said 32 something very similar. Ms. Richardson-Pinto, a well-educated, worldly woman—a doctor, and a two-time Olympic gold medalist in women's softball—listened to me intently, nodded politely, began to form a question, and then, thinking better of it, looked at me for a moment longer before turning back to the President. She'd had a choice what—or rather whom—to believe; and she'd made it.

4.

Saddam would never have disarmed.
—George W. Bush, first presidential debate, September 30, 2004

Seven o'clock on the evening of Election Day and the office of the election 33 supervisor in downtown Jacksonville was mobbed, encircled by a raggedy line of hundreds and hundreds of late voters. In the street in front an enormous crowd of Democrats chanted, cheered, and sang, filling every inch of space and spilling out into the streets. Car after car, horns blaring, made its way carefully through the crowd, the drivers leaning out to administer high fives and to cheer, and cheer again. When word of the early exit-poll numbers seeming to confirm an overwhelming Kerry victory swept through the crowd, hundreds broke into song, to the tune of the old civil rights classic, "Ain't Gonna Let Nobody Turn Me Around":

> Ain't gonna let nobody steal my vote
> Steal my vote, steal my vote
> Ain't gonna let nobody steal my vote. . . .

It had been Jacksonville where in 2000 the infamous "caterpillar bal- 34 lot" had led officials to discard tens of thousands of votes, votes cast overwhelmingly by African-Americans. As I stood watching the dancing and the celebration—"We gonna *elect* one, not *select* one!"—the sense people had of justice finally being done was vivid. I had felt it all day as I went from polling place to polling place in the downtown neighborhoods of the city—they were overwhelmed with voters, and overwhelmed with a sense that a wrong would be righted.

What I didn't find was any sense of strong support for John Kerry as a 35 politician or a leader, or even a feeling of familiarity with him. The personality of Bush seemed vivid among voters, whether they admired him or hated him; the personality of Kerry was faint, indistinct, and where I found its mark most strongly was among those Bush voters who saw the Massachusetts senator, or the depiction of him that the Bush campaign had succeeded in creating, as a threat to their security. To counteract this Kerry would have had to become a known quality, trusted, *familiar;* but even after the hundreds of millions spent on advertising and his strong performance in the debates, for most voters he seemed a distant figure. He never entered that great stock company of celebrities—the "Oprah touring company"—that ordinary Americans welcome into their living rooms and believe they have somehow come to know. Love him or hate him, the President had long since taken his place as a recognizable, powerful personality in that company; John Kerry never did.

I had seen Kerry speak two nights before in Tampa, before a crowd fully 36 as delirious as the one that had greeted George W. Bush the night before. Though the Kerry crowd was recognizably younger and, for lack of a better word, "hipper," most of those present would not have seemed out of place at either event. Partly hidden behind a forest of yellow "Two More Days!" signs, Kerry, by far the tallest person on stage, stretched and shifted as he was introduced, raising and lowering himself on the balls of his feet:

he was plainly exhausted. Nonetheless he gave a powerful, well-crafted speech, though built around the uninspired phrases "a fresh start" and "first we must choose." And then he turned to Iraq:

> The President tells us that in Iraq, his "strategy is succeeding. . . ." But every day on our TV screens, we see the hard truths. We see the consequences of this President's decision to rush to war without a plan to win the peace: the loss of over 1,100 of our brave men and women in uniform. A cost of $225 billion with billions more on the way. Entire regions controlled by insurgents and terrorists. By pushing our allies aside, George Bush's catastrophic mismanagement of this war has left America to bear almost 90 percent of the costs and 90 percent of the coalition casualties. We relied on Afghan warlords instead of American troops to hunt down Osama bin Laden, and the man responsible for murdering more than three thousand Americans walked away. . . . On Tuesday, we have the opportunity to set a new course in Iraq . . . open up a new chapter in our relationship with the rest of the world . . . and do whatever it takes to defend America and keep our troops safe. . . . When I'm president, I will bring other nations to our side and train Iraqis so that we can succeed and bring our troops home. As president, I will fight a tougher, smarter, more effective war on terror. We will hunt down, capture, and kill the terrorists wherever they are. I defended this country as a young man and I will defend it as president.

Kerry's indictment of Bush's stewardship of the war was strong, but he offered little by way of an alternative; his "new course in Iraq" amounted to bringing "other nations to our side" to train Iraqis. He would "do whatever it takes to defend America"—a broad, empty assertion that depended entirely on the trust a prospective voter was willing to grant him. And though Kerry struggled to separate Iraq and the war on terror, not just the imagery of the war—the descent of Iraq into a kind of terrorism that, ironically enough, seemed to confirm the President's insistence that it was in fact "the central front of the war on terror"—but Kerry's own discussion of Iraq and terrorism only seemed to bring them together. 37

For Kerry, this proved fatal. If Bush had succeeded in joining Iraq and terrorism and then wrestling to the very center of the election his chosen question—whom do you trust to protect you and your family from terrorism?—he had also succeeded, for too many of those famous "swing voters," in providing the answer. The exit polls make this clear: nearly six in ten voters said they trusted Bush to "handle terrorism." Nearly six in ten said they did not trust Kerry to do the same. 38

Of course it is easy to say, as many have, that Kerry's policy on Iraq and terrorism was inadequate or incoherent. It is much harder to say what that policy should have been. Kerry, it is true, did not prove himself a very 39 creative or resourceful candidate, and the Bush campaign was ruthless and brilliant in seizing on his missteps—his mention of a "global test" for United States intervention abroad, for example, and his unfortunate statement that "I actually voted for the $87 billion before I voted against it"—and using them to color in vivid tones the picture they wanted to paint of the senator.[9] Kerry gave them a good deal of help, particularly by focusing on Vietnam, and attempting to make his heroic service as a naval officer there a central part of his campaign while avoiding discussion of his more controversial leadership in the antiwar movement after he returned. The so-called Swift Boat Veterans for Truth, incensed by the antiwar Kerry, did great damage to the reputation of heroic warrior Kerry, and thereby did much to bolster the point that the Bush campaign, with the help of tens of millions of dollars in television and radio ads, had sought to drive home to American voters: that Kerry was inauthentic, untrustworthy, and "unfit to lead."

But Kerry's mistakes, however costly, in fact concealed a deeper problem, which was that Democrats themselves, haunted by the traditional charge of "weakness on national security" (which of course helped lead to Kerry's nomination), were deeply divided on what should be done about the Iraq war, with as many favoring withdrawal as not.[10] This is not surprising: the war itself, a costly, tangled, unending mess, admits of no obvious solution. The war may well be President Bush's greatest wound; but for candidate Bush the ability to depict Iraq as "the central front of the war on terror" and trumpet his willingness to confront the war and "stay the course" to victory was an audacious and astonishing act of political legerdemain. He took what looked to be his greatest weakness and made it his opponent's. 40

Kerry might have done better to declare early on that Iraq and the war on terror could no longer be separated, and to argue, forcefully and consistently, that Bush had conducted both incompetently—so incompetently, in fact, that four more years of his leadership would put Americans at ever greater risk. But to have been convincing, such a strategy, at least implicitly, would have meant accepting the necessity of going to war in Iraq—a position that many committed Democratic voters strongly disputed and that Kerry's own past statements tended to contradict. And it would have meant demonstrating the kind of single-mindedness, relentlessness, and rigor that the Bush campaign managed but the Kerry forces never did. Either way, as long as Bush was able to succeed in melding Iraq and the war on terror and placing them firmly at the center of the campaign, Kerry faced an incumbent "war president" who, whatever his missteps, Americans would be hesitant to abandon—without a very good reason for doing so. Kerry never produced that reason. 41

At about half past eight, as I stood amid the roiling sea of jubilant 42
Democrats outside that election supervisor's office in downtown Jacksonville, I began to hear, through the civil rights songs and the laughter and cheers, a distant, booming, amplified chant. One by one people in the crowd before me heard it, and began turning to look down the street whence the chanting came, and then to look at one another. The voices grew louder and louder, and finally we saw their source: a group of twenty or so young men—they looked like football players—led by a beefy fellow holding high a blue Bush/Cheney sign, and chanting through a megaphone in a deep baritone:

Bush Won the State! Bush Won the State! Bush Won the State!

The dream of a Democratic victory had been fueled by the enormous 43
turnout and by a handful of faulty exit polls. Everyone had believed it, even those distinctly downcast Republicans I'd visited at their Jacksonville headquarters earlier that afternoon. But the dream had ended.

The Democrats had come remarkably close. They had matched the Re- 44
publicans in fund-raising dollar for dollar and had mounted an unprecedented "ground game." On election day they managed the impressive feat of bringing eight million more voters to the polls than they had four years before. But the Republicans managed to bring in eleven million additional voters. George W. Bush, having gained half a million fewer votes than Al Gore in 2000, defeated John Kerry by three million votes.[11]

Still, the victory was "narrow but clear," as William Kristol described 45
it, with candor rare among Republicans after the election. For all the talk of "moral values," had 60,000 Ohioans made a different choice on election day, we would now be discussing the unpopularity of the Iraq war and the President's failed economic policies. After his narrow but clear victory, George W. Bush remained a popular leader promoting unpopular policies. And though he managed to convince enough Americans that Iraq was "the central front in the war on terror," the truth remains that he has saddled himself and the country he leads with a worsening, increasingly unpopular shooting war that offers no obvious means of escape.

Now he faces a newly emboldened set of claimants. Though several mil- 46
lion more evangelical voters turned out in 2004, and thus were critical to Bush's victory, they do not seem to have formed a higher percentage of Republican voters than they had four years before.[12] Still, having accounted, in their increased numbers, for a third of Bush's margin of victory, the evangelicals unquestionably form the Republican Party's most reliable and aggressive base of supporters. Their leaders have been quick and aggressive in claiming full credit for the triumph and the press has been happy to play along. As so often in politics, the appearance, through repetition, becomes its own reality.

Leaders like the unabashedly direct Reverend Bob Jones III now demand,   47
in the name of moral values and the political redemption they claim to have
brought the President, that Bush "pass legislation defined by Biblical norms"
and that he "leave an imprint of righteousness upon this nation that brings
with it the blessings of Almighty God." This is a tall order, and one fraught,
like the war, with considerable political peril—from moderate voters, who,
for example, support outlawing "partial-birth abortion" but oppose outlawing abortion itself; and even, perhaps, from Democrats who may one day
come to focus on what they have gained in this election rather than what they
have lost. After all the recriminations and all the analyses of how the party
must change, the fact remains that the Democrats came very close to bringing off an almost unprecedented achievement: turning out an incumbent
president in a time of war. They failed, but not entirely; they now confront a
narrowly reelected president, encumbered with a grim and intractable war,
constrained by a huge deficit of his own creation, and faced with increasingly
extreme demands that will be satisfied only at great political cost.
   —December 15, 2004

Notes

[1]See *The Road to Illegitimacy: One Reporter's Adventures in the 2000
Florida Vote Recount* (Melville House, 2004), based on "The Road to Illegitimacy," *The New York Review,* February 22, 2001.

[2]In 1996 Bill Clinton, the last president to win reelection, won by 8.5 percent and 220 electoral votes; in 1964 Lyndon Johnson—who like Theodore
Roosevelt had not been elected but took office after the death of an incumbent—won by 22 percent and 434 electoral votes. To find an elected incumbent who won by nearly as narrow a margin as George W. Bush, one must
look back nine decades, to 1916, when Democrat Woodrow Wilson won by
3.2 percent and 23 electoral votes.

[3]Because of population gains recorded in the 2000 Census some states, like
Arizona, Florida, and Georgia, were accorded more electoral votes in 2004,
while others, like New York, Pennsylvania, and Wisconsin, were accorded
fewer. This process favored the Republicans, with their base in the growing
states of the South and Southwest; the same states they had won in 2000
were worth seven more votes in 2004.

[4]These figures are drawn from Michael McDonald of George Mason University and the United States Election Project. His turnout figures represent the
percentage of people eligible to vote (VEP)—thus eliminating noncitizens,
felons, etc.—rather than the more common, but less accurate, percentage of
people of voting age (VAP). See <elections.gmu.edu/voter_turnout.htm>.

[5]These numbers are all drawn from *The New York Times*/CBS News Poll, taken in mid- to late October, with most, though not all, of the polling done between October 28 and 30.

[6]Ralph Reed, who had directed Bush's campaign in the Southeast, made this point repeatedly, explicitly comparing Bush's rhetoric on terrorism and the Middle East to Reagan's on communism. See *The Charlie Rose Show*, December 13, 2004.

[7]See Steven Kull et al., *The Separate Reality of Bush and Kerry Supporters* (PIPA/Knowledge Networks, October 21, 2004), p. 13.

[8]See Matt Bai, "Kerry's Undeclared War," *New York Times Magazine*, October 10, 2004.

[9]See especially "How He Did It," *Newsweek*, November 15, 2004, p. 70, for an excellent account of the Bush campaign's handling of the $87 billion gaffe.

[10]See, among others, Ron Brownstein, "Kerry Feels Squeeze on Iraq Policy," *Los Angeles Times*, May 27, 2004. As Brownstein points out, polls had shown nearly half of Democratic voters favoring immediate withdrawal, a position that, if adopted, would likely have doomed Kerry's candidacy.

[11]Half of those votes came from the President's loyal supporters in the "deep red" states—especially Texas, Georgia, Alabama, and Tennessee—and a third from stronger support for Bush in the deep blue states, especially New York and New Jersey. The remainder came from the so-called purple states, and half of these from Florida—where the President, with a spectacular effort to register new voters in the outer suburbs, increased his margin from 537 to more than 370,000.

[12]Much less noticed, and in many ways more dramatic, was the upsurge in Catholics voting for Bush, which was a true shift from four years ago. Kerry, a Catholic, received 5 percent fewer Catholic votes than Al Gore, a Southern Baptist, and these votes were critical in several swing states, especially Ohio, where 55 percent of Catholic voters cast their ballots for Bush. According to Sidney Blumenthal, who reported these figures, the reason can be traced to the aggressive position that many in the Catholic hierarchy took against John Kerry. With the Catholic Church in America "in crisis," writes Blumenthal, "electing a liberal Catholic as president would have been a severe blow" to the Church and its conservative leadership. Because of this, Kerry faced aggressive opposition from many in the hierarchy, including some bishops who openly denounced the candidate and threatened to deny him communion or even to ex-communicate him. See Sidney Blumenthal, "The Lowest Ignorance Takes Charge," *The Guardian*, November 11, 2004.

Thinking Critically

1. Aside from length, what other key distinctions can you make between Mark Danner's approach here in "How Bush Really Won" and Deborah Caldwell's rhetorical strategies later in this chapter in "Dispatches from Lancaster: Getting Out the Vote in a Conservative Christian County"? Compare the audiences for Danner's and Caldwell's articles. Are you surprised by any similarities in these two articles?

2. What use does Mark Danner make of radio commentaries, political commercials, and other media in shaping his argument?

3. In Danner's assessment, what two issues did the media argue were foremost in the minds of voters in the 2004 American presidential election? How does Danner define those two issues, and what evidence does he use to argue about their real influence on the election's results?

Writing Critically

1. Danner's article is a close and careful analysis of the results of the 2004 presidential election, but his first-person reporting seems to be telling another story as well. How did the events of September 11, 2001, change the social, political, and economic concerns of your own family or community? In an essay that draws on your own experience and observations, as well as on interviews with individuals in your family and community, support an argument about how the events of 9/11 fundamentally changed some aspect of your public or civic life.

2. Write a narrative of your own involvement with—or disengagement from—a major civic event, such as a recent election, an important demonstration, or an act of civil disobedience. How fair and accurate were news accounts of that event, in comparison with your own direct experience?

3. What specific predictions does Danner make about the impact of the 2004 American presidential election? In an analytical essay, evaluate Danner's prescience about a particular issue. Your task here is not to say whether he is "wrong" or "right," but rather to build on Danner's conclusions and draw on the same kinds of evidence he used to trace the continued evolution of an ongoing event, issue, or problem.

The Day the Enlightenment Went Out

GARY WILLS

An adjunct professor of history at Northwestern University and the author of *Under God: Religion and American Politics* (1990) and *Why I Am a Catholic* (2002), Gary Wills has published extensively on faith, politics, and culture, from perspectives both academic and personal. An acclaimed historian, Wills was awarded the 1993 Pulitzer Prize for General Nonfiction for *Lincoln at Gettysburg.* Discussing his book *A Necessary Evil: A History of American Distrust of Government* (1999) on the PBS program *The NewsHour with Jim Lehrer,* Wills observed that "I think the way we have to go is to say government is dangerous, so we have to control it. But it's not a necessary evil, it's a necessary good." "The Day the Enlightenment Went Out" appeared on the op-ed page of the *New York Times* on November 4, 2004.

This election confirms the brilliance of Karl Rove as a political strate-   1
gist. He calculated that the religious conservatives, if they could be turned out, would be the deciding factor. The success of the plan was registered not only in the presidential results but also in all 11 of the state votes to ban same-sex marriage. Mr. Rove understands what surveys have shown, that many more Americans believe in the Virgin Birth than in Darwin's theory of evolution.

This might be called Bryan's revenge for the Scopes trial of 1925, in   2
which William Jennings Bryan's fundamentalist assault on the concept of evolution was discredited. Disillusionment with that decision led many evangelicals to withdraw from direct engagement in politics. But they came roaring back into the arena out of anger at other court decisions—on prayer in school, abortion, protection of the flag and, now, gay marriage. Mr. Rove felt that the appeal to this large bloc was worth getting President Bush to endorse a constitutional amendment banning gay marriage (though he had opposed it earlier).

The results bring to mind a visit the Dalai Lama made to Chicago not   3
long ago. I was one of the people deputized to ask him questions on the stage at the Field Museum. He met with the interrogators beforehand and asked us to give him challenging questions, since he is too often greeted with deference or flattery.

The only one I could think of was: "If you could return to your country, 4
what would you do to change it?" He said that he would disestablish his religion, since "America is the proper model." I later asked him if a pluralist
society were possible without the Enlightenment. "Ah," he said. "That's the
problem." He seemed to envy America its Enlightenment heritage.

Which raises the question: Can a people that believes more fervently in 5
the Virgin Birth than in evolution still be called an Enlightened nation?

America, the first real democracy in history, was a product of Enlight- 6
enment values—critical intelligence, tolerance, respect for evidence, a regard for the secular sciences. Though the founders differed on many
things, they shared these values of what was then modernity. They addressed "a candid world," as they wrote in the Declaration of Independence, out of "a decent respect for the opinions of mankind." Respect for
evidence seems not to pertain anymore, when a poll taken just before the
elections showed that 75 percent of Mr. Bush's supporters believe Iraq either worked closely with Al Qaeda or was directly involved in the attacks
of 9/11.

The secular states of modern Europe do not understand the fundamen- 7
talism of the American electorate. It is not what they had experienced from
this country in the past. In fact, we now resemble those nations less than
we do our putative enemies.

Where else do we find fundamentalist zeal, a rage at secularity, reli- 8
gious intolerance, fear of and hatred for modernity? Not in France or
Britain or Germany or Italy or Spain. We find it in the Muslim world, in
Al Qaeda, in Saddam Hussein's Sunni loyalists. Americans wonder that
the rest of the world thinks us so dangerous, so single-minded, so imper-
vious to international appeals. They fear jihad, no matter whose zeal is being expressed.

It is often observed that enemies come to resemble each other. We torture the torturers, we call our God better than theirs—as one American
general put it, in words that the president has not repudiated.

President Bush promised in 2000 that he would lead a humble country, 9
be a uniter not a divider, that he would make conservatism compassionate.
He did not need to make such false promises this time. He was re-elected
precisely by being a divider, pitting the reddest aspects of the red states
against the blue nearly half of the nation. In this, he is very far from Ronald
Reagan, who was amiably and ecumenically pious. He could address more
secular audiences, here and abroad, with real respect.

In his victory speech yesterday, President Bush indicated that he would 10
"reach out to the whole nation," including those who voted for John Kerry.

But even if he wanted to be more conciliatory now, the constituency to which he owes his victory is not a yielding one. He must give them what they want on things like judicial appointments. His helpers are also his keepers.

The moral zealots will, I predict, give some cause for dismay even to 11 nonfundamentalist Republicans. Jihads are scary things. It is not too early to start yearning back toward the Enlightenment.

Thinking Critically

1. What is the Enlightenment? Given your understanding of American social and political history, to what extent do you think the nation reflects Enlightenment ideals? In your study of American history at the high school or college level, were the ideas of the Enlightenment covered? How about the role of religion or faith in the founding of postrevolutionary America?

2. How does Garry Wills characterize American religious fundamentalists? Do you agree or disagree with his assessment? Base your response on direct evidence or experience—whether from your own family and community background or from your exposure to the news and entertainment media.

3. Wills seems to draw a parallel between American religious fundamentalism and al-Qaeda. Is this comparison fair either to American fundamentalists or to mainstream Muslims? In what ways does the rhetorical form of the op-ed essay allow for this kind of claim to be made?

Writing Critically

1. What, for Wills, is the significance of the Dalai Lama's response to Wills's question? Write an essay in which you explore the question of whether a "pluralistic society were possible without the Enlightenment" (paragraph 4). As part of your research and drafting, be sure that you grasp the connotations of the phrase "pluralistic society" and understand the historical, cultural, and philosophical significance of the Enlightenment. (Obviously, you won't be able to address the entirety of the Enlightenment in one essay. But you can select as the basis for your argument a specific author or a particular event or circumstance associated with the Enlightenment.)

2. The text of the Declaration of Independence is available online at <http://www.law.emory.edu/FEDERAL/independ/declar.html>. What did the authors of the Declaration mean by "a candid world"? In what ways is the United States today a "candid" nation—or not—in a candid (or not) world?

The Political Conversion of New York's Evangelicals

ANDREA ELLIOTT

> *New York Times* reporter Andrea Elliott began her career as a journalist at her high school newspaper, going on to receive an M.S. in journalism at Columbia University's Graduate School of Journalism. Her first "real job" as a journalist was as a producer of a documentary filmed in Chile. She joined the staff of the *Miami Herald* in 1999, covering local government, Hispanic affairs, crime, and other stories of the urban beat. Elliott joined the staff of the *New York Times* as a reporter on the metro desk in 2003. In an essay on the website of the American Society of Newspaper Editors, Elliott writes of her career: "The greatest thing about journalism is how it inserts us—often uncomfortably, sometimes unforgettably—into the world. We look, we listen and we share the story of life. The story is almost always larger than we are, but without us, who would tell it?" This article appeared in the *New York Times* on November 14, 2004.

The signs are all around. Storefront churches dot the commercial land- 1
scapes of the Bronx and Queens. Twice as many churchgoers—about 15,000—pray weekly at the Christian Cultural Center in Brooklyn, compared with five years ago. Some 200,000 New Yorkers tune in daily to Radio Vision Cristiana, an AM radio station. And last March, thousands of evangelicals gathered on the steps of the State Supreme Court in the Bronx to protest the idea of same-sex marriage.

Evangelism is flourishing not just in the red states of the nation's heart- 2
land, but in the urban, liberal stronghold of New York City, where thousands of evangelical churches are anchored in working-class neighborhoods. Whether it will evolve into a local political force, as it has nationally, remains an open question. But a range of interviews with pastors, congregants and religious experts suggests that a new debate—and perhaps a political conversion—is taking place in parts of the city's minority neighborhoods, swaths that Democrats have long claimed as their own.

It is a conversion that prompted Jeanmarie Salazar, a Puerto Rican 3
mother of four in the Bronx, to vote for President Bush even though his economic policies troubled her. And a conversion that caused Harold

Thompson, an African-American from Flatbush who lived through the civil rights movement, to part with a lifetime of voting Democratic, citing the "immorality that is destroying our country."

Both Ms. Salazar and Mr. Thompson belong to evangelical churches 4 whose leaders have spread a single but potent message: Faith trumps everything else, even traditional party alignments.

"They're beginning to think about the social transformation of New York 5 City," said Tony Carnes, a sociologist of religion at Columbia University.

Precisely determining the number of people who consider themselves mem- 6 bers of evangelical churches or movements is difficult. Mr. Carnes said that he conducted a census of the city's evangelical churches and estimated that 1.5 million New Yorkers attend them. A separate study, conducted in 2000 by the Association of Statisticians of American Religious Bodies, put the number of evangelical New Yorkers closer to 1 million, said Vivian Klaff, a professor of sociology at the University of Delaware who analyzed the study's data.

If a fully accurate count of evangelicals in the city is difficult to achieve, 7 it is even harder, at the moment, to define the voting patterns of evangelicals. But the number of Protestant New Yorkers who cast ballots for a Republican president more than doubled in the last four years, to nearly a quarter of those surveyed at polling sites by Edison Media Research and Mitofsky International. And a recent study by Mr. Carnes suggested that a majority of evangelical church leaders in the city were breaking with tradition and voting Republican: of 1,006 ordained ministers surveyed last year, Mr. Carnes found, 55 percent said they planned to vote for Mr. Bush.

About 30 percent of the ministers were black and 30 percent Hispanic, re- 8 flecting the demographic breakdown of the religious group, Mr. Carnes said.

"It's a significant development," said Randall Barnes, a professor of 9 American religious history at Barnard College. But, he added, the Republican Party in New York City is "still a decade or two away from making significant inroads into that community."

Any measuring of the political clout of evangelicals in the city, now or 10 in the future, is complicated by the fact that a sizable portion of them are from other countries, and some are not eligible to vote, said Mr. Carnes, who conducted his study with a team of pollsters at the International Research Institute on Values Changes, an independent research group in New York City. The study was financed by the Christian Cultural Center, a charismatic evangelical church.

But the results indicated a shift to the right among voting evangelicals. 11 In a separate study he did in 1997, Mr. Carnes said, only 22 percent of the city's evangelical church leaders surveyed identified themselves as "politically conservative."

In the past 5 years, membership has doubled at the Christian Cultural Center in East New York, Brookly

In the aftermath of the election, an increasingly complex image has   12
emerged of the Christian electorate—one that is not entirely captured under the religious right rubric. In New York City, there are the evangelicals
who consider themselves liberal and voted for Kerry but find that they are
missing from the mainstream image of their faith.

But then there are those, like Mr. Thompson, who broke with tradition   13
for the first time to vote Republican.

And while many New Yorkers have loudly voiced their sense of alien-   14
ation from the faith-based vote of the red states, the city's evangelicals, in
numerous interviews, said they felt a similar invisibility in the Democratic
stronghold they call home.

"You feel like you're alone," said Abraham Lopez, 19, as he stood on   15
a recent Saturday outside the Assemblies of United Christian Churches on
Third Avenue in the South Bronx.

Perhaps no single event better captures the group's presence than a   16
same-sex marriage protest on March 14 in the South Bronx.

Led by State Senator Rubén Diaz, 150 Bronx churches closed for the   17
day. They sent their congregants to the steps of the State Supreme Court on
the Grand Concourse where thousands of people—estimated at 8,000 by
Mr. Carnes, who used two methods to count the crowd—filled the streets.
A large banner hung between two pillars, reading, "No to Homosexual
Marriage."

"We said, 'Sunday nobody goes to church; we'll go to the street,' " said   18
Mr. Diaz, one of the most noted of the city's Hispanic evangelicals. Mr.
Diaz, whose South Bronx district includes about 250,000 people, is both
an evangelical pastor and a registered Democrat.

"I am a conservative Democrat," Mr. Diaz, 61, said in a telephone in-   19
terview from Puerto Rico. "When it comes to education, when it comes to
health, when it comes to jobs, I'm a Democrat. When it comes to moral issues—marriage, abortion—I'm not a Democrat."

Mr. Diaz has a history of stirring controversy with his conservative stands   20
on same-sex marriage and abortion. In 1994, after he organized a voter drive
for Mayor Rudolph W. Giuliani, Mr. Diaz, then a city councilman, vocally
criticized the Gay and Lesbian Olympic Games. Mr. Giuliani then issued a
statement distancing himself from Mr. Diaz's views. In 2003, Mr. Diaz filed
a lawsuit, which is still pending, against the city over the opening of a small
public school for gay students. He defends his positions unflinchingly, saying things like he "cannot wait" for the reversal of *Roe v. Wade* and eagerly
admitting that gay rights activists have picketed his church.

Several political strategists who have worked with Republicans and   21
Democrats said that no one with Mr. Diaz's conservative views would be
able to win a citywide or statewide office. But in local city politics, like
races for the State Assembly and the City Council, the faith-driven agenda
might have greater impact.

"In a Democratic primary where you take the party affiliation question   22
out of play, then I think it could become a more powerful influence," said
Kieran Mahoney, a Republican political strategist whose clients have included Gov. George E. Pataki.

Pedro Espada Jr., who lost to Mr. Diaz in the primary this year, said he had   23
no doubt that the evangelical movement could sway local politics. Mr. Espada,
who was ousted from his Senate seat by Mr. Diaz in 2002, tried to reach out
to evangelical voters by visiting Bronx churches.

"They would say, 'Espada, we would vote for you but you are not a 24
Christian,' " Mr. Espada said. But other politicians were more skeptical
that the group's members would be driven by religion when they entered
the voting booth.

Fernando Ferrer, the former Bronx borough president who is running 25
for mayor, said, "Issues of faith and family matter, but so do issues of how
we support our families, equal access and opportunity, housing, education,
health care, jobs."

While Hispanics and African Americans in New York City have tradi- 26
tionally voted Democratic, those who attend evangelical churches may feel
a different pull.

José Casanova, a professor of sociology who specializes in religion and 27
politics at New School University and has studied evangelicals around the
world, said that even if they are poor, they tend to vote for conservative
candidates.

"They do not so much identify with their economic position right now, 28
but with the one they ought to have with the help of God," he said. "They
are very conservative and pro-market and do not expect the government to
help them."

It is not clear how pervasive this view has been in New York City's 29
evangelical community. But the Rev. A. R. Bernard has made a point of
preaching economic independence and social conservatism at the Christian
Cultural Center, where more than 90 percent of congregants are African
Americans or black immigrants.

"We are teaching them self-reliance," Mr. Bernard said. "We have a 30
whole new generation of people of color who have grown up without legal and racial barriers. They have experienced unprecedented wealth, unprecedented education, a position in the marketplace. So once you have
something to conserve, you become more conservative."

Mr. Bernard, who said he voted for President Bush, does not publicly 31
endorse candidates. However, he did tell his congregants that they should
question the tendency to vote along traditional party lines.

Two of his church's members, Raina and Robert Bundy, said they de- 32
cided to vote for Mr. Bush by following the news, watching the debates
and, ultimately, praying over their choice. Like many African Americans,
they said they were brought up to vote Democratic, but now compared the
tradition to their mothers' old recipes for collard greens.

"We don't use fatback, it's all about olive oil now," Mrs. Bundy said. 33
"You don't keep cooking something even though you know it's not good
for you."

Thinking Critically

1. Why does Andrea Elliott consult sociologists for perspective and evidence? What kinds of issues do sociologists study, and how do they gather and evaluate evidence? What are the similarities between journalism and sociology?

2. What factors make an exact tally of evangelical Christians in New York particularly difficult? How might those same factors influence the politics of urban evangelical Christians?

3. How is a "faith-driven agenda" defined in this article, and who does the defining?

Writing Critically

1. Elliott quotes an African American religious leader, the Reverend A. R. Bernard, as noting of his congregation that "once you have something to conserve, you become more conservative" (paragraph 30). In an essay, use Rev. Bernard's observation as the basis for an extended definition of what you consider to be "conservative." Whether you agree or disagree with Rev. Bernard's definition, be sure to cite examples from *Many Americas,* current events, or your own experience to illustrate your definition.

2. How do the news media or popular culture stereotype evangelical Christians (or some other faith tradition)? Describe several specific examples of what you believe to be stereotyping, and argue clearly why you think those stereotypes are inaccurate and whether they might be racist, classist, or otherwise harmful.

3. In some communities, churches and faith-based organizations provide health care, social services, child care, and education. Do you think their outreach and support should include political action? Why, or why not?

Dispatches from Lancaster: Getting Out the Vote in a Conservative Christian County

DEBORAH CALDWELL

Deborah Caldwell is the religion producer for <Beliefnet .com>, an online religion and spirituality magazine that serves as a reference resource, community center, and news service for a wide range of religions and faiths. As a Beliefnet journalist, Caldwell has worked closely with ABC News to produce multimedia, interactive reports on the intersection of religion, culture, and politics in

America. Before joining Beliefnet in 1999, Caldwell was a reporter for the *Dallas Morning News,* covering religion. Of making the switch from newspaper journalism to an online magazine, Caldwell notes that "journalism on the Web is different in that I have many more tools at my disposal than words and pictures to tell a story. And this is what I love about it most . . . Probably the biggest difference between what we do and what traditional print journalists do is the interactivity between us and what we call our 'users.' " Caldwell is also a contributor to the magazine *The Lutheran,* and is a member of that church.

12:30 P.M. Mount Hope United Methodist Church, Ephrata, Pa.

When Republican committeewoman Anna Mae Ressler arrived at the   1
polling place here off a busy two-lane highway at 6:30 A.M., a line of voters was already snaking around the church. By noon, 800 of the precinct's 1,600 voters had already cast their ballots—about double a normal presidential election. But of course this is not a normal election.

"We've been hitting the election really hard at church," Ressler said, de-   2
scribing the voter guides and church bulletin announcements she'd helped provide her congregation. Indeed, the local GOP also provided two conservative Christian voter guides to people walking into the precinct to vote on Tuesday. One was provided by the Pennsylvania Family Institute, which billed it as an "impartial, non-partisan guide." The other was prepared by Lancaster County ACTION.

Beyond the voter guides, there was no public display of religious fervor   3
by evangelical Christians at the precinct. But Ressler says the fervor is definitely there. As she made phone calls to remind local Republicans to vote, she prayed with them over the election's outcome, hoping for a Bush win. If he does win reelection, Ressler said, God has "answered our prayers and given us another chance."

And if Kerry wins? To prepare for that possibility, Ressler has been   4
reading the Book of Jeremiah. "When that nation got so bad, the Lord sent them into captivity," she explained. "We've done an awful lot of things in this country that are displeasing to God."

Kerry, she says, will be a punishment to the nation.   5

1:15 P.M. Dove Christian Fellowship, Ephrata, Pa.

Dove Christian Fellowship sits down the road from an Agway outlet and   6
Martin's Country Store and across from a strip shopping mall on the edge of a rolling expanse of farmland.

Here, Diana Sheehan kept a solitary vigil as part of a round-the-clock 7
prayer session for the election sponsored by the church. She paced back
and forth, Bible in hand, in the fourth-grade classroom, praying for "a
godly man to be elected to office. We're praying for the future of this country. And we're praying that it's an honest election."

Sheehan had a dream five years ago that jolted her to political awareness. 8
It included an ostrich with its head in the sand, a lion advancing against it,
an American flag in the background, and a letter that read: "America, this is
a wakeup call." She believes the ostrich represents American Christians,
who've "turned our backs on what is going on in politics in this nation."

For the last four months, Sheehan's been leading a weekly prayer group 9
whose sole task is to pray about the election. And in the last 40 days, she's
participated in a no-sugar fast sponsored by Intercessors for America,
which is encouraging millions of conservative Christians to do the same.

If the prayer and fasting work, she says, Bush will be reelected, and God 10
will signal that "he's giving us more time to get our act together. I think this
nation is going down the tubes very quickly."

If Kerry wins? "I don't know what that means," she said, drawing in her 11
breath. "I'll be praying a whole lot more because I think it's a spiritual battle."

At the same time, she said, "I'm not really afraid. I know who's in con- 12
trol and his banner over us is love. My trust is in Him, not in who is President of the United States."

2:30 P.M., Martindale Volunteer Fire Co., Martindale, Pa.

Getting to Martindale, in the heart of Mennonite and Amish farm country, 13
involves swerving around hairpin turns while passing horses and buggies,
porch swings, acres of grazing cows, trees turned burnished autumn gold,
and even an occasional hen strutting near the side of the road.

In this tranquil place, Philip Weaver sat assisting the day's trickle of voters— 14
216 by mid-day out of 610 registered. He wore a T-shirt emblazoned with "One
Nation Under God," and said: "As a Christian, I really don't think there's much
of an option who we vote for."

Weaver is a member of the Church of the Brethren, one of the historic 15
"peace churches." But he is not a pacifist. He believes in "non-resistance,"
meaning that Christians shouldn't be involved in war. Yet he supports the
war in Iraq and says most of his congregation agrees. His support of President Bush stems primarily from his pro-life views. "That's an innocent
life," he said, "where war is a totally different situation."

As we spoke, Lucy Zimmerman, a 22-year-old member of an Old Or- 16
der Mennonite community, stepped up to vote for the first time, her heart
pounding from nervousness. She voted for Bush, she said quietly, her voice

heavily accented with her native Pennsylvania German dialect—"for the freedom of our people," meaning Mennonites and Amish, and because Bush supports private schools.

Zimmerman got a ride to the poll from her boss, like Stoltzfus, reared 17 Amish but now a member of the politically active Worship Center in nearby Leola. His church held an aggressive voter registration drive and a three-week voter education program with conservative Christian and Republican speakers. When he heard politically active grassroots Republicans talk about "the power of one"—motivating just one extra person to vote Republican—he convinced Zimmerman to register and vote.

3:30 P.M. East Earl Township Building, East Earl, Pa.

George Platt, the cheerful township election judge, stepped into the cur- 18 tained partition of a voting machine with a black-bonneted Old Order Mennonite woman and her husband. It was their first try at voting, and they didn't know what to do. Platt patiently showed them how to press the levers to register their votes, then stepped aside as they walked into the machine and cast their ballots.

Earlier in the day, an Amish family pulled up in a horse and buggy. But 19 they spoke no English—only Pennsylvania German—and had to be led through the process by an election volunteer in order to cast their ballots.

4:45 P.M. New Life Assembly of God Church, East Lampeter, Pa.

A two-hour wait was in store for the hundreds of people pouring into the 20 mobbed parking lot at this polling place off Lancaster's main highway. Police officers directed traffic, and the local television station parked a truck in front of the church building. Of the precinct's 5,000 registered voters, about half had voted so far, and there was no sign of a let-up.

Gene Frey of Lancaster waited in the line—his third try at voting today. 21 He'd arrived at 6:50 to find a huge line, tried again at 1 P.M. to find a similarly long line, and finally at 4:30 resigned himself to waiting. "I'm not going to pass up this election," he said. "I want conservative politicians so my grandchildren don't have to live in a liberal country."

A Bush voter, Frey was particularly swayed by the president's stance 22 against gay marriage. Frey is a Mennonite, but he is not a pacifist. "Some people say Mennonites don't vote Republican, but thousands do," Frey said.

He called himself a pacifist in personal relationships—but believes support- 23 ing the war is moral because war is waged by governments, not individuals.

If Kerry is elected, Frey said, he will not be happy, but he will also not 24 be afraid. "I got through eight years with Bill Clinton, so I can wait another eight years."

Both inside and outside the church, there was no Christian political 25
activity—just some volunteers handing out campaign literature. But once
voters cast their ballots, they followed an exit sign past the church's sanctuary. A huge sign that read "Jesus" hung on the wall, and an elaborate
grouping of musical instruments spanned the stage.

The doors were flung open, awaiting meditative voters. No one was inside. 26

Thinking Critically

1. Visit <www.beliefnet.com> and spend some time touring the different features of the site. Who is the primary audience for Beliefnet, and how can
   you tell? In what ways does Deborah Caldwell's article appeal to Beliefnet's
   audience?

2. How do the people Caldwell cites strike you? For example, some might be
   surprised or even appalled by the quote from Diana Sheehan; in Caldwell's
   context as a reporter, however, Sheehan's perspective is as valid as any
   other subject's.

3. In what ways does Caldwell's article follow the conventions of newspaper
   reporting? Consider the form of the article, the number of sources cited
   and the way they're cited, the presence (or absence) of Caldwell herself. In
   what ways is this article different from the election coverage you read in a
   mainstream newspaper or media source? (You should consult the electronic archives of a major television news network or daily newspaper in order to give your response more depth and context.)

Writing Critically

1. The American political system, at least in its ideal version, allows any eligible citizen to vote for any candidate based on any number of personal or
   political litmus tests. For example, no one is barred from voting because of
   their religious beliefs or practices (or lack thereof). However, a brief survey
   of candidates for major political offices in the history of the United States
   is overwhelmingly populated by Christians. How does the religious faith or
   background of a political candidate influence your vote, and why? (Your response need not be defensive – although, if your first impulse is to defend
   your voting patterns and belief systems, you might want to explore the issue of why you feel the need to defend yourself.) Do you feel that the American political system fairly represents people of your faith community or
   belief system? Should it?

THE LAST SECULAR HUMANIST
IS FLUSHED FROM HIS SPIDER HOLE

Right from the Beginning: The Roots of American Exceptionalism

JOHN MICKLETHWAIT AND ADRIAN WOOLDRIDGE

This selection is an excerpt from John Micklethwait and Adrian Wooldridge's book *The Right Nation: Conservative Power in America* (2004). Both authors are reporters for the British weekly newsmagazine *The Economist,* founded in 1843. Their approach to the historical role of religion in American political culture has been praised for its "degree of dispassionate clarity" and called "a bold and impressive analysis of modern American conservatism" that benefits from the authors' European perspective. John Micklethwait and Adrian Wooldridge were educated at Oxford University. Both have lived in and written about the United States for *The Economist,* which covers international business and politics.

In God's Name

Why are Americans so religious? The obvious reason is that religion played such a prominent role in both the creation and shaping of the country. The earliest American colonies were settled by Puritans, dissenters who saw the new land as an opportunity to escape from religious persecution and practice their religious faith as vigorously as they could. The constitution's First Amendment specifically guaranteed the "free expression" of religion. By and large, the new country lived up to this promise, but those who did still feel discriminated against, notably the Mormons, helped to spearhead the move westward in the nineteenth century. 1

The other reason for America's religiosity is perhaps more surprising: it is the fact that America was founded as a secular state. The same First Amendment that guarantees the free exercise of religion also prohibits Congress from making any law "respecting an establishment of religion." The separation of church and state distinguishes America from European "confessional states." Many religious conservatives complain that this separation unjustly excludes religion from the public square. Many of the most vigorous supporters of the separation are liberals. But in fact the separation of church and state has done more than anything else to preserve religion as a vigorous (and usually conservative) force in American life. 2

The disestablishment of religion injected market forces into American   3
religious life. Religious organizations could not rely on the state for subsidies in the same way as, say, the Church of England. They had to compete
to survive. This was exactly as Jefferson, one of the most vigorous supporters of disestablishment, predicted. In his notes for a speech to the leg-
islature in 1776 he argued that religious freedom would strengthen the
church because it would "oblige its ministers to be industrious [and] ex-
emplary."[1] American religion was always throwing up new churches that
could market the Word better than the competition. During the Great
Awakening of the 1840s, for example, revivalists dispensed with Latinate
sermons ("all *hic haec hoc* and no God in it") and invented rousing gospel
songs.[2] Disestablishment also lifted a huge burden from religion. What better way to distort faith than to make it dependent on the whims of politicians? And what better way to debilitate faith than to link it to the pursuit
of sinecures and preferments? America was mercifully free from the local
equivalents of Trollope's parsons, who were constantly maneuvering for
official preferment. It was also free from the power struggles that debili-
tated the Catholic Church: remember that Lord Acton's injunction that
power corrupts and absolute power corrupts absolutely comes from his description of the medieval papacy. American churches had nothing to rely
on to ensure their survival other than their own spiritual strength.

The religious groups that survived best in America's competitive envi-   4
ronment were the most "enthusiastic": the ones that took their faith most
seriously and preached it most vigorously. Even today, Americans swap religions quickly: around 16 percent of the population has changed denominations and the proportion rises the more fundamental the creeds get, with
one study showing that half the pastors in megachurches having moved
from another denomination.[3] Some people think America is currently in
the middle of its Fourth Great Awakening,[4] but the truth is that these great
awakenings have been so frequent and prolonged that there has never been
a period of sleep from which to awake. Revivalism does not need to be revived; rather, it is a continuous fact of American life.

America's penchant for religion hasn't exclusively benefited conserva-   5
tives. One of the most religious groups in the country is also one of the
most Democratic: African-Americans. Two of the most prominent left-
wing politicians, Jesse Jackson and Al Sharpton, are both reverends (Sharpton was ordained at the tender age of ten). Throughout American history,
protest movements have had a religious component. The underground rail-
way, which helped slaves to the North and freedom, was run by holy criminals. The father of populism, William Jennings Bryan, was a lay preacher.
Religious people were in the forefront of the struggle for civil rights for

women and blacks. During the 2000 election campaign Al Gore talked about using "faith-based organizations" to help solve America's social problems almost as enthusiastically as George Bush.

But throughout its history America's religiosity has encouraged Americans to see problems in terms of individual virtues and vices. It has also encouraged Americans to try to solve society's ills through voluntary activity rather than state action. Calvin Colton, a Briton who visited America in the 1830s, noted that the separation of church and state had given rise to "a new species of social organization before unknown in history."[5] In America voluntary organizations took on functions that, in Europe, were performed either by the state or by state-financed churches. Religious groups set up elaborate systems of voluntary welfare. The Catholic Church, for example, established a separate welfare state, a parallel universe with its own schools, hospitals and provisions for the indigent and unfortunate. Many of these voluntary groups were highly suspicious of government interference. In 1931 the chairman of the Red Cross's central committee went before Congress to discuss a proposed federal appropriation of $25 million for relief of drought victims. "All we pray for," he said, "is that you let us alone and let us do the job."[6]

Religion has also reinforced America's patriotism. From the first the religious groups who fled to America had a strong sense that they were settling in a special place with a special role in God's plan—a city on a hill, a beacon to the rest of the world. America has long regarded itself as a redeemer nation. "Nation after nation, cheered by our example, will follow in our footsteps till the whole earth is freed," said Lyman Beecher, a nineteenth-century cleric. Patriotism and religion are mutually reinforcing. This is why, during Eisenhower's presidency, religious groups got the phrase "under God" (Lincoln's phrase from the Gettysburg address) added to the Pledge of Allegiance, whose original version, conservatives note, was written by Francis Bellamy, a socialist educator.[7]

The Mighty Dollar

If God has predisposed America to conservatism, then so has Mammon. Why throw in your lot with radicals when you can simply move farther West? Why agitate for revolution when you are doing so well out of the established system? As Werner Sombart famously put it, the ship of American socialism ran aground on "shoals of roast beef and apple pie."

America has always been a feast of plenty. From the sixteenth century onward, visitors have waxed lyrical about the country's abundance of everything: abundance of space which allows people to own their own homes and support their own families; abundance of food that makes them the most generously fed people in the world; and abundance of opportunities for upward mobility. In Europe, too many people were always chasing too few opportunities. In America, there were always too few people to exploit everything the country had to offer. In the 1780s J. Hector St. John de Crèvecoeur, a visiting Frenchman, noted that "there is room for everybody in America. . . . I do not mean that everyone who comes will grow rich in a little time; no, but he may procure an easy, decent maintenance, by his industry." In 1817, William Cobbett, a British critic of the establishment, commented on American dietary excesses: "You are not much pressed to eat and drink, but such an abundance is spread before you . . . that you instantly lose all restraint." In 1831 Alexis de Tocqueville, the first person to meditate at any length on American exceptionalism, remarked that fortune offered "an immense booty to the Americans."[8]

These differences became more marked with the invention of mass production. Americans simply possessed more *stuff* than anybody else: more cars, more telephones, more radios, more vacuum cleaners, more electric lights, more bathtubs, more supermarkets, more movie theaters, more of any new invention or innovation that would make life more endurable. In *The Future in America* (1906), H. G. Wells noted that even in the "filthy back streets of the East Side" of New York people were much better off than their peers in London.[9] During his stay in New York in 1917, Leon Trotsky was astonished by the facilities in his cheap apartment in the East Bronx: "electric lights, gas cooking-range, bath, telephone, automatic service elevator, and even a chute for the garbage." All this won his children over to New York.[10] Franklin D. Roosevelt said that if he could place one American book in the hands of every Russian, he would choose the Sears, Roebuck catalogue.[11]

Just as important as the abundance of material goods was the abundance of opportunity. For most of America's history, most of its inhabitants could expect to get richer during their lifetimes—and expect that their children would get richer still. In 1909–1929 consumer expenditure per head rose almost 45 percent in real terms, and then rose another 52 percent from 1929–1960.[12] The twin engines of economic expansion—geographical expansion into new lands in the West and technological expansion into new realms of production—created a constant supply of new opportunities. And at the same time a relentless supply of new immigrants stood ready to take the places that were being vacated at the bottom of the ladder. Everybody in the country—old or new, immigrant or settled, middle class or lumpen proletarian, Italian godfather or WASP patrician—seemed to be moved by the same motives: the desire to make a profit, to accumulate dollars, to get ahead in the world and flaunt your wealth as a sign that you had got ahead.

It was only fitting that a people of plenty should put their trust not in   12
the state, but in the providers of plenty—the businessmen. Capitalism came
to America with the first settlers. The country was founded by profit-
obsessed corporations: the Virginia Company, the Massachusetts Bay
Company and, more darkly for the country's future, the slave-trading
Royal African Company (New York was named after the latter's president,
James, Duke of York).[13] The Puritans, who came for religious rather than
commercial reasons, also had a distinctly capitalist frame of mind. There
have always been exceptions to this enthusiasm for capitalism, such as the
Southern Agrarians, the Populists and Michael Moore, but in general
America has had little use for the European contempt for business. Americans celebrate the creative genius of business people in much the same way
that the French celebrate the creative genius of artists and intellectuals.
Ronald Reagan captured this attitude perfectly when, as a flack for General Electric in the 1950s, he liked to say that the company's primary product was progress.[14] American school textbooks recounted tales of the
practical genius of men like Henry Ford and Thomas Edison (and will no
doubt one day celebrate the practical genius of Bill Gates). The first instinct
of policy makers has generally been to stand back and give businesspeople
the room that they need to exercise their creative genius.

America has been much more inclined to let public work be covered by   13
private philanthropy than Europe has. The country's landscape is littered
with monuments to business philanthropy: great universities like Stanford
and Chicago; great galleries like the Getty and the Frick; great medical research centers like Rockefeller University. Every one of these monuments is
the product of a large private fortune translated into a large public good.
And for each of these great monuments there are a thousand small-scale
charities bent on repairing the fractured raiment of society. Andrew
Carnegie, John D. Rockefeller Sr. and the rest of the robber barons were
hard-faced men who destroyed their competitors and crushed trade unions.
But they were also great philanthropists. Carnegie talked about the religion
of philanthropy. His dictum that "the man who dies rich dies disgraced"
created a fashion among his fellow robber barons for pouring money into
universities, art galleries and medical schools, a fashion that survives with
today's new tech billionaires.

The idea that wealth entails responsibility went much deeper than bil-   14
lionaires. Americans of all degrees of wealth have been unusually generous
with their money. Even while he was a poor clerk in Cleveland, Rockefeller
gave away a fixed proportion of his income. More important still, Americans have been unusually generous with their time. Voluntary organizations designed to solve society's problems have flourished more lavishly in

the United States than perhaps any other country. Today American philanthropic contributions account for about 1 percent of national income, compared with between 0.2 percent and 0.8 percent in Europe.[15] Crucially, Americans much prefer to give away their money themselves, rather than let their government do it; foreign aid is a pathetic portion of government spending.

This tradition of philanthropy encouraged America to tackle its social 15
problems without building a European-style welfare state, and to embrace modernity without abandoning its traditions of voluntarism, decentralization and experiment. The country did a remarkable job of creating a national infrastructure before the introduction of the federal income tax in 1913. And, even as the federal government grew in the 1930s and 1940s, boosted by war, depression and idealism, America took the conservative attitude that the public sector should not be allowed to crowd out the voluntary one.

The Lure of the West

The roots of American conservatism are embedded in the most fundamen- 16
tal thing about any country: its geography. America is the world's fourth largest country, and, unusually for such a large place, two-thirds of it is habitable. It is a land of wide-open spaces—a place where rugged individualism can become a philosophy rather than just a hopeful cliché, where reinvention is always possible and where conservation can become a much more optimistic—even sometimes utopian—creed than it has been anywhere else.

Geography helps to explain why immigration, so often a source of dis- 17
content in more crowded places, has usually had the opposite effect in America. The history of every big city in America has been littered with fights between the established inhabitants and new arrivals. But immigrants have repeatedly replenished the supply of devotees to the American capitalist dream. (An old Ellis Island motto: "The cowards never came, and the weak died on the way.") Most immigrants saw—and still see—America as a land of milk and honey compared with their old homelands. Most have embraced their new country with the enthusiasm of converts and followed the path of upward mobility: starting off in ethnic enclaves (which also had the effect of diluting working-class solidarity) and then eventually making it into the suburbs and the great American middle class. It cannot be a mere coincidence that the most consistently left-wing group in America has been blacks—the only people who did not come to the country voluntarily.

And once people arrived in America, they kept on moving. Internal mi- 18
gration has been one of the secrets of America's economic success. One of

Margaret Thatcher's cabinet ministers once famously exhorted Britain's unemployed to "get on their bikes" to look for work; that advice has never been needed in America, where there has always been somewhere better to go. The Left is correct to point out that some economic migrations have been desperate affairs: think of Tom Joad and the hapless Okies in *The Grapes of Wrath*. But the truth for most migrants over time has been more enriching. "The western wilds, from the Alleghenies to the Pacific, constituted the richest free gift that was ever spread out before civilized man," Frederick Jackson Turner wrote in his paper "The Significance of the Frontier in American History" (1893). "Never again can such an opportunity come to the sons of men." A senior Republican in California, surveying the prosperous elderly white faces at his party's state convention, says that one word comes to his mind: Okies. (He means it as an insult, but it also shows that Tom Joad's descendants have not done badly.)

The migrants left their past behind, along with all the accumulated traditions of the Old World. Many migrants were identified not by their family names but by their given names and preferably by their nicknames—a tradition that still thrives in Texas (and can be seen in George W. Bush's habit of giving everybody he knows a pet name).[16] Daniel Boorstin produces a wonderful quotation from a Texas pioneer: "Truly this is a world which has no regard for the established order of things, but knocks them sky west and crooked, and lo, the upstart hath the land and its fatness."[17]   19

The modern equivalent of this homestead is the suburb. Ask Americans where they want to live, and only 13 percent say they would like to live in a city; the biggest number—37 percent—say a small town, and 25 percent say the suburbs.[18] Most Americans seem to expect, in their heart of hearts, that they will end up living in a sun-blessed subdivision.[19] And they are right to do so. More than half the population now lives in a suburb of some sort; by contrast, two thirds of the population in Europe is categorized as urban. And American suburbs are different: the new Edge cities include far more offices and workplaces, far more immigrants, far more space and far more variety in terms of rich suburbs and poor suburbs than the standard middle-class dormitory "commuter belts" of the sort you see round big European cities.   20

The New World's capacity to reinvent itself—to summon up ever newer worlds from its vast expanse of space—has reinforced the odd mixture of individualism and traditionalism at the heart of American conservatism. The Sun Belt that burst into prominence in the Reagan era might almost be regarded as a new nation. Its towns began without any of the palaces, cathedrals, archives and monuments that weigh people down with memories of the past. It is a nation of sprawling cities, a slash-and-burn social   21 policy and incessant reinvention, a nation of strip malls and megachurches, of country-and-western music and NASCAR racing.

Yet many of the rootless people of the new frontier combined this rein-   22
vention with a fierce thirst for the solace of religion. This religion was much more hard-edged than the sort that flourished back on the East Coast, let alone back in Europe. It saw money not as something that needed to be apologized for but as a sign that you had worked hard and earned the Lord's blessing—an idea that survived long after wagon trains gave way to Jeep Cherokees. In June 1981 Ronald Reagan's deputy counsel, Herbert Ellingwood, told a "financial success seminar" in Anaheim, California, that "economic salvation and spiritual salvation go side by side."[20] One of us once rather merrily suggested to a group of Christian conservatives in Colorado that Jesus Christ was really something of a socialist—and then had to spend the next half hour in what might be described as emergency Bible study. In the South in particular this religion can be fiercely judgmental. The mystical vision of the New Testament about forgiving people their trespasses has held less appeal than Old Testament pragmatism; if you do bad things, bad things happen to you. As T. R. Fehrenbach, Texas's leading modern chronicler, observes, the passages in the Bible that made more sense to his state were "the parts in which the children of Israel saw the sweetness in a harsh land and piled up the foreskins of their enemies."[21]

Meanwhile, the frontier also inured Americans to violence. Guns were   23
essential to people who were taming a wild frontier. Frontier societies easily turned to the ultimate punishment—execution—to preserve a precarious order or indeed to grab the land in the first place. The people who built Texas, such as Jack Hays and L. H. McNelly, saw themselves as warriors, not murderers. In the spirit of the West, writes Fehrenbach, "Hays, who shot many a squaw outside her teepee, was no more a killer than a bombardier who dropped his armaments on crowded tenements in World War II."[22] Even once the land was grabbed, the burden of self-defense in disputes lay with the individual. (If they were too wimpish to do so, tough luck: they should have stayed at home.) The prospect of prosperity and the permanent threat of anarchy: what could be more conducive to conservative thinking than that?

So America has always had conservative elements. But it did not really   24
have a Right Nation until the mid-twentieth century. Since then a set of conservative inclinations and prejudices have hardened into something more substantial. For most of its history, America didn't need a conservative movement because it was a fundamentally conservative nation. This movement sprang up in the 1950s when conservative Americans began to react against the advances that "big government liberalism" had made in

the past two decades, and it roared into life in the 1960s when Johnson's Democrats tried to drag the country dramatically to the Left. Even today hostility to liberalism—be it Southern churchgoers protesting against gay marriage or Bill O'Reilly harrying the European axis of weasel on Fox News—forms a strong part of American conservatism. But American conservatism plainly has metamorphosed into something far more formidable than knee-jerk reaction; at home and abroad it is an ideology that is characterized as much by aggressive preemption as by defensive reaction.

Notes

[1]Garry Wills, *Under God: Religion and American Politics* (New York: Simon & Schuster, 1990), p. 370.

[2]James A. Morone, *Hellfire Nation: The Politics of Sin in American History* (New Haven: Yale University Press, 2003), p. 127.

[3]John Parker, "Survey of America," *Economist,* November 8, 2003, p. 14.

[4]See Robert Fogel, *The Fourth Great Awakening and the Future of Egalitarianism* (Chicago: University of Chicago Press, 1999).

[5]Quoted in Seymour Martin Lipset, "American Exceptionalism Reaffirmed," in *Is America Different? A New Look at American Exceptionalism,* ed. Byron Shafer (Oxford: Clarendon Press, 1991). p. 25.

[6]Ibid., p. 26.

[7]Gene Healy, "What's Conservative About the Pledge of Allegiance?" Cato Institute, November 4, 2003, <http://www.cato.org/dailys/11-04-03.html>.

[8]David M. Potter, *People of Plenty. Economic Abundance and the American Character* (Chicago: University of Chicago Press, 1954), p. 80.

[9]H. G. Wells, *The Future in America* (New York: Harper and Brothers, 1906), pp. 105–6.

[10]Seymour Martin Lipset and Gary Marks, *It Didn't Happen Here: Why Socialism Failed in the United States* (New York: W. W. Norton, 2000), p. 27.

[11]Potter, *People of Plenty,* p. 80.

[12]Seymour Martin Lipset, *The First New Nation: The United States in Historical and Comparative Perspective* (London: Heinemann, 1963), p. 325.

[13]John Micklethwait and Adrian Wooldridge, *The Company: A Short History of a Revolutionary Idea* (New York: Modern Library, 2003).

[14]H. W. Brands, *The Strange Death of American Liberalism* (New Haven: Yale University Press, 2001), p. 139.

[15]"In Praise of the Unspeakable." *Economist,* July 20, 2002.

[16]Daniel J. Boorstin, *The Americans: The National Experience* (New York: Vintage Books, 1965). p. 91.

[17]Ibid., p. 113.

[18]Gallup poll results cited in "Live with TAE," *The American Enterprise,* October/November 2002, p. 17.

[19]Andres Duany quoted in "Live with TAE," *The American Enterprise,* October/November 2002, p. 18.

[20]Kevin Phillips, *Post-Conservative America: People, Politics and Ideology in a Time of Crisis* (New York: Random House, 1982), p. 141.

[21]T. R. Fehrenbach, *Lone Star: A History of Texas and the Texans,* updated edition (New York: Da Capo, 2000), p. 716.

[22]Ibid., p. 711.

Thinking Critically

1. How can you tell—if you can tell—that this essay was written from an international perspective? What is the authors' tone toward "America," both in the abstract and in their discussion of contemporary American culture and politics?

2. Prepare a glossary to accompany this essay in which you offer very brief definitions or biographies of key people, events, and terms to which the authors refer.

3. How do chronology and narrative shape the authors' argument? Are chronology and narrative always the most effective choices for an analytic essay that offers historical perspective on a contemporary issue? What are the challenges of writing history in a chronological framework? (Recall the Latin phrase *post hoc, ergo propter hoc,* discussed on page 34.)

Writing Critically

1. What do Micklethwait and Wooldridge have to say about philanthropy in American culture? Much of Chapter 2 deals with issues of community. Is the idea of philanthropy ever discussed in the selections in that chapter? What kinds of communal values are attached to philanthropy (be sure to distinguish philanthropy from "charity")? Who tends both to practice philanthropy and to uphold it as a virtue?

2. What is the authors' opinion about the role of the suburbs in American culture? How do other authors in this book agree or disagree with this interpretation?

3. "The prospect of prosperity and the permanent threat of anarchy: what could be more conducive to conservative thinking than that" (paragraph 23)? How do the authors arrive at this interpretation of the American frontier experience? Identify a "prospect of prosperity" or a "threat of anarchy" that you think might cause someone (or some community) to support more "conservative" values and elect "conservative" candidates to public office today. Be sure to support your argument with *specific* illustrations from the news media or your own experience.

The Real Danger Behind the Christian Right: Beware of Conservative Ecumenism

WENDY KAMINER

Wendy Kaminer brings tremendous intellectual curiosity and expertise to her journalism. A contributing editor to the *Atlantic Monthly* since 1991 and a senior correspondent for the *American Prospect,* Kaminer, a lawyer by training and a contrarian by temperament, is likely to take the least expected but most cleverly argued perspective on a subject. From feminism to psychoanalysis, from "therapy culture" to gun control, Kaminer's contributions to the national conversation are always provocative and often quoted by other writers. Her book *Sleeping with Extra-Terrestrials: The Rise of Irrationalism and the Perils of Piety* (1999) was eerily prescient of the cultural turmoils surrounding the 2004 presidential election and its cultural fallout. A reviewer for the *Boston Globe* noted that "Wendy Kaminer is hard to place on the left-right political spectrum—and that is what imbues her work with originality. She relishes the clang of a good argument." "The Real Danger Behind the Christian Right" appeared in the October–November 2003 issue of *Free Inquiry,* a publication of the Council for Secular Humanism. Although the magazine has a relatively small circulation, its regular contributors include many of the most important and controversial social critics and journalists of our times. As the magazine's statement of purpose declares: "Our best guide to truth is free and rational inquiry; we should therefore not be bound by the dictates of arbitrary authority, comfortable superstition, stifling tradition, or suffocating orthodoxy. We should defer to no dogma—neither religious nor secular—and never be afraid to ask 'How do you know?' " The website of the Council for Secular Humanism is at <http://www.secularhumanism.org/>.

How do you measure the influence of evangelicals on public life? Ask a   1
culturally conservative Christian if America is a Christian country and you're apt to hear a series of complaints about sexual permissiveness, sexually explicit media, gambling, gay rights, abortion, divorce, and other alleged sins of our godless, sinful culture. From this perspective, the assertion that we are a Christian country is a form of wishful thinking. Ask a secularist if America is a Christian country, or an increasingly religious one, and you'll hear a different series of complaints, about government-funded sectarianism, references to God in official documents and proclamations, and the Supreme Court's increasing hostility toward separation of church and state. From this perspective, it's wishful thinking to regard America as excessively secular.

These conflicting responses don't simply reflect conflicting perspectives   2
and agendas. There is no short answer to questions about the power of the religious Right, from any perspective. Its influence on policy and law can be quantified with relative ease: at least we can catalogue the allocation of public funds to sectarian groups, the rise of creationism in public schools, and other markers of conservative Protestantism in government. But the religious Right's influence on American culture is harder to assess, particularly in light of our general cultural complexity. Consumerism and the mass media may unite us, but American culture still reflects contradictory strains of Puritanism and libertarianism, conformity and individualism, freedom and authoritarianism, rationalism and superstition, religiosity and secularism. While we can identify dominant social trends, they are never singular. That's what makes this country interesting. It's culturally diverse and conflicted; you can find some truth in many opposing complaints from secularists and evangelicals.

Let's start with the secular lament: there's no question that the country   3
has been in the midst of a religious revival for some fifteen years. The culture of disbelief that Stephen Carter famously attacked in his best-selling book of the early 1990s was actually a small, relatively insignificant subculture; indeed, if secularists were dominant, if the premise of his book had been true, it would never have been a bestseller. By the 2000 presidential election, both Democrats and Republicans were advertising their godliness, as Al Gore along with George Bush stressed his personal relationship with Jesus. Right and Left, conventional wisdom proclaimed religious belief essential to virtue. It was, by the way, interesting to hear "virtuecrats" qualify their routine

equation of religion with virtue after the faith-based initiative of September 11. Some quickly began distinguishing between bad religions and good.

In the United States, Christianity is naturally considered as one of the   4 "good" religions—if not the very best—so in general the American public doesn't seem to regard the religiosity of the Bush administration and the church-state partnerships it favors as even remotely theocratic. I suspect many people associate theocracies with the official adoption of religions they don't like. Similarly, the deadly fanaticism of Islamic fundamentalism doesn't seem to have aroused public anxiety about fundamentalism in general; instead, the public seems more likely to worry about Islam in particular and people from Islamic countries. A closely divided Supreme Court is increasingly inclined to allow state sponsorship of sectarian activities, as its 2002 decision upholding the channeling of tax dollars to religious schools showed. There's no question that secularists are right when they complain the constitutional wall between church and state is crumbling.

In the realm of law and policy, the Christian Right enjoys clearly in-   5 creased power. It's not exercised through previously prominent interest groups like the Christian Coalition or the Moral Majority. Instead the perspectives and concerns of right-wing Christians have been incorporated into the Republican Party leadership. So while its organizations appear to be in decline, the Christian Right has more political power than ever. You don't need lobbying groups to petition the government when your cohort runs the government. Moreover, Pat Robertson and Jerry Falwell were divisive, nasty, nutty figures who often embarrassed conservatives with their unapologetic extremism; George W. carefully promotes an image of religious tolerance. Under his leadership, right-wing Christianity seems more likely to be associated with compassionate conservativism than mean fundamentalism.

So Christian conservatives now help shape a broad range of government   6 policies, especially on the domestic front, in the areas of science, social policy, and social services. The president repeatedly refers to the power of faith to cure social ills, and examples of sectarian policymaking and grantmaking abound. The Bush administration was not deterred when its legislative proposals for funding sectarian social services were initially rejected by Congress (because of opposition to provisions exempting publicly funded religious organization from federal anti-discrimination law). What the administration could not accomplish by legislation it began to accomplish by fiat: federal rules for housing, community service, and substance abuse programs were rewritten to provide federal funding of sectarian religious groups, even if they engage in employment discrimination. We're also seeing an increase in government-funded sectarian social engineering, aimed at combating such sins as divorce and premarital sex or extramarital sex. In Florida, for example, a state public health agency has distributed an AIDS education pamphlet consisting largely of Bible verses and references to Jesus.

It's possible, therefore, to substantiate the secularist complaint about 7 the increased influence of the Christian Right on law and policy. But it's also important to acknowledge that the political success of the Christian Right is not unmitigated by failure. In June 2003, the Supreme Court struck down laws against same-sex sexual relations, observing that gay people "are entitled to respect for their private lives." (In a dissent that will resonate with the Christian Right, Justice Scalia complained that the Court "has largely signed on to the so-called homosexual agenda.") In previous years, the Court has struck down laws prohibiting indecency on the Internet, as well as a ban on virtual child porn and the practice of officially sanctioned student prayers at high school football games. These rulings represent significant political defeats for the religious Right. So does its repeated failure to pass a constitutional amendment allowing official prayer in public schools; so do decades of state and federal civil rights laws prohibiting sex discrimination in higher education and the workplace.

While the Christian Right has enjoyed a mixed record of success in the 8 sphere of law and policy, in the cultural sphere, it has suffered some prominent failures. Only a pathologically paranoid secularist would imagine that the Christian Right dominates American culture. While Christians are still in the majority, their dominance is challenged by the growth of other world religions, not to mention splits within their own ranks—both political and theological—and not to mention the New Age movement, which the Vatican recently felt the need to critique. And while the Christian Right has obtained significant government sponsorship for its sermonizing, Americans don't generally practice what it preaches.

Whether you focus on the divorce rate, the relative success of the gay 9 rights movement and feminism, sexual activity among young teens (as well as older ones), the growth of the gambling industry, the persistence of the porn industry, prostitution, recreational drug use, sex and violence on prime-time television, or the ubiquity of half-naked women on city streets every summer, you'd be hard pressed to characterize popular culture as a product of Christian conservativism. For all the money spent on abstinence-only sex ed, for example, some 20 percent of teens have had sexual intercourse before their fifteenth birthdays, according to a recent report.[1] As the Christian Right has discovered, it's easier to obtain political power, even in a pluralistic country, than it is to eradicate sin.

So when you consider American culture—the entertainment culture in 10 particular—the complaints of conservative Christians about excessive secularism are not unrealistic. They have reason to feel besieged by culture, just as non-Christians are apt to feel besieged by Christmas. Secular liberals may scoff at their tirades against the sexual revolution or sexual explicitness in the media; we may dismiss them as Puritans—but we might also sympathize with the sincere concern of some about their prospects for salvation. Conservative Christians are apt to fear that, once captured by popular culture, their children will go to hell, quite literally. Personally I don't believe in hell, or censorship, or abstinence-only sex ed; I'm simply pointing out that calls for censorship and the official adoption of sectarian moral codes shouldn't simply be dismissed as meanness or narrow-mindedness. Conservative Christians who feel threatened by popular culture should not be dismissed as delusional.

But complicating the cultural divide is a growing Christian entertainment culture. It's most evident in Christian rock, some of which crosses over—and has merited a parody in the online humor magazine *The Onion*. "Bassist Unaware Rock Band Christian" was the headline of a May 28, 2003, article. It proclaimed: "Brad Rolen, the new bassist for Pillar of Salt, remains oblivious to the fact that he is in a Christian rock band, sources reported Tuesday. 'Pillar's great,' said Rolen, 22, who is unaware of his band mates' devotion to Christ . . . 'I've only been with these guys for three months but I feel like it's the perfect fit for me.' He does go on to complain, however, that he's having trouble finding groupies: 'Whenever I ask them to come back to the bus with me, they say, 'I can't do that—that's not right.' I'm like, 'Come on, this is rock and roll.' "

Pop Christian literature has crossed over as well; its commercial appeal 12 has been confirmed by the hugely popular *Left Behind* series—mass-market Christian thrillers that offer a story of the final days. You can find pop Christianity in best-selling self-help books, especially those that preach the gospel of success. (Self-help books have long combined secular strivings for success and self-improvement with religious faith, in various forms.) You can read Christian computing, car, and travel magazines. You can laugh at or with Christian parodies of Christian culture. Stephen Bates reviewed this phenomenon in an excellent December 2002 article in *The Weekly Standard*.[2] He characterizes the Christian retail trade as a "4 billion-dollar-a-year business with bestsellers and Grammys and trademark lawyers."

This industry seems to have begun, Bates suggests, as a kind of Christian 13 separatism. Disgusted with secular pop culture, the Christian Right created its own. But its success has obscured where Christian culture ends and mainstream secular culture begins, especially if you're in the aisles of Wal-Mart. Is the marketplace changing Christianity or is Christianity changing the marketplace? God knows. Bates notes that the Jesus market includes both separatists and integrationists—performers and merchandisers who confine themselves to Christian audiences with explicitly Scripture-laden messages,

and those who peddle a softer version of Christianity, palatable in the mainstream. Think of the difference between Pat Robertson and George W. Bush.
The president is the Christian Right's most successful crossover pop star.

Wal-Mart may be the Christian Right's most powerful marketer. With   14
100 million customers per week and highly ideological retailing policies,
Wal-Mart exerts a powerful influence on pop culture. It is notorious for
selling only "clean" or cleaned-up versions of pop music, books, and films;
and, according to the *New York Times,* Wal-Mart and other discount
chains now account for "more than 50 percent of the sales of a best-selling
album, more than 40 percent for a best-selling book, and more than 60 percent for a best-selling DVD."[3] The Left Behind series owes its phenomenal
success partly to Wal-Mart's marketing.

The effect of national chain stores and media conglomeration on cul-   15
tural and political diversity has long been a concern for writers, artists, and
civil libertarians. Corporate media tends to be cautious and centrist (when
not downright conservative), and as the culture moves to the right the media moves with it, exacerbating our rightward trend. This is all good news
for conservative Christians, since the right wing in this country leans toward sectarianism, or at least against secularism.

Still, we should never underestimate the power of sin and hypocrisy, or   16
the allure of social freedom—the right to define vice and virtue for yourself and choose between them. When an avowed absolutist like Bill Bennett
disagrees with fellow virtuecrats about the morality of gambling, even he
has to admit that notions of virtue and vice may be relative. If we can all
agree that murder is wrong, we will still disagree about the morality of
abortion, same-sex marriage, or pre-marital sex, among other issues. It's
hard to imagine many Americans ever consistently practicing what the
Christian Right preaches. Besides, the religious impulse itself can be difficult to channel. It can send people to yoga class or channeling sessions as
often as it sends them to church. It creates saints out of pop stars, as pop
culture sanctifies celebrities. At its most hysterical and extreme, celebrity
worship turns Elvis into a Jesus figure and Graceland into a shrine. Even
in its more moderate form, the cultural obsession with celebrities can inspire quasi-spiritual quests—positing fame and fortune as a holy grail. You
can see the curious mix of materialism, the desire for fame, and religiosity
on *American Idol,* where the contestants thank God for getting them on
television; you'd think he had nothing better to do.

I suppose secularists might consider our amen culture a victory for religious   17
conservatives, but I'm not sure most religious conservatives would agree. This
is religion infected with secularism. This is religion that equates doing good
with doing well and doesn't quite focus on saving souls. This is religion that

can justify self-centeredness, exhibitionism, and virtually any form of worldly ambition. If it sanctifies such circuses as *American Idol,* it poses no threat to other less "wholesome" reality television shows like *The Bachelor* or *Married by America* which give viewers the thrill of watching half-clothed real people engaging in sexual foreplay on TV, just like actors in prime time. The kind of religion that flourishes in the marketplace is amorphous, adaptable, ceremonial; it's banal, undemanding "In God We Trust" religiosity which, in some ways, undermines religion more effectively than secularism.

I doubt that a right-wing Christian moral code will ever dominate American popular culture. Women are not going to retreat from the workplace into the kitchen anymore than they are going to cover their hair and hide their bodies in public. Gay people are not going back into the closet. People are not going to stop gambling or enjoying sexually explicit media. Teenagers are not going to stop having sex. Married couples are not going to stop committing adultery. And, even if abortions become generally illegal once again, women will not stop having them. No one will be stoned for any of these offenses. 18

I suspect that, in the end, even Christian merchandising will have a greater effect on politics than pop culture. In other words, it is likely to affect how people vote more than how they live. This is not exactly good news. 19

The primary threat facing secularists and liberals is not the rise of a traditional theocracy that turns a conservative Christian moral code into law. It's not the reversal of the Sexual Revolution or the end of social permissiveness. It's not even the allocation of government funds to sectarian social programs, although I'm not dismissing the dangers and indignities these pose to thousands of people. 20

The most serious threat we face is not conservative Christianity but conservative ecumenism. What worries me more than the ideological purists on the religious Right are the pragmatists. What worries me are the compromises that right-wing Protestants are willing to make in order to acquire and maintain power. What worries me is the president's crossover appeal. It is, in part a tribute to the individualistic, therapeutic religiosity that unites born again Christians with nonsectarian Twelve Step groups. George Bush made friends with Jesus while recovering from alcoholism, as innumerable other Americans made friends with other higher powers in recovery. Whether or not they are Christian, graduates of Twelve Step groups may recognize a fellow traveler in Bush. 21

The president's cross-denominational appeal also testifies to alliances formed during the 1990s between conservative Protestants, Catholics, and Jews. (Someday socially conservative but assimilated Muslims may join with them.) Secularism was their common enemy; conservative Christians and Jews were also drawn together by common concern about Israel. This 22 new conservative ecumenism was exemplified by the selection of Joe Lieberman as a Democratic vice presidential candidate in 2000. Lieberman ran on a platform of personal piety, having won the vice presidential slot because of, not in spite of, his religious beliefs. Secularized Christians who rarely attend church are electable nationally, but not Jews who never go to shul. Orthodox people of different faiths are apt to feel more threatened by the secular state than by church-state partnerships.

So while we need to defend religious freedom and separation of church   23 and state vigorously, we ought not become fixated on the dangers posed by evangelical Christians. Worry less about the evangelical influence on public life and more about the power of conservative ecumenism and the political threat it poses. Don't exacerbate that threat by picking fights over trivial ceremonial pieties strongly supported by large nonsectarian majorities. I imagine that religious conservatives thank God for the lawsuit over the words "under God" in the Pledge of Allegiance. If it doesn't result in a Supreme Court ruling affirming the constitutionality of official references to God, it may well result in a constitutional amendment that erodes prohibitions on establishing religion. The religious Right is probably salivating at the prospect; consider the usefulness of an "under God" Amendment as an organizing tool. Religious conservatives have chosen power; secularists ought not consign themselves to purity.

Notes

[1]Tamar Lewin, "1 in 5 Teenagers Has Sex Before 15, Study Finds," *New York Times*, May 20, 2003.

[2]Stephen Bates, "The Jesus Market," *Weekly Standard*, December 16, 2002. (Also available on the *Standard* website.)

[3]David Kirkpatrick, "Shaping Cultural Tastes at Big Retail Chains," *New York Times*, May 18, 2003.

Thinking Critically

1. Explore the connotations of each key word in Wendy Kaminer's title: danger, beware, conservative, ecumenism. How closely does her title mirror her thesis and approach?

2. Kaminer's argument proceeds from an important distinction between American politics and American culture. What is that distinction? Offer examples from your own experience and observation to support (or refute) this distinction.

3. According to Kaminer, what is the "most serious threat" facing "secularists and liberals"? How do you feel about her use of terms such as "threat," "worries," "danger," and "beware"? How might an evangelical Christian respond to Kaminer's rhetoric? What would the reaction be if a magazine or newspaper were to discuss the "dangers" and "threats" of Jewish or Buddhist or Muslim beliefs, and their "threats" to American secularism?

Writing Critically

1. Read the quotation from *Free Inquiry* magazine's statement of purpose in the headnote for this essay. Should that declaration be a guiding principle for all journalists? With reference to at least two other essays in this book, discuss how this principle is demonstrated (or refuted by) each author.

2. Many writers in this book (see Chapters 2 and 5 in particular) describe and analyze the intersection of popular culture and religious faith in America. Using Kaminer and at least one other essay from this book, discuss how the commercialization of religion and spirituality could happen only in America. If you have lived in another country, consider how religion and popular culture intersected there, and compare those observations with what you've seen in the United States.

Scholars Infuse Religion with Cultural Light

ALAN WOLFE

In the weeks preceding and following the presidential election of 2004, political pundits, scholars, talk-show hosts, and comedians joined a growing chorus of voices seeking to explain the role of religious faith in American political life. For Alan Wolfe, a professor of political science at Boston College and director of the Boisi Center for Religion and American Life, the presence of religion in American cultural and political life was no surprise. The recipient of grants from the Russell Sage Foundation, the Templeton Foundation, and the Lilly Endowment, Wolfe has twice conducted programs under the auspices of the U.S. State Department that bring Muslim scholars to the United States to learn about separation of church and state. In his 2003 book *The Transformation of American Religion: How We Actually Practice Our Faith,* Wolfe, who admits that he himself does not practice any particular religion, addresses secularists and liberal intellectuals: "As modern Americans with distinctly tolerant sensibilities, you pride yourselves on your willingness to change, yet religious believers, even the most conservative among them, have adopted themselves to modern society far more than you have changed your views about what they are really like. You have made the whole country more sensitive to the inequalities of race and gender. Now it is time to extend the same sympathy to those who are different in the sincerity of their belief." This petition to readers who are skeptical about, or fearful of, the impact of religion on American civic life informs the following essay. The *Chronicle of Higher Education,* where this essay appeared in October 2004, is a weekly newspaper and website for academic scholars and administrators.

Religion is playing a major role in the 2004 campaign for the presidency. 1 Conservative faiths are growing rapidly, in the United States as well as abroad. While a clash of civilizations may not be taking place, religious conflict—primarily, but not exclusively, in the Middle East—is a major cause of global instability.

All of those statements are not only true but testify to the importance 2 of religion in the contemporary world. They also raise the question of whether scholarship on religion is up to the task of offering Americans insights on the controversies that surround them.

Thirty years ago, the answer to that question would have been nega- 3 tive. Religion had been instrumental in the founding of at least two academic disciplines: sociology, because of the focus of Max Weber and Émile Durkheim on the role of religion in maintaining social order, and anthropology, because of its interest in ritual and symbols. Yet persuaded that the world was becoming increasingly secular and dedicated to value-free scholarship ill equipped to deal with passionate and irreconcilable beliefs, social scientists from the 1960s until the 1980s treated religion as marginal to their concerns. Combined with the conviction on the part of many natural scientists that religion was hostile to their enterprise and a turn in the humanities away from actual texts like *Paradise Lost* in favor of theories about how such works can or should be read, that left American academics outside of divinity schools unready for the religious revival that seemed to take on new life in the 1990s, particularly the rise of evangelical religions and the decline of mainline ones.

The academic study of religion, having badly missed the boat on one of 4 the most profound social transformations of our time, has a lot of catching up to do. The good news is that the process has started, as a plethora of books and scholarly articles dealing with religion has begun to appear. There may even be an advantage to the late start in academic scholarship on the role of religion in American life: Scholars have been able to incorporate recent approaches that show considerable promise.

One involves ethnographic description of individuals and the groups 5 with which they affiliate. Looking under the conventional labels used to depict religious believers, ethnographers and cultural historians are uncovering some unexpected findings. We know, for example, that religious conservatives are likely to vote Republican, but what, exactly, does it mean to be a religious conservative? If the scholarship of historians like R. Marie Griffith or sociologists like Gerardo Marti is any indication, it does not necessarily mean turning one's back on the modern world. Griffith's *Born Again Bodies: Flesh and Spirit in American Christianity,* published this month, places the popularity of diet and fitness books among American believers, many of them conservative, in the context of earlier attempts to achieve spiritual renewal through mind control or self-discipline. Marti's *A Mosaic of Believers: Diversity and Innovation in a Multiethnic Church,* to be published next month, offers a case study of a Los Angeles–based church that is at one and the same time Southern Baptist in affiliation and conservative theologically and attractive to a young, primarily single Hollywood clientele working at cutting-edge cultural jobs in the entertainment industry.

As such books illustrate, the ethnographic trend overlaps with interest 6 in the complexities of religion and American culture and their intersection. While religion has certainly done its share to shape American culture, it is also the case that American culture shapes religion, and in very powerful ways. For example, the 350th anniversary of the arrival of the first Jew on North American soil marks the publication of Jonathan D. Sarna's magisterial *American Judaism: A History.* Sarna's recent book documents the many ways American Jews adapted themselves to American practices, not only in the obvious case of transforming Hanukkah into a holiday resembling Christmas but also by revising Judaism to help suburban parents with child rearing or to appeal to increasingly assertive Jewish women. At the same time, Sarna also shows the importance of movements designed to resist American culture in the name of Jewish renewal, including the return to Orthodoxy on the part of highly educated Jews who once might have been considered candidates for assimilation.

Jews belong both to an ethnic and a religious category, and, as such, 7 their history reflects the ways in which not only national culture but the specific cultures of America's many ethnic groups influence the religious composition of the nation. The forthcoming *Themes in Religion and*

American Culture, edited by Philip Goff and Paul Harvey, offers a synthesis of the work of primarily younger scholars who examine the ways in which Latinos, Native-Americans, and African-Americans, among others, have shaped a contemporary religious environment in the United States that would have been unrecognizable to a Jonathan Edwards or a Henry Ward Beecher, however much they may have admired its energy and authenticity.

No other scholar in America has explored the relationship between eth-   8 nicity and religion with the insight of Robert A. Orsi, whose classic work, *The Madonna of 115th Street: Faith and Community in Italian Harlem 1880–1950,* published in 1985, brought to life the visibly celebratory and public world of Italian-American Roman Catholicism (while comparing it to the more cerebral and dourly Calvinistic Irish-American variety). In his *Between Heaven and Earth: The Religious Worlds People Make and the Scholars Who Study Them,* due out soon, Orsi combines personal reflections on his own family with a historical analysis of the relationships Catholics have formed with the Virgin Mary.

As in all his work, Orsi shows religious believers as people who are very   9 much like everyone else in their concerns with pain, suffering, and getting by, yet also unlike secularists because they really do believe that supernatural forces shape the course of the lives they lead. Orsi also demonstrates how slippery even some of our basic religious categories can be, for while the term "Catholic" conjures up for many Americans a universal church led by a pope in Rome, the worship experiences of a Latino in New Mexico may have so little to do with those of a German-American in Milwaukee that applying the same term to both is not going to tell us much about how Catholics will vote or even about what they believe.

What do religious people believe in when they believe? Monotheistic re-   10 ligions emphasize the centrality of one God, but people themselves, even those devoted to monotheist faiths, are often more capacious in their understanding than that. Indeed, if the work of a cultural historian like Stephen R. Prothero is any indication, Christians believe in Jesus while Buddhists, or at least significant numbers of them, believe in—Jesus. In *American Jesus: How the Son of God Became a National Icon,* published last year, Prothero finds people continually defining and redefining Jesus to accommodate their needs. If one believes that belief itself is or ought to be fixed, universal, and demanding, one comes away from Prothero's book convinced that something is rotten in the state of faith. If one admires people for their ingenuity, as well as their determination to make religion meaningful to themselves, one comes away impressed by the many forms belief can take.

When it comes to politics, ethnographic and historical accounts of reli-   11 gious experiences supplement surveys and polling data, but they do not entirely supplant them. If anything, quantitative studies of the role that religion plays in American voting have increased in both their methodological sophistication and their understanding of religion since political scientists began in the 1950s to pay attention to political behavior in addition to political institutions. Of all the scholars who offer journalists and others interested in the role religion plays in American politics relevant data, no one is more frequently cited than John C. Green, a political scientist at the University of Akron. And with good reason. Green, who happens to live and work in the crucial swing state of Ohio, never allows his political views, whatever they are, to color his analysis.

At a recent retreat for political journalists held in Key West, Fla., under 12 the auspices of the Ethics and Public Policy Center, Green presented the findings of a study, "The American Religious Landscape and Political Attitudes: A Baseline for 2004," which offered a number of conclusions that support the ethnographic approach to the study of religion. For example, evangelical Protestants, who, according to Green, constitute 26.3 percent of the American population, are by no means unanimously Republican in their political outlook. And that is because evangelicals come in many forms, some more traditional than others. In fact, Green shows, of those usually considered by the news media to be associated with the "religious right," traditionalist evangelicals (12.6 percent of the population) represent a smaller group than the combined centrist (10.8 percent) and modernist (2.9 percent) evangelicals. Since the latter two groups are not as likely to identify as Republican as the former, George W. Bush would be wrong to take the evangelical vote for granted in the 2004 election.

Sometimes the new scholarship on religion directly relates to the issues 13 facing Americans as they vote for candidates or take positions on matters of public policy. Consider Robert Wuthnow's recent book *Saving America?: Faith-Based Services and the Future of Civil Society*. Wuthnow, America's most distinguished sociologist of religion in the generation that has followed Peter Berger and Robert N. Bellah, points out that both President Bush, who defends providing public funds to religious-based charities, and his critics, who worry that such financing may violate the Establishment Clause of the U.S. Constitution, know very little about how America's faith-based organizations actually work. Based on surveys he and others have taken, as well as his own study of the Lehigh Valley area in Pennsylvania, Wuthnow has concluded that congregations are unlikely to increase the charitable work they already do if additional federal funds come their way through faith-based initiatives; that even strongly religious national organizations devoted to charitable provision frequently play down their religious character; and that recipients of public provision are more likely to trust providers if they view them as motivated by faith. Wuthnow does not tell Americans what they should believe about Mr. Bush's proposals, but he does offer them empirically grounded findings that can help them reach their own conclusions.

There are other ways to have an impact on society besides direct en-   14 gagement with its preoccupations. The study of religion will always, and should always, include those who examine the theologies of different faith traditions, write biographies of important religious figures, or study the psychological templates of belief. But by focusing on culture, examining the actual practices of believers, and demonstrating a willingness to explore widely used, but often misunderstood, categories, much of the new scholarship on religion enables Americans to recognize that a revival of religion need not lead to the creation of a theocracy or that the religious conflict so evident around the world need not be played out within the United States. Religion is here to stay. What form it takes and how it will continue to interact with culture and politics is very much open to discussion.

Thinking Critically

1. To whom does Alan Wolfe address this essay? Does he anticipate a friendly, an indifferent, or a hostile audience? How can you tell?

2. At one point in his essay, Wolfe notes that many terms used to describe certain religions and people of faith are "slippery" or inadequate, given the complexity of American religious faith. Drawing on some of the terms in other essays in this book, discuss ways in which broad religious or spiritual labels oversimplify the presence and impact of both individuals and groups.

Writing Critically

1. Wolfe names several academic scholars who are doing surprising work in the fields of religion and popular culture. At the reference desk of your campus or local library, ask for assistance in compiling an annotated bibliography of new academic research on religion and American culture. Focus on books and articles published within the last five years, and try to cover as many academic disciplines as possible.

2. Wolfe refers to a study by political scientist John C. Green, "The American Religious Landscape and Political Attitudes: A Baseline for 2004." The entire report is available online at <pewforum.org/publications/surveys/green-full.pdf>. Use this report as evidence to support or refute an argument made by Wolfe or by any other writer in Chapter 3. How can an ethnographic, objective, numerically based approach enhance our understanding of such a complex and personal issue?

What the Religious Right Can Teach the New Democrats: Extremists Aside, America's Evangelicals Have a Message We All Need to Hear

JON MEACHAM | Journalist and historian Jon Meacham has been recognized by his peers as one of the most important editors and writers in contemporary American media. At the age of twenty-nine, Meacham became the managing editor of *Newsweek;* the *New York Times* described him as "one of the most influential editors in the news magazine business." Meacham directed *Newsweek's* coverage of the events of September 11, 2001, winning a National Magazine Award for the magazine's coverage. His writings about American history and his analysis of American culture and current events appear in the *Los Angeles Times Book Review* and the *Washington Monthly.* A member of the Council of Foreign Relations, Meacham is a frequent guest on cultural and political talk shows across the political spectrum, from *The Charlie Rose Show* to *The O'Reilly Factor.* Jon Meacham is also a respected and accomplished historian. His book *Franklin and Winston: An Intimate Portrait of an Epic Friendship* (2003) draws on previously undiscovered archives as well as his own interviews with surviving members of Franklin Roosevelt's and Winston Churchill's staffs. The following essay appeared in the April 1993 issue of *Washington Monthly* magazine.

Sneering at the Religious Right of his day—Tennessee Holy Rollers who 1 campaigned to ban the teaching of evolution in the 1920s—H. L. Mencken famously called evangelical Christianity "a childish theology" "rounded upon hate" for "half-wits," "morons," "rustic ignoramuses," and "yokels from the hills." And that was just for starters.

In March, when Michael Frederick Griffin, a prolife activist, murdered a 2 physician behind a Florida abortion clinic—try to reconstruct the logic of that—he could have walked straight out of Mencken's acidic dispatches from the Scopes Trial. A barbaric act, informed by twisted religious fervor: Griffin is the stereotypical Religious Right adherent brought to life. I happened to grow up near the Tennessee hills that Mencken skewered, but I'm neither an evangelical nor a fundamentalist; at best, I'm a desultory Episcopalian. And although I'm quick to roll my eyes at Tammy Faye Bakker and would never vote for Pat Robertson, the evangelicals I knew—Southern Baptists, Presbyterians, a few Roman Catholics—weren't exotic yokels or extremists. They were ordinary people, no different from anybody else except when religion came up.

In those moments, evangelicals would show their colors and speak 3 quite seriously of how they enjoyed "a personal relationship with Jesus Christ." And if politics came up, they were generally, but not fanatically, Republican. There was nothing crazy about these people, nothing that suggested apocalyptic inclinations or theocratic ambitions. If anything, they were annoyingly nice, not threatening.

But the mainstream has so thoroughly accepted the Menckenite version 4 of conservative Christianity that the Griffins of the world are taken to be the rule, not the exception. It's a caricature that's alive and flourishing even outside the usual liberal op-ed suspects: After all, it's not news when Anthony Lewis snipes at the Religious Right. These days, the caricature is more widespread than that. In a *Washington Post* news story about evangelical opposition to President Clinton's lifting the ban on gays in the military, reporter Michael Weisskopf tossed off an unattributed generalization that had none of Mencken's flair but all of his prejudice: He called followers of Robertson, Jerry Falwell, and Co. "poor, uneducated, and easy to command."

When asked about his source, Weisskopf explained that though he had 5 talked with several experts about the Religious Right, "I try not to have to attribute every point in the story if it appears to be universally accepted. You don't have to say, 'It's hot out, according to the weatherman.'" The assumption is that you no more need an authority to tell you the Religious Right is witless than you need a weatherman to tell you a hot day is hot. Everyone, Weisskopf implies, knows these folks dwell at the bottom of the social and political food chains.

Such dismissive cultural assumptions, ill-founded and blithely propa- 6 gated, are keeping liberals, moderates, and even conservatives from realizing what the millions-strong movement is actually right about. Look past the obsession with homosexuals and abortion—what we might call pelvic sins—and there's a fairly sensible cultural vision and a not unreasonable policy agenda that's as neoliberal as it is fundamentalist.

Take crime, for example. Noting the backbreaking costs of large pris- 7 ons, the National Association of Evangelicals suggests punishing nonviolent offenders through community service and restitution—an idea rooted in biblical law and neoliberal gospel. Democrats like Clinton and Sam

Nunn have been working on this for years. In Georgia, first-time, nonviolent drug offenders are sent to boot camps for structured rehabilitation, an approach Clinton wants to make national. It's hard to argue, believer or atheist, that calisthenics, strict discipline, and stern sermons cloaked in the vocabulary of "self-esteem" wouldn't do malefactors some good.

Where the Religious Right is really right, however, is on family issues. Discourage teen pregnancy, welfare dependency, and divorce? Force deadbeat dads to pay up? Make schools instill values? Encourage community service? These are Religious Right favorites—old-time moral causes that are now progressive causes.   8

Clinton and Al Gore, two Southern Baptists, campaigned as traditionalists. William Galston, who is now deputy assistant to the president for domestic policy, defined traditionalism this way in 1991: "We cannot be indifferent to fundamental (and decidable) questions of right and wrong, and we violate no one's rights by putting public authority in the service of what is right." So, if the New Democrats have already picked up on these themes, why should anyone care about the Religious Right? Because the Right is far more comfortable with the conversation about families, hard work, and responsibility than the Democrats are. And where the Religious Right has the right ideas, the neoliberals have the right plan. Pursuing those plans in the face of an establishment with Mencken's reservations about religion will be difficult. Whenever the president feels reluctant to do moral battle, he ought to draw on both gospels—political and evangelical.   9

There's a world of cultural baggage to conquer first. For years, the establishment has feared the Religious Right. The most recent terror began with the Moral Majority's rise with Reagan in 1980—a phenomenon that led the National Abortion Rights Action League (NARAL) to declare that the movement had the "potential for [the] destruction of our political, religious, and legal institutions."   10

Here's a sketch of the people everybody's so hot about. Evangelicals— about 35 million Americans—believe that they have a personal, immediate relationship with Jesus Christ; that the Bible is the strict word of God; and that they have an obligation to share the "good news" of the gospel.   11

Across the board, 38 percent of Americans say they are born again or evangelical Christians, and 87 percent say religion is either very important or fairly important in their lives, according to Gallup Religious Research. The values that the Right holds dear—patriotism, integrity, traditional definitions of familial and sexual roles—are essentially the mainstream values of the thirties and forties and fifties. They're the values that won World War II. The worst that can be said of the Religious Right is that it's dramatically out of step—not out of its mind.   12

In this sense, the Religious Right does not include the snakehandlers of 13
southern Appalachia or truly extreme figures like David Koresh, the Waco,
Texas, cult leader—the "Wacko of Waco," as he's come to be called. It is,
instead, made up of those evangelicals who take anti-abortion, anti-
homosexual, and antifeminist positions on political questions. Not all are
Protestants, of course: Some Catholics, most notably Patrick Buchanan, are
allies. There are five million Religious Right activists: people who campaign,
donate money, contact public officials, or attend political meetings. And
while these activists are slightly less well-educated and well-off than non-
evangelical political activists—a group that could include NARAL activists,
for instance—the differences are hardly of, well, biblical proportions.

According to a 1992 University of Akron Survey Research Center poll, 14
17 percent of Christian activists had postgraduate degrees, compared to
15 percent for non-evangelical activists. While that's probably due to the
number of ministers in the Religious Right's ranks, a more realistic picture
emerges from other statistics. Nineteen percent of the Religious Right's activists are college graduates, compared to 24 percent of non-evangelical
activists. And while 30 percent of non-evangelical activists didn't go beyond high school, 39 percent of Religious Right activists didn't make it
that far. But "uneducated"? Doesn't look like it.

Financially, it's hard to say which of the activist camps does better. More 15
non-evangelical activists than Religious Right activists are on the poorest end
of the scale, making less than $25,000 a year. The Religious Right also leads
in the $25,000 to $50,000 range. Then, in the $50,000 to $75,000 range, it's
a dead heat, 21 percent to 21 percent. Over $75,000, non-evangelical ac-
tivists have an edge, 14 percent to 11 percent. Because the Religious Right
draws a majority of its activists from the South—fully 53 percent—even the
differences are understandable. "Although it's changing, the South is a region
with traditionally lower levels of income and education anyway," says Lyman Kellstedt, a director of the Akron survey and a political scientist at
Wheaton College. "That accounts for some of the disparity, because the non-
evangelical activists are evenly dispersed geographically."

Until about 1968, conservative Christians, assuming the world to be 16
beyond temporal redemption, kept religious crusading and politics separate. In 1965, an obscure Baptist minister named Jerry Falwell said, "Believing in the Bible as I do, I would find it impossible to stop preaching the
pure saving Gospel of Jesus Christ, and begin doing anything else—
including fighting communism . . . Preachers are not called to be politicians
but to be soul winners." Spurred on by the social chaos of the late sixties,
the old notion that a Christian's duty was to the private sphere of family
and church—not to the public sphere of politics and government—broke

down. A similar sense of disorder from that era, incidentally, would turn some Democrats into Republicans and some liberals into neoliberals.

It didn't take long for the Religious Right's Holy Roller rhetoric to frighten those who professed to protect Jefferson's much-vaunted (and vaulted) "wall of separation between church and state." Says Robert Maddox, a Carter White House religious liaison and speechwriter who is also a former head of Americans United for the Separation of Church and State: "Robertson, Falwell, and the other key players—including people you don't hear about—are angry and feel threatened by the culture. With them, there's no gray area, no toleration, and I find that very dangerous. I don't know that I could stay in the same room with most of them." That's true of many people, and it underscores the cultural divide between the unctuous preachers and the broad middle.   17

Disappointed by the end of the Reagan-Bush dynasty and by the apparent invulnerability of abortion fights, the Religious Right has turned to what it calls "pro-family" issues. That shift in emphasis reassures none of the movement's old foes. "The Religious Right of the nineties is much stronger, more sophisticated, and will, as a result, probably be much more successful in its lobbying," says Arthur Kropp, executive director of People for the American Way. "The movement builds itself by dividing America. I think that's poisonous: The way they play the game is damaging, and their agenda is threatening." Robert Peck of the American Civil Liberties Union hastens to defend the movement's right to participate, then homes in: "We think that much of their agenda is out of step with traditional American principles and liberties, and we feel an obligation to oppose them when they try to trample on those things."   18

Even Clinton worries about protecting his liberal credentials. He did hold one meeting with ministers in Little Rock during the transition, and Billy Graham gave the benediction at the inauguration. But when the five-million-member National Association of Evangelicals, as moderate a part of the Religious Right as there is, invited Clinton to speak to its national convention in March, the president didn't acknowledge the invitation. "I think those extreme forces on the Religious Right are going to find themselves irrelevant," the Rev. Benjamin F. Chavis, vice president of the National Council of Churches and a Clinton transition team member, told *The Los Angeles Times*. "It's not because anyone is shutting the door in their face, but because their ideology increasingly does not apply to the American condition."   19

But on family policy, can you tell the difference between what Marshall Wittmann, legislative director of the conservative Christian Coalition, says and what William Galston and Elaine Kamarck wrote in *Mandate for Change,* the Clinton policy blueprint?   20

"We want public policy in this country that is pro the Sermon on the Mount. So wouldn't it make sense to make divorce for couples with children   21 more difficult?" The Galston/Kamarck plan would impose a nine-month cooling-off period between filing and going to court, giving parents the chance to ponder the implications of breaking up a household.

The plan, similar to one proposed by Britain's Law Commission, is on   22 target: Since 1960, the U.S. divorce rate—the highest in the world—has increased 250 percent. "Unless you're in a radical state of denial, you simply have to acknowledge that kids raised where the marriage is intact grow up more confident, happier, and more stable," says James Davison Hunter, a University of Virginia sociologist. According to the Census Bureau, the gross income of a child and the custodial parent drops 37 percent immediately after a divorce and rises only slightly 16 months later. To press for something as sweeping as divorce reform would require a revival not unlike the Great Awakening, and the Democrats, outside that one chapter in *Mandate*, have been silent about it. That's no surprise: Restricting divorce is restricting, from the left's point of view, an exercise of liberty. It's hard to imagine what, outside of a pro-life button, could be less fashionable among the professional baby boomer set.

In areas like family or divorce policy, the Religious Right helps bring   23 the moral element of a problem into focus. Its agitation forces politicians of the left and the right to address concerns—however large, however uncomfortable—that traditional liberals think too intrusive. When liberals read the gloomy statistics and wonder why everything's falling apart, they don't make the obvious connection. "The Right does raise issues and forces us to talk about things we might otherwise not talk about," says Maddox, the former Carter aide. "They do serve a purpose, however heavy-handed and occasionally unpleasant: They're kind of like castor oil."

There are other potential points of contact. William Bennett, a conser-   24 vative Republican, spoke out at the GOP convention against "rampant promiscuity." The Progressive Policy Institute, speaking through Galston and Kamarck, says, "The president should use the full force of his office to wage an all-out campaign against teenage pregnancy and out-of-wedlock births." A good way to do that is to speak out against "rampant promiscuity," which is not a little relevant to the pregnancy rate. In 1989, a quarter of all infants in the United States were born out of wedlock. And while 60 percent of black babies were illegitimate, illegitimacy is rising fastest among white children. Teenage girls give birth to 500,000 babies a year, and those infants are four times as likely as children in other families to be poor.

Traditional liberals are caught in a curious irony on this. While they are   25 terribly reluctant to condemn promiscuity for fear of appearing intolerant, they are equally reluctant to link personal behavior (promiscuity) and social ills (poverty, dropout rates, welfare dependency). At the same time, these reluctant liberals aren't encouraging their own children to act irresponsibly, and it's cynical not to discourage dangerous behavior in others.

As Mickey Kaus noted recently in *The New Republic,* Marian Wright 26
Edelman, a Clinton intimate and president of the Children's Defense Fund,
has cried out against "our obsession with the motivation and behavior of the
poor—their sexual as well as their work behavior." That's precisely where
part of the problem lies, though. Sexual and work behavior euphemisms for
producing out-of-wedlock children and going on the dole instead of working—is what the Religious Right speaks to. Now, it's the president's turn.

Of course, much of the Religious Right's rhetoric can be simplistic and 27
unrealistic. Its fascination with sex moves many of us in the middle to angry distraction and repels people like Edelman from hearing it out. "I have
always believed that the center of gravity in American opinion is tolerant
traditionalism," says Galston. "People really do embrace traditional values,
but people are very, very wary of using the state apparatus to enforce those
values. Both parties would do well to attend to that center of gravity."

One way to do that is to promote values-based education in public 28
schools. The phrase terrifies liberals who fear responsive readings from the
Psalter and endless kindergarten Passion plays. But the National Commission on Children, Senator Jay Rockefeller's bipartisan panel that included
Clinton and every ideological type from evangelicals to Edelman, recommends promoting community service as a value. Maryland now requires
75 hours of such service to graduate from high school. That speaks powerfully to ancient religious concerns: It's as close as we will ever get to codifying the Golden Rule. Writing about teenagers—the kids who could,
alternatively, be out conceiving illegitimate children—Rockefeller's commission says: "They can staff soup kitchens, tutor their peers and younger
children, visit shut-ins and the elderly, and improve their neighborhoods
through construction and cleanup projects."

These are not ill-placed priorities: 61 percent of high school students 29
confess to cheating on tests; assaults on teachers are up 700 percent since
1978; each month, 282,000 students are attacked in schools. Teaching values as broadly defined as not beating up your teacher seems to be in order.
Civility and responsibility are consummately religious values. So are "compassion" and "truth," two of the values that a community council in Baltimore County, using the Constitution and the Bill of Rights, decided were
nonsectarian and worthy of teaching. These aren't new ideas: St. Augustine
had a good bit to say about charity and conduct; even a pagan like Aristotle meditated on the tension between rights and responsibilities.

Out in Colorado Springs, where Dr. James Dobson's vast Focus on the 30
Family Christian organization is headquartered, 500 staffers field 200,000

calls a month from people bewildered by the brutal business of modernity. Mothers call for childrearing tips, others for a dissection of Clinton's tax plan. They worry about violence, about drugs, about what's on television, and they turn to the religious outfit for guidance. I personally wouldn't telephone a "Christian ministry" founded on inspirational videotapes, direct mail, and Bible radio shows; most in the middle probably wouldn't, either. What brings others to do it is the same impulse that holds together inner-city churches, or Girls and Boys Clubs, or midnight basketball leagues: the impulse for community in a broken world. "We have our hands full with the problems of hurt and pain that are being heaped on the family by the culture and by the economy," says Rob Gregory, a Focus on the Family spokesman. They are words that could echo across the worst city street.

Rockefeller's commission confronted an uncomfortable truth that neo- 31 liberals and conservative Christians acknowledged long ago: "Today, too many young people seem adrift, without a steady moral compass to direct their daily behavior or to plot a thoughtful and responsible course for their lives." Speaking to that requires encouraging neoliberal favorites like community service and values education, and institutions like the draft and public schools to foster democratic instincts. These are practical matters that significantly overlap with the Religious Right's agenda, which is focused, too, on renewing a world where people appreciate and care for one another. "Evangelicals are not retreating from society," says Allan Carlson, president of the conservative Rockford Institute in Illinois. "We are trying to rebuild a sense of community block by block."

There are unhappy signs that the Democratic family revival won't come 32 off: Already, Donna Shalala, the secretary of Health and Human Services, has downplayed the work component of welfare reform. In 1991, as a gesture toward the Right's views, Rockefeller's commission called for funding abstinence-based sex education equally with teenage family planning (birth control); neither the Bush administration, nor the Congress, nor the Clinton administration responded. Thus far, there have been few wise words from the White House about responsibility and personal conduct—too few.

The culture wars between the left and the Religious Right sometimes 33 have all the sophistication of a backyard dogfight. On public property in California, for example, the evergreens draped with colored lights and tinsel during December aren't "Christmas trees" anymore. Instead, they're called "community trees" or "city holiday trees" to avoid religious conflicts. In New York, a Queens school district provoked the latest fracas in the most enduring Religious Right cause: school prayer. The district's school board voted in a "moment of reflection" to let students, in the words of the school superintendent, "focus their thoughts, calm down, and get ready for the day's learning activities." Nevertheless, the New York Civil Liberties Union and other organizations are squawking about the move.

Part of the cultural opposition to school prayer is based in liberal snob- 34 bery: Only reactionaries trapped by naive allegiance to religion, an old liberal argument goes, would really care about school prayer. Nobody ought to seriously suggest kicking off a public school day with the Lord's Prayer—the courts have clearly held that to be unconstitutional. By the same token, there's nothing wrong with asking children to observe a moment of silence. In 26 states, there are laws on the books that would permit the ritual. A kid can worry about a baseball game or the Pauline accounts of the Resurrection—either way, the choice is the child's. The Religious Right would be pacified, and the establishment, by conceding a nonsectarian moment of silence, would demonstrate that it shares the same values and concerns. A moment of silence has never kept a family together or taught a kid to read, but resolving this would give us an idea of how to find common ground between the Religious Right, the left, and the broad middle.

There is a very great difference between the jingoism of the Religious 35 Right and the tolerant traditionalism that most of us intuitively accept. Some conservatives are slowly recognizing that: "The Religious Right does have to learn to be more tolerant in their public rhetoric, and there's a theological reason for that," says Michael Cromartie, director of the Evangelical Studies Project at the Ethics and Public Policy Center. "Religious conservatives understand their own essential brokenness; they should understand that everybody is fallen."

So when Pat Robertson next suggests that Clinton has "a radical plan 36 to destroy the traditional family," get angry, roll your eyes, fulminate. That's reasonable, because Robertson's dead wrong. But remember to pause when Robertson or someone of his ilk suggests something quaint about keeping families together or minding one's manners. Pause, because from preachers and from presidents, those are words many people need to hear.

Thinking Critically

1. Jon Meacham wrote this essay in 1993. At the time, President Bill Clinton and Vice President Al Gore were both open about their Southern Baptist faith, and the previous two terms of the Ronald Reagan presidency had brought the Religious Right to general attention as both a cultural phenomenon and a political force. In what ways does this essay seem prescient about the 2004 presidential election?

2. How does Meacham describe the "mainstream" view of conservative Christianity? Although he doesn't use the "red" and "blue" labels, which of the values that Meacham assigns to different groups of people might be termed "red" or "blue"?

3. What kinds of evidence does Meacham use to support his argument? Which of his evidence do you find most convincing?

Writing Critically

1. Both Alan Wolfe (page 145) and Jon Meacham argue that the "liberal intelligentsia," including academics and the news media, need to be more open-minded and have a tolerant approach toward American religious fundamentalists and evangelicals. On what points do Wolfe and Meacham agree? Where do they disagree? What are your own opinions about the influence of the Religious Right on American politics and civic life?

2. Meacham considers some of the broad stereotypes of American evangelical Christians, offering both his own experience growing up in the South and the findings of a 1992 research poll to refute those stereotypical images. Of course, evangelical Christians are not the only religious group that is stereotyped and condescended to by the American media; this book is full of essays about how uncomfortable the American mainstream media are with people of *any* religious or spiritual background. Write a researched paper in which you trace the stereotyping of a religious faith or spiritual practice in American popular culture.

3. In areas ranging from family and divorce policy to punishing nonviolent offenders, Meacham suggests common ground between Clinton-era Democrats and activists on the Religious Right. Write an essay in which you argue for "common ground" on a contentious social or political issue. Be sure that you avoid stereotyping or simplifying the views of the side with which you are most inclined to disagree. For a model of such "common ground" work go to the website of the Religious Coalition for Reproductive Choice, at <http://www.rcrc.org>.

Vote or Lie

HUA HSU

Hua Hsu is a student and writer living in Cambridge, Massachusetts. He writes about music, film, books, and politics for *Slate,* the *Village Voice, Wired,* and *Blender,* among other publications. Formerly an editor at *URB* magazine, he currently writes a column for *The Wire.* Hua is pursuing a Ph.D. in the History of American Civilization program at Harvard University. He hopes to complete his dissertation on China's place in the American cultural imagination by the time you graduate from college. He also moonlights as a DJ and is one-fourth of the Stickershock collective. If you enter his name into Google, you can find out more about all of the above. This article appeared in the *Village Voice* in October 2004.

Few people remember the Public Affairs Act of 1975. The legislation 1 noiselessly received all the appropriate votes and knowing backslaps, skimming along with little fanfare until a group of University of Cincinnati researchers started asking questions. Led by a political scientist named George Bishop, the researchers asked Americans across the country the same question: "Do you favor or oppose the Public Affairs Act of 1975?" For some reason, the act that nobody scrutinized yielded surprisingly divisive views now that it had been codified—the research team discovered that about one-third of respondents expressed a definitive preference one way or another on this heretofore uncontroversial legislative throw-away. Naturally, nothing happened.

The act lived unspectacularly for the next 20 years until a *Washington* 2 *Post* poll asked a similar question: What did Americans think now that the act was poised for repeal? Did it matter that it was the "Republican Congress" that wanted to roll back the act's obscure gains? What about President Clinton's support of the repeal? Again, the public voiced a fierce split. Again, nothing happened.

The thing is, the Public Affairs Act of 1975 never existed. It was a fab- 3 rication of Bishop's team designed to prove a point: People prefer feigning authority to admitting ignorance. Those who study polling call these phantom opinions "non-attitudes" since they are the product of harried, on-the-spot guessing rather than actual deliberation. Now you can paw over this and conclude that social scientists are dry blowhards fixated on quantifying collective dullness, or you can come clean and admit that you retreated to Google before the second paragraph so you could ready an opinion. It's that time again. Every four years, we come together as a nation to commission a new leader, and every time it turns into another referendum on how misinformed, gullible, or just plain dumb we the people can be. The greatest symptoms? Apathy, poor showings on man-on-the-street late-night TV segments, and that dreaded thing known as "low voter turnout."

Before we slump our shoulders and start talking declension, let's think 4 about that last thing. If we refer back to the archival footage, we find that only 6 percent of the nation's population voted for George Washington. This astonishingly tiny sum has a lot to do with the fact that only adult white males were eligible for the vote, but during the entire colonial period turnout was still dreadfully low. Participation grew steadily through the 19th century as roughly three-quarters of eligible voters made their way to the booth, whether it was by horseback or as part of an elaborate, flowery parade. The numbers dipped again in the 20th century. In 2000, about half of eligible voters made it to the polls—which isn't so bad, considering the turnout percentage was similar in the early 20s. The figure is sure to be higher this time, though our registration and turnout numbers will still pale in comparison to many of our esteemed democratic peers.

It's a commonly held misperception that Americans don't vote. Americans love to vote. The problem is that we vote for inane things. We vote on competing but really conspiring blends of Coca-Cola. We vote on who we believe will win the World Series or whether a given coach bungled a crucial third down. We vote people to the zenith of prefab pop stardom, often over the objections of bona fide talent scouts. We vote on issues of other people's matrimony and during the commercial breaks, Internet providers and cable music video channels mainline election-year imagery and jockey for our "votes." We are quizzed in the streets, on the Web, and on television for our views. The language of "voting" is everywhere when, in reality, it usually amounts to nothing more than a bar graph and the threat of future spam. Democracy? The free expression of ideas? Civil society? Sometimes it seems like Americans can't get enough of it.

Public life brims with opportunities to take part in collective decision-making. I mean, reality television seems far more like "direct democracy" than the presidential contests, which still have to travel the arcane thruways of the electoral college for their legitimacy. There is no electoral college on Fox; they want to know what I think, not what some distant secondary representative does on my behalf. Consider this very unscientific anecdote. Approximately 100 million voters turned out to elect Al Gore in 2000. In a similarly tight race, roughly 65 million votes were cast during the final episode of this year's *American Idol,* in which Fantasia Barrino emerged victorious over Diana DeGarmo. Of course, most of the *Idol* votes came from kids punching in early and often, but is this not the sign of a healthy democracy, to care so much about an outcome that one resorts to cheating?

In a weird way, the noted sociologist Robert Putnam got it wrong. In his splashy 2000 book *Bowling Alone,* he tracked the decline of the American community by looking at how isolated people had become. The feeling of mutuality—the thing Alexis de Tocqueville pointed to as the preservative of our political culture—had seemingly evaporated as fewer Americans were joining clubs, mingling with friends, or, worse yet, bowling in leagues.

But mutuality has never felt stronger, and I'm not just talking about 8
how the current regime basically bombed the masses out of apathy. Everywhere you turn, there are opportunities to voice some kind of civic sentiment or join a modest, imagined nation of fellow travelers. What is more
Athenian than the convenience of choosing between two options on your
Sprint PCS phone? What better polis than linking to funny, like-minded
blogs from the comfort of my own futon? The participatory impulses of the
masses are as strong as ever—Americans are getting down with a whole
gamut of activities that resemble politics and ape the shape, form, and logic
of democracy, and it has all helped foster an illusion that politics, like
choosing a setup man out of the bullpen, is easy. Think about how John
Kerry is scolded for thinking too much about issues usually framed in
strict, Manichaean terms.

But there's something missing in all of this: deliberation. The prolifera- 9
tion of outlets badgering us for opinions or flattering us as experts has produced a great deal of noise but little actual discourse. How do I know
which of these tubby redheads would make a better Danny Bonaduce? I'm
voting for the one with the better shoes. We have grown used to cavalierly
expressing "non-attitudes" rather than thinking through possible choices
or imagining better alternatives. Whether all of this practice voting has prepared us to make an educated choice next month is a wholly different matter. And even if it doesn't, that's why the framers wisely included the
safeguarding provisions of Article II of the Public Affairs Act.

Thinking Critically

1. What was the Public Affairs Act of 1975? (Yes, this is a trick question.)
2. What is Hua Hsu's claim about Americans and voting behavior, and how
   does he support that claim?
3. What's the difference between a "non-attitude" and an opinion, and why
   does it matter?

Writing Critically

1. Which is preferable voter behavior: apathy, "non-attitude," ignorance, or
   prayer? If we guarantee pretty much everyone over the age of eighteen a
   vote, is it fair to expect everyone to be judicious, deliberate, and considerate about voting?
2. What was the last thing you voted for? How many opportunities are available to you, right now, online or on television or somewhere else in the media, to "vote"?

3. Read Leslie Savan's essay "Did Somebody Say 'Community?'" (see pp. 77–81). According to Savan's thesis, are people who participate in the kind of "voting" or "democracy" that Hsu describes maybe just looking for community? What would Hsu and Savan find either pitiable or understandable in that impulse?

Arguing the Cultural Divides

1. In an analytical essay, discuss the ways in which American voters reach their decisions. Is a cultural divide evident in the ways in which Americans make their voting decisions? It's an oversimplification to divide the country into voters and nonvoters. On the basis of this chapter and other selections in this book, develop a more subtle set of criteria for distinguishing between groups of voters.

2. Is it possible to keep religion out of the civic and political arenas? What about profound ethical and moral issues, such as abortion, the death penalty, or the allocation of health care? Would you prefer to have such decisions argued and legislated by people who have no religious or spiritual tradition or convictions? Why, or why not? Should public officials check their religious beliefs at the office door? You might use John Micklethwait and Adrian Wooldridge's "Right from the Beginning" as historical context, and you should consider the observations, experiences, and opinions of at least two other sources from this book.

3. During and after the 2004 election there was a great deal of chatter about "values"—one of those vague words, like "community" and "democracy," that essayists Leslie Savan and Hua Hsu, among others, enjoy deconstructing and dissecting. In an essay that uses extended definition and comparison and contrast, propose a definition of the word *values* based in real actions and consequences rather than empty rhetoric and advertising.

The Home Front: Who Is the American Family?

Money Changes Everything: Coming to Terms with Father's Day

TED RALL

Ted Rall is an editorial cartoonist, a radio commentator, an illustrator, and an essayist. First a physics and then a history major at Columbia University in the 1980s, Rall was inspired to draw by the ecstatic, politically engaged New York street artist Keith Haring. If Rall has a hero as an editorial cartoonist, it would be the nineteenth-century muckraker Thomas Nash, whose editorial cartoons in *Harper's Weekly* exposed the realities of Civil War battlefields and the depredations of Tammany Hall's political scandal. An abolitionist, Nash also supported the rights of Chinese immigrant workers and Native Americans. Rall's political cartoons carry on Nash's fearless pursuit of social justice and mockery of political folly. Rall's radio journalism is equally fearless. He aired the first live American radio talk shows from Cuba and Uzbekistan, and he broadcast live dispatches from Afghanistan after America invaded that country in pursuit of terrorists. Ted Rall is the author of four graphic novels, including *Real Americans Admit: The Worst Thing I've Ever Done!*

(1996) and *Revenge of the Latchkey Kids* (1998). "Money Changes Everything: Coming to Terms with Father's Day" was published in *Killed: Great Journalism Too Hot to Print* (2004). In a prologue, Rall explains how this essay came about and why it was eventually "killed" (rejected) by the *New York Times Magazine*.

Some years ago, the *New York Times Magazine* began running "Lives," a column on its last page. Ordinary readers were invited to submit essays about events that changed them, but I noticed that in practice, many of the pieces that appeared in the section were by professional writers like me.

I called a hip young *Times* editor to pitch "Lives," which posited that my generation's resentment of its elders (Baby Boomers and other assorted codgers) stemmed from their penchant for irresponsible behavior. I thought that dissing my dad in a piece that ran on Father's Day would make an amusing counterpoint to the litany of "aren't fathers just the best?" pap that usually gets published on that *Hallmark* holiday. And I hoped that it would communicate to other children of divorce that they weren't alone.

After I filed, my editor called with good news: the Magazine's editorial committee had signed off on the piece, which was scheduled for publication in June as I had suggested.

Weeks passed. Finally my editor called to say they were killing the piece. I heard that it had made some influential people on West Forty-third Street feel "uncomfortable."

As a writer I've often been surprised by what topics editors consider too hot to handle. We live in a nation with a 50 percent divorce rate, yet the media still ferociously defends the sacred myth of the rock-solid nuclear family. When I called one of my collections of essays "Kill Your Parents Before They Kill You," buyers for major chains that carried books about bestiality and terrorism refused to stock it unless I agreed to change its title. (I did.)

The Census Bureau reports that 27 percent of all American children live in single-parent households. They're more likely to grow up poor, become criminals, and get divorced themselves. Divorce is a major issue, but the mainstream media seems scared to admit that *Leave It to Beaver* is dead. At least during the '90s publications occasionally referenced children of divorce as part of pieces about Generation X (remember them?). Now they almost never do. You read more editorials and features about the problems of children in Afghanistan and Iraq than you do about those right here in the United States.

When I was a kid, I always dreaded the week before the third Sunday in June.   1

The Hallmark store in our local shopping center was larger than Kettering, Ohio, deserved, but I could never find the right Father's Day card for the man I saw during court-ordered visits.   2

Nevertheless, my mother insisted that our shattered-rump family at-   3
tempt to maintain appearances, to retain a vestige of normality despite the
facts. That meant dropping a few dollars on a card for "Dad."

Money and my father had been symbiotic words as long as I could re-   4
member. Mom and I didn't have and couldn't get it. Dad had more than he
knew what to do with but wouldn't part with any.

I was two when my parents split up. Dad moved to a high-rise apartment   5
in downtown Dayton with abstract art on the walls and a pool on the roof.
Mom found a job teaching high-school French. In a ritual familiar to tens of
millions of Americans, a county family court judge ordered my mom to turn
me over to my father on alternating Saturdays and Sundays, 1:00 to 7:00 PM,
plus two consecutive weeks in August. Dad stuck to the judge's schedule with
the pinpoint precision that he'd picked up at MIT, cutting his latest new car—
he was partial to Pontiacs—into our driveway at the exact moment that the
news on his radio came on at the top of the hour. We spent most of the ensu-
ing six hours at the mall, watching action-adventure films, feeding quarters
into pinball machines, and shopping for (his) stereo equipment. He never held
my hand, put his arm around my shoulder or referred to me by name. "Son,"
he'd say, "don't ever wear your heart on your sleeve." It was good advice.

The stuff of day-to-day parenting—school assemblies, Boy Scouts—fell   6
to mom. She taught me how to swim, worried about bullies, and unraveled
the mysteries of fractions, angles, and logarithms. Dad didn't exist during
the week. He never called. Dad was like James Garner in *The Rockford
Files*. Both came on every weekend; neither felt real.

Dad, an aeronautical engineer, had been working on a supersonic   7
bomber project for the Air Force when he left my mom. Only four prototypes were built, yet it turned out to be his biggest triumph. He invented
the plane's movable nose, a feature later incorporated into the Concorde. I
think about him whenever I see it.

He bought furniture and more art as he did better at work. Every time   8
I saw his new stuff on those alternating Saturdays and Sundays, I hated him
a little more.

One morning, Dad broke routine. He appeared with the principal of my   9
elementary school at the door of my classroom. "You're going with your
dad," the principal said. My first thought was that mom had died. As we
left, Dad broke into a rare grin. "How about box seats to the World Series?" he asked, waving two tickets. It was a magical afternoon. The Reds
beat the Sox. Reds shortstop David Concepcion signed my ball. For half a
day, I forgot that Dad was usually late with the child support. ("Thank
God it's too little to matter," my mom joked.) I nearly felt something like
love for my father.

A few months later, Dad remarried.   10

Dad bought a sprawling new split-level to house the five stepchildren   11
he'd acquired through Mrs. Rall II. Every alternating Saturday and Sunday
he exposed me to the lavish upper-middle-class lifestyle that might have
been mine if not for my parents' divorce. Dad and his new wife merged her
children's photos with mine on the wall of the new house's family room, but
my picture appeared on the bottom right-hand corner of the arrangement.

After the remarriage mom and I spent many weekdays downtown in   12
family court, trying to force Dad to honor the divorce decree he'd signed
back in 1968. First he refused to pay for my braces, an expense he had
agreed to bear. Knowing that he didn't stand a chance in court, he showed
up at my orthodontist's office a day before the hearing. He slammed fifteen
hundred-dollar bills on the receptionist's desk and stormed out.

Although we never discussed money when we were together, I couldn't   13
ignore Dad's latest rancid court maneuvers during visitations. I'd come home
incensed at nothing in particular, unable to articulate my rage, my head
throbbing for hours as I stared at the patterns in the paint on the ceiling.

After I got my first job, bagging groceries in a supermarket, I asked my   14
boss to schedule me for as many weekend afternoon shifts as possible. I saw
my father less frequently. Oddly, I felt guilty that I didn't miss him. Mom
and I fought the battles of my rebellious teens, with others and against each
other. She was always there, providing the moral grounding that my irresponsible father couldn't or wouldn't give.

In the divorce decree, Dad had promised to pay my tuition at the college   15
of my choice. He didn't indicate that he planned to welch until the last minute.
As I was packing to leave for Columbia, Dad called Mom's lawyer to say he
refused to pay more than the equivalent of in-state tuition at Ohio State. I
went to Columbia anyway. I paid $850 a month in student loans for ten years.

At age twenty-nine, I was still seething at my dad. I mailed him a nine-   16
page letter listing my complaints. For the first time, he called. At his suggestion we met for a bizarre weekend summit at an Embassy Suites on the
I-270 loop outside Columbus, Ohio. During the course of two day-long
sessions, Dad admitted that he had never felt emotional responses. Love,
hate, fear, regrets—they were all strangers. He blamed his own distant,
Methodist parents for his coldness. Great: my dad, the sociopath.

His take on his cheapness was: "I can't do anything about it. That's all   17
in the past now."

"You *could* pay off my student loans," I suggested, knowing full well   18
that he would never try to repent for his neglect. And he didn't. Upon my
return to New York I found a newsy letter from Dad in the letterbox. He
obviously believed that we were friends now, that we could start afresh

without revisiting the past. I haven't spoken to him since, nor have I thought about sending him a Father's Day card.

But I've reconsidered that holiday lately. Just because my dad wasn't a 19
father doesn't mean I didn't have a father. This year on Father's Day, I'm calling my *real* dad. I'm calling Mom.

Thinking Critically

1. What about this take on fatherhood does Ted Rall believe made the editors at the *New York Times Magazine* "uncomfortable"?

2. At least two significant subjects are compared and contrasted in this essay. How does Rall use comparison and contrast to shape his essay? Why is this a particularly effective rhetorical choice, given Rall's subject matter?

3. One challenge about telling a story from a child's perspective is that you have an unreliable narrator. Huckleberry Finn is perhaps the best-known example of an unreliable narrator in American fiction. In what ways is Rall an unreliable narrator in this essay? Does he ever admit to being, at least at some points, an unreliable narrator? What's the emotional impact of reading a story told by an unreliable narrator?

Writing Critically

1. Although Rall is writing about a deeply personal and emotionally difficult experience, his intent was obviously to reach a larger audience. What is Rall's purpose in sharing these personal experiences? How does a "personal narrative" become an essay that has greater relevance and a larger civic, cultural, or political purpose?

2. Revisit an essay that you wrote earlier in this course, or perhaps for another class, in which you didn't (for whatever reason) use the first person. Can you rewrite the essay from a first-person point of view, including your own experiences and observations? How does that change the way you structure your overall argument and select your evidence? Does it change your audience? Does it change your commitment to the topic?

3. Suppose your child, your parent, or someone very close to you told you one day that he or she was publishing an essay about his or her relationship with you. How would you respond? Would you be angry? Demand to see a copy before publication? Threaten to sue? In general, you would have no legal recourse—especially if you were not named in the essay (notice that Ted Rall never names either his mother or his father). Who has the "right" to tell your story? In an essay, create a hypothetical situation or use an actual event—perhaps you were interviewed in the media, or your former girl- or boyfriend turned up on a talk show and spilled all kinds of intimate though anonymous details—in which the rights to your "story" are challenged.

Why the M Word Matters to Me

ANDREW SULLIVAN

Journalist, essayist, blogger, and broadcaster Andrew Sullivan gets stuck with all sorts of labels by the media. He's the person you call if you want a conservative, a gay man, or a gay conservative man to comment on current political and cultural events. Born in England in 1963, Sullivan won a fellowship to Harvard University. While he earned a Ph.D. in political science, Sullivan began freelancing for the *New Republic,* the *New York Times,* the *Wall Street Journal,* and other newspapers and magazines. In 1991 Sullivan was appointed editor of the *New Republic,* a weekly magazine of intelligent, provocative, and politically independent views on literature, culture, and current events. Sullivan tested positive for the HIV virus in 1993, and he has candidly written about what it means to live with HIV. He was one of the first journalists to maintain a regular blog; (www.andrewsullivan.com) is one of the most widely read blogs in the United States. The intersection of his private life and his public journalism has led to some ugly confrontations. After an anonymous blogger posted details about Sullivan's sex life, the resulting scandal led to Sullivan being "barred indefinitely" from writing anymore for the *New York Times Magazine.* Nevertheless, Sullivan continues to be a bold and public advocate for gay rights, using his media presence and contacts to continue pressing for gay rights and to challenge politicians whose views on the subject are contradictory, spiteful, uninformed, or willfully ignorant. Sullivan is much in demand as a speaker at college campuses, and he appears frequently on radio and television talk shows across the political spectrum. "Why the M Word Matters to Me" appeared in *Time* magazine in February 2004.

As a child, I had no idea what homosexuality was. I grew up in a tradi- 1 tional home—Catholic, conservative, middle class. Life was relatively simple: education, work, family. I was raised to aim high in life, even though my parents hadn't gone to college. But one thing was instilled in me. What mattered was not how far you went in life, how much money you earned, how big a name you made for yourself. What really mattered was family and the love you had for one another. The most important day of your life was not graduation from college or your first day at work or a raise or even your first house. The most important day of your life was when you got married. It was on that day that all your friends and all your family got together to celebrate the most important thing in life: your happiness—your ability to make a new home, to form a new but connected family, to find love that put everything else into perspective.

But as I grew older, I found that this was somehow not available to me. 2 I didn't feel the things for girls that my peers did. All the emotions and so-cial rituals and bonding of teenage heterosexual life eluded me. I didn't know why. No one explained it. My emotional bonds to other boys were one-sided; each time I felt myself falling in love, they sensed it, pushed it away. I didn't and couldn't blame them. I got along fine with my buds in a nonemotional context, but something was awry, something not right. I came to know almost instinctively that I would never be a part of my fam-ily the way my siblings might one day be. The love I had inside me was un-mentionable, anathema. I remember writing in my teenage journal one day, "I'm a professional human being. But what do I do in my private life?"

I never discussed my real life. I couldn't date girls and so immersed my- 3 self in schoolwork, the debate team, school plays, anything to give me an excuse not to confront reality. When I looked toward the years ahead, I couldn't see a future. There was just a void. Was I going to be alone my whole life? Would I ever have a most important day in my life? It seemed impossible, a negation, an undoing. To be a full part of my family, I had to somehow not be me. So, like many other gay teens, I withdrew, became neu-rotic, depressed, at times close to suicidal. I shut myself in my room with my books night after night while my peers developed the skills needed to form real relationships and loves. In wounded pride, I even voiced a rejection of family and marriage. It was the only way I could explain my isolation.

It took years for me to realize that I was gay, years more to tell others and 4 more time yet to form any kind of stable emotional bond with another man. Because my sexuality had emerged in solitude—and without any link to the idea of an actual relationship—it was hard later to reconnect sex to love and self-esteem. It still is. But I persevered, each relationship slowly growing longer than the last, learning in my 20s and 30s what my straight friends had found out in their teens. But even then my parents and friends never asked the question they would have asked automatically if I were straight: So, when are you going to get married? When will we be able to celebrate it and affirm it and support it? In fact, no one—no one—has yet asked me that question.

When people talk about gay marriage, they miss the point. This isn't 5 about gay marriage. It's about marriage. It's about family. It's about love. It isn't about religion. It's about civil marriage licenses. Churches can and should have the right to say no to marriage for gays in their congregations, just as Catholics say no to divorce, but divorce is still a civil option. These family values are not options for a happy and stable life. They are necessities. Putting gay relationships in some other category—civil unions, domestic partnerships, whatever—may alleviate real human needs, but by their very euphemism, by their very separateness, they actually build a wall between gay people and their families. They put back the barrier many of us have spent a lifetime trying to erase.

It's too late for me to undo my past. But I want above everything else   6
to remember a young kid out there who may even be reading this now. I want to let him know that he doesn't have to choose between himself and his family anymore. I want him to know that his love has dignity, that he does indeed have a future as a full and equal part of the human race. Only marriage will do that. Only marriage can bring him home.

Thinking Critically

1. Who is the audience for *Time* magazine, and how does Andrew Sullivan shape his thesis, his tone, and his evidence to accommodate that audience?

2. When it comes to significant social and cultural issues like gay marriage, why do the media present first-person accounts and opinion pieces? What kind of authority do such first-person accounts have that might be missing from more objective news analysis?

3. Is there a recognizable arc or structure to the coming-out story? Do you recognize that arc in narratives about other kinds of experiences?

Writing Critically

1. Use a database or an online search engine to locate at least three additional articles from 2003 through 2005 that offer diverse first-person views on the Defense of Marriage Act, gay marriage in Massachusetts, California, or Canada, or civil unions. What do these first-person accounts have in common? Is it easier to find first-person accounts that support gay marriage or that oppose it? In an analytical essay, compare and contrast the different personal arguments for or against gay marriage.

2. Do you agree with Sullivan that "only marriage" can guarantee "a future as[1] a full and equal part of the human race" (paragraph 6)? What does that mean for people—gay *or* straight—who simply don't want to get married or who can't find anyone to marry? What does it imply for people (gay *or* straight) whose marriages failed? In what way is Sullivan's argument "conservative" in its view of marriage?

Jill and Jill Live on the Hill, but One Must Boil the Water

TZIVIA GOVER

Tzivia Gover received her M.F.A. in creative writing from Columbia University. A freelance writer, editor, and educator, Gover is the author of *Mindful Moments for Stressful Days* (2002) and gives workshops and lectures about finding ways to create joy and meaning in everyday life. Her essays on religion, spirituality, and health have appeared in the *Christian Science Monitor* and the *Boston Globe*. Gover has studied the Bible, Buddhism, and Jewish mysticism, and she is a frequent contributor to *Beliefnet.com*. Gover is a poetry instructor at The Care Center in Holyoke, Massachusetts, a program for pregnant and parenting teenagers that prepares them to take the GEDs. "Jill and Jill Live on the Hill, but One Must Boil the Water" appeared in the "Modern Love" column of the *New York Times* Sunday "Styles" section in November 2004.

My straight male friends don't believe it when I tell them, but it happens. I'll be lunching with some women who are grousing about their husbands: perfectly nice guys who will never just listen to their problems but always have to solve them, who won't write a thank-you note—even to their own mothers—and who give their child one bath and think they deserve a medal. At some point these women look wistfully in my direction and say, "I'd be a lesbian too, if I could!" 1

I wallow in their Lesbian Envy for as long as I can. But eventually I want to blurt, "Look, it's not a male-female issue; it's about testosterone overload, and a person of any gender can have that." 2

Granted this isn't a scientifically proven point. But what else could explain the fact that I find myself living, with my lesbian partner, in a gender-bent Ozzie and Harriet reality? How else to explain the fact that every time my partner and I get into a car she sits in the driver's seat and that I cook the dinners but she handles the barbecues? Or that while I chauffeur my 16-year-old daughter to and from endless pointe classes and spend hours hanging out rows of her pink tights to dry, my partner listens to the Red Sox game and cleans the gutters? How, I wonder, did I fail so miserably at my goal of becoming a liberated woman? 3

By age 12, I had determined that being a traditional woman meant trading your goals and priorities for a man's. Marriage for women, it seemed 4 to me, meant accepting dominion over the kitchen and laundry room, and forfeiting the right to pursue adventure and success outside. Case in point: my mother, after high school, enrolled in an elite college with dreams of traveling to Europe and studying history—but rather than graduate with a diploma, she left with a marriage license, and for years her dreams of Europe were reduced to drilling me on the verb *être* before French quizzes.

To avoid this fate, I began systematically to refuse to learn to do laundry or mop a floor. During a required home economics class, I sewed meandering seams on my yellow tennis dress. It was at about this time, too, when the tectonic plates of affection holding my parents in close proximity, touching but never quite joined, began to slide apart. This confirmed my suspicion that marriage and happiness were mutually exclusive concepts, especially for the woman, who gives up so much the day she says "I do."   5

I carry an image of my parents from that time: They are frozen as statues, as if the two figures that top a wedding cake had repositioned themselves 16 years later, refrozen at the close of the marriage. My father is caught mid-stride, as he climbs the steps from the back door of our suburban home to the kitchen. He is wearing his Brooks Brothers suit, minus the red and blue striped tie, which is balled up in one hand. His mouth is puckered slightly, as if for a kiss; but really he is about to utter the two syllables that pull us all into his rigid orbit: "I'm home."   6

My mother is standing at the kitchen counter, the handset of the phone pressed to her ear. The phone cord is draped around her like a beauty queen's sash. Her head is cocked to one side, lips slightly parted, and in the instant before she speaks, one might think she is being flirtatious or coy. Instead, she is apologizing. "Sorry," she tells her friend, "I've got to go."   7

"Sorry," she says to my father, to us.   8

"Sorry," she says, about everything.   9

From that moment to the actual divorce was a reverse courtship that would take a year or two. During that time, I suspect, my mother pretended not to notice my anti-marriage maneuvers, while secretly cheering me on. I graduated from high school blissfully ignorant of how to broil a steak, remove grass stains or compose a proper party invitation. I believed that I had succeeded in maturing into a young woman who was utterly unfit for becoming anyone's mother or wife.   10

I was baffled, therefore, when my first few serious boyfriends, with whom I had unabashedly shared my objections to being Mrs. Anyone, persisted in bringing up the subject of marriage. The fact that nothing I said or did seemed to convince men I was unmarriageable may have been the reason I allowed myself to be swept off my feet by a tall, dark, handsome woman I met in the college cafeteria my first semester away from home.   11

Not long after, I called my mother from a pay phone in my dormitory 12
with the news that I was gay. She paused. I waited nervously. "I'm glad
you're in love," she said finally. "I'm only sorry you won't have children."
This was 1982, before the lesbian baby boom, before *Will & Grace* and
back when a Boston marriage was something that would never be recorded
by a clerk in City Hall. I managed not to say, "That's the point, Mom!"

Meanwhile, in my Feminism 101 class we were debating whether biol- 13
ogy is destiny. I was opposed to the idea that a modern woman had to be
slave to her reproductive capability; that just because one could have a
child didn't mean she had to sublimate her other goals in favor of motherhood. But somehow I seemed unable to escape at least part of this fate. My
next lover sat me down shortly into our relationship and announced that
she wanted to have a baby.

At first I resisted. But eventually I gave in. Being a mother in an equal 14
relationship, I reasoned, could be more radical than not being a mother at
all. So when my partner gave birth, we tried to split the family duties down
the middle. Confronted by the inherent inequality of the biological bond
that nursing the baby would create, I purchased a device for adoptive
mothers that lets women "breast-feed" with the help of a tiny tube laid
alongside the breast and attached to a pouch of formula.

We traded off night feedings and diaper changings, and we divided the 15
responsibility for earning an income. We agreed that I'd freelance from
home so I could watch the baby while I worked. It was while I was typing
at my word processor with the baby balanced on my lap that the idea of a
division of labor based on male and female responsibilities crossed my
mind. This time the concept seemed wildly appealing.

But before I could explore this idea, the relationship between my 16
partner and me failed. At this point strict equality would have meant
having our 2-year-old daughter spend half the week in each of our
apartments, which seemed unfair to her. Instead, I settled into the role
of divorced father, seeing her on weekends and holidays and helping out
with the finances as best I could.

Meanwhile, I fell in love again, this time with Chris, a woman who 17
could drive a nail like nobody's business. She looked sexy with a tool belt
slung across her hips, and after the devastation of my breakup, I welcomed
the feeling of security that comes when someone you love seems able to fix
anything: a stopped-up toilet, a leaking roof, a weary heart.

But I soon found that she also refused to stop and ask directions if we 18
were lost, and she thought it perfectly natural that I should wash dishes and
she should take out the trash. Still reeling from the ache of separation from
my daughter's daily life, and the searing pain of my recent breakup, I found

surprising comfort in the illusion that I was sheltered by the rooms of our new home and by the more predictable tasks inside of it. I was—perhaps not unlike some traditional wives—content to let someone else handle the less wieldy problems that required power tools, steel-toed work boots or, simply, exposure to the elements. No, it wasn't perfect. But at the time, it worked.

Then one day as we were driving (she at the wheel, of course) I heard 19 her mutter in disgust at the car in front of us, "Women drivers!"

"That, of course, would include you," I pointed out. She rolled her eyes 20 and shrugged.

Later, during an argument in which I was all emotion and had lost my 21 grasp on logic, she spat, "You're acting like such a girl."

"You can't say that!" I sputtered. "You're one, too." 22

Being a lesbian, I now saw, hadn't shielded me from the sexism I once 23 feared would suffocate me. Rather, I learned that gender roles aren't as simple as biology. Every successful relationship requires its own hard-won formula for accepting the people we are, and for pushing to outgrow limits.

Decades have passed since my parents split up. My mother has had her 24 chance at a career of her own, and my father has had time to fall in love again and learn to love the people around him while letting them live their own lives.

And in the 14 years since Chris and I have been together, I have learned 25 that her sexist outbursts are as painful to her as they are to me. After all, in the world beyond our front lawn she is subject to the same prejudice I am. We grapple with what it means to be a woman without being trapped in a stereotype. I have come to see that a clean floor really can be something to be proud of. But I also don't forget that I know, too, how to shingle a roof, milk a goat and paddle a canoe through white water.

The other day when my best friend, who has a special fondness for be- 26 stowing nicknames, called just as Chris and I were on our way to play tennis, she said, "You two are Venus and Serena today." I quickly corrected her: "Try Billie Jean and Bobby."

On the court that afternoon, Chris and I laughed at the absurd aptness 27 of my remark. Joking aside, I did put an extra spin on the ball. After all, I didn't want to be accused of playing like a girl, and I really wanted to win.

Thinking Critically

1. How does Tzivia Gover define the "traditional woman"? What factors contributed to her understanding of this ideal?

2. One challenge for any writer who draws on personal experience to support his or her thesis is selecting the most relevant details and presenting them in an interesting fashion. What other challenges do writers who use their personal lives to support public arguments face?

3. Which stereotypes does Gover challenge? How does your thinking about certain stereotypes change after reading this essay?

Writing Critically

1. Compare the courtship and relationship dynamics of your generation with those of the generation immediately before or after you. How do personal relationships, especially romantic relationships, change in response to the larger social and political climate?

2. Gover mentions the long-running argument over whether "biology is destiny." The phrase originated with the psychoanalyst Sigmund Freud, who was speaking specifically about women. Find Freud's original discussion of "biology is destiny" either online or at the library. Do you agree or disagree that "biology is destiny" for either men or women?

Grieving Our Infertility

DAN SAVAGE

"Savage Love," Dan Savage's syndicated sex and relationship advice column, first appeared in Seattle's alternative newspaper *The Stranger* in 1991. The column has set a new standard for candor, humor, and honesty in the way many younger Americans talk and think about sexuality, romance, and relationships. "Savage Love" often deals with untraditional variations on love and romance, and the problems readers describe and the counsel Savage gives can be quite graphic. You're far more likely to find his column in alternative newspapers than in the mainstream press, and a Google search for "Dan Savage" and "Savage Love" will easily turn up archives of his columns. Now the editor of *The Stranger,* Savage has shown no fear when it comes to exposing the hypocrisy and homophobia of some politicians. He was rather famously charged with voter fraud when he revealed in an article that, in an effort to subvert the 2000 presidential campaign of right-wing, anti-gay Republican Gary Bauer, he had posed as a volunteer for Bauer's Iowa campaign and had licked doorknobs, staplers, and pens in Bauer's Iowa campaign office in an attempt to give Bauer the flu. Although Savage is willing to be outrageous when he believes outrage is called for, his quest to settle down with his longtime boyfriend and adopt a baby made for one of the sweetest, funniest chronicles of parenthood of the late twentieth century.

"Grieving Our Infertility" is a chapter from Savage's memoir *The Kid: What Happened After My Boyfriend and I Decided to Go Get Pregnant* (2000).

The director of the agency officially welcomed all of us to the two-day seminar, "Adoption: A Lifelong Process," rousing me from my paranoid fantasies. Ruth had headed the agency for three years, but first she was a client. She showed us a picture of her adopted son and told us she knew what we were going through. Ruth had a look of practiced empathy on her face. We saw this look a lot over the next two days, from the counselors, lawyers, and adoptive parents who came to share their experiences and answer our questions. Doubtless, Ruth's concern was genuine, but she'd probably given this speech thirty-six times already. She'd probably heard a similar speech herself before she adopted her son through the agency. Empathy had become a mark she hit.

Ruth was in her early thirties, attractive, with curly brown hair; she had that contradictory mix of concern and distance that sets social workers apart from mere mortals. The parent-wannabes sitting around the table were not quite abstractions to her, but we were pretty close—we were clients. As she spoke, Ruth made it clear that she and the agency cared very deeply about each and every one of us. But her tone communicated that she wouldn't be getting involved in our private dramas. She had too much work to do. Her overt message was compassion, but her covert message was "You're here, you're adopting, get used to it."

Apparently it took some getting over for the straight couples, who in agency-speak had "come to" or "arrived at" adoption, as if it were a physical destination. I was unprepared for the funereal tone of the seminar's first day. And as Ruth's opening comments picked up steam, Terry and I began to feel more out of place, and even more conspicuous than we had when we first walked through the door.

I opened my ten-pound notebook and peeked at the agenda: "Grieving Your Infertility." "Coping with Infertility." "Infertility and Its Impact on Adoption." "Losses Inherent in Adoption." I nudged Terry and slid the notebook over. His eyebrows shot up. Infertility was never an issue for us, just a fact, so we hadn't spent much time thinking about it, let alone learning to cope with it. And there were no "losses inherent in adoption" for us, but only victory. When I came out in 1980, it didn't occur to me that one day I would be able to adopt a child. I assumed, incorrectly, that it was illegal for gay men to adopt children. After all, gay men didn't have families—we were a threat to families.

My boyfriend passed me a note: "Maybe they should have let us skip the first day."

Ruth walked the group through our infertility issues. "Infertility can   6
sabotage the adoption process," Ruth explained. "You felt you had no control over your fertility, so you may attempt to impose control over this
process. Or you may come to resent the child you adopt because it isn't
your dream biological child. You're successful people, with successful lives
and successful relationships—having a child is probably the first thing you
have not succeeded at, your first failure as individuals."

At this point, we were positive we should have skipped the first day. The   7
boyfriend and I had accepted our infertility a long time ago, and sitting with
the straight couples, we felt our very presence was mocking their "loss."

"If you need to feel sad or angry about not having your 'own' biological   8
children—that's fine," Ruth continued. "But do not let those feelings dominate
your life. Enter parenting from a place of abundance, not a place of need. . . ."

In high school and college, my straight friends would point out the many   9
disadvantages of being gay; it was supposed to be a joke, but they sounded
serious. Their understanding of sexuality was pretty limited, and so was mine
at the time, and they were trying to talk me out of being gay. They didn't
want to lose my friendship, and they assumed they would if I "turned"
gay. In 1980, being gay still meant going off and joining a secret society, moving away and becoming someone else. They would spot me on a street corner years later, wearing leather pants and a teal T-shirt, waiting for a bus. To
prevent this fate, my friends would warn me that gays couldn't get married,
or hold certain jobs, or live where we wanted to. And we couldn't have kids.

I would respond by pointing out the many advantages of being gay, as   10
I saw them at the time. Before he got the boot, Jimmy Carter showed Iran
he meant business by making high school–age boys register for the draft.
When Ronald Reagan became president, it looked like he'd be declaring
war on the Sandinistas any day and calling us up. Advantage, gay: they did-
n't take my kind in the army, so I wouldn't get shot up in Central America.
But the ultimate advantage of being gay in 1980 was that it freed me from
having to worry about birth control. For my straight friends, birth control
was a major headache; first they had to worry about getting it, then they
had to worry about hiding it from their parents. Advantage, gay: I didn't
have to worry about the pill, or condoms, or missed periods, or babies, or
abortions. On this one point they agreed that being gay was better than being straight. Then the tables turned, of course, and I was spending more
time worrying about death control than my straight friends ever spent worrying about birth control. And if their birth control failed and they got
pregnant, they could always have abortions; if my death control failed, and
I got infected, there was no way to abort the virus. I would die. Advantage,
straight.

After years of careful birth control it must have come as a shock to the 11
straight couples around the table to learn that they needn't have bothered.
Unable to have "their own" kids, they'd had to reconcile themselves to
having someone else's before they could walk into this conference room.
As we went around the table and introduced ourselves, everyone put on
brave faces, trying to get to Ruth's "place of abundance," but it was clear
from some watery eyes and thrust-out chins that having to sit in this room
represented a painfully humiliating defeat. Each told or hinted at horror
stories: tens of thousands of dollars spent on unsuccessful fertility treatments, in-vitro this, test-tube that, egg harvesting. Years wasted. Even calm
and centered Ruth had pumped money and drugs into her uterus in a failed
attempt to have her own bio-kid.

Ruth explained how infertility placed an enormous strain on her marriage, 12
and how during treatments she fell into a deep depression. One day, at the end
of her rope, she read about the side effects of an infertility drug she'd been taking. Third on the list was "mild insanity." She decided that having her own biological child was not worth her sanity, and stopped taking the drugs. This was
how Ruth "arrived at" adoption, and her story was very similar to the others
we heard that day as we went around the table telling our stories.

When it came time for Terry and me to introduce ourselves, what were we 13
supposed to say? "Thrilled to be here, couldn't be happier?" We couldn't
seem too upbeat, but we *were* feeling pretty up. When I came out, my
straight friends told me I'd never have kids; a guy I knew to be gay in 1980
(we slept together) told me he'd never come out because he wanted a family.
He died in 1986, never having come out, and never having that family he
wanted. In Florida it's illegal for gays to adopt, and soon it may be illegal
in other states. In some, our bio-kids are taken from us by homophobic
courts in cahoots with homophobic relatives.

So sitting in this room, looking into adoption, living in a free state, be- 14
ing taken seriously by this agency—this was no defeat for us. This was a
great, big, honkin' victory. A triumph. And while adoption was where the
straight couples at the table ended up after a long and painful journey, it
was practically where we began. So what did we say?

The wrong thing, naturally. When I'm under pressure and feeling awk- 15
ward, my mouth opens and something idiotic, something totally Tourette's-y,
drops right out. This day was no exception. We were the next-to-last couple
to speak, and we'd heard five very sad stories. Some wayward synapse in my
pea-brain told me a joke might be in order, something to lighten the mood and
cheer up the straight folks.

"Hi, I'm Dan, and this is Terry, and as you can see, we have some fer- 16
tility issues of our own."

If there was any way to take it back, I would. No one laughed, no one 17
smiled—and why should they? Thankfully, the couple after us, Carol and
Jack, cracked a couple of jokes, too. Jack was an engineer, Carol a business
executive. They'd spent years trying to get pregnant, to no avail.

"We're here," Jack explained, "because I finally scored a zero on a test." 18

Heterosexual identity is all wrapped up in the ability of heterosexuals to 19
make babies. Straight sex can do what gay sex cannot, make "miracles." The
straights at our seminar had expected to grow up, fall in love, get married,
make love for fun, and sooner or later make love to make life. Infertility did
more than shatter their expectations; it undermined their sexual identities.

Straight sex can be recreational or procreational—or both—but gay sex 20
can only ever be recreational. Gay sex is never a means, only an end, and
the end is pleasure. Homophobes use this to justify their hatred of gays and
lesbians: straight sex, since it can make a baby, is "natural"; gay sex, since
it can only make a mess, is not. Babies make straight sex more important
than gay sex, so straights are therefore more important than gays. Babies
underpin all hetero-supremacism, from "Adam and Eve, not Adam and
Steve" to "Gays don't have children, so they have to recruit yours." Even
when straights are using birth control, procreation still sanctifies straight
sex. Even when straights are having sex that couldn't possibly make babies
(oral, anal, phone, cyber), the fact that these two people *could* make babies
under other circumstances or in other positions legitimizes straight sex.

This is pounded into the heads of gay people and straight people alike. 21
Gays grow up believing their desires, pleasures, and loves are illegitimate;
and straights who fall for the hype believe they gotta work that magic, gotta
make that baby, or . . . what? A straight person who can't make a baby isn't
really a straight person at all. And if you're not straight, you must be . . .
what? You're like my boyfriend and me. Suddenly your sex is all recreational, like gay sex, delegitimized and desanctified. Straight sex absent fertility has no larger significance. Oh, it's an expression of love—but so is gay
sex, and that never made gay sex okay. No babies means no miracles, no
magic. The sex you're having may still be pleasurable, but in a sex-hating
(and consequently sex-obsessed) culture, pleasure is not a good enough reason, otherwise gay and lesbian sex would never have been stigmatized.

I sympathized with the straight people sitting around the conference 22
table. I understood what they must have been going through. I had been
through it myself, a long time ago. When I hit puberty, I got the news that
I was functionally infertile. But the straight couples at the seminar had only
recently gotten that news, and they were still adjusting to it. How much we
had in common with them was driven home by the rhetoric the counselors
used during the seminar. It was the rhetoric of coming out. The straight

couples were encouraged to accept what they could not change. In time, they'd see their "problem" as a blessing. It was important to tell family and friends the truth, even if they might not understand at first. They might in their ignorance ask hurtful questions, but be patient and try to answer. And while it is possible to live a lie, possible to adopt a child and pass it off as your biological child, no one can spend a lifetime in the closet.

Now we all had some common ground.   23

While the straight couples at the seminar were getting a little gay by 24
coming out to themselves and each other about their infertility, my boyfriend and I were getting a little straight. Terry and I would be giving up certain things that, for better or worse, define what it means to be gay. Good things, things we enjoyed and that had value and meaning for us. Like promiscuity. Safely and respectfully done, whorin' around, like travel, is broadening. One night in Amsterdam, I met a guy in a leather bar, a twenty-eight-year-old German student. We had a beer, left the bar, and went back to his apartment. We messed around, nothing serious, and when we were done, talked all night about German reunification, what it was like growing up in the East, and what his grandparents had been up to during the Second World War.

The next day, he showed me parts of Amsterdam I would never have 25
found on my own; then he walked me back to my hotel, gave me a kiss, and said good-bye. I never saw him again, and I don't remember his name, but it was a beautiful experience. And certainly not one unique to gay people; heterosexuals have been known to get laid now and then while traveling, too. But this experience was made easier for both of us by certain assumptions we shared as gay men. On the basis of where we met, we knew about how long this relationship was destined to last (ten hours), what we were "into," and on what terms we would part.

My Amsterdam affair wasn't an experience I was prepared to deny 26
or denigrate in an effort to make myself better parental material in the eyes of the agency, the court, or my mom. But I did know that by becoming a parent I was limiting myself, cutting myself off from similar experiences in the future. But who said I had to become a hypocrite, too? I inhaled all sorts of things: men, makeup, drink, drugs. Could I be honest about these experiences, treasure their memory, and still be a good parent? I thought so.

Terry and I wanted to adopt; we didn't want to hide or lie about who 27
we were. But we did realize the kid meant no more Amsterdams, not for a while. Terry and I had talked about having a three-way sometime (actually, I talked about it, Terry listened, nothing happened), but once we had a kid in the house, it was unlikely we ever would. When sexually adven-

turous straight people go through this (the loss of certain sexual possibilities), I think it's called settling down. Probably, neither of us would ever have a good ol'-fashioned big-gay-slut phase again. I got sad when I thought about that, because I'd enjoyed my last couple of slutty phases quite a lot.

What else were we giving up? Well, it looked as if we were never going 28 to make it to a circuit party. And if we ever did use recreational drugs again, it would have to be on a vacation, with the kid at home with my mother. For years, I'd indulged myself (once you've gone and kissed boys, there isn't anything you're afraid of), and I'd lived to tell the tale. If we got a kid, I'd be giving indulgence up, and so would Terry. So there were losses inherent in adoption for Terry and me, too, and perhaps we'd end up doing some grieving. But unlike the straight couples in the room, we chose this loss; it was not imposed on us.

Thinking Critically

1. What are the different reasons why gay and straight couples decide to adopt? How does the adoption agency Dan Savage and his boyfriend consulted address those issues?

2. Savage suggests a parallel between the way some people perceive gays and the ways in which infertile or voluntarily childless straight couples are stigmatized. On what basis does he make this comparison? What kind of evidence does he offer in support of this parallel?

Writing Critically

1. Savage asserts that "Heterosexual identity is all wrapped up in the ability of heterosexuals to make babies" (paragraph 19). Do you agree or disagree? (You might consider Tzivia Gover's reflection, in this chapter; on Freud's claim that "biology is destiny" as you draft your essay.)

2. The "rhetoric of coming out" and the "rhetoric" used by adoption counselors helping infertile straight couples is, Savage argues, fundamentally similar—that is, it tells the same kind of story. In this book are many examples of this kind of rhetoric, such as Andrew Sullivan's specifically "coming-out" narrative and Ted Rall's coming to terms with his father's deficiencies as a parent (both in this chapter). What do these kinds of stories have in common, in both structure and their content? In a comparative essay, examine at least three examples (at least one of which should be from this book) of a coming-out or coming-to-terms narrative. Do the authors have a shared purpose in telling their stories? How do they make their very personal narratives relevant for a larger section of society?

Opening Marriage: Do Same-Sex Unions Pave the Way for Polygamy?

CATHY YOUNG

Reason magazine and its online component *Reason Online* are published by the Reason Foundation. The foundation, through the magazine and the Reason Public Policy Institute, works to "shape public opinion in favor of individual liberty in all areas of human activity." Although the Reason Foundation and its offshoots are politically independent, their views can be described as libertarian. *Reason* magazine, in which "Opening Marriage: Do Same-Sex Unions Pave the Way for Polygamy?" appeared in March 2004, covers culture, politics, and current events. Cathy Young, the author of this essay, is a contributing editor to *Reason,* a columnist for the *Boston Globe,* and the author of *Ceasefire! Why Women and Men Must Join Forces to Achieve True Equality* (1999) and *Growing Up in Moscow: Memories of a Soviet Girlhood* (1989). Cathy Young was born Ekaterina Jung to a nonpracticing Soviet Jewish family who lived a comfortable and artistic life in Moscow. Like many Jewish families of the Brezhnev era, Young's family emigrated to the United States in 1980, when she was seventeen years old. In her column in the *Boston Globe* and her work for *Reason,* she often argues for academic, personal, and cultural freedom—earning the ire of readers on both the left and the right of the political spectrum. Young is also the vice president of the Women's Freedom Network, a nonprofit think tank that, in its own words, "views women's issues in light of a philosophy that defines women and men as individuals and not in terms of gender" as an alternative to "extremist ideological feminism and the anti-feminist traditionalism."

The debate over same-sex marriage moved closer to center stage last 1 November, after the Massachusetts Supreme Judicial Court ruled that denying marriage rights to gay couples violated the state constitution.

To a large extent, the debate is now less about homosexuality than it is 2 about marriage. Except on the far right, objections to same-sex marriage are rarely couched in terms of moral objections to homosexual relationships.

Historically in our culture, the argument goes, marriage has meant the union of one man and one woman. Change it to include a union of two men, and who's to say that it shouldn't be redefined further to include one man and two women, two women and three men, or any other possible combination?

At first glance, this argument may seem like a red herring. Yet it is taken 3 seriously by noted legal scholars who are hardly hostile to equal rights for gays, such as Richard A. Posner of the U.S. Court of Appeals for the 7th Circuit and Eugene Volokh of UCLA Law School. Volokh, who supports same-sex marriage but believes the issue should not be settled by the courts, cautions that "slippery slope" arguments should not be dismissed lightly.

Not long ago, warnings that the Equal Rights Amendment or laws pro- 4 hibiting discrimination on the basis of sexual orientation would lead to the legalization of gay marriage were dismissed as "hysterical" scare tactics. Yet the Massachusetts court relied precisely on such provisions to strike down the same-sex marriage ban as discriminatory.

The Massachusetts ruling states that the right to "marry the person of 5 one's choice" is a fundamental right, albeit "subject to appropriate gov- ernment restrictions in the interests of public health, safety, and welfare." Could it include the right to marry more than one person?

In the recent book *Same-Sex Marriage and the Constitution*, political 6 scientist and lawyer Evan Gerstmann argues that polygamy is different since the would-be polygamist can still marry the person of his *first* choice. Yet one may counter that having multiple spouses *is* the polygamist's first choice—or that, as Posner notes in his review of Gerstmann's book in *The New Republic*, the woman who wants to be the polygamist's *second* wife is barred from marrying the person of her first choice. (Most commenta- tors seem to equate polygamy with polygyny.)

Indeed, gay marriage proponents have offered no substantive argu- 7 ments to show that the reasoning used to assert the right to same-sex mar- riage could not be extended to plural marriage as well. They merely point out that at present there is no push to legalize polygamy. Likewise, the Massachusetts court majority dealt with the issue by stating that the plain- tiffs in this case "do not attack the binary nature of marriage."

Yet a polygamy rights movement could certainly gather cultural and 8 political momentum in the future. If that happens, Volokh suggests, some courts may discover a constitutional right to plural marriage, "citing the Massachusetts decision as an eminently logically applicable precedent."

Would that be such a terrible thing? If someone has two, three, or six 9 spouses of either sex, they are presumably all consenting adults; if they are harming anyone, it is only themselves. My own belief is that polygamous re- lationships are likely to involve imbalances of power and even psychological abuse, and that they carry a high risk of instability and stress. "Polyamory" advocates talk a lot about transcending sexual jealousy, but plural marriages are rife with jealousy and tension even in cultures where polygamy is a long-standing tradition. (One reason plural marriage may prove far harder to legalize than same-sex marriage is that people who have been personally hurt by polygamy will be available to speak out against it.) But if that's what some people want, should the state restrict their choices for their own good?

On the other hand, legalizing polygamy would alter the state of mar- 10 riage in general far more than gay marriage could. Allowing Jane to marry Ann does not in any tangible way change Sally's marriage to Bill; allowing Sally and Bill to marry other people while remaining married to each other changes it drastically. Even if they never exercise this option, the mere possibility of it could cause enough anxiety to destabilize a marriage subtly.

While legalizing same-sex unions is extremely unlikely to entice any het- 11 erosexual man to leave his wife and marry another man, having multiple partners could potentially be a temptation for anyone, though it's likely that social disapproval would still discourage plural marriage for most people.

Then again, the potentially harmful consequences of polygamy could 12 exist without legalized plural marriage. Open marriages and de facto plural marriages already exist. Such relationships may even receive a measure of legal recognition: In 2000 the longtime mistress of married television correspondent Charles Kuralt won a court dispute with his widow over a property he owned in Montana.

The primary issue is not the legal benefits for multiple spouses but the 13 perception that the state, and by implication we as a people, will be giving sanction to something a majority of Americans regard as morally objectionable—which, of course, is also at stake in the debate over gay marriage.

One proposed solution is simply to get the state out of the marriage busi- 14 ness. As the Cato Institute's David Boaz asked in a 1998 article for *Slate,* "Why should the government be in the business of decreeing who can and cannot be married?" Boaz suggested that people could simply enter private marriage contracts, either standard or personalized, and the government could enforce these contracts like any other agreement, with no differential legal treatment on the basis of marital status. Meanwhile, religious institutions could decide what kind of unions to solemnize.

Boaz explicitly proposed the privatization of marriage as a solution to 15 the gay marriage debate: "It would put gay relationships on the same footing as straight ones, without implying official government sanction. No one's private life would have official government sanction—which is how it should be." At the same time, his article is based on the assumption that privatized marriage will still be a union of "two individuals."

Boaz confirms that he would indeed favor such a limitation. "Two peo- 16 ple seems like a good number for a marriage," he says. "People should be allowed to make just about any contracts they want among themselves. But the laws that relate to 'marriage' reflect society's desire to support marriage as an element of stability in social order and the raising of children." For that purpose, he believes, the government has a right to place some restrictions on which contracts it will recognize as marriages—at least as long as special laws related to marriage continue to exist.

But that brings us back to square one in the gay marriage debate: Rec- 17 ognizing the legality of a marriage implies its endorsement by society. A partial deregulation of marriage is unlikely to satisfy either conservatives or libertarians. But then, true privatization of marriage would likely generate furious opposition as well. Conservatives would see it as the final destruction of the family. Meanwhile, many advocates of same-sex marriage would no doubt feel that the marriage rights they had won were reduced to an empty prize. They might even suspect that the heterosexual majority was willing to destroy the institution of marriage rather than open it to gays.

Whatever the philosophical merits of such a proposal, the chances of 18 privatizing marriage in the foreseeable future are virtually nil. Far from being depoliticized, marriage is likely to remain a major battlefield in the culture wars.

Thinking Critically

1. How provocative is the title of Cathy Young's argument? Is her essay provocative in its content or its tone?

2. Why does Young, and why do many of the legal scholars she cites, think it so critical to consider the implications of polygamy when considering the legality of same-sex marriage? Paraphrase these complex legal arguments.

3. How does Young conclude her essay? What are the implications of her conclusion?

Writing Critically

1. Young points out in paragraph 13 that the critical issue in this argument is neither polygamy nor same-sex marriage but "the perception that the state, and by implication we as a people, will be giving sanction to something a majority of Americans regard as morally objectionable" (that is, either polygamy or gay marriage). Could you argue, however, that the state already sanctions or supports practices and policies that large groups of Americans find "morally objectionable"? To what extent should the state be involved in making or mandating "morals" or "ethics"?

2. How would Andrew Sullivan respond to Cathy Young's argument? How would Cathy Young respond to Andrew Sullivan? (You might also consider whether, rhetorically, it's wholly fair to compare these two arguments. Sullivan's also appears in this chapter.)

3. In an essay, describe a working, compassionate relationship (married or not) to which you have been a witness. In what ways did that relationship contribute to the larger community? Alternatively, if you have been a witness to a destructive marriage, what was the impact of that marriage on the larger community?

Taking Leave

JOE MICELI

This starkly eloquent narrative was submitted to the National Story Project sponsored by National Public Radio's *Weekend All Things Considered* program. Novelist Paul Auster proposed the idea to NPR listeners in 1999, inviting anyone to send in a short, "true" story. As Auster recalled in his introduction to a published collection of these stories, *I Thought My Father Was God and Other True Tales from NPR's National Story Project* (2001), "What interested me most, I said, were stories that defied our expectations about the world, anecdotes that revealed the mysterious and unknowable forces at work in our lives, in our family histories, in our minds and bodies, in our souls." Some four thousand people responded, sending in stories ranging from a few sentences to several pages. Auster read several of the stories each month on *All Things Considered*. Many listeners responded to what they heard with still more stories of their own. *I Thought My Father Was God* includes 179 of the thousands of submitted stories (some of them too long to broadcast). "Taking Leave," Joe Miceli's narrative, is one of three stories from the collection included in this book. The other two are B.C.'s essay "Homeless in Prescott, Arizona" (see pp. 289–92) and Rachel Watson's narrative "My Story" (see pp. 354–59).

For the last fifteen years I've been confined to a nine-by-seven cage of   1
solid steel bars, squeezed between walls I can touch with my fingertips if I stretch my arms. On my right is my bed. Its mattress is as flat as a pancake, and next to it is a ceramic toilet, which is covered with a wooden board to keep the stench out.

Ghost town Many small shops on the main street of Albany, Missouri (pop. 1,865) have been shut down since a Wal-Mart opened nearby. Rural communities and small towns across the Midwest have rapidly been losing population as the farm economy crashes and other job opportunities are lost.

Considering the Image

1. How are America's small towns depicted in popular culture? What is missing from this photograph that you would expect to see in a movie or television image of small-town America?

2. For demographic information about Albany, Missouri, go to <http://www.city-data.com/city/Albany-Missouri.html>. How does this image illustrate that demographic data? At the same site, do a search for Litchfield, Minnesota, the hometown of Sarah Anderson (p. 259). What demographic features do these two towns have in common? What does this suggest about the impact of a loss of local businesses on a rural community?

Anywhere, USA The fastest-growing communities in America are "exurbs" – new planned communities many miles from a major urban area, or former small towns some distance from a major urban area that have been rezoned and redeveloped for significant new housing and large-scale shopping and commercial districts. Many of these communities lack a central "Main Street" or sidewalks, and are served by the same retail chains, restaurant franchises, and "superstores" from coast to coast.

Considering the image

1. Compare the architecture of these buildings in a Santee, California suburban shopping district with the buildings of Albany, Missouri, on the previous page. What does a building's physical appearance suggest about its purpose and use?

2. What's missing from both of these photographs? What story could you tell about that absence?

3. Which image best represents the America where you grew up? The America where you shop?

Fighting the law In 2003, a U.S. District Judge ordered this monument of the Ten Commandments removed from public view in the Alabama Judicial Building in Montgomery, Alabama.

Considering the Image

1. Describe the composition of this image. What is in the center? How are the figures arranged? Does the arrangement and shape of this image remind you of another iconic image? Do you think that resemblance was deliberate on the part of the photographer?

2. Which essay in Chapter 3 does this image best illustrate, and why?

Praying for victory The election of 2004 deeply divided some faith communities over issues such as the morality of war, the distribution of wealth, the death penalty, abortion, and gay marriage. Candidate John Kerry, a Roman Catholic, was challenged by clergy and laymen alike over some of his positions.

He's got the whole world in his hands In his first presidential campaign in 2000, George W. Bush was photographed at a Christian based home for teenagers in Iowa.

Considering the Images

1. Why do people use buttons, bumper stickers, lawn signs, T-shirts, and similar ephemera to declare their political beliefs? How do these materials use the conventions of consumer advertising to get their message across?

2. Candidates and their handlers are often very cautious about how, where, and in what context a candidate is photographed. What are some of the advantages and disadvantages for the Bush campaign (or any political campaign) of an image like that seen here of Bush?

One mission, many faiths For the first time in memory, a Buddhist monk presided over a military funeral at Arlington National Cemetery in April 2003. Marine Cpl. Kemaphoom Chanawongse, of Waterford, Conn., was killed during operations on the outskirts of Nasiriyah, Iraq.

Considering the Image

1. Many levels of paradox—visual, emotional, contextual—make this image particularly compelling. Describe how paradox is at work in this image.

2. In 2003 and 2004, it was rare to see images of flag-draped coffins or wounded American soldiers in the media. Why was that?

3. How might an image such as this one be used to make an argument against the war in Iraq? How might it be used to uphold the argument for America's presence in the Middle East?

Silent but politically incorrect night Many communities, weary of annual conflicts between various interest groups, have given up on any public display for any religious holiday at all. Mission Viejo, CA, still hosts an inclusive holiday display with a giant lighted menorah and a Christmas crèche.

Considering the Image

1. How is light used in this image? Would the image make a different argument, or tell a different kind of story, if it was shot in daylight?

2. Would the image tell a different story if the photographer had foregrounded the crèche instead of the menorah? How so?

Having and holding In 2004, San Francisco became one of the first communities in the nation to allow same-sex marriage. These two men, fathers of twin daughters, took their vows in San Francisco's City Hall. Later in the year, the California Supreme Court annulled these weddings, and the issue continues to be debated in the California courts.

Considering the Image

1. Often, a news photograph is like a film still from a movie; all of the critical elements of the story are captured in the frame. What story does this image tell about gay marriage? How is the photo composed to best illustrate that this is a marriage ceremony?

2. The context in which an image is placed often determines a reader's response to the image. Think about this image in relation to the essays by Ted Rall, Andrew Sullivan, Dan Savage, Cathy Young, Francis Fukuyama, and Stephanie Coontz in Chapter 4. For each essay, rewrite the caption for this image so that it directly reflects a key claim or idea in the essay.

Mmmmm . . . . donuts The highly acclaimed animated series *The Simpsons* affectionately subverts the ideals of the American nuclear family as it satirizes political and social issues across the ideological spectrum.

Considering the image

1. How do the characters relate to one another in this image? In what ways does this image reflect or mimic other representations of family in advertisements or entertainment?

2. Even if you're not a fan of *The Simpsons*, what guesses can you make about who in this image plays what role in the family? Does this particular image poke fun at or satirize any particular aspect of American society?

3. *The Simpsons* has been on the air since 1989. Search for reviews of and articles about the show from its first season. What did critics and writers think then of the show's depiction of the American family? How accurate were their assessments and opinions?

I was in bed, on the verge of falling asleep, when my cell gate cracked. 2
Any time it opened was a welcome relief. I jumped up, stepped out on the
gallery, and called to the officer at the control booth a hundred feet away.

"The chaplain wants to see you. Get dressed," he said. I laced my boots, 3
snatched my jacket, and hurried outside. A call from the cleric's office usually meant bad news. As I whizzed past my neighbor's crib I heard him say,
"Is everything all right. Joe?"

"I hope so," I said. "I think I'm going to make an emergency phone call." 4

As I hurried across the snow-covered yard, groups of prisoners huddled to- 5
gether against the freezing wind. Blacks, whites, and Latinos bundled in multicolored hoods, hats, gloves, and mittens. Some were familiar, but most were just
faces in a vast sea of lonely insignificance. A few walked endless laps around
the yard, others stared at one of four TVs. Most were lost in self-imposed distractions, doing the best they could to kill time the only way they knew how.

At the wire gate leading to the guidance unit; I shoved my pass into the 6
tiny slot of the guard's wooden shack. The officer scrutinized it like a suspicious cashier looking at a counterfeit fifty-dollar bill. Then, dismissing
me like a foreigner at a border crossing, he said, "Go ahead." Relieved, I
sprinted toward the building. At last I was going to speak with my grandmother, a tough eighty-year-old lady who could curse you out in a minute
if you got her angry.

We had not spoken in several weeks, because my father, who had just com- 7
pleted a ten-year federal sentence, had disconnected the three-way service at
Nan's house as a condition of his parole. When I spoke to my father, he said.
"Your grandmother's in the hospital, but she should be back in three days."

Although her health was deteriorating. I never expected such a sudden 8
decline. I remembered our last conversation, when she had cried and complained about her swollen legs.

"Nan, you got to try and walk around, stretch your legs and get some 9
exercise," I pleaded.

"I do. You don't understand. My legs are no good anymore. Last week 10
I went to the bank and fell down on the sidewalk."

I tried to ease her pain by talking about the good old days, when we lived 11
on Ninety-eighth Street and when Grandpa was alive. I pictured myself in
the kitchen, watching her open the oven to peek at the golden-brown loaves
of Sicilian bread she baked for me and my grandfather. Back then one of my
favorite treats was a hot round loaf of homemade bread stuffed with chicken
roll and washed down with a tall glass of milk. Those were great times, and
now, here I was, clinging to them the same way my grandmother was.

But even as we spoke about the happy times, she had still cried bitterly. 12
Her greatest fear was that she'd be forced to live in an old-age home.

"I want to die in my own house. I don't want to live with strangers." 13

"Nan, I promise no one's going to stick you in a home. Don't worry, 14 when I get out I'll take care of you."

"Did you talk to the lawyer?" 15

"Yes, they're still working very hard." 16

"I hope to God you come home before I go." 17

"I will, Nan, you just take care of yourself." Although I was able to reas- 18 sure her, my feelings of guilt lingered in my mind like the taste of spoiled milk.

Now, as I arrived at the chaplain's office, an officer said, "The imam 19 wants to see you." The imam? I said to myself. Randazzo, my counselor, must have made arrangements with him to call my grandmother. Inside the small room, four Muslims were busy filling tiny bottles with scented oils. The room smelled like jasmine, musk, and coconut incense, penetrating and pungent, like the fragrance of head shops in the '60s. Imam Khaliffa was talking on the telephone. He removed the receiver from his ear and cupped the mouthpiece. In a soft voice he told the men to leave the room.

As they filed past me, he continued talking on the phone while I impa- 20 tiently scanned the room. Although his desk was cluttered with bottles and papers, my eyes were drawn to one particular document that seemed out of place. On it I noticed my name written in bold letters above my grand-mother's. It was a business letter from the Francisco Funeral Home.

The imam hung up the phone, and I asked, "What's going on?" 21

"Your brother Buddy called. He needs to speak with you." 22

Two days later, at 6:00 A.M., I was awakened by a young officer named 23 Rizzo. He was thin, had short-cropped black hair, and a voice that spoke with the soothing calm of a priest in a confessional booth. Perhaps he also knew what it felt like to experience the loss of a loved one. I was grateful.

When we crossed the yard, it was windy, dark, and pouring with rain. 24 Inside the administration building, a burly Irishman with blond hair and rosy cheeks approached me and said, "I'm sorry to hear about your grand-mother." I put on the garments given to me by the prison for the trip: blue jeans, a white shirt, and a tan jacket. I wore my own sneakers. I glanced at myself in the mirror and was disgusted by my reflection.

At last we climbed into a specially equipped van with a thick Plexiglas par- 25 tition separating me from the officers, who carried .38-caliber pistols strapped to their hips in black leather holsters. My legs were shackled by a twelve-inch dog chain, secured tightly at each ankle. I was also handcuffed with a belly chain. This was fastened to my cuffs with a master lock. To eat I had to bend forward and strain my neck to peck at a sandwich clasped in my fingers.

I had not been outside the stone walls of the prison for fifteen years. We 26 drove past mountains, trees, and farms with black-and-white cows grazing leisurely on the grass. I felt like I was part of a surreal three-dimensional photograph. Soon we entered a valley that was covered in thick fog. It consumed us like the smoke in woods after a smoldering forest fire. Suddenly a deer darted from the mist. It leapt onto the highway and into the front end of the pickup truck that was ahead of us. The driver didn't have a chance to swerve. I whipped my neck around and slid to the edge of my seat.

"Did you see that?" Officer Warren asked. 27

I peered out the side window, through beads of raindrops scurrying 28 across the glass, and saw the deer sprawled on the perimeter of the roadway. As I strained forward in my seat, my shackles and restraints dug deep into my flesh. The deer's tongue dangled from her soft furry jaw, and her mouth was slightly open as she exhaled nervous, panting puffs of steam.

"*It's still alive!*" I exclaimed. 29

"Yeah, but she don't look good," Officer Warren said. I wanted to see 30 her sprint back into the woods. Instead she lay motionless, as still as the fog hanging over the valley, as stiff as the trees.

By midafternoon trees were replaced by apartment houses and commercial 31 brick buildings with an assortment of bubble-shaped, multicolored, bright bold letters. Some of the structures were boarded up. Finally we exited Lexington Avenue, passed the piers of Manhattan, crossed the Brooklyn Bridge, and emerged on Atlantic Avenue. The city was vaguely familiar, dreamlike.

I imagined myself in the old days, leaning on the armrest of my black 32 1983 Ninety-Eight Oldsmobile. I'd be listening to music with a thick joint burning in the ashtray. Inhaling the smoke of the sweet sticky weed, its pungent aroma drifting through a crack in the moonroof in swirling plumes. Once I had had it all.

On Atlantic Avenue there were rows of stores and bodegas and people 33 buzzing everywhere. Beautiful women wearing tight pants, platform shoes, and leather jackets strolled by, swinging shopping bags. They swayed their hips in sync with the seductive rhythm and style that spelled attitude with a capital A in the barrio. There were furniture shops with sofas outside, a black homeless man begging, and an amputee in a wheelchair hurrying across the street.

When we pulled up in front of the funeral home, Officer Warren said, 34 "Hold on, I have to check it out."

Two minutes later he appeared and nodded to his partner. Then, with 35 Rizzo's assistance, I carefully climbed out of the van. "Wait," Rizzo said, stopping me in midstride. "Let's take the belly chain and cuffs off first."

He inserted a key into the master lock and with a quick, practiced twist 36 snapped it open. He reached around my back, unwrapped the chain, and then removed the handcuffs. I stretched and rubbed my wrists. They were swollen and red and had deep creases in them. Followed by Rizzo, I limped inside the lobby, taking slow, even steps to avoid tripping on the tether still attached to my ankles.

My brother Buddy appeared. He was tall and broad and impeccably   37
dressed in a fine black suit. I could tell he was shocked and glad to see me. We shook hands and kissed. Then my uncle, whom I hadn't seen in fifteen years, sauntered in. He looked much older, seemed shorter, and was as round as a wine barrel. He paused for a second, studying me the same way I pondered him. Fifteen years was a long time.

"Joey," he said in his distinctive Sicilian brogue.   38

I wrapped my arms around him. "It's great to see you, Uncle Charlie."   39

"I'm a grandfather now," he said, proudly slipping a photo from his   40
wallet. "Your cousin Joey and his wife had a boy. His name is Cologero."

I took the picture and glanced at it and wondered where all the years   41
had gone. I remembered my cousin Joey when he was a teenager wearing a football jersey rushing out of his house in College Point to play two-hand touch. Now he was a father. I handed the photo back to my uncle and said, "Congratulations."

I stepped into the viewing room and encountered my sisters, Gracie and   42
Maria. Both were drowned in black clothes. We hugged and kissed and each cried on my shoulder. I was quickly surrounded by other family members, including my father, whom I had not seen in ten years. His hair was pure white and as fine as rabbit's fur.

"You made it," he said: 43

We embraced. "Yeah, Dad, security cleared me."   44

Because of restrictions, I had not spoken to my father while he was   45
away. I stood there and scrutinized him, searching for the man I had last seen on a visit ten years ago. I knew I'd never find him again.

The room was still and quiet. Chairs lined one wall and a sofa the   46
other. There were tables with lamps on them, and others that held crystal bowls filled with mints. At the rear of the room my grandmother lay lifeless, surrounded by an assortment of colorful floral arrangements. As I approached I could smell the familiar fragrance of freshly picked roses. I placed my hand on the edge of her bronze casket and gazed at her face. She was thinner than the last time I had seen her, five years ago. Her skin was pale and colored with a thick coat of makeup that made her look unnatural. She wore a smile that seemed more like a contrived grin. On her wrist was the same gold bracelet that she always wore on special occasions. It was heavy and adorned with several medals that jingled like bells when she walked. Now the charms—large solid-gold hearts and diamond-studded medallions inscribed with dates and heartfelt expressions—hung stiffly from her frozen wrist. She was dressed in a beautiful silk and lace

pink gown that stretched to her ankles. On her feet she wore tiny pink shoes the color of seashells.

All these years I had expected this day. I just never thought it would happen so damn suddenly. Now all I had left were memories. Fragmented remnants of our lives scattered on the lid of her coffin. One was a picture of my grandmother taken in 1984, the year I went away, standing by the dock of our home in Howard Beach. Boats adorned with flags, some with fly bridges as tall as our house, floated on the surface of calm waters, waiting to cast off. She's wearing a pair of shorts and sneakers and has a huge grin on her face. And there beside her are the rosebushes she raised, exploding in brilliant full bloom. 47

At our house my grandmother usually kept large bowls of warm food in the oven. Pans of chicken cutlets and pasta, or meat and white potatoes, were always available for visitors who wanted to sit down and eat. On Sundays Nan always cooked a huge meal, large pastel-colored bowls filled with pasta, marinara sauce, garlic, and freshly picked basil. Then we passed around trays of meatballs, sausages, and meats stacked a foot high. I would wipe the sauce from my lips between mouthfuls of food and gulps of red wine mixed with 7Up. My grandfather wore a napkin tucked into his shirt and a pen in his pocket; he would busily grate a chunk of fresh ricotta cheese onto his macaroni. His arm moved in round, sweeping, circular motions. When he was finished, I took the cheese from him and did the same. 48

When I used to come home after junior high school to a house filled with the aroma of sauce simmering on the stove, I'd snatch a loaf of semolina bread, tear off a hunk, and soak it in the sweet red gravy. Before long, I'd hear my grandmother say, "Get outa here, will you?" She didn't say it in a mean way, she said it proudly, delighted by the thought of how much I loved her cooking. 49

The time to leave arrived with a nod from Officer Warren. Everyone surged forward to kiss me good-bye. My uncle and I grasped each other one last time, and he said, "You were your grandmother's world, she loved you more than anything." Then my father held me and exploded into a violent, shuddering convulsion of sobs. We stood there clinging to each other like passengers on a plane about to crash; hurtling toward the ground. At that moment, with my dad's tears falling on my shoulder, I felt like I was his father and he was my son, and in the solace of my arms he discovered the safety I had once sought in his. 50

I walked to the van and extended my hands to Officer Rizzo to have the cuffs clamped on my wrists again. Instead, he said, "We'll put them on later, after we eat." This surprised me. I hopped into the van, slid close to the window, and peered out one last time hoping to freeze this moment that would have to last as a picture in my mind forever. I watched my uncle reach into his jacket pocket, pull out a cigar, and light it up, taking short, quick puffs. As we rolled away, I waved to him and wondered if my expression betrayed my sadness. 51

Thinking Critically

1. What are Joe Miceli's "family values"? In what ways does his prison experience reflect or affect those values?

2. Miceli wrote this narrative from prison, as he makes clear in his very first sentence. What might his purpose have been in writing this narrative? Why would he want to share it with a national audience?

3. Explain the haunting image of the dying deer. How do Miceli and the accompanying prison guards react to the sight?

Writing Critically

1. The popular television series *The Sopranos* has been accused of glamorizing violence and promoting stereotypes about Italian Americans. In what ways does Miceli's story challenge those stereotypes? In what ways does it reinforce them? How does Miceli's heritage sustain him despite his lengthy prison sentence?

2. Elijah Anderson's essay "The Black Inner-City Grandmother in Transition" (the next selection in this chapter) takes a more objective, sociological approach to describing the role played by grandmothers in a particular community. Compare and contrast the significance of Miceli's grandmother in his family and community with the roles that black inner-city grandmothers have in their communities. If you find strong similarities between the expectations about and significance of grandmothers in these ethnically different communities, how do you account for those similarities?

3. How would you describe the relationship between Miceli and his father? What does Miceli learn about his father over the course of this story? In an essay, describe the relationships between fathers and sons in your own community or extended family. What challenges to the father-son relationship are posed by society?

The Black Inner-City Grandmother in Transition

ELIJAH ANDERSON

In *Code of the Street: Decency, Violence, and the Moral Life of the Inner City* (1999), from which this essay is excerpted, University of Pennsylvania social sciences professor Elijah Anderson offers a detailed, honest, and compassionate ethnographic study of a particular African American community in Philadelphia. Anderson's work won the Eastern Sociological Society's Komarovsky Book

Award. William Julius Wilson, an African American
professor at Harvard University, called *Code of the
Street* "powerful and poignant" and described it as
"must reading for those who want to understand the
problem of urban violence and how it can be corrected." Cornel West, a professor of religion at Princeton University and a renowned African American public
intellectual and fearless provocateur, called Anderson's
book "the best treatment we have of the tormented
inner life of young people wrestling with nihilism in a
society indifferent to their plight and predicament." In a
1999 interview in *Atlantic Unbound,* the online component of the *Atlantic Monthly,* Anderson acknowledged the concerns some members of the community
had about publicizing their troubles: "Certainly some
people have been concerned that white people who read
this could get the wrong message, or could use the reality to hurt black people. Feathers sometimes get ruffled,
because people may be ashamed or may not want to
have the word get out. But the idea is to represent these
places as accurately as I can. I believe it's very important to tell the truth so we can deal with these issues
forthrightly."

From slavery onward, in the most trying of circumstances, the mother—   1
and by extension, the grandmother—has been an extremely important
source of support for the black family.[1] Correspondingly, the black grandmother holds a special place among her people, both in folklore and in real
life. Through the generations, many have characterized her as the anchor
holding in place the family and indeed the whole kinship structure.
E. Franklin Frazier summed her role up nicely:

> In her explanation of why the responsibility of "her chillen" falls upon
> her, this old woman [a seventy-seven-year-old ex-slave] expresses the
> characteristic attitude of the grandmother in her role as "oldest head"
> in the family. Where the maternal family organization assumes such
> importance as among a large section of the Negro population, the old-
> est woman is regarded as the head of the family. Some of these grand-
> mothers will tell you of their courting, which sounded very much like
> that of the granddaughters' today [1939]. Often, instead of having
> been a prelude to marriage, it culminated in motherhood and the re-
> sponsibilities which it imposed. Even when they married, sometimes
> marriage was of short duration, and the responsibility of rearing and
> supporting their children fell upon them. Thus it has been the grand-
> mother who has held the generations together when fathers and even
> mothers abandoned their offspring.[2]

This chapter seeks both to paint an ethnographic picture of this traditional   2
pillar of strength in the black community and to indicate the reasons, structural and personal, for the grandmother's resilience through changing forms
of adversity, from slavery through the impoverishment of today's inner city.
The lack of jobs brought about by the economic shift from a manufacturing
to a service base and by the growth of the global economy—particularly widespread joblessness and the appearance of crack cocaine as a central feature of
the ghetto underground economy—has greatly exacerbated the problems
with which the grandmother has been called upon to do battle. How she has
been able to manage and why her position is now more threatened than perhaps it has ever been sheds light on the very nature of the black community
and what is necessary to sustain and nourish it. For although the network of
grandmothers continues to form a communal safety net, that net is weakened
and imperiled. Young women are still maturing into the traditional grandmother role, but their increasingly small numbers are making their obstacles
proportionately greater.

The Role of the Grandmother: Then and Now

In the days of slavery and then of sharecropping, when black men generally   3
were unable to achieve economic independence, the black grandmother was
often a heroic figure whose role required great sacrifice. The black man was
frequently, but not always, emasculated, weakened, or simply neutralized
by the social control efforts of the wider white society, and was thus reduced
as a competitive force in a male-dominated society.[3] But the black woman
was not usually perceived to be as much a threat to the hegemony of the
white man as the black man was. According to folklore, such women were
then allowed to develop into strong, independent, willful, wise, and omnis-
cient matriarchs who were not afraid to compete with men when necessary.

With the advent of the industrial economy, black men became better   4
able to support themselves and their women and children and began to
function less ambiguously as head of the family.[4] Accordingly, over time the
grandmother's traditional role was diminished but never completely dis-
mantled. Even in the "good old" days of available jobs at decent wages, the
grandmother was there in a crisis to pick up the slack when difficulties
arose,[5] and at times she even competed with the man for dominance within
the family (see Alice Walker's *The Color Purple* for a fictional treatment of
the theme). Traditionally, her meager savings and her home were at the disposal of family members during temporary hard times.

Today, with the loss of well-paying manufacturing jobs and the intro-   5
duction of drugs (particularly crack) and the violent drug culture into the
ghetto, the black grandmother is once again being called upon to assume

her traditional role.[6] As in the past the heroic grandmother comes to the aid of the family, taking responsibility for children abandoned by their own parents, asserting her still considerable moral authority for the good of the family, and often rearing the children herself under conditions of great hardship.

The grandmother's central role has become institutionalized in the black community and carries with it a great deal of prestige but also a great deal of stress.[7] However, because this role is imbued with such prestige and moral authority and is so firmly entrenched in the culture, many of those who assume it see it as highly rewarding and necessary, if not critical, for the survival of the black inner-city family.   6

A review of the literature on grandparenthood reveals that the existence of the institutionalized grandmother role is a major feature of black family life, particularly among the poor. Among inner-city blacks, because of this strong tradition, it appears to be a mandatory role with established rights, obligations, and duties,[8] and those who refuse it may be judged by many in the local black community as having abdicated a vital responsibility. Hence, when called upon, black grandmothers appear constrained to play out their role.   7

Traditionally, grandmothers have served as "kin keepers" for the extended family. This function seems much greater among poor blacks[9] and is deemphasized among the middle and upper classes.[10] Extensive kinship networks in general are more in evidence among poor black families[11] and tend to diffuse with upward mobility. Even so, women appear on the whole to be resilient, protective of home life and culture, and much more important to the working of the family than many men are wont to acknowledge. The stereotype of the meddling mother-in-law, which has become well established in general popular culture—for blacks, it finds comedic expression in the Sapphire figure and her mother in *Amos and Andy* or, more recently, in *The Jeffersons*—reflects this important, yet sometimes resented, position. However, such popular portrayals represent a very small part of the black female's actual familial role.[12]   8

Because the role of grandmother has such communal support—even public acknowledgment and expectation—unmarried teenage mothers of fifteen or sixteen easily turn to their own mothers for help, which is generally forthcoming.[13] In this social context, depending on the age of maturity of the new mother, the experienced grandmother may take over the care of the newborn, partly because she lacks full confidence in her daughter's ability to be a mother and an adult and partly to help keep her daughter from being as deviant as she would be otherwise, at times even helping her to resume her social life. In addition, the grandmother may take pleasure and pain in revisiting the role of a mother in a more than simply vicarious way. For these reasons a girl tends to achieve a new, if provisional, status in her mother's eyes once she becomes an unwed mother.[14] At the same time,   9 through the trials and tribulations of motherhood, such girls often gain a new appreciation of their mother,[15] as well as of themselves.

Moreover, the community is prepared to make a conceptual distinction be- 10 tween a biological and a "real" mother. A common neighborhood saying goes that any women can have a baby, but it takes caring, love, and "mother wit" to be a real mother. Regardless of the circumstances, the birth of a baby is considered to be a truly blessed event. Accordingly, a profound female bonding takes place as the mother begins to pass her wisdom and experience down to the daughter. At social gatherings neighbors, relatives, and friends often augment this knowledge with their own fond remembrances and tales of maternity, attempting effectively to socialize the new mother into the preferred role of real mother. At the same time they try to prepare her to survive on her own terms, with or without a man. Given that families dissolve at a high rate among poor inner-city blacks and that women then prevail upon their extended family members and friends—often other females—for moral, emotional, practical, and financial support, the familial experience among the poorest may be described as matriarchal. Kinship ties, fictive or real, cemented through the grandmother, thus become the backbone of the inner-city extended family and, by implication, of young children in particular. The grandmother fills an important, perhaps the preeminent, domestic female role in the community.

The community consistently looks to the mother or grandmother to play 11 or strongly support this mothering role, a duty handed down to her through tradition and by her own socialization. Typically, a young girl with a limited outlook and sense of options for the future is easily enlisted for this role. In conditions of persistent poverty, she may look forward to the rewarding roles of mother and, by extension, of grandmother. Young men sometimes come to expect such young women to bear their children and to make few claims on them in the process; at the very least, they view birth control as the woman's responsibility, as a matter of "taking care of herself." A common notion in the inner-city poor community is that bearing and raising children is the business of women and that men should be involved only marginally except in matters of discipline and finances, which are almost always in short supply.

Today the grandmother increasingly emerges as a hero who was waiting 12 in the wings and has now been activated by the social and economic crises besetting the poor black family.[16] When more options become available to poor blacks, and the miseries of poverty, drugs, and violence recede, the heroic grandmother may once again retire to the wings, because her role is perceived to be less necessary, socially and economically. Hers, then, is a role that has been nurtured, supported, and legitimated over time, because of the ghetto family's chronic lack of resources, its subsequent vulnerability, and particularly the inability—or unwillingness, in many cases—of young men to fulfill their parental obligations and responsibilities.

In many cases vulnerable family members turn to their families and 13
close friends when they are threatened by predators. The grandmother often provides the most reliable support. Given her traditional role, it is generally believed that she cares and that she will marshal family resources,
call the authorities, and even mobilize the community for an organized
protest against those plying the local drug trade. In any event, she will
know what to do. These beliefs shape the conception that family members
as well as community residents tend to have of her role. Today, in playing
her positive community roles, some of these women actually lead marches
down the street and picket crack houses. In a literal sense, they fight to preserve their neighborhood and especially the lives of its children.

This social context is important to an understanding of the grandmother's 14
role, which, as we noted, has a long tradition but has at times been diminished. If it is resurgent now, that is largely because the social context—the
dearth of able male breadwinners, the rise of crack-addicted daughters and
male predators, and the general encroachment of the street culture into the
fabric of the community—demands it. In her traditional role, the grandmother may really be viewed, romantically at least, as a selfless savior of the
community. Her role may be compared to a lifeboat. If she is pressed into
service, it is because the ship is sinking. And, to many residents, the inner-
city ghetto community does seem to be sinking into ever more entrenched
poverty and to be increasingly undermined by the realities of the street culture as the mainstream culture slips further away. The ideal traditional
grandmother is generally viewed as decent, or a "real" grandmother, and
thus close to mainstream society. The one who shirks her expected role is
considered a nothing, but particularly if she is associated with the street.
How far grandmothers deviate from the traditional role may be an indication of how far the social type is itself falling victim to persistent poverty and
to present realities. It may also indicate the diminished ability of the community to produce citizens who can function adequately in the wider society.

Conceptually, two types of grandmothers may be discerned: the decent and 15
the street-oriented. The decent one tends to be much better off financially. Accordingly, she is able to marshal various props of decency and to make claim
on wider values like the work ethic, propriety, and church and to gain affirma-
tion of a sort through these connections, which further serve to enhance their
authority. She is very far from the street, and generally likes it that way. She
tends to be somewhat suspicious of and careful with most anonymous black
people she encounters for the first time; her doubts begin to dissipate only when
she gets to know them better and determines they are more decent than street.

Along with church and religion, she espouses abstinence, and often she 16
does not drink or smoke. She takes religion very seriously, and pictures of

Jesus, Martin Luther King Jr., and sometimes John F. Kennedy grace her walls. An aura of decency hangs about her, and these emblems attest to her decency, as anyone who visits her quickly learns. The word "decency" is an important part of her vocabulary and conversation. In her presence everyone defers. She usually has a solid financial position. Whatever its sources— whether from a pension, Social Security, or welfare—she has an income and tends to manage her money well enough that she is known to have a "stash." This reputation enables her to exert some leverage over family members. Depending on how they behave, she metes out favors, giving them things, tangible and intangible. Her grown children may make more money than she does, but they tend to run through it more quickly. Carefully managing her money, she tends to be thrifty and wise and able to live within her means, so the little she has may seem like a lot and go a long way.

In addition, in times of family distress or real trouble, this grandmother 17 is often able to assume the role of an activator.[17] Not only does she have resources of her own to commit to family needs; she has the moral authority to prod other members of the family to commit their own resources of time, money, and care to aid the family member in trouble or need. In one family I interviewed, when a daughter became addicted to crack, her siblings initially responded simply with expressions of "shame, shame" and little more. But their mother was able to prevail on them to help out materially and even to take in one of the daughter's children. And she "went to work" on the girl, counseling her strongly and offering "tough love."

Thanks to their normally better educational background, the decent peo- 18 ple usually have more resources than the street-oriented people, and this goes for grandmothers as well. Such grandmothers are more able to obtain help from the system. They are the ones who can deal with the welfare agency and have their addicted daughter's benefit checks diverted to them so that the money actually goes to the children and not for drugs. They not only provide help themselves but know to whom to turn in order to get even more.

Racism, the changing economy, unemployment, and changing social 19 values all affect the people in the community. But the grandmother, particularly if middle-aged or elderly, often takes an ideologically conservative view and tends to have little tolerance for structural explanations. Given her prior experience in the local community in the days of the manufacturing economy, in matters of idleness and unemployment she is ready to blame the victim, because she feels that there is work to be had for those who are willing to do it and that people can abstain from doing wrong if they want to. It is her belief that the various social problems plaguing the community stem more from personal irresponsibility than from any flaw in the wider system. At times she feels she is paying the price for the failures of family members. As one seventy-eight-year-old grandmother rather vehemently expressed herself,

> Well, I don't have too much sympathy about these drugs. Everything is drugs, drugs, if it wasn't for the drugs. As long as someone is not hold- ing you down, prying your mouth open, and pourin' it down your throat, you don't have to take it. So you take it because you want to take it. And nobody else has beat the habit, so what makes you think you're stronger than the other fellow? You see what it has done to his life. Now, if you're forced into it, then you're a victim of circumstance.

Certain other women who wake up one day and find themselves in the grandmother's role are at best ambivalent about it. They are, however, con- strained to try to enact it because of the forces of tradition and the present- day circumstances. What else can they do? Not to do something would be seriously to abdicate their responsibility to their kin. With very limited re- sources, they may experience bitterness and stress, at times resenting their daughters and grandchildren, yet they work to help their kin because that is their place, which they largely accept. 20

Still other women completely abdicate, or are indifferent to, their tra- ditional responsibility with respect to their grandchildren and this role. Often, though not always, they are associated with the street. These street grandmothers are much more at the mercy of circumstances beyond their control. They tend to be deeply invested in the "rough" street culture. They are apt to drink, smoke, take drugs, cavort with men, and generally engage in behavior that discredits them in the eyes of others, who then say things like, "She's weak," or "She's not ready," readily measuring her with respect to the ideal traditional grandmother role—which is loving and de- cent. The label "weak" or "not ready" may simply be describing the in- ability to define oneself according to the role. Even those who shirk the grandmother role know that they have deviated from a norm. Some feel enormous guilt, which often prods them to attempt to play this positive role as best they can in spite of their personal circumstances. Hence the traditional grandmother role has become something of a standard, a con- ceptual touchstone of the value system into which many young girls are initiated and actively grow. 21

All of this has resulted in a core cadre of black women in poor inner- city neighborhoods who are fountains of strength, reservoirs of resilience. In these communities they play out this strong decent role, becoming rock- solid figures others have learned to depend on and even to mythologize. When the family is intact, this woman is often the person other family members praise and look to for authority and direction; she gives advice and others take it. If the family is broken, she keeps the pieces at least 22 loosely together. She may have few material resources, but she has enormous moral authority and spiritual strength.

On the average, a woman becomes a grandmother at about the age of [23] thirty-seven; some do so at thirty-three or thirty-four, though some are, of course, elderly. Typically single, she may have a steady boyfriend or sporadic male company. Thus some semblance of nuclear family life is apparent, but there may be no formal domestic ties. Her home is a social center, a kind of nest for the family, where her grown children regularly come and go. Generally, her daughters are still living with her when they begin to have babies, further complicating the home's social activity. The woman herself may be employed but often in a low-level service or clerical occupation, such as that of nurse's aide, while the daughters may be working at a fast-food restaurant. By pooling their resources, they cope, but barely. Concerned about helping out the family, the grandmother buys clothes and toys for the kids, takes responsibility for child care, and when necessary gives moral support to the mothers. In addition, the grandmother draws social sustenance from her female friends, her church, and her neighborhood. At local coffee and liquor gatherings, they sometimes exchange the latest gossip about others in the neighborhood and share accounts of their own family problems. They discuss who's going with whom, who's working, and whose child is "on the pipe" (attested to by a clear loss of weight). In the course of such talk, important social and moral lessons are drawn, and children are carefully instructed in the rules of right and wrong. Children who grow up in this kind of household learn the rules and values of communal family support and are strongly encouraged to be "good" and "sweet." Rooted in this tradition, if they successfully negotiate the hazards of the neighborhood street culture, they have a chance to achieve social stability in the ghetto culture.

Notes

[1]Faustine C. Jones, "The Lofty Role of the Black Grandmother," *The Crisis* 80, no. 1 (1973): 41–56; Herbert Gutman, *The Black Family in Slavery and Freedom* (New York: Vintage Books, 1976).

[2]E. Franklin Frazier, *The Negro Family in the United States* (Chicago: University of Chicago Press, 1939), 150.

[3]See Gutman, *Black Family;* Kenneth M. Stampp, *The Peculiar Institution: Slavery in the Ante-bellum South* (1956; reprint, New York: Vintage Books, 1989); John Blassingame, *The Slave Community* (New York: Oxford University Press, 1971); Frank F. Furstenberg Jr., Theodore Hershberg, and John

Modell, "The Origins of the Female-Headed Black Family: The Impact of the Urban Experience," in *Philadelphia: Work, Space, Family, and Group Experience in the 19th Century,* ed. Theodore Hershberg (New York: Oxford University Press, 1981), 435–54; Nicholas Lemann, *The Promised Land: The Great Black Migration and How It Changed America* (New York: Knopf, 1991).

[4]Frazier, *Negro Family;* William Julius Wilson, *The Truly Disadvantaged: The Inner City, the Underclass, and Public Policy* (Chicago: University of Chicago Press, 1987); Gerald David Jaynes, *Branches Without Roots: Genesis of the Black Working Class in the American South* (New York: Oxford University Press, 1986).

[5]Jones, "Lofty Role"; Jaquelyne J. Jackson, "Aged Blacks: A Potpourri in the Direction of the Reduction of Inequities," *Phylon* 32 (1971): 260–80.

[6]Wilson, *Truly Disadvantaged;* William Julius Wilson, *When Work Disappears: The World of the New Urban Poor* (New York: Knopf, 1996); Theodore Hershberg, "Free Blacks in Antebellum Philadelphia," in *The Peoples of Philadelphia: A History of Ethnic Groups and Lower-Class Life, 1870–1940,* ed. Allen F. Davis and Mark H. Haller (Philadelphia: Temple University Press, 1973), 111–33; Elijah Anderson, *Streetwise: Race, Class, and Change in an Urban Community* (Chicago: University of Chicago Press, 1990).

[7]Jaquelyne J. Jackson, "The Blacklands of Gerontology," *Aging and Human Development* 2 (1971): 156–71; Jasper C. Register and Jim Mitchell, "Black-White Differences in Attitudes Toward the Elderly," *Journal of Minority Aging* 7, nos. 3–4 (1982): 34–36.

[8]Linda M. Burton and Vern L. Bengtson, "Black Grandmothers: Issues of Timing and Continuity of Roles," in *Grandparenthood,* ed. Vern L. Bengtson and Joan F. Robertson (Beverly Hills: Sage Publications, 1985), 61–77; Vern L. Bengtson, "Diversity and Symbolism in Grandparental Roles," ibid., 11–85; Jackson, "Aged Blacks."

[9]Bengtson, "Diversity"; Andrew J. Cherlin and Frank F. Furstenberg Jr., *The New American Grandparent* (New York: Basic Books, 1986); Lillian E. Troll, "The Family of Later Life: A Decade Review," *Journal of Marriage and the Family* 33 (1971): 263–90.

[10]Arthur Kornhaber and Kenneth L. Woodward, *Grandparents, Grandchildren: The Vital Connection* (Garden City, N.Y.: Doubleday/Anchor Books, 1981).

[11]St. Clair Drake and Horace R. Cayton, *Black Metropolis: A Study of Negro Life in a Northern City* (New York: Harper & Row, 1962); William C. Hays and Charles H. Mindel, "Extended Kinship Relations in

Black and White Families," *Journal of Marriage and the Family* 35 (1973): 51–57; Carol Stack, *All Our Kin* (New York: Harper & Row, 1974); Jerold Heiss, *The Case of the Black Family* (New York: Columbia University Press, 1975).

[12]Doris Y. Wilkinson, "Play Objects as Tools of Propaganda: Characterizations of the African American Male," *The Journal of Black Psychology* 7, no. 2 (August 1980): 1–16.

[13]Patricia J. Dunston et al., "Black Adolescent Mothers and Their Families: Extending Services," in *The Black Adolescent Parent*, ed. Stanley F. Battle (New York: Haworth Press, 1987); Harriet B. Presser, "Sally's Corner: Coping with Unmarried Motherhood," *Journal of Social Issues* 36 (1980): 107–29.

[14]Constance W. Williams, *Black Teenage Mothers: Pregnancy and Child Rearing from Their Perspective* (Lexington, Mass.: Lexington Books/D. C. Heath, 1991).

[15]Annette U. Rickel, *Teen Pregnancy and Parenting* (New York: Hemisphere Publishing, 1989).

[16]See Doris Y. Wilkinson, "Traditional Medicine in American Families: Reliance on the Wisdom of Elders," *Marriage and Family Review* 11, nos. 3–4 (1987).

[17]See Doris Y. Wilkinson, "Afro-American Women and Their Families" in *Women and the Family: Two Decades of Change*, Beth B. Hess and Marvin B. Sussman, eds. (New York: Haworth Press, 1984).

Thinking Critically

1. Ethnography is a way of doing research, and it is an invaluable though challenging practice that enhances the work of anthropologists and social scientists. Ethnology, when conducted ethically and systematically, balances a day-to-day understanding of a community's relationships, circumstances, values, and practices with an objective review of statistical data, historical documents, and other sources of information. Read through Elijah Anderson's essay and name the different kinds of information and authority he uses to describe the role of the black inner-city grandmother. How does Anderson balance different kinds of information and authority?

2. Be sure to include Anderson's endnotes in your reading and rereading of his essay. What do these notes contribute to your understanding of his argument and your confidence in his authority and research? How do you use endnotes or footnotes in your own academic writing?

3. Anderson makes a distinction, based on the ways in which members of the community he studies describe themselves, between "street" values and "decent" values. List the attributes of each set of values. What kinds of

judgments do members of the community make about people who are "street" and people who are "decent"? Does Anderson himself seem to make judgments (as opposed to describing and naming behaviors, in keeping with the practice of ethnology)?

Writing Critically

1. Compare the role of the black inner-city grandmother, as described by Anderson, and the role of the grandmother in Joe Miceli's Italian American family (in the preceding essay). How do the very different audiences and purposes of Anderson's and Miceli's writing affect the ways in which each man describes the role of the grandmother? In an analytical essay, compare and contrast the role of the grandmother in the communities described by each writer.

2. In an essay that combines the personal narrative approach of Joe Miceli and the ethnographic approach of Elijah Anderson, describe the role played by a relative in your family and the ways in which that role has larger significance in your community.

3. Anderson describes the political views held by many "middle-aged or elderly" inner-city black grandmothers. How do those views compare with the views described by Andrea Elliot in "The Political Conversion of New York's Evangelicals" (see pp. 116–20)?

How to Re-Moralize America

Francis Fukuyama

Francis Fukuyama is the Bernard L. Schwartz Professor of International Political Economy at Johns Hopkins University. He received his B.A. from Cornell University in classics and his Ph.D. from Harvard in political science. He was a member of the Political Science Department of the RAND Corporation, an independent public policy research group, from 1979 to 1980, 1983 to 1989, and 1995 to 1996. Fukuyama was a member of the Policy Planning Staff of the U.S. Department of State, at first specializing in Middle East affairs and then serving as deputy director for European political-military affairs. In 1981–1982 Fukuyama was a member of the U.S. delegation to the Egyptian-Israeli talks on Palestinian autonomy. In *The End of History and the Last Man* (1992), Fukuyama advances the controversial argument that before the end of the Cold War human history was marked by ideological conflict but since the resolution of that conflict there has been steady movement toward liberal democracy. Since 1992, Fukuyama's argument has been challenged by the emergence of religious fundamentalism worldwide, as well as by the impact of environmental degradation and the dangerous potential of biotechnology. In a later book, *Our Posthuman Future: Consequences of the Biotechnology Revolution* (2002), Fukuyama acknowledges the limits of his argument in *The End of History:* "we hadn't reached the end of history because we hadn't yet reached the end of science." In 2002, Fukuyama was named by President George W. Bush to serve on the President's Council of Bioethics. "How to Re-Moralize America" appeared in the Summer 1999 issue of the *Wilson Quarterly,* a publication of the Woodrow Wilson International Center for Scholars. The Center, established as a "living memorial" to President Wilson, supports the collaboration of academic research and public policy.

In 1994, William J. Bennett published a book called *The Index of Lead-* 1 *ing Cultural Indicators,* which brought together a variety of statistics about American social trends. Between the mid-1960s and the early 1990s, Bennett showed, there was a shocking deterioration of America's social health. By the 1990s, one American child out of three was being born to an unmarried mother, nearly a third of African American men between the ages of 20 and 29 were involved in some way with the criminal justice system, and scores on standardized tests of educational achievement had dropped America to the bottom of the pack among industrialized countries. While we were materially richer than at any time in history, Bennett argued, we were becoming morally poorer at an alarming rate.

In the brief period since Bennett's *Index* appeared, we have experienced 2 what seems to be a remarkable turnaround. Crime, including violent crimes and those against property, has decreased by more than 15 percent nationally; the murder rate in New York City has declined to levels not seen since the mid-1960s. Divorce rates, which had already begun a downward trend in the 1980s, continue on that path. Starting in 1995, the illegitimacy rate ceased its upward climb and began to decline slightly. The teenage pregnancy rate dropped eight percent between 1991 and 1996; among black teenagers, it fell 21 percent. Welfare caseloads have dropped by as much as a quarter nationally, and states at the forefront of welfare reform, such as Wisconsin, have seen astonishing reductions of up to 75 percent. Americans' general level of trust in their institutions and in one another, though difficult to gauge, has risen. In 1991, for example, only 15 to 20 percent of Americans said they trusted the federal government to do the right thing most of the time; by the end of the decade that percentage had rebounded to between 25 and 30 percent.

What are we to make of these improvements? Are Americans at century's end being blessed not only with a booming stock market and a near full-employment economy but a restoration of cultural health as well? Many conservatives, notably social scientist Charles Murray and historian Gertrude Himmelfarb, don't think so. The changes, they argue, are too shallow and recent; they may be the product of more jails and stiffer sentencing rather than any true improvement in moral behavior. One conservative activist, Paul Weyrich of the Free Congress Foundation, was thrown into such despair last summer by the public's refusal to repudiate President Bill Clinton despite a sex scandal and impeachment proceedings that he publicly declared that Americans have never been more degenerate than they are today.

But conservatives are wrong to dismiss the good news contained in the social statistics. In fact, there has been a shift back to more traditional social values, and they should take credit for helping to bring it about. It would be a mistake to become complacent, or to think that our social and cultural problems are now behind us. But there is good reason to think that American society is undergoing a degree of moral regeneration. There is still a great deal of confusion over the sources of moral decline, however, and over the nature of moral renewal. Liberals need to confront the reality of moral decline and the importance of socially beneficial, less self-centered values. Conservatives have to be realistic and recognize that many of the developments they dislike in contemporary society are driven by economic and technological change—change brought about by the same dynamic capitalist economy they so often celebrate.

Moral decline is not a myth or a figment of the nostalgic imagination. Perhaps the most important conservative achievement over the past couple of decades was to convince the rest of American society that these changes had occurred, that they reflected a disturbing shift in values, and that consequently not every social problem could be addressed by creating a new federal program and throwing money at it.

This reconception of social problems began with two large government-funded studies published in the mid-1960s: Daniel Patrick Moynihan's report, *The Negro Family: The Case for National Action* (1965), and James Coleman's *Equality of Educational Opportunity* (1966). Moynihan, then working for the U.S. Department of Labor, argued that family structure, and in particular the absence of fathers in many African American homes, was directly related to the incidence of crime, teenage pregnancy, low educational achievement, and other social pathologies. Coleman's study showed that student educational achievement was most strongly affected not by the tools of public policy, such as teacher salaries and classroom size, but by the environment a child's family and peers create. In the absence of a culture that emphasizes self-discipline, work, education, and other middle-class values, Coleman showed, public policy can achieve relatively little.

Once published, the Moynihan report was violently attacked. Moyni-   7
han was accused of "blaming the victim" and seeking to impose white values on a community that had different but not necessarily inferior cultural norms. Liberals at first denied the reality of massive changes in family structure, and then fell back on the argument that single-parent households are no worse from the standpoint of child welfare than traditional ones—the kind of argument Moynihan was later to label "defining deviancy down." By the early 1990s, however, conservatives had largely won the argument. In 1994, the publication of Sara McLanahan and Gary Sandefur's book *Growing Up with a Single Parent* (1994) made the social science community's shift more or less official. The two well-respected sociologists found that a generation's worth of empirical research supported Moynihan's basic conclusion: growing up in a single-parent family is correlated with a life of poverty and a host of other social ills.

Few Americans understand that they were not alone in experiencing   8
these changes. All of the industrialized countries outside Asia experienced a massive increase in social disorder between the 1960s and '90s—a phenomenon that I have called the Great Disruption of Western social values. Indeed, by the 1990s Sweden, the United Kingdom, and New Zealand all had higher rates of property crime than the United States. More than half of all Scandinavian children are born to unmarried mothers, compared with one-third of American children. In Sweden, so few people bother to get married that the institution itself probably is in long-term decline.

While conservatives won their case that values had changed for the   9
worse, they were on shakier ground in their interpretation of why this shift had occurred. There were two broad lines of argument. The first, advanced by Charles Murray in his landmark book *Losing Ground* (1984), argued that family breakdown, crime, and other social pathologies were ultimately the result of mistaken government policies. Chief among them was Aid to Families with Dependent Children (AFDC), which in effect subsidized illegitimacy by paying welfare benefits only to single mothers. But there were other causes, such as new court-imposed constraints on police departments won by civil libertarians. In this interpretation, any improvement in social indicators today must be the result of the unwinding of earlier social policies through measures such as the 1996 welfare reform bill.

The second conservative line of argument held that moral decline was 10
the result of a broad cultural shift. Former federal judge Robert Bork, for
example, blamed the 1960s counterculture for undermining traditional
values and setting the young at war with authority. Others, such as philosopher John Gray, reached further back in time. They revived the arguments
of Edmund Burke and Joseph de Maistre, tracing moral decay to an Enlightenment commitment to replacing tradition and religion with reason
and secular humanism.

While there is more than a germ of truth in each of these interpreta- 11
tions, neither is adequate to explain the shift in values that occurred during the Great Disruption. Detailed econometric studies seeking to link
AFDC to illegitimacy have shown that although there is some causal connection, the relationship is not terribly strong. More important, illegitimacy is only part of a much broader story of family breakdown that
includes divorce, cohabitation in place of marriage, declining fertility, and
the separation of cohabiting couples. These ills cut across the socioeconomic spectrum and can hardly be blamed on a federal poverty program.

The second line of argument, which sees moral breakdown as a conse- 12
quence of a broad cultural shift, is not so much wrong as inadequate. No
one who has lived through the last several decades can deny that there has
been a huge shift in social values, a shift whose major theme has been the
rise of individualism at the expense of communal sources of authority, from
the family and neighborhood to churches, labor unions, companies, and
the government. The problem with this kind of broad cultural explanation
is that it cannot explain timing. Secular humanism, for example, has been
in the works for the past four or five hundred years. Why all of a sudden
in the last quarter of the 20th century has it produced social chaos?

The key to the timing of the Great Disruption, I believe, is to be found 13
elsewhere, in changes that occurred in the economy and in technology. The
most important social values that were shaken by the Great Disruption are
those having to do with sex, reproduction, and the family. The reason the
disruption happened when and where it did can be traced to two broad
technological changes that began in the 1960s. One is the advent of birth
control. The other is the shift from industrial to information-based
economies and from physical to mental labor.

The nuclear family of the 1950s was based on a bargain that traded the 14
husband's income for the wife's fertility: he worked, she stayed home to
raise the family. With the economy's shift from manufacturing to services
(or from brawn to brains), new opportunities arose for women. Women began entering the paid labor force in greater numbers throughout the West
in the 1960s, which undid the old arrangement. Even as it liberated women

from complete dependence on their husbands, it freed many men from responsibility for their families. Not surprisingly, women's participation in
the labor force correlates strongly with divorce and family breakdown
throughout the industrialized world.

The Pill reinforced this trend by shifting the burden of responsibility for   15
the consequences of sex to women. No longer did men need to worry
greatly if their adventures led to pregnancy. One sign of this change was
found by economists Janet Yellen, George Akerlof, and Michael Katz. Between the 1960s and '90s, the number of brides who were pregnant at the
altar declined significantly. The shotgun wedding, that ultimate symbol of
male accountability, is increasingly a thing of the past.

Humans share a fundamental trait with other animal species: males are   16
less selective in their choice of sexual partners than females, and less attached to their children. In humans, the role that fathers play in the care
and nurture of their children tends to be socially constructed to a significant degree, shaped by a host of formal and informal controls that link men
to their families. Human fatherhood is therefore more readily subject to
disruption. The sexual revolution and the new economic and cultural independence of women provided that disruption. The perfectly reasonable
desire of women to increase their autonomy became, for men, an excuse to
indulge themselves. The vastly increased willingness of men to leave behind
partners and children constitutes perhaps the single greatest change in
moral values during the Great Disruption. It lies at the core of many of the
period's social pathologies.

What are the chances of a moral renewal? What are its potential   17
sources? Renewal must be possible. While conservatives may be right that
moral decline occurred over the past generation, they cannot be right that
it occurs in every generation. Unless we posit that all of human history
has been a degeneration from some primordial golden age, periods of
moral decline must be punctuated by periods of moral improvement.
Such cycles have occurred before. In both Britain and the United States,
the period from the end of the 18th century until approximately the middle of the 19th century saw sharply increasing levels of social disorder.
Crime rates in virtually all major cities increased. Illegitimacy rates rose,
families dissolved, and social isolation increased. The rate of alcohol consumption, particularly in the United States, exploded. But then, from the
middle of the century until its end, virtually all of these social indicators
reversed direction. Crime rates fell. Families stabilized, and drunkards
went on the wagon. New voluntary associations—from temperance and
abolitionist societies to Sunday schools—gave people a fresh sense of
communal belonging.

The possibility of re-moralization poses some large questions: Where do 18
moral values come from, and what, in particular, are the sources of moral values in a postindustrial society? This is a subject that, strangely, has not received much attention. People have strong opinions about what moral values
ought to be and where they ought to come from. If you are on the left, you
are likely to believe in social equality guaranteed by a welfare state. If you are
a cultural conservative, you may favor the authority of tradition and religion.
But how values actually are formed in contemporary societies receives little
empirical study. Most people would say that values are either passed along
from previous generations through socialization (which fails to explain how
change occurs) or are imposed by a church or other hierarchical authority.
With the exception of a few discredited theories, sociologists and cultural anthropologists haven't had much to contribute. They have had much more success in describing value systems than in explaining their genesis.

Into this breach in the social sciences have stepped the economists, 19
who have hardly been shy in recent years about applying their formidable
methodological tools to matters beyond their usual realm. Economists
tend to be opponents of hierarchy and proponents of bargaining—individuals, they say, act rationally on their own to achieve socially productive ends. This describes the market. But Friedrich A. Hayek (among
others) suggested that moral rules—part of what he called the "extended
order of human cooperation"—might also be the product of a similar decentralized evolutionary bargaining process.

Take the virtues of honesty and reliability, which are key to social co- 20
operation and that intangible compound of mutual trust and engagement
called "social capital." Many people have argued that such virtues have religious sources, and that contemporary capitalist societies are living off the
cultural capital of previous ages—in America, chiefly its Puritan traditions.
Modern capitalism, in this view, with its amoral emphasis on profits and
efficiency, is steadily undermining its own moral basis.

Such an interpretation, while superficially plausible, is completely 21
wrong. A decentralized group of individuals who have to deal with one another repeatedly will tend as a matter of self-interest to evolve norms of
honesty and reliability. That is, reputation, whether for honesty or fair
dealing or product quality, is an asset that self-interested individuals will
seek to acquire. While religion may encourage them, a hierarchical source
of rules is not necessary. Given the right background conditions—especially
the need for repeated dealings with a particular group of people—order and
rules will tend to emerge spontaneously from the ground up.

The study of how order emerges spontaneously from the interaction of 22
individual agents is one of the most interesting and important intellectual

developments of the late 20th century. One reason it is interesting is that the study is not limited to economists and other social scientists. Scientists since Charles Darwin have concluded that the high degree of order in the biological world was not the creation of God or some other creator but rather emerged out of the interaction of simpler units. The elaborate mounds of some species of African termites, taller than a human being and equipped with their own heating and air conditioning systems, were not designed by anyone, much less by the neurologically simple creatures that built them. And so on, throughout the natural world, order is created by the blind, irrational process of evolution and natural selection. (In the 1980s, the now famous Santa Fe Institute was created to support studies of just this type of phenomenon, so-called complex adaptive systems, in a wide variety of fields.)

Indeed, there is a good deal more social order in the world than even 23 the economists' theories would suggest. Economists frequently express surprise at the extent to which supposedly self-interested, rational individuals do seemingly selfless things: vote, contribute to charities, give their loyalty to employers. People do these things because the ability to solve repeated dilemmas of social cooperation is genetically coded into the human brain, put there by an evolutionary process that rewarded those individuals best able to generate social rules for themselves. Human beings have innate capabilities that make them gravitate toward and reward cooperators who play by the community's rules, and to ostracize and isolate opportunists who violate them. When we say that human beings are social creatures by nature, we mean not that they are cooperative angels with unlimited resources for altruism but that they have built-in capabilities for perceiving the moral qualities of their fellow humans. What James Q. Wilson calls the "moral sense" is put there by nature, and will operate in the absence of either a lawgiver or a prophet.

If we accept the fact that norms have spontaneous as well as hierarchi- 24 cal sources, we can place them along a continuum that extends from hierarchical and centralized types of authority at one end to the completely decentralized and spontaneous interactions of individuals at the other. But there is a second dimension. Norms and moral rules can be the product of rational bargaining and negotiation, or they can be socially inherited or otherwise a-rational in origin.

In order to clarify the origins of re-moralization, I have constructed a ma- 25 trix (below) that organizes these alternatives along two axes. Different types of moral rules fall into different quadrants. Formal laws handed down by governments belong in the rational/hierarchical quadrant; common law and spontaneously generated rules concerning, say, honesty in market relations,

The Universe of Norms

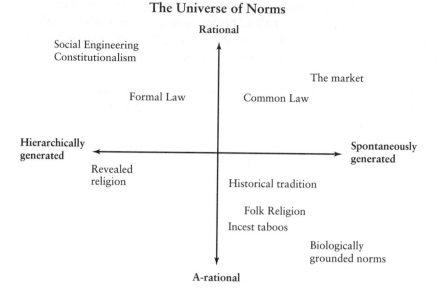

fall in the rational/spontaneous quadrant. Because, according to most recent research, incest taboos have biological origins, they are a spontaneous, a-rational norm. Revealed religion—Moses bringing the Ten Commandments down from Mount Sinai, for example—occupies the a-rational hierarchical quadrant. But folk religions—a cult of rock worshipers, for example—may be a species of spontaneous, a-rational order.

This taxonomy gives us a basis for at least beginning a discussion of where norms in a postindustrial society come from. Economists, following their rational, nonhierarchical bent, have been busy populating the upper-right quadrant with examples of spontaneously generated rules. A case in point is the database of more than 5,000 cases of so-called common pool resource problems compiled by Elinor Ostrom. Such problems confront communities with the need to determine rules for sharing common resources such as fisheries or pastureland. Contrary to the expectation that the self-interest of each individual will lead to the depletion of the resources—the famous "tragedy of the commons"—Ostrom finds many cases in which communities were able to spontaneously generate fair rules for sharing that avoided that result.

Max Weber, the founder of modern sociology, argued that as societies 27 modernize, the two rational quadrants, and particularly the hierarchical quadrant, tend to play a strong role in the creation of norms. Rational bureaucracy was, for him, the essence of modernity. In postindustrial societies, however, all four quadrants continue to serve as important sources of norms. Modern corporations, for example, have discovered that they cannot organize complex activities and highly skilled workers in a centralized, formal, top-down system of bureaucratic rules. The trend in management is to reduce formal bureaucracy in favor of informal norms that link a variety of firms and individuals in networks.

We now have a framework in which to discuss how the socially corrosive 28
effects of the Great Disruption are being overcome, and what continuing possibilities for change there might be. In the quest for the source of authoritative new rules, one starting point is the rational-hierarchical quadrant, which is the sphere of public policy. Crime rates are down across the United States today in no small measure because government is embracing better policies, such as community policing, and spending more on law enforcement, prisons, and punishment.* But the fact that tougher policies have brought crime rates down would not be regarded by most people as evidence of moral renewal. We want people to behave better not because of a crackdown but because they have internalized certain standards. The question then becomes, Which of the three remaining quadrants can be the source of moral behavior?

Many cultural conservatives believe that religion is the sine qua non of 29
moral values, and they blame the Great Disruption on a loss of religious values. Religion played a powerful role in the Victorian upsurge during the second half of the 19th century, they note, and, therefore, any reversal of the Great Disruption must likewise depend on a religious revival. In this view, the cultural conservatives are supported (in a way) by Friedrich Nietzsche, who once denounced the English "flathead" John Stuart Mill for believing that one could have something approximating Christian values in the absence of a belief in the Christian God.

Nietzsche fatuously argued that God was on his deathbed and inca- 30
pable, in Europe at least, of being resuscitated. There could be new religions, but they would be pagan ones that would provoke "immense wars" in the future. Religious conservatives can reply that, as an empirical matter, God is not dead anywhere but in Europe itself. A generation or two ago, social scientists generally believed that secularization was the inevitable byproduct of modernization, but in the United States and many other advanced societies, religion does not seem to be in danger of dying out.

---

*A highly salient issue often is not what the government does, but what it refrains from doing, since an overly large and centralized state can rob individuals and communities of initiative and keep them from setting norms for themselves. During the 1960s and '70s, the American court system decriminalized many forms of petty deviance such as panhandling and public drunkenness. By limiting the ability of urban middle-class neighborhoods to set norms for social behavior, the state indirectly encouraged suburban flight and the retreat of the middle class into gated communities. To the extent that these kinds of policies can be limited or reversed, social order will increase.

Some religious conservatives hope, and many liberals fear, that the prob- 31
lem of moral decline will be resolved by a large-scale return to religious orthodoxy—a transformation as sudden as the one Ayatollah Khomeini
wrought 20 years ago by returning to Iran on a jetliner. For a variety of reasons, this seems unlikely. Modern societies are so culturally diverse that it is
not clear whose version of orthodoxy would prevail. Any true form of orthodoxy is likely to be seen as a threat to important groups and hence would
neither get very far nor serve as a basis for widening the radius of trust. Instead of integrating society, a conservative religious revival might only increase social discord and fragmentation.

It is not clear, moreover, that the re-moralization of society need rely on 32
the hierarchical authority of revealed religion. Against Nietzsche's view that
moral behavior inevitably rests on dogmatic belief, we might counterpose
Adam Smith, the Enlightenment philosopher with perhaps the most realistic
and highly developed theory of moral action. Harking back to a kind of Aris-
totelian naturalism, Smith argued that human beings are social and moral
creatures by nature, capable of being led to moral behavior both by their natural passions and by their reason. The Enlightenment has been justly criticized
for its overemphasis on human reason. But reason does not have to take the
form of a bureaucratic state seeking to engineer social outcomes through the
wholesale rearrangement of society. It can also take the form of rational individuals interacting with one another to create workable moral rules, or, in
Smith's language, being led from a narrowly selfish view of their interests to
the view of an "impartial spectator" exercising reasoned moral judgment.

Religious conservatives, in other words, underestimate the innate ability of 33
human beings to evolve reasonable moral rules for themselves. Western societies underwent an enormous shock during the mid-20th century, and it is not
surprising that it has taken a long time to adjust. The process of reaching a rational set of norms is not easy or automatic. During the Great Disruption, for
example, large numbers of men and women began to behave in ways that
ended up hurting the interests of children. Men abandoned families, women
conceived children out of wedlock, and couples divorced for what were often
superficial and self-indulgent reasons. But parents also have a strong interest in
the well-being of their children. If it can be demonstrated to them that their behavior is seriously injuring the life chances of their offspring, they are likely to
react rationally and want to alter that behavior in ways that help their children.

During the Great Disruption, there were many intellectual and cultural 34
currents at work obscuring from people the consequences of their personal
behavior for people close to them. They were told by social scientists that
growing up in a single-parent family was no worse than growing up in an
intact one, reassured by family therapists that children were better off if the

parents divorced, and bombarded by images from the popular culture that glamorized sex. Changing these perceptions requires discussion, argument, even "culture wars." And we have had them. Today Barbara Dafoe Whitehead's controversial 1993 assertion that "Dan Quayle was right" about the importance of families no longer seems radical.

What would the re-moralization of society look like? In some of its   35 manifestations, it would represent a continuation of trends that have already occurred in the 1990s, such as the return of middle-class people from their gated suburban communities to downtown areas, where a renewed sense of order and civility once again makes them feel secure enough to live and work. It would show up in increasing levels of participation in civil associations and political engagement. And it would be manifest in more civil behavior on college campuses, where a greater emphasis on academics and more carefully codified rules of behavior are already apparent.

The kinds of changes we can expect in norms concerning sex, repro-   36 duction, and family life are likely to be more modest. Conservatives need to be realistic in understanding how thoroughly the moral and social landscapes have been altered by powerful technological and economic forces. Strict Victorian rules concerning sex are very unlikely to return. Unless someone can figure out a way to un-invent birth control, or move women out of the labor force, the nuclear family of the 1950s is not likely to be reconstituted in anything like its original form.

Yet the social role of fathers has proved very plastic from society to soci-   37 ety and over time, and it is not unreasonable to think that the commitment of men to their families can be substantially strengthened. This was the message of two of the largest demonstrations in Washington during the 1990s, the Nation of Islam's Million Man March and the Promise Keepers' rally. People were rightly suspicious of the two sponsors, but the same message about male responsibility can and should be preached by more mainstream groups.

There is also evidence that we are moving into a "postfeminist" age that   38 will be friendlier to families and children. Feminism denigrated the work of raising children in favor of women's paid labor—an attitude epitomized by Hillary Clinton's dismissive response to questions about her Arkansas legal career that she could have just "stayed home and baked cookies." Many women are indeed now working—not as lawyers or policymakers but as waitresses and checkers at Wal-Mart, away from the children they are struggling to raise on their own after being abandoned by husbands or boyfriends. Many women like these might choose to stay at home with their children during their early years if the culture told them it was okay, and if they had the financial means to do so. I see anecdotal evidence all around me that the well-to-do are already making this choice. This does not represent a return of the housewife ideal of the 1950s, just a more sensible balancing of work and family.

Women might find it more palatable to make work and career sacrifices   39
for the sake of children if men made similar sacrifices. The postindustrial economy, by undermining the notion of lifetime employment and steady movement up a career ladder for men, may be abetting just such a social change. In the industrial era, technology encouraged the separation of a male-dominated workplace from a female-dominated home; the information age may reintegrate the two.

Religion may serve a purpose in reestablishing norms, even without a   40
sudden return to religious orthodoxy. Religion is frequently not so much the product of dogmatic belief as it is the provider of a convenient language that allows communities to express moral beliefs that they would hold on entirely secular grounds. A young woman I know does not want to have sex until she is married. She tells her suitors that she follows this rule out of religious conviction, not so much because she is a believer but because this is more convincing to them than a utilitarian explanation. In countless ways, modern, educated, skeptical people are drawn to religion because it offers them community, ritual, and support for values they otherwise hold. Religion in this sense is a form of a-rational, spontaneous order rather than a hierarchical alternative to it.

Re-moralizing a complex, diverse society such as the United States is not   41
without pitfalls. If a return to broad orthodoxy is unlikely, re-moralization for many will mean dropping out of mainstream society—for example, by home-schooling one's children, withdrawing into an ethnic neighborhood or enclave, or creating one's own limited patch of social order. In his science fiction novel *The Diamond Age,* Neal Stephenson envisions a future world in which a group of computer programmers, realizing the importance of moral values for economic success, create a small community called New Atlantis. There they resurrect Victorian social values, complete with top hats and sexual prudery. The "Vickies" of New Atlantis do well for themselves but have nothing to say to the poor, disorganized communities that surround them. Re-moralization may thus go hand in hand with a sort of miniaturization of community, as it has in American civil society over the past generation. Conversely, if these small communities remain reasonably tolerant and open, they may light the way to a broader moral revival, just as Granges, Boy Scout troops, immigrant ethnic associations, and the other myriad small communities of the late 19th century did.

The reconstruction of values that has started in the 1990s, and any   42
renorming of society that may happen in the future, has and will be the product of political, religious, self-organized, and natural norm building.

The state is neither the source of all our troubles nor the instrument by which we can solve them. But its actions can both deplete and restore social capital in ways large and small. We have not become so modern and secularized that we can do without religion. But we are also not so bereft of innate moral resources that we need to wait for a messiah to save us. And nature, which we are constantly trying to evict with a pitchfork, always keeps running back.

Thinking Critically

1. What does Francis Fukuyama consider to be good news, and what kind of evidence does he offer to support his claim?

2. A responsible argument includes discussion of opposing viewpoints and a reasonable, well-supported refutation of the opposition's stance. Who is Fukuyama's opposition? How much exposition does he give to the opposing point of view, and what is his attitude about his opposition? How does he go about refuting the opposition's arguments?

3. How does Fukuyama define "moral decline"? What, in his opinion, would be necessary for a "moral renewal"?

Writing Critically

1. At the midpoint of his argument (in paragraph 18), Fukuyama asks a key question: "Where do moral values come from, and what, in particular, are the sources of moral values in a postindustrial society?" How does Fukuyama answer that question? Do you agree or disagree with his answer? Support your argument with reference to any of the other readings in this book. You might also consult some of the economists, policy makers, and social scientists that Fukuyama mentions.

2. Should a civic or political agenda have anything to do with "morals"? Fukuyama proposes a continuum of social interaction that generates moral rules ranging from the rational/hierarchical to the rational/spontaneous. Where on Fukuyama's matrix would you locate the ideal balance between civic responsibility and personal morals? Support your argument with specific examples of the intersection of private morals and the public good.

3. Fukuyama seems to offer a comforting response to those who fear that a "large-scale return to religious orthodoxy" will resolve the "moral decline" of Western culture. In the years since this article was first published, have circumstances changed in such a way to either support Fukuyama's claim or refute it?

"First Comes Love, Then Comes Marriage, Then Comes Mary with a Baby Carriage": Marriage, Sex, and Reproduction

STEPHANIE COONTZ

> Stephanie Coontz teaches history and family studies at Evergreen State College in Olympia, Washington. *The Way We Never Were: American Families and the Nostalgia Trap,* the book in which "First Comes Love . . ." appears, was published in 1992 at the height of election-year debates about "family values." The 1992 presidential election set Democrat Bill Clinton against incumbent Republican president George H. W. Bush. Dan Quayle, the incumbent vice president, publicly spoke out against the decision of an unmarried television sitcom: character, Murphy Brown, to become a single mother. In subsequent books, including *The Way We Really Are: Coming to Terms with America's Changing Families* (1997) and *Marriage, a History: From Obedience to Intimacy or How Love Conquered Marriage* (2005), and in numerous magazine and newspaper articles and media appearances, Coontz has become a formidable advocate for the rights of American working families. Of particular interest to her in recent years is the need for universally available, safe, and affordable child care for working parents. Coontz is the director of research and public education for the Council on Contemporary Families, which she chaired from 2001 to 2004, and she has testified about her research before the House Select Committee on Children, Youth and Families in Washington, DC. A former Woodrow Wilson Fellow, in 1995 Coontz received the Dale Richmond Award from the American Academy of Pediatrics for her "outstanding contributions to the field of child development."

In 1963, I worked for a time at a mental hospital in Washington state. Although the psychiatrist and psychologist in charge were men, 90 percent of the rest of the staff, from the lowest-paid attendant counselors to the more highly trained occupational therapists and researchers, were women. Despite our different pasts and trajectories—some of us going on to college,

1

some likely to work at the hospital for life; some young and unmarried, others older women with children in school—we exchanged confidences that now seem rare among people of such different racial, class, and age backgrounds. What bridged the gap between us was our sense that we all shared, or would share, a common life course—a predictable pattern in which women fell in love, got married, had sex, and bore children. Sometimes, granted, they had sex first, but they eventually married; if they did not, any children that resulted were adopted into a family that had proceeded in the accepted manner. Marriage, after all, was central to everyone's establishment of adult status and identity, and since we were women, marriage and childrearing would occupy the bulk of our active adult lives.

Jeri,* the physical therapist, married since 1951, had three children. She 2 had gone "all the way" with her future husband while in college, a fact he often threw up to her when they argued over whether she could bring friends home from work. Sue, who dropped out of high school in 1952 to get married, had a similar sexual and marital history, though her fights with her husband were usually triggered by his infidelities. Sherry and Gwen had had sex with a couple of other men before their marriages in the late 1950s, but they would never admit this to their husbands. Camilla had been a virgin at marriage in 1961, and she now regretted it. Carol and Willie Lee did not expect to be virgins when they married and claimed they would never put up with Jeri's husband's attitudes, but they did think I was too "young and innocent" to hang out with Annette, the "wild" one in the bunch. Still single at twenty-four, she had a tendency to develop huge crushes on men who stood out from the crowd in any way, from hospital administrators to the lead singer in the band at the local bar. If the only way she could spend some time with them was in a one-night stand, so be it. Annette was hardly permissive, however. She joined the older women in condemning the counselor who had gotten pregnant a few years earlier, put her baby up for adoption, and come back "pretending nothing had happened."

In 1983, I went to a twenty-year reunion of people who had worked in 3 our ward. Many of the older women still worked there, although half were divorced and one had died. Of the younger ones, almost a quarter remained unmarried, two with children out of wedlock; another quarter had been divorced at least once. Annette, after admitting to herself that she had never been sexually attracted to men anyway, had finally settled down in a monogamous, long-term relationship: She and an older divorced woman had been together for eleven years. Willie Lee's husband had had a vasectomy in his previous marriage, so they were trying to adopt a baby.

*I have changed the names of these women for obvious reasons.

The breakdown of the expectations of these women was not excep-   4
tional, nor was it caused by willful abandonment of traditional family roles
and values. None of the women I spoke with was quite sure how she got
where she was today. Yet even those who had experienced the most pain in
their transitions saw no way of going back to older patterns, either for
themselves or for their children.

The breakdown of the tight links and orderly progression we had once as-   5
sumed to exist between marriage, sex, reproduction, and childrearing provides
compelling evidence for those who contend that a "revolution" has occurred
in family life. Marriage, for example, is no longer the major transition into
adulthood. The average age for marriage has risen by six years since 1950.
More than three-quarters of today's eighteen- to twenty-four-year-old men and
women have never married, and the majority of young adults today leave their
parental homes and establish themselves in jobs well before marriage. Marriage also is less likely to last until death. About 50 percent of first marriages,
and 60 percent of second ones, can be expected to end in divorce. In 1988, sixteen out of every thousand children under age eighteen saw their parents divorce, down from nineteen in 1980, but still twice as many as in 1963. As a
result of both the rising age for marriage and the frequency of divorce, men
and women spend, on average, more than half their lives unmarried.[1]

Men and women also live more of their lives alone. Despite recent in-   6
creases in the number of grown children who live with one or both of their
parents, the number of single-person households has risen dramatically. Almost four times as many Americans between the ages of thirty-five and
forty-four live alone today as did so in 1970.[2]

Childrearing is no longer as tightly linked to marriage as in the past.   7
Approximately three-quarters of a million unmarried couples in America
are raising children together. In 1990, a quarter of all new births were out
of wedlock; in half of them, there was no identified father. Since parenthood has ceased to inhibit divorce the way it did as late as 1970, more than
half of American children will live in a single-parent household for some
period during their childhood.[3]

Sex is far more likely to occur outside of marriage than at any time during   8
recent history. By the mid-1980s, 75 percent of American women were sexually
active before marriage. There are 2.9 million cohabitating couples in America
today, an increase of 80 percent since 1980. People also are initiating sex at an
earlier age. The percentage of women aged fifteen to nineteen who had had sexual intercourse at least once increased by one-third between 1971 and 1979.[4]

The separation of sex, marriage, and childrearing is most dramatically   9
demonstrated in the new legal and social definitions of family that have
emerged over the past two decades. Many states and cities have adopted

"domestic partner" laws, allowing unmarried heterosexual or homosexual couples certain privileges that used to be accorded only to traditional married couples. In 1989, New York's highest court ruled that the surviving member of a gay couple held the same legal rights to the apartment they had shared as would a surviving wife or husband—the relationship had been exclusive, long-lasting, committed, self-sacrificing, and public enough to qualify as a family.[5]

There are more than two million gay mothers and fathers in America. 10 Although most of their children come from earlier heterosexual relationships, up to 10,000 lesbians have borne children through sperm donations or other such procedures, and many gay and lesbian couples have won the right to adopt children.[6]

Compared to the first sixty years of the twentieth century, then, there is now 11 an increasing diversity of family types in America. The male-breadwinner family no longer provides the central experience for the vast majority of children, but it has not been replaced by any new modal category: Most Americans move in and out of a variety of family types over the course of their lives—families headed by a divorced parent, couples raising children out of wedlock, two-earner families, same-sex couples, families with no spouse in the labor force, blended families, and empty-nest families.[7]

Something Old . . .

Throughout most of this book, I have emphasized that many recent innova- 12 tions in family behaviors have deep roots in our past, and many so-called traditional norms never really existed. It would be easy, from one perspective, to organize this chapter along the same lines. None of these changes, taken by itself, is unprecedented or qualitatively new. While comparisons between 1960 and 1990 show enormous discontinuities in patterns of marriage, sex, and reproduction, 1960 represented the end year of a very deviant decade.

Today's diversity of family forms, rates of premarital pregnancy, pro- 13 ductive labor of wives, and prevalence of blended families, for example, would all look much more familiar to colonial Americans than would 1950s patterns. The age of marriage today is no higher than it was in the 1870s, and the proportion of never-married people is lower than it was at the turn of the century. Although fertility has decreased overall, the actual rate of childlessness is lower today than it was at the turn of the century; a growing proportion of women have at least one child during their lifetime. Many statistics purporting to show the eclipse of traditional families in recent years fail to take into account our longer life spans and lower mortality rates. As one author asks: "Are an eighty-year-old husband and wife really to be counted as 'nontraditional' just because they've lived long enough to see all their children leave home?" Even though marriages today are more likely to be interrupted by divorce than in former times, they are much less likely to be interrupted by death, so that about the same number of children spend their youth in single-parent households today as at the turn of the century, and fewer live with neither parent.[8]

The 1960s generation did not invent premarital and out-of-wedlock 14 sex. Indeed, the straitlaced sexual morality of nineteenth-century Anglo-American societies, partly revived in the 1950s, seems to have been a historical and cultural aberration. Anthropologist George Murdock examined cultural rules concerning sexual behavior in 250 societies and found that only 3 shared our "generalized sex taboo" on sexual behavior of any type outside marriage. Nor is there evidence that homosexual or lesbian activity is more frequent now than it was in the past; the claim that increased toleration of such activity portends reproductive doom does not mesh with the fact that two-thirds of the historical societies for which evidence is available have condoned homosexual relations.[9]

America's Founding Fathers were not always married: In Concord, Mass- 15 achusetts, a bastion of Puritan tradition, one-third of all children born during the twenty years prior to the American Revolution were conceived out of wedlock; during the 1780s and 1790s, one-third of the brides in rural New England were pregnant at marriage. A study of illegitimacy in North Carolina found that out-of-wedlock birth rates for white women were approximately the same in 1850 as in 1970, though the pattern was more indicative of class exploitation than it is today: The fathers tended to be well-off heads of intact families, while the mothers lived in poor, female-headed households.[10]

In nineteenth-century America, the "age of consent" for girls in many 16 states was as low as nine or ten, which rather makes a mockery of the term. What one author calls "the myth of an abstinent past" stems in part from lower fecundity and higher fetal mortality in previous times, making early sexual activity less likely to end up in pregnancy or birth. The proportion of fecund fifteen-year-old girls in America increased by 31 percent between 1940 and 1968 alone. In 1870, only 13 percent of European girls were fully fecund at age 17.5, compared to 94 percent of American girls the same age today.[11]

It is also estimated that there was one abortion for every five live births 17 during the 1850s, and perhaps as many as one for every three in 1870. Although abortion and birth control were criminalized in the 1880s, and the age of consent for girls was raised, the triumph of the "purity" movement was short-lived. America experienced a sexual revolution in the 1920s that was every bit as scandalous to contemporaries as that of the past few decades.[12]

Even the 1950s were hardly asexual. My modern students, who accept 18 premarital sex between affectionate partners quite matter-of-factly, are profoundly shocked when they read about panty raids and the groups of college boys who sometimes roamed through a campus chanting, "We want girls! We want sex!" Much of the modern sexual revolution, indeed, consists merely of a decline in the double standard, with girls adopting sexual behaviors that were pioneered much earlier by boys. This has led to a remarkable decrease in at least one form of extramarital sexual activity: Prostitution is far less widespread than it was in the nineteenth century, when New York City contained one prostitute for every sixty-four men and the mayor of Savannah estimated his city to have one for every thirty-nine men.[13]

And Something New . . .

I do not, however, want to make a case that nothing has changed. Taken to- 19
gether, the rearrangements in marriage, childrearing, intergenerational relations and responsibilities, sexuality, and reproduction have been tremendous, far-reaching, and unprecedented. For many cultural conservatives, the framework that best describes and explains these changes is summed up in the words permissiveness and self-indulgence. For cultural liberals, less pejorative terms reflect an equally linear view of change: New family patterns are the result of pluralism, increased tolerance, and the growth of informed choice. I will argue that neither the notion of "permissiveness" nor that of "enlightenment" captures the complexity and breadth of the demographic and attitudinal changes we have experienced. To assess the opportunities and problems posed by these changes, we must accurately describe the full range of the new social and demographic territory through which modern men, women, and children are required to make their way.

The Changing Role of Marriage and Childrearing in the Life Course

Perhaps the most visible rearrangement of family terrain is that both mar- 20
riage and childrearing occupy a smaller proportion of adults' lives than they did at any time in American history. They define less of a person's social identity, exert less influence on people's lifecourse decisions, and are less universal, exclusive, and predictable than ever before. (The one seeming exception to the declining salience of marriage—that divorce is now a stronger predictor of poverty for women and children than any other factor—is true only in the short run. Even in the short run, the causative role of divorce and illegitimacy in poverty has been greatly overstated. . . .)

A white woman can now expect, on the average, to spend only 43 per- 21
cent of her life in marriage, while a black woman can expect marriage to occupy only 22 percent of her life. Marriage has ceased to be the main impetus into or out of other statuses, and it increasingly coexists for women, as it has long done for men, with several other roles. The orderly progression

from student to single jobholder to wife to mother to married older worker that prevailed from the 1920s to the 1960s, for example, is now gone. Modern women take on these functions in different orders or occupy all of them at once. In 1967, half of all women in their thirties were married mothers who remained at home full-time; by 1982, only a quarter of all women in their thirties could be found specializing in this way.[14]

Despite the high value that Americans continue to attach to marriage and   22 family, there is a new tolerance for alternative life courses. In 1957, 80 percent of Americans polled said that people who chose not to marry were "sick," "neurotic," and "immoral." By 1977, only 25 percent of those polled held such views. In 1962, the overwhelming majority of mothers believed that "almost everyone should have children if they can"; by 1985, only a minority agreed. Most women still want children but feel less pressure to get married first. A national survey conducted in 1989 found that 36 percent of the single women polled had seriously considered raising a child on their own.[15]

Parenthood, like marriage, is a less salient, central, and long-lasting part   23 of life than it used to be. Parents are having fewer children than they had in most decades of American history and are spacing them somewhat closer. At the beginning of this century, most women saw their last child married when they were fifty-six and then lived, on average, only ten or fifteen years longer. Today, despite the "boomerang" child phenomenon, the average woman has forty years to live after her children leave home. A couple who stays together after their kids depart faces more than a third of a century with no other company in the household besides each other, compared to the short time of child-free years experienced by couples in previous centuries. Men, who are more likely to let their contact with children lapse after a divorce, live an even greater proportion of their lives today without involvement in childrearing. In 1960, men aged twenty to forty-nine spent an average of 12.3 years in families with children under age eighteen; by 1990, that had fallen to 7 years.[16]

This decline in the centrality of marriage and parenthood for adults has   24 been building for 150 years, with only a partial and temporary interruption during the 1950s. Changes in the life course of American youth, less linear, appear especially dramatic because the first sixty years of the twentieth century saw an increase in the centrality of family formation for young people and in the predictability of patterns of schooling, work, marriage, and parenthood.

Notes

[1]U.S. Department of Health and Human Services, National Center for Health Statistics, *Monthly Vital Statistics Report 39* (May 1991); *Wall Street Journal,* 20 February 1990, p. B1; *Wall Street Journal,* 31 May 1990, p. B1; *Seattle Weekly,* 17 October 1990, p. 12; Gannett News Service release, 4

February 1991; *Newsweek Special Issue,* Winter/Spring 1990; Frank Mac-
chiarola and Alan Gartner, eds., *Caring for American Children* (New York:
Academy of Political Science, 1989), pp. 4–19; Sylvia Hewlett, *When the
Bough Breaks: The Cost of Neglecting Our Children* (New York: Basic
Books, 1991), p. 12; Nicholas Zill and Carolyn Rogers, "Recent Trends in
the Wellbeing of Children in the United States and Their Implications for
Public Policy," in *The Changing American Family and Public Policy,* ed.
Andrew Cherlin (Washington, D.C.: Urban Institute Press, 1988), p. 39.

[2]William Chafe, *The Paradox of Change: American Women in the 20th Century* (New York: Oxford University Press, 1991), pp. 220–22; *New York
Times,* 7 June 1991, p. A18.

[3]Dept. of Health and Human Services, *Monthly Vital Statistics Report 39;
The Olympian,* 26 September 1991; *New York Times,* 30 January 1991;
New York Times, 14 March 1991; *Seattle Times,* 26 September 1991,
p. A12; *Los Angeles Times,* 23 March 1992, p. A3.

[4]Elise Jones et al., *Teenage Pregnancy in Industrialized Countries* (New
Haven: Yale University Press, 1986), pp. 37–66; Macchiarola and Gartner,
Caring for American Children, pp. 14–19; *Los Angeles Times,* 23 March
1992, p. A3. See also note 15.

[5]*New York Times,* 31 August 1989, pp. C1 and C6; "The 21st Century Family," *Newsweek,* Winter/Spring 1990, p. 38; *U.S. News & World Report,* 21
August 1989, p. 13.

[6]"The 21st Century Family," p. 39; *New York Times,* 4 July 1990, pp. 1, 10.

[7]Howard Hughes, "Family Members in the Work Force," *Monthly Labor
Review,* March 1990, p. 14.

[8]Warren Sanderson, "Below-Replacement Fertility in Nineteenth-Century
America," *Population and Development Review 13* (1987); Stewart Tolnay
and Avery Guest, "Childlessness in a Transitional Population: The United
States at the Turn of the Century," *Journal of Family History 7* (1982); Heidi
Hartmann, *Demographic and Economic Trends: Implications for Family
Life and Public Policy* (Paper prepared for the American Council on Educa-
tion, Women Presidents' Summit, Institute for Women's Policy Research,
Washington, D.C., 5–7 December 1990), p. 9; Vivian Fox and Martin Quitt,
*Loving, Parenting and Dying: The Family Cycle in England and America,
Past and Present* (New York: Psychohistory Press, 1980), p. 33; Kain, *Myth
of Family Decline,* p. 37; Dorrian Sweetser, "Broken Homes: Stable Risk,
Changing Reasons, Changing Forms," *Journal of Marriage and the Family*
(August 1985); Ben Wattenberg, *The Good News Is the Bad News Is Wrong*
(New York: Simon & Schuster, 1985), pp. 283–84.

[9]Kain, *Myth of Family Decline*, p. 127; John Gillis, "From Ritual to Romance: Toward an Alternative History of Love," in *Emotion and Social Change: Toward a New Psychohistory,* ed. Carol and Peter Stearns (New York: Holmes and Meier, 1988), p. 94; Martin Duberman, Martha Vicinus, and George Chauncey, eds., *Hidden from History: Reclaiming the Gay and Lesbian Past* (New York: NAL Books, 1989), p. 10; David Greenberg, *The Construction of Homosexuality* (Chicago: University of Chicago Press, 1988).

[10]Sar Levitan, *What's Happening to the American Family?* (Baltimore: Johns Hopkins University Press, 1981), p. 66; Jack Larkin, *The Reshaping of Everyday Life, 1790–1840* (New York: Harper & Row, 1988); Susan Newcomer, "Out of Wedlock Childbearing in an Ante-Bellum Southern County," *Journal of Family History 15* (1990).

[11]Phillips Cutwright, "The Teenage Sexual Revolution and the Myth of an Abstinent Past," *Family Planning Perspectives 4* (1972): 24, 26; Jane Lancaster and Beatrix Hamburg, eds., *Schoolage Pregnancy and Parenthood: Biosocial Dimensions* (New York: Aldine, 1986).

[12]Howard Bahr, "Changes in Family Life in Middletown, 1924–77," *Public Opinion Quarterly 44* (1980); James Mohr, *Abortion in America: The Origins and Evolution of National Policy, 1800–1900* (New York: Oxford University Press, 1978); Kain, *Myth of Family Decline*, p. 121; Ellen Dubois and Linda Gordon, "Seeking Ecstasy on the Battlefield: Danger and Pleasure in Nineteenth-Century Feminist Sexual Thought," *Feminist Studies 9* (1973): 15.

[13]Beth Bailey, *Sexual Containment* (Paper given at "Ike's America, a conference on the Eisenhower Presidency and American Life in the 1950s," University of Kansas, Lawrence, 4–6 October 1990), p. 2; John D'Emilio and Estelle Freedman, *Intimate Matters: A History of Sexuality in America* (New York: Harper & Row, 1988), pp. 65, 133–34.

[14]Heidi Hartmann, "Changes in Women's Economic and Family Roles in Post–World War II United States," in *Women, Households, and the Economy,* ed. Lourdes Beneria and Catharine Stimpson (New Brunswick: Rutgers University Press, 1987), p. 37; Kingsley Davis, "The Future of Marriage," in *Contemporary Marriage: Comparative Perspectives on a Changing Institution,* ed. Kingsley Davis (New York: Russell Sage, 1986); Judith Blake, "Structural Differentiation and the Family: A Quiet Revolution," in *Societal Growth: Processes and Implications,* ed. Amos Hawley (New York: Free Press, 1979); Steven McLaughlin et al., *The Changing Lives of American Women* (Chapel Hill: University of North Carolina Press, 1988), pp. 5, 45, 188–89, 198–99.

[15]McLaughlin et al., *Changing Lives,* p. 188; Doug Honig, "Altered States," *Pacific Northwest,* May 1987, p. 33; *The Olympian,* 29 May 1989.

[16]Robert Wells, "Demographic Change and the Life Cycle of American Families," in *The Family in History: Interdisciplinary Essays,* ed. Theodore Rabb and Robert Torberg (New York: Harper & Row, 1973); Hewlett, *When the Bough Breaks,* p. 12; *Washington Post,* 16 December 1990; Kain, *Myth of Family Decline,* pp. 72–73; Philip Elmer-Dewitt, "The Great Experiment," *Time,* Fall 1990, p. 75.

Thinking Critically

1. In 1963 what expectations did Stephanie Coontz's female colleagues have about the trajectory of their lives? Twenty years later, how had those expectations played out? How does Coontz use the examples of these women to make a larger argument?

2. What words does Coontz use to describe the decade *ending* with 1960? In what sense does she use these words, and what are their additional connotations?

3. What are some of the key arguments that Coontz makes, as a social scientist, about the interpretations of statistics that show the "eclipse of traditional families"?

Writing Critically

1. Select one aspect of American family life that Coontz addresses in this essay. In her view, what is it about that issue that has been used or misinterpreted in a political fashion? What is the source of the evidence that she cites to refute that interpretation? In an analytical essay, select one of the family-based issues described by another writer in Chapter 4. According to the evidence Coontz offers, how "traditional" or "nontraditional" is this particular family issue? Be sure to consult Coontz's original sources for her data, listed in the endnotes for this essay.

2. What does the word *traditional* mean in the context of American political discourse? What values and lifestyles are considered "traditional"? Is there an argument to be made that one of the American cultural divides is based on a distinction between "traditional" and "nontraditional" values? In your essay, be sure to distinguish between what other writers label "traditional" or "nontraditional" and the way you yourself define the terms for the purposes of *your* argument.

3. In a research paper, examine how some of the traditional or nontraditional values described by Coontz have been represented in American popular culture. Possible topics include the Hays Code; the "purity" movement of 1886–1914; the "housewife" in television sitcoms of the 1950s; a comparison of marriage announcements in a major newspaper such as the *New York Times* in 1955 and in 2005.

Suffering the Pornographers

JOHN LELAND | *New York Times* reporter and cultural critic John Leland is the author of *Hip: The History* (2004), a former columnist at *SPIN* magazine, and editor-in-chief of *Details* magazine. *Village Voice* called him "the best American postmod critic (the best new American rock critic period)." A *Village Voice* review by Leland of the rap group Public Enemy's first album so annoyed rapper Chuck D. that the nastier parts of a later Public Enemy track, "Bring the Noise," are about Leland. In an interview about *Hip: The History*, Leland notes that "Hip forces change on the culture, freeing us from the stasis we try to create for ourselves. So hip is the onrush of intelligence that comes from new ideas and desires, not simply the latest cool products." "Suffering the Pornographers," which appeared in the *New York Times* in October 2004, is a good example of the kind of cultural change and clash of marketing cool and genuine inspiration that Leland chronicles.

RIVERSIDE, Calif.

Craig Gross and Mike Foster, two young pastors from California, were 1 looking for direction when one day in 2001, Mr. Foster said, God came to him in the shower and said one word: "Pornography." Mr. Foster, 33, said he did not often get such visits, and so he treated it as a divine calling. Since it came with no further instructions, the two reasoned that it was up to them to figure out what to do next.

And so it came to be that on a Sunday afternoon three years later, 2 Mr. Gross, 28, and Mr. Foster were tooling around a mall parking lot here in a black Scion xB festooned with ads declaring, "XXXChurch.com: The No. 1 Christian Porn Site." An air freshener with an image of Jesus dangled above the dash.

"You can see people checking us out," Mr. Gross said. 3

For Mr. Gross and Mr. Foster, who sometimes refer to themselves as "the 4 goofballs," it was just another day of 21st century ministry, combining technology, self-promotion, sensationalism and humor to address what they see as an equally up-to-date scourge on modern society: Internet pornography. Their approach bears little resemblance to what most people think of as church.

The two started their online ministry, XXXChurch.com, shortly after 5 Mr. Foster's experience in the shower. Instead of posting Scripture online, they flashed, "Porn. Sex. Girls. Guys," in order to reach the people who wanted to

see pornography, not ban it. Once the curious visit the site, they can download
a free computer program called X3watch, one of several "accountability" programs designed for people who want to stop looking at Internet pornography
but cannot do so on their own. Whenever a user visits a pornographic Web
site, the program alerts his or her designated "accountability partner."

So far, Mr. Gross and Mr. Foster said, 100,000 people have down- 6
loaded X3watch, including all of the pastors at the church Mr. Gross at-
tends. In his own case, his wife gets a list of every site he visits.

"Filters don't work," Mr. Gross said, speaking of programs that block 7
Internet pornography. "Kids are smarter than that. Filters don't bring up
conversation. A filter avoids the topic. Accountability forces you and another person to talk about what you're looking at. That's hard. We would
have more downloads if it was a filter."

Mr. Gross and Mr. Foster have also set up booths at pornography trade 8
shows and handed out postcards that said, "Jesus Loves Porn Stars." They
joined with a pornography director to produce a public service announcement aimed at keeping the materials away from children.

Then there is the Porn Mobile. 9

As a couple approached the car at the mall, demanding an explanation, 10
Mr. Gross took the lead. He had studs in both ears, and surfer bangs with
streaked highlights.

"We're pastors," he said. "We're trying to get people to talk about the 11
issue of pornography."

"Awesome," said the woman, Cindy Mosher, 40, who said she had just 12
come from church. "My previous husband was involved in porn, and that
was one factor that destroyed our marriage."

"I'm in marketing, and you have to go for extremes," Ms. Mosher 13
added. "Christian churches are quite traditional. To bring people in, maybe
we have to go to extremes."

Internet pornography is one of the vexing issues for churches today, es- 14
pecially those that take strict moral lines on sexuality. Some consider viewing pornography a form of adultery; others decry erotic images as addictive
and destructive to marriage.

Pastors, like school officials, often face severe punishment if they are 15
found to have looked at Internet pornography. In 2000 *Christianity Today*
magazine surveyed its readers (anonymously) and found that more than a
third of the pastors who responded said they viewed pornographic Web
sites, a number only slightly lower than their parishioners.

Even this figure is low, said Archibald D. Hart, a senior professor of psy- 16
chology at Fuller Theological Seminary in Pasadena, Calif. "I do conferences
for 3,000 pastors a year, and this is a biggie wherever I go," Mr. Hart said.

In response, churches and lay Christians have created a circuit of "sex-   17
ual addiction" seminars, 12-step programs and even residential treatment
centers, modeled on drug or alcohol detox centers, where people can stay
for months at a time. Most address pornography as psychologically damaging rather than as a sin, Mr. Hart said.

Mr. Hart, who surveyed pastors for his 1995 book, *The Sexual Man,*   18
said that most pastors and church members used Internet pornography at
one time or another.

"In some of the more conservative denominations it is silent, it's a se-   19
cret, no one talks about it," he said. "And those pastors are frankly in denial about the impact of pornography."

For Mr. Foster and Mr. Gross, who were both involved with conserva-   20
tive churches, the issue called for a generational break: not condemning
pornography from on high, but forming relationships with both the producers and its consumers, including pastors.

Neither draws a salary from XXXChurch.com. Mr. Foster is also the com-   21
munications pastor at Crossroads Christian Church, a nondenominational

Craig Gross and Mike Foster, founders of online ministry XXXchurch.com, with their Porn Mobile.

church in Corona, Calif. Mr. Gross speaks to Christian youth groups around the country as a founding partner in Fireproof Ministries, a non-denominational youth ministry.

Their unorthodox calling is the subject of *Missionary Positions,* a doc- 22 umentary film made by Bill Day, a secular filmmaker. The documentary is rated R and includes profanity and suggestions of nudity.

On an autumn afternoon in Los Angeles, Mr. Gross and Mr. Foster at- 23 tended a screening of the film, along with an audience that included James DiGiorgio, the pornographer who directed their public service announcement, and Ryan Dobson, the son of James Dobson, founder of the conservative Christian group Focus on the Family.

"The church has gotten prissy in not going to the porn conventions," 24 said the younger Mr. Dobson, 34, who runs a ministry for surfers and skateboarders. "God bless Craig and Mike for doing it. I don't want to do it."

"I loved the movie today," he added. "I wouldn't play it in my church. 25 But if you beeped out the swear words and covered up some of the nudity, I'd totally play it in my church." He said that the senior pastor at his church uses X3watch software and talks about it from the pulpit.

"He talks about his struggle with pornography," Mr. Dobson said. "He 26 says, 'I have X3watch on my computer, and my wife is one of my accountability partners. Why? Because I struggle. And I know people out there struggle as well.' I flock to a guy like that, because he's honest about it. We struggle together."

Mr. DiGiorgio, whose films include *Bodyshop Girls* and *Punished in* 27 *Plaid,* and who works under the name Jimmy D, took a different view of his unlikely collaborators. He appreciated that they did not preach at him, as other ministers had, he said. But mainly he liked their nose for publicity.

"These guys are like guerrilla marketers, they recognized right away 28 that a controversial relationship would spark interest in the media," he said. "They saw it as I saw it."

In the movie Mr. DiGiorgio is seen filming a sexual act that he says he 29 finds repugnant. But of his collaboration with Mr. Gross and Mr. Foster, he said: "I didn't do it for any kind of Christian value. I respect their faith, and so far they've respected my lack of it. I'm the first guy to admit that I'm sometimes conflicted about what I do. I've expressed that to them. But have they tried to minister to me? No, not really."

To Mr. Foster and Mr. Gross, their relationship with Mr. DiGiorgio, 30 like their attendance at pornography events, gives them leverage to address the people scared away by church. "If Jesus were around today," Mr. Gross said, "he would be at porn shows. But most Christians would rather preach to Jimmy D, and if he doesn't accept Christ, move on to the next person. And you might reach more people, but Jesus worked with 12 people."

In the mall parking lot, Lana Olsen, 54, said she did not appreciate the 31 shock tactics. "To me that is crossing the line," she said of the car. "I decided this was a porn person trying to make fun of the church. My son, an atheist, would think that's the enemy's greatest tool."

But Andy Allman, 19, who worked in the mall Starbucks, liked the car. 32 "You guys are anti-porn, right?" he asked. When Mr. Gross explained that they were pastors, Mr. Allman, was interested. "Really?" he said. "Because I've been looking for a church. Can you recommend one?"

Thinking Critically

1. No, this isn't a parody. But if you didn't know that this article appeared in the *New York Times,* would anything about it seem suspicious to you? Explain your answer.

2. What kinds of material details does John Leland use in this report? What additional information or subtext do these details provide?

3. What is Leland's implied argument about the relationship between ministry and marketing?

Writing Critically

1. Why are the most private and intimate aspects of our lives so subject to civic and religious scrutiny? Why are the private lives of public figures, from actors and models to senators and presidents, so salaciously served up as moralizing entertainment?

2. What is the function of X3watch? Several of the essayists in Chapter 11, including Deborah Pearlstein (see pp. 630–35), Adam Gopnik (pp. 640–48) and David Cole (pp. 649–62), discuss ways in which the monitoring of personal communications and private life is becoming a national security issue. The users of X3watch voluntarily install the program on their computer; many Americans voluntarily or implicitly (by the way they vote) support the federal communications monitoring permitted by the Patriot Act. Is spying on a family member a legitimate way to maintain "safety" and security within a family? Is it a legitimate way to maintain "homeland security"?

3. Does a religious faith need to market itself? Does a corporation need to create a sense of community and "faithfulness" to ensure consumer loyalty? Consider "cult" brands such as Apple, Coca-Cola, or Nike, or mission-driven companies such as The Body Shop or Whole Foods.

Arguing the Cultural Divides

1. In a research paper, discuss the origins of the political catchphrase "family values." What has this phrase come to represent? Who uses it? Are its supporters blue-staters or red-staters? Draw from the essays in this chapter to closely examine what both "family" and "values" mean in contemporary American society. Finally, read George Orwell's 1946 essay "Politics and the English Language," which is available online at <http://eserver.org/langs/politics-english-language.txt. What would Orwell have to say about the term "family values" and its function in contemporary political discourse?

2. Choose two first-person essays from this chapter or elsewhere in the book (or another first-person account approved by your instructor) that in *your* opinion exemplify a "family value." If you believe there never has been such a thing as the "traditional" American family portrayed on *Leave It to Beaver,* do you think talk of "family values" unfairly excludes groups of people from an ideal America? Should your personal choices and family circumstances leave you open to societal condemnation? Should personal choices that seem harmful or destructive be tolerated as "nontraditional" choices? If, as Hillary Rodham Clinton famously said, "It takes a village to raise a child," should the village have set standards and "values" to which everyone needs to conform?

Getting and Spending: Shopping, Working, and Values

Migrants No More

MAGGIE JONES

Maggie Jones, a Los Angeles–based journalist, writes about social, health, and women's issues. She is a frequent contributor to *Mother Jones,* where "Migrants No More" appeared in the November/December 2004 issue; her articles have also appeared in the *New York Times Magazine,* the *Washington Post, Salon.com, Mirabella,* and the *Philadelphia Inquirer Magazine.* In 1997, Jones was a finalist for a National Magazine Award and received the Exceptional Merit Media Award for feature writing from Radcliffe College and the National Women's Political Caucus. Jones wrote "Migrants No More" while on a journalism fellowship in child and family policy from the University of Maryland. In 2001, as a Fellow at the Pew International Journalism Program, Jones reported on women's and children's issues in Thailand. A former contributing editor for *Glamour* magazine, she received an EMMA (Exceptional Merit Media Award) from the National Women's Political Caucus and Radcliffe College for feature writing. *Mother Jones* magazine, founded in 1976, is committed to promoting social justice through in-depth

> investigative journalism. The magazine won the 2001 Na-
> tional Magazine Award in General Excellence and was
> nominated for National Magazine Awards nine times
> (winning four times). The magazine is named for Mary
> Harris "Mother" Jones, an elderly widowed Irish immi-
> grant who in the early twentieth century transformed her-
> self into a leading activist for working people. For more
> on Mother Jones—the woman, the magazine, and the
> website—go to <http://motherjones.org/index.html>.

I t is night when the day begins.   1

At 4:30 A.M. in a dusty farming town in California's San Joaquin Valley,   2
the lights are on in a one-room house no bigger than a garage. Inside, Isabel
makes tortillas and beans for the workday ahead, while her husband, Vicente,
puts on his farmworker's uniform of long pants, long-sleeved shirt, work
boots, and a baseball cap. Much of the town of Arvin is awake by now: The
local *panaderias*—Mexican bakeries—open at 5 A.M., as do the small markets
where farmworkers buy gas and pick up coffee before heading to the fields.

By 5:40, Isabel and Vicente have joined a caravan of more than 40 cars,   3
vans, and pickup trucks, with their lights on, rolling past acres of grapes,
potatoes, and onions. The road turns from potholed concrete to sand before dead-ending at a line of cherry trees that seems to stretch for miles. As
some 200 farmworkers, in groups of three and four and five, walk down a
dirt path into the fields, Isabel secures the shield of bandannas she wears
to protect her skin from the sun and dust: One ties around the top of her
head while the second falls down the back of her neck, like a tent flap. The
third is fastened bandit-style, high and tight over her nose and mouth.

Vicente will spend the day on a 12-foot ladder, pulling bunches of cher-   4
ries from the tops of the trees, while Isabel twists the fruit off the branches
below. Over the next seven hours, with one 15-minute break, Vicente will
pick more than 100 pounds of cherries, dumping them into deep trays har-
nessed to his shoulders. His pay will depend on how quickly he can fill the
trays. No matter how fast he works, it's often less than minimum wage.

It wasn't supposed to be this way. John Steinbeck's *The Grapes of*   5
Wrath, which portrayed the struggles of Okie migrants at Weedpatch
Camp just a few miles from Arvin, drew national attention to the plight of
California farmworkers in the 1930s. In the '60s, Cesar Chavez and the
United Farm Workers made the problems of the fields a part of dinner-table
conversations nationwide. But though some union victories of the 1970s
remain in place, conditions for farmworkers have grown more bleak in the

past two decades. Real farm wages have fallen a full 10 percent since the '80s; in 1998, when the most recent survey was conducted, the average field worker made $7,500 a year and had no health insurance or other benefits.

Vicente is 30 years old, short and strong, with a small mustache, a straight-ahead gaze, and a kind, slightly reserved manner; like the other farmworkers interviewed for this story, he didn't want his last name used. For 14 years, he has worked blueberries, cherries, grapes, oranges, watermelons, and onions. A scar wraps around his left index finger from the time he cut it to the bone with pruning shears. His ankle bears another scar, from the day he stepped on a blade in the onion fields. One summer he slept atop a flattened cardboard box in a vineyard. Another year, he lived in a two-room house near Santa Barbara with about 50 other men—"lined up like pigs," he says with a small smile. For eight years, Vicente followed the migratory route that Mexicans have traveled since they first came to the California fields in the 1940s: He would enter the United States for the harvest and return to Oaxaca each winter to be with his family and build a house.

But that changed six years ago, when Vicente paid a coyote $1,200 and filled a backpack with gallon jugs of water, tortillas, canned beans, and two changes of clothes for himself and Isabel, who was 14 years old and five months pregnant. They left behind photos and mementos. ("If they catch you," Vicente says of the Border Patrol, "they'll take anything from you, even pennies.") Along with about 30 other migrants, Vicente and Isabel hiked across Arizona's Sonoran Desert for three nights, sleeping and hiding out during the day, when temperatures can reach 110 degrees.

The Sonoran Desert has been called "the cruelest place on earth." Last year, 409 immigrants died trying to get across—a sevenfold increase since 1995. Heightened border controls that began under the Clinton administration and escalated after 9/11 have effectively shut down migrant crossings near San Diego and El Paso, pushing migrants to ever more remote routes. Yet even now, with the Border Patrol's budget and manpower at an all-time high, about 800,000 undocumented immigrants arrive in the United States annually, up from 500,000 a decade ago, according to the Urban Institute in Washington, D.C. A full 60 percent of them come from Mexico.

Many of those immigrants, like Vicente and Isabel, have no plans to go home again. "In the last 10 years, the rate of return to Mexico has fallen through the floor," says Douglas S. Massey, codirector of the Mexican Migration Project at Princeton University. "The risk of crossing isn't high enough not to come at all, but it's made immigrants think twice about going back and forth." In 2000, only 1 in 10 undocumented immigrants returned to Mexico within a year, according to the Public Policy Institute of

6

7

8

9

California, a San Francisco think tank—almost 50 percent fewer than in 1992. In its effort to lock people out, the U.S. government has instead locked them in.

Initially, Vicente and Isabel did plan to return to Mexico, once they 10 saved enough money. But then they had children—a son, now five, and two daughters, ages four and three—and migrating home became too expensive (coyote fees have tripled, to more than $3,000 per person, since Vicente first crossed in the early 1990s) and too dangerous. The longer the family stayed in the United States, the less they wanted to leave.

Their story is like those of tens of thousands of farmworkers who once 11 shuttled between Mexico and the United States. Migrants have settled because of the tighter borders, because of a 1986 amnesty program that legalized 1.1 million farmworkers, and because of changes in agriculture: The fruits and vegetables consumers now demand—strawberries, lettuce, broccoli—are more labor-intensive than the rice and cotton that once dominated the fields. And new harvesting methods have allowed growers to plant multiple crops in succession, providing work in some places for nine months or more each year.

In California, the settling of farmworkers and the growth of immigrant 12 families have reshaped an entire landscape. The San Joaquin Valley—240 miles of the nation's richest farmland, stretching from Bakersfield in the south to Stockton in the north—has doubled in population, to 3.3 million, in the past three decades. Small farming towns that were largely Anglo for more than 100 years are now as much as 98 percent Latino, and bulging at the seams. In Arvin, where Vicente and Isabel live, the population has tripled in the last 30 years. Sixty miles farther north, the community of Lost Hills—overrun with dilapidated trailers and almond groves—has grown by a full 60 percent in just 10 years, becoming the most crowded community in all of California, with an average of 5.6 people in every home.

With the booming population of farmworkers has come a deep-seated 13 poverty. Observers have dubbed the Valley the "Appalachia of the West." Actually, the per capita income in Appalachia is $24,000, about 80 percent of the national average. In Arvin, whose statistics are typical of small farming towns in the region, the per capita income is less than $7,500.

Juan Vicente Palerm, an anthropologist at the University of California 14 at Santa Barbara who has surveyed 200 rural farmworker communities like Arvin, says it's important to realize that the towns are "not overgrown labor camps, like some people believe," but real communities where people are making their homes and putting down roots. Still, he warns, with more and more working families subsisting far below the poverty level, the San Joaquin Valley is becoming home to "a new rural underclass."

Thinking Critically

1. Why does Maggie Jones approach the plight of Mexican migrant workers by focusing on one family?

2. Go to the *Mother Jones* website at <http://motherjones.org/index.html>. What kinds of stories are reported by the magazine and the website? What is the mission of *Mother Jones*? How do Maggie Jones's (no relation to Mother Jones) subject and perspective meet the expectations of her *Mother Jones* audience?

3. What is Maggie Jones's purpose in writing this article? Do a search at the *Mother Jones* website for this article. What kinds of additional features and resources are offered at the online version of this article? What kinds of expectations does *Mother Jones* have of its readers?

Writing Critically

1. Do a database or online search for other articles by Maggie Jones, using the biographical details in the headnote to be sure that you're finding articles by the right person. How would you describe Maggie Jones's work as a reporter and journalist? Is it possible to combine a mission, or a profound political or ideological commitment, with objectivity? In an essay, describe Jones's approach in at least five or six articles (preferably from different magazines and newspapers). To enrich this assignment, compare her work on several subjects with mainstream news media coverage or with reporting from more conservative writers, journals, and magazines. What is the distinction between journalism and advocacy? Should there be a distinction?

2. Compare Vicente and Isabel's "family values" with those of the families (and politicians) described in Chapter 4. To what extent do Vicente and Isabel exemplify the political model of "family values"? Anything ironic about that?

3. Read, or reread, John Steinbeck's novel *The Grapes of Wrath* (1939). Why does Jones suggest a parallel between immigrant Mexican farmworkers and the "Okies" whom Steinbeck described in the 1930s?

Buyer's Remorse

DANIEL AKST

As a columnist for the *New York Times,* Daniel Akst explores the tangled relationships between money and culture. His financial journalism also appears in the *Los Angeles Times* and the *Wall Street Journal.* As a features writer for newspapers and magazines across the country, Akst writes observantly and often humorously about everything from the perils of home renovation to computer-generated fiction. In his

> nonfiction book *Wonder Boy,* Akst recounts the
> amazing story of a twenty-one-year-old California con
> man, Barry Minkow, who epitomized the greed of the
> 1980s. The magazine *BusinessWeek* called *Wonder Boy*
> one of the best books of 1990. "Buyer's Remorse"
> appeared in the Winter 2004 issue of *Wilson Quarterly,*
> a journal published by the Woodrow Wilson
> International Center for Scholars.

There are two things at which Americans have always excelled: One is gen-   1
erating almost unimaginable material wealth, and the other is feeling bad
about it. If guilt and materialism are two sides of a single very American coin,
it's a coin that has achieved new currency in recent years, as hand-wringing
and McMansions vie for our souls like the angels and devils who perch on the
shoulders of cartoon characters, urging them to be good or bad.

When Princeton University researchers asked working Americans   2
about these matters a decade ago, 89 percent of those surveyed agreed that
"our society is much too materialistic," and 74 percent said that materialism is a serious social problem. Since then, a good deal has been written
about materialism, and magazines such as *Real Simple* (filled with advertising) have sprung up to combat it. But few of us would argue that we've
become any less consumed with consuming; the latest magazine sensation,
after all, is *Lucky,* which dispenses with all the editorial folderol and devotes itself entirely to offering readers things they can buy.

The real question is, *Why* should we worry? Why be of two minds   3
about what we buy and how well we live? Most of us have earned what we
possess; we're not members of some hereditary landed gentry. Our material success isn't to blame for anyone else's poverty—and, on the contrary,
might even ameliorate it (even Third World sweatshops have this effect,
much as we might lament them). So how come we're so sheepish about possessions? Why do we need a class of professional worrywarts—a.k.a. the
intelligentsia—to warn us, from the stern pulpits of Cambridge, Berkeley,
and other bastions of higher education (and even higher real estate prices)
about the perils of consumerism run amok?

There are good reasons, to be sure. If we saved more, we could proba-   4
bly achieve faster economic growth. If we taxed ourselves more, we might
reduce income inequality. If we consumed less, our restraint might help the
environment (although the environment mostly has grown cleaner as
spending has increased). Then, too, there's a personal price to be paid for
affluence: Because we're so busy pursuing our individual fortunes, we endure a dizzying rate of change and weakened community and family ties.

There is merit in all these arguments, but while I know lots of people who are ambivalent about their own consumerism, hardly any seem to worry that their getting and spending is undermining the economy or pulling people off family farms. No, the real reason for our unease about possessions is that many of us, just like the makers of Hebrew National franks, still seem to answer to a higher power. We may not articulate it, but what really has us worried is how we think God wants us to behave.

And on that score, materialism was making people nervous long before there was an America. In the Bible, the love of money is said to be the root of all evil, and the rich man has as much of a shot at heaven as a camel has of passing through the eye of a needle. On the other hand, biblical characters who enjoy God's blessings have an awful lot of livestock, and other neat stuff as well. Though Job loses everything while God is testing him, he gets it all back when he passes the test. Perhaps even God is of two minds about materialism. Here on earth, however, traditional authorities have always insisted that materialism is a challenge not just to the social order but to the perfection of God's world. James B. Twitchell, a student of advertising and a cheerful iconoclast on materialism, has observed that sumptuary laws were once enforced by ecclesiastical courts "because luxury was defined as living above one's station, a form of insubordination against the concept of *copia*—the idea that God's world is already full and complete."

America represents the antithesis of that idea. Many of the earliest European settlers were motivated by religion, yet by their efforts they transformed the new land—God's country?—into a nation of insubordinates, determined not so much to live above their station as to refuse to acknowledge they even had one. Surely this is the place Joseph Schumpeter had in mind when he wrote of "creative destruction." America was soon enough a nation where money could buy social status, and American financial institutions pioneered such weapons of mass consumption as the credit card. Today, no other nation produces material wealth on quite the scale we do—and citizens of few other affluent countries are allowed to keep as much of their earnings. In America, I daresay, individuals have direct control of more spending per capita than in just about any other nation.

If affluence is a sign of grace, is it any wonder that Americans are more religious than most other modern peoples? Twitchell is right in observing that the roots of our ambivalence about materialism are essentially religious in nature. They can be traced all the way back to Yahweh's injunction against graven images, which might distract us from God or suggest by their insignificant dimensions some limits to his grandeur. Over the centuries the holiest among us, at least putatively, have been those who shunned material possessions and kept their eyes on some higher prize.

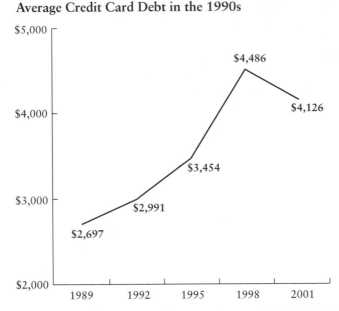

Average Credit Card Debt in the 1990s

Based on Demos's calculations from the Survey of Consumer Finances, 1989, 1992, 1995, 1998, and 2001.
Source: Demos: A Network for Ideas and Action.

Will that be cash or charge? Monthly balances on American credit cards almost doubled over a ten-year period. The economy boomed in the mid- and late 1990s, as technology stocks soared, but still people carried larger and larger balances from one month to the next.

From that elevated perspective, material goods, which are essentially transient, seem emblems of human vanity and gaudy memento mori. Unless you happen to be a pharaoh, you can't take it with you; there's a much better chance that your kids will have to get rid of it at a garage sale. Ultimately, our love-hate relationship with materialism reflects the tension between our age-old concern with the afterlife and our inevitable desire for pleasure and comfort in this one.

The Puritans wrestled this contradiction with characteristic intelligence   9
and verve, but our guilt about materialism is probably their legacy. They understood that there was nothing inherently evil in financial success, and much potential good, given how the money might be used. The same work ethic, Protestant or otherwise, powers the economy today. Americans take less time off than Europeans, for instance, and there is no tradition here of the idle rich. But the Puritans also believed that poverty made it easier to get close to God. Worldly goods "are veils set betwixt God and us," wrote the English Puritan Thomas Watson, who added: "How ready is [man] to terminate his happiness in externals."

Leland Ryken, a biblical scholar and professor of English at Wheaton   10
College who has written extensively about Christian attitudes toward
work and leisure, shrewdly observes that the Puritans regarded money as
a social good rather than a mere private possession: "The Puritan outlook
stemmed from a firm belief that people are stewards of what God has en-
trusted to them. Money is ultimately God's, not ours. In the words of the
influential Puritan book *A Godly Form of Household Government,* money
is 'that which God hath lent thee.'" So who are you to go buying a Jaguar
with that bonus check?

As if to dramatize Puritan ambivalence about wealth, New England   11
later produced a pair of influential nonconformists, Horatio Alger Jr.
(1832–99) and Henry David Thoreau (1817–62), whose work embodies
sharply contrasting visions of material wealth; for better or worse, we've
learned from both of them. Alger's many novels and stories offered an
ethical template for upward mobility, even as they gave him a sanitized outlet for his dangerous fantasies about young boys. Thoreau, meanwhile,
came to personify the strong disdain for materialism—what might be called
the sexual plumage of capitalism—that would later be expressed by commentators such as Thorstein Veblen and Juliet Schor.

Alger and Thoreau had much in common. Both were from Massachu-   12
setts, went to Harvard, and lived, in various ways, as outsiders. Their lives
overlapped for 30 years. Both struggled at times financially, and both apparently were homosexual.

The popular image of Thoreau is of the lone eccentric contemplating   13
nature at Walden Pond. In fact, he spent only two years and two months
there, and while he always preferred to be thinking and writing, he spent
much of his life improving his father's pencil business, surveying land, and
otherwise earning money. Of course, Thoreau scorned business as anything
more than a means to an end. His literary output, mostly ignored in his lifetime, won a wide audience over the years, in part, perhaps, because of the
triumph of the materialism he so reviled. Thoreau's instinctive disdain for
moneymaking, his natural asceticism and implicit environmentalism, his
embrace of civil disobedience, and his opposition to slavery all fit him well
for the role of patron saint of American intellectuals.

Alger's work, by contrast, is read by hardly anyone these days, and his   14
life was not as saintly as Thoreau's. When accusations of "unnatural" acts
with teenage boys—acts he did not deny—forced him from his pulpit in
Brewster, Massachusetts, the erstwhile Unitarian minister decamped for
New York City, where he became a professional writer. It was in venal New
York that he made his name with the kind of stories we associate with him
to this day: tales of unschooled but goodhearted lads whose spunk, industry,

and yes, good looks, win them material success, with the help of a little luck and their older male mentors. Alger's hackneyed parables are tales of the American dream, itself an accumulation of hopes that has always had a strongly materialistic component. The books themselves are now ignored, but their central fable has become part of our heritage. "Alger is to America," wrote the novelist Nathanael West, "what Homer was to the Greeks."

If Thoreau won the lofty battle of ideology, Alger won the war on the   15
ground. This tension is most clearly visible among our "opinion leaders," who identify far more easily with Thoreau than with, say, Ragged Dick. One reason may be that few writers and scholars seem to have Alger stories of their own. I rarely meet journalists or academics from poor or even working-class families, and even the movie business, built by hardscrabble immigrants from icy Eastern Europe, is run today by the children of Southern California sunshine and prosperity.

Hollywood aside, journalists, academics, and intellectuals have already   16
self-selected for anti-materialist bias by choosing a path away from money, which may account for why they're so down on consumerism (unless it involves Volvo station wagons). In this they're true to their ecclesiastical origins; monasteries, after all, were once havens of learning, and intellectuals often operated in a churchly context. Worse yet, some intellectuals, abetted by tenure and textbook sales, are doing very well indeed, and they in turn can feel guilty about all those itinerant teaching fellows and underpaid junior faculty whose lives suggest a comment by Robert Musil in his novel *The Man Without Qualities*: "In every profession that is followed not for the sake of money but for love," wrote Musil, "there comes a moment when the advancing years seem to be leading into the void."

There are no such feelings in the self-made man (or woman). Once a   17
staple of American life and literature, the self-made man is now a somewhat discredited figure. Like the Puritans, knowing moderns doubt that anyone really can be self-made (except maybe immigrants), though they're certainly not willing to assign to God the credit for success. Besides, more of us now are *born* comfortable, even if we work as hard as if we weren't, and this change may account for the persistence of minimalism as a style of home décor among the fashionable. The perversely Veblenesque costliness of minimalist design—all that glossy concrete, and no cheap clamshell moldings to slap over the ragged seams where the doorways casually meet the drywall—attests to its ascetic snob appeal. So does the general democratization of materialism. Once *everybody* has possessions, fashion can fulfill its role, which is to reinforce the primacy of wealth and give those in the know a way of distinguishing themselves, only by shunning possessions altogether.

"Materialism," in this context, refers to somebody else's wanting what 18
you already have. When my teenage nephew, in school, read Leo Tolstoy's
"How Much Land Does a Man Need?"—a parable about greed whose grim
answer is: six feet for a burial plot—nobody told the students that Tolstoy
himself owned a 4,000-acre estate (inherited, of course). We have plenty of
such well-heeled hypocrites closer to home. John Lennon, for example, who
lugubriously sang "imagine no possessions," made a bundle with the Beatles
and lived at the Dakota, an unusually prestigious and expensive apartment
building even by New York City standards. And before moving into a $1.7
million house in New York's northern suburbs, Hillary Rodham Clinton told
the World Economic Forum in Davos that without a strong civil society, we
risk succumbing to unbridled materialism. "We are creating a consumer-
driven culture that promotes values and ethics that undermine both capitalism and democracy," she warned. But Mrs. Clinton soon suspended her
concerns about capitalism and democracy to accept a controversial avalanche
of costly china and other furnishings for the new house.

Heck, Thoreau could never have spent all that time at Walden if his 19
friend Ralph Waldo Emerson hadn't bought the land. It's fitting that getting and spending—by somebody—gave us our most famous anti-
materialist work of literature. Getting and spending by everyone else
continues to make the intellectual life possible, which is why universities
are named for the likes of Carnegie, Rockefeller, Stanford, and Duke. Every
church has a collection plate, after all, even if the priests like to bite the
hands that feed them.

Thinking Critically

1. What are the opposing perspectives on material wealth that Daniel Akst
   describes? How would you characterize the behaviors and beliefs of each
   perspective?
2. To what factors does Akst ascribe American ambivalence about materialism? Do you agree with him? In light of your own spiritual traditions or life
   experiences, how would you challenge Akst's perspective?
3. What paradox in the behavior of the people in our culture who are most
   likely to deplore materialism does Akst describe? Refer to other essays in
   this book to support or challenge his perspective.

Writing Critically

1. Are you surprised by Akst's assessment of Henry David Thoreau? Why
   does Akst refer to Thoreau as the "patron saint of American intellectuals"

(paragraph 13)—and does he mean that title as a compliment? Read Thoreau's 1854 essay *Walden, or Life in the Woods,* which is available from the University of Virginia Electronic Text Center at <http://etext.lib.virginia.edu/toc/modeng/public/ThoWald.html>. What is it about Thoreau's perspective that, in Akst's view, "opinion leaders" of today "identify far more easily with"?

2. Without consulting any critical or scholarly essays about his work, read Horatio Alger's 1868 novel *Ragged Dick, or, Street Life in New York* (the full text is available online at <http://etext.lib.virginia.edu/toc/modeng/public/AlgRagg.html>). How would you describe Alger's attitude toward material wealth and American capitalism? Akst says that Alger's books are "ignored" in contemporary American culture. Why do you think they are ignored?

Alt.Everything: The Youth Market and the Marketing of Cool

NAOMI KLEIN

Canadian-born journalist and activist Naomi Klein writes extensively on consumer culture, with a particular interest in the burgeoning worldwide antiglobalization movement. She contributes a regular column to the *Globe and Mail* in Canada and the *Guardian* in Britain. "Alt.Everything" appeared in her 2000 book chronicling the antiglobalization movement, *No Logo: Taking Aim at the Brand Bullies.* In a 2002 interview with *Index Magazine* about the book, Klein described how college students in the mid-1990s were beginning to react against corporate advertising: "What they wanted from advertising was not for it to be more progressive, or for it to represent them accurately. They just wanted advertising to shut up once in a while. It was the beginnings of an articulation of a politics about reclaiming public space, as opposed to changing the pictures." Klein's essay "America Is Not a Hamburger: America's Attempt to 'Re-Brand' Itself Abroad Could Be a Worse Flop than New Coke" appears in Chapter 12 (see pp. 698–702).

It's terrible to say, very often the most exciting outfits are from the poorest people.
—Designer Christian Lacroix in *Vogue,* April 1994

In our final year of high school, my best friend, Lan Ying, and I passed   1
the time with morbid discussions about the meaninglessness of life when
everything had already been done. The world stretched out before us not
as a slate of possibility, but as a maze of well-worn grooves like the ridges
burrowed by insects in hardwood. Step off the straight and narrow career-
and-materialism groove and you just end up on another one—the groove
for people who step off the main groove. And that groove was worn indeed
(some of the grooving done by our own parents). Want to go traveling? Be
a modern-day Kerouac? Hop on the Let's Go Europe groove. How about
a rebel? An avant-garde artist? Go buy your alterna-groove at the secondhand bookstore, dusty and moth-eaten and done to death. Everywhere we
imagined ourselves standing turned into a cliché beneath our feet—the stuff
of Jeep ad copy and sketch comedy. To us it seemed as though the arche-
types were all hackneyed by the time our turn came to graduate, including
that of the black-clad deflated intellectual, which we were trying on at that
very moment. Crowded by the ideas and styles of the past, we felt there was
no open space anywhere.

Of course it's a classic symptom of teenage narcissism to believe that the   2
end of history coincides exactly with your arrival on earth. Almost every
angst-ridden, Camus-reading seventeen-year-old girl finds her own groove
eventually. Still, there is a part of my high-school globo-claustrophobia
that has never left me, and in some ways only seems to intensify as time
creeps along. What haunts me is not exactly the absence of literal space so
much as a deep craving for metaphorical space: release, escape, some kind
of open-ended freedom.

All my parents wanted was the open road and a VW camper. That was   3
enough escape for them. The ocean, the night sky, some acoustic guitar . . .
what more could you ask? Well, actually, you could ask to go soaring off
the side of a mountain on a snowboard, feeling as if, for one moment, you
are riding the clouds instead of the snow. You could scour Southeast Asia,
like the world-weary twenty-somethings in Alex Garland's novel *The
Beach*, looking for the one corner of the globe uncharted by the Lonely
Planet to start your own private utopia. You could, for that matter, join a
New Age cult and dream of alien abduction. From the occult to raves to ri-
ots to extreme sports, it seems that the eternal urge for escape has never enjoyed such niche marketing.

In the absence of space travel and confined by the laws of gravity, how-   4
ever, most of us take our open space where we can get it, sneaking it like
cigarettes, outside hulking enclosures. The streets may be lined with billboards and franchise signs, but kids still make do, throwing up a couple of
nets and passing the puck or soccer ball between the cars. There is release,

too, at England's free music festivals, and in conversions of untended private property into collective space: abandoned factories turned into squats
by street kids or ramped entrances to office towers transformed into skate-
boarding courses on Sunday afternoons.

But as privatization slithers into every crevice of public life, even these in-   5
tervals of freedom and back alleys of unsponsored space are slipping away.
The indie skateboarders and snowboarders all have Vans sneaker contracts,
road hockey is fodder for beer commercials, inner-city redevelopment projects are sponsored by Wells Fargo, and the free festivals have all been
banned, replaced with the annual Tribal Gathering, an electronic music festival that bills itself as a "strike back against the establishment and clubland's
evil empire of mediocrity, commercialism, and the creeping corporate capitalism of our cosmic counter-culture"[1] and where the organizers regularly
confiscate bottled water that has not been purchased on the premises, despite
the fact that the number-one cause of death at raves is dehydration.

I remember the moment when it hit me that my frustrated craving for   6
space wasn't simply a result of the inevitable march of history, but of the
fact that commercial co-optation was proceeding at a speed that would have
been unimaginable to previous generations. I was watching the television
coverage of the controversy surrounding Woodstock '94, the twenty-fifth-
anniversary festival of the original Woodstock event. The baby-boomer
pundits and aging rock stars postured about how the $2 cans of Woodstock
Memorial Pepsi, festival key chains and on-site cash machines betrayed the
anticommercial spirit of the original event and, incredibly, whined that the
$3 commemorative condoms marked the end of "free love" (as if AIDS had
been cooked up as a malicious affront to their nostalgia).

What struck me most was that the debate revolved entirely around the   7
sanctity of the past, with no recognition of present-tense cultural challenges.
Despite the fact that the anniversary festival was primarily marketed to
teenagers and college students and showcased then-up-and-coming bands
like Green Day, not a single commentator explored what this youth-culture
"commodification" might mean to the young people who would actually be
attending the event. Never mind about the offense to hippies decades after
the fact; how does it feel to have your culture "sold out" now, as you are
living it? The only mention that a new generation of young people even existed came when the organizers, confronted with charges from ex-hippies
that they had engineered Greedstock or Woodshlock, explained that if the
event wasn't shrink-wrapped and synergized, the kids today would mutiny.
Woodstock promoter John Roberts explained that today's youth are "used
to sponsorship. If a kid went to a concert and there wasn't merchandise to
buy, he'd probably go out of his mind."[2]

Roberts isn't the only one who holds this view. *Advertising Age* reporter 8
Jeff Jensen goes so far as to make the claim that for today's young people,
"Selling out is not only accepted, it's considered hip."[3] To object would be,
well, unhip. There is no need to further romanticize the original Woodstock. Among (many) other things, it was also a big-label-backed rock festival, designed to turn a profit. Still, the myth of Woodstock as a sovereign
youth-culture state was part of a vast project of generational self-
definition—a concept that would have been wholly foreign to those in attendance at Woodstock '94, for whom generational identity had largely
been a prepackaged good and for whom the search for self had always been
shaped by marketing hype, whether or not they believed it or defined themselves against it. This is a side effect of brand expansion that is far more
difficult to track and quantify than the branding of culture and city spaces.
This loss of space happens inside the individual; it is a colonization not of
physical space but of mental space.

In a climate of youth-marketing feeding frenzy, all culture begins to be 9
created with the frenzy in mind. Much of youth culture becomes suspended
in what sociologists Robert Goldman and Stephen Papson call "arrested
development," noting that "we have, after all, no idea of what punk or
grunge or hip hop as social and cultural movements might look like if they
were not mined for their gold . . ."[4] This "mining" has not gone unnoticed
or unopposed. Both the anticorporate cultural journal *The Baffler* and the
now-defunct *Might* magazine brilliantly lampooned the desperation and
striving of the youth-culture industry in the mid-nineties. . . . For the most
part, however, branding's insatiable cultural thirst just creates more marketing. Marketing that thinks it is culture. . . .

Cool Hunters: The Legal Stalkers of Youth Culture

While the change agents were getting set to cool the corporate world from 10
the inside out, a new industry of "cool hunters" was promising to cool the
companies from the outside in. The major corporate cool consultancies—
Sputnik, *The L. Report,* Bureau de Style—were all founded between 1994
and 1996, just in time to present themselves as the brands' personal cool
shoppers. The idea was simple: they would search out pockets of cutting-
edge lifestyle, capture them on videotape and return to clients like Reebok,
Absolut Vodka and Levi's with such bold pronouncements as "Monks are
cool."[5] They would advise their clients to use irony in their ad campaigns,
to get surreal, to use "viral communications."

In their book *Street Trends,* Sputnik founders Janine Lopiano-Misdom 11
and Joanne De Luca concede that almost anyone can interview a bunch of
young people and make generalizations, "but how do you know they are

the 'right' ones—have you been in their closets? Trailed their daily routines? Hung out with them socially? . . . Are they the core consumers, or the mainstream followers?"[6] Unlike the market researchers who use focus groups and one-way glass to watch kids as if they were overgrown lab rats, Sputnik is "one of them"—it is in with the in-crowd.

Of course all this has to be taken with a grain of salt. Cool hunters and   12 their corporate clients are locked in a slightly S/M, symbiotic dance: the clients are desperate to believe in a just-beyond-their-reach well of untapped cool, and the hunters, in order to make their advice more valuable, exaggerate the crisis of credibility the brands face. On the off chance of Brand X becoming the next Nike, however, many corporations have been more than willing to pay up. And so, armed with their change agents and their cool hunters, the superbrands became the perennial teenage followers, trailing the scent of cool wherever it led.

In 1974, Norman Mailer described the paint sprayed by urban graffiti   13 artists as artillery fired in a war between the street and the establishment. "You hit your name and maybe something in the whole scheme of the system gives a death rattle. For now your name is over their name . . . your presence is on their Presence, your alias hangs over their scene."[7] Twenty-five years later, a complete inversion of this relationship has taken place. Gathering tips from the graffiti artists of old, the superbrands have tagged everyone—including the graffiti writers themselves. No space has been left unbranded.

Hip-Hop Blows Up the Brands

As we have seen, in the eighties you had to be relatively rich to get noticed   14 by marketers. In the nineties, you have only to be cool. As designer Christian Lacroix remarked in *Vogue,* "It's terrible to say, very often the most exciting outfits are from the poorest people."[8]

Over the past decade, young black men in American inner cities have been   15 the market most aggressively mined by the brandmasters as a source of borrowed "meaning" and identity. This was the key to the success of Nike and Tommy Hilfiger, both of which were catapulted to brand superstardom in no small part by poor kids who incorporated Nike and Hilfiger into hip-hop style at the very moment when rap was being thrust into the expanding youth-culture limelight by MTV and *Vibe* (the first mass-market hip-hop magazine, founded in 1992). "The hip-hop nation," write Lopiano-Misdom and De Luca in *Street Trends,* is "the first to embrace a designer or a major label, they make that label 'big concept' fashion. Or, in their words, they 'blow it up.'"[9]

Designers like Stussy, Hilfiger, Polo, DKNY and Nike have refused to   16 crack down on the pirating of their logos for T-shirts and baseball hats in the inner cities and several of them have clearly backed away from serious attempts to curb rampant shoplifting. By now the big brands know that profits from logowear do not just flow from the purchase of the garment but also from people seeing your logo on "the right people," as Pepe Jeans' Phil Spur judiciously puts it. The truth is that the "got to be cool" rhetoric of the global brands is, more often than not, an indirect way of saying "got to be black." Just as the history of cool in America is really (as many have argued) a history of African-American culture—from jazz and blues to rock and roll to rap—for many of the superbrands, cool hunting simply means black-culture hunting. Which is why the cool hunters' first stop was the basketball courts of America's poorest neighborhoods.

The latest chapter in mainstream America's gold rush to poverty began   17 in 1986, when rappers Run-DMC breathed new life into Adidas products with their hit single "My Adidas," a homage to their favorite brand. Already, the wildly popular rap trio had hordes of fans copying their signature style of gold medallions, black-and-white Adidas tracksuits and low-cut Adidas sneakers, worn without laces. "We've been wearing them all our lives," Darryl McDaniels (a k a DMC) said of his Adidas shoes at the time.[10] That was fine for a time, but after a while it occurred to Russell Simmons, the president of Run-DMC's label Def Jam Records, that the boys should be getting paid for the promotion they were giving to Adidas. He approached the German shoe company about kicking in some money for the act's 1987 Together Forever tour. Adidas executives were skeptical about being associated with rap music, which at that time was alternately dismissed as a passing fad or vilified as an incitement to riot. To help change their minds, Simmons took a couple of Adidas bigwigs to a Run-DMC show. Christopher Vaughn describes the event in *Black Enterprise:* "At a crucial moment, while the rap group was performing the song ["My Adidas"], one of the members yelled out, 'Okay, everybody in the house, rock your Adidas!'—and three thousand pairs of sneakers shot in the air. The Adidas executives couldn't reach for their checkbooks fast enough."[11] By the time of the annual Atlanta sports-shoe Super Show that year, Adidas had unveiled its new line of Run-DMC shoes: the Super Star and the Ultra Star—"designed to be worn without laces."[12]

Since "My Adidas," nothing in inner-city branding has been left up to   18 chance. Major record labels like BMG now hire "street crews" of urban black youth to talk up hip-hop albums in their communities and to go out on guerrilla-style postering and sticker missions. The L.A.-based Steven Rifkind Company bills itself as a marketing firm "specializing in building word-of-mouth in urban areas and inner cities."[13] Rifkind is CEO of the rap label Loud Records, and companies like Nike pay him hundreds of thousands of dollars to find out how to make their brands cool with trend-setting black youth.

So focused is Nike on borrowing style, attitude and imagery from black 19 urban youth that the company has its own word for the practice: *bro-ing*. That's when Nike marketers and designers bring their prototypes to inner-city neighborhoods in New York, Philadelphia or Chicago and say, "Hey, bro, check out the shoes," to gauge the reaction to new styles and to build up a buzz. In an interview with journalist Josh Feit, Nike designer Aaron Cooper described his bro-ing conversion in Harlem: "We go to the playground, and we dump the shoes out. It's unbelievable. The kids go nuts. That's when you realize the importance of Nike. Having kids tell you Nike is the number one thing in their life—number two is their girlfriend."[14] Nike has even succeeded in branding the basketball courts where it goes bro-ing through its philanthropic wing, P.L.A.Y (Participate in the Lives of Youth). P.L.A.Y sponsors inner-city sports programs in exchange for high swoosh visibility, including giant swooshes at the center of resurfaced urban basketball courts. In tonier parts of the city, that kind of thing would be called an ad and the space would come at a price, but on this side of the tracks, Nike pays nothing, and files the cost under charity.

Tommy Hilfiger: To the Ghetto and Back Again

Tommy Hilfiger, even more than Nike or Adidas, has turned the harness- 20 ing of ghetto cool into a mass-marketing science. Hilfiger forged a formula that has since been imitated by Polo, Nautica, Munsingwear (thanks to Puff Daddy's fondness for the penguin logo) and several other clothing companies looking for a short cut to making it at the suburban mall with inner-city attitude.

Like a depoliticized, hyper-patriotic Benetton, Hilfiger ads are a tangle 21 of Cape Cod multiculturalism: scrubbed black faces lounging with their wind-swept white brothers and sisters in that great country club in the sky, and always against the backdrop of a billowing American flag. "By respecting one another we can reach all cultures and communities," the company says. "We promote . . . the concept of living the American dream."[15] But the hard facts of Tommy's interracial financial success have less to do with finding common ground between cultures than with the power and mythology embedded in America's deep racial segregation.

Tommy Hilfiger started off squarely as white-preppy wear in the tradi- 22 tion of Ralph Lauren and Lacoste. But the designer soon realized that his clothes also had a peculiar cachet in the inner cities, where the hip-hop philosophy of "living large" saw poor and working-class kids acquiring status in the ghetto by adopting the gear and accoutrements of prohibitively costly leisure activities, such as skiing, golfing, even boating. Perhaps to better position his brand within this urban fantasy, Hilfiger began to associate his clothes more consciously with these sports, shooting ads at yacht clubs, beaches and other nautical locales. At the same time, the clothes themselves were redesigned to appeal more directly to the hip-hop aesthetic. Cultural theorist Paul Smith describes the shift as "bolder colors, bigger and baggier styles, more hoods and cords, and more prominence for logos and the Hilfiger name."[16] He also plied rap artists like Snoop Dogg with free clothes and, walking the tightrope between the yacht and the ghetto, launched a line of Tommy Hilfiger beepers.

Once Tommy was firmly established as a ghetto thing, the real selling 23 could begin—not just to the comparatively small market of poor inner-city youth but to the much larger market of middle-class white and Asian kids who mimic black style in everything from lingo to sports to music. Company sales reached $847 million in 1998—up from a paltry $53 million in 1991 when Hilfiger was still, as Smith puts it, "Young Republican clothing." Like so much of cool hunting, Hilfiger's marketing journey feeds off the alienation at the heart of America's race relations: selling white youth on their fetishization of black style, and black youth on their fetishization of white wealth.

Indie Inc.

Offering *Fortune* magazine readers advice on how to market to teenage girls, 24 reporter Nina Munk writes that "you have to pretend that they're running things. . . . Pretend you still have to be discovered. Pretend the girls are in charge."[17] Being a huge corporation might sell on Wall Street, but as the brands soon learned on their cool hunt, "indie" was the pitch on Cool Street. Many corporations were unfazed by this shift, coming out with faux indie brands like Politix cigarettes from Moonlight Tobacco (courtesy of Philip Morris), Dave's Cigarettes from Dave's Tobacco Company (Philip Morris again), Old Navy's mock army surplus (the Gap) and OK Cola (Coke).

In an attempt to cash in on the indie marketing craze, even Coke itself, 25 the most recognizable brand name on earth, has tried to go underground. Fearing that it was too establishment for brand-conscious teens, the company launched an ad campaign in Wisconsin that declared Coke the "Unofficial State Drink." The campaign included radio spots that were allegedly broadcast from a pirate radio station called EKOC: Coke backward. Not to be outdone, Gap-owned Old Navy actually did launch its own pirate radio station to promote its brand—a microband transmitter that could only be picked up in the immediate vicinity of one of its Chicago billboards.[18] And in 1999, when Levi's decided it was high time to recoup its lost cool, it also went indie, launching Red Line jeans (no mention of Levi's anywhere) and K-1 Khakis (no mention of Levi's or Dockers).

Ironic Consumption: No Deconstruction Required

But Levi's may have, once again, missed a "paradigm shift." It hasn't taken 26 long for these attempts to seriously pitch the most generic of mass-produced products as punk-rock lifestyle choices to elicit sneers from those ever-elusive, trend-setting cool kids, many of whom had already moved beyond indie by the time the brands caught on. Instead, they were now finding ways to express their disdain for mass culture not by opting out of it but by abandoning themselves to it entirely—but with a sly ironic twist. They were watching *Melrose Place*, eating surf 'n' turf in revolving restaurants, singing Frank Sinatra in karaoke bars and sipping girly drinks in tiki bars, acts that were rendered hip and daring because, well, *they* were the ones doing them. Not only were they making a subversive statement about a culture they could not physically escape, they were rejecting the doctrinaire puritanism of seventies feminism, the earnestness of the sixties quest for authenticity and the "literal" readings of so many cultural critics. Welcome to ironic consumption. The editors of the zine *Hermenaut* articulated the recipe:

> Following the late ethnologist Michel de Certeau, we prefer to concentrate our attention on the independent use of mass culture products, a use which, like the ruses of camouflaged fish and insects, may not "overthrow the system," but which keeps us intact and autonomous within that system, which may be the best for which we can hope. . . . Going to Disney World to drop acid and goof on Mickey isn't revolutionary; going to Disney World in full knowledge of how ridiculous and evil it all is and still having a great innocent time, in some almost unconscious, even psychotic way, is something else altogether. This is what de Certeau describes as "the art of being in-between," and this is the only path of true freedom in today's culture. Let us, then, be in-between. Let us revel in Baywatch, Joe Camel, *Wired* magazine, and even glossy books about the society of spectacle [touché], but let's never succumb to the glamorous allure of these things.[19]

In this complicated context, for brands to be truly cool, they need to 27 layer this uncool-equals-cool aesthetic of the ironic viewer onto their pitch: they need to self-mock, talk back to themselves while they are talking, be used and new simultaneously. And after the brands and their cool hunters had tagged all the available fringe culture, it seemed only natural to fill up that narrow little strip of unmarketed brain space occupied by irony with pre-planned knowing smirks, someone else's couch commentary and even a running simulation of the viewer's thought patterns. "The New Trash brands," remarks writer Nick Compton of kitsch lifestyle companies like Diesel, "offer inverted commas big enough to live, love and laugh within."[20]

Pop Up Videos, the VH1 show that adorns music videos with snarky 28 thought bubbles, may be the endgame of this kind of commercial irony.

It grabs the punchline before anyone else can get to it, making social commentary—even idle sneering—if not redundant then barely worth the expense of energy.

Irony's cozy, protected, self-referential niche is a much better fit than attempts to earnestly pass off fruit drinks as underground rock bands or sneakers as gangsta rappers. In fact, for brands in search of cool new identities, irony and camp have become so all-purpose that they even work after the fact. It turns out that the so-bad-it's-good marketing spin can be deployed to resuscitate hopelessly uncool brands and failed cultural products. Six months after the movie *Showgirls* flopped in the theaters, for instance, MGM got wind that the sexploitation flick was doing okay on video, and not just as a quasi-respectable porno. It seemed that groups of trendy twenty-somethings were throwing *Showgirls* irony parties, laughing sardonically at the implausibly poor screenplay and shrieking with horror at the aerobic sexual encounters. Not content to pocket the video returns, MGM decided to relaunch the movie in the theaters as the next *Rocky Horror Picture Show.* This time around, the newspaper ads made no pretense that anyone had seriously admired the film. Instead, they quoted from the abysmal reviews, and declared *Showgirls* an "instant camp classic" and "a rich sleazy kitsch-fest." The studio even hired a troupe of drag queens for the New York screenings to holler at the crowd with bullhorns during particularly egregious cinematic moments. 29

With the tentacles of branding reaching into every crevice of youth culture, leaching brand-image content not only out of street styles like hip-hop but psychological attitudes like ironic detachment, the cool hunt has had to go further afield to find unpilfered space and that left only one frontier: the past. 30

What is retro, after all, but history re-consumed with a PepsiCo tie-in, and breath-mint and phone-card brand extensions? As the re-release of *Lost in Space,* the *Star Wars* trilogy, and the launch of *The Phantom Menace* made clear, the mantra of retro entertainment seems to be "Once more with synergy!" as Hollywood travels back in time to cash in on merchandising opportunities beyond the imagination of yesterday's marketers. 31

Sell or Be Sold

After almost a decade of the branding frenzy, cool hunting has become an internal contradiction: the hunters must rarefy youth "microcultures" by claiming that only full-time hunters have the know-how to unearth them—or else why hire cool hunters at all? Sputnik warns its clients that if the cool trend is "visible in your neighborhood or crowding your nearest mall, the learning is over. It's too late. . . . You need to get down with 32 the streets, to be in the trenches every day."[21] And yet this is demonstrably false; so-called street fashions—many of them planted by brandmasters like Nike and Hilfiger from day one—reach the ballooning industry of glossy youth-culture magazines and video stations without a heartbeat's delay. And if there is one thing virtually every young person now knows, it's that street style and youth culture are infinitely marketable commodities.

Besides, even if there was a lost indigenous tribe of cool a few years   33
back, rest assured that it no longer exists. It turns out that the prevailing legalized forms of youth stalking are only the tip of the iceberg: the Sputnik vision for the future of hip marketing is for companies to hire armies of Sputnik spawns—young "street promoters," "Net promoters," and "street distributors" who will hype brands one-on-one on the street, in the clubs and on-line. "Use the magic of peer-to-peer distribution—it worked in the freestyle sport cultures, mainly because the promoters were their friends. . . . Street promoting will survive as the only true means of personally 'spreading the word.'"[22] So all arrows point to more jobs for the ballooning industry of "street snitches," certified representatives of their demographic who will happily become walking infomercials for Nike, Reebok and Levi's.

By fall 1998 it had already started to happen with the Korean car man-   34
ufacturer Daewoo hiring two thousand college students on two hundred campuses to talk up the cars to their friends. Similarly, Anheuser-Busch keeps troops of U.S. college frat boys and "Bud Girls" on its payroll to promote Budweiser beer at campus parties and bars.[23] The vision is both horrifying and hilarious: a world of glorified diary trespassers and professional eavesdroppers, part of a spy-vs.-spy corporate-fueled youth culture stalking itself, whose members will videotape one another's haircuts and chat about their corporate keepers' cool new products in their grassroots newsgroups.

Notes

[1]Mean Fiddler promotional material obtained by author.

[2]"Woodstock at 25" (editorial), *San Francisco Chronicle*, 14 August 1994, 1.

[3]"Hits replace jingles on TV Commercials," *Globe and Mail*, 29 November 1997.

[4]Robert Goldman and Stephen Papson, *Sign Wars: The Cluttered Landscape of Advertising* (New York: Guilford Press, 1996), 43.

[5]Robert Sullivan, "Style Stalker," *Vogue*, November 1997, 182, 187–88.

[6]Janine Lopiano-Misdom and Joanne De Luca, *Street Trends: How Today's Alternative Youth Cultures Are Creating Tomorrow's Mainstream Markets* (New York: HarperCollins Business, 1997), 11.

[7]Norman Mailer, "The Faith of Graffiti," *Esquire*, May 1974, 77.

[8]"Off the Street . . . ," *Vogue*, April 1994, 337.

[9]Lopiano-Misdom and De Luca, *Street Trends*, 37.

[10]Erica Lowe, "Good Rap? Bad Rap? Run-DMC Pushes Rhyme, Not Crime," *San Diego Union-Tribune*, 18 June 1987, E-13.

[11]Christopher Vaughn, "Simmons' Rush for Profits," *Black Enterprise*, December 1992, 67.

[12]Lisa Williams, "Smaller Athletic Firms Pleased at Super Show; Shoe Industry Trade Show," *Footwear News*, 16 February 1987, 2.

[13]*Advertising Age*, 28 October 1996.

[14]Josh Feit, "The Nike Psyche," *Willamette Week*, 28 May 1997.

[15]*Tommy Hilfiger 1997 Annual Report*.

[16]Paul Smith, "Tommy Hilfiger in the Age of Mass Customization," in *No Sweat: Fashion, Free Trade, and the Rights of Garment Workers*, edited by Andrew Ross (New York: Verso, 1997), 253.

[17]Nina Munk, "Girl Power," *Fortune*, 8 December 1997, 137.

[18]"Old Navy Anchors Micro-Radio Billboard," *Chicago Sun-Times*, 28 July 1998.

[19]Editorial, *Hermenaut #10: Popular Culture*, 1995.

[20]Nick Compton, "Who Are the Plastic Palace People?" *Face*, June 1996, 114–15.

[21]Lopiano-Misdom and De Luca, *Street Trends*, 8–9.

[22]Ibid., 110.

[23]James Hibberd, "Bar Hopping with the Bud Girls," *Salon*, 1 February 1999.

Thinking Critically

1. What is the significance of "open space" to Naomi Klein, and why does she begin her essay with this concept?

2. An implied definition or an extended definition is a way of structuring an argument around a concept and creating a definition or context for that concept through the use of examples and illustrations. In your own words, describe

Klein's definition of *culture*. How consistently does she use the term *culture* in her argument? What, to your mind, constitutes a "culture"? Even the title of this book, *Many Americas: Reading and Writing Across the Cultural Divides,* depends on common understanding of the concept of "culture." Is Klein's definition of *culture* similar to the definition implied by this textbook's title?

3. How does Klein define *ironic* consumption? Compare her description of *irony* in contemporary American consumer culture with Eric S. Cohen's view of irony in "To Wonder Again" (see pp. 331–43). In what ways does "irony," either in attitude or in consumer behavior, seem to suggest a deeper spiritual hunger? (You might return to Daniel Akst's "Buyer's Remorse," in this chapter, for additional perspective.)

Writing Critically

1. How was status determined in your high school, or, if you're a parent, how is status determined among your child's friends and peers? Where did you get the knowledge about what was or wasn't cool? Klein argues that advertising firms, marketing specialists, and consumer-goods merchants are becoming increasingly sophisticated about determining what's "cool" in youth culture and how to make a profit from that knowledge. If you were working for one of the "corporate cool consultancies," how would you recommend they go about marketing a product to your senior class?

2. In her argument about the commodification of cool, Klein describes efforts by Nike, Tommy Hilfiger, record company promoters, and others to capitalize on hip-hop culture. In an analytical essay, describe how consumer goods and an attitude toward materialism are portrayed in music videos of a specific genre (hip-hop, alternative, country—your choice). For example, how often do artists in a particular genre mention specific brand names in songs or show them in videos? What values are implied by these links between consumer goods and a genre's image?

3. How does your campus market itself? Examine and compare the marketing tools and messages your campus brings to different groups of people, such as alumni donors, students of color, and athletes. Where do those images and tools come from? (For example, compare a brochure from a campus "development office" intended to solicit alumni contributions with a "viewbook" or other recruitment publication created by the admissions department.) In what ways are students on your campus used, either implicitly or explicitly, to "market" or promote your college's programs and interests?

Wal-Mart's War on Main Street

SARAH ANDERSON

Journalist and activist Sarah Anderson is the director of
the Global Economy Project at the Institute for Policy
Studies, a progressive think tank in Washington, D.C.
Her work for the IPS Global Economy Project includes
researching the impact of financial globalization on issues of social justice and environmental sustainability.
Anderson, who holds a master's degree in international
affairs from American University in Washington, D.C.,
and a B.A. in journalism from Northwestern University,
worked as a consultant to the U.S. Agency for International Development from 1989 to 1992, when she
joined the Institute for Policy Studies. She sits on the
steering committee of the Alliance for Responsible
Trade and is a board member of the Coalition for Justice in the Maquiladoras. Anderson's investigations into
the social and environmental impact of corporation-
friendly political policies have been published in many
magazines and journals, including *The Progressive*,
where "Wal-Mart's War on Main Street" appeared in
1994. Founded in 1909 as "a magazine of progress, social, intellectual, institutional," *The Progressive* has for
nearly a century been an advocate for "democracy,
peace, social justice, civil rights, civil liberties, and environmental awareness," according to its website:
<http://www.progressive.org/>.

The basement of Boyd's for Boys and Girls in downtown Litchfield, Min- 1
nesota, looks like a history museum of the worst in children's fashions. All
the real duds from the past forty years have accumulated down there: wool
pedal-pushers, polyester bell-bottoms, wide clip-on neckties. There's a big box
of 1960s faux fur hats, the kind with the fur pompon ties that dangle under a
girl's chin. My father, Boyd Anderson, drags all the old stuff up the stairs and
onto the sidewalk once a year on Krazy Daze. At the end of the day, he lugs
most of it back down. Folks around here don't go in much for the retro look.

At least for now, the museum is only in the basement. Upstairs, Dad 2
continues to run one of the few remaining independent children's clothing
stores on Main Street, USA. But this is the age of Wal-Mart, not Main
Street. In 1994, the nation's top retailer plans to add 110 new U.S. stores
to its current total of 1,967. For every Wal-Mart opening, there is more
than one store like Boyd's that closes its doors.

259

Litchfield, a town of 6,200 people sixty miles west of Minneapolis, 3
started losing Main Street businesses at the onset of the farm crisis and the
shopping-mall boom of the early 1980s. As a high-school student during
this time, I remember dinner-table conversation drifting time and again toward rumors of store closings. In those days, Mom frequently cut the conversation off short. "Let's talk about something less depressing, okay?"

Now my family can no longer avoid the issue of Main Street Litchfield's 4
precarious future. Dad, at sixty-eight, stands at a crossroads. Should he retain his faith in Main Street and pass Boyd's down to his children? Or
should he listen to the pessimists and close up the forty-one-year-old family business before it becomes obsolete?

For several years, Dad has been reluctant to choose either path. The 5
transition to retirement is difficult for most people who have worked
hard all their lives. For him, it could signify not only the end of a working career, but also the end of small-town life as he knows it. When
pressed, Dad admits that business on Main Street has been going downhill for the past fifteen years. "I just can't visualize what the future for
downtown Litchfield will be," he says. "I've laid awake nights worrying
about it because I really don't want my kids to be stuck with a business
that will fail."

I am not the aspiring heir to Boyd's. I left Litchfield at eighteen for the 6
big city and would have a tough time readjusting to small-town life. My
sister Laurie, a nurse, and my sister-in-law Colleen, who runs a farm with
my brother Scott, are the ones eager to enter the ring and fight the retail
Goliaths. Both women are well suited to the challenge. Between them, they
have seven children who will give them excellent tips on kids' fashions.
They are deeply rooted in the community and idealistic enough to believe
that Main Street can survive.

My sisters are not alone. Across the country, thousands of rural peo- 7
ple are battling to save their local downtowns. Many of these fights have
taken the form of anti-Wal-Mart campaigns. In Vermont, citizens'
groups allowed Wal-Mart to enter the state only after the company
agreed to a long list of demands regarding the size and operation of the
stores. Three Massachusetts towns and another in Maine have defeated
bids by Wal-Mart to build in their communities. In Arkansas, three independent drugstore owners won a suit charging that Wal-Mart had
used "predatory pricing," or selling below cost, to drive out competitors. Canadian citizens are asking Wal-Mart to sign a "Pledge of Corporate Responsibility" before opening in their towns. In at least a dozen
other U.S. communities, groups have fought to keep Wal-Mart out or to
restrict the firm's activities.

By attacking Wal-Mart, these campaigns have helped raise awareness   8
of the value of locally owned independent stores on Main Street. Their concerns generally fall in five areas:

> *Sprawl Mart:* Wal-Mart nearly always builds along a highway
> outside town to take advantage of cheap, often unzoned land.
> This usually attracts additional commercial development, forc-
> ing the community to extend services (telephone and power
> lines, water and sewage services, and so forth) to that area, de-
> spite sufficient existing infrastructure downtown.
>
> *Wal-Mart channels resources out of a community:* Studies have
> shown that a dollar spent on a local business has four or five
> times the economic spin-off of a dollar spent at a Wal-Mart,
> since a large share of Wal-Mart's profit returns to its Arkansas
> headquarters or is pumped into national advertising campaigns.
>
> *Wal-Mart destroys jobs in locally owned stores:* A Wal-Mart-
> funded community impact study debunked the retailer's claim
> that it would create a lot of jobs in Greenfield, Massachusetts.
> Although Wal-Mart planned to hire 274 people at its Green-
> field store, the community could expect to gain only eight net
> jobs, because of projected losses at other businesses that would
> have to compete with Wal-Mart.
>
> *Citizen Wal-Mart?* In at least one town—Hearne, Texas—Wal-
> Mart destroyed its Main Street competitors and then deserted
> the town in search of higher returns elsewhere. Unable to attract
> new businesses to the devastated Main Street, local residents
> have no choice but to drive long distances to buy basic goods.
>
> *One-stop shopping culture:* In Greenfield, where citizens voted to
> keep Wal-Mart out, anti-Wal-Mart campaign manager Al Norman
> said he saw a resurgence of appreciation for Main Street. "People
> realized there's one thing you can't buy at Wal-Mart, and that's
> small-town quality of life," Norman explains. "This community
> decided it was not ready to die for a cheap pair of underwear."

So far Litchfield hasn't been forced to make that decision. Nevertheless,   9
the town is already losing at least some business to four nearby Wal-Marts,
each less than forty miles from town. To find out how formidable this enemy is, Mom and I went on a spying mission to the closest Wal-Mart,
twenty miles away in Hutchinson.

Just inside the door, we were met by a so-called Wal-Mart "greeter"   10
(actually the greeters just say hello as they take your bags to prevent you
from shoplifting). We realized we knew her. Before becoming a greeter, she
had been a cashier at a downtown Litchfield supermarket until it closed

early this year. I tried to be casual when I asked if she greets many people from Litchfield. "Oh, a-a-a-ll the time!" she replied. Sure enough, Mom immediately spotted one in the checkout line.

Not wanting to look too suspicious, we moved on toward the children's   11
department, where we discreetly examined price tags and labels. Not all, but many items were cheaper than at Boyd's. It was the brainwashing campaign that we found most intimidating, though. Throughout the store were huge red, white, and blue banners declaring BRING IT HOME TO AMERICA. Confusingly, the labels on the children's clothing indicated that they had been imported from sixteen countries, including Haiti, where an embargo on exports was supposed to be in place.

Of course, Wal-Mart is not Main Street's only foe. Over coffee at the   12
Main Street Cafe, some of Litchfield's long-time merchants gave me a litany of additional complaints. Like my dad, many of these men remember when three-block-long Main Street was a bustling social and commercial hub, with two movie theaters, six restaurants, a department store, and a grand old hotel.

Present-day Litchfield is not a ghost town, but there are four empty   13
storefronts, and several former commercial buildings now house offices for government service agencies. In recent years, the downtown has lost its last two drugstores and two supermarkets. As a result, elderly people who live downtown and are unable to drive can no longer do their own shopping.

My dad and the other merchants place as much blame for this decline   14
on cutthroat suppliers as on Wal-Mart. The big brand names, especially, have no time anymore for small clients. Don Brock, who ran a furniture store for thirty-three years before retiring in 1991, remembers getting an honorary plaque from a manufacturer whose products he carried for many years. "Six months later I got a letter saying they were no longer going to fill my orders."

At the moment, Litchfield's most pressing threat is a transportation de-   15
partment plan to reroute the state highway that now runs down Main Street to the outskirts of town. Local merchants fear the bypass would kill the considerable business they now get from travelers. Bypasses are also magnets for Wal-Mart and other discounters attracted to the large, cheap, and often unzoned sites along the bypass.

When I asked the merchants how they felt about the bypass, the table   16
grew quiet. Greg Heath, a florist and antique dealer, sighed and said, "The bypass will come—it might be ten years from now, but it will come. By then, we'll either be out of business or the bypass will drive us out."

The struggles of Main Street merchants have naturally created a growth   17
industry in consultants ready to provide tips on marketing and customer

relations. Community development experts caution, though, that individual merchants acting on their own cannot keep Main Street strong. "Given the enormous forces of change, the only way these businesses can survive is with active public and government support," says Dawn Nakano, of the National Center for Economic Alternatives in Washington, D.C.

Some of the most effective efforts at revitalization, Nakano says, are 18 community development corporations—private, nonprofit corporations governed by a community-based board and usually funded in part by foundation and government money. In Pittsburgh, for example, the city government and about thirty nonprofit groups formed a community development corporation to save an impoverished neighborhood where all but three businesses were boarded up. Today, thanks to such financing and technical assistance, the area has a lively shopping district.

Although most community development corporations have been cre- 19 ated to serve low-income urban neighborhoods, Nakano feels that they could be equally effective in saving Main Streets. "There's no reason why church, civic, and other groups in a small town couldn't form a community development corporation to fill boarded-up stores with new businesses. Besides revitalizing Main Street, this could go a long way towards cultivating a 'buy local' culture among residents."

The National Main Street Center, a Washington, D.C.–based nonprofit, 20 provides some of the most comprehensive Main Street revitalization services. The Center has helped more than 850 towns build cooperative links among merchants, government, and citizens. However, the Center's efforts focus on improving marketing techniques and the physical appearance of stores, which can only do so much to counter the powerful forces of change.

No matter how well designed, any Main Street revitalization project will 21 fail without local public support. Unfortunately, it is difficult for many rural people to consider the long-term, overall effects of their purchases, given the high levels of rural unemployment, job insecurity, and poverty. If you're worried about paying your rent, you're not going to pay more for a toaster at your local hardware store, no matter how much you like your hometown.

Another problem is political. Like those in decaying urban neighbor- 22 hoods, many rural people have seen the signs of decline around them and concluded that they lack the clout necessary to harness the forces of change for their own benefit. If you've seen your neighbors lose their farms through foreclosure, your school close down, and local manufacturing move to Mexico, how empowered will you feel?

Litchfield Mayor Ron Ebnet has done his best to bolster community 23 confidence and loyalty to Main Street. "Every year at the Christmas lighting ceremony, I tell people to buy their gifts in town. I know everyone is sick of hearing it, but I don't care." Ebnet has whipped up opposition to the proposed bypass, with strong support from the city council, chamber of commerce, the newspaper editor, and the state senator. He also orchestrated a downtown beautification project and helped the town win a state redevelopment grant to upgrade downtown businesses and residences.

Ebnet has failed to win over everyone, though. Retired merchant Don 24 Larson told me about a local resident who drove forty miles to get something seventeen cents cheaper than he could buy it at the Litchfield lumberyard. "I pointed out that he had spent more on gas than he'd saved, but he told me that 'it was a matter of principle.' I thought, what about the principle of supporting your community? People just don't think about that, though."

Mayor Ebnet agrees, "Many people still have a 1950s mentality," he 25 says. "They can't see the tremendous changes that are affecting these small businesses. People tell me they want the bypass because there's too much traffic downtown and they have a hard time crossing the street. And I ask them, but what will you be crossing to? If we get the bypass, there will be nothing left!"

Last summer, with the threat of the bypass hanging over his head, Dad 26 became increasingly stubborn about making a decision about the store. His antique Underwood typewriter was never more productive, as it banged out angry letters to the state transportation department.

My sisters decided to try a new tactic. While my parents were on vaca- 27 tion, they assaulted the store with paintbrushes and wallpaper, transforming what had been a rather rustic restroom and doing an unprecedented amount of redecorating and rearranging.

The strategy worked. "At first, Dad was a bit shocked," Laurie said. 28 "He commented that in his opinion, the old toiletpaper dispenser had been perfectly fine. But overall he was pleased with the changes, and two days later he called for a meeting with us and our spouses."

"Your dad started out by making a little speech," Colleen said. "The 29 first thing he said was, 'Well, things aren't how they used to be.' Then he pulled out some papers he'd prepared and told us exactly how much sales and profits have been over the years and what we could expect to make. He told us what he thinks are the negative and the positive aspects of the job and then said if we were still interested, we could begin talking about a starting date for us to take over."

Dad later told me, "The only way I could feel comfortable about Lau- 30 rie and Colleen running the store is if it was at no financial risk to them. So I'm setting up an account for them to draw from—enough for a one-year trial. But if they can't make a good profit, then that's it—I'll try to sell the business to someone else. I still worry that they don't know what they're getting themselves into. Especially if the bypass goes through, things are going to be rough."

My sisters are optimistic. They plan to form a buying cooperative with   31
Main Street children's clothing stores in other towns and have already drafted a customer survey to help them better understand local needs. "I think we're going to see a big increase in appreciation of the small-town atmosphere," Colleen says. "There are more and more people moving to Litchfield from the Twin Cities to take advantage of the small-town way of life. I think they might even be more inclined to support the local businesses than people who've lived here their whole lives and now take the town for granted."

Small towns cannot return to the past, when families did all their shop-   32
ping and socializing in their hometown. Rural life is changing and there's no use denying it. The most important question is, who will define the future? Will it be Wal-Mart, whose narrow corporate interests have little to do with building healthy communities? Will it be the department of transportation, whose purpose is to move cars faster? Will it be the banks and suppliers primarily interested in doing business with the big guys? Or will it be the people who live in small towns, whose hard work and support are essential to any effort to revitalize Main Street?

In my hometown, there are at least two new reasons for optimism.   33
First, shortly before my deadline for this article, the Minnesota transportation department announced that it was dropping the Litchfield highway bypass project because of local opposition. (My dad's Underwood will finally get a rest.) The second reason is that a new teal green awning will soon be hanging over the front of Boyd's—a symbol of one family's belief that Main Street, while weary, is not yet a relic of the past.

Thinking Critically

1. Sarah Anderson makes it clear that Wal-Mart is just one of many causes of the decline of rural Main Streets in her hometown and across America. What other causes for the decline of Main Street does she describe?

2. Why does Anderson choose to draw from her personal experience and to write in the first person? You know, from the headnote to this essay, that she is a professional journalist and public policy researcher. Given that she is an experienced writer and researcher, what does her choice of the first person bring to her argument?

3. Anderson suggests ways in which Main Street revitalization projects can be supported and made effective. What other reasons does she express— either implicitly or explicitly—for the revitalization of Main Streets?

Writing Critically

1. Several writers in Chapter 2, including Blake Hurst (see pp. 58–65), Jedediah Purdy (pp. 66–77), and Bill McKibben (pp. 82–91), describe challenges to the values and lifestyles of small towns and rural communities. In what ways do the problems that Sarah Anderson describes support the observations of Hurst, Purdy, or McKibben? What is the relationship between financial and commercial support for small towns and the "values" of the small town's community? (For inspiration, rent a DVD of the great 1946 James Stewart movie *It's a Wonderful Life,* and pay particular attention to the role that the bank plays in Bedford Falls as compared with the bank's role in Pottersville.)

2. Anderson describes the efforts made by Litchfield's Mayor Ron Ebnet to "bolster community confidence and loyalty to Main Street." In what ways do these efforts reflect the values of Litchfield's community? What is the "principle" that retired merchant Don Larson describes, and how does that principle reflect community values? What is the "small-town way of life" that people from urban areas, such as the Twin Cities, expect to enjoy when they move to smaller communities like Litchfield? Is it reasonable or fair to expect citizens of a small town to uphold certain communal values if doing so means sacrificing certain personal benefits?

3. Sinclair Lewis described a fictional but quintessential Minnesota small town in his 1920 novel *Main Street,* which is available online from the University of Virginia Electronic Text Center at <http://etext.lib.virginia.edu/toc/modeng/public/LewMain.html>. What "Main Street" values described by Lewis are reflected in Anderson's essay? Compare the attitudes toward those values reflected in Lewis's novel and in Anderson's essay. You might also include in your discussion one of the selections from Chapter 2.

Serving in Florida

BARBARA EHRENREICH

This chapter from Barbara Ehrenreich's book *Nickel and Dimed: On (Not) Getting By in America* (2001), reflects Ehrenreich's extraordinarily engaged and compassionate approach to her work as a journalist. For *Nickel and Dimed,* Ehrenreich spent several months working low-wage jobs in Maine, Minnesota, and Florida, attempting to live solely on her earnings from her work as a waitress, a housekeeper, and a Wal-Mart salesperson, among other jobs. Her chronicle of the daily injustices faced by America's working poor—and her portraits of individual men and women who maintain their dignity despite these obstacles—was a *New*

York Times bestseller. A self-described socialist and feminist, Ehrenreich, who holds a Ph.D. in biology from Rockefeller University, uses her scientific training to investigate a broad range of social issues. As a journalist and social critic, she frequently explores (and exposes) what she considers to be issues of social injustice, especially as they affect women and the poor. Her work appears frequently in *Salon.com*, *Time*, the *New York Times Magazine*, *Z Magazine*, *The Nation*, and *The Progressive*, and she is a contributing editor to *Ms.* and *Mother Jones*.

Picture a fat person's hell, and I don't mean a place with no food. Instead there is everything you might eat if eating had no bodily consequences— the cheese fries, the chicken-fried steaks, the fudge-laden desserts—only here every bite must be paid for, one way or another, in human discomfort. The kitchen is a cavern, a stomach leading to the lower intestine that is the garbage and dishwashing area, from which issue bizarre smells combining the edible and the offal: creamy carrion, pizza barf, and that unique and enigmatic Jerry's scent, citrus fart. The floor is slick with spills, forcing us to walk through the kitchen with tiny steps, like Susan McDougal in leg irons. Sinks everywhere are clogged with scraps of lettuce, decomposing lemon wedges, water-logged toast crusts. Put your hand down on any counter and you risk being stuck to it by the film of ancient syrup spills, and this is unfortunate because hands are utensils here, used for scooping up lettuce onto the salad plates, lifting out pie slices, and even moving hash browns from one plate to another. The regulation poster in the single unisex rest room admonishes us to wash our hands thoroughly, and even offers instructions for doing so, but there is always some vital substance missing—soap, paper towels, toilet paper—and I never found all three at once. You learn to stuff your pockets with napkins before going in there, and too bad about the customers, who must eat, although they don't realize it, almost literally out of our hands.

The break room summarizes the whole situation: there is none, because there are no breaks at Jerry's. For six to eight hours in a row, you never sit except to pee. Actually, there are three folding chairs at a table immediately adjacent to the bathroom, but hardly anyone ever sits in this, the very rectum of the gastroarchitectural system. Rather, the function of the peri-toilet area is to house the ashtrays in which servers and dishwashers leave their cigarettes burning at all times, like votive candles, so they don't have to waste time lighting up again when they dash back here for a puff. Almost everyone smokes as if their pulmonary well-being depended on it—the multinational mélange of cooks; the dishwashers, who are all Czechs here;

the servers, who are American natives—creating an atmosphere in which oxygen is only an occasional pollutant. My first morning at Jerry's, when the hypoglycemic shakes set in, I complain to one of my fellow servers that I don't understand how she can go so long without food. "Well, I don't understand how *you* can go so long without a cigarette," she responds in a tone of reproach. Because work is what you do for others; smoking is what you do for yourself. I don't know why the antismoking crusaders have never grasped the element of defiant self-nurturance that makes the habit so endearing to its victims—as if, in the American workplace, the only thing people have to call their own is the tumors they are nourishing and the spare moments they devote to feeding them.

Now, the Industrial Revolution is not an easy transition, especially, in my   3 experience, when you have to zip through it in just a couple of days. I have gone from craft work straight into the factory, from the air-conditioned morgue of the Hearthside directly into the flames. Customers arrive in human waves, sometimes disgorged fifty at a time from their tour buses, peckish and whiny. Instead of two "girls" on the floor at once, there can be as many as six of us running around in our brilliant pink-and-orange Hawai-

Poverty Rates by Age: 1959 to 2003

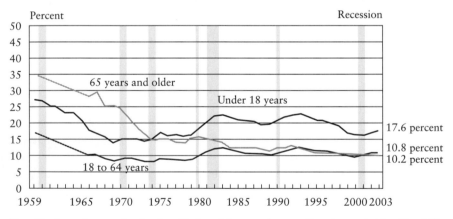

Note: The data points are placed at the midpoints of the respective years. Data for people 18 to 64 and 65 and older are not available from 1960 to 1965.

Source: U.S. Census Bureau, Current Population Survey, 1960 to 2004 Annual Social and Economic Supplements.

Just getting by Almost eleven percent of people in the United States of working age—18 to 64— live in poverty today, a rate that has hardly fluctuated since the late 1960s. According to the Department of Health and Human Services, in 2005 the definition of poverty for a single person with no children is an annual income of $9,570.

ian shirts. Conversations, either with customers or with fellow employees, seldom last more than twenty seconds at a time. On my first day, in fact, I am hurt by my sister servers' coldness. My mentor for the day is a supremely competent, emotionally uninflected twenty-three-year-old, and the others, who gossip a little among themselves about the real reason someone is out sick today and the size of the bail bond someone else has had to pay, ignore me completely. On my second day, I find out why. "Well, it's good to see *you* again," one of them says in greeting. "Hardly anyone comes back after the first day." I feel powerfully vindicated—a survivor—but it would take a long time, probably months, before I could hope to be accepted into this sorority.

I start out with the beautiful, heroic idea of handling the two jobs at once, 4 and for two days I almost do it: working the breakfast/lunch shift at Jerry's from 8:00 till 2:00, arriving at the Hearthside a few minutes late, at 2:10, and attempting to hold out until 10:00. In the few minutes I have between jobs, I pick up a spicy chicken sandwich at the Wendy's drive-through window, gobble it down in the car, and change from khaki slacks to black, from Hawaiian to rust-colored polo. There is a problem, though. When, during the 3:00–4:00 o'clock dead time, I finally sit down to wrap silver, my flesh seems to bond to the seat. I try to refuel with a purloined cup of clam chowder, as I've seen Gail and Joan do dozens of time, but Stu catches me and hisses "No *eating*!" although there's not a customer around to be offended by the sight of food making contact with a server's lips. So I tell Gail I'm going to quit, and she hugs me and says she might just follow me to Jerry's herself.

But the chances of this are minuscule. She has left the flophouse and her 5 annoying roommate and is back to living in her truck. But, guess what, she reports to me excitedly later that evening, Phillip has given her permission to park overnight in the hotel parking lot, as long as she keeps out of sight, and the parking lot should be totally safe since it's patrolled by a hotel security guard! With the Hearthside offering benefits like that, how could anyone think of leaving? This must be Phillip's theory, anyway. He accepts my resignation with a shrug, his main concern being that I return my two polo shirts and aprons.

Gail would have triumphed at Jerry's, I'm sure, but for me it's a crash 6 course in exhaustion management. Years ago, the kindly fry cook who trained me to waitress at a Los Angeles truck stop used to say: Never make an unnecessary trip; if you don't have to walk fast, walk slow; if you don't have to walk, stand. But at Jerry's the effort of distinguishing necessary from unnecessary and urgent from whenever would itself be too much of an energy drain. The only thing to do is to treat each shift as a one-time-only emergency: you've got fifty starving people out there, lying scattered on the battlefield, so get out there and feed them! Forget that you will have to do this again tomorrow, forget that you will have to be alert enough to dodge the drunks on the drive home tonight—just burn, burn, burn! Ideally, at some point you enter what servers call a "rhythm" and psychologists term a "flow state," where signals pass from the sense organs directly to the muscles, bypassing the cerebral cortex, and a Zen-like emptiness sets in. I'm on a 2:00–10:00 P.M. shift now, and a male server from the morning shift tells me about the time he "pulled a triple"—three shifts in a row, all the way around the clock—and then got off and had a drink and met this girl, and maybe he shouldn't tell me this, but they had sex right then and there and it was like *beautiful*.

But there's another capacity of the neuromuscular system, which is   7
pain. I start tossing back drugstore-brand ibuprofens as if they were vitamin C, four before each shift, because an old mouse-related repetitive-stress injury in my upper back has come back to full-spasm strength, thanks to the tray carrying. In my ordinary life, this level of disability might justify a day of ice packs and stretching. Here I comfort myself with the Aleve commercial where the cute blue-collar guy asks: If you quit after working four hours, what would your boss say? And the not-so-cute blue-collar guy, who's lugging a metal beam on his back, answers: He'd fire me, that's what. But fortunately, the commercial tells us, we workers can exert the same kind of authority over our painkillers that our bosses exert over us. If Tylenol doesn't want to work for more than four hours, you just fire its ass and switch to Aleve.

True, I take occasional breaks from this life, going home now and then   8
to catch up on e-mail and for conjugal visits (though I am careful to "pay" for everything I eat here, at $5 for a dinner, which I put in a jar), seeing *The Truman Show* with friends and letting them buy my ticket. And I still have those what-am-I-doing-here moments at work, when I get so homesick for the printed word that I obsessively reread the six-page menu. But as the days go by, my old life is beginning to look exceedingly strange. The e-mails and phone messages addressed to my former self come from a distant race of people with exotic concerns and far too much time on their hands. The neighborly market I used to cruise for produce now looks forbiddingly like a Manhattan yuppie emporium. And when I sit down one morning in my real home to pay bills from my past life, I am dazzled by the two- and three-figure sums owed to outfits like Club Body Tech and Amazon.com.

Management at Jerry's is generally calmer and more "professional"   9
than at the Hearthside, with two exceptions. One is Joy, a plump, blowsy woman in her early thirties who once kindly devoted several minutes of her time to instructing me in the correct one-handed method of tray carrying

but whose moods change disconcertingly from shift to shift and even within one. The other is B.J., aka B.J. the Bitch, whose contribution is to stand by the kitchen counter and yell, "Nita, your order's up, move it!" or "Barbara, didn't you see you've got another table out there? Come *on,* girl!" Among other things, she is hated for having replaced the whipped cream squirt cans with big plastic whipped-cream-filled baggies that have to be squeezed with both hands—because, reportedly, she saw or thought she saw employees trying to inhale the propellant gas from the squirt cans, in the hope that it might be nitrous oxide. On my third night, she pulls me aside abruptly and brings her face so close that it looks like she's planning to butt me with her forehead. But instead of saying "You're fired," she says, "You're doing fine." The only trouble is I'm spending time chatting with customers: "That's how they're getting you." Furthermore I am letting them "run me," which means harassment by sequential demands: you bring the catsup and they decide they want extra Thousand Island; you bring that and they announce they now need a side of fries, and so on into distraction. Finally she tells me not to take her wrong. She tries to say things in a nice way, but "you get into a mode, you know, because everything has to move so fast."[1]

I mumble thanks for the advice, feeling like I've just been stripped 10 naked by the crazed enforcer of some ancient sumptuary law: No chatting for *you,* girl. No fancy service ethic allowed for the serfs. Chatting with customers is for the good-looking young college-educated servers in the downtown carpaccio and ceviche joints, the kids who can make $70–$100 a night. What had I been thinking? My job is to move orders from tables to kitchen and then trays from kitchen to tables. Customers are in fact the major obstacle to the smooth transformation of information into food and food into money—they are, in short, the enemy. And the painful thing is that I'm beginning to see it this way myself. There are the traditional asshole types—frat boys who down multiple Buds and then make a fuss because the steaks are so emaciated and the fries so sparse—as well as the variously impaired—due to age, diabetes, or literacy issues—who require patient nutritional counseling. The worst, for some reason, are the Visible Christians—like the ten-person table, all jolly and sanctified after Sunday night service, who run me mercilessly and then leave me $1 on a $92 bill.

1. In *Workers in a Lean World: Unions in the International Economy* (Verso, 1997), Kim Moody cites studies finding an increase in stress-related workplace injuries and illness between the mid-1980s and the early 1990s. He argues that rising stress levels reflect a new system of "management by stress" in which workers in a variety of industries are being squeezed to extract maximum productivity, to the detriment of their health.

Or the guy with the crucifixion T-shirt (SOMEONE TO LOOK UP TO) who complains that his baked potato is too hard and his iced tea too icy (I cheerfully fix both) and leaves no tip at all. As a general rule, people wearing crosses or WWJD? ("What Would Jesus Do?") buttons look at us disapprovingly no matter what we do, as if they were confusing waitressing with Mary Magdalene's original profession.

I make friends, over time, with the other "girls" who work my shift: 11
Nita, the tattooed twenty-something who taunts us by going around saying brightly, "Have we started making money yet?" Ellen, whose teenage son cooks on the graveyard shift and who once managed a restaurant in Massachusetts but won't try out for management here because she prefers being a "common worker" and not "ordering people around." Easygoing fiftyish Lucy, with the raucous laugh, who limps toward the end of the shift because of something that has gone wrong with her leg, the exact nature of which cannot be determined without health insurance. We talk about the usual girl things—men, children, and the sinister allure of Jerry's chocolate peanut-butter cream pie—though no one, I notice, ever brings up anything potentially expensive, like shopping or movies. As at the Hearthside, the only recreation ever referred to is partying, which requires little more than some beer, a joint, and a few close friends. Still, no one is homeless, or cops to it anyway, thanks usually to a working husband or boyfriend. All in all, we form a reliable mutual-support group: if one of us is feeling sick or overwhelmed, another one will "bev" a table or even carry trays for her. If one of us is off sneaking a cigarette or a pee, the others will do their best to conceal her absence from the enforcers of corporate rationality.[2]

But my saving human connection—my oxytocin receptor, as it were—is   12
George, the nineteen-year-old Czech dishwasher who has been in this country exactly one week. We get talking when he asks me, tortuously, how much cigarettes cost at Jerry's. I do my best to explain that they cost over a dollar more here than at a regular store and suggest that he just take one

2. Until April 1998, there was no federally mandated right to bathroom breaks. According to Marc Linder and Ingrid Nygaard, authors of *Void Where Prohibited: Rest Breaks and the Right to Urinate on Company Time* (Cornell University Press, 1997), "The right to rest and void at work is not high on the list of social or political causes supported by professional or executive employees, who enjoy personal workplace liberties that millions of factory workers can only dream about. . . . While we were dismayed to discover that workers lacked an acknowledged right to void at work, [the workers] were amazed by outsiders' naïve belief that their employers would permit them to perform this basic bodily function when necessary. . . . A factory worker, not allowed a break for six-hour stretches, voided into pads worn inside her uniform; and a kindergarten teacher in a school without aides had to take all twenty children with her to the bathroom and line them up outside the stall door while she voided."

from the half-filled packs that are always lying around on the break table. But that would be unthinkable. Except for the one tiny earring signaling his allegiance to some vaguely alternative point of view, George is a perfect straight arrow—crew-cut, hardworking, and hungry for eye contact. "Czech Republic," I ask, "or Slovakia?" and he seems delighted that I know the difference. "Vaclav Havel," I try, "Velvet Revolution, Frank Zappa?" "Yes, yes, 1989," he says, and I realize that for him this is already history.

My project is to teach George English. "How are you today, George?" I 13 say at the start of each shift. "I am good, and how are you today, Barbara?" I learn that he is not paid by Jerry's but by the "agent" who shipped him over—$5 an hour, with the agent getting the dollar or so difference between that and what Jerry's pays dishwashers. I learn also that he shares an apartment with a crowd of other Czech "dishers," as he calls them, and that he cannot sleep until one of them goes off for his shift, leaving a vacant bed. We are having one of our ESL sessions late one afternoon when B.J. catches us at it and orders "Joseph" to take up the rubber mats on the floor near the dishwashing sinks and mop underneath. "I thought your name was George," I say loud enough for B.J. to hear as she strides off back to the counter. Is she embarrassed? Maybe a little, because she greets me back at the counter with "George, Joseph—there are so many of them!" I say nothing, neither nodding nor smiling, and for this I am punished later, when I think I am ready to go and she announces that I need to roll fifty more sets of silverware, and isn't it time I mixed up a fresh four-gallon batch of blue-cheese dressing? May you grow old in this place, B.J., is the curse I beam out at her when I am finally permitted to leave. May the syrup spills glue your feet to the floor.

I make the decision to move closer to Key West. First, because of the drive. 14 Second and third, also because of the drive: gas is eating up $4–$5 a day, and although Jerry's is as high-volume as you can get, the tips average only 10 percent, and not just for a newbie like me. Between the base pay of $2.15 an hour and the obligation to share tips with the busboys and dishwashers, we're averaging only about $7.50 an hour. Then there is the $30 I had to spend on the regulation tan slacks worn by Jerry's servers—a setback it could take weeks to absorb. (I had combed the town's two downscale department stores hoping for something cheaper but decided in the end that these marked-down Dockers, originally $49, were more likely to survive a daily washing.) Of my fellow servers, everyone who lacks a working husband or boyfriend seems to have a second job: Nita does something at a computer eight hours a day; another welds. Without the forty-five minute commute, I can picture myself working two jobs and still having the time to shower between them.

So I take the $500 deposit I have coming from my landlord, the $400 15 I have earned toward the next month's rent, plus the $200 reserved for emergencies, and use the $1,100 to pay the rent and deposit on trailer number 46 in the Overseas Trailer Park, a mile from the cluster of budget hotels that constitute Key West's version of an industrial park. Number 46 is about eight feet in width and shaped like a barbell inside, with a narrow region—because of the sink and the stove—separating the bedroom from what might optimistically be called the "living" area, with its two-person table and half-sized couch. The bathroom is so small my knees rub against the shower stall when I sit on the toilet, and you can't just leap out of the bed, you have to climb down to the foot of it in order to find a patch of floor space to stand on. Outside, I am within a few yards of a liquor store, a bar that advertises "free beer tomorrow," a convenience store, and a Burger King—but no supermarket or, alas, Laundromat. By reputation, the Overseas park is a nest of crime and crack, and I am hoping at least for some vibrant multicultural street life. But desolation rules night and day, except for a thin stream of pedestrians heading for their jobs at the Sheraton or the 7-Eleven. There are not exactly people here but what amounts to canned labor, being preserved between shifts from the heat.

In line with my reduced living conditions, a new form of ugliness arises   16 at Jerry's. First we are confronted—via an announcement on the computers through which we input orders—with the new rule that the hotel bar, the Driftwood, is henceforth off-limits to restaurant employees. The culprit, I learn through the grapevine, is the ultraefficient twenty-three-year-old who trained me—another trailer home dweller and a mother of three. Something had set her off one morning, so she slipped out for a nip and returned to the floor impaired. The restriction mostly hurts Ellen, whose habit it is to free her hair from its rubber band and drop by the Driftwood for a couple of Zins before heading home at the end of her shift, but all of us feel the chill. Then the next day, when I go for straws, I find the dry-storage room locked. It's never been locked before; we go in and out of it all day—for napkins, jelly containers, Styrofoam cups for takeout. Vic, the portly assistant manager who opens it for me, explains that he caught one of the dishwashers attempting to steal something and, unfortunately, the miscreant will be with us until a replacement can be found—hence the locked door. I neglect to ask what he had been trying to steal but Vic tells me who he is—the kid with the buzz cut and the earring, you know, he's back there right now.

I wish I could say I rushed back and confronted George to get his side   17 of the story. I wish I could say I stood up to Vic and insisted that George be given a translator and allowed to defend himself or announced that I'd find a lawyer who'd handle the case pro bono. At the very least I should have testified as to the kid's honesty. The mystery to me is that there's not much worth stealing in the dry-storage room, at least not in any fenceable quantity: "Is Gyorgi here, and am having 200—maybe 250—catsup packets. What do you say?" My guess is that he had taken—if he had taken anything at all—some Saltines or a can of cherry pie mix and that the motive for taking it was hunger.

So why didn't I intervene? Certainly not because I was held back by the 18 kind of moral paralysis that can mask as journalistic objectivity. On the contrary, something new—something loathsome and servile—had infected me, along with the kitchen odors that I could still sniff on my bra when I finally undressed at night. In real life I am moderately brave, but plenty of brave people shed their courage in POW camps, and maybe something similar goes on in the infinitely more congenial milieu of the low-wage American workplace. Maybe, in a month or two more at Jerry's, I might have regained my crusading spirit. Then again, in a month or two I might have turned into a different person altogether—say, the kind of person who would have turned George in.

But this is not something I was slated to find out. When my monthlong 19 plunge into poverty was almost over, I finally landed my dream job— housekeeping. I did this by walking into the personnel office of the only place I figured I might have some credibility, the hotel attached to Jerry's, and confiding urgently that I had to have a second job if I was to pay my rent and, no, it couldn't be front-desk clerk. "All *right*," the personnel lady fairly spits, "so it's *housekeeping*," and marches me back to meet Millie, the housekeeping manager, a tiny, frenetic Hispanic woman who greets me as "babe" and hands me a pamphlet emphasizing the need for a positive attitude. The pay is $6.10 an hour and the hours are nine in the morning till "whenever," which I am hoping can be defined as a little before two. I don't have to ask about health insurance once I meet Carlotta, the middle-aged African American woman who will be training me. Carlie, as she tells me to call her, is missing all of her top front teeth.

Thinking Critically

1. Some of Barbara Ehrenreich's most compelling reporting in *Nickel and Dimed* comes from her efforts to get by on the very low wages paid to the "working poor" in America. In Key West, for example, she scrapes together the funds to rent a trailer in the Overseas Trailer Park—practically the only housing option for working-class people in that expensive resort community. What does she mean when she notes (in paragraph 15) that "By reputation, the Overseas park is a nest of crime and crack, and I am hoping at least for some vibrant multicultural street life"?

2. Who is Ehrenreich's audience for "Serving in Florida"? What clues indicate who her audience is? What does she hope her audience learns from or does with her reporting?

3. If you've worked in a restaurant, comment on the accuracy of Ehrenreich's observations. How would you, as a current or former restaurant worker, respond to some of the conflicts and circumstances that she describes?

Writing Critically

1. What is Ehrenreich's attitude toward her fellow employees, her boss, and her customers? In her tone or her choice of words, does she ever emphasize the differences between herself (a professional, acclaimed writer) and the people she describes here? How would you characterize her attitude toward members of her own social class, based on her tone and language? Does her attitude toward her "old life" change through her experience waitressing at Jerry's?

2. British rock band Pulp released one of its biggest hits, "Common People," in 1995. The sleeve of the single carried the message "There is a war in progress—don't be a casual(ty). The time to decide whose side you're on is here. Choose wisely. Stay alive in '95." Download the song (legitimately, please), and search online for the lyrics (do a Google search for "Jarvis Cocker" "Common People" "lyrics"). What's the message of this song, and how might it apply, in a way, to Barbara Ehrenreich's project? Find at least one other example in popular culture of "slumming," and in an analytical essay discuss the ethical tensions of crossing class borders—whether out of curiosity or as a social worker, law enforcement officer, or journalist.

3. "My project is to teach George English," says Ehrenreich (paragraph 13). How would you characterize her attitude toward George, and in what ways does she treat him differently than she does other workers at Jerry's? What is really going on in her brief confrontation with B.J., and in her reaction to the news that George was caught stealing?

The Myth of the Working Poor

Steven Malanga

In this analytical essay published in the Autumn 2004 issue of *City Journal*, financial journalist Steven Malanga takes a critical look at Barbara Ehrenreich's methodology in *Nickel and Dimed: On (Not) Getting By in America* and challenges the conclusions she draws from her experiences. A contributing editor of *City Journal* and a Senior Fellow at the Manhattan Institute, a conservative think tank, Malanga was executive editor of *Crain's New York Business*, a publication to

which he also contributed a weekly column. He has
won awards for his journalism exposing the intersections of private and nonprofit organizations and their
influence on public policy. Malanga has also contributed to the *Wall Street Journal, New York Daily
News,* and *New York Post,* among other publications.
The Manhattan Institute is a market-oriented research institute that provides support for research
into public policy and urban affairs. To learn more
about it, visit <http://www.manhattan-institute.org/html/
about_mi.htm>.

Forty years ago a young, radical journalist helped ignite the War on Poverty　1
with his pioneering book *The Other America.* In its pages, Michael Harrington warned that the recently proclaimed age of affluence was a mirage,
that beneath the surface of U.S. prosperity lay tens of millions of people stuck
in hopeless poverty that only massive government intervention could help.

Today, a new generation of journalists is straining to duplicate Harrington's feat—to convince contemporary America that its economic sys-　2
tem doesn't work for millions and that only government can lift them out
of poverty. These new journalists face a tougher task than Harrington's
though, because all levels of government have spent about $10 trillion on
poverty programs since his book appeared, with disappointing, even counterproductive, results. And over the last four decades, millions of poor people, immigrants and native-born alike, have risen from poverty, without
recourse to the government programs that Harrington inspired.

But brushing aside the War on Poverty's failure and the success of so　3
many in climbing America's economic ladder, this generation of authors
dusts off the old argument for a new era. Books like Barbara Ehrenreich's
Nickel and Dimed and David Shipler's *The Working Poor* tell us that the
poor are doing exactly what America expects of them—finding jobs, rising
early to get to work every day, chasing the American dream—but that our
system of "carnivorous capitalism" is so heavily arrayed against them that
they can't rise out of poverty or live a decent life. These new anthems of despair paint their subjects as forced off welfare by uncompassionate conservatives and trapped in low-wage jobs that lead nowhere. They claim, too,
that the good life that the country's expanding middle class enjoys rests on
the backs of these working poor and their inexpensive labor, so that prosperous Americans *owe* them more tax-funded help.

Steve Malanga, author of *The New, New Left,* is a contributing editor at the Manhattan Institute's
City Journal (www.city-journal.org), from whose Autumn 2004 issue this article is reprinted.

Though these books resolutely ignore four decades' worth of lessons   4
about poverty, they have found a big audience. The commentariat loves
them. Leftish professors have made them required course reading. And
Democratic candidates have made their themes central to the 2004 elections. So it's worth looking closely at what these tomes contend, and at the
economic realities that they distort.

To begin with, they follow Harrington's 1962 classic by seeing the poor   5
as victims of forces over which they have no control. From the hills of Appalachia to the streets of Harlem, Harrington had found a generation of
impoverished former sharecroppers whose jobs had been replaced by
mechanization. For them, the advances that enriched everyone else spelled
disaster: "progress is misery" and "hopelessness is the message." Unprepared for life off the farm, many could never find productive work, Harrington argued, and would need perpetual government aid.

But the new thinkers quickly veer to the left of Harrington, following   6
some of his more radical acolytes whose theories produced the War on
Poverty's most spectacular disasters. Harrington had seen the poor as victims
because they could find no work; his more radical allies, especially a group
associated with Columbia University's social-work school, argued that compelling the demoralized inner-city poor to work or take part in training that
would fit them for work, instead of giving them unconditional welfare, was
itself victimization. Richard A. Cloward and Frances Fox Piven, for example, argued that America's poverty programs—"self-righteously oriented toward getting people off welfare" and making them independent—were
violating the civil rights of the poor. Journalist Richard Elman claimed that
"vindictive" America was "humiliating" welfare recipients by forcing them
to seek entry-level work as taxi drivers, restaurant employees, and factory la-
borers, instead of giving them a guaranteed minimum income.

Sympathetic mayors and welfare officials responded to Cloward and   7
Piven's call, boosting benefits, loosening eligibility rules, and cutting investigations of welfare cheating. Welfare rolls soared, along with welfare
fraud and illegitimate births. The result was a national backlash that
sparked the Reagan administration's welfare spending cuts.

But the Columbia crew left its enduring mark on welfare policy, in the   8
principle that welfare, once a short-term program to help people get back
on their feet, should be continuous and come with few restrictions and no
stigma. A welfare mother, screaming at New York mayor John Lindsay (responsible for much of the city's rise in welfare cases), expressed the system's
new philosophy: "It's my job to have kids, Mr. Mayor, and your job to take
care of them." It was a philosophy that bred an urban underclass of non-
working single mothers and fatherless children, condemned to intergenerational poverty, despite the trillions spent to help them.

Like communists who claim that communism didn't fail but instead 9
was never really tried, Barbara Ehrenreich made her public debut with an
attempt to brush aside the War on Poverty's obviously catastrophic results.
The 46-year-old daughter of a Montana copper miner-turned-business executive, she joined Cloward and Piven to co-author a 1987 polemic, *The
Mean Season: The Attack on the Welfare State.* The War on Poverty had
failed so far, the book claimed, not because of its flawed premises but because the government hadn't done enough to redistribute the nation's
wealth. America needed an even bigger War on Poverty that would turn the
country into a European-style social welfare state. Pooh-poohing the work
ethic and the dignity of labor, the authors derided calls for welfare reform
that would require recipients to work, because that would be mortifying to
the poor. "There is nothing ennobling about being forced to please an employer to feed one's children," the authors wrote, forgetting that virtually
every worker and business owner must please someone, whether boss or
customer, to earn a living. Welfare's true purpose, the book declared,
should be to "permit certain groups to opt out of work." (The authors
never explained why all of us shouldn't demand the right to "opt out.")

The Mean Season's argument gained little traction, but as the nineties 10
dawned, Ehrenreich found a way to bring Cloward and Piven's socialistic
themes successfully into the new decade and beyond. Her 1989 book, *Fear
of Falling: The Inner Life of the Middle Class,* blamed poverty's continued
existence in America partly on the Me Generation, which Tom Wolfe had
so brilliantly made interesting to the nation. America's emerging professional middle class had started out hopefully in the 1960s, Ehrenreich
claims, the inheritor of a liberating cultural revolution. But because that
class depended on intellectual capital to make its living, rather than on income from property or investments, it felt a sharp economic insecurity,
which by the late 1980s had made it "meaner, more selfish," and (worse
still) "more hostile to the aspirations of the less fortunate," especially in its
impatience with welfare.

The book vibrates with Ehrenreich's rage toward middle-class Ameri- 11
cans. The middle class, she sneers, obsessively pursues wealth and is abjectly
"sycophantic toward those who have it, impatient with those who do not."
To Ehrenreich, "The nervous, uphill climb of the professional class accelerates the downward spiral of society as a whole: toward cruelly widening inequalities, toward heightened estrangement along class lines, and toward
the moral anesthesia that estrangement requires." Ironically, Ehrenreich's
economic prescription for a better America was for government to create
one gigantic bourgeoisie: "Tax the rich and enrich the poor until both
groups are absorbed into some broad and truly universal middle class. The

details are subject to debate." *Time* magazine, the voice of the bourgeoisie, made her a regular columnist.

If the Reagan era could provoke Ehrenreich to such anger, it's no sur- 12 prise that the 1996 welfare reform heightened her fury. Passed by a Republican-controlled Congress and signed into law by Democratic president Bill Clinton, the legislation ended welfare as an automatic federal entitlement and required states to oblige able-bodied recipients to work. The law put a five-year limit on welfare (the average stay on the rolls had been 13 years) but exempted 20 percent of the cases—roughly equivalent to the portion of the welfare population believed too dysfunctional ever to get off public assistance. After President Clinton signed the bill, Ehrenreich claimed that she had seen the betrayal coming: she'd presciently cast a write-in vote for Ralph Nader in 1992's presidential election. She castigated the Left for its muted response to the new welfare law, though she later praised National Organization for Women president Patricia Ireland's hunger strike protesting the bill.

Ehrenreich's anger propelled her to write *Nickel and Dimed*. Beginning 13 life as a piece of "undercover journalism" for *Harper's,* the 2001 book purports to reveal the truth about poverty in post-welfare reform America. "In particular," Ehrenreich asks in the introduction, how were "the roughly four million women about to be booted into the labor market by welfare reform . . . going to make it on $6 or $7 an hour?"

Nickel and Dimed doesn't fuss much with public-policy agendas, messy 14 economic theories, or basic job numbers. Instead, it gives us Ehrenreich's first-person account of three brief sojourns into the world of the lowest of low-wage work: as a waitress for a low-priced family restaurant in Florida; as a maid for a housecleaning service in Maine; and as a women's-apparel clerk at a Minneapolis Wal-Mart. In her journeys, she meets a lively and sympathetic assortment of co-workers: Haitian busboys, a Czech dishwasher, a cook with a gambling problem, and assorted single working mothers. But the focus is mostly on Ehrenreich, not her colleagues.

The point that *Nickel and Dimed* wants to prove is that in today's econ- 15 omy, a woman coming off welfare into a low-wage job can't earn enough to pay for basic living expenses. Rent is a burden, Ehrenreich discovers. In Florida, she lands a $500-a-month efficiency apartment; in Maine, she spends $120 a week for a shared apartment in an old motel (she turns down a less expensive room elsewhere because it's on a noisy commercial street); in Minneapolis, she pays $255 a week for a moldy hotel room. These seem like reasonable enough rents, except perhaps for Minneapolis, judging from her description of the place. But with her entry-level wages—roughly the minimum wage (when tips are included) as a waitress, about $6 an hour as a maid, and $7 an hour to start at Wal-Mart—Ehrenreich quickly finds that she'll need a second job to support herself. This seems to startle her, as if holding down two jobs is something new to America. "In the new version of supply and demand," she writes, "jobs are so cheap—as measured by the pay—that a worker is encouraged to take on as many as she possibly can."

What's utterly misleading about Ehrenreich's exposé, though, is how she   16
fixes the parameters of her experiment so that she inevitably gets the outcome that she wants—"proof" that the working poor can't make it. Ehrenreich complains that America's supposedly tight labor market doesn't produce entry-level jobs at $10 an hour. For people with no skills, that's probably true in most parts of the country; but everywhere, the U.S. economy provides ample opportunity to move up quickly. Yet Ehrenreich spends only a few weeks with each of her employers, and so never gives herself the chance for promotion or to find better work (or better places to live).

In fact, few working in low-wage jobs stay in them long. And most   17
workers don't just move on quickly—they also move on to better jobs. The Sphere Institute, a California public-policy think tank founded by Stanford University professors, charted the economic path of workers in the state from 1988 to 2000 and found extraordinary mobility across industries and up the economic ladder. Over 40 percent of the lowest income group worked in retail in 1988; by 2000, more than half of that group had switched to other industries. Their average inflation-adjusted income gain after moving on: 83 percent, to over $32,000 a year.

The workers who stayed in retail, moreover, were usually the higher   18
earners, making about $10,000 more a year than the leavers. They had already started improving their lots back in 1988, in other words, and probably elected to stay because they rightly saw further opportunity in retailing, though the study doesn't say what happened to them. The same dynamic occurs in other industries where low-wage jobs are concentrated, the study found: those who do well stay and watch earnings go up; those who feel stuck often depart and see earnings rise, too, as they find more promising jobs. In total, over 12 years, 88 percent of those in California's lowest economic category moved up, their incomes rising as they gained experience on the job and time in the workforce, two things that the marketplace rewards.

Such results are only the latest to confirm the enormous mobility that the   19
U.S. economy offers. As a review of academic, peer-reviewed mobility studies by two Urban Institute researchers put it: "It is clear that there is substantial mobility—both short-term and long-term—over an average life-cycle in the United States." Perhaps most astonishingly, mobility often occurs within months. The Urban Institute report points out that several mobility studies based on the University of Michigan's Panel Study of Income

Dynamics, which has traced thousands of American families since 1968, show that about 20 percent of those in the lowest economic quintile rise at least one economic class within a year. If Ehrenreich had given herself 12 months in her low-wage stints, instead of a week or two, she might have worked her way into the lower middle class by the end of her experiment.

This mobility explains why poverty rates didn't soar in the 1990s, even   20 though some 13 million people, most of them dirt-poor, immigrated here legally. In fact, the country's poverty rate actually fell slightly during the nineties—which could only happen because millions already here rose out of the lowest income category.

Confidence in the American economy's capacity to foster income mo-   21 bility helped impel the 1996 welfare reform in the first place. Most former welfare recipients entering the workforce, reformers believed, would over time improve their lives—at least if other handicaps such as drug or alcohol addiction and serious mental deficiencies didn't hold them back. Everything we've subsequently learned about welfare reform shows that the reformers were right, rendering Ehrenreich's book oddly dated from the outset.

Since welfare reform passed, employment among single mothers who'd   22 never previously worked has risen 40 percent. More important, child poverty in single-mother households fell to its lowest point ever just three years after welfare reform became law. Except for a hiccup at the end of the last recession, the poverty rate among those households has continued to drop, down now by about one-third. The *New York Times* recently reported that "lawmakers of both parties describe the 1996 law as a success that moved millions of people from welfare to work and cut the welfare rolls by 60 percent, to 4.9 million people." Those results belie the hysterical warnings of welfare advocates, Ehrenreich among them, that reform would drastically worsen poverty.

Given that such data subvert Ehrenreich's case against the U.S. economic   23 system, she unsurprisingly puts statistics aside in *Nickel and Dimed* and instead seeks to paint the low-wage workplace as oppressive and humiliating to workers forced by reformers to enter it. But given the author's self-absorption, what the reader really gets is a self-portrait of Ehrenreich as a longtime rebel with an anti-authoritarian streak a mile wide, who can't stomach the basic boundaries that most people easily accept in the workplace.

At Wal-Mart, for instance, she's "oppressed by the mandatory gentility"   24 that the company requires of her, as if being nice to customers and co-workers were part of the tyranny of capitalism. (I suspect that most customers, if they encountered a snarling Ehrenreich as a clerk while shopping, would flee for the exit.) Told to scrub floors on her hands and knees by the maid service, she cites a "housecleaning expert" who says that this technique is ineffective. Ehrenreich then theorizes that the real reason that the service wants its employees down on their hands and knees is that "this primal posture of submission" and "anal accessibility" seem to "gratify the consumers of maid services." Never has the simple task of washing a floor been so thoroughly Freudianized.

In Ehrenreich's looking-glass world, opportunity becomes oppression. 25 Hired by Wal-Mart shortly after applying, she weirdly protests that "there is no intermediate point [between applying and beginning orientation] . . . in which you confront the employer as a free agent, entitled to cut her own deal." Though she admits that in such a tight labor market, "I would probably have been welcome to apply at any commercial establishment I entered," she still feels "like a supplicant with her hand stretched out."

Unable to understand why her fellow workers don't share her outrage, 26 this longtime socialist and radical feminist turns on the very people with whom she's trying to sympathize, imagining that they can only accept their terrible exploitation because they've become psychologically incapable of resisting. Why are the maids so loyal to the owner of the cleaning service? she asks. They're so emotionally "needy" that they can't break free, she speculates. Why do Wal-Mart workers accept their place in "Mr. Sam's family" instead of rising in a tide of unionization against the company? The Waltons have hoodwinked them, she surmises, misunderstanding completely the appeal to employees of Wal-Mart's opportunity culture, where two-thirds of management has come up from hourly-employee store ranks and where workers own a good chunk of company stock.

Responsibility for America's shameful economic injustice rests not only 27 with exploitative businesses like Wal-Mart, in Ehrenreich's view, but also with the rich and—you guessed it—the middle class. Going beyond even *Fear of Falling*, *Nickel and Dimed* hangs a huge guilt trip on the middle class. Actually, guilt "doesn't go anywhere near far enough," Ehrenreich says. "[T]he appropriate emotion," she claims, "is shame—shame at our own dependency, in this case, on the underpaid labor of others." After all, Ehrenreich tells us, it's the middle class and its irritation with the poor that led to the catastrophe of welfare reform. "When poor single mothers had the option of remaining out of the labor force on welfare, the middle and upper middle class tended to view them with a certain impatience, if not disgust," she maintains.

Like some of Ehrenreich's earlier work, *Nickel and Dimed* is contemptu- 28 ous of ordinary Americans. Cleaning the homes of middle-class families, she snoops in bookcases and finds mostly writers on the "low end of the literary spectrum"—you know, Grisham, Limbaugh, those kinds of authors. "Mostly though, books are for show," she clairvoyantly concludes. A woman whose home furnishings suggest that she is a Martha Stewart "acolyte" comes in for particularly withering scorn. "Everything about [her home] enrages me," Ehrenreich snaps. She's only slightly less condescending toward the lower middle class. She mocks Wal-Mart's customers for being obese—or at least the "native Caucasians" among them. Ehrenreich doesn't say what she thinks about the body types of middle-income blacks, Latinos, or Asians.

Ehrenreich's disparagement of the middle class, Wal-Mart, Martha 29 Stewart, and various other targets of the Left these days doubtless has a lot to do with *Nickel and Dimed*'s remarkable success. The book rode the *New York Times* hardcover bestseller list for 18 weeks and has been on the paperback bestseller list for nearly two years now. So far, it has sold upward of a half-million copies in the U.S.

The left-leaning professoriat is helping drive the sales. *Nickel and* 30 *Dimed* is standard fare in many freshman-orientation reading programs, in which schools require an entire incoming class to read one particular book. Among the 20 or so schools that have picked *Nickel and Dimed* for such programs are Ohio State (14,000 freshmen), the University of California, Riverside (nearly 20,000 freshmen), and Ball State (8,000-plus freshmen). Some of the schools, including Mansfield University in Pennsylvania (freshman class, about 1,600), have bought the book for students, just to ensure that the kids don't miss out on its wisdom. Since the book's publication, Ehrenreich enthuses, she's lectured at more than 100 universities.

Not everybody is taking this force-feeding of leftist propaganda sitting 31 down. Conservative students at the University of North Carolina at Chapel Hill protested the freshman-orientation reading committee's choice of *Nickel and Dimed*, bringing in local conservative groups and state legislators to try to force greater ideological balance on the school's reading program. What students objected to, explains Michael McKnight, a UNC grad who helped lead the protest, was the book's biased and misleading depiction of the American workplace, along with UNC's failure to provide any counterweight, such as critical reviews of the book. Says McKnight, "The freshman-orientation package of resources on the book included nothing but glowing reviews of it and lists of Ehrenreich's awards."

There's other evidence that students aren't buying Ehrenreich's pes- 32 simistic line on the U.S. economy. Professor Larry Schweikart, who teaches U.S. economic history at the University of Dayton, assigns his students *Nickel and Dimed* along with other books that paint a brighter picture of the American economy. Schweikart says that many students quickly grasp what's wrong with Ehrenreich's book. "Many of these kids have worked in the low-wage marketplace, so they are more familiar with it than their professors or media reviewers. They tell me that there are better jobs out there than the ones Ehrenreich stuck herself with, that those jobs aren't long-term, and that they understand that she didn't give herself any time to find better work or advance."

If the holes in Ehrenreich's argument are clear even to some college kids, 33 the logical gaps gape even wider in the 2004 book that hopes to succeed *Nickel and Dimed* as the definitive left statement on the oppressiveness of low-wage work: *The Working Poor,* by former *New York Times* reporter David Shipler. To his credit, Shipler, unlike Ehrenreich, cares enough about the workers who are his subjects to try to give a comprehensive account of their struggles to make it, delving into their lives and addressing important economic and cultural issues head-on. Following Ehrenreich, however, Shipler wants to blame an unjust U.S. economy for the plight of the poor. Yet his own evidence proves a very different, and crucial, point: it's often dysfunctional behavior and bad choices, not a broken economy, that prevent people from escaping poverty.

Consider some of the former welfare recipients Shipler profiles in his 34 chapter called "Work Doesn't Work." Christie, a day-care worker, describes herself as "lazy" for never finishing college (her brother, who did, is an accountant, and her sister is a loan officer). She has had several children out of wedlock with various men, and now lives with one of them— Kevin, an ex-con—in public housing. Christie can't make ends meet, but that's partly because, having never learned to cook, she blows her $138-a-month food-stamp allocation on "an abundance of high-priced, well-advertised snacks, junk food, and prepared meals."

Then there's Debra, who had her first illegitimate child at 18. Forced to 35 work by welfare reform, Debra actually lands a job in a unionized factory— the holy grail of low-wage work to the Left. Unfortunately, she can't adjust to work in the shop, has nightmares about the assembly line, and imagines that the bosses prefer the Hispanic workers to her, since she's black. Shipler understands that with such attitudes, she is unlikely to move up.

Or how about Caroline, who spent years on welfare and has worked var- 36 ious jobs, including at Wal-Mart? She actually owns her own house, though, as Shipler ominously mentions, "it is mostly owned by the bank." (Welcome to the club, Caroline.) Caroline is a victim of the "ruthlessness of the market system," Shipler informs us, because she can't seem to land a promotion. We eventually learn from her caseworkers, however, that she doesn't bathe regularly and smells bad, that when she first divorced she refused her in-laws' offer of help, that she then married a man who beat her (she later left him), and that she keeps managing to get hired but then loses one job after another.

How has the U.S. economy let these workers down? In each of these 37 cases, bad choices have kept someone from getting ahead.

Shipler's grim chapter headings are often wildly at odds with the stories 38 he tells. One chapter, "Harvest of Shame," describes Hispanic seasonal farmworkers, who toil long hours for little money, often live in substandard

temporary quarters, yearn for their families, and—because many are here
illegally—don't qualify for government benefits. Again, though, is the U.S.
economic system really exploiting these workers, as Shipler thinks? We soon
learn that many of the illegals have come here to support families back in
Mexico. They send home 70 percent of what they earn and plan to return
south when they've amassed enough wealth (by Mexican standards).

True, since they're illegals, they can't get mainstream jobs with the po-   39
tential for promotion and benefits. Yet for them, this low-wage work pays
off. Pedro earns nine times more working illegally on a North Carolina
farm than he did toiling in a Mexican slaughterhouse. He sends from $300
to $500 a month home to his folks. If he works just two more years on the
farm, he figures, he'll have enough to build a house in Mexico, and it'll be
time to go home. Like many of his countrymen, Pedro is temporarily using
America to make up for the Mexican economy's deficiencies. This hardly
represents a failure of our economy. Shipler nonetheless finds puzzling the
"absence of anger" among these immigrants.

Pointing to illegals like Pedro, who can't take advantage of the larger   40
opportunities that our economy offers, or to people like Debra and
Christie, who, every time they start to climb the economic ladder, do something self-destructive that causes them to fall back a few rungs, Shipler
claims that economic mobility is vanishing from the United States. Today,
he says, low-wage workers can only better themselves if they benefit from
a "perfect lineup of favorable conditions."

The Tran family is just such an exception, Shipler thinks. Everything   41
works for these Vietnamese immigrants. Within four months of arriving in
the U.S. in 1998, three family members were working, earning $42,848 in
their first year in the country. Within five months, the family had earned
enough to buy two used cars. Within two years, two children had registered for college. This is a "heroic" success story, in Shipler's view, because
for low-wage workers in today's America, "there is no room for mistake or
misfortune—not for drugs, not for alcohol, not for domestic violence."

But what the Trans have done, admirable as it is, isn't heroic—or even un-   42
usual. In 1990s California, where the Trans did so well, recall that nearly nine
out of ten low-wage workers moved up, presumably avoiding the drugs, alcohol, and violence that Shipler wrongly sees as endemic to poverty. The average
real income of the low-wage workers in the Sphere Institute study doubled
over that time to more than $27,000 a year. Nor is there any evidence, statis-
tically or anecdotally, that such mobility is disappearing from the U.S.

For Shipler, as for Ehrenreich, the U.S. always shortchanges the poor.   43
Education is a prime example, he says. He tours Washington, D.C.'s public schools, where student scores are abysmal and dropout rates are inex-

cusably high, and—noticing the classrooms' shortages of supplies and books and the nonexistent computers—says that lack of money is to blame. But the notorious failure of D.C.'s public schools has nothing to do with money. Those schools spend some $13,500 per pupil a year—not as much as rich suburban districts, true, but far above the national average and well above what many private schools spend to educate kids effectively. As for the missing supplies and computers, blame a corrupt, dysfunctional system that wastes the more-than-adequate funds. There's no hint of this ongoing scandal in Shipler's book, even though for years the local papers have chronicled it extensively and, in desperation, Mayor Williams and the U.S. Congress have set up a voucher plan to address it.

Shipler's obliviousness to the real causes of poverty also characterizes 44 the latest addition to the "working poor" canon: Joanna Lipper's *Growing Up Fast*. A sometime documentary filmmaker, Lipper traveled to the once-thriving industrial town of Pittsfield, Massachusetts, in order to chronicle the lives of a generation of teenage unwed mothers. Because many of these young women are daughters of blue-collar workers who lost their jobs as General Electric gradually pulled out of Pittsfield during the 1980s, Lipper blames G.E. and, more broadly, globalization for the social pathology evident in the town today—not just the teen pregnancies but also the rising crime and drug-abuse rates that she says followed G.E.'s departure. The town's youth "have been excluded from the American dream," she writes.

Yet as the tale of Pittsfield and its teens unfolds, a different story emerges, 45 even if Lipper—like Shipler in this regard—seems not to grasp the meaning of her own evidence. We learn, for example, that the town's drug problem actually began in the early 1980s, before G.E. left, after social-services providers opened government-funded drug-treatment centers in the area and imported hundreds of addicts from New York City and elsewhere to receive treatment. Many of these addicts, released from the programs but not fully detoxed, stayed on. They then brought friends and relatives to town and started dealing drugs around local fast-food joints and other spots where teens hung out. Not that all the buyers were kids, let alone "excluded" ones. Fueling the market, we learn, were "doctors from Williamstown and well-to-do people."

The teens get pregnant, as Lipper tells it, because they've got nothing 46 better to do. They feel trapped, because "the major institutions of American life," the job market heading the list, "are not working for them," Lipper says. "[H]ope is the ingredient missing" from their lives. Yet one teen mother, Jessica, confides: "I had so much going for me before I got pregnant." Another, Shayla, herself born to teen parents long before job woes came to Pittsfield, says that she wanted to attend college but didn't work hard enough in high school to get in.

It never occurs to Lipper that teen pregnancy doesn't naturally flow from 47
economic status. After all, millions of impoverished immigrants came to
America from Europe in the early twentieth century without illegitimacy getting out of hand, thanks to strong religious traditions that stigmatized illegitimacy. What's really missing from the lives of Pittsfield's unwed mothers
isn't hope; it's shame about teenage sex or out-of-wedlock pregnancy. The
teens talk openly of early sexual escapades, and matter-of-factly pose for
book photos with their illegitimate kids—unsurprising in a culture that glo-
rifies sex and in which movie stars and rock musicians proudly flaunt their
out-of-wedlock offspring. The demise of shame is a far more plausible explanation for Pittsfield's teen-pregnancy problem than is economic distress.

Like Shipler, in other words, Lipper has reversed cause and effect. She 48
sees social dysfunction in Pittsfield and blames it on poverty. But it typically is personal failure and social dysfunction that create poverty. To stay
out of poverty in America, it's necessary to do three simple things, social
scientists have found: finish high school, don't have kids until you marry,
and wait until you are at least 20 to marry. Do those three things, and the
odds against your becoming impoverished are less than one in ten. Nearly
80 percent of everyone who fails to do those three things winds up poor.

That's a crucial truth that left-wing social thinkers have tried to deny 49
from the earliest days of the welfare-rights movement. And as these books
show, even after the conclusive failure of the War on Poverty and the re-
sounding success of welfare reform, they are still at it.

Thinking Critically

1. In your own words, summarize Steven Malanga's historical overview of political responses to American poverty, particularly as that overview relates
   to the working poor. What conclusions based solely on Malanga's overview
   do you draw? What do you know about the War on Poverty and the work of
   Michael Harrington, Richard A. Cloward and Frances Fox Piven, and Richard
   Elman? Working on your own or with a peer group, find and briefly summarize the work of those journalists and describe the War on Poverty. How
   does acquaintance with, and understanding of, those journalists and the
   War on Poverty programs influence your reading of "The Myth of the Working Poor"? Given that Malanga places allusions and references to them in
   the first few paragraphs of his essay, speculate about what he expects of
   his audience. How do those expectations differ from what Barbara Ehrenreich
   assumes about her audience for *Nickel and Dimed*?

2. How does Malanga specifically refute Ehrenreich's methodology and conclusions? Having read "Serving in Florida," the excerpt from *Nickel and Dimed*
   included in this chapter, how fair and accurate do you think Malanga's challenges are?

3. What kinds of evidence does Malanga use to support his own arguments and refute Ehrenreich's work? In what way do the sources that Malanga relies on differ from the sources that Ehrenreich uses?

Writing Critically

1. Malanga notes that many colleges and universities require Ehrenreich's *Nickel and Dimed* as part of a "freshman-orientation" program. Why would a four-year college require students to read such a book? What does Malanga think is behind this requirement? What impact does the excerpt "Serving in Florida" make on you as a college student?

2. Along with *Nickel and Dimed,* Malanga also challenges the methodology and argument of journalist David Shipler in his book *The Working Poor: Invisible in America* (2004). Read Shipler's book and Ehrenreich's *Nickel and Dimed.* In a comparative essay, describe what these two books have in common and indicate how fair and accurate you think Malanga's criticism of them is. (You might also, with a bit of research, compare the backgrounds of Ehrenreich and Shipler with the lives of the people they document.)

3. Malanga refers a few times in his essay to "leftish professors" and the "left-leaning professoriat." How was Malanga's essay brought to your attention in this class? Other essayists in this collection, including Mark Bauerlein (see pp. 518–25) and John Tierney (pp. 496–99) in Chapter 9, argue that college faculties are dominated by liberal or left-wing perspectives. Based on your experience, do you agree or disagree? Is it possible to consider and compare the work of Barbara Ehrenreich and Steven Malanga solely on its rhetorical merits?

Homeless in Prescott, Arizona

B.C.

This first-person account was a contribution to novelist Paul Auster's National Story Project. Auster proposed the idea to NPR listeners in 1999, inviting anyone to send in a short, "true" story. In his introduction to a published collection of these stories, *I Thought My Father Was God and Other True Tales from NPR's National Story Project* (2001), Auster recalled: "What interested me most, I said, were stories that defied our expectations about the world, anecdotes that revealed the mysterious and unknowable forces at work in our lives, in our family histories, in our minds and bodies, in our souls." Some four thousand people responded, sending in stories ranging from a few sentences to several pages. Two other contributions appear in *Many Americas:* Joe Miceli's memoir "Taking Leave" (see pp. 188–94) and Rachel Watson's narrative

"My Story" (see pp. 354–59). Auster read several of the stories each month on *All Things Considered*. Many listeners responded to what they heard with still more stories of their own.

Last spring I made a major life change, and I wasn't suffering from a midlife crisis. At fifty-seven I'm way beyond that. I decided I could not wait eight more years to retire, and I could not be a legal secretary for eight more years. I quit my job, sold my house, furnishings, and car, gave my cat to my neighbor, and moved to Prescott, Arizona, a community of thirty thousand, nestled in the Bradshaw Mountains with a fine library, community college, and a beautiful town square. I invested the proceeds from selling everything and I now receive $315 a month in interest income. That is what I live off of. 1

I am anonymous. I am not on any government programs. I do not receive any kind of welfare, not even food stamps. I do not eat at the Salvation Army. I do not take handouts. I am not dependent on anyone. 2

My base is downtown Prescott, where everything I need is within a radius of a mile and a half—easy walking. To go farther afield, I take a bus that makes a circuit of the city each hour and costs three dollars for a day pass. I have a post-office box—cost, forty dollars a year. The library is connected to the Internet, and I have an e-mail address. My storage space costs twenty-seven dollars a month, and I have access to it twenty-four hours a day. I store my clothes, cosmetic and hygiene supplies, a few kitchen items, and paperwork there. I rent a secluded corner of a backyard a block from my storage area for twenty-five dollars a month. This is my bedroom, complete with arctic tent, sleeping bag, mattress, and lantern. I wear a sturdy pack with a water bottle, flashlight, and Walkman, toiletries and rain gear. 3

Yavapai College has an Olympic-size pool and a women's locker room. I take college classes and have access to these facilities; cost, thirty-five dollars a month. I go there every morning to perform my "toilet" and shower. I go to the Laundromat with a small load of clothes whenever I need to; cost, fifteen dollars a month. Looking presentable is the most important aspect of my new lifestyle. When I go to the library, no one can guess I'm homeless. The library is my living room. I sit in a comfortable chair and read. I listen to beautiful music through the stereo system. I communicate with my daughter via e-mail and type letters on the word processor. I stay dry when it's wet outside. Unfortunately, the library does not have a television, but I've found a student lounge at the college that does. Most of the time I can watch *The News Hour, Masterpiece Theater,* and *Mystery.* To further satisfy my cultural needs, I attend dress rehearsals at the local amateur theater company, free of charge. 4

Eating inexpensively and nutritiously is my biggest challenge. My budget   5
allows me to spend two hundred dollars a month for food. I have a Coleman burner and an old-fashioned percolator. I go to my storage space every
morning and make coffee, pour it into my thermos, load my backpack, go
to the park, and find a sunny spot to enjoy my coffee and listen to *Morning
Edition* on my Walkman. The park is my backyard. It's a beautiful place to
hang out when the weather is clement. I can lie on the grass and read and
nap. The mature trees provide welcome shade when it's warm.

My new lifestyle has been comfortable and enjoyable so far because the   6
weather in Prescott during the spring, summer, and fall has been delightful,
though it did snow Easter weekend. But I was prepared. I have a parka,
boots, and gloves, all warm and waterproof.

Back to eating. The Jack in the Box has four items that cost one dollar—   7
Breakfast Jack, Jumbo Jack, a chicken sandwich, and two beef tacos. After I
enjoy my coffee in the park, I have a Breakfast Jack. There's a nutrition program at the adult center where I can eat a hearty lunch for two dollars. For
dinner, back to the Jack in the Box. I buy fresh fruit and veggies at Albertson's. Once in a while I go to the Pizza Hut—all you can eat for $4.49. When
I return to my storage space in the evening, I make popcorn on my Coleman
burner. I only drink water and coffee; other beverages are too expensive.

I've discovered another way to have a different eating experience and   8
to combine it with a cultural evening. There's an art gallery downtown, and
the openings of the new shows are announced in the newspaper. Two weeks
ago I put on my dress and panty hose, went to the opening, enjoyed eating
the snacks, and admired the paintings.

I've let my hair grow long, and I tie it back in a ponytail like I did in   9
grade school. I no longer color it. I like the gray. I do not shave my legs or
underarms and do not polish my fingernails, wear mascara, foundation,
blush, or lipstick. The natural look costs nothing.

I love going to college. This fall, I'm taking ceramics, chorale, and cul-   10
tural anthropology—for enrichment, not for credit. I love reading all the
books I want to but never had enough time for. I also have time to do absolutely nothing.

Of course there are negatives. I miss my friends from back home.   11
Claudette, who works at the library, befriended me. She was a feature
writer for the local newspaper and is adept at getting information from
people. Eventually, I told her who I was and how I live. She never pressures
me to live differently, and I know she's there for me if I need her.

I also miss my Simon cat. I keep hoping that a cat will come my way,   12
particularly before winter sets in. It would be nice to sleep and snuggle with
a furry body.

I hope I can survive the winter. I've been told that Prescott can have lots   13
of snow and long stretches of freezing temperatures. I don't know what I'll
do if I get sick. I'm generally an optimist, but I do worry. Pray for me.

Thinking Critically

1. In what ways does B.C. either refute or exemplify the "values" expressed
   by other writers in *Many Americas*? What adjectives would you use to describe B.C.'s life?

2. How can you tell B.C.'s gender? In what ways does knowing—or thinking
   you know—the writer's gender determine your response to this essay?

3. Would you categorize B.C. as having blue-state or red-state values? Is the
   lifestyle B.C. has chosen "conservative" or "liberal"? How do your own political, cultural, or religious values influence your response to "Homeless in
   Prescott, Arizona"?

Writing Critically

1. How does B.C. define "anonymous"? What advantages might there be to
   this anonymity? Could you be anonymous in the same way if you wanted
   to? What would it take?

2. Why does B.C. make an inventory of possessions and an accounting of
   costs? How does this inventory structure B.C.'s essay? Keep a log of a
   week's worth of expenses. In an essay that borrows the structure of
   "Homeless in Prescott, Arizona," discuss your spending habits and priorities and what values they reflect.

3. Does B.C.'s essay challenge your understanding of what it means to be
   "homeless"? How are the homeless usually depicted in the news media, in
   popular culture, or in political rhetoric? (Another essay, much-anthologized,
   that is similar to "Homeless in Arizona" in content and structure is Lars
   Eighner's "On Dumpster Diving." You can find it in Eighner's book *Travels
   with Lizbeth* [1993].)

Common Wealth

SCOTT RUSSELL SANDERS

Scott Russell Sanders is Distinguished Professor of English at Indiana University. His many publications include novels, short stories, creative nonfiction, and
books for children. He has received fellowships from
the Guggenheim Foundation, the National Endowment
for the Arts, and the Lilly Endowment, as well as the
Associated Writing Programs Award in Creative Non-

fiction, the Kenyon Review Award for Literary Excellence, the Great Lakes Book Award, and the Ohioana Book Award. In his work, Sanders often explores relationships between fathers and sons, the pleasures of physical work, and the interplay between humans and the natural world. In a 2000 interview with the literary journal the *Kenyon Review,* he discussed how his teaching influences his essay writing: "In essays I speak earnestly about matters close to my heart, not because I wish to dictate how my readers should think, but to call up in them an equal passion and earnestness. As a college teacher, I make great demands on my students. I push my students and my readers to examine their own minds and their own lives." "Common Wealth" first appeared in the November–December 2003 issue of *Tikkun* magazine. *Tikkun* is a Hebrew word that means "to heal, to repair." Founded in 1986 as a liberal and spiritual alternative to conservative Jewish thinking as well as to "deadness" and materialism in American culture as a whole, *Tikkun* works to promote social justice as well as a more spiritual approach to the legal system, health care, and other issues beyond Judaism. Learn more at <http://www.tikkun.org/>.

1 Let me tell you two stories, then invite you to decide which of them points toward the country where you'd rather live.

2 In one story, a man I'll call Sam wakes up in his luxurious condo. Hearing sirens tear through a nearby street, he fights off a feeling of panic by remembering the fences and guards protecting his place from the riffraff of the city. The windows are sealed shut, of course, because the air outside is foul with fumes, but Sam is comforted by the whirring of an air purifier in his bedroom.

3 In the kitchen, not trusting what flows from the tap, he drinks bottled water that his cash has brought here from France. He thinks with satisfaction of the way those numbers in his bank account make things appear and disappear, like magic. As he eats, the TV advises him what he can do with his money. He doesn't pay attention until a good ad comes on—like one for an exercise machine that will turn your body hard in fifteen minutes a day. He glances at the sports pages but ignores the rest of the newspaper, which is too depressing.

4 Instead, he reads the cereal box. On the back are instructions telling how he could win a Caribbean cruise for his family, but he can't imagine going anywhere with his ungrateful kids, even if his ex-wife would let them out of her clutches. He doesn't recognize most of the ingredients listed on the box,

although he's sure they must have been scientifically approved. Finished eating, he leaves the dishes on the table as he left the towels in the shower and yesterday's clothes on the bedroom floor, for the maid to clean up.

Then Sam climbs into his SUV and pushes through morning traffic, the other cars making way for his bulky vehicle. On the drive, he calls his broker to discuss a few stock tips, calls his accountant to review an offshore tax shelter, calls his ex to argue over the kids' tuition. He lays on the horn when anyone fills the lane in front of him, and he gives no quarter to the few, harried pedestrians trying to cross the street.

As he walks from the parking garage, a sweat breaks out on his forehead. Already the day seems unseasonably hot, and Sam wonders for a moment about the global warming business. Entering the arctic cool of his office, however, he brushes the worries aside. The employees greet him, and he sees in their eyes admiration for the fit of his suit, the shape of his haircut, the authority in his stride.

His secretary has laid out the day's tasks on his desk. It will be a lot to get through before he leaves at 6:00 to see his shrink, but he'll manage; he always does. The trick is to make your decisions and not look back. Sam isn't sure how he'll fill the evening—maybe try out the new sushi bar. Before opening the first folder, he glances in a mirror to straighten his tie. The man gazing back at him is happy, secure, fulfilled, his life charged with meaning. It is a man blessed with everything that money can buy.

You see variations on that story every day on television and billboards, in magazines and malls, and you hear upbeat versions of it from pundits and politicians. Before I say anything more about it, let me tell you another story, one you rarely hear in public but one I suspect you know in your bones.

A man I'll call John wakes in the small house that he and his wife, Kate, have been slowly fixing up. Soon their daughter will start babbling in her crib. Their son is already awake, singing as he draws. Through open windows John hears the calls of crickets and birds. Kate breathes peacefully beside him. A dog barks, a hammer rings, and from downtown comes the whistle of a train. Since the conversion to fuel cells and electric motors, the traffic hardly makes a sound, and the air smells of flowers instead of exhaust.

Because Kate was up late the night before rehearsing with the community band, John tiptoes from the bedroom. After a few minutes of meditation, he bows to the morning, and goes to take a shower. The water, heated by panels on the roof, drains from the tub into an irrigation system in the yard, which is planted in wildflowers and prairie grasses. Like the garden, the light he shaves by is powered by the sun, from photoelectric shingles.

As he is drying off, John hears his daughter's waking cry. While he changes her diaper, the two of them talk, John in a playful speech he learned from his own parents, the baby in a musical prattle. He is feeding her pureed carrots when Kate comes into the kitchen, smelling of shampoo. She kisses him, and they talk over plans for the day. She'll walk their son to school, then bicycle to her lab. He'll take the baby to daycare at the library, where she can play while he works a shift at the circulation desk. Since he's working half-time while the children are young, John can do the rest of his job by computer from home. On her way home, Kate will stop by the farmers' market to collect salad makings for a pitch-in supper with neighbors.

After the meal, if there's enough light, John and Kate and the children 12 will tend their plot in the community garden, or they'll visit with Kate's parents and arrange for some weekend babysitting. After the children go to sleep, John and Kate may watch a documentary on PBS, or may crawl into bed early and read for an hour before sleep.

It will be a full day—but then all their days are full. As he pushes the baby 13 in her stroller toward the library, John thinks of the riches they enjoy. The nation is at peace. The city is a humane and handsome place, with abundant green space, decent housing for everyone, and programs to serve the needs of children and the elderly. He and Kate work at secure and useful jobs. They share a snug house, with friends nearby and neighbors who look out for them.

Nearing the library, John takes a path through a prairie that occupies 14 land reclaimed from a former oil depot beside the river. The river, once filthy, is now clean enough for swimming. As a member of the local land trust, John played a small role in restoring this place, and that work makes him proud. He is admiring the dance of leaves and light on the prairie when he notices the baby has grown still. Following her gaze, he sees a goldfinch bobbing on a coneflower. The bird lets loose a song, which makes the baby clap her hands and laugh, and John laughs with her.

Having heard both stories, you may think I've made the first one too dark, 15 the second too bright. But if I've exaggerated the differences between these two views of the good life, it's only because we're being fed sugarcoated versions of the first story every waking hour, and we rarely taste the second story at all.

The dominant media in our society—including most television pro- 16 grams, films, magazines, Internet sites, and advertisements—tell us that happiness, meaning, and security are to be found through piling up money and buying things. Whatever troubles us, shopping can fix it; whatever hollowness we feel, shopping can fill it. A recent billboard for cigarettes used the slogan, "Get More Stuff," and that might serve as the motto for our entire commercial culture.

Our political culture delivers pretty much the same message—which isn't 17 surprising, since the corporations that flood the media with their ads also fund political campaigns. After the September 11 attacks, when Americans longed to know how we could help our country, politicians told us to run up some debt on our charge cards. When Americans wondered how we could reduce our dependence on oil, and thus our entanglement with despotic regimes in the Middle East, our leaders told us to hit the roads and fill the airports. As we look around at this richest of nations and see public debt piling up, hospitals closing, schools failing, forests dying, prison populations swelling, farmland disappearing under subdivisions and malls, children going without medical care, and countless people sleeping on the streets, our leaders offer us a tax cut, so we'll have more money in our pockets. And 40 percent of those cuts will go to the richest 1 percent of Americans, who already have more money in their pockets than they know what to do with.

For the past two decades, U.S. politics has been dominated by efforts to   18 ransack the commons, increasing the wealth of a few at the expense of the many. This plundering might take the form of clear-cutting in national forests, drilling in wildlife refuges, grazing on public lands at below market costs, tax subsidies for the nuclear industry and agribusiness, pork barrel highway projects, industrial pollution of air and water and soil. The looting of the commons has been carried out through the privatizing of prisons, the use of tax dollars for religious schools, the commercial ripoff of the airwaves and the Internet, the scouring of the oceans by factory ships, the draining of aquifers for development, the opening of parks to snowmobiles, the patenting of organisms, the elimination of the estate tax, and so on. The net result of all this plundering is to diminish the wealth we hold in common.

Our politicians, manufacturers, and merchants seem not to notice that   19 we hold any wealth in common. The story they tell is almost entirely about private wealth and private solutions. If the streets are unsafe, instead of reducing the poverty that causes crime, buy an alarm system, move into a gated community, pack a gun. If the public schools are failing, instead of fixing them, put your kids in private schools. If the water is tainted, don't work to end pollution; buy your own supply in bottles. If the roads are clogged, don't push for public transportation; buy a bigger car. If cancer is epidemic, instead of addressing the causes, try the latest therapies. If Social Security looks insecure, instead of overhauling the system to safeguard everyone, funnel the dollars into private accounts, so those who guess right on the market will win and those who guess wrong will lose.

A week before the September 11 anniversary, a two-page ad in the *New*   20 *York Times* for a cell phone service used the slogan, "Get More," and then listed two dozen things you would get more of by purchasing this product, including more laughs, more party invites, and more second glances; with this phone you'd also get more friendly, available, motivated, and involved; you'd get more time with your kids, more of what you want, "more and more and more." Those claims are almost entirely false, of course, and we could laugh them off if they weren't beamed at us, on behalf of one product or another, through every channel of communication, twenty-four hours a day.

Viewed against this background, my opening story about Sam, though 21 plenty dark, should not seem exaggerated. Sam is the ideal consumer, the un-bridled ego wooed by all the ads. He thinks only about himself—his ap-pearance, pleasure, and power. He feels no gratitude to the countless people, living and dead, whose labors support him. He is scarcely aware that he lives on a planet along with millions of other species, nor that he draws every drop of his existence from the wellspring of Nature. He looks no deeper for mean-ing than his own cravings. While the world decays around him, he tries to buy his way to happiness and health, as if he could withdraw inside a cocoon of money. Sam's story is dark because it is demented, a self-centered fantasy that leads to loneliness for the individual and disaster for the world.

By contrast, my story about John may sound too good to be true, yet noth- 22 ing in his life is beyond our reach. He measures his wealth by the well-being of his family, friends, and neighbors. He understands that his own health and the health of everyone he loves depends on the health of his community, its air and water, its parks and schools, its councils and courts. He sees himself as belonging not merely to a city but to a watershed, a bioregion, and ulti-mately to the Earth. Rather than defining himself as a consumer, he seeks to be a conserver. Rather than chasing after fashion, he savors everyday gifts. He finds joy in the voice of a child or a bird, in music and books, in gardening and strolling, in sharing food and talk. He finds meaning in caring for other people and for his place. It's clear that many of John's fellow citizens embrace this vision, for their city is infused with a spirit of cooperation, compassion, and ecological wisdom. To live in such a way, people need not be saints nor sages; they need simply be awake to the real sources of the good life.

I'm guessing that everyone reading these lines has at least glimpsed this 23 vision—which is why I suspect you know John's story in your bones. You've dreamed of living in a household and a neighborhood suffused with love and respect. You've dreamed of living in a community that is just, beautiful, har-monious, and durable, a community that values all its citizens, that makes room for other species, that draws energy from wind and sun, that meets many of its own needs from local sources, that nourishes learning and the arts, and that protects these blessings for future generations. You've dreamed of belonging to a nation of such communities, and to a world of such nations.

The work of creating wise and loving communities begins with cherish- 24 ing our common wealth. I speak of it as "common" because it's ordinary and because it's shared. By "wealth" I don't mean money, but the actual sources of well-being. I mean the soils, waters, and atmosphere; the oceans and prairies and forests; the human gene pool and the plenitude of species. I mean language in all its forms, including mathematics and music; every kind of knowledge, from folklore to physics; and all manner of artifacts, from satellites to shoes. I mean the practical arts such as cooking, building, herding, and farming; the art of medicine; the traditions of civil liberty and democratic government. I mean wildlife refuges, national parks, and wilderness areas, as well as museums, libraries, and other public spaces.

You won't see these treasures for sale in the mall. You won't see them 25 advertised on TV. You won't discover them in corporate balance sheets or the Gross National Product. You'll rarely hear them spoken of with pride by politicians, who seem hell-bent on auctioning off everything that might have the word "public" attached to it.

Where you're likely to hear people talking about our common wealth 26 is at a block party, a union meeting, a street festival, a concert in the park. You're likely to hear such talk among people cleaning up a river, planting trees on a ravaged hillside, reclaiming an abandoned rail yard for a playground, turning a trash-filled lot into a community garden. In short, you'll hear testimony to our shared wealth wherever people come together to preserve, restore, or create something for the good of the community, and not merely for their own private advantage.

What's being sold to us every day as the "American way of life" is 27 mostly a cheat and a lie. It's an infantile dream of endless consumption, endless novelty, and endless play. It's a pacifier for the ego to suck on. It's bad for us and bad for the Earth.

We need a new vision of the good life. We need a dream worthy of 28 grown-ups, one that values simplicity over novelty, conservation over consumption, harmony over competition, community over ego.

Fortunately, many people sense this need. Across our country and around 29 the world, people are shaping a new story about the sources of peace and plenty. You can see the story come alive in farmers' markets, Habitat for Humanity building sites, food coops, town theaters, land trusts. You can witness the story unfolding in citizen forums and simple living collectives, in hospices, in shelters for abused women and children, in efforts to restore eagles or wolves. Those who are acting out this new story are recovering wisdom known to our ancestors but largely forgotten in our hectic, narcissistic age.

Love of our common wealth is the root impulse behind the countless 30 acts of gratitude and kindness that ordinary people perform every day. We all feel it, but we don't always know how to speak of it, or we speak of it so quietly that our story is drowned out by the blare of consumerism.

We need to speak up, to say boldly why we fight for good schools, why 31 we build houses for the homeless, why we protect open space, why we look after the ailing and the elderly, why we pay taxes without grumbling, why we honor government as a defender of the common wealth. In a culture drunk on private greed, we need to declare why we're committed to the public good. In a society obsessed with competition, we need to say why we practice cooperation. In a culture addicted to instant gratification, we need to champion long-term healing and the welfare of future generations.

Again, I'm not saying that such ways of thinking and acting mean we're   32 paragons of virtue; they only mean we're awake to the sources of well-being. In spite of what the media tell us, we know that the good life is not for sale. We understand that the good life is something we make together in households and communities, in partnership with other people and in harmony with Nature. We realize that happiness, health, security, and meaning come to us largely as gifts, and we feel called to preserve those gifts, enhance them if we can, and pass them on.

The glorification of private wealth will go on around the clock, in every   33 medium, without any help from us. We need to counter that chorus by lifting our voices in praise of the wealth we share, recalling how our lives depend on one another, on generations past and future, on the bountiful Earth and all its creatures, on the spirit that lifts us into being and sustains us through every moment and reclaims us in the end.

Thinking Critically

1. What rhetorical strategy does Scott Russell Sanders use to structure his essay? Compare his use of this strategy with the way many of the writers in Chapter 2 use the same strategy.

2. What is a hypothetical situation? In what ways is a hypothetical situation useful to an argument, and in what ways can it weaken an argument? Refer specifically to "Common Wealth" as you consider your answer.

3. The title of this essay is a pun. What are the multiple meanings, both connotative and denotative, of the title? How does Sanders explore those many meanings in his essay?

Writing Critically

1. In which of the two communities described by Scott Russell Sanders would you rather live, and why? Could you envision moving back and forth between the two communities at different stages of your life?

2. Does "Common Wealth" illustrate or exaggerate certain divisions in contemporary American culture? Your response should focus on just two or three key divisions. Refer to other selections in *Many Americas* to support your argument.

3. What, to Sanders's mind, is the key distinction between private wealth and public wealth? What values does he ascribe to people who seek private wealth, as opposed to those who promote public wealth? Adapt the structure of Sanders's argument to an essay in which you describe your own ideal community, one that reflects both your private and your communal values. In what ways do "politicians, manufacturers, and merchants" currently reflect your values? In what ways would they challenge your ideal community?

God Is in the Retails

OMRI ELISHA

In this review of two scholarly books about American evangelical Christian culture, anthropologist Omri Elisha draws from his own "field research" at Christian music festivals to bring context and perspective to his argument. (Some other essays in *Many Americas* also are "book reviews" that go beyond simply discussing the books at hand to explore a larger cultural, political, or social issue.) Elisha is a member of the Center for Religion and Media at New York University. His doctoral research is on the role of philanthropy in the communities of three American "mega-churches." *The Revealer,* the online journal where "God Is in the Retails" appeared in December 2004, is published by the Center for Religion and Media and updated daily. According to its website, *The Revealer* has three basic premises: "(1) Belief matters, whether or not you believe. Politics, pop culture, high art, NASCAR—everything in this world is infused with concerns about the next. As journalists, as scholars, and as ordinary folks, we cannot afford to ignore the role of religious belief in shaping our lives. (2) The press all too frequently fails to acknowledge religion, categorizing it as either innocuous spirituality or dangerous fanaticism, when more often it's both and inbetween and just plain *other.* (3) We deserve and need better coverage of religion. Sharper thinking. Deeper history. Thicker description. Basic theology. Real storytelling." The website for *The Revealer* is at <http://www.therevealer.org/>.

I first witnessed a Christian music festival in the summer of 1988. I re-   1
member standing in a sea of born-agains as they waved their raised arms, swayed their bodies, and bobbed their heads, while rock bands with big hair belted out pop-rock anthems in the name of Jesus.

Like most of the audience, I was a teenager at the time, but I did not at- 2
tend the Creation Festival as a Christian (in fact, in a crowd of almost 40,000
people I was probably the only Jew for miles). I was working as correspondent for a short-lived PBS news magazine affiliated with Children's Express,
a youth journalism organization (known today as Children's PressLine). I
covered the four-day festival in its entirety with a small production crew. We
interviewed event organizers, merchandisers, youth groups, and performers,
such as Steve Taylor and the band Whiteheart, who have since faded into the
special cultural obscurity reserved for Christian rock veterans.

My producer pressured me to ask questions about the money angle: How 3
was the festival paid for? Where did all the proceeds go? How much money
do Christian rock stars make? My producer was baffled that so much consumerism could take place at a religious festival. She believed that there had
to be a hidden story behind it, something provocative, something scandalous. It was the 1980s after all, a time when televangelism was marred by
high-profile scandals involving embezzlement and illicit sex. When it came
to evangelicals, the national media was interested in little else.

Our reporting turned up nothing much to raise an eyebrow, other than 4
the fact that Christian music records, concert tickets, and t-shirts cost
money, and that born-again teenagers don't mind spending it. I even managed to offend an interviewee who worked for the festival by my repeated
questions about the money trail. He was right. I was beating a dead horse
that probably didn't run very fast in the first place.

Fortunately, my coverage did not completely neglect other, richer angles 5
on what was going on. In the finished segment that we aired on PBS, the
most memorable interviews by far were with two young festival-goers. The
first was Jesse, a long-haired teenage metal-head with ripped jeans who
played guitar and listened to mainstream bands like Metallica at home. He
came to Creation Festival because he liked the "scene." He was drawn to
the music first, then to the fact that so many different types of kids—punks,
hippies, metal-heads—were all there together. He also met a girl at one of
the campsites, and they hooked up. Jesus was alright and all, but Jesse had
his mind on other cool things.

The second was 19-year-old Tom, who was heavily into drugs and whose 6
lifestyle, by his own admission, was far from pious. I don't know how he came
to the festival, but on the morning I met him he had decided to change his life.
He said he was "moved by the Spirit" during one of the performances the night
before, and decided to participate in a lakeside baptism—his first—and dedicate himself to Christ. I interviewed him on camera as he emerged from the
frigid lake. I will never forget the image of his soaked and shivering body telling
me, with his eyes closed, "I feel so much better, I can feel Christ inside me."

I have always found it puzzling whenever nonevangelicals—whether in   7
the media or in casual conversation—express shock and surprise over the
commercialization of Christian religiosity through popular media and
commodities. That shock suggests that even the most secularized among us
remain susceptible to an essentially religious axiom: that the sacred and the
profane must be kept separate as a matter of proper moral order. Even people who do not believe in Christ the Redeemer still want to believe in a Jesus who throws a fit when money-changers show up at the temple. And
they want evangelicals to believe in that Jesus first and foremost, as well.

But why should the entrepreneurialism of popular evangelical media seem   8
so aberrant to nonevangelicals, when evangelicals themselves have long since
gotten over it? This is not to say that contemporary Christian media, whether
at is most tempered or most fiercely evangelistic, does not have its share of detractors among the faithful. This is precisely the point. The way people use
and evaluate media is not only meaningful but also highly variable and often
hotly contested within cultural groups, including the throngs of evangelical
Christians in America whom we habitually misrecognize as homogenous.

What makes Christian media so fascinating may not be the extent to   9
which it undermines moralistic standards of religious authenticity that, paradoxically, preoccupy the secular world. Instead, we should be drawn to the
fact that Christian media producers and consumers, as they aspire toward
the ideal of being "in the world but not of the world," are caught up in their
own labyrinth of moral ambiguity over the merits of media technologies as
vehicles for spreading the Word, and over the aesthetic quality of Christian
media once produced. Believers may be profoundly moved by a compelling
piece of Christian music, film, or fiction. They may just as likely be offended
by such "worldly" things, seeing them as dilutions or distortions of the
Gospel. Lest we underestimate their capacity for self-consciousness, it's also
worth pointing out that many evangelicals recognize, as others do, that
Christian media all too often tends to be laughable kitsch at best.

Such insight is gained from Heather Hendershot's *Shaking the World for*   10
Jesus, an impressive and thorough work of cultural history and media analysis. Hendershot covers a wide range of evangelical Christian media, including
contemporary Christian music, pro-chastity magazines and anti-gay videos
directed at teenagers, creationist science films from the postwar era, and
contemporary children's videos, such as the popular *VeggieTales* and the
scripture-based superhero series, *Bibleman.* In every case we see the dilemmas
and tensions—ideological, theological, and aesthetic—that are defining characteristics of American evangelicalism. The revivalist spirit of evangelicalism
has always had to reconcile itself with compromises and contradictions as it
engages with the lost and fallen world that it seeks to lead to redemption.

Hendershot makes many astute observations, but none is more critical 11
to the understanding of Christian media fields than her argument about
their persistent ambiguities. As evangelicals seek to integrate Christian messages into mass culture, they also attempt to balance marketing strategies
with missionary desires. They make conscious choices about how best to
convey religious content, or whether to convey it explicitly at all. The result,
as Hendershot points out, is that different Christian media convey different
levels of evangelical intensity.

The case of contemporary Christian music (CCM) is particularly illus- 12
trative, as Hendershot demonstrates in a chapter that makes apt use of
Christian music icon Larry Norman's famous quip, "Why Should the Devil
Have All the Good Music?" Contemporary Christian musicians and video
makers who want to break out into the mainstream recognize that they
cannot wear their religion on their sleeves. That usually means they must
avoid explicit references to God and Jesus, and play down the message of
salvation in favor of vague and indirect appeals to religious sentimentality
and moral fortitude. Popular cross-over bands such as P.O.D. (Payable on
Death), DC Talk, Sixpence None the Richer, and Jars of Clay have replaced
the Strypers and Amy Grants of old, and their rising success is marked by
their ability to reach a wider audience by "watering-down" Christian elements in their songs while also appealing to young Christian consumers
who are looking for competent musical alternatives to Metallica and Eminem that they won't feel embarrassed to listen to.

"On a practical level," writes Hendershot, "[CCM] artists are making a 13
strategic response to a secular world that assumes all evangelicals are Jim
Bakker clones. On a spiritual level, such artists are planting seeds, softening
hearts, spreading messages that, if not overtly about God, at least are not
about Satan, sex, parental disobedience, and other Christian bogeyman."

For CCM artists and producers, watering-down the message is a mar- 14
keting sacrifice, and in this sense can be frustrating. But they also rationalize
it as a way to advance the gospel. As CCM music producer Cindy Montano
tells Hendershot, "'the thing is, if you want to reach people who are searching, you can't come on too strong with the whole Christian-y, spiritual
mumbo jumbo, so to speak. Because it doesn't mean anything to them.'"

There are, of course, CCM artists for whom coming on too strong is 15
their stock in trade, and anything less is seen as "selling out," pure and simple. Hendershot's exemplar of the "hard-sell" evangelism in the CCM
world is the strangely indomitable recording artist, Carman, whose unam-
biguously Christian songs and videos—including one called "Satan Bite the
Dust," in which he defeats a cowboy Satan with a Holy Spirit gun—are so
"painfully literal" in their missionary zeal that they are impossible to miss.

Then again, unless you happen to be steeped in the evangelical subculture and make a habit of watching music videos on Trinity Broadcasting Network (TBN), you probably will miss them. But this hasn't stopped Carman from being an adamant crusader of the evangelical cause and a prolific marketer of Christ-centered entertainment.

What Hendershot reveals in all this is that what some evangelicals view   16 as excessive propaganda, others see as true ministry. Conversely, a process that evangelical purists view as mainstream Christian artists selling out, others see as reaching out to nonbelievers who otherwise would never pay attention to religiously inspired media. In either case, a great deal of appropriation of mass culture occurs, whether it's in the form of P.O.D.'s crafted goatees, tattoos, and dredlocks, or Carman's awkward attempts at homiletic hip-hop. Hendershot makes a convincing case that such appropriation is part of a common ambition among evangelicals to Christianize mass culture rather than to merely mimic it. At the same time, such aspirations contribute in no small part to the ambiguity and confusion that pervades the Christian media industry.

There is another angle to the story, however, which is Hendershot's sec-   17 ond key observation. This relates to the heartfelt desires of white, middle-class evangelicals, the people to whom much Christian media is targeted, to be recognized as active participants in a modern consumer economy. "To purchase Christian products," she writes, "is to declare one's respectability in a country in which people are most often addressed by mass culture not as citizens but as consumers." Respectability has been a hallmark of American evangelicalism since the postwar emergence of neo-evangelicalism, a movement in which evangelicals like Carl Henry and Billy Graham carved a space in public culture for more "world-friendly" forms of evangelical engagement. Over subsequent decades, born-again religiosity became increasingly prominent among America's educated and "respectable" middle class.

While Hendershot deals primarily with the production and content of   18 Christian media, the "reception" angle is dealt with more fully in Amy Johnson Frykholm's *Rapture Culture: Left Behind in Evangelical America* (2004), a study based on interviews with a cross-sample of readers of *Left Behind,* the immensely popular series of post-rapture adventure novels by Timothy LaHaye and Jerry Jenkins. Frykholm is the quintessential "insider-outsider." She is a feminist literary scholar who rejected the conservative evangelical subculture in which she was raised, but for whom the prophetic narratives of dispensational premillennialism remain intimately familiar. She reads *Left Behind* and finds it shallow, propagandistic, and boring, but she readily imagines a worldview in which apocalyptic fiction of this kind is rich and meaningful.

Then again, according to Frykholm, all Americans are "insider-outsiders" 19 when it comes to rapture culture. Our national consciousness is deeply rooted in millennialist and apocalyptic imaginings that have defined our history. Frykholm builds her case on an understanding of American evangelicalism as defined by its "porous" boundaries vis-à-vis mass culture. Evangelicals and their ways of thinking are never as far removed from the mainstream as they or anyone else might think.

Accordingly, Frykholm does not confine her study to churchgoing evan- 20 gelical readers alone, whose motives for reading the books and responses to them are diverse enough as it is, but also interviews a number of nonevangelical readers (religious as well as secular), many of whom receive *Left Behind's* message of salvation on their own terms, either by rejecting it or reforming it to suit their worldviews.

Rapture Culture is a book about reading, and about how texts are 21 made meaningful through particular lenses, and in particular social contexts. With *Left Behind,* reading occurs through the dual lens of literary fiction merged with biblical or prophetic "truth." The process of making meaning here is especially dynamic and complicated. Frykholm writes: "*Left Behind's* status as a fictional purveyor of truth gives it an unusual cultural authority for readers—one that is both undermined and reinforced by the book's status as fiction." Social contexts (such as family, community, and church) greatly influence how readers interpret these symbolically loaded texts.

Frykholm's discussion of reading practices is enhanced by her empha- 22 sis on listening. Although she provides ample space for her own content analysis and critique, she listens to her subjects with a careful and empathetic ear. This convention seems obvious, but is easily overlooked if we are content to say that Christian media forms merely entertain, edify, or proselytize, without ever asking people who consume them how this happens, or if it happens.

In Frykholm's account, we learn of readers who credit *Left Behind* for 23 helping them cope with personal and spiritual crises, readers who praise the series as a vehicle of prophetic truth but question its literary quality, and readers who reject its dispensationalist theology and conservative ideology but embrace the texts as colorful escapism or even spiritual therapy.

To their credit, neither Frykholm nor Hendershot delve too deeply into 24 the political issues, because the concerns of Christian media producers and consumers are rarely explicitly political. However, political implications are never far from the surface. Focus on the Family and other conservative Christian groups obtain government support for pro-chastity media, Hendershot notes, by subsuming religious messages under the banner of public health. Frykholm observes that apocalyptic fiction is always tied up with political ideology, and that readers of *Left Behind* become engaged with a powerful form of rhetoric that offers a graphic script with which to view the political and social world around them.

More than politics per se, the question of evangelism itself is a fasci- 25 nating undercurrent in these two studies. The authors discuss evangelism indirectly for the most part, and we are repeatedly reminded that most of the Christian media being discussed is marketed primarily to those who are already believers. Still, we see through all the case studies that the missionary impulse of evangelical Christianity is always a factor—and often a contentious one at that—in the production, commodification, and reception of Christian media. Being an evangelical means being a believer, but it also means becoming a bearer of "the good news," and media forms provide one more aspect of everyday life through which evangelicals can fulfill the mandate.

We should begin to look more closely at media forms that are even far- 26 ther outside the mainstream, and even more explicit as pieces of evangelism targeting nonbelievers. Jack Chick's ubiquitous Bible tracts and Campus Crusade for Christ's famed *Jesus Film Project* come readily to mind. For the time being, however, Hendershot and Frykholm offer a critical opportunity for us to recognize there is more to Christian media than novelty, fanaticism, and kitsch, and that Christian consumers are a mixed bunch of people who can be as ambivalent as they are assertive about pursuing the fruits of their faith in the marketplace of earthly delights.

Thinking Critically

1. Examine the structure of this essay. How does Omri Elisha integrate a review of two books with his own experiences and commentary? Identify places in the essay where he summarizes the ideas of book authors Heather Hendershot and Amy Johnson Frykholm and where he discusses his own observations and experiences.

2. What information does Elisha provide about the content, argument, and approach of each of the books he reviews? Who is his audience for this book review, and what is his persuasive purpose in writing this review?

Writing Critically

1. In what other ways have spiritual symbols, practices, and beliefs been commercialized? (Think about Madonna's involvement with Kabbalah, or the use of Buddhist statues and symbols as home decoration.) Do you agree

with Elisha that "even the most secularized among us remain susceptible to an essentially religious axiom: that the sacred and the profane must be kept separate as part of proper moral order" (paragraph 7)?

2. Elisha notes that some Christian music groups view the dilution of their spiritual message in order to reach a broader market as "selling out." Read Naomi Klein's essay "Alt.Everything: The Youth Market and the Marketing of Cool," also in this chapter. In an analytical essay, discuss what "selling out" implies. Who does the "selling," and who does the "buying"?

3. One of the books Elisha reviews is Amy Johnson Frykholm's *Rapture Culture: Left Behind in Evangelical America* (2004). Read *The Economist* article "The End of the World: A Brief History" (see pp. 382–87). In an analytical essay, discuss an aspect of American culture that Elisha, Frykholm, and the writer for *The Economist* find to be "apocalyptic." This is *not* a theological argument—that is, your work here is to argue neither for nor against the possibility of "rapture" or "apocalypse." Rather, your challenge in this essay is to define and discuss an aspect of American popular, social, or political culture that in some way exemplifies an apocalyptic belief. (For example, in 1999 a general panic spread among computer users and systems engineers that "Y2K"—or the inability of older computers to understand dates that didn't begin with "19"—would lead to a meltdown of the world's computer networks. It didn't.)

Dreams in the Line: A Day at the Antiques Roadshow

RONALD BISHOP | Communications professor Ronald Bishop writes extensively about media coverage of popular culture, ranging from topics such as the 1997 death of Princess Diana, the seeming inability of journalists to be objective about *Mister Rogers' Neighborhood*, and the biases revealed in coverage of athletes who hold out for higher salaries in contract talks. The *Journal of Popular Culture*, where this article appeared in 2001, is a bimonthly scholarly publication of the Popular Culture Association. The academic study of popular culture is rooted in the 1960s and involves scholars from many different disciplines. The website for *Journal of Popular Culture* notes that the "popular culture movement was founded on the principle that the perspectives and experiences of common folk offer compelling insights into the social world. . . . *The Journal of Popular*

Culture continues to break down the barriers between so-called 'low' and 'high' culture and focuses on filling in the gaps a neglect of popular culture has left in our understanding of the workings of society." *Antiques Roadshow* is an enormously popular American version of a BBC Television program. For more information on *Antiques Roadshow,* go to <http://www.pbs.org/wgbh/pages/roadshow/>.

Now in its fourth season, the *Antiques Roadshow* is the Public Broad-   1
casting System's top-rated show, attracting 10 million viewers each week (Prisant 109). Each year, the *Roadshow* embarks on a multi-city tour, spreading the gospel of collecting to a growing number of viewers. The program encourages individuals to search their attics and basements for two items that they can bring to a *Roadshow* stop for free appraisals by one of the show's roving band of 85 appraisers. . . .

Let me frame my analysis of the *Roadshow* with a short discussion of why   2
so many of us collect and how our zeal for collecting changes us and the items we seek. More than 20 million of us collect something (Milford D-10)—from Beanie Babies and other made to be collected items to everything from dime store novels and motel room keys to old bank checks. Baby boomers, armed with disposable income and a substantial amount of leisure time, and possessed by a strong sense of nostalgia, are at the heart of the collecting boom. Some argue that "media hype" (D-11), which includes the *Roadshow,* has helped swell the ranks of collectors. But the *Roadshow* is only the most visible impetus that has sent so many of us scrambling into our basements and attics looking for items that might be worth a tidy sum. As Jean Baudrillard might argue, there are deeper reasons why we are in the process of becoming our collections. We collect, he claims in "The System of Objects," in an attempt to reconnect to the past, to "divinity, to nature, to primitive knowledge" (76). Antiques represent "absolute reality" and "symbolize an inward transcendence, that phantasy of a centre-point in reality which nourishes all mythological consciousness, all individual consciousness—that phantasy whereby a projected detail comes to stand for the ego, and the rest of the world is then organized around it" (79). An item, Baudrillard notes, has two functions: "to be put to use and to be possessed" (86). If an item no longer has a function, or use value, it "takes on a strictly subjective status: it becomes part of a collection" (86). In the end, all objects are roughly the same. This poses quite a dilemma for collectors: they seek items for their collection chased by the knowledge that there is a potentially endless string of items left to collect. Eventually, the only satisfaction comes from repeating the act of collecting—the "hunt," as some collectors would call it. . . .

How the Roadshow Works

Participants began arriving for the *Roadshow* at 8 P.M. the evening before 3
the taping. By 6 A.M. the next morning, when my wife and I arrived in Baltimore, the line of prospective participants encircled the Convention Center, wound along a sizable part of a concrete skyway that connects many
of Baltimore's downtown buildings, and spilled out on to several adjoining
streets. Several *Roadshow* staff members would say later in the day that the
show's producers did not expect such a large turnout. *Roadshow* staff
members gave out timed tickets that allowed attendees on to the floor of
the Convention Center for appraisals at 8 A.M., 11 A.M., and 2 P.M. About
2,000 people were allowed in for each wave of appraisals. Many would be
turned away. The "hunt," as described earlier, was in full swing. Once inside, participants stood in a cordoned queue, waiting to get into what Peter Cook, the show's senior producer, calls "triage": the first round of item
appraisals. Participants were sent to a numbered table, where volunteers
wearing gray shirts featuring the *Roadshow* logo distributed small, rectan-
gular red tickets that let participants know into which category their item
fell. More gray-shirted volunteers shepherded participants to these areas,
where small groups of *Roadshow* appraisers waited to make the first round
of appraisals. Participants were asked to give a brief history of the item,
and to explain how they came to own it and whether the value of the item
has ever been established. The appraiser then offered his or her opinion of
the item, along with an estimate of its value. If the item was deemed worthy of an on-camera appraisal, the appraiser sent a runner to alert a member of the program's production staff. The staff member asked if a similar
item has been appraised on a previous show; it thus becomes the appraiser's job to lobby for an appraisal of the item. A second appraisal is
then taped. Of the thousands of people who bring items to a typical *Roadshow* taping, only about 50 will be taped, according to Cook. Of those appraisals, 15 will be included in the episode of the show based on the stop.
Attendees whose items are not selected leave the appraisal area and head
home with their items; some were quite disappointed with the opinions offered by the *Roadshow* appraiser.

When we arrived, the mood of the attendees was relaxed and positive. The 4
event had the feel of young people waiting in line for tickets for a rock concert. A steady stream of attendees emerged with their items from nearby parking lots and parking garages. Some carried their items, some pushed them
along on wagons, hand trucks, and baby carriages, while others relied on family members and friends to help them transport their items. Among the larger
items was a cart with forged metal wheels used by newsboys to carry copies
of the defunct Philadelphia *Evening Bulletin* to their corners. It should be

noted at the outset that all of the individuals interviewed for the paper were cooperative; most were anxious to share the history of their item(s) and their love for the *Roadshow*. Our observations during our time on line revealed several primary themes; a brief discussion of each theme follows.

Pure Curiosity

For many of the attendees, curiosity—about their items and the items   5
brought by others—was the primary motivation for coming to Baltimore.
Seated against a Skyway wall, Rose Slutz, an elderly woman from Alexandria, Virginia, said she was interested in seeing what people brought to the event—to see where the items came from, and to hear the stories about them. With a bit of coaxing, Rose dug through a small black bag and pulled out the items she had brought to be appraised: a Christmas greeting card to her father-in-law, Edwin Young, a Pittsburgh banker, from President Calvin Coolidge (Coolidge and Young were fraternity brothers), and a tea set whose pieces all were shaped like melons. "It's a monstrosity," Rose said. As she struggled with the teapot, Rose told of her strong desire to learn the history of her items. "How many melon-shaped tea pots are there—have you ever seen one?" she asked. Rose's research revealed that the McCormick Company manufactured the sets as a premium item. The Christmas greeting card featured the names of all of Coolidge's cabinet members. "I'm anxious to know what to do with it," Rose said. She said she wasn't sure if it was a collectible, especially since Coolidge was not a popular president. Rose's comments were a nod to the authority held by the *Roadshow* appraisers—the "magical agents," as Propp* might call them. Only the appraisers could give Rose a clear idea of what to do with the tea pot and the greeting card—an idea based on the item's monetary value rather than any sentimental connection Rose might have felt to them.

"It's fun just to see the process," said M. M. Schneck of Dundalk,   6
Maryland. Clad head to toe in denim, Schneck carried her items in a camouflage satchel, picking it up and putting it down each time the line lurched forward. During the interview, Schneck spoke with great energy and enthusiasm about the *Roadshow*. "If I don't come down, I'm stupid. This is something you'll be able to talk about to your children," she said. Schneck recalled looking through many items of her father's before settling on a Brownie camera given to her when she was a child, a clock, and a leather-bound copy of the book *A Man Without a Country*. Even though Schneck said she would still enjoy the items if they were not worth a lot of money,

---

*Vladimir Propp (1895–1970), Russian structuralist scholar who studied folktales and fairy tales.

the opinion of the *Roadshow* appraisers was important, at least in determining whether she would appear on camera: "I don't think I could show it if it was shot down."

Craig Ball, a television producer from Virginia, said he was convinced   7 that it was "absolute stupidity and craziness," not curiosity, that drove so many people to attend the taping. As we spoke, the line had grown to the point where pockets of people were heading back for their cars. Dorothy Howatt, perhaps the most enthusiastic person interviewed by the author, gushed when she said the *Roadshow* was "an adventure." She loved to see the "interesting pieces of Americana" and to find out "what the price ranges are." Dorothy stressed that interest in the history of their items was as important to the individuals who brought items to the *Roadshow* as their value. It was the unusual items that would find their way, along with their owners, on to the program, she predicted.

Sue and Steve Benigni claimed that taking part in the taping was more   8 important than the significance of the items they brought. Sue Benigni said they came "just to be part of something interesting." The *Roadshow,* Sue said, is significant because the program "has high entertainment and educational value." Still, the Benignis said they were intrigued at the possibility of learning the value of their items: wooden candlesticks given to them by Sue's grandmother, a turn of the century ceramic gorilla, and an event program signed by General "Black Jack" Pershing for Sue's great-grandfather. "It would be interesting to find out, [even if we're] given 20 seconds with these people," Steve said.

Christine Magee, a Maryland resident, said her motivation was hope—   9 her father's hope—that the dusty violin she brought to the *Roadshow* in a tattered leather case was a Stradivarius. "He doesn't believe us, so maybe he'll believe an appraiser," she said. Christine's husband, Jim, carried four family portraits. Like Rose Slutz, Magee was placing her faith in the "magical agent" whose work is at the heart of the *Roadshow.* "We've got the family history here," he said, tapping the paintings through several layers of brown paper wrapping. One of the portraits depicted Magee's great-great-great grandfather, who worked 150 years ago as the trainmaster at Camden Yards, where the Baltimore Orioles' sparkling ballpark now sits. "We're across from his station," Magee said with reverence. "The stationmaster is home."

Dolores Fisher-Jenkins of Arlington, Virginia, focused on how far people   10 would go to appear on the program, all "in the hopes that [an item] will be valuable or unusual." A devout *Roadshow* fan, Fisher-Jenkins, one of only a handful of African-Americans in the line, said she watches the show to improve her skills as an interior designer. Friends and co-workers urged Fisher-Jenkins to bring her item, a Civil War–era book that includes contributions by many who fought in the war, to the taping. The potential for a high appraisal was lost on Fisher-Jenkins, who said that she had planned to keep the book or donate it to a museum. When she took it to work, nearly everyone had the same reaction: "Their eyes lit up—they said 'I'll take it!'" if Fisher-Jenkins chose not to go.

The Treasure Hunt

The second major theme that emerged from the interviews was the excitement felt by the attendees about the possibility that their items might be valuable. Whatever use value the items still had was no longer important. "It's like standing in line with a lottery ticket," Ball said. Steve Benigni took a more idealistic view: "There are a lot of dreams in this line," Steve said, casting a glimpse at the participants. The lottery theme would recur throughout the morning's interviews. "It's like finding buried treasure," said Annapolis resident Ralph Petragnani. A short, stocky man, Petragnani brought two paintings to the *Roadshow*—the first from his grandmother's house, the second bought years ago to furnish an apartment. The *Roadshow* appraisers would be able to tell him if the paintings were "junk" or "something important." Petragnani said he had rejected offers to have the paintings appraised. He changed his mind when he heard that the *Roadshow*—"with its name recognition"—was coming to Baltimore. Petragnani touched on the universality of collecting encouraged by the *Roadshow*. "Everybody's looking for that hidden Picasso, that hidden Michelangelo, that hidden copy of the Declaration of Independence," he said. But Petragnani, like Ball, said the taping had the feel of a lottery: "It's the lottery, it's the jackpot." This caused the author to wonder if the tapings of the *Roadshow,* like most state lotteries, draw predominantly lower- and middle-income people. At that moment, the line resembled a line for Powerball tickets.

Such optimism was not limited to fans of the show, just as the desire to win the lottery is not limited to diehard players. Pennsylvania resident R. Edward Wallace, who said he had seen the *Roadshow* only two times, brought a Victorian painting called "Death of Cleopatra" to the taping. Wallace placed the painting in a closet, where it remained until he accidentally pierced it with an umbrella. Despite his misfortune, Wallace said he was buoyed by the hope that his damaged painting still might be worth something. "If you doubt people are optimistic," he said, motioning to the throngs in line. "It's a wonderful game show—who's the winner, who's the loser—and how will they squirm," he said, referring to individuals whose items would not bring high appraisals.

Elizabeth Stuart, who came to the *Roadshow* with Ball and Betty Bainhouse, admitted that she did not know a lot about the African mask she brought to the taping, but said she hoped to learn more about it from an appraiser. In addition, she was sure that the appraisers had never seen anything like it. "I've never seen it on the *Roadshow,*" she said, proudly showing the mask to the author. The impact of the *Roadshow,* she said, is that it makes more people wonder "what's in their attic." Joe and Jamie Duchynski were not entirely convinced that standing on line for hours was a productive way to spend a Saturday morning. A sporadic *Roadshow* viewer, Joe said the program did make him wonder if they had anything valuable. "It's either the mother lode or the big fizzle," Joe said. The end result is that more of us will be following the *Roadshow* all over the country "with a bag of items, checking for value." Pursuing high value estimates is like "the Holy Grail," Duchynski said. Linda Sceurman, who attended the taping with the Duchynskis, was less philosophical, especially when it came to talking about whether an appraisal of her item would add anything to the program: "Who cares if it adds to the show if it adds to your pocket?" Learning not to bypass potential treasure was another important lesson taken away from the *Roadshow* by some attendees; Sue Benigni said she would now carefully examine an item before getting rid of it. "I know now that if you see something that's hideously ugly, you shouldn't naturally assume that it could go out at a garage sale for $2," she said. Walter Gainer of Ellicott City, Maryland, had few kind words for some of the items he had seen in the line. "I think my piece is valuable, but the rest of the stuff looks like Appalachia junk," he said mockingly. What motivates attendees is what Gainer called the program's "Disneyland approach"—the feel of a theme park, complete with what seems to be a never-ending queue. "One more corner and you'll be there," he said, gesturing at the Convention Center entrance.

"Line Stars"

Looking with amazement at the variety of methods used by individuals to   14 transport their items to the taping, Stuart, Ball, and Bainhouse seemed relieved that they had "kept it conservative," by only bringing items that were easy to carry. They soon spotted a short, stout cabinet owned by James Mullican and began guessing what it was. Speculation about the item took over this section of the line. Ball was convinced that Mullican's item would be selected for a taped appraisal: "This guy's obviously going to be taped," he said confidently. For his part, Mullican was not entirely convinced that his item, a dwarf cabinet, would be of much interest to *Roadshow* producers. His sister, Dorothy Howatt, was more optimistic. Built in the 1840s, the cabinet held the family Bible, and, according to Howatt, many secrets. Howatt said that James Forbes, a well-known citizen of Baltimore, raised her great-grandfather. He inherited the cabinet when Forbes died. It made its way through the family: Dorothy "was the unlucky one to get this monstrosity," her brother said, wheeling it around a corner and into a sun-drenched area of the Convention Center grounds. The dwarf cabinet was just one of several "line stars" (a term coined by my wife) observed in the line. Participants would gather around these items, talk about them, ask questions of their owners, and return to the line to discuss them further. Some individuals acted as scouts; they would wander through the line to find out about a "line star," then come back and tell participants in their part of the line about it in glowing detail. The line star also represented the last stage in the dissolution of solidity discussed by Agnew (70). The use value and personal history attached to these newly anointed items dissolved as attendees gave more and more weight to the characteristics that would lead to a high value estimate, and, perhaps, an appearance on the *Roadshow*.

A Public Service

Ball admitted that he enjoyed watching what he called the "forgeries"— 15 *Roadshow* appraisals that reveal that the item is a fake or a reproduction. "It's the look on their faces," Ball said, referring to the reactions of the item's owner when given the bad news. Indeed, the emotional reactions of the item owners are what drew Stuart to the program. She recalled a segment featuring an appraisal of a violin owned by a man whose father had traded a horse for it so that his son could take lessons. "It wound up a forgery," Stuart said with a look of genuine disappointment. The man was "completely crestfallen," Stuart said.

By identifying forgeries, many attendees argued, *Roadshow* appraisers 16 were performing a genuine public service. Dorothy Howatt noted that *Roadshow* helped collectors of all stripes by "showing the general public what's fake," with the result that people are now better able to "pick the age of something." It's important, she said, to be made aware of the things one has—"whether they have value, or if it's just sentimental value." For Bainhouse, the program's appraisers seemed more reliable than those one might encounter in a typical appraisal situation. "You can never tell when someone's trying to snow you," she said. There is no ulterior motive on the part of the *Roadshow* appraisers—attendees would receive "a fair assessment in this type of arena," Bainhouse concluded. The appraisers reveal forgeries "to get folks to be careful about items," said Steve Benigni. "It's a tough thing to see the disappointment in their faces," Steve said of those participants whose items are proven to be fake. "They're always smiling, but you can see it in their eyes. You have to look behind their reaction to see what they're feeling," he said. The stories of forgeries reflected the almost blind faith that the attendees had in the appraisers. The fact that most of the appraisers own and operate successful antique and collectible galleries, and thus had a vested interest in appearing on the *Roadshow,* was immaterial. In fact, the appraisers were treated like celebrities. Applause had rippled through the line when Leslie and Leigh Keno—twin brothers and perhaps the *Roadshow*'s most popular appraisers—emerged from their car, in search of the Convention Center entrance.

Production Values

Rose Slutz harbored few illusions about her chances for being selected to appear in a taped appraisal, and even fewer about her chances for ending up in an episode of the *Roadshow.* "They photograph a lot [of items]," she said. "I'd probably end up on the cutting room floor. It won't make for good television. I'm not very photogenic." Nevertheless, if selected, Rose was ready. "I'll just have to remember to say 'wow,'" she said, when the value of the item is announced. Rose had figured out a batting order for her appraisals: "I guess I'll give Dad's card in first; it's more interesting than the teapot." She then discussed her history as a collector. Once a regular in antique stores, Rose now only visits when the store has something she truly wants. "I comparison shop," Rose said. "Everything is worth something to someone." 17

Many attendees freely and proudly shared their knowledge of how the show is produced. "They want something unique, something that catches their eye," Ball said. The story told by the item's owner is important, but secondary. Complicating matters for the show's production team are individuals "who aren't camera-friendly and who don't react," Ball said. "You look at all those folks and you get a dud—that has to stink." This problem, in Ball's estimation, was not limited to the item owners; at times, the appraisers "are as unanimated as the furniture they examine," he said. Soon, Ball and Stuart began recalling favorite *Roadshow* segments—for example, the little girl who brought an old bellows to a taping and who shouted "That's a lot of money!" when she was told of its value. 18

Ball recalled a segment that would turn out to be quite popular—almost a legend—with other interviewees: a woman brought a Colonial table to a *Roadshow* taping. Leigh and Leslie Keno appraised the table, purchased by the woman for $25, for $250,000. The Kenos' estimate turned out to be conservative, Ball recalled; the piece brought $490,000 at a recent Sotheby's auction. Stuart said "Life would never be the same" if she received that much money for an item—and she would be happy to sell it, "unless it were handed down." But Ball was just as impressed by the Kenos as by the price fetched by the table: "I just want to meet these guys," he said. "I'd shake hands, get their card, and leave—that would suit me just fine." Ball and Stuart later 19 admitted to watching the *Roadshow* and guessing what the items were worth—and speculating whether they would sell or hold on to the item.

Dorothy Howatt proudly told the author that she, Mullican, and Mul- 20 lican's wife, Mary, had brought "family pieces," including some clothing, and an icebox that served as a salesperson's sample, to the taping. Howatt said she hoped that these pieces would impress the *Roadshow* appraisers enough so that they would select her to appear on the show. "They'll fall in love right away," Mullican said with more than a touch of sarcasm. Like Stuart, Howatt said she was convinced that the fact the *Roadshow* had never featured an item like hers would weigh in her favor—that and the fact that the piece has local roots: "It is an unusual piece—it's a Baltimore piece from a Baltimore home," she said. Even if she didn't get in, Howatt would continue to watch the *Roadshow* and continue to talk with her friends about items that have appeared on the show—"at least once a week or more," she said. A former resident of New Hope, Pennsylvania—a town well known for its antique stores—Dorothy said she still gets excited when someone from that area pops up on the *Roadshow*. Like Ball, Howatt is an unabashed fan of the Keno twins. "The way they will explain something— they seem genuinely interested in what you have to say," Dorothy said. Sue and Steve Benigni also showed extensive knowledge about how the show is produced. Steve recalled that the "big stuff"—the most valuable items— usually are reserved for the final 20 minutes of the show. Further, the Benignis had selected items that they hoped would "make their eyes light up." Sue noted Rockwood Pottery was one such collectible. "That's one of the things they'll stand up and take notice of," she said. Still, they said they had no expectations about appearing on television; even if they didn't appear, it would still be "neat to see it after we've been there," Steve said. The Benignis' politeness was somewhat disingenuous. One could see the hope on their faces.

Jim and Christine Magee said they were sure their story about the sta- 21 tionmaster would add to the program, but added that they would be satisfied to learn the style in which the artists painted. Christine said she was drawn to "the trauma and the drama, the agony and the ecstasy" seen in the *Roadshow* appraisals. It is fascinating, she said, "to see people's faces drop" when they are told an item is valuable. According to Jim, an appearance on the *Roadshow* is like "trying for one stab at immortality" for the folks who frequent yard and garage sales. While the show focuses on the rich history of an item, the producers are well aware, Jim said, that viewers want to see the valuable items—and the forgeries. "They're looking for the make or break deal—like someone who bought their item for 25 cents at a yard sale," he said. The Magees also discussed the favorite pastime of *Roadshow* viewers: item handicapping, or guessing the value of an item before the *Road-*

show appraiser utters the key phrase, "Do you have any idea what this is worth?" Jim said his improved knowledge of antiques and collectibles has helped him become pretty good at this game. "It's kind of like antique *Jeopardy*," he said. "The show has really piqued my interest [in antiques]. I'm a hound now." But Jim also recognized that the information provided by the *Roadshow* does have a downside. "A little knowledge can be dangerous," he said, echoing a warning heard elsewhere in line. "Everyone now thinks 'that dusty curio cabinet' or 'my grandmother's corset pin' is valuable."

The Common Man

The *Roadshow*, Petragnani said, touches everyone; we all "have something   22 [we] want to know about—what it's worth." For Petragnani, the *Roadshow* empowers individuals; it levels the antique playing field. It's about "the common man—the common person," he said. Sue and Steve Benigni contended that *Roadshow* offers its viewers and participants "a feeling of inclusion." We all like to be part of a group, Steve said. Gathering for a *Roadshow* taping allowed participants to rediscover—for the moment—a lost sense of community. "We've become so isolated in recent years. We don't know our neighbors," he said. Steve said he felt "a strong sense of belonging" among the participants. The *Roadshow*, he said, "is the common bond." Unlike the antique business, which caters to wealthy individuals, the *Roadshow* "is not elitist at all—all of America is in this line," Steve said. The key to the show is that it "brings out special items of historical significance," a theme that the producers go to great lengths to weave into the program. "They really take viewer interest into account" by featuring a wide range of items, he said. The Benignis, who said they obtained much of their information on the taping from the Internet and from newsgroup postings, said they believed that it is the desire to become educated about items that brings "the antique buffs and everyday people" together. "Everyone can learn," Steve said.

Conclusions

Attending a *Roadshow* taping, one is struck by the similarity to standing   23 in line to buy lottery tickets—and to attending a revival meeting. Participants bring their ailing items to the appraisers, in the hopes of having them healed by the "laying on" of the appraiser's knowledge. . . .

Like the lottery, the *Roadshow* seems to present an opportunity for in-   24 dividuals to attain a quickly realized temporary membership in the "elite." This conclusion comes in spite of comments by participants that the taping brought together people from all walks of life, and from all socioeconomic groups, and the quality of the items, which even to an untrained observer, did not for the most part appear to be valuable. In fact, one random check of 100 participants done by the author and his wife found only nine African-Americans and two Latinos. Indeed, there were signs of elitism in the line—the ascent of the "line stars" comes to mind, those items that many participants agreed would end up appearing on television, either because they were strange and potentially valuable, or just potentially valuable. It is worth noting that the "line stars" were built on the attendees' ostensibly sound knowledge of the show's production values. Attendees were well aware of what the producers looked for in an item, and selected their items for the trip to Baltimore with that in mind. But just as the lottery gives the illusion one will eventually win if one plays frequently, the *Roadshow* creates the illusion that with enough participation in the discourse of collecting—enough digging, enough collecting—we all will eventually stumble upon a valuable item. Althusser* might argue that the visit to a taping further interpellates fans of the show (a process begun by watching the program on television); they (and their items) have become subjects of the discourse about collecting—meaning is made through their participation in the program. In an earlier paper, I argued that an appearance on the *Roadshow* converts an owner's narrative about an item from one based on sentimentality to one based on value. It is at this point, Debord would argue, that "the commodity has attained the total occupation of social life" (qtd. in Best and Kellner 6). Collectors no longer talk about the emotional reasons for beginning their collections and obtaining items. Their narratives begin to revolve around that history of an item as a commodity and its value in relation to other collectibles—and other items seen on the *Roadshow*. While none of the individuals interviewed for the paper were "converted," we were able to observe as individuals—almost as they moved closer to the appraisal area—slowly dropped the sentimentality and adopted the discourse of commodity. Most participants do not come away from the *Roadshow* with exorbitantly high value estimates—just as most of us don't win the lottery. But for many, the sentimentality with which one once viewed the item does not return. Recall the woman with the communion box; unhappy with her appraisal (and with the appraiser) she was certain the item was worth more money. Perhaps when the participants return home, and put their items back in their basements and attics, the sentimentality may reemerge. . . .

. . . The amount of knowledge exhibited by the participants and their love for the show were not the key issues to emerge from our observations   25 of the line. It is far more revealing to consider how the participants deployed that knowledge and that love. It seemed that the participants knew

---

*Louis Althusser (1918–1990), Marxist philosopher who examined the ways in which institutions create ideologies that participants internalize—sometimes without being aware of the process.

that acting like a fan was part of the process—part of "getting on TV," the cost, so to speak, of participating in the discourse of collecting. For the observer, it was like being part of fraternity or sorority rush. Participants knew they had to act that way—which was fine, so long as they were able to take part, and, perhaps, able to appear on camera. It is fitting, then, that a spectacle like the *Roadshow* provides the backdrop against which this occurs. As Debord notes, "the spectacle corresponds to the historical moment at which the commodity completes its colonization of social life. It is not just that the relationship to commodities is now plain to see—commodities are now all that there is to see" (29). Applying ethnographic research techniques allowed us to see this transformation unfold.

Works Cited

Agnew, Jean-Christophe. "The Consuming Vision of Henry James." *The Culture of Consumption.* Eds. Richard Wightman Fox and T. J. Jackson Lears. New York: Pantheon, 1983. 65–101.

Baudrillard, Jean. *The System of Objects.* London: Verso, 1996.

Best, Steven, and Douglas Kellner. "Modernity, Commodification, and the Spectacle from Marx Through Debord into the Postmodern." 1996. Online. Internet. 1 Oct. 1997.

Cook, Peter. Personal interview. 16 Feb. 1998.

Debord, Guy. *The Society of the Spectacle.* New York: Zone Books, 1995.

Milford, Maureen. "Our Collecting Mania." *Wilmington News Journal* 23 Feb. 1997: D-10, D-11.

Prisant, Carol. "Collecting." *House Beautiful* 1 Jan. 1999: 101–02, 109.

Thinking Critically

1. "Dreams in the Line: A Day at the Antiques Roadshow" was originally published in an academic journal (the version reprinted here was edited for length). What clues can you find in the structure and language of this argument that indicate its academic audience and purpose? If you were to edit Ronald Bishop's article for a more general audience (a weekly magazine, for example), what changes would you suggest, and why?

2. Bishop notes that he uses "ethnographic research techniques" to gather the necessary evidence to support his hypothesis about *Antiques Roadshow.* What is Bishop's hypothesis? In what ways are his ethnographic research techniques similar to, or different from, the information-gathering strategies of other writers in *Many Americas*? What other sources of information or authority does Bishop consult to support his hypothesis?

3. Watch an episode of *Antique Roadshow.* The show's website at <http://www.pbs.org/wgbh/pages/roadshow/> lists viewing times for stations

across the country. How effective, accurate, or compelling is Bishop's hypothesis about *Antiques Roadshow*? Why is a television program like *Antiques Roadshow* a useful subject for academic study?

Writing Critically

1. Choose an object that has some personal significance in your family. Describe the object both objectively (giving as much detail as possible, as if you were an auction-house appraiser) and subjectively (explaining its significance to your family's story). Then interview members of your family about the object's significance and provenance. (*Provenance* is a term of unique importance to collectors and curators. You'll want to use it in your essay, so be sure to look it up and use it accurately.) Finally, create a visual document that presents the object as though it were a "line star," explaining its worth and significance to viewers of *Antiques Roadshow*.

2. In what ways does participation in *Antiques Roadshow* create a sense of "community"? Read Leslie Savan's essay "Did Somebody Say 'Community'?" (see pp. 77–81); then, in an essay, determine how Savan's argument about the meaning of "community" in contemporary American culture is supported (or refuted) by Bishop's findings at an *Antiques Roadshow* taping.

3. What gives material possessions their worth? Discuss how Bishop and at least two other writers in Chapter 5 define material worth. Can something have worth but not value? Or, conversely, have value but not worth?

National Museum of the Middle Class Opens in Schaumburg, IL

THE ONION

The Onion: America's Finest News Source was founded in 1988 by two students in Madison, Wisconsin. Appearing weekly in both print and online editions, *The Onion* provides a satirical take on the news as well as "real" reviews of popular and alternative culture. A book by the staff of *The Onion, Our Dumb Century: The Onion Presents 100 Years of Headlines from America's Finest News Source*, won the 1999 Thurber Prize for American Humor. Read more at <http://theonion.com/>.

Schaumburg, IL

The Museum of the Middle Class, featuring historical and anthropological exhibits addressing the socioeconomic category that once existed between the upper and lower classes, opened to the public Monday.

"The splendid and intriguing middle class may be gone, but it will never 2
be forgotten," said Harold Greeley, curator of the exhibit titled "Where the
Streets Had Trees' Names." "From their weekend barbecues at homes with
backyards to their outdated belief in social mobility, the middle class will
forever be remembered as an important part of American history."

Museum guests expressed delight over the traditions and peculiarities 3
of the middle class, a group once so prevalent that entire TV networks were
programmed to satisfy its hunger for sitcoms.

"It's fascinating to think that these people once drove the same streets 4
as we do today," said Natasha Ohman, a multimillionaire whose husband's
grandfather invented the trigger-safety lock on handguns. "I enjoyed learning how the middle class lived, what their customs were, and what sorts of
diversions and entertainment they enjoyed. Being part of this middle class
must have been fascinating!"

During the modern industrial age, the middle class grew steadily, reach- 5
ing its heyday in the 1950s, when its numbers soared into the tens of millions. According to a study commissioned by the U.S. Census Bureau,
middle-class people inhabited great swaths of North America, with settlements in the Great Plains, the Rocky Mountains, the Pacific Northwest,
and even the nation's urban centers.

"No one predicted the disappearance of the middle class," said 6
Dr. Bradford Elsby, a history professor at the University of Pennsylvania.
"The danger of eliminating workers' unions, which had protected the middle class from its natural predators for years, was severely underestimated.
We believe that removal of the social safety net, combined with rapid
political-climate changes, made life very difficult for the middle class, and
eventually eradicated it altogether."

One of the 15 permanent exhibits, titled "Working for 'The Weekend,'" 7
examines the routines of middle-class wage-earners, who labored for
roughly eight hours a day, five days a week. In return, they were afforded
leisure time on Saturdays and Sundays. According to many anthropologists, these "weekends" were often spent taking "day trips," eating at chain
family restaurants, or watching "baseball" with the nuclear family.

"Unlike members of the lower class, middle-class people earned enough 8
money in five days to take two days off to 'hang out,'" said Benson Watercross,
who took a private jet from his home in Aspen to visit the museum. "Their adequate wages provided a level of comfort and stability, and allowed them to enjoy diversions or purchase goods, thereby briefly escaping the mundanity."

Many museum visitors found the worldview of the middle class—with 9
its reliance on education, stable employment, and ample pensions—difficult
to comprehend.

Thirty-five Booker T. Washington Junior High School seventh-graders, 10
chosen from among 5,600 students who asked to attend the school's annual
field trip, visited the museum Tuesday. Rico Chavez, a 14-year-old from the
inner-city Chicago school, said he was skeptical of one exhibit in particular.

"They expect us to believe this is how people lived 10 years ago?" Chavez 11
asked. "That 'Safe, Decent Public Schools' part was total science fiction. No
metal detectors, no cops or dogs, and whole classes devoted to art and music? Look, I may have flunked a couple grades, but I'm not that stupid."

Others among the 99 percent of U.S. citizens who make less than 12
$28,000 per year shared Chavez's sense of disbelief.

"Frankly, I think they're selling us a load of baloney," said laid-off tex- 13
tile worker Elsie Johnson, who visited the museum Tuesday with her five
asthmatic children. "They expect us to believe the *government* used to help
pay for college? Come on. The funniest exhibit I saw was 'Visiting the Family Doctor.' Imagine being able to choose your own doctor and see him
without a four-hour wait in the emergency room. Gimme a friggin' break!"

While some were incredulous, others described the Museum of the 14
Middle Class as "a trip down memory lane." William Harrison, a retired
social worker with middle-class heritage, said he was moved to tears by
several of the exhibits.

"You wouldn't know it to look at me, but my parents were middle class," 15
Harrison said. "Even though my family fell into poverty, I cherish those roots.
Seeing that section on middle-class eating habits really brought it all back: the
Tuna Helper, the Capri Sun, and the cookie dough in tubes. Oh, and the 2-
percent milk and reduced-cholesterol butter spread! I was thankful for the
chance to rediscover my past, even if the middle class *is* gone forever."

The Museum of the Middle Class was funded primarily by the Ford 16
Foundation, the charitable arm of the Ford automotive company, which
sold cars to the middle class for nearly 100 years.

Thinking Critically

1. What is the distinction between parody and satire? How does "National Museum of the Middle Class Opens in Schaumburg, IL" exemplify both?

2. If you didn't know that this article was first printed in *The Onion,* would it
   still strike you as funny? Why, or why not?

3. Satire uses humor to make a larger, usually political, point. What's the political point of this article? How effectively is that point made?

Writing Critically

1. What benefits and values does this article attribute to the extinct "middle class"? Choose one of these values or benefits, and discuss whether or not it really is endangered. For example, compare what "laid-off textile worker Elsie Johnson" says about health care with Tamara Odisho's "A Night in the Emergency Room" (see pp. 438–40), or the comments of "Rico Chavez" with Whitney Joiner's essay "One Strike and You're Out of School" (see pp. 509–18).

2. Political satirists, such as Jon Stewart and the editors of *The Onion,* are credited (or blamed) for an alternatively engaged voice in the American political process. Follow the way an issue or news event is covered both by the mainstream press and by one (or more) of these satirical outlets. To what extent do mainstream and satirical news outlets depend on one another? What are the benefits, to media consumers, of getting news and commentary from both kinds of outlets?

Arguing the Cultural Divides

1. What does "class" mean in twenty-first-century American popular culture? What are key indicators of "class" today—material possessions, moral or spiritual values, political beliefs, or some combination of the three? Draw from at least two of the essays in Chapter 5 as you build your argument.

2. It is often impossible to separate a discussion of class from a discussion of race. Choose two or three selections from Chapter 5 that deal either implicitly or explicitly with the intersection of race and class. In contemporary American culture, are the deepest divisions based on class or on race? Who has the most at stake in creating and maintaining—or reaching across and blurring—those divisions?

3. If your house were on fire, what material possession (not people or pets) would you try hardest to save? What does that possession mean to you? What does it say about you? Now, suppose that you took this possession to *Antiques Roadshow* and it turned out to be incredibly rare and valuable. Would you sell it? At what price? Use the findings of Ronald Bishop, the hypothetical situations of Scott Russell Sanders, and the reflections of Daniel Akst as you draft your response.

6

CHAPTER

Faith and Reason: What Do We Believe?

My God Problem and Theirs

NATALIE ANGIER

New York Times science writer Natalie Angier won a Pulitzer Prize in 1999 for her science reporting. She is the author of numerous books, including *Natural Obsessions* (1988), *The Beauty of the Beastly* (1995), and *Woman: An Intimate Geography* (1999). As an undergraduate at Barnard College in the 1970s, Angier studied literature, physics, and astronomy. She joined the science magazine *Discover* in 1980, first as a researcher and then as a writer, with particular interests in biology and behavior. Angier joined the *New York Times* in 1984. In 1992 she received the Science Journalism Award from the American Association for the Advancement of Science. Angier also writes and speaks about her atheism and the particular challenges of raising a child to think freely and critically in a society that increasingly values faith over reason. "My God Problem" appeared first in the *American Scholar* and was reprinted in *Free Inquiry*. The *American Scholar* is a quarterly published by the academic honor society Phi Beta Kappa. The bimonthly magazine *Free Inquiry* presents both scholarly and popular articles relating to the separation of church and state, the rights of religious minorities, and other issues.

It is published by the Council for Secular Humanism. For more information, go to <http://www .secularhumanism.org/fi/>.

In the course of reporting a book on the scientific canon and pestering hundreds of researchers at the nation's great universities about what they see as the essential vitamins and minerals of literacy in their particular disciplines, I have been hammered into a kind of twinkle-eyed cartoon coma by one recurring message. Whether they are biologists, geologists, physicists, chemists, astronomers, or engineers, virtually all my sources topped their list of what they wish people understood about science with a plug for Darwin's dandy idea. Would you please tell the public, they implored, that evolution is for real? Would you please explain that the evidence for it is overwhelming and that an appreciation of evolution serves as the bedrock of our understanding of all life on this planet? 1

In other words, the scientists wanted me to do my bit to help fix the terrible little statistic they keep hearing about, the one indicating that many more Americans believe in angels, devils, and poltergeists than in evolution. According to recent polls, about 82 percent are convinced of the reality of heaven (and 63 percent think they're headed there after death); 51 percent believe in ghosts; but only 28 percent are swayed by the theory of evolution. 2

Scientists think this is terrible—the public's bizarre underappreciation of one of science's great and unshakable discoveries, how we and all we see came to be—and they're right. Yet I can't help feeling tetchy about the limits most of them put on their complaints. You see, they want to augment this particular figure—the number of people who believe in evolution—without bothering to confront a few other salient statistics that pollsters have revealed about America's religious cosmogony. Few scientists, for example, worry about the 77 percent of Americans who insist that Jesus was born to a virgin, an act of parthenogenesis that defies everything we know about mammalian genetics and reproduction. Nor do the researchers wring their hands over the 80 percent who believe in the resurrection of Jesus, the laws of thermodynamics be damned. 3

No, most scientists are not interested in taking on any of the mighty cornerstones of Christianity. They complain about irrational thinking, they despise creationist "science," they roll their eyes over America's infatuation with astrology, telekinesis, spoon bending, reincarnation, and UFOs, but toward the bulk of the magic acts that have won the imprimatur of inclusion in the Bible, they are tolerant, respectful, big of tent. Indeed, many are quick to point out that the Catholic Church has endorsed the theory of evolution and that it sees no conflict between a belief in God and the divinity 4

of Jesus and the notion of evolution by natural selection. If the pope is buying it, the reason for most Americans' resistance to evolution must have less
to do with religion than with a lousy advertising campaign.

So, on the issue of mainstream monotheistic religions and the irra-   5
tionality behind many of religion's core tenets, scientists often set aside
their skewers, their snark, and their impatient demand for proof, and instead don the calming cardigan of a kiddie-show host on public television.
They reassure the public that religion and science are not at odds with one
another, but rather that they represent separate "magisteria," in the words
of the formerly alive and even more formerly scrappy Stephen Jay Gould.
Nobody is going to ask people to give up their faith, their belief in an everlasting soul accompanied by an immortal memory of every soccer game
their kids won, every moment they spent playing fetch with the dog. Nobody is going to mock you for your religious beliefs. Well, we might if you
base your life decisions on the advice of a Ouija board; but if you want to
believe that someday you'll be seated at a celestial banquet with your long-
dead father to your right and Jane Austen to your left—and that she'll want
to talk to you for another hundred million years or more—that's your private reliquary, and we're not here to jimmy the lock.

Consider the very different treatments accorded two questions presented   6
to Cornell University's "Ask an Astronomer" Web site. To the query, "Do
most astronomers believe in God, based on the available evidence?" the astronomer Dave Rothstein replies that, in his opinion, "modern science
leaves plenty of room for the existence of God . . . places where people who
do believe in God can fit their beliefs in the scientific framework without
creating any contradictions." He cites the Big Bang as offering solace to
those who want to believe in a Genesis equivalent and the probabilistic
realms of quantum mechanics as raising the possibility of "God intervening
every time a measurement occurs" before concluding that, ultimately, science can never prove or disprove the existence of a god, and religious belief
doesn't—and shouldn't—"have anything to do with scientific reasoning."

How much less velveteen is the response to the reader asking whether as-   7
tronomers believe in astrology. "No, astronomers do not believe in astrology," snarls Dave Kornreich. "It is considered to be a ludicrous scam. There
is no evidence that it works, and plenty of evidence to the contrary." Dr.
Kornreich ends his dismissal with the assertion that in science "one does not
need a reason not to believe in something." Skepticism is "the default position"
and "one requires proof if one is to be convinced of something's existence."

In other words, for horoscope fans, the burden of proof is entirely on   8
them, the poor gullible gits; while for the multitudes who believe that, in
one Way or another, a divine intelligence guides the path of every leaping

lepton, there is no demand for evidence, no skepticism to surmount, no need to worry. You, the religious believer, may well find subtle support for your faith in recent discoveries—that is, if you're willing to upgrade your metaphors and definitions as the latest data demand, seek out new niches of ignorance or ambiguity to fill with the goose down of faith, and accept that, certain passages of the Old Testament notwithstanding, the world is very old, not everything in nature was made in a week, and (can you turn up the mike here, please?) Evolution Happens.

And if you don't find substantiation for your preferred divinity or your most cherished rendering of the afterlife somewhere in the sprawling emporium of science, that's fine, too. No need to lose faith when you were looking in the wrong place to begin with. Science can't tell you whether God exists or where you go when you die. Science cannot definitively rule out the heaven option, with its helium balloons and Breck hair for all. Science in no way wants to be associated with terrifying thoughts, like the possibility that the pericentury of consciousness granted you by the convoluted, gelatinous, and transient organ in your skull just may be the whole story of you-dom. Science isn't arrogant. Science trades in the observable universe and testable hypotheses. Religion gets the midnight panic fêtes. But you've heard about evolution, right?

So why is it that most scientists avoid criticizing religion even as they decry the supernatural mind-set? For starters, some researchers are themselves traditionally devout, keeping a kosher kitchen or taking Communion each Sunday. I admit I'm surprised whenever I encounter a religious scientist. How can a bench-hazed Ph.D., who might in an afternoon deftly purée a colleague's PowerPoint presentation on the nematode genome into so much fish chow, then go home, read in a two-thousand-year-old chronicle, riddled with internal contradictions, of a meta-Nobel discovery like "Resurrection from the Dead," and say, gee, that sounds convincing? Doesn't the good doctor wonder what the control group looked like?

Scientists, however, are a far less religious lot than the American population, and, the higher you go on the cerebro-magisterium, the greater the proportion of atheists, agnostics, and assorted other paganites. According to a 1998 survey published in *Nature*, only 7 percent of members of the prestigious National Academy of Sciences professed a belief in a "personal God." (Interestingly, a slightly higher number, 7.9 percent, claimed to believe in "personal immortality," which may say as much about the robustness of the scientific ego as about anything else.) In other words, more than 90 percent of our elite scientists are unlikely to pray for divine favoritism, no matter how badly they want to beat a competitor to publication. Yet only a flaskful of the faithless have put their nonbelief on record or publicly criticized religion, the notable and voluble exceptions being Richard Dawkins of Oxford University and Daniel Dennett of Tufts University. Nor have Dawkins and Dennett earned much good will among their colleagues for their anticlerical views; one astronomer I spoke with said of Dawkins, "He's a really fine parish preacher of the fire-and-brimstone school, isn't he?"

So, what keeps most scientists quiet about religion? It's probably something   12 close to that trusty old limbic reflex called "an instinct for self-preservation." For centuries, science has survived quite nicely by cultivating an image of reserve and objectivity, of being above religion, politics, business, table manners. Scientists want to be left alone to do their work, dazzle their peers, and hire grad students to wash the glassware. When it comes to extramural combat, scientists choose their crusades cautiously. Going after Uri Geller or the Raëlians is risk-free entertainment, easier than making fun of the sociology department. Battling the creationist camp has been a much harder and nastier fight, but those scientists who have taken it on feel they have a direct stake in the debate and are entitled to wage it, since the creationists, and more recently the promoters of "intelligent design" theory, claim to be as scientific in their methodology as are the scientists.

But when a teenager named Darrell Lambert was chucked out of the Boy   13 Scouts for being an atheist, scientists suddenly remembered all those gels they had to run and dark matter they had to chase, and they kept quiet. Lambert had explained the reason why, despite a childhood spent in Bible classes and church youth groups, he had become an atheist. He took biology in ninth grade, and, rather than devoting himself to studying the bra outline of the girl sitting in front of him, he actually learned some biology. And what he learned in biology persuaded him that the Bible was full of . . . short stories. Some good, some inspiring, some even racy, but fiction nonetheless. For his incisive, reasoned, scientific look at life, and for refusing to cook the data and simply lie to the Boy Scouts about his thoughts on God—as some advised him to do—Darrell Lambert should have earned a standing ovation from the entire scientific community. Instead, he had to settle for an interview with Connie Chung, right after a report on the Gambino family.

Scientists have ample cause to feel they must avoid being viewed as   14 irreligious, a prionic life-form bent on destroying the most sacred heifer in America. After all, academic researchers graze on taxpayer pastures. If they pay the slightest attention to the news, they've surely noticed the escalating readiness of conservative politicians and an array of highly motivated religious organizations to interfere with the nation's scientific enterprise— altering the consumer information Web site at the National Cancer Institute to make abortion look like a cause of breast cancer, which it is not, or stuffing scientific advisory panels with anti-abortion "faith healers."

Recently, an obscure little club called the Traditional Values Coalition 15 began combing through descriptions of projects supported, by the National Institutes of Health and complaining to sympathetic congressmen about those they deemed morally "rotten," most of them studies of sexual behavior and AIDS prevention. The congressmen in turn launched a series of hearings, calling in institute officials to inquire who in the Cotton-pickin' name of Mather cares about the perversions of Native American homosexuals, to which the researchers replied, um, the studies were approved by a panel of scientific experts, and, gee, the Native American community has been underserved and is having a real problem with AIDS these days. Thus far, the projects have escaped being nullified, but the raw display of pious dentition must surely give fright to even the most rakishly freethinking and comfortably tenured professor. It's one thing to monkey with descriptions of Darwinism in a high-school textbook. But to threaten to take away a peer-reviewed grant! That Dan Dennett; he is something of a pompous leafblower, isn't he?

Yet the result of wincing and capitulating is a fresh round of whacks. 16 Now it's not enough for presidential aspirants to make passing reference to their "faith." Now a reporter from *Newsweek* sees it as his privilege, if not his duty, to demand of Howard Dean, "Do you see Jesus Christ as the son of God and believe in him as the route to salvation and eternal life?" In my personal fairy tale, Dean, who as a doctor fits somewhere in the phylum *Scientificus,* might have boomed, "Well, with his views on camels and rich people, he sure wouldn't vote Republican!" or maybe, "No, but I hear he has a Mel Gibson complex." Dr. Dean might have talked about patients of his who suffered strokes and lost the very fabric of themselves and how he has seen the centrality of the brain to the sense of being an individual. He might have expressed doubts that the self survives the brain, but, oh yes, life goes on, life is bigger, stronger, and better endowed than any Bush in a jumpsuit, and we are part of the wild, tumbling river of life, our molecules were the molecules of dinosaurs and before that of stars, and this is not Bulfinch mythology, this is corroborated reality.

Alas for my phantasm of fact, Howard Dean, M.D., had no choice but 17 to chime, oh yes, he certainly sees Jesus as the son of God, though he at least dodged the eternal life clause with a humble mumble about his salvation not being up to him.

I may be an atheist, and I may be impressed that, through the stepwise rigor 18 of science, its Spockian eyebrow of doubt always cocked, we have learned so much about the universe. Yet I recognize that, from there to here, and here to there, funny things are everywhere. Why is there so much dark matter and dark energy in the great Out There, and why couldn't cosmologists have given them different enough names so I could keep them straight? Why is there something rather than nothing, and why is so much of it on my desk? Not to mention the abiding mysteries of e-mail, like why I get exponentially more spam every day, nine-tenths of it invitations to enlarge an appendage I don't have.

I recognize that science doesn't have all the answers and doesn't pretend   19
to, and that's one of the things I love about it. But it has a pretty good notion of what's probable or possible, and virgin births and carpenter rebirths just aren't on the list. Is there a divine intelligence, separate from the universe but somehow in charge of the universe, either in its inception or in twiddling its parameters? No evidence. Is the universe itself God? Is the universe aware of itself? We're here. We're aware. Does that make us God? Will my daughter have to attend a Quaker Friends school now?

I don't believe in life after death, but I'd like to believe in life before   20
death. I'd like to think that one of these days we'll leave superstition and delusional thinking and Jerry Falwell behind. Scientists would like that, too. But for now, they like their grants even more.

Thinking Critically

1. Natalie Angier examines the ways in which astronomers respond to two different questions. What, to Angier's mind, is the most glaring inconsistency between the answers given to these questions? How does this example illustrate Angier's main thesis or claim?

2. How would you describe Angier's tone? Go online and examine the tone and content of the two publications in which this essay first appeared. How does Angier meet or challenge (or both) the expectations of their audiences? Find a few of the articles Angier wrote for the *New York Times,* and evaluate their tone. What strategies does this particular writer use to modulate her tone for specific audiences?

3. The writers throughout Chapter 6 struggle with the ambivalence, ambiguity, and occasional hostility between science and faith (especially in American culture). Does Angier believe that it is possible for a scientist to have religious faith? Does she distinguish between mainstream religious faiths and other supernatural beliefs? Revisit and refine your answer as you read other selection's in this chapter.

Writing Critically

1. Angier states that "Science isn't arrogant." Do you agree or disagree? Be prepared to support your answer with specific, well-researched examples. (This is an exercise in subtlety, too. Notice that Angier does *not* claim that *scientists* aren't "arrogant." What's the difference?)

2. Why, in Angier's view, are "most scientists quiet about religion"? To what extent do you feel that you should keep "quiet" about your own spirituality, faith, or religious beliefs (or lack thereof)? Whether or not your reasons are the same as those held by scientists (in Angier's view), describe situations in which you feel that sharing any spiritual beliefs or information is either inappropriate or unsafe.

3. Setting aside all questions of religion and spirituality, what do you personally believe in or have faith in that cannot be easily explained by either religion or science? What does it mean to "believe" something that cannot be quantified, or to have "faith" in something (or someone) even if there's no tangible evidence for it?

To Wonder Again

ERIC S. COHEN

Eric S. Cohen was for many years on the editorial staff of *The Public Interest,* a Washington, D.C.–based quarterly on politics and culture. "To Wonder Again" first appeared in the May 2000 issue of *First Things: A Monthly Journal of Religion and Public Life,* published by the neoconservative Institute on Religion and Public Life. For more information on *First Things,* go to <http://firstthings.com>. The liberal watchdog group Right Web discusses the roots and the influence of the Institute on Religion and Public Life at <http://rightweb.irc-online.org/org/irpl.php>.

Modern societies are the best-equipped in history at satisfying man's immediate desires: food is fast and plentiful; shelter is comfortable and extravagant; gadgets and devices simplify our lives; the Internet puts a worldwide market at our fingertips; modern medicine prolongs life, eases suffering, and even dulls, at least temporarily, psychological despair; birth control all but guarantees sex without responsibility; and television supplies endless varieties of ready-made entertainment. Modern man is safe (except in certain parts of certain cities or when madmen strike in unsuspecting places), mobile, and autonomous; and his civilization is the most democratic, the most advanced, and the most prosperous in human history—leading some scholars to ponder whether mankind has reached "the end of history." 1

And yet, pessimists abound on both the right and the left. Robert Bork 2 laments the erosion of America's moral fabric at the hands of corrosive liberalism. In *Earth in the Balance,* Al Gore assails American society as "corrupt" and "inauthentic" and compares the modern age to an ecological

Holocaust. Feminists decry the oppression of women and multiculturalists decry the oppression of minorities. Men and women of faith condemn the secular culture that pushes biblical morality from the public square. Conservatives bemoan the cultural elite's assault on American values, only to criticize the American public for its lack of outrage during the impeachment of President Clinton. Everyone seems angry or insulted about something, even as a majority of Americans are too busy, too happy, or too cynical to vote. And even those who declare the end of history do so with a note of despair, fearing that man has given up on the higher ideals and grand questions that fueled the great clashes, but also the greatness, of the past.

Obviously, we cannot judge modernity by its material achievements   3
alone; and it is always wise to take social critics with a grain of salt, since they frequently lack the moderation to appreciate the complexity of their surroundings. For the fact is that modernity embraces and promotes multiple human types. The question—Who is the quintessential character of our civilization? Is he someone to be admired or lamented?—suggests numerous, often contradictory, answers. Is it the high-tech entrepreneur or the organization man? The soccer mom or the pregnant teenager? The little-boy killers at Littleton or the martyr who gave her life instead of renouncing her faith in God? The millions of children on Ritalin and Prozac or the ambitious overachievers who flock to SAT preparation courses? The spirited or the apathetic? The unforgiving ideologues or the nonjudgmental relativists?

Plato said that the human city is the soul writ large, and so it should not surprise us that the city, like man, is mired in these and other contradic-   4
tions. But among the confusions of modernity certain human types can, I think, be identified. In prosperous times, the "middling" sort prevails. He is neither totally aimless nor totally satisfied. He struggles to balance the gifts of modernity with its lack of answers to man's permanent questions. He is, as Tocqueville noted 150 years ago, "restless amidst abundance." And thus he is susceptible to certain maladies of the soul: debased irony and cynicism, which reduce life to absurdity; a therapeutic ethic, which deifies the self and devalues virtue and transcendence; the revolutionary spirit, which denies the fact of human limitation or rebels against all tradition and restraint; and, most common, the life of the bourgeois egoist, who is decent and practical but spiritually unsatisfied.

The old orthodoxies of modernity are exhausted. The only question is   5
whether these sad wanderings will lead man to terminal trivialization and despair or to a rediscovery of his transcendent, eternal, and revealed purpose.

In *The Closing of the American Mind*, Allan Bloom indicts American   6
youth as languid, empty, and adrift. "They can be anything they want to be," writes Bloom, "but they have no particular reason to want to be any-

thing in particular. . . . Why are we surprised that such unfurnished persons should be preoccupied principally with themselves and with finding means to avoid permanent free fall?" The moral drifter has no responsibilities, no hope, and no purpose. He is free from all commitments and tries not to concern himself with the perilous questions of life and death. He is a stranger, a tourist, an indifferent observer. He is the television-watcher, the apathetic consumer, the college student who stares blankly for four years from the back of the classroom, waiting, he says, for real life to begin.

The drifter is homeless. Nothing is stable or binding in his life, and so he   7
always expects the arbitrary and the fleeting. Divorced from tradition, nature, and the old responsibility of upholding the family name, the drifter does what advertisers tell him or what his urges urge him. He has sex when it's convenient but never falls in love. His parents are divorced or distant, and his home life is dominated by the anxious extremes of yelling and silence.

When it comes to politics, culture, and morality, the drifter is tolerant   8
by default. He does not judge others because he is unwilling, afraid, or unable to judge himself. His life boils down to the defensive statement, "I'm not bothering anyone." He focuses almost entirely on himself, and yet he is, at bottom, ambivalent toward himself, holding no strong opinions one way or another. This is not humility, since humility affirms a transcendent good—a God—that is a source of wonder, forgiveness, and guidance. Indifference is just the opposite: it destroys the sacred altogether, taking all things as equal and as equally nonbinding.

To the drifter, everything is at best a game, a joke, an ironic play. If he is   9
not entirely humorless, the sadness of the drifter is softened by easy pleasures, repackaged humor, and childish naughtiness. He sits for hours in front of the television, remote control in hand, flipping from station to station, sitcom to sitcom, with nothing in particular to watch and nothing in particular to do. He is not horribly sad, but he is bound by nothing, loves nothing, reveres nothing. He is totally passive, and dislikes himself, but only vaguely, and not enough to do anything about it, since he really has no idea what he ought to do. His laughs are short, and he does not make jokes; he only retells them.

Ironic distance is the drifter's last recourse—the snide filter that reduces   10
all things big and small to one sad unobtrusive monotone. Humans are ridiculous creatures, and we have always been smart enough to laugh at our foibles, our shortcomings, and our failure to live up to the better parts of our natures. This gap between man the stumbler and man the exalted is the heart of all irony and humor, from Shakespeare and Aristophanes to *The Simpsons* and *Saturday Night Live*. And yet there is a crucial difference between low irony and high, between an irony that narrowly debunks and one that points out the distance between the high and the low, the sacred and the profane.

The low irony of our age has nothing to contribute beyond the obser- 11
vation that life is absurd. It is all debunking; it leads men nowhere. High
irony, by contrast, is funny precisely because it retains a memory of man's
seriousness. It points man toward higher meanings by pointing out the absurdity, the baseness, and the limits of the low. To the high ironist, everything is not a game, and so he often treads dangerously on sacred ground;
to the low ironist, by contrast, nothing is sacred, reverence is impossible,
and the only salvation is that others are crazier than you are. Which explains, in part, why so many people watch daytime talk shows—the infamous *Jerry Springer Show,* for example—that turn men's basest instincts
into public spectacles.

The cynic, like the ironist, sees only the absurd and nothing beyond. 12
Irony and cynicism are variations on a theme, which is why cynics are typically quite funny to the rest of us (at least for a while), if only partially so
to themselves. The cynic expects the dark before even looking. He is blind
to joy, blind to transcendence, blind even to the simplest goodness. The
cynic's heart has contracted, and his intellect is cold. The exacting cynic can
be rather useful, since he sees through utopian schemes and sentimental solutions. He recognizes the limits of man but sees none of the possibilities.
He offers no basis for restoration, no direction, no hope. All he sees is a
world worthy of resentment, a world that brings only suffering and
hypocrisy, a world that is ultimately silent and empty.

Dark irony—the irreverent blend of irony and cynicism—is the domi- 13
nant sensibility in American popular culture. It combines the debunking
style of the ironist with the cynical sense of life and death as profane fodder for amusement—a genre aptly titled "pulp fiction." In the recent film
by that name, for example, professional killers engage in trivial repartee as
they load their weapons and head upstairs to do their work. Once inside,
one of the killers (Samuel Jackson) admires the tastiness of a soon-to-be
victim's fast food burger and beverage, then immediately switches into the
role of a dark prophet, reciting a passage about vengeance from the biblical book of Ezekiel before killing everyone in the room. In the wildly popular cartoon show and movie *South Park* the running joke is that one of
the children dies every episode, which his friends find wildly amusing. The
show's first episode—a bloody fight between Santa Claus and Jesus over
who is the real Christmas hero—became a cult hit and led to cover stories
in *Newsweek* and *Rolling Stone.*

The morality behind both *Pulp Fiction* and *South Park* is the same: 14
death is funny, nothing is sacred, and everything is absurd. The thirst for
meaning, order, and wholeness—which marked the philosophical absurdity
of Samuel Beckett and Albert Camus—is gone. There are only fragments of

sacred traditions, which are cut and pasted together with postmodern triv-
ialities. There is no tragedy, because there is no longing for something better; there is only darkness, and the futile laughter of a trivializing culture.

Nor is this simply a chimerical culture without consequences. Eric Harris 15
and Dylan Klebold, the Littleton killers, "whooped and hollered like it was a
game" (in the words of one of the survivors) as they acted out the "Gothic"
roles glamorized by popular culture and murdered twelve of their classmates.
The same nation that mourns over the mayhem at Littleton chuckles at the
pop nihilism that comes out of Hollywood—and sees no contradiction.

Meanwhile, the philosophers teach us that art and reality are the same, 16
since "reality," including moral reality, is just an arbitrary construct. The
deconstructionists and postmodernists who rule over the academy are simply ironists and cynics in different guises. The deconstructionist actively
(and spitefully) debunks order and tradition. He attempts to show that
morality and reason are illusions. Postmodernists, for their part, celebrate
the splintering of morality as the happy emancipation of the mature self,
who is left to cut and paste reality as he desires. "Postmodern ironists,"
says Richard Rorty, are "never quite able to take themselves seriously" because they are "always aware that the terms in which they describe themselves are subject to change, always aware of the contingency and fragility
of their final vocabularies, and thus themselves." Many postmodernists
celebrate the Internet as the structural underpinning of the postmodern
world, since it allows individuals to adopt multiple personae, switch gen-
ders, and indulge whatever fantasies.

The college freshman, whose moral sensibilities have been shaped largely 17
by the darkly ironic world of popular culture, arrives at the university with
already diminished expectations. Instead of being led out of the cave, or at
least pointed in the right direction, his professors tell him that irony is all
there is, that his unsatisfying instincts are the summit of human understanding, that he has already arrived, because the destination is "nowhere and
anywhere." They tell him that "reality" is simply the "prisonhouse of language"; that life is merely an empty struggle between oppressors and oppressed; that eccentricity, revolution, and irony are the only "authentic"
ways to live in the "abyss." Most students, thankfully, settle for irony, which
they already know. And in the end, the distance between philosophy and
conventional sensibilities collapses: students leave just as they began—darkly
ironic, with any vestiges of hope and wonder slowly dying inside them.

Therapy attempts to console such empty and wayward souls. In the ther- 18
apeutic universe, the goal of human life is not virtue or grace but sanity and
self-esteem. Therapy displaces the moral categories of good and evil, the
philosophical categories of truth and falsehood, and the spiritual categories

of reverence and faith. As sociologist James Nolan explains, "Where older moral orders looked to a transcendent being, to a covenantal community, to natural law, or to divine reason to provide the substantive basis for culture's moral boundaries, the therapeutic ethos establishes the self as the ultimate object of allegiance." This new focus on the self is not self-examination in the Socratic sense, since that would require some ultimate criteria, such as truth, God, or reality. Rather, the turn inward is wholly self-regarding; it is, at bottom, an act of desperation in the face of an empty culture.

For while postmodernists may celebrate the great divorce of the self   19 from ultimate criteria, the ineradicable fact of suffering and death and the inherent human longing for meaningful order and social attachment dictate that some moral vocabulary will fill the void. Man cannot stand alone in the face of eternity: he needs the comfort of purpose, the peace of forgiveness, and the confidence of truth. The therapeutic ethic has attempted to fill the void by, as Anthony Giddens puts it, "dispensing with the great riddles of life in exchange for a modest and durable well-being." It attempts to build an anesthetized Garden of Eden, redefining both sadness (now called "depression") and sinfulness (now called "mental illness" or "addiction") as chemical or psychological pathologies, thus recasting the cause of the primordial fall as a psychiatric disorder. Freud, who reinterpreted the panorama of human experience in pathological terms, provided the moral and cultural vocabulary for this fundamental shift in human self-understanding. In Freud's universe, sanity is the best one can hope to achieve—an empty category when compared with biblical holiness, Christian grace, or philosophical ascent.

In the most sympathetic interpretation, the therapeutic ethic is a hu-   20 manitarian, well-meaning effort to restore meaning and purpose to people's lives by establishing the self as the "ultimate object of allegiance." Therapy today attempts to overcome Freud's tragic conclusion—namely, that the primal self conflicts with the demands of civilization—by freeing the self from all demands, restraints, responsibilities, and anxieties. Individuals turn inward, define themselves entirely by their subjective emotions, and become responsible only to themselves. The only external reference points are the interpretive frameworks of the therapists, who pathologize anxiety and transgression as a series of illnesses, such as "Impulse Control Disorder" and "Adjustment Disorder with Anxious Mood." These classifications are taken from the *Diagnostic and Statistical Manual of Disorders,* put out by the American Psychiatric Association, which estimates that "one in four adults will suffer from a mental illness or substance abuse disorder in any [given] year." According to a recent Surgeon General's report, one-half of all Americans will suffer from a mental illness in their lifetime.

But while therapy may temporarily pacify its patients, it does not in- 21
form man's truest, most persistent longings; it does not help the "self" address the most important human questions. Instead, it creates a moral
universe where nothing is demanded of individuals, who are reduced to
mere creatures of appetite, prone to "emotional imbalances," and so totally dependent on therapeutic drugs and experts.

By redefining responsibility inward, the therapeutic ethic devalues 22
virtue, transcendence, and duty to others. The individual is left on shaky,
unsatisfying ground, while all the worst features of modern society—
atomization, fragmentation, sentimental response—are bolstered by a new
class of therapists and counselors. Man is subdued but not saved, quieted
but not answered, excused but not forgiven. And in the end, the therapeutic self—like the ironist, the cynic, and the drifter—cannot help but be
moved by his own self-conscious mortality, by his experience of smallness,
or by his ineradicable, as yet unanswered, spiritual needs. The humanness
of human beings inevitably revolts. But without the old maps to guide
them, the old traditions to direct them, or the old ideals to awaken them to
their better angels, such revolt is either self-indulgent or utopian; and it
leads only to disruption and despair.

Revolt has taken many forms in the modern age, but three predominate: 23
revolt against the ordinary, against the political order, and against the transcendent. The first—revolt against the ordinary—spans human experience
from the mundane to the drastic: tattoos, body piercings, daredevil stunts,
abnormal eroticism. Of course, when informed by some noble purpose, an
honest spirit, and the humility that befits man's estate, this thirst for the extraordinary can lead to creativity and insight. But when transgression becomes a desperate act, a camouflaged cry in the wilderness, it corrupts both
the individual and the city. The revolutionary screams out for a unique place
in the universe, for meaning and purpose, for the thrill of extremes. But
without any basis to discriminate, without reverence or humility, the revolutionary denies that much of what is ordinary is good. That, or his pride
leads him to deny that norms, nature, or tradition apply to him.

Political revolt exaggerates the will to greatness or mere recognition 24
into a social program. Having abandoned transcendent truths or the notion of God the Redeemer, revolutionaries embrace an apocalyptic politics.
They claim to hold the secret—indeed, the destiny—to deliver man from
wretched imperfection to this-worldly utopia.

Following Marx, the revolutionary frames his apocalyptic vision in 25
populist terms; he promises to liberate the oppressed from the status-quo
power structure. And yet, the typical revolutionary has nothing but contempt for the "small-minded morality" of ordinary people, who fail to join

the revolution and instead place their hope in God and family. The revolutionary frames his program as the march of progress, the new beginning. But its reality is dark, as repeatedly failed attempts at the perfection or liberation of man lead to increasingly unsavory methods—what Lenin unapologetically called "cracking the eggs."

The revolutionary is spiritually and metaphysically sick, which explains the   26
desperation of his politics. He cannot accept the fact of human limitation, because he has rejected—or lost—the moral, philosophical, and religious ways of knowing that make limitation bearable and meaningful. He cannot accept the imperfectability of man or the apparent smallness of his own place in the universe. He cannot accept the slow, imperfect business of political reform or the anonymity of altruism; he wants, instead, to be the liberator of mankind. The revolutionary's soul is hardened; he lacks what G. K. Chesterton called the "wondrous vision of the child." Instead, he wants "peak experiences"—such as acid trips or the momentary god experience of defying death. He has no time for kindness and no gratitude for life's blessings or even life itself.

As with the therapeutic ethic, the revolutionary ethic recasts the theol-   27
ogy of good and evil as a secular struggle: the power elite versus the oppressed; affirmative action supporters versus hate-mongers and racists; friends of the environment versus environmental Nazis; tolerant multiculturalists versus ethnocentric imperialists. And again, as with therapy, ideologies of liberation appeal to the desperate, the cynical, and those who simply long for the moral self-congratulation that seems to be missing from their modern cosmopolitan lives. As Vaclav Havel observed:

> Ideology offers human beings the illusion of an identity, of dignity, and
> of morality while making it easier to part with them. As the repository
> of something "supra-personal" and objective, it enables people to de-
> ceive their conscience and conceal their true position and their inglori-
> ous modus vivendi, both from the world and from themselves. . . . It
> is a veil behind which human beings can hide their own "fallen exis-
> tence," their trivialization, and their adaptation to the status quo.

In an age of moral anomie, ideology promises order; it channels anxi-   28
ety and especially resentment into a full-fledged moral, political, and tele-
ological program. It gives extremism the appearance of heroism and
ignores inconvenient facts in favor of unforgiving revolutionary action.
The retreat into ideology splits the social world into irreconcilable camps,
where public discourse becomes an impossible war of all against all and
ideals become hollow tools of party and power. For those who fall prey to
it, ideology really offers no dignity at all; it cannot speak to the deepest human longings in a satisfying way. It offers only struggle, and ends up reducing life to empty categories, constant revolution, and a quest for power

only thinly veiled behind the utopian rhetoric of justice. The final revolt is against the very ideas of good and evil; it is the last act in the modern drama of liberation, and Nietzsche is its playwright. Nietzsche's superman accepts no truth that is not of his own making. He is a creator, a comic poet. He is totally free, bound by nothing except his own imagination, his shamelessness, and his creative transgression. In the end, however, he challenges mortality and loses. He closes the pathway to transcendence, and therefore eliminates the meaning of death—since, at best, he leaves an ambiguous mark on a world that he has defined as transient, arbitrary, and empty. He resents the silence of the universe; he resents the God who doesn't exist; and so he attempts to become a god himself—and fails.

The revolutionary spirit thrives in certain pockets of American society: 29 the university, the environmental movement, the bitter politics of race, large segments of the art world. Together with therapy, it is the false cure for the most self-hating members of the bourgeoisie—the comfortable winners, who feel guilty about their success and doubt the purpose of their lives. And so they tolerate revolutionary ideas, even celebrate them, as a way to supply their own ambition with a moral justification, their own cynicism with a program, and their own wealth and power with the nobility it seems to lack.

But the corrosive influence of the revolutionary ethic (especially the revolt 30 against morality) extends far beyond the so-called cultural elite. For while most Americans still embrace notions of right and wrong, they are less willing and less able than ever before to judge between them. Most such men and women lead watered-down versions of the old bourgeois lives. But they take no particular pride in doing so and would never impose their "lifestyles" on others. They cling to the leftover capital of traditional morality, but they are less steadfast in defending virtue against those who zealously deny its claim.

Most Americans, thankfully, are neither revolutionaries nor drifters, the 31 two deadening extremes of modern man's spiritual sickness. They waver but do not fall (at least not too far). They occasionally shrug off the apparent meaninglessness of their lives, and so retreat into prosaic amusements and blank stares. They occasionally seek revolutionary answers to their spiritual problems. But for the most part, Americans chart a middle course. The problem, as Irving Kristol has observed, is that "the full range of man's spiritual nature . . . makes more than middling demands upon the universe, and demands more than middling answers."

Most Americans are decent, if at times morally lazy, a touch self-absorbed, 32 and deficient in gratitude for the comforts they have come to think of as rights. They are loyal friends, coworkers, and teammates; they care about their children (which, in the age of divorce, often means making tolerable arrangements with their former spouses), take pride in their homes, and show up to work on

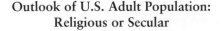

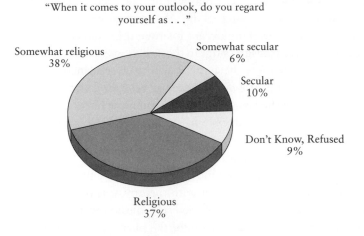

Outlook of U.S. Adult Population:
Religious or Secular

"When it comes to your outlook, do you regard
yourself as . . ."

Somewhat religious
38%

Somewhat secular
6%

Secular
10%

Don't Know, Refused
9%

Religious
37%

American Religious Identification Survey, 2001

One nation, under God(s) Of all the respondents to this survey, a clear majority described themselves as at least "somewhat" religious. Additional information about the 2001 American Religious Identification Survey, conducted by the Graduate Center of the City of New York, is online at http://www.christianitytoday.com/ct/2002/100/33.0.html.

time. Most Americans meet the demands of the day, even if they stumble occasionally. They are eminently practical, even if they sometimes seem oblivious to the deeper meanings that such practical wisdom ought to preserve.

In the balancing act of means and ends, the nation's scales are tipped to- 33 ward the means, which is perhaps the way it must be in stable and prosperous regimes. Americans are, with relatively few exceptions, well-housed, well-fed, and well-entertained, and thus rarely are they faced sharply with the fact of human limitation, except in sickness, tragedy, or war. (Though even war has become a distant, technological affair, especially for Americans, who have come to expect victories without losses and who have a diminishing memory of the experience of warfare.)

Americans embrace irony in their entertainments and cynicism when 34 it's fashionable. They never criticize their friends who see therapists or take Prozac, since they know, heaven forbid, that they could be next. They are cavalier, even-tempered, and comfortable. But there is a spiritual restlessness about them, a vague disquiet with business as usual. They are short on gratitude but have "volunteer" written down somewhere on a things-to-do list. They always send a check to their favorite charity, when they are not worn down by "compassion fatigue."

In short, most Americans are realists and egoists—not the cold, con- 35 temptuous individuals portrayed by Ayn Rand, but the considerate sort, who open doors, help with the dishes, and take pride in being kind and generous, assuming the sacrifice is not too great. Such individuals are rationally moral—they do what's right because it's right, ultimately, but also because it preserves the right appearances. Egoists are ambitious; they seek prestige, originality, and influence as the most important achievements. But they are also realists; they are worldly and calculating, and tend to preserve and build (usually wealth) rather than deconstruct. They are not, at bottom, driven by a love of material goods (though they are attentive consumers), but by the desire for autonomy—and specifically, the desire to build for themselves and their families a suburban air-conditioned shelter from the uncertainties and impersonalities of modern life. Their ultimate goal is to retire early so that they can "do what they really want to do"—which is usually something admirable, such as spend time with their families, or something harmless, such as play golf.

For most such egoists, pursuit of self-interest is moderated by other 36 longings—a real desire to do good, love of family and friends, a sense of honor and decency. In short, most egoists have limits, and the drives of their ego are tempered by the realization that life alone, even life at the top, is lonely and unsatisfying. The torment of the egoist is in trying to balance what often appear to him as competing goods—between work and family, success and leisure, ambition and virtue. The egoist struggles to see the good, and often experiences life as an endless calculation of means and ends, where both the efficacy of the means and the meaning of the ends are perpetually uncertain. He is often torn between his hardened worldly self and his wish to lead a more charitable life. He struggles with the periodic realization of his own limits, the pangs of his conscience, and his longing for deeper meanings. He wavers between satisfaction and angst, all the while making sure not to lose ground in the social world of reputation and reward, always making sure to get things done, even if he is never certain why he does them and is never entirely satisfied with the results.

The instincts of the bourgeoisie are to be admired, not criticized. But 37 these instincts are not enough for a complete life; they are the means, not the end; the tools, not the design. Many Baby Boomers, now in their forties and fifties, have begun to realize that comfort and security are important but limited. Confronted ever more clearly with the fact of their own mortality, they are beginning to consider the fundamental questions of existence, which they have ignored, feared, or actively forgotten for much of their lives. They are beginning to realize, in a deeper way, their own limits—not just the final limit of death, but their own growing anxiety about the "why" of existence and the robustness of their souls.

The spiritual searches of Baby Boomers have taken many directions,   38
some admirable and ennobling, others drastic and destructive. Some renounce the world as fallen and proclaim themselves as among the few who will be saved—the Denver-based "Concerned Christians" cult, for example, whose members were deported from Israel last year for plotting a gunfight in the belief that it would hasten the apocalypse. Others are sentimental; they celebrate the "oneness of all things" and the "inner child" who can do no wrong. Some want to spiritualize their workaday lives—evident in best-selling books like *The Tao of Abundance* and *What Would Buddha Do? 101 Answers to Life's Daily Dilemmas*. Others have abandoned modern life altogether; they retreat to ashrams in the Himalayas, wellness centers, or underground swamis. Or they join strange, often ruinous cults, such as the Raelians and Heaven's Gate.

But the best among them, the true seekers, just want to be better human   39
beings; they are, as philosopher Peter Emberley puts it, "simply looking for a little grace and an opportunity to express indebtedness, fidelity, and reverence." They seek, above all, a source of forgiveness for their shortcomings and a source of strength in their quest for self-renewal, which neither irony nor cynicism, therapy nor revolution, can ever truly provide.

The modern age is tremendous for its accomplishments: wealth, com-   40
fort, more equal opportunity, scientific discovery. But despite its achievements, modernity lacks answers to man's fundamental questions; it lacks the transcendent vision that makes life joyful and death meaningful; and, as Daniel Bell and others have observed, its very success often undermines its virtues. Wealth degenerates into indulgence; tolerance degenerates into unthinking relativism; science without philosophy reduces man to a laboratory study; technology without humility tempts him into dangerous projects, such as cloning, and into the illusion of divinity and immortality. For all his accomplishments, modern man needs his ancient forebears, who provide better answers to his most enduring questions.

Indeed, as Leon Kass and others have argued, the prospect of genetic   41
engineering brings modernity to a crossroads. It raises once inconceivable questions: Do humans have to die? Is the purpose of knowledge to overcome death? To the scientists and technologists on the "cutting edge," immortality is the final triumph of man over nature; man becomes the irreverent creator, the technological superman (or at least some men do, while the rest of us, like it or not, are condemned to live in the dystopian world they are creating).

The ancients knew better, and it is to their old wisdom that modern man   42
must return. In both the classical and biblical vision, death awakens man
to the preciousness of life; mortality awakens him to the possibility of transcendence; and constant recognition of his own imperfection reminds him
of the need for restraint and repentance.

In his misplaced quest for autonomy—freedom from want, freedom from   43
morality, freedom from death—modern man has forgotten how to see; he
has turned his back on his essential nature. He treats the human experience
of incompleteness—the fact of suffering, alienation, and death—as a problem to be solved, a sickness to be cured, a stirring to be forgotten. And so he
forgets what his wise and wondering ancestors remembered—that man is
not fully of this world; that the beginning of wisdom is not only realizing the
limits of one's knowledge but the ultimate meaning of one's limits.

Reverence is not dead in America, as the religious response to the Lit-   44
tleton massacre, the continuing strength of faith in the most degraded parts
of America's inner cities, and the recent surge of public-policy interest in
faith-based organizations all demonstrate. The military code still honors
and preserves the virtues of courage, discipline, and temperance. The motto
"In God We Trust" remains at the center of American self-understanding.

Even as the disorders of the age continue to worsen, there are signs of   45
an awakening. The modern age of religious wandering is approaching the
top (or bottom) of its (inverse) crescendo: some, thankfully, want to live
again or for the first time by different notes, better notes, older notes. They
want to restore the tattered old maps that they know to exist. It is too soon
to tell whether the spiritual seekers of our age can restore modernity from
within, or even restore faithful platoons inside the spiritual desert: the
crescendo may be too loud, the wandering may continue indefinitely. But
that is no reason not to hope, no reason not to wonder, no reason not to
yearn for holiness in a disenchanted age.

Thinking Critically

1. Eric Cohen suggests many divisions in American culture, surprisingly few of
   them conservative. What, in Cohen's opinion, are the qualities or viewpoints dividing American culture? Are the examples and illustrations he offers for these qualities and viewpoints satisfactory?

2. How does Cohen describe the following personality types: the revolutionary, the
   cynic, the drifter, the egoist, the Baby Boomer? What values does he ascribe to
   each of these types? Does he ever cross the line from type to *stereo*type?

3. Cohen uses classification to structure his essay. What is the broad subject
   of his essay, and how does he use classification to divide and explain that
   subject?

Writing Critically

1. In an essay that, like "To Wonder Again," uses classification to provide its structure, describe the different ways in which students on your campus (or people in your community) engage or keep aloof from social and political events. You may borrow or adapt Cohen's terms, but be sure to define and illustrate them from your own context and perspective.

2. In paragraph 4, Cohen identifies four "maladies of the soul" that he says are common in contemporary American culture. Select one of these "maladies" and, in an argumentative essay, discuss its causes and its attributes and propose a remedy. (Conversely, you might argue that what Cohen calls a "malady" is in fact not a malady at all but rather something useful and even spiritual.)

3. What is the "middle course" (paragraph 31), described by Cohen? Throughout *Many Americas,* in ways both explicit and implicit, essayists suggest and reporters describe ways in which people live a "middle course." Cohen describes such people as "realists and egoists." In an essay, compare Cohen's "middle course" with that described or suggested by at least one other writer in *Many Americas.*

Do the Spirits Move You?

JILL NEIMARK

New York City–based journalist Jill Neimark reports with eloquence, wit, and candor on the intersections of science and spirituality in American culture. She is writer and features editor for *Psychology Today,* where "Do the Spirits Move You?" appeared in 1996. In 2003 Neimark joined the magazine *Science & Spirit* as articles editor. For more information about *Science & Spirit,* go to <http://www.science-spirit.org>.

I have always had a secret and embarrassing love of psychics. But I'm an unfaithful lover, I wander from one to the next, infatuated and then disillusioned, on the hunt for something I can hardly set a name to. A cosmic compass in this crazy world? My own wiretap on God? Or just the scoop on an old boyfriend?   1

There have been some uncanny, spinetingling "hits"—psychic parlance for accurate predictions—in my psychic readings over the years, and just as   2 many misses. It's the hits that keep me coming back, jockeying between faith and doubt. The moment I sit for a reading, I am admitting a whole starry night of possibilities: that my life has narrative force and heft; that time may not travel in a straight line; that there is sacred order in seeming disorder.

Even stopping by the table of a blue-haired, red-lipsticked tarot card 3
reader in New York City's East Village, I am on a half-acknowledged quest. As physician Larry Dossey, M.D., author of *Prayer Is Good Medicine,* puts it, "I have a passion for psychic phenomena, because they tell us we may have to think in new ways about how consciousness behaves."

He's not alone in his passion. As of this writing, Betty J. Eadie's *Em-* 4
braced by the Light has been on the best-seller list for 93 weeks. Televi-sion's cult hit, *The X Files,* reels in 8 million households per show. And *Many Lives, Many Masters,* the book in which psychiatrist Brian Weiss, M.D., describes the benefits of past-life therapy, has now been printed in 17 languages. At California Pacific Medical Center in San Francisco, Eliz-abeth Targ, M.D., is overseeing a national study to determine the effect of remote prayer on healing AIDS patients. A previous study showed results that were promising enough to warrant further research.

Even the CIA came out of the closet last year with its abashed confession 5
that the government agency had spent $20 million on psychic research in the last two decades. Gallup polls show that 69 percent of Americans believe in angels, half believe they have their own guardian angels, and 48 percent be-lieve UFOs are real. Last April, Robert Miller, the governor of Nevada, re-named State Route 375 the Extraterrestrial Highway, supposedly because of the frequency of UFO sightings. Dionne Warwick's Psychic Friends Network logs 4 million minutes a month at $3.99 a minute and last spring celebrated its 10 millionth caller. Even that wonderful relic of my childhood, the Magic 8-Ball, has resurfaced, reaching record-breaking sales of a million balls a year.

Not that our culture hasn't always had a mystical bent; think Emerson 6
and the transcendentalists. But why are we now turning to oracles in huge numbers? Who is this new "vast middle-class of credulous neospiritualists"—as *Newsweek* so aptly referred to them in a recent cover story?

Traveling Through the Twilight Zone

As a serial monogamist, I've always been able to preserve the illusion that 7
my psychics were better than they actually were. I got to know and like them. Above all—probably like most of us—I tended to sift out and re-member only the remarkable moments. There was the time a healer and clairvoyant named Jason Schulman sat across the room from me and with-out knowing a single fact about my history, described down to the point of a pinhead exactly where pain was throbbing in my body, despite no outward

sign to clue him in. There was the morning my friend called me before and after a phone reading with a psychic named Rochelle. He said the first words out of the visionary's mouth were, "What's this about Romania?" He and I marveled over the peculiarity of extrasensory perception—it was I who was flying to Romania the following week, not he. Had our talk about my trip that morning lingered around him, in some electromagnetic corona around his head, one that she'd picked up but not precisely?

For this article I wantonly sampled readings—eight of them in a single 8 week—culled from friends, recommendations, books, and newspaper articles. I followed a reporter's mandate for objectivity, and so prepared myself by talking to skeptics as well as believers. And, for the first time in my life, even with a glut of readings, I came up nearly empty-handed.

I had never before compared and contrasted readings; but as soon as I 9 did it became clear they were like verbal Rorschach prints, their interpretation dependant on the beholder. They were all different; they could all have been at least somewhat true. Then, because the senior editor of this magazine emphatically declared that he was "horrified" to see this subject taken seriously, we assembled a list of simple questions for the intuitives to answer: How many siblings do I have? What does my uncle do for a living? Almost uniformly, they either got the facts wrong or claimed their "guides" did not allow them to see such trivia because it had no spiritual significance. Even if I give professional seers leeway, for working creatively and intuitively, for accessing a part and not a whole, I can't help wondering why it was hard for them to retrieve such simple information.

Two of the eight seemed to hit the bull's-eye several times. One was 10 Mary Jo McCabe, a New Orleans clairvoyant and author of *Learn to See*, a book about developing your own intuitive ability. I'd had a reading from her a few months earlier on the phone. In her previous reading, she'd correctly predicted the amount of money I'd be offered for a job (she was proved right the following week). In my "test" reading of her, she saw that in September of 1994 I'd moved, and that the move was very hard for me (both true). She also saw bookends coming together in 1993—the year my first novel was published. When I asked her what our senior editor had been doing in September of 1995, she saw "a roomful of furniture covered with sheets and all of a sudden he's taking off the sheets. He has a new placement in life." As it turns out, he had also moved into a new home then. "There were no sheets on the furniture," he said, "but my wife and I spent most of October unpacking." Ever the joking nonbeliever, he added "Maybe the previous family kept sheets on their furniture."

Another reader, Carolyn Myss, a "medical intuitive," has worked 11 closely with Norman Shealy, M.D., Ph.D., a Missouri physician and founding president of the American Holistic Medical Association, and Christiane Northrup, M.D., a Maine doctor specializing in women's health. Both physicians have referred patients to Myss for readings that confirmed their own, independent medical diagnoses. Myss diagnosed me by phone, correctly identifying portions of my medical history. While Myss didn't get the whole picture, she seemed to genuinely "see" things.

It seems that even the best readers are like radio stations in a lightning 12 storm, picking up an occasional signal perfectly, yet transmitting a lot of static as well. Dr. Dossey—who early in his career had experienced three detailed precognitive dreams but who has not had one since—respects those rare, perfect signals for the questions they make us ask about space and time: "In my case, it was like, Dossey here's the message: Time is not linear. You got it? Yup, I've got it."

The Illogic of Belief

Yet our capacity for credulity is large, and too often we see clothes the Em- 13 peror isn't wearing. Ray Hyman, Ph.D., a psychologist at the University of Oregon and perhaps the field's most relentless debunker of all things psychic, worked as a palm reader when he was a college student, and was deeply convinced of its accuracy. Then, at a friend's suggestion, he started telling clients the opposite of what he "saw" in their palms. They were as enthusiastic as those who'd come before, and Hyman was sufficiently shaken to switch his major from journalism to psychology. "My specialty is human error," he says today.

The tendency for people to agree with what they've been told at read- 14 ings has been dubbed the Barnum effect, in honor of P. T. Barnum's line, "There's a sucker born every minute." A legendary test of the Barnum effect was offered in Paris in the 1970s, by Michel Gauquelin, who placed an ad offering free personal horoscopes. Later, 94 percent of the recipients rated their horoscope accurate. Each person had received the same horoscope, that of one of France's most notorious mass murderers.

The Barnum effect is heightened incredibly in one-on-one readings, 15 simply because of the way most psychics approach them. Many offer a kind of messianic authority that both elevates and deflates the listener, and that may veer from warmly embracing to hostile—an all-knowing blend of mother's milk and a slap in the face.

When I began responding to what one visionary was saying to me, she cut 16 me off. . . . "I don't like any help in someone's file, so butt out." Another said my father was very protective; when I disagreed, she retorted, "You don't know your father. You've never known your father." When a world-renowned seer told me I wanted to move west, I assured him that I had tried that the year before and discovered I was deeply attached to New York. I never wanted to leave again. He replied, "That's your head talking. Your heart wants to move."

I suspect it's this psychic hubris that catapults some readers to fame. 17 This isn't as benign as it may sound. "I've known my share of psychic casualties," Mark Matousek wrote in a controversial *Common Boundary* magazine article entitled "Painting Devils." "A few years ago," he wrote, "an otherwise brilliant, politically active liberal I know actually followed his psychic teacher's brainstorm to buy Krugerrands while apartheid was still being practiced in South Africa. Someone else was told by a psychic that he was about to embark on the most important love affair of his life, then had his bones jumped by that same wacko."

What is really at work in a psychic reading? Why do some of the psy- 18 chics get it right some of the time? And why do "ordinary" folks sometimes come up with uncannily accurate predictions themselves? After a thoroughly disappointing session with a tarot card reader, I traded tarot card readings with the art director at this magazine. We don't know each other well, but I was able to tell her that she'd recently given the boot to two men in her life, which she had actually done the week before; and she was able to describe my emotional state as accurately as I could have myself.

"All people frequently take advantage of subtle cues," explains Joe 19 Nickell, a former stage magician and private investigator, and editor at the *Skeptical Inquirer,* a magazine devoted to debunking the paranormal and pseudoscience. What many of us call intuition may simply be a finely tuned antenna, decoding subtle signals. Many psychics have perfected that ability, as well as a few less-than-respectable techniques.

- During a first, cold reading, many psychics begin by stating the few facts they already know or by offering generalities. They closely monitor their clients' reactions—eye movements, facial expressions, any noticeable response—and take their cue from those signals.

- Psychics often speak in a stream-of-consciousness style, piling on impressions. According to one 1982 study, when the abilities of psychic sleuths who worked with detectives were tested against college students and homicide detectives, none of the three groups scored better than they would have if left to chance, but the psychics produced 10 times as much information, increasing their likelihood of a chance hit.

- Psychics tend to shift away from their errors in midstream. For example, one reader asked me, "Were you recently married? No? Do you know anybody going through a divorce? No? Well one of your friends is going to divorce in the future and they'll need you to be a buffer."

- Psychics are adept at reinterpreting their pronouncements after the fact. This is called retrofitting. For instance, they will come up with numbers

They went that-a-way In 1996 the Nevada Commission on Tourism installed signs along the so-called "Extraterrestrial Highway" in a remote area of the state. Many people have claimed to see UFOs along this stretch of State Route 375.

supposedly related to a specific crime, and later say those numbers qualify as accurate hits when they correspond to anything from the birthday of a suspect's friend to a significant date, time of day, or telephone number.

Saved by Science

Why are we seeing a sudden surge of interest in the paranormal, especially now, in this so-called age of science? Is it a kind of backlash? "Paradise has been lost, not to sin but to science," contends Stuart Kaufmann, Ph.D., a physicist at the Santa Fe Institute and pioneer in the field of complexity. In his book, *At Home in the Universe,* Kaufmann delineates the ways science has shattered our sense of importance. First came Copernicus, who proved that we were not the center of the universe; then came Newton, who proved that gravity, not God, made the arrow arc toward its target; and the final blow was struck by Darwin, who, says Kaufmann, showed us that we are merely "the result of a chain of accidental mutations, sifted by a law no more noble than survival of the fittest."

In the words of Roger Walsh, Ph.D., professor of psychiatry and phi- 21
losophy at the University of California at Irvine, "Science enlarged the
scope of our known universe from leagues to light years, but paradoxically
we ended up as meaningless blobs of protoplasm adrift on a little speck of
dust in some uncharted galaxy. In response to this we're seeing a real thirst
for direct spiritual experience." Toss a little millennial fever into the brew
and, says Walsh, you've got more and more people turning to psychics,
moving back to magical views of reality.

Psychics themselves recognize the power of science, and many casually 22
borrow its language. In the course of my readings, I heard statements like
"I'm picking up some chronic illness in your DNA," or "I go into the chemical, metabolic, and electromagnetic fields of a person to access privileged
information." To the scientists who are actually studying the paranormal,
these statements are infuriating. "If those psychics were pressed to explain
what they mean, you would discover they don't know what they're talking
about," complains Dean Radin, Ph.D., director of the Consciousness Research Laboratory at the University of Nevada.

At laboratories like Radin's, along with the pioneering Princeton Engi- 23
neering Anomalies Research lab (PEAR), founded by rocket engineer Robert
Jahn, Ph.D., in 1979, psychic ability is studied in carefully designed and re-
peatable studies. These scientists have staked out a narrow and mesmerizing
band of reality where science and the "mystical" begin to merge.

"When the history of consciousness in the twentieth century is writ- 24
ten," contends Dr. Dossey, "it will be the studies at these laboratories that
mark the turning point." It is in these labs, at this moment, that science
may actually be demonstrating that consciousness is nonlocal; that is, it's
not limited to specific points in space or time—or even to the brain itself.

And so it was, paradoxically, the scientists who rescued me from my 25
withering faith. Scientists themselves are apparently encouraged of late because of a new form of statistical analysis called meta-analysis. Using computers, researchers can compare and sift out masses of data from a vast
archive of different studies.

Two of the most robust areas of scientific research are telepathy and 26
telekinesis (mind over matter). In the first, a "sender" tries to connect with
a "receiver," though they are isolated from each other. The sender may
look at a "target" (a visual image) randomly selected by the researchers,
while a receiver in another room tries to identify or describe that target. Or
a sender may try to alternately calm and excite a receiver at random intervals, simply via his thoughts and own state of being; the receiver's skin con-
ductance and galvanic skin response (indications of arousal) are measured.
Studies repeatedly demonstrate significant results.

"The results are surprisingly positive," notes Walsh. Marcello Truzzio, 27 Ph.D., a sociologist at the University of Michigan, agrees. "Some areas have borne up remarkably well when they are re-analyzed."

The O. J. Simpson Effect

Mind over matter emerges as the most electrifying area of research. It 28 seems that human intention can influence machines—even at a distance, when no influence seems possible. Researchers are both enthralled and puzzled by the data, which makes no sense. Studies thus far have examined machines that randomly produce positive or negative electrical pulses, or measure random radioactive decay, or randomly generate numbers. By concentrating, subjects try to influence the machines in one direction or another. After more than 14 million trials, Jahn has found constant, significant influence of humans on the performance of machines, and the odds of this happening are 1 in 5,000. Other studies have shown that people can influence not only the random generator they are concentrating on, but hidden generators they don't even know about.

The actual shift is small, but to understand it requires a stunning leap of perspective. Something is at work here that indicates our world may be far more fluid and interconnected than we ever imagined. Inspired by Jahn's research, Radin tested five different random generators on October 4, 1995, the day the O. J. Simpson verdict was delivered. At 10 A.M. Pacific time, when 44 million Americans were tuned in to television and radio, the random generators all became significantly less random. The shift lasted for 50 seconds. Radin believes that "the movement of mind does affect matter. It influences everything you can imagine, including mind itself. If 44 million minds are focused on one thing, that coherence spreads out, and influences even machines."

Other researchers have tried to find flaws in the studies. "We've wondered 30 if influence varies with distance, or with data rate, or with the voltage of the machine," says physicist Michael Ibison, Ph.D., a visiting scholar at PEAR. "It doesn't." So, says Ibison, you start musing on the mysteries of quantum physics, where mind and matter don't seem so separate and divided. "When cooled to zero degrees Kelvin," he says, "matter exhibits very weird behavior at great distances, as if the whole system is a single, unified, unbroken, organic thing, and instantaneous changes are visible everywhere. But that's still just a metaphor. All we really know is that what you are thinking now can actually be correlated with what is happening over there in a machine."

Or in another mind. Perhaps the strangest phenomenon in the world of 31 parapsychology research is the fact that a researcher who is a "believer" will get positive results while a skeptical researcher will often come up with nothing. One would assume the believers are simply skewing their data by interpreting them with a generous and uncritical eye. But these absolutely contradictory findings have occurred even when researchers double up on the same study.

Marilyn Schlitz, Ph.D., an anthropologist who is research director at   32 the Institute of Noetic Sciences, a think tank, conducted an experiment with psychologist Richard Wiseman, Ph.D., at Cambridge University. "It was a study in remote staring," recalls Schlitz, "with a closed-circuit TV setup." In this type of study, two people are put into separate rooms. A video camera is pointed at one person and connected to a television monitor in the other room. Half the time, at random intervals, the camera is on and the person in the second room can see an image of the first person. During the "on" times, the second person stares at the image and tries to mentally get the attention of the first.

"I did two such experiments with physicist Ed May, and got significant re-   33 sults in both," says Schlitz. "Richard [Wiseman] is a skeptic, and wasn't able to replicate my results, so he invited me over [to England] to run the same experiment at the same time. Everything was identical. I worked with half the people and got significant results, and he got no effect. I wonder what this means about the mind of the researcher and how that may influence data."

Schlitz suggests that the whole notion of a truly double-blind proce-   34 dure, the supposed hallmark of pristine science, is questionable. "Can any experimenter be truly objective and detached from his object of inquiry?" she wonders.

It's possible, then, that the world we live in truly is a web without a   35 weaver, that each strand in that web vibrates alone, and yet in consonance with the whole. As science inches along that web with its newly designed studies, we seem to illuminate a strand here, a strand there, just as real rainwater and light bring a spider's silk into sudden, brilliant relief when you wander onto your back porch on a summer morning.

I think back to the clairvoyant who years ago described to me exactly   36 where I felt pain in my body. He told me that he was able to travel back in time, and one day I asked him to try this. I wanted to know about my first year of life, when my mother suffered from agoraphobia and couldn't leave the house. He was still for a long time and then asked, "Did you move when you were three?" I nodded, we'd moved from a town house to a ranch house. Again he was still. But then he shook his head. "Something is stopping me. I can't go back to before you were three." Make of it what you wish; I believed him. He knew more than he should, but not as much as I wanted.

There's no question that our fascination with the paranormal is here to   37 stay. "It's one of the most ancient human attractions," notes Dr. Dossey, "part of the legacy of the human species, part of our original nature."

And so the mystery remains—blinking on and off somewhere between 38 infinity and now, as strange and fluctuating as the random numbers the scientists measure and that our minds nudge now to coherence, now to randomness. It's a question, not an answer, but one of the more meaningful questions we can ask.

I Was a Psychic Spy

David Morehouse's *Psychic Warrior,* to be published in November [1996] 39 by St. Martin's Press, sounds more like a sequel to the sci-fi film *Strange Days* than real life. After being tapped for the CIA's psychic espionage program—now known as Star Gate—he spent eight months, eight hours a day, being trained in the practice known as "remote viewing," by which individuals are taught to transcend space and time to access people, places, and things remote from them; to go forward and backward in time; and to use their five senses to taste, smell, touch, hear, and see the details of their target.

"The trainers tried to take our emotions to an extreme, to calibrate our 40 senses," says Morehouse. "We might find ourselves crawling in the ovens of Dachau or at ground zero at Hiroshima, weeping openly, suffering the emotional trauma that is locked into that specific time and place. On another day I might find myself traveling to a garden with a Shinto shrine, attuned to the subtle nuances of a cherry blossom."

A typical assignment, says Morehouse, was to access the mind of an en- 41 emy test pilot in order to get detailed information about fighter planes, "Let's say we wanted to find out the capabilities of a new Soviet MIG21. I'd concentrate on the test pilot, step in behind his eyes, and hear his thoughts, feel the aircraft and whether it had enough power in a turn or if the seat was too small or gauges vibrated too violently." The information was correlated with other surveillance programs.

Though the CIA claims it has abandoned the program because of lack 42 of success, Morehouse and his remote viewing colleagues believe Star Gate is as active as ever but has gone further undercover. They also believe the government is taking this technique into the realm of weaponry, training individuals in "remote influence"—accessing another human mind to inflict harm on it, anything from nausea to confusion to physical illness. Morehouse says remote influence was used against Saddam Hussein in the Gulf War. "Later, on CNN, I saw him accuse the U.S. of using psychics to attack him."

Now that Morehouse has gone public about a top-secret program, does 43 he continue to use remote viewing in his everyday life? "Once the channels are open you can't close them," he says. "Remote viewing is like entering an altered state that is very euphoric. Access to pure information is like a morphine flow that the brain craves and wants." After years of the experience, his brain won't stop. "At night I can't sleep without the TV blaring, just to shut out all the internal data."

Look for a $70 million movie from Interscope Pictures. Tune in and try   44 some remote viewing to see who will star.

Thinking Critically

1. Why is it especially important for Jill Neimark that she "followed a reporter's mandate for objectivity" for this article? What was it about that objectivity that made reporting and writing this article especially challenging for Neimark?

2. What happens to a "reporter's mandate for objectivity" when a reporter's subject is inherently subjective or requires a leap of faith? How does Neimark negotiate this conflict?

3. How does Neimark use figurative language (simile and metaphor) in her article? In "objective" writing, what purpose does figurative language serve?

Writing Critically

1. Anthropologist Marilyn Schlitz is quoted by Neimark as wondering if "any experimenter [can] be truly objective and detached from his object of inquiry." (The same question might be asked of a journalist.) In an essay, describe a situation in which your efforts to remain objective were overcome by something irrational or subjective—an emotion, a belief or opinion, or some other factor. For example, you may have been advised to "trust your gut instincts," or you may have been teased for relying on "female intuition."

2. Consider the reasons Dr. Roger Walsh and Dr. Stuart Kaufmann give Neimark for the increase in American's credulity when it comes to psychics and other supernatural occurrences. In an essay, compare their perspective to the arguments of Eric S. Cohen and/or Natalie Angier, both in this chapter.

My Story

RACHEL WATSON

This is one of three narratives included in *Many Americas* from the novelist Paul Auster's collaboration with National Public Radio's National Story Project. Auster invited NPR listeners to send in a short, "true" story. In his introduction to a published collection of these stories, *I Thought My Father Was God and Other True Tales from NPR's National Story Project* (2001), Auster recalled: "What interested me most, I said, were stories that defied our expectations about the world, anecdotes that revealed the mysterious and unknowable forces at work in our lives, in our family histories, in our minds and bodies, in our souls." Some four thousand people responded, sending in stories ranging from a few sentences to several pages. The other two contributions appearing in *Many Americas* are Joe Miceli's memoir "Taking Leave" (see pp. 188–93) and B.C.'s essay "Homeless in Prescott, Arizona" (see pp. 289–92). Auster read several of the stories each month on *All Things Considered*. Many listeners responded to what they heard with still more stories of their own.

1   Here is my story, the story I tell you when I know you well enough. I am twenty-three as I write this; when these things happened, I was nineteen, on the verge of twenty.

2   After my sophomore year of college, I got a summer job working for the forest service in California. I didn't want to drive all the way from Georgia by myself, so I convinced Anna, my best friend of ten years, to ride with me and then fly back home. Neither one of us had ever been across the country. My father filled the car with pounds and pounds of emergency equipment for the road: an axe, a baby-blue "do-it-herself" tool set, flares, emergency lights that would last for thirty-six hours, a fancy jack, a gallon of water, a bent coat hanger (in case the muffler fell off), a small first-aid kit, and a cellular phone that could be plugged into the cigarette lighter. He spent several nights awake, thinking of ways to protect us from everything that could possibly happen to us on the trip.

3   We set off in early June, driving fast to get out of the Southeast. We began to relax a little when we reached the prairie edge of the western mountains and took our sweet time when we rolled into the deserts of the Southwest. I remember driving between the golden sandstone formations in the heat and Anna putting her palms flat against the windshield and exclaiming that it felt like she was holding the sunshine in her hands. That night, we stopped in a tiny Utah town called Blanding. In the hotel, we charted out our route on the map and decided that we would wake up early, speed south through Arizona, and reach Las Vegas by the following night.

4   We started out just after dawn, heading south on Highway 81. It was a two-lane highway, and as soon as we left Blanding, there wasn't much to look at but sagebrush and distant red hills. I was driving, and Anna was running the video camera. Just before we turned it off that morning, I remarked on how horrific it would be to have a car accident out there—the

isolation was palpable, the treeless landscape felt merciless. I was looking forward to seeing trees again.

Suddenly, there was the figure of a man ahead of us on the right side of   5
the road. He seemed to have emerged from the low embankment and was waving his arms at us.

"Oh, Jesus," I said, thinking of my mother's talk-show stories of   6
women being ambushed on the road, "what the hell is this?"

"Rachel," Anna said, her hand on her window, "do you see his face?   7
Do you see that car?"

I turned and I looked. It was the last thing I wanted to see.   8

The man's face was half-covered with blood. About forty feet behind him   9
was a truck, turned upside down and smashed flat in the sand. I saw bodies scattered around the sagebrush, some as far as fifty feet from the road.

Anna rolled down her window. The man said that there had been a ter-   10
rible accident and that they needed help. I pulled the car over and punched on the hazards, while Anna called 911 on the cell phone. I had noticed a sign a moment before; we were five miles north of the Arizona border. Anna asked the man how many people were down there. I heard her tell the tiny phone, "I think it's about fifteen people." There was no one else around and nothing in sight for miles. We had not seen another car since starting out that morning. When Anna hung up the phone, it was only us and them. The man said his name was Juan.

The first emergency vehicles would arrive about forty minutes later.   11
Over the course of the morning, they would come one by one, running out of tape and backboards and room for bodies. A few people would stop to help. It was a one-car accident, a covered truck carrying seventeen Mexican immigrants that had been traveling all night. Three of them died that day, and fourteen suffered internal injuries, lacerations, and broken bones.

I got out of the car and made my way down the embankment, trem-   12
bling, carrying the little water we had. As I reached the flat ground, a girl my age came running at me. She was the only woman in the group, and she had sprung up from the side of a young man who was stretched out on his back on the ground. There was blood on her face and her mouth and she had a crazed look in her eyes. She was speaking in Spanish, and she took the water from me. Her long black hair flowed behind her. I followed her back to him and knelt beside her as she poured water over his face, screaming something over and over in Spanish. I looked up for a second. Other men lay silently on their stomachs in the sand. The young man's breathing was labored and clogged, and something told me that his insides were completely broken. I ran back to the car to get our supplies.

When I reached the car and pulled out the prepackaged first-aid kit, 13 which was about the size of two baking potatoes, I started to laugh. I unzipped it and looked at the small, wrapped gauze pads and the Band-Aids, and I was gripped by a sudden, overwhelming feeling of self-hatred. I imagined myself crawling under the car and waiting for the ambulances to arrive. This moment seemed to last, but it couldn't have. Another feeling rushed up from a different place and lifted me out of myself, and I knew that I would go down there, and that nothing I would see could make me turn away.

For the next four hours. Anna and I ran from one body to another, us- 14 ing Juan as an interpreter, telling men to be still or asking if they were cold. Anna and I pulled out all the towels and blankets that I had packed for the summer, tucking them around the men who were beginning to shake from shock. There were several gruesome sights. I found myself putting my face in the sand to make eye contact and moving my hands softly over backs and heads, speaking English in what I hoped were soothing tones, knowing instinctively that if you feel alone, it is easier to decide to die.

When the ambulances arrived we helped the paramedics load the men 15 onto backboards, tried to keep the sand off the tape, and stayed with the

A light in the darkness In the days and weeks after the terrorist attacks of September 11, 2001, makeshift shrines appeared all over New York City. One of the largest was at Union Square, where Annabelle Banievicz, and her son, Oriel Vanega, 7, attended a candlelight vigil.

men who had to wait on the side of the road for the next round. One man's breathing sounded nearly impossible, his eyes were like glass marbles, and his mouth was coated with blood. I positioned my face directly above his and gently rubbed his chest, encouraging him to keep breathing.

The boy who was broken died while I watched his nineteen-year-old   16 wife screaming and pushing up on his lips and gums as if looking for life in his mouth. I sat still for a moment, stunned and paralyzed. When I understood that he was dead, I ran to another silent body turned face-down in the sand.

As I put my head down to speak to one man who was lying crushed on   17 his stomach and whose forearm was snapped in half, I glanced up and saw the deeply lined face of an old man with long gray hair staring at me, his head resting on the sand. I scrambled to get there and shut his eyes, to get one of the sheets to put over him, to do anything for him so he was not just lying there dead and unnoticed.

There was a boy who had been thrown farther than anyone else, who   18 was being strapped to a backboard by the paramedics. I spoke to him, smiling brightly and assuring him that he was going to be FINE! His eyes and mouth were filled with blood, but he seemed to see me and he seemed to smile back. He died later in the helicopter that was taking him to Grand Junction.

By the time all the others had been taken away, Anna and I had fallen   19 in love with our interpreter, Juan. He was twenty-seven years old, spoke perfect English, and had a head of thick, dark curls. As a female Navajo paramedic tended to him with Anna and me on either side, he said he was embarrassed that he had gone so long without a haircut. Anna went and got his bag out of the crushed truck, a plastic grocery bag with socks in it. He had four lacerations on the top of his head; his thick hair had helped control the bleeding. He was heading into delirium when they finally loaded him into the ambulance. When he realized that we were being separated, panic came into his eyes and he reached out to me from the stretcher.

"Where are you going?" he asked, and I had to say that we were get-   20 ting back on the road. I said it because I didn't know what else I could do. I couldn't follow him into the world of the hospital. I had had enough. I was ready to return to the world of safety, to blood and bones neatly contained within bodies, to trees and comfort and mercy.

"I cannot pay you," Juan said, "but God will repay you."   21

The smell of the man stayed with me, despite repeated washing. I could   22 smell it emanating from my wrists while I drove, the bitter smell of old sweat and poverty. Our leg muscles cramped up in the night from the hours of tremulous running back and forth across an incline of sand, and the sand mixed with my own sweat is still embedded in the sandals I was wearing that day.

Anna and I reached Las Vegas that night, exhausted and shaken. I 23 wept on the phone to my father, saying over and over, "It was so awful." That was the only time I cried about the accident. One year later, I woke up in a cold sweat in the middle of the night with a voice pounding inside my head, repeating over and over the phrase, "You have seen a man die."

What is to be done with that? What is to be done with the events of that 24 morning, swallowed back up into time as we drove away, things never to be heard of again—no segment on the nightly news, no articles in any paper we ever saw. It might as well have been a dream we both had.

What do you do with a story like that? There is no lesson, no moral, barely 25 even an ending. You want to tell it, hear it told, but you don't know why.

Thinking Critically

1. Knowing what you do about the National Story Project, what is especially surprising or compelling about the very first sentence of "My Story"?

2. In paragraph 4, Rachel Watson includes a seemingly casual remark. What is the narrative and dramatic effect of that remark? If you read Jill Neimark's essay "Do the Spirits Move You?" (the preceding selection), what new shades of meaning does Watson's remark seem to take on?

3. Why do you think Watson told this story?

Writing Critically

1. What is an epiphany? In what way is Rachel Watson's story an epiphany?

2. Why is "My Story" included in a chapter on faith and reason? Tell your own story about a moment when what you would call faith or reason was either challenged or affirmed.

3. Jill Neimark in paragraph 35 of "Do the Spirits Move You?" suggests that "the world we live in truly is a web without a weaver." What did she mean? How does Rachel Watson's story exemplify or defy that metaphor? If you're feeling particularly literary, look up Robert Frost's poem "Design" and include it in your reflections.

Earth Music

DAVID JAMES DUNCAN

Teacher and essayist David James Duncan, a native of
Oregon, now lives and works in rural Montana. In recent years he has reflected on his writing, and his teach-
ing of writing, as a kind of passionate political dissent.
His lifelong commitment to environmental conservation
(especially in his beloved American West) makes his writ-
ing about the environmental policies of the George
W. Bush administration particularly eloquent in its rage.
An expert fly-fisher, Duncan is the author of the classic
novel *The River Why* (1983) and the essay collection *My
Story as Told by Water* (2001). He has worked to protect
Montana's Blackfoot River, made famous by Norman
Maclean's novel *A River Runs Through It* (1983).
Duncan received a Lannan Fellowship, the 2001 Western
States Book Award, and an honorary doctorate for public service from the University of Portland. During an interview with *weber studies,* a quarterly journal about the
contemporary American West, Duncan was asked to define a writer's obligation to ulture. He replied, "To be a
penultimate pessimist but an ultimate optimist. I feel
there's a spark in our children that can't be killed, and
I'm optimistic because of that. But I'm pessimistic about
the ruin of their world." "Earth Music" first appeared in
the Fall 2003 issue of *Portland Magazine,* a literary quarterly published by the University of Portland in Oregon.

I hold the thing we call "nature" to be the divine manuscript. I hold the 1
infinite wilds to be the only unbowdlerized book we possess of the
Authorship that gives and sustains life. Human industry is shredding
this book like an Enron document. Some call this shredding "economics" and "freedom." It's not quite a lie. But the freedom to shred the divine manuscript is not an economics any lover of neighbor, self, or
Earth wishes to practice.

A spiritual hero told me when I was young that "true happiness lies in 2
making others happy." Having found no happiness seeking it for myself, I
tried seeking the happiness of others, and found this unlikely statement to
be true. The formula was not without side-effects, however, once self-
giving starts to give you joy, you grow bewildered by the spectre of self-
ishness, fall out of the nationalist/capitalist loop, and limp about in search
of healthier hopes. A new source of hope for me: the growing reverence for
nature and its mysteries among scientists.

360

Though science itself never caged us, until recently the sciences were ³
committed to mechanistic paradigms and an obsession with the physically
measurable that made reverence possible only by disconnecting spirituality
and scientific thought. The so-called "Enlightenment" and its empirical
thinking led, sans spirit, to the effective naming of things, cataloguing of
things, dissecting, extracting, and reconstruction of things, to create the
modern world as we know it. By the late twentieth century, the same divorce between spirituality and science had led to genetically warping even
the most sacred living things, filing corporate copyrights on ancient living
things, and raping, monoculturizing, extincting, and abstracting ourselves
from living things as if we were not living things ourselves.

I see two chief causes for the countering outburst of reverence in science—one ⁴
famous, the other infamous. The infamous cause: suffering. How many biologists, botanists, ethnologists, anthropologists, have been forced to renounce
their fields in mid-career because their living objects of study have died out
before their eyes? How many more have been so dismayed by the world's bar-
rios, biological dead or disease zones, slave job and oil war zones, that they've
abandoned their disciplines to become peace activists or humanitarians?

The famous cause of the new reverence among scientists: the new ⁵
physics. Quantum mechanics have changed the way we see the universe.
The old proton/neutron/electron atom, for instance, is as unfit for describing matter as we now understand it as a Model T Ford is unfit for
negotiating a contemporary freeway. Atomic particles are now said to derive from "immaterial wave packets"; space is now said to have had ten
original dimensions that collapsed, at the beginning of time, to form the
"superstrings" of which subatomic particles consist. Field theory. Mor-
phogenesis. It's hard to keep up with all the ways that physics is telling
us that Space, Time, and Matter derive from something infinitely subtler
and greater than all three.

One upshot of all this has been a sea-change in the kind of thinking that ⁶
we can now call scientific. Reason, though still a crucial tool, is no longer
Science's despot king. Intuition, imagination, poetry, humility, and reverence now also play their roles, leading to the possibility of scientific statements such as these:

> WILLIGIS JAGER: "There aren't two kinds of laws: matter and
> mind. Rather, there is a single continuous law for both matter
> and mind. Matter is the domain of space in which the field is
> extremely dense."
>
> ALBERT EINSTEIN: "In the new physics, there is no place for both
> field and matter, because field is the only reality."

TEILHARD DE CHARDIN: "Concretely speaking, there is no matter and spirit. There exists only matter that is becoming spirit."

FREDERICK SOMMER: "Spirit is the behavior of matter. Perception does not take spiritedness into a state of affairs that does not already have it."

My daily work is reflection, imagination, and story-telling. The recent sea-change in science has returned the modifier "scientific" to a place of honor in this work. When, for example, I first read in my teens of medieval cosmologists referring to a "music of the spheres," my reason howled in protest because its "education in science" had trained it to do so. Despite reason's howling, though, my heart at the time told me: *You have heard such music.* The science of today adds that if "field is the only reality" and "there exists only matter that is becoming spirit," it is scientific not only to ask my heart where I heard spheric music, but to try to hear it again.

Exploring my heart, I recalled that, years ago, I read the *Upanisadic* description of a state in which "the soul perceives infinite hugeness and infinite smallness as one and the same," and felt a strong intuitive resonation. Then, years later, I found in the Koran the statement, "All Creation in the hands of the Merciful One is smaller than a mustard seed," and felt the same resonation. Then last year I learned of a mathematician, Georg Cantor, who proved in demonstrable mathematical fashion that infinities come in an infinite range of sizes, and that any Infinity, being a unity and hence complete within itself, must include itself, and be a member of itself, "and thus can only be known through a flash of mystical vision." And then one morning last spring, while cleaning my study, I opened a dusty *National Geographic* and found a Hubble Space photo of 150,000 galaxies swirling in a jot of universe "the size of a grain of sand held at arm's length," and tears rose because, in an instant, the entire preceding series of scriptual and mathematical images swept through me, filling me with the *profundo* hum of an indescribable music.

That night, after watching the movie *Captain Corelli's Mandolin*, I dreamed that I was shot dead by a hundred machine guns, shot so many times that a dark bullet-driven wind blew my soul irrevocably away from even my dead body and I was invisible and afraid and had neither breath nor voice with which to call out to my God. I called out in bodiless desire anyway, and a spheric point pierced the wall of the grim gray world in which I drifted, the point expanded, tore that world's wall apart like so much wet Kleenex, a light poured through, and I saw my Beloved's cheek and brilliant eye peeking at me through the hole, just that much of Him, yet there was such love in that eye, such *What-a-trick-I've-pulled!* glee, that a posthumous existence without need of this body felt not just possible but certain, and I woke with a jolt of joy, hearing the same kind of music. So when, the next day, I read Annie Dillard writing, "There is no less holiness at this time—as you are reading this—than there was the day the Red Sea parted. . . . There is no whit less might in heaven or on earth than there was the day Jesus said, 'Maid, arise' to the centurion's daughter, or the day Peter walked on water, or the night Mohammed flew to heaven on a horse. . . . In any instant you may avail yourself of the power to love your enemies; to accept failure, slander, or the grief of loss; or to endure torture. . . . 'Each and every day the Divine Voice issues from Sinai,' says the Talmud. Of eternal fulfillment, Tillich said, 'If it is not seen in the present, it cannot be seen at all.'" I felt an urge to shout: *Hallelujah, Annie! You're singin' the morpho-genetic gospel now!*

If field is the only reality and all matter is becoming spirit, I daresay this 10 shout can be called scientific.

The sensations of field, of palpable presence, of *hum*, still come over me 11 walking the mountains or cities, wading the traffic or trout streams. I don't seek such sensations. They just unfold, unlooked for, in the course of what comes. A spring aspen leaf might brush my face, and I'll close my eyes and find myself feeling the tiny, self-contained universe that is a spring-green aspen cell suddenly making two of itself, and growing, *because it loves to.* I'll witness "fruitful multiplication" in our Montana-winter-blighted fruit trees or the year's brood of Bantam chicks, the creek's insects or the river bottoms' whitetail fawns, the newborn wood-ducks, the kingfishers, the killdeers, and wonder comes upon me in the form of music as the densities, unions, and divisions of love are made palpable. I'll stand by the ocean, see the slight curve of horizon, feel the ocean's hum, and see: *the very seas are a single spherical note.* I'll have the sense, standing in running water, that I've been not just close to the molecules flowing round me but *inside* them: that I've experienced, in the womb or aeons earlier, the coming together and breaking apart of spheric particles of H and of O. I'll witness the aging, sickness, and deaths of plants, animals, family, friends, self, the migrations to new climes, transmigrations into unknowns, jolts into new awareness or bodies, slow breakdowns by organic or industrial attrition, transformations of earth, water, matter, energy, clouds, leaves, souls—and a vast pulsing harmony and an anguish of joy will fill the bit of me left unabsorbed.

It's time I stopped building sentences now and stepped down to the creek, 12 as I've done half my life come evening. This time of year I'll look for the rainbows that migrate up from the bigger rivers to spawn. And I'll find a pair, if this spring is like the last eight, in a tiny side channel a quarter mile downstream. As I approach them on my belly I'll be crawling across spheroid grains of white granitic sand. I'll then lie like a Muslim, watching a female trout an arm's length from my eyes beat her body against gold-colored pebbles, build a stone nest, and fill it with a thousand lit-from-within orange spheres. I'll watch the male ease over like one of the gray-black snow clouds above. And when the milt pours down, each nested sphere will suddenly love to divide and divide till it's a sphere no longer but a tiny, sphere-eyed trout. I'll encounter the same trout over the slow course of summer, drifting down toward the rivers, growing by dividing, defeating time; I'll catch them now and then, release most, eat a few, and the survivors will return in twelve or sixteen seasons, bearing the milt clouds, glowing spheres, and hidden fields that carry the genius of trout toward my children's children's world. There's not much more to discuss here. Either fields beyond matter exist or they don't, the kingdom of heaven is within us or it isn't, and each and every day the Divine Voice issues from Sinai, every inch of Creation is pierced by Its song, and every point, cell, particle, field is so moved by the Music that it loves to sing, swell, shrink, leap, divide, and bear all fruit and all life and all death and all regeneration in response, or It doesn't.

But my honest experience is: *It does, it does!*   13

I have no rational idea "what it means" when consciousness revs up and   14 perceives mystery or field amid mind, amid life, amid matter, but oh do I have perceptions of what it means. And if I am ever to rise to the Beauty that is Truth, I must describe these *perceptions* as consciousness Truly perceives them. I therefore confess lifelong love for a wilderness found outside myself, till once in a while I encounter it within—a wilderness entered, it seems, through agenda-less alertness at work, rest, or play in the presence of language, rivers, mountains, music, plants, creatures, rocks, moon, sun, dust, pollen grains, dots, spheres, galaxies, grains of sand, stars, every sort of athletic ball, cells, DNA, molecules, atomic particles, and immaterial forces, till it suddenly "inside-outs" me, leading to the perception and adoration of synergies and harmonies that leave my mind wondrous happy but far, far behind my heart. It's a wilderness my dog, Reason, will never succeed in sniffing out, chomping up, or rationally defining, yet a wilderness I've been so often and gratefully assailed by that I've lost all but comic interest in my good dog's sniffing and suspect that even the dog begins to enjoy itself when we get flipped into wilderness's heart.

I believe—based on hydrogen clouds giving birth to stars, exploded   15 stars to planets, spring stormclouds to snow, snowbanks to rivers, orange orbs to trout; I believe based on lives collapsing into ashes and dust, and dust bursting back to life; I believe based on spheric shapes singing, dividing, creating cells, plants, creatures, creating my children, sunflowers, sun, self, universe, by constantly sacrificing all that they are in order to be reconfigured and reborn forever and ever—that when we feel Love's density, see its colors, feel its pulse, it's time to quit worrying about reason and words and cry: *"My God! Thanks!"*

If I stake my life on one field, one wild force, one sentence issuing from   16 Sinai, it is this one: *There is no goal beyond love.*

Thinking Critically

1. How does David James Duncan use the term *reverence*? When he refers to "spirituality," what does he mean?

2. In "Earth Music," Duncan uses comparison and contrast to structure his argument. What two concepts or ways of thinking does he compare? Why is comparison and contrast a useful strategy for his overall argument?

3. Duncan cites four "scientific statements" in paragraph 6. Who are the four speakers? Are they all "scientists"? Can a person have a scientific approach to the world without "being" a scientist or "doing" science? Is it possible to have a spiritual worldview without following any particular faith tradition?

Writing Critically

1. Eric S. Cohen never once mentions the natural world in his essay "To Wonder Again" (also in this chapter). Is there any common ground between Cohen and Duncan? For example, notice that Cohen also uses the term "reverence" to describe something waning in American culture. How does his use of the term compare with Duncan's? In an essay that consists of an extended definition, refer to Cohen and Duncan as you develop your own definition of *reverence* and explain why your concept of "reverence" could help address a cultural, social, or spiritual divide.

2. In an essay using comparison and contrast, describe two different (though not necessarily opposed) ways of understanding the natural world. Like Duncan, you could draw from your own experiences of nature to inform your argument. Another possibility would be to research different spiritual approaches to the natural world.

3. In this essay Duncan refers to the Koran, the *Upanishads,* and the Talmud. Although he does not specifically mention the Christian Bible, he frequently makes allusions to Christian tenets. Yet he begins his essay by referring to "nature" as "the divine manuscript," the "only unbowdlerized book we possess." Read Rachel Watson's "My Story" (the preceding selection). What story that can't be explained or justified by any written word have you "read" from your own lived experience or in the "book" of the natural world? Watson seems to suggest that there is no ending, no reconciliation. Duncan confesses (in paragraph 14) that he has "no rational idea 'what it means' when consciousness revs up." At what point do you give up searching for meaning in the story of your life?

The Science and Religion Wars

MANO SINGHAM

Physicist Mano Singham is the director of the University Center for Innovation in Teaching and Education at Case Western Reserve University. A native of Sri Lanka, he earned an M.S. and Ph.D. in theoretical nuclear physics from the University of Pittsburgh. Singham is deeply concerned with the state of science education in America. He has conducted workshops nationwide for science teachers at the precollege and college levels and worked as a scientist-educator with the National Science Foundation's Project Discovery, an outreach program to improve science education for children from kindergarten through high school. Singham's recent research interests are in education, theories of knowledge, and physics and philosophy. An antiwar activist, Singham participated in teach-ins and other protest activities against the recent war with Iraq. In an opinion piece published in the June 2000 issue of the online journal *Physics Today,* he reflects on the paradoxes of teaching complex and still-theoretical concepts such as relativity and quantum mechanics and expects students to accept such propositions out of faith in his authority as a teacher: "The best that I can hope for is to enable my students to think critically, to detect propaganda and reject intellectual coercion, even when I am the one doing it. What troubles me is the assumption by some scientists that it would be quite admirable if people believed what we say and rejected the views of those who disagree with us, even though most people have no real basis for preferring one view over the other. If scientists want the spirit of true inquiry to flourish, then we have to accept—and even encourage—public skepticism about what we say, too. Otherwise, we become nothing but ideologues." This essay appeared in the journal *Phi Delta Kappan* in 2000.

A casual (and even not-so-casual) observer of the science/religion debate   1
can be excused for being confused as to whether or not there actually is a conflict between the two. On the one hand, newspapers report that the 1999 Templeton Prize for Religion was awarded to a physicist who promotes dialogue between science and religion, and in 1998 *Newsweek* determined that "Science Finds God" was worthy of being a featured cover story.

On the other hand, there are the recurrent heated conflicts about ques-   2
tions such as whether evolution or creationism better explains the origins
of life in all its forms and which world view should be taught in schools.
The push by some groups to obtain equal treatment of both views in school
science classes led to state laws (in Louisiana and Arkansas in 1981) mandating such teaching. That such laws have been overturned by appeals
courts and by the U.S. Supreme Court may have settled the legal issue of
what can be taught in schools (at least for the time being), but the acrimonious nature of the discussion has not changed.

In order to be able to discuss the issue without creating undue antago-   3
nism, it is necessary to have an understanding of what drives the reasoning
of the leading characters in this conflict.

To the casual observer, the conflict seems to be about deciding between   4
two fairly straightforward but dissonant propositions. Proponents of one
side advocate the view that both creation science and evolution are unproven theories and that simple fairness requires either teaching or omit-
ting both from the school science curriculum. Those who support the other
side argue that creation science is a religion-based belief, while evolution is
not, and so the establishment clause of the First Amendment to the U.S.
Constitution justifies the exclusion of the former from the public school
curriculum and the inclusion of the latter.

The fact that both sides believe fiercely in the rightness of their positions   5
should give us a clue that the underlying issues involving science and religion are not really so simple. In fact, these issues do involve subtle and complex questions, drawing upon knowledge from many disciplines. It is often
said that politics makes strange bedfellows, but perhaps nowhere can
stranger bedfellows be found than in the controversies surrounding science
and religion. Scientists, theologians, creationists, postmodernists, social
constructivists, feminists, multiculturalists, philosophers, and historians of
science all play key—and often surprising—roles in this contentious debate.

To understand how these strange coalitions are formed, a good place to   6
start is by looking at the discussions of scientific literacy that periodically
take place among elite opinion makers. Three features of such discussions
are entirely predictable.

The first is that everyone will lament the sorry state of scientific literacy   7
in the U.S. and predict dire consequences if the situation is not improved.

The second is the inevitable listing of all the deplorable things that the   8
general public believes in (e.g., aliens, alternative medicine, astrology, psychokinesis, superstitions, and the like) and that allegedly contribute to this
illiteracy. For convenience, I will lump all these alternative beliefs under the
label of "fringe beliefs," not because they are held by only a few people (some

of them may actually be held by a majority of the population), but because they lie on the fringes of elite opinion. These fringe beliefs are considered disreputable and labeled with such pejoratives as "pseudoscience" or "non-science" or "nonsense."

The third predictable feature of discussions of scientific literacy is   9
harder to observe because, like the dog that did not bark in the night in the Sherlock Holmes story, it involves noticing what is not said. No one raises the question as to what fundamental difference, if any, exists between these supposedly non- (or even anti-) science fringe beliefs and those of mainstream religions. And it is this silent issue that must be confronted if we are to understand the often bizarre coalitions that form and re-form around the science/religion issue.

In the triangle formed by science, mainstream religion, and fringe be-   10
liefs, it is the conflict between science and fringe beliefs that is usually the source of the most heated, acrimonious, and public debate. The other two relationships (between science and mainstream religion and between mainstream religion and fringe beliefs) are usually ignored. But we must examine the mutual relationships of all three knowledge structures if we are to make any sense of the problem because the entire debate ultimately boils down to two key questions: (1) Is it possible to set up a hierarchy of belief structures with science and mainstream religions at the top (and thus respectable) and with fringe beliefs at the bottom (and thus disreputable)? (2) What makes elite opinion makers feel that science is compatible with mainstream religious beliefs but incompatible with fringe beliefs?

Part of the confusion in dealing with these questions arises from trying   11
to lump everything under a single label—either science or religion. Following the suggestion of theologian Langston Gilkey, it is perhaps more enlightening to split each of the two belief structures into two subgroups (elite and popular science and elite and popular religion) and then to examine the relationships between the resulting four subgroups.[1]

Elite science encompasses the consensus belief structures of the scien-   12
tific establishment, as represented in the departments of science at universities and research institutes and as published in mainstream scientific journals. Members of this group have a fundamentally naturalist belief in the idea that each and every physical phenomenon must have a scientific explanation, with no arbitrariness allowed. The eminent paleontologist George Gaylord Simpson (who had some personal reservations about the belief that everything in the universe can be explained naturalistically) captured the essence of the naturalistic position when he said, "The progress of knowledge rigidly requires that *no non-physical postulate ever be ad-*

mitted in connection with the study of physical phenomena. We do not know what is and what is not explicable in physical terms, and the researcher who is seeking explanations must seek physical explanations only" (emphasis added).[2]

Popular science, on the other hand, represents the widely held beliefs of 13 people in superstitions, astrology, magic, witchcraft, psychokinesis, extrasensory perception, and the like, all of which can be categorized as what I have called fringe beliefs. People who believe these things view as quaint the notion that everything must have a scientific explanation. They have no difficulty believing that there are extraphysical entities capable of violating the laws of science at will.

Elite religion represents those views held by theologians of mainstream 14 religions. In the theistic religions, this view holds that, while a creator exists, the creator does not directly intervene (or intervenes only rarely) to change the course of everyday events, thus violating scientific laws. Changes are usually achieved indirectly, by changing the minds of people and causing them to act in different and better ways.

Popular religion, on the other hand, incorporates beliefs in a personal 15 God, a creator who can and does intervene when and if the creator sees fit, and thus can be induced to intervene to change the course of everyday events by prayer and other supplications. The fundamentalist strains of most major religions fall into this category.

So who is fighting with whom? Popular science and popular religion gen- 16 erally have no problems with each other (and I place both under the umbrella label of fringe beliefs). After all, both groups have no difficulty in accepting the occurrence of phenomena that defy scientific explanations. This does not mean that they always agree. For example, fundamentalist Christians are adamantly opposed to witchcraft, which falls into the category of popular science. But such disagreements concern issues of moral right and wrong and of good versus evil and have nothing to do with the issue being addressed here of whether it is possible that events may violate scientific laws.

Similarly, elite and popular religions are usually not in open conflict 17 since the major religions can encompass both viewpoints under their umbrellas. The mass of believers tends to adopt popular religious views about an interventionist deity, while the elite tends to believe that God works in indirect and subtle ways that are not easily attributable.

Elite science and popular science, on the other hand, have had a long 18 history of conflict, ever since (around the time of Galileo) science became an established field of study, with its own protocols for judging evidence and establishing truths. Even now, the constant calls for increasing scientific literacy are a symptom of the scientific community's exasperation with the fact that, after many years of mass science education, large numbers of people still believe in all sorts of things that the scientific community views as wholly irrational. For example, fairly recent surveys show that 55% of American teenagers believe that "astrology works" and 38% of college students believe that human life originated in the Garden of Eden.[3]

The nature of all three of the above relationships has remained stable   19
over the years. However, there has been a dramatic change in the fourth relationship, the relationship between elite science and elite religion. In the early days of science, this relationship was one of hostility, as scientific inquiry grew and rapidly dethroned religion as the source of authoritative knowledge about the world. From the days of Copernicus and Galileo through Darwin's publication of *On the Origin of Species,* elite religion battled the scientific community to see which world view would be dominant.

The well-publicized Scopes "monkey trial" in 1925 is a good example.   20
The outcome of the case was technically a defeat for the scientific establishment because a court in Tennessee convicted teacher John Scopes of violating a law banning the teaching of Darwin's theory of evolution in public schools. But the case is popularly perceived as a victory because Clarence Darrow (the attorney defending Scopes), assisted by the establishment press, managed to bring into ridicule Biblical theories of the Earth's origin, as propounded by prosecuting attorney William Jennings Bryan, and to persuade at least elite opinion of the day that the Biblical story of creation was not very credible as a scientific account of the history of the Earth and the origin of species. The supporters of Darwinian evolutionary theory thus achieved a major public relations victory, even as they suffered a legal defeat. The explosive growth of science and technology in the middle of this century seemed to consolidate the feeling (at least among the elite) that science, not religion, had the answers to questions about the origins of life and the universe.

The relationship between elite science and elite religion nowadays is   21
dramatically different and can be well characterized by the Cold War term "peaceful coexistence." In its political context, this term referred to the recognition of separate spheres of influence over which each side in the Cold War held unquestioned supremacy. This avoided endless border skirmishes that might have precipitated a major conflict. In the science/religion context, the philosophical basis for this coexistence can be called the "two worlds model"; the physical realm, comprising all phenomena accessible via the senses, belongs to the world of science; the spiritual realm, dealing with moral and ethical questions and the soul and the afterlife, belongs to the world of religion. This formulation is aptly captured in a statement by

the council of the prestigious National Academy of Sciences, which says, "Religion and science are *separate and mutually exclusive realms* of human thought whose presentation in the same context leads to misunderstanding of both scientific theory and religious belief" (emphasis added).[4]

Most noncombatants in the science/religion wars subscribe to some 22 version of this statement and thus see no conflict between scientific and religious belief structures because each deals with one of two distinct worlds that do not overlap. This group comprises a large number of people, scientists and nonscientists alike, who are respectful of science and its accomplishments but also believe in a deity and are active members of churches, temples, and mosques. Such people view the creation narratives in their religious texts as figurative and metaphorical—not as records of actual historical events. Such people also tend to view the periodic legal and political skirmishes between the creationist and naturalist camps as the work of overzealous extremists, both religious and scientific, who are attempting to mix together things that should properly be kept separate.

But is this "middle ground" viewpoint intellectually robust enough to 23 achieve amity between the scientific and religious world views? In other words, are religious views about the workings of the world in *fundamental* conflict with known scientific laws? Or does this middle ground survive by not posing awkward questions?

One awkward question that is avoided deals with the miraculous events 24 that are central to every theistic religious tradition and that seem to violate directly the laws of science. Are they purely the result of natural laws (of which we may currently be unaware), thus ceasing to be miracles in any meaningful sense of the word, or are they singular events that occur in direct contradiction of natural laws?

For example, take the well-known Biblical story of the parting of the Red 25 Sea. In the orthodox religious view this is a miracle pure and simple, an act that occurs in clear contradiction of natural laws. So does it belong only to the world of religion? Yet it is an event that is supposed to have occurred in the physical world, so should it not also belong to the world of science? How can the National Academy of Sciences' sharp distinction between the spiritual and the physical worlds be sustained? One solution is to reject the idea that the parting of the Red Sea ever occurred as described, thus denying it historical status. Another is to look for evidence that some unusual, but wholly natural, combination of causes resulted in something that seemed to be miraculous to the naive observer of that time. The key consequence of both these explanations is to remove the event from the realm of the miraculous. The evolution of knowledge throughout history has been precisely in this direction, replacing "miraculous" occurrences with scientific explanations.

But can every single event that is commonly believed to be miraculous   26
be explained away in this manner? The committed naturalist would argue
that this must be so; otherwise, the entire framework of science will collapse. The scientific establishment starts with the assumption that all natural phenomena should be explainable by natural laws that can be discovered
using the methods of science. It does not allow for even one deviation from
these natural laws. Miracles, by definition, have no place in this framework.

The evolutionary geneticist Richard Lewontin put it clearly and   27
bluntly: "We cannot live simultaneously in a world of natural causation
and of miracles, for if one miracle can occur, there is no limit."[5] His point
is well-taken. If the scientific community concedes even one miraculous
event, then how can it credibly contest the view that the world (and all its
fossilized relics) was created in one instant just 6,000 years ago? Robert
Park, director of public affairs for the American Physical Society, goes even
further when he says that "to attribute natural events to supernatural
forces is not merely lazy, it defines anti-science."[6] Although both these
comments were specifically aimed at creationists, they undermine traditional mainstream religions as well. If there is to be no divine intervention
at all, what is left for religion? Is it just a system of beliefs that have no tangible consequences whatsoever? John Horgan in *The End of Science*[7]
quotes cosmologist Stephen Hawking asking rhetorically, "What place,
then, for a creator?" There is no place, was Hawking's own reply; a final
theory would exclude God from the universe—and with him all mystery.
Hawking "hoped to rout mysticism, vitalism, creationism from their last
refuge, the origin of the universe."

Another awkward question is also avoided: While we can readily see   28
that the physical world exists, is there any tangible evidence that a
moral/ethical/spiritual world also exists?

If the answer is no (so that the existence of the moral/ethical/spiritual   29
world is to be simply believed and not experienced in any way), that means
its existence does not have any consequences that affect the physical world.
Then of what use is this supernatural world? What would be the point of
believing in a deity if the spiritual world occupied by the deity could have
no influence whatsoever on the physical world we actually live in? This answer seems to imply that we can dispense entirely with the spiritual world,
a position that is surely not the intention of those advocating the "two
worlds" model.

If the answer is yes, how can we still maintain the clear distinction be-   30
tween the two worlds? After all, tangible evidence is something that belongs to the physical world, and so such evidence for the existence of a
spiritual world must imply that the two worlds overlap.

In fact, it quickly becomes clear that this middle ground that treats "re- 31 ligion and science [as] separate and mutually exclusive realms of human thought" contains a basic internal contradiction. The middle ground seems to start by saying that there is a self-contained world of natural laws and another self-contained world of spiritual laws. But then it goes on to imply (since moral and ethical values presumably influence human behavior) that these two worlds do overlap, which means that they are not self-contained after all.

Why is it that this middle ground is so popular and its shaky founda- 32 tions relatively immune from close questioning? It is possible that, wearied by the historical baggage of such conflicts as those involving Galileo and Darwin, the elite scientific community has reached an unspoken agreement with mainstream religions that they will not attack each other. The physical/ spiritual distinction provides a useful escape route for both groups. Pope John Paul II's statement in 1996 that "fresh knowledge [which he failed to specify] leads to recognition of the theory of evolution as more than just a hypothesis" can be viewed as further consolidating this alliance. The Pope did reserve some area for religion by emphasizing that "if the human body has its origins in living material which preexists it, the spiritual soul is immediately created by God," thus showing that he too is an advocate of the "two worlds model" endorsed by the National Academy of Sciences.

Thus elite science is allowed to interpret the physical world, while elite 33 religions interpret the spiritual world, and both sides agree not to stray onto each other's turf. This tacit agreement then allows the elites to combine forces and attack those who brazenly mix the two worlds together, such as upstart creationist believers and those who put their faith in other unorthodoxies, such as astrology, witchcraft, New Age mysticism, and the like. For example, in the 1981 Arkansas "balanced treatment" case, the witnesses against the law mandating that creationism be taught alongside evolution in the public schools were from both the mainstream religions and the scientific establishment.

Understandably, creationists are not happy with the development of 34 this alliance, since it makes them vulnerable to attack on two fronts. To continue with the war metaphor, creationists look on the deal as appeasement by the elite religionists who have been duped by the scientific elite into thinking they have negotiated a long-term peace, when what the elite religionists have really done is to lose the war by allowing the scientific community complete hegemony over the physical world.

To understand the creationists' argument, we must go beyond the super- 35 ficialities that are frequently used in describing them.[8] If there is one common thread that all creationists share, it is the view that the world as we know it now is too complex and subtle to have come about without the active and repeated intervention of an external agent or a deity, acting outside the laws of science. It is this unifying belief (rather than any specific model or religious tradition) that I will characterize as the "creationist point of view," and it is the source of the fundamental conflict with elite science. When we formulate our description of creationists in this way, we see that creationism is not some narrow sectarian grouping but incorporates major elements of mainstream Christianity, Judaism, Hinduism, Islam, and other theistic religions. They differ only in their beliefs about the extent and nature of this divine intervention.

(One other model that should be mentioned is that in which the creator   36 is a sort of prime mover who creates the universe and all its laws of evolution at one instant at the beginning of the universe but never intervenes thereafter, allowing the universe to evolve in a manner consistent with the laws of science. This model has a creator in it, but it is not creationist as defined above because there is no subsequent intervention in any form to change the natural course of events. Thus this model does not lead to any conflict with elite science.)

Nowadays, elite religion has tacitly (if not openly) conceded the under-   37 standing of the physical world to science, reserving for itself the moral/ ethical/spiritual realm. The creationists argue that the elite religionists' strategy of retreating to the moral and ethical sphere puts them in an extremely weak position that can be easily overrun by the advancing scientific hordes. After all, it is quite possible that neurobiology may someday be able to pinpoint specific areas in the brain that are the source of moral and ethical impulses and spiritual feelings. Neuroscience may even be able to locate the neurons that trigger good and bad impulses or generate moral decisions.

Creationists realize that such developments will result in the total sub-   38 jugation of religious beliefs to scientific hegemony. Thus it should not be surprising if some of the most incisive critiques of the naturalist view have come from creationists, who see in it a real threat to their own religious belief structure. But rather than try to fight border skirmishes with science in order to eke out a larger sphere of influence for religion, these creationists have gone for broke, waging an all-out counterattack on elite science.

The attack has been two-pronged. On one front, creationists try to drive   39 a wedge between elite science and elite religion by arguing that, at a fundamental level, the scientific and religious world views are incompatible and that both cannot be believed simultaneously. Some creationists have sought to win back elite religion to their side by pointing out to followers of mainstream religions that their beliefs too are undermined if the naturalists' claims to be the sole authorities for knowledge of the physical world are allowed to pass unchallenged. They argue that the very same arguments that are used to assert that creationism is incompatible with science can also be used to argue that mainstream religious beliefs are inconsequential, because the spiritual world has no influence whatsoever on the physical world. In other words, the creationists argue that all the naturalists who reject creationism as either irrelevant or wrong are actually (though not openly) implying the same thing about mainstream religious beliefs as well.

Phillip Johnson, a creationist, recently wrote a book titled *Darwin on* 40
Trial,[9] which makes the by-now familiar claims that Darwinism is a poor theory both on logical grounds ("survival of the fittest" as a mechanism for change is tautologous and lacks any predictive power) and on evidentiary grounds (the evidence is sparse for the existence of intermediate forms of life, and the rate at which micromutations can occur is not rapid enough to explain the current diversity in life forms). But in addition, he goes on to charge explicitly that beliefs in evolution and a creator are fundamentally incompatible.

The response to Johnson's book was fierce. Paleontologist Stephen Jay 41
Gould responded with an extremely vitriolic review in *Scientific American.*[10] Disposing swiftly of the logical and evidentiary arguments (which he had encountered many times before), he directed his attention to the claim that beliefs in science and God are mutually exclusive. It was clear that Johnson's charge had stung. For example, Gould says, "Either half my colleagues are enormously stupid, or else the science of Darwinism is fully compatible with conventional religious beliefs—and equally compatible with atheism." Or later, "To say it for all my colleagues and for the umpteenth millionth time . . . science simply cannot (by its legitimate methods) adjudicate the issue of God's possible superintendence of nature. We neither affirm it nor deny it; we simply can't comment on it as scientists. . . . Science can work only with naturalistic explanations; it can neither affirm nor deny other types of actors (like God) in other spheres (the moral realm, for example)."

Gould also states that science and religion "should not conflict because 42
science treats factual reality, while religion struggles with moral reality" and asserts that there is a "consensus that science and religion are separate and equally valuable." Both of these assertions are reformulations of the National Academy of Sciences' "two realms" statement. The key point that Gould does not address is the nature of the "moral reality" he refers to. If by this he means that religious beliefs can influence our behavior, then that resulting behavior must be part of the physical "factual reality," and hence the two realities are not separate.

Gould is certainly correct when he asserts that many scientists are also 43
religious believers. Surveys conducted in 1996 and 1998 found that about

40% of scientists believe in a personal God as defined by the statement "a God in intellectual and affirmative communication with man . . . to whom one may pray in expectation of receiving an answer."[11] Despite the explosive growth of science in the 20th century, this figure of 40% has remained stable since previous surveys done in 1914 and 1933. The figure would undoubtedly be much higher if belief in a nonpersonal God (some sort of prime mover who acted only through natural laws) were included as well.

There are two interesting features about Gould's review. One is the extreme harshness of the response. Gould is one of the more open-minded of well-known scientists and usually understanding of heterodox views. Creationists frequently use his frank views on the ambiguities and problems of evolution to attack the theory, much to his chagrin. But here he unequivocally lays down the scientific party line against creationism. The second interesting feature is that, instead of countering Johnson's views with careful arguments, Gould responds by simply asserting that the two belief systems must be compatible because many scientists are also religious people. Gould seems to be saying that his position that science and religion are compatible must be correct simply because he and many other scientists believe it to be correct.

In a subsequent book, Gould expands on this position, trying to further the case for the "two worlds model."[12] He reserves all explanations of physical phenomena for the realm of science (explicitly ruling out the possibility of any miraculous events), while leaving the moral and ethical realm for religion. But he still does not address the issue of the source of moral and ethical feelings. Do they originate within the brain and achieve their effects via commands that originate from the brain? If so, surely they lie within the realm of science, since the brain is a part of the physical world and thus subject to the investigations of science. However, if moral and ethical feelings transcend the brain, then how can they have any influence on people who live in the physical world?

Evolutionary biologist Francisco Ayala (president of the American Association for the Advancement of Science in 1994 and one of the expert witnesses against the creationist position at the 1981 Arkansas trial) also tries Gould's approach of arguing that science and religion must be compatible because famous intellectuals believe they are. Whereas Gould points to the religious beliefs of scientists, Ayala looks to the scientific views of famous theologians. Speaking at a symposium titled "Anti-Science/Anti-Evolution," he examined what Saint Augustine and Saint Thomas Aquinas had to say about the Bible and creation. Ayala concluded that "the point is that the two greatest thinkers of Christianity could find no reason based on the Bible that species could [not] find their origin in causes other than God."[13] He goes on to quote two popes (Leo XIII and John Paul II) to the effect that the Bible should not be interpreted literally or serve as a source of scientific understanding.

Both Gould and Ayala seem to argue that the fact that eminent scien- 47 tists and eminent theologians do not see a conflict between science and religion must mean that there is no such conflict. But all it might mean is that such people want to maintain peace between elite science and elite religion and are not keen to provoke a split.

As the targets of this alliance between elite religion and elite science, 48 creationists have no such interest in papering over any fundamental conflicts that might exist between the two. In this, they receive support from an unlikely source in biologist Richard Dawkins. Dawkins is a fervent advocate of Darwinian natural selection, the very theory that creationists love to hate. He has spent a great deal of time and effort refuting the claims of creationists that it is very highly improbable that natural selection could have led to the diversity, complexity, and sophistication of present-day life forms.[14] But Dawkins joins forces with Johnson in pouring scorn on the "two worlds model" of the National Academy of Sciences, calling it "a cowardly cop-out. I think it's an attempt to woo the sophisticated theological lobby and to get them into our camp and put the creationists into another camp. It's good politics. But it's intellectually disreputable."[15]

The second front opened up by the creationists in their war with elite 49 science is a direct attack on the very foundations of the scientific world view, which is that science is the sole source of authoritative knowledge about the physical world. And in this attack too creationists have found some unlikely allies, namely philosophers and historians of science and postmodern social constructivists of knowledge.

Philosophers of science, following in the tradition of Thomas Kuhn, 50 Karl Popper, Imre Lakatos, and Paul Feyerabend,[16] have long tried to understand the basis from which scientific knowledge derives its success and authority. It seems plausible that this success can come about only because the methods of science are leading toward truth. But notions of truth and objective reality have been extraordinarily difficult to pin down. Although these philosophers of science are, by and large, supporters of science and admirers of its achievements, they have regretfully concluded that there is no compelling reason to believe that scientific progress is leading to the truth about the physical world or even that there is such a thing as the truth or objective reality.

Postmodern philosophers have expanded upon this last point. Social 51 constructivists have argued that all knowledge, including scientific knowledge, is filtered and interpreted through the lenses of the observer and is thus inevitably colored by those lenses. What this means is that, when I directly experience something through my senses (say, I see a pencil), I make sense of that experience using my prior knowledge (what a pencil looks like, feels like, and does) and embed the new experience in my existing knowledge frameworks, modifying those frameworks in the process. Each person does the same thing, but since each person's history is different, his or her understanding of the same phenomenon must also differ. The unfiltered truth about a pencil (independent of any particular observer's interpretation) is thus impossible to discern. The best we can hope for is to negotiate a shared meaning so that we can communicate with one another.

Therefore, some social constructivists argue that modern scientific 52 knowledge is the product of the people (primarily male and Western) who were involved in its creation and that there might be equally valid alternative scientific world views, depending on the perspective of the people who engage in the creation of such alternative views.[17] Thus science cannot claim that its knowledge structure is objective and unique, and this has led to the discussion of possible alternatives, such as feminist science and multicultural science, in contrast to the present "orthodox" science.[18]

Scientists employ positivism (the view that the only things we can talk 53 about are those that we can show to exist by making measurements) to both understand and interpret scientific theories (especially difficult ones like quantum mechanics) and to attack fringe beliefs and creationism (since those beliefs involve phenomena that elude systematic observation). Taking a leaf from positivist science, however, radical social constructivists have argued that there can be no objective reality at all since one can never detect its existence independently of the interpretations of the observer. This illustrates another of the many ironies in the science wars in which one of the pillars of the scientific world view (positivism) is used to undermine another pillar (the belief in an objective reality).

Some creationists have used the arguments of all these groups to argue 54 that elite science, rather than being the imposing body of knowledge its supporters claim, has feet of clay and that its claim to sole authoritative knowledge about the physical world is unjustified. In particular, creationists assert that the views of elite science on the issue of evolution (a subject close to the heart of creationists) should not be accepted unquestioningly.

The scientific community has been somewhat flummoxed by the wide- 55 ranging nature of the criticisms it has received. The assault against its authority by an unexpected convergence of creationists, philosophers of science, postmodernists, social constructivists, feminists, and multiculturalists (groups that share little in common other than their skepticism of the scientific community's claims to special authority about the physical world)—coupled with the refusal of large segments of the public to give up their beliefs in astrology and the like—has caused considerable despair within the scientific community. Members of the elite scientific community decry what they see as the exploitation of widespread scientific illiteracy to create a growing anti-science sentiment.

The response to this situation by the more moderate members of the 56 elite science community has been to call for more investment in science education in order to improve science literacy. Those in this group feel that the problem arises because of popular misunderstanding and ignorance about the nature of the scientific enterprise. They feel that, if people really understood what science is and how its knowledge is acquired, they would be more supportive of science and more skeptical of alternative beliefs.

However, the more militant members of elite science see a more sinister 57 anti-science conspiracy at work and have launched a vigorous counterattack. In the vanguard of this initiative have been Paul Gross and Norman Levitt, who in *Higher Superstition*[19] rail against philosophers, feminists, postmodernists, and all the other people (whom they dub the "academic left") within the academy who, they feel, are willfully undermining the authority of science in an attempt to dethrone science from its position of prestige within the academy. Their polemic is a bitter and often mean-spirited attack on anyone they see as an enemy of science.

They followed the publication of their book by convening a conference 58 in New York in 1995 and publishing the papers presented as *The Flight from Science and Reason*.[20] About 200 scholars were invited to lead the charge against the perceived danger to science from both within and outside the academy, and the rhetoric was heated. Philosopher Mario Bunge said, "Walk a few steps away from the faculties of science, engineering, and medicine. Walk towards the faculty of arts. Here, you will meet another world, one where falsities and lies are manufactured in industrial quantities. . . . We should expel these charlatans from the university." According to philosopher Barry Gross, "The sole remedy at our disposal is to quarantine the anti-science brigades and inoculate the rest of the population against them. Scientists will have to devote some of their energy to systematic confrontation with the enemies of science."[21]

But the very vehemence of this counterattack may be backfiring on sci- 59 ence. Rather than coming across as reasonable defenders of the scientific world view, these scientists risk being perceived as arrogant elitists who sneer at those who do not understand them and adopt a scorched-earth policy in dealing with those who disagree with them.

At present, there seems to be very little attempt by any of the soldiers 60 in the science/religion wars to try really to understand what the other groups are saying. The debate is often cast in apocalyptic terms, with both sides determined to "win" the hearts and minds of the general public and forecasting dire consequences if they "lose." In the view of elite science, a "win" for fringe beliefs will mark the end of civilization as we know it, with rampant ignorance and superstition eventually driving out science from decision making, giving respectability to astrologers and other charlatans, and replacing reason with gullibility and foolishness. In the view of creationists, if they "lose," it will also mark the end of civilization as we know it and constitute the first step in the march toward rampant atheism, moral degeneracy, and, of course, secular humanism.

Given that this engagement is ostensibly a battle for public acceptance 61 of competing world views, the vitriolic tactics that have been adopted by both sides seem more likely to alienate people than to win them over. Rather than being convinced by one side or the other, the public is more likely to wish a plague on both their houses and tune out the debate. That would be a pity because the issues raised are deeply interesting and have profound implications for anyone who seeks an understanding and synthesis of science, religion, and philosophy. The subject is ripe for fresh insights, but new ideas are often delicate and ambiguous and require nurturing. This is unlikely to occur in the present climate.

In this war, as in any other war, the question that is always immediately 62 posed is "Which side are you on?" And deeper questions about whether the war itself makes any sense or should be fought at all get shunted aside. As long as the debate continues in its present adversarial form, we are unlikely to make much progress. What is clear, however, is that a solution to this seeming incompatibility between the scientific and religious world views remains extremely elusive.

Notes

[1]Ronald L. Numbers, *The Creationists: The Evolution of Scientific Creationism* (New York: Knopf, 1992).

[2]George Gaylord Simpson, *Tempo and Mode in Evolution* (New York: Columbia University Press, 1944), p. 76.

[3]William Hively, "How Much Science Does the Public Understand?," *American Scientist*, September/October 1988, p. 439.

[4]*Science and Creationism: A View from the National Academy of Sciences, Committee on Science and Creationism* (Washington, D.C.: National Academy Press, 1984), p. 6.

[5]Richard C. Lewontin, Introduction to Laurie R. Godfrey, ed., *Scientists Confront Creationism* (New York: Norton, 1983), p. xxvi.

[6]Robert Park, *What's New,* electronic newsletter of the American Physical Society, 27 December 1996, http://www.aps.org/WN/WN96/wn122796.html.

[7]John Horgan, *The End of Science* (Reading, Mass.: Addison-Wesley, 1996).

[8]For a careful and thorough review of the creationist movement, see Numbers, op. cit.

[9]Phillip E. Johnson, *Darwin on Trial* (Washington, D.C.: Regnery Gateway, 1991).

[10]Stephen Jay Gould, "Impeaching a Self-Appointed Judge," *Scientific American,* July 1992, p. 118.

[11]Edward J. Larson and Larry Witham, "Scientists Are Still Keeping the Faith," *Nature,* April 1997, p. 435.

[12]Stephen Jay Gould, *Rocks of Ages: Science and Religion in the Fullness of Life* (New York: Ballantine, 1999).

[13]Newsletter, Ohio Academy of Science, Spring 1995, p. 5.

[14]Richard Dawkins, *Climbing Mount Improbable* (New York: Norton, 1996).

[15]Edward J. Larson and Larry Witham, "Scientists and Religion in America," *Scientific American,* September 1999, p. 88.

[16]Thomas Kuhn, *The Structure of Scientific Revolutions* (Chicago: University of Chicago Press, 1970); Karl R. Popper, *Conjectures and Refutations: The Growth of Scientific Knowledge* (New York: Harper Torchbooks, 1965); Imre Lakatos, *The Methodology of Scientific Research Programmes* (Cambridge: Cambridge University Press, 1986); and Paul K. Feyerabend, *Against Method* (London: Verso, 1978).

[17]David Bloor, *Knowledge and Social Imagery* (London: Routledge & Kegan Paul, 1976).

[18]Nancy Tuana, ed., *Feminism and Science* (Bloomington: Indiana University Press, 1989).

[19]Paul R. Gross and Norman Levitt, *Higher Superstition: The Academic Left and Its Quarrels with Science* (Baltimore: Johns Hopkins University Press, 1994).

[20]Paul R. Gross, Norman Levitt, and Martin W. Lewis, eds., *The Flight from Science and Reason* (New York: Academy of Sciences, 1996).

[21]Franklin Hoke, "Scientists See Broad Attack Against Research and Reason," *The Scientist,* 10 July 1995, p. 1.

Thinking Critically

1. Write an outline of Mano Singham's argument. How does he explain and accommodate the opposing view of the "leading characters" in the argument about teaching creationism? At what point does Singham express his own views?

2. Singham makes a distinction between "fringe beliefs" and "elite opinion." What attributes does he assign to each category?

3. Singham's carefully constructed argument relies on classification to clearly delineate different ways of thinking or believing. Create a chart or graph that names Singham's categories, and list the attributes he assigns to each. Then draw a model of the "triangle" Singham proposes to frame the debate. Where on this triangle would you locate each of those categories of belief?

Writing Critically

1. Singham proposes a surprising relationship between "popular science" and "popular religion." What is surprising about this relationship? How would Jill Neimark and Natalie Angier respond to Singham on this point? Their essays also appear in this chapter.

2. Singham quotes the National Academy of Sciences statement, which says, "Religion and science are separate and mutually exclusive realms of human thought whose presentation in the same context lead to misunderstanding of both scientific theory and religious belief." In an essay that draws on at least two readings from this chapter, discuss whether or not you agree with this statement. Is there room for common ground between "religion" and "science," as implied by this statement? If so, where does it lie, and what are the stakes?

3. Compare what Singham calls "middle ground" with the "middle course" suggested by Eric S. Cohen in "To Wonder Again" (see paragraph 31 of Cohen's essay, in this chapter).

The End of the World: A Brief History

THE ECONOMIST

The Economist is a weekly print magazine founded in 1843 that covers international business and politics. Interesting features of *The Economist* are the anonymity of its articles and the collaborative nature of its editorial viewpoint. As explained on its website, "The main reason for

anonymity . . . is a belief that what is written is more
important than who writes it. As Geoffrey Crowther,
editor from 1938 to 1956, put it, anonymity keeps the
editor 'not the master but the servant of something far
greater than himself. You can call that ancestor-worship
if you wish, but it gives to the paper an astonishing momentum of thought and principle.'" *The Economist* is
indeed independent and sometimes surprising in its politics. It supported both Ronald Reagan and Bill Clinton
and has been an advocate for progressive causes ranging
from the abolition of the death penalty to the rights of
gays to marriage. The website of *The Economist* is at
<http://www.economist.com>. "The End of the
World: A Brief History" appeared in the issue of
December 16, 2004.

A VeriChip is a tiny, implantable microchip with a unique identification   1
number that connects a patient to his medical records. When America's Food and Drug Administration recently approved it for medical use in
human's, the news provoked familiar worries in the press about privacy-
threatening technologies. But on the notice boards of raptureready.com,
the talk was about a drawback that the FDA and the media seemed to have
overlooked. Was the VeriChip the "mark of the beast"?

Raptureready.com runs an online service for the millions of born-again   2
Christians in America who believe that an event called the Rapture is coming soon. During the Rapture, Christ will return and whisk believers away
to join the righteous dead in heaven. From there, they will have the best
seats in the house as the unsaved perish in a series of spectacular fires, wars,
plagues and earthquakes. (Raptureready.com advises the soon-to-depart to
stick a note on the fridge to brief those left behind—husbands, wives and
in-laws—about the horrors in store for them.)

Furnished with apocalyptic tracts from the Bible, believers scour news   3
dispatches for clues that the Rapture is approaching. Some think implantable chips are a sign. The Book of Revelation features a "mark" that
the Antichrist makes everybody wear "in their right hand, or in their foreheads." Rapturists have more than a hobbyist's idle interest in identifying
this mark. Anyone who accepts it spends eternity roasting in the sulphurs
of hell. (And, incidentally, the European Union may be "the matrix out of
which the Antichrist's kingdom could grow.")

Christians have kept faith with the idea that the world is just about   4
to end since the beginnings of their religion. Jesus Himself hinted more
than once that His second coming would happen during the lifetime of

His followers. In its original form, the Lord's Prayer, taught by Jesus to his disciples, may have implored God to "keep us from the ordeal."

Men have been making the same appeal ever since. In 156 A.D., a fel- 5 low called Montanus, pronouncing himself to be the incarnation of the Holy Spirit, declared that the New Jerusalem was about to come crashing down from the heavens and land in Phrygia—which, conveniently, was where he lived. Before long, Asia Minor, Rome, Africa and Gaul were jammed with wandering ecstatics, bitterly repenting their sins and fasting and whipping themselves in hungry anticipation of the world's end. A bit more than a thousand years later, the authorities in Germany were stamping out an outbreak of apocalyptic mayhem among a self-abusing sect called the secret flagellants of Thuringia. The disciples of William Miller, a 19th-century evangelical American, clung ecstatically to the same belief as the Montanists and the Thuringians. A thick strand of Christian history connects them all, and countless other movements.

Don't Get Left Behind

Apocalyptic belief renews itself in ingenious ways. Belief in the Rapture, 6 which enlivens the familiar end-of-time narrative with a compellingly dramatic twist, appears to be a modern phenomenon: John Nelson Darby, a 19th-century British evangelical preacher, was perhaps the first to popularise the idea. (Darby's inspiration was a passage in St. Paul's letter to the Thessalonians, which talks about the Christian dead and true believers being "caught up together" in the clouds.) It is not easy to say how many Americans believe in Darby's concept of Rapture. But a dozen novels that dramatise the event and its gripping aftermath—the "Left Behind" series— have sold more than 40m. copies.

New apocalyptic creeds have even sprung from those sticky moments 7 when the world has failed to end on schedule. (Social scientists call this "disconfirmation.") When the resurrected Christ failed to show up for Miller's disciples on the night of October 22nd 1844, press scribblers mocked the "Great Disappointment" mercilessly. But even as they jeered, a farmer called Hiram Edson snuck away from the vigil to pray in a barn, where he duly received word of what had happened. There had been a great event after all—but in heaven, not on Earth. This happening was that Jesus had begun an "investigative judgment of the dead" in preparation for his return. Thus was born the Church of Seventh-day Adventists. They were not the only ones to rise above apparent setbacks to the prophesies by which they set such store: the Jehovah's Witnesses of the persistently apocalyptic Watchtower sect survived no fewer than nine disconfirmations every few years between 1874 and 1975.

Which Way to Armageddon?

Why do end-of-time beliefs endure? Social scientists love to set about this 8
question with earnest study of the people who subscribe to such ideas. As
part of his investigation into the "apocalyptic genre" in modern America,
Paul Boyer of the University of Wisconsin asks why so many of his fellow
Americans are "susceptible" to televangelists and other "popularisers."
From time to time, sophisticated Americans indulge the thrillingly terrify-
ing thought that nutty, apocalyptic, born-again Texans are guiding not just
conservative social policies at home, but America's agenda in the Middle
East as well, as they round up reluctant compatriots for the last battle at
Armageddon. (It's a bit south of the Lake of Galilee in the plain of Jezreel.)

Behind these attitudes sits the assumption that apocalyptic thought 9
belongs—or had better belong—to the extremities of human experience.
On closer inspection, though, that is by no means true.

Properly, the apocalypse is both an end and a new beginning. In Chris- 10
tian tradition, the world is created perfect. There is then a fall, followed by
a long, rather enjoyable (for some) period of moral degeneration. This cul-
minates in a decisive final battle between good (the returned Christ) and
evil (the Antichrist). Good wins and establishes the New Jerusalem and
with it the 1,000-year reign of King Jesus on Earth.

This is the glorious millennium that millenarians await so eagerly. Mil- 11
lenarians tend to place history at a moment just before the decisive final
showdown. The apocalyptic mind looks through the surface reality of the
world and sees history's epic, true nature: "apocalypse" comes from the
Greek word meaning to uncover, or disclose.

Norman Cohn, a British historian, places the origin of apocalyptic 12
thought with Zoroaster (or Zarathustra), a Persian prophet who probably
lived between 1500 and 1200 B.C. The Vedic Indians, ancient Egyptians
and some earlier civilisations had seen history as a cycle, which was for ever
returning to its beginning. Zoroaster embellished this tepid plot. He added
goodies (Ahura Mazda, the maker and guardian of the ordered world),
baddies (the spirit of destruction, Angra Mainyu) and a happy ending (a
glorious consummation of order over disorder, known as the "making
wonderful," in which "all things would be made perfect, once and for all").
In due course Zoroaster's theatrical talents came to Christians via the Jews.

This basic drama shapes all apocalyptic thought, from the tenets of 13
tribal cargo cults to the beliefs of UFO sects. In 1973, Claude Vorilhon, a
correspondent for a French racing-car magazine, claimed to have been
whisked away in a flying saucer, in which he had spent six days with a green
chap who spoke fluent French. The alien told Mr. Vorilhon that the Frenchman's real name was Rael, that humans had misread the Bible and that,

properly translated, the Hebrew word *Elohim* (singular: *Eloha*) did not mean God, as Jews had long supposed, but "those who came from the sky."

The alien then revealed that his species had created everything on Earth 14 in a space laboratory, and that the aliens wanted to return to give humans their advanced technology, which would transform the world utterly. First, however, Rael needed financial contributions to build the aliens an embassy in Jerusalem, because otherwise they would not feel welcome (a bit lame, this explanation). Although the Israeli government has not yet given its consent, the Raelians—those persuaded by Rael's account—continue to welcome donations in anticipation of a change of heart.

The Raelians' claim to be atheists who belong to the secular world must 15 come as no surprise to Mr. Cohn, who has long detected patterns of religious apocalyptic thought in what is supposedly rational, secular belief. He has traced "egalitarian and communistic fantasies" to the ancient-world idea of an ideal state of nature, in which all men are genuinely equal and none is persecuted. As Mr. Cohn has put it, "The old religious idiom has been replaced by a secular one, and this tends to obscure what otherwise would be obvious. For it is the simple truth that, stripped of their original supernatural sanction, revolutionary millenarianism and mystical anarchism are with us still."

Nicholas Campion, a British historian and astrologer, has expanded on 16 Mr. Cohn's ideas. In his book, *The Great Year,* Mr. Campion draws parallels between the "scientific" historical materialism of Marx and the religious apocalyptic experience. Thus primitive communism is the Garden of Eden, the emergence of private property and the class system is the fall, the final gasps of capitalism are the last days, the proletariat are the chosen people and the socialist revolution is the second coming and the New Jerusalem.

Hegel saw history as an evolution of ideas that would culminate in the 17 ideal liberal-democratic state. Since liberal democracy satisfies the basic need for recognition that animates political struggle, thought Hegel, its advent heralds a sort of end of history—another suspiciously apocalyptic claim. More recently, Francis Fukuyama has echoed Hegel's theme. Mr. Fukuyama began his book, *The End of History,* with a claim that the world had arrived at "the gates of the Promised Land of liberal democracy." Mr. Fukuyama's pulpit oratory suited the spirit of the 1990s, with its transformative "new economy" and free-world triumphs. In the disorientating disconfirmation of September 11th and the coincident stockmarket collapse, however, his religion has lost favour.

The apocalyptic narrative may have helped to start the motor of capi- 18 talism. A drama in which the end returns interminably to the beginning leaves little room for the sense of progress which, according to the 19th-century social theories of Max Weber, provides the religious licence for material self-improvement. Without the last days, in other words, the world might never have had 65-inch flat-screen televisions. For that matter, the whole American project has more than a touch of the apocalypse about it. The Pilgrim Fathers thought they had reached the New Israel. The "manifest destiny" of America to spread its providential liberty and self-government throughout the North American continent (not to mention the Middle East) smacks of the millennium and the New Jerusalem.

Science treasures its own apocalypses. The modern environmental 19 movement appears to have borrowed only half of the apocalyptic narrative. There is a Garden of Eden (unspoilt nature), a fall (economic development), the usual moral degeneracy (it's all man's fault) and the pressing sense that the world is enjoying its final days (time is running out: please donate now!). So far, however, the green lobby does not appear to have realised it is missing the standard happy ending. Perhaps, until it does, environmentalism is destined to remain in the political margins. Everyone needs redemption.

Watch This Spacesuit

Noting an exponential acceleration in the pace of technological change, fu- 20 turologists like Hans Moravec and Ray Kurzweil think the world inhabits the "knee of the curve"—a sort of last-days set of circumstances in which, in the near future, the pace of technological change runs quickly away towards an infinite "singularity" as intelligent machines learn to build themselves. From this point, thinks Mr. Moravec, transformative "mind fire" will spread in a flash across the cosmos. Britain's astronomer royal, Sir Martin Rees, relegates Mr. Kurzweil and those like him to the "visionary fringe." But Mr. Rees's own darkly apocalyptic book, *Our Final Hour,* outdoes the most colourful of America's televangelists in earthquakes, plagues and other sorts of fire and brimstone.

So there you have it. The apocalypse is the locomotive of capitalism, the 21 inspiration for revolutionary socialism, the bedrock of America's manifest destiny and the undeclared religion of all those pseudo-rationalists who, like *The Economist,* champion the progress of liberal democracy. Perhaps, deep down, there is something inside everyone which yearns for the New Jerusalem, a place where, as a beautiful bit of Revelation puts it:

> God shall wipe away all tears from their eyes; and there shall be no more death, neither sorrow, nor crying, neither shall there be any more pain; for the former things are passed away.

Yes, perhaps. But, to be sure, not everyone agrees that salvation, when 22 it comes, will appear clothed in a shiny silver spacesuit.

Thinking Critically

1. Using Mano Singham's classifications, determine which parts of "The End of the World: A Brief History" deal with elite or popular religious beliefs, and elite or popular science. (Singham's essay precedes this one.)

2. Why do the British writers of "The End of the World: A Brief History" find apocalyptic thinking to be particularly American? How many different kinds of examples and sources of evidence do they offer to support this claim?

3. How would you characterize the tone of "The End of the World: A Brief History"? Is it similar in tone to any other selections in Chapter 6?

Writing Critically

1. Compare the apocalyptic scenarios in Paul Roberts's "Over a Barrel" (see pp. 414–17) or Adam Gopnik's "The Unreal Thing" (see pp. 640–48). What other recent or ongoing events in American culture seemed apocalyptic, either to you personally or as described in the news media? Set this event in a larger social or historical context using "The End of the World: A Brief History."

2. Define *disconfirmation,* and describe a recent news or cultural event that is an example of disconfirmation.

3. In an essay, describe a particular kind of apocalyptic thinking that turns up frequently in popular culture. Be careful and specific about how you define *apocalyptic,* remembering that the term has many different political and cultural as well as religious connotations.

But Will the Klingons Understand Deuteronomy?

CARRIE DOLAN

This article first appeared in the "middle column" of the front page of the *Wall Street Journal* in June 1994. The *Wall Street Journal* is the most authoritative daily business newspaper in the United States, and its front page (which never includes photographs) is usually a mix of current affairs and business news. The middle column of the front page has historically been the home of more offbeat feature reporting, including this article. Carrie Dolan has been a writer for the *Wall Street Journal* since 1982.

Citing deep philosophical differences with fellow scholars, Glen   1
Proechel has resigned from his Bible-translation group.

"We have very, very different goals," says Prof. Proechel, a language in-   2
structor at the University of Minnesota. The rift will result in two translations of the Good Book for a civilization that, until now, has lacked the
Word in its own language: the Klingon language.

Klingons, for those who have been off the planet for the past 30 years,   3
are a fictitious alien race from television's *Star Trek* series. Prof. Proechel
is now working alone on his Klingon translation, a paraphrase of the New
Testament. Rivals are writing a literal translation of the entire Bible.

"It's not going to make any sense," Prof. Proechel says of the literal Klin-   4
gon version. "It will be describing things that don't exist in their culture."

But Klingon literalists disagree. "You don't mess around with the   5
Bible," even if the warrior-like Klingon vocabulary is void of biblical concepts like mercy and compassion, says Dr. Lawrence Schoen, a linguist
overseeing the literalist translation.

Klingons, and *Star Trek,* have been on TV since 1965. But it was in 1984   6
that a linguist invented an official Klingon language for the movie *Star Trek
III: The Search for Spock,* and it has been used in subsequent movies and
TV episodes. For reasons that might escape some humans, Klingon has been
picked up by avid earthling students, religious and otherwise.

The second annual Interstellar Language School, including a festival of   7
Klingon poetry readings, will take place next month in Minnesota. There
are Klingon newsletters, Klingon Internet conversation groups and audio
cassettes with titles like "Conversational Klingon" and "Power Klingon."
Weddings have been performed in Klingon. An estimated quarter-million
copies of the Klingon Dictionary have been sold.

"Klingon is the first artificial language to be adopted by popular culture,"   8
says Dr. Schoen, a professor of psycholinguistics at Chestnut Hill College in
Philadelphia and founder of the nonprofit Klingon Language Institute. The
three-year-old KLI, which claims 750 members, is working on several Klingon projects, including language correspondence courses and translations of
all Shakespeare's works. (It will soon publish a Klingon *Hamlet.*)

Speaking Klingon, Dr. Schoen says, "is no more bizarre than sports   9
trivia, or knowing the details of engines of cars that haven't been manufactured in 20 years."

The KLI, based in Flourtown, Pa., is heading the Klingon Bible project,   10
which could take up to five years. It involves ten scholars, led by a gradu-

ate of Yale Divinity School. They are getting help from a Lutheran Bible group; far from seeing the project as blasphemous, the group hopes it will draw attention to the challenges of translating the Bible for real people.

The scholars are translating directly into Klingon from Greek and other   11 original biblical languages. Among the hurdles: the fact that the Klingons have no word for "God" or "holy," says Prof. Proechel. Conveying even basic concepts has proven difficult. "Their mode of thought is quite different," he says. "Things that are part and parcel of the Judeo-Christian faith—forgiveness, atonement—don't fit into Klingon thinking." (Klingon thinking does, however, allow for words like "choljaH," a ponytail holder, and "butlh," a phrase meaning "dirt under fingernails.")

Until recently, Prof. Proechel was part of the team, but he has since   12 strayed from the flock. He is working on what he calls a "retelling of the New Testament in the world which the Klingons understand."

Consider the line from Mark "We have five loaves and two fishes." Klin-   13 gon doesn't have words for loaves or fish. The literal camp uses the Klingon "tIrSoj," which means "grain food," and "bIQHa'DIbah," or "water animal." Prof. Proechel, translating the same sentence using things with which the Klingons are familiar, uses the Klingon "vagh 'Iwchab cha' ghargh wIghaj," meaning, "We have only five blood pies and two serpent worms."

That's where the rift developed. With only 2,000 words in the Klingon   14 vocabulary to chose from, translators often disagree on the Klingon term closest to the meaning of the original. For instance, there are plenty of lambs in the Bible, but none in the Klingon world, so Prof. Proechel uses the word "targh"—a vicious, ugly, piglike animal. "But it is the most important animal to the Klingons, so it gets the message across," he explains.

Literalist scholars object to such substitutions, however in tune with   15 Klingon culture they might be. "A targh bears about as much resemblance to a lamb as a charging rhino does," says Kevin Wilson, general editor of the KLI Bible project.

The Bible has undergone other unorthodox translations, of course. The   16 American Bible Society says it has been translated into 337 of an estimated 6,000 languages and dialects spoken on earth. There are also rap translations, feminist versions, Cajun editions and a multimedia version in an MTV-like format. There are two versions of the Gospels in Esperanto, a turn-of-the-century language whose inventors hoped would become a universal tongue. (It hasn't.)

"A multitude of curious things have been done with Scripture," notes Ger-   17 ald Studer, president of the International Bible Collectors Society. Mr. Studer has over 5,000 versions of the Bible, including the Gospels written in Liverpool slang, the New Testament supposedly corrected by spirits and the Book of Psalms written on 166 pages of animal skin. He eagerly awaits the Klingon translation.

TV's Klingons may not be particularly articulate, but Klingon's earthly 18 scholars are quite picky about the Klingon language. Like the French government, they are dead set against polluting the alien tongue with earthly borrowings. "We are sort of like the Académie Française," the French agency charged with guarding the purity of French, says Dr. Schoen. "We're doing what we can to keep it pure." When faced with the need for a new Klingon word, translators are encouraged to simply recast the sentence using some of the 2,000 existing words. At last summer's Klingon language camp, for instance, players at a softball game had to work around Klingon's lack of equivalents for "safe" and "out." The solution: "yIn," which is Klingon for "to live," and "Hegh," Klingon for "to die."

Sometimes literalists break their rules. With no good substitute for 19 "lamb," they are quietly using "SIp," Klingonifying the English "sheep."

When things get really desperate, scholars turn to Dr. Marc Okrand, 20 Klingon's creator. Dr. Okrand has studied native American tongues, Chinese and Southeast Asian languages, but says Klingon's "collection of grammatical elements is unique. This is not an earth language."

Officially, the Klingon dictionary is limited to words acquired through in- 21 terviews with a Klingon prisoner named Maltz captured in the 23rd century, says Dr. Okrand, who works at the National Captioning Institute in Falls Church, Va. But, in a pinch, Dr. Okrand can beam up a few new phrases. "From time to time," admits Dr. Schoen, the Klingon purist, Dr. Okrand "has agreed to review our wish lists and discover new words."

Thinking Critically

1. What is the key difference between the two translations of the Bible into Klingon that Carrie Dolan describes?

2. The creation of an artificial language is a unique opportunity to create—or not create—values, beliefs, and concepts. Considering what's missing from the Klingon language, what conclusions can you draw about Klingon values?

Writing Critically

1. What kind of story does science fiction tell a culture about itself? How does *Star Trek,* obviously a classic bit of American science fiction, compare to, say, the Raelians discussed in "The End of the World: A Brief History" (the preceding selection)?

2. In paragraph 4 of "To Wonder Again" (in this chapter), Eric S. Cohen classifies several distinct "maladies of the soul" afflicting contemporary Americans.

Where do fans of science fiction fit in his classification scheme, if they fit at all? In a research paper, trace the origins of popular science fiction in American culture. What does science fiction respond to? From what does it offer an escape?

Arguing the Cultural Divides

1. Mano Singham, Jill Neimark, Eric S. Cohen, Natalie Angier, and other writers in this chapter examine why Americans are so likely to believe in things that cannot be scientifically proved (or that have been conclusively disproved). In an essay, discuss what you think such beliefs reveal about the American character or about American society.

2. Elsewhere in *Many Americas* you will find specific examples of a kind of collision between faith and politics, or church and state. For example, Chapter 3 examines the role of religion in American politics, and Chapter 9 looks more closely at the creationism versus evolution debate in public schools. Writers in this chapter take a broader view of what it means to have faith, and what happens when faith and reason (what David James Duncan calls "my dog Reason") can't be reconciled. Some of the writers in this chapter (like Duncan) celebrate this conflict; others, like Mano Singham and Jill Neimark, look hopefully toward a kind of peaceful, though tentative, accord between reason and faith. In a personal essay, chronicle the ways in which your own faith and reason have been challenged, supported, refuted, or renewed by your education. Do you find it more personally rewarding to balance faith and reason, to keep them in conflict, or to completely give over to one and not the other? Be sure to draw on at least two of the writers in this chapter to support and illustrate your position.

3. Are you more impressed by a political candidate's profession of faith or confession of doubt? In your answer, you can refer to the actions of a specific politician, or you can reflect more broadly on what qualities you associate with faith and doubt and whether or not you consider those qualities consistent with leadership. Be sure to make reference to the diverse conceptions of faith, reason, skepticism, reverence, or doubt illustrated by the selections in Chapter 6.

America the Beautiful: Wilderness or Resource?

Cultivating the Butterfly Effect

ERIK ASSADOURIAN

Erik Assadourian is a staff researcher at the World-watch Institute, a nonpartisan independent research group founded in 1974 to, in its own words, promote "an environmentally sustainable and socially just society." Among the Institute's researchers and members are activists and scientists specializing in a range of environmental issues and fields. "Cultivating the Butterfly Effect" first appeared in the January–February 2003 issue of *World Watch* magazine, published bimonthly by the Institute for a general audience. The Institute also publishes research papers, books, and other materials for specialized audiences. Assadourian graduated from Dartmouth with a combined degree in psychology, religion, and anthropology. Before joining Worldwatch in 2002, he worked for the U.S Public Interest Research Group, traveled in India, and did development work in the Dominican Republic. His research interests at Worldwatch include overconsumption, sustainability, and social change. Assadourian has made numerous contributions to Worldwatch Institute publications, and he has been interviewed about overconsumption issues on CNN, National Public Radio, the Voice of America, and the BBC.

Chaos theorists suggest that the waving wings of even a single butterfly   1
affect the weather around the world. All life affects all life. And so, in a
vastly larger way, does the growth of even the smallest home or neighborhood garden. The millions of gardens growing around the globe are having
a powerful cumulative effect on people, communities, and the environment.

Monarchs, anise swallowtails, gulf fritillaries: these are just 3 of the 15   2
species of butterflies that now inhabit the 2nd Street Elementary School
Garden. Begun 10 years ago in a few flowerboxes, the garden has expanded to the size of two classrooms. Kids who walk into it find themselves
sharing space not only with butterflies, but with sunflowers, ladybugs, and
yellow-rumped warblers. The National Wildlife Federation has even designated this little plot a certified wilderness area.

This would be a commendable achievement for any garden, but it's es-   3
pecially impressive for one that is contained on all sides by freeways, and is
located in an inner-city Los Angeles neighborhood that suffers from a severe
degree of gang-violence. The garden has become a refuge of green within the
gray smog-filled junction of Interstate 5, Interstate 10, and Route 60, with
chirping birds now defying the rumble of downshifting trucks that exit the
I-5—the freeway whose retaining wall is shared by the school parking lot.

Like countless other gardens around the world, the 2nd Street Elemen-   4
tary School Garden is having noticeable effects on its community. While it
can't quite neutralize the smog of the three major highways or the aggression of nearby gangs, it has brought a new vitality to both the school and
its neighborhood—restoring a piece of the local environment, fostering a
sense of community, and providing the school with fresh vegetables and a
fresh approach to education.

Brandyn Scully, the teacher who started the garden in 1992, says the   5
project has become the students' "reason to learn," and is consistently
voted their favorite part of school. "It helps me teach," she says. For example, it provides a creative way to discuss the intricacies of math and science, as when the kids investigate the life cycle of flies that grow in
marigold seed pods. For students who are just beginning to learn English,
that kind of hands-on setting also helps to reduce the difficulties of learning only in a classroom setting. It has fostered a newfound respect for the
environment, as teachers and students become partners in restoring a natural system that balances the needs of the environment—like milkweed for
the monarchs—with the needs of humans.

The 2nd Street Elementary School is one of about 3,000 California   6
schools that have maintained gardens with the encouragement, materials,

Source: Worldwatch Institute, *Worldwatch Magazine*, Jan/Feb 2003. Reprinted by permission.

and funding of a state Department of Education program, "A Garden in Every School." A primary mission of the program, which began in 1995, is to provide "an opportunity for children to learn about nutrition, healthy eating, and basic food preparation." According to the program's coordinator, Deborah Tamannaie, the program is working. "Instead of eating junk food, the children are eating what they grow," she says.

One indication of the program's success comes from a recent study of 97 children, conducted by Jennifer Morris and her colleagues at the University of California at Davis. Morris found that the 48 children who learned about nutrition and worked in a garden throughout the school year were significantly more willing to try new vegetables than were those of a control group, who did not have gardens or nutrition education.

Critics might question whether school systems that are financially stretched can really afford gardens. But in fact, these gardens address a rather urgent need. In the United States, with obesity having reached epidemic proportions, the health of the school-age population is at stake. About 13 percent of American kids are overweight or obese, and only one percent meet the daily U.S. Food Pyramid Guide recommendations for all five standard food groups. As they grow older, if their eating habits remain poor, their vulnerability to getting fat is likely to rise dangerously. Already, a record 61 percent of the adult population is overweight or obese. According to a 2001 report by the U.S. Surgeon General, this epidemic contributes to 300,000 deaths per year—just shy of the 400,000 deaths associated with tobacco.

School gardens also help to counter the damage done by two other notorious trends in U.S. schools: cutting back on physical education classes, and signing sales contracts with soft-drink companies and fast-food restaurants. Gardening may not be as strenuous as soccer or tennis, but it gets the kids outdoors doing something physically active. And the pleasure of eating a sun-ripened tomato or fresh carrot may offer a refreshing alternative to processed potatoes, which currently make up about a fifth of the vegetables consumed by Americans.

. . . In the United States, while saving individual families hundreds of dollars in food costs per year, gardens also supply food to local poverty assistance programs. In Huntsville, Alabama, more than a thousand volunteers help to grow food at the CASA (Care Assurance System for Aging and Homebound) community garden. In 2001, volunteers harvested and delivered almost 9 tons of vegetables to elderly and homebound people in the surrounding area. The CASA garden is part of a national program, Plant a Row for the Hungry, which since 1996 has mobilized community gardeners to donate a portion of each year's harvest. So far, the program has supplied over 800 tons of fresh produce to local assistance programs.

The potential, of course, is vastly greater than that. During World War 11
II, 20 million community and home gardens across the United States provided more than 40 percent of the fresh vegetables consumed by civilians,
so that farms could feed the troops. If gardening could be done on that
scale again, local food security could be improved while freeing surpluses
to assist in areas suffering from food shortages caused by political or environmental instability.

The kind of land-use shift required to grow gardens on that scale could 12
have an ecological and health benefit far beyond that of providing fresher,
more chemical-free food. At present, the largest "crop" in the United States
is lawns, which cover 10 million hectares. By one estimate, the average U.S.
lawn (about one-eight of a hectare or one-third of an acre) absorbs up to
4.5 kilograms of pesticides, 9 kilograms of fertilizers, and 773,000 liters of
water annually—along with the countless hours of labor and liters of gasoline consumed by mowing. Even converting just 1 percent of these lawns
into organic gardens would reduce the toxic pesticide exposure to families
and wildlife by up to 3.4 million kilograms per year, while also helping to
reduce reliance on energy-intensive commercial food transport. Along with
reducing nutritional value and creating vast amounts of packaging waste,
shipping food over long distances—by ship, truck, or plane—leads to increased production of carbon dioxide emissions. In the United Kingdom,
agricultural products traveled an average of 125 kilometers in 1999, producing 4 million tons of carbon dioxide in the process. Yet, 125 kilometers
is relatively short; in the United States, the average food product travels
from 2,400 to 4,000 kilometers, more than 20 times as far as in the U.K....

Finally, there is a benefit of urban gardens that is too often overlooked 13
by urban planners and government officials. People often congregate to
work, relax, and enjoy communal spaces, and through these interactions
build community. In a study of community gardens in upstate New York,
Donna Armstrong of the State University of New York at Albany found
that in 54 of 63 gardens surveyed, people worked to some degree cooper-
atively—sharing tools, work, or harvest. Having a garden often helped to
foster pride in the neighborhood, evidence of which could be seen in
reduced littering rates and improved maintenance of other properties in the
neighborhood. Further, in one-third of the gardens, more expansive community empowerment initiatives were generated by participants—initiatives
that included the creation of a new park and the establishment of a neighborhood crime-watch program.

Along with empowering communities, gardens can also help to inte- 14
grate them—facilitating interactions between diverse populations. La Plaza
Cultural, a garden founded in 1974 in New York City's Lower East Side,

functions as a cultural center and performance space—holding regular performances that range from *King Lear* to Sufi dancing. At the same time, it provides organic produce to local food shelters and, like the 2nd Street Elementary School garden, serves as a registered wildlife habitat.

Gardens can be venues for community building and empowerment, either by providing a communal space, cultural activities, or—sometimes—by providing a common cause when the garden itself is threatened. Often, as gardens transform previously rubble-littered vacant lots into green havens, they attract not just butterflies but bulldozers, sent to convert the now pristine land into new developments. In the United Kingdom, about one-third of the half-million allotment gardens that existed in the mid-twentieth century have been destroyed.

La Plaza Cultural is another of these threatened gardens. For many years, a developer wanted to build a senior citizen housing complex on its city-owned lot in Manhattan. When public housing and open space come into conflict, the former is usually regarded as the more urgent of the two—and the garden is lost. In New York, a city known for both its beautiful gardens as well as its 18-year-long conflict between the city government and gardening community, these two constituencies reached a major compromise this past autumn, resulting in an agreement that preserves 391 of the 838 contested gardens. While some (including La Plaza Cultural) are not covered, the settlement dramatizes how much the social value of gardens has grown. If these spaces can survive in a city where real estate is some of the most expensive in the world, they can thrive anywhere.

Thinking Critically

1. Visit the website of the Worldwatch Institute at <http://www.worldwatch .org/> and the website of the U.S. Public Interest Research Group at <http://www.uspirg.org/>. How would you characterize the political position of these two entities? What does an understanding of the purposes and goals of these groups contribute to your reading of "Cultivating the Butterfly Effect"? How would your own reading patterns (either casual or academic) change if you routinely paid close attention to the associations and affiliations of publications and authors?

2. How does Erik Assadourian use the concept of the "butterfly effect" to bring coherence to his argument? Take note of places in his essay where he describes things that seem to exemplify the butterfly effect, even if he doesn't explicitly use that term.

3. Create an outline of "Cultivating the Butterfly Effect" that traces every causal relationship Assadourian suggests. What kinds of evidence does he supply to connect each cause with its effect?

Writing Critically

1. Create a presentation for your school's board of regents (or other governing board) arguing for the construction of a public garden on your campus. Use as a model the kinds of gardens that Assadourian describes, paying attention to the ways in which a garden would enhance the quality of life for different groups of people on and around your campus. What kinds of funding and other resources would you need to request for such a garden? Who would be responsible for maintaining the garden? Consider the power of visual images, the accessibility of PowerPoint, and other media and tools that could help you create a powerful argument.

2. Many of the writers in Chapter 2 discuss ways in which "community" can be created, enhanced, or eroded by various cultural and economic factors. Use "Cultivating the Butterfly Effect" and at least one of the readings in Chapter 2 in an essay describing how community gardens can help to foster a sense of community.

3. Among the many troubles plaguing American education described in Chapter 9, the inability to grow a good tomato is not mentioned. How would a cooperative school garden help to address any of the issues discussed in Chapter 9?

Why I Hunt

RICK BASS

In a 1994 interview with the online journal *weber studies,* Rick Bass said he hoped that the audience for his nature writing "will be touched by the land and behave in such a way that will not bring it harm and in fact will be inspired to fight their hearts out for it. That would be the kind of person I would want to encourage with my writing. . . . I see more wild people trying to go out and find similar places for themselves, finding them, becoming engaged in them, falling in love with them, and fighting the rest of their lives to protect those things from being wiped off the face of the earth." Before moving to the remote Yaak Valley on the Montana-Canada border, Bass worked as an oil and gas geologist in America's Deep South, work he documented in his 1979 book *Oil Notes.* As a writer and a committed activist, Bass has written about and been a public advocate for the preservation of America's wild places. "Why I Hunt" appeared in the July/August issue of *Sierra* magazine, published by the Sierra Club. Bass grew up in the Texas hill country and learned to hunt from his grandfather. His widely acclaimed first book,

The Deer Pasture (1985), is a collection of essays about the Texas hill country, the allure of the hunt, and the necessity of a good hunting dog. The Sierra Club, of which Bass is an active member, was founded in 1892 and is America's oldest grassroots environmental organization. For more information, go to <http://sierraclub.com/>.

I was a hunter before I came far up into northwest Montana, but not to the degree I am now. It astounds me sometimes to step back, particularly at the end of autumn, the end of the hunting season, and take both mental and physical inventory of all that was hunted and all that was gathered from this life in the mountains. The woodshed groaning tight, full of firewood. The fruits and herbs and vegetables from the garden, canned or dried or frozen; the wild mushrooms, huckleberries, thimbleberries, and strawberries. And most precious of all, the flesh of the wild things that share with us these mountains and the plains to the east—the elk, the whitetail and mule deer; the ducks and geese, grouse and pheasant and Hungarian partridge and dove and chukar and wild turkey; the trout and whitefish. Each year the cumulative bounty seems unbelievable. What heaven is this into which we've fallen? 1

How my wife and I got to this valley—the Yaak—15 years ago is a mystery, a move that I've only recently come to accept as having been inevitable. We got in the truck one day feeling strangely restless in Mississippi, and we drove. What did I know? Only that I missed the West's terrain of space. Young and healthy, and not coincidentally newly in love, we hit that huge and rugged landscape in full stride. We drove north until we ran out of country—until the road ended, and we reached Canada's thick blue woods—and then we turned west and traveled until we ran almost out of mountains: the backside of the Rockies, to the wet, west-slope rainforest. 2

We came over a little mountain pass—it was August and winter was already fast approaching—and looked down on the soft hills, the dense purples of the spruce and fir forests, the ivory crests of the ice-capped peaks, and the slender ribbons of gray thread rising from the chimneys of the few cabins nudged close to the winding river below, and we fell in love with the Yaak Valley and the hard-logged Kootenai National Forest—the way people in movies fall with each other, star and starlet, as if a trap door has been pulled out from beneath them: tumbling through the air, arms windmilling furiously, and suddenly no other world but each other, no other world but this one, and eyes for no one, or no place, else. 3

Right from the beginning, I could see that there was extraordinary bounty in this low-elevation forest, resting as it does in a magical seam be- 4 tween the Pacific Northwest and the northern Rockies. Some landscapes these days have been reduced to nothing but dandelions and fire ants, knapweed and thistle, where the only remaining wildlife are sparrows, squirrels, and starlings. In the blessed Yaak, however, not a single mammal has gone extinct since the end of the Ice Age. This forest sustains more types of hunters—carnivores—than any valley in North America. It is a predator's showcase, home not just to wolves and grizzlies, but wolverines, lynx, bobcat, marten, fisher, black bear, mountain lion, golden eagle, bald eagle, coyote, fox, weasel. In the Yaak, everything is in motion, either seeking its quarry, or seeking to avoid becoming quarry.

The people who have chosen to live in this remote valley—few phones,   5
very little electricity, and long, dark winters—possess a hardness and a dreaminess both. They—we—can live a life of deprivation, and yet are willing to enter the comfort of daydreams and imagination. There is something mysterious happening here between the landscape and the people, a thing that stimulates our imagination, and causes many of us to set off deep into the woods in search of the unknown, and sustenance—not just metaphorical or spiritual sustenance, but the real thing.

Only about 5 percent of the nation and 15 to 20 percent of Montanans   6
are hunters. But in this one valley, almost everyone is a hunter. It is not the peer pressure of the local culture that recruits us into hunting, nor even necessarily the economic boon of a few hundred pounds of meat in a cash-poor society. Rather, it is the terrain itself, and one's gradual integration into it, that summons the hunter. Nearly everyone who has lived here for any length of time has ended up—sometimes almost against one's conscious wishes—becoming a hunter. This wild and powerful landscape sculpts us like clay. I don't find such sculpting an affront to the human spirit, but instead, wonderful testimony to our pliability, our ability to adapt to a place.

I myself love to hunt the deer, the elk, and the grouse—to follow them   7
into the mouth of the forest, to disappear in their pursuit—to get lost following their snowy tracks up one mountain and down the next. One sets out after one's quarry with senses fully engaged, wildly alert: entranced, nearly hypnotized. The tiniest of factors can possess the largest significance—the crack of a twig, the shift of a breeze, a single stray hair caught on a piece of bark, a fresh-bent blade of grass.

Each year during such pursuits, I am struck more and more by the conceit   8
that people in a hunter-gatherer culture might have richer imaginations than those who dwell more fully in an agricultural or even post-agricultural environment. What else is the hunt but a stirring of the imagination, with the quarry, or goal, or treasure lying just around the corner or over the next

rise? A hunter's imagination has no choice but to become deeply engaged, for it is never the hunter who is in control, but always the hunted, in that the prey directs the predator's movements.

The hunted shapes the hunter; the pursuit and evasion of predator and prey are but shadows of the same desire. The thrush wants to remain a thrush. The goshawk wants to consume the thrush and in doing so, partly become the thrush—to take its flesh into its flesh. They weave through the tangled branches of the forest, zigging and zagging, the goshawk right on the thrush's tail, like a shadow. Or perhaps it is the thrush that is the shadow thrown by the light of the goshawk's fiery desire. 9

Either way, the escape maneuvers of the thrush help carve and shape and direct the muscles of the goshawk. Even when you are walking through the woods seeing nothing but trees, you can feel the unseen passage of pursuits that might have occurred earlier that morning, precisely where you are standing—pursuits that will doubtless, after you are gone, sweep right back across that same spot again and again. 10

As does the goshawk, so too do human hunters imagine where their prey might be, or where it might go. They follow tracks hinting at not only distance and direction traveled, but also pace and gait and the general state of mind of the animal that is evading them. They plead to the mountain to deliver to them a deer, an elk. They imagine and hope that they are moving toward their goal of obtaining game. 11

When you plant a row of corn, there is not so much unknown. You can be fairly sure that, if the rains come, the corn is going to sprout. The corn is not seeking to elude you. But when you step into the woods, looking for a deer—well, there's nothing in your mind, or in your blood, or in the world, but imagination. 12

Most Americans neither hunt nor gather nor even grow their own food, nor make, with their own hands, any of their other necessities. In this post-agricultural society, too often we confuse anticipation with imagination. When we wander down the aisle of the supermarket searching for a chunk of frozen chicken, or cruise into Dillard's department store looking for a sweater, we can be fairly confident that grayish wad of chicken or that sweater is going to be there, thanks to the vigor and efficiency of a supply-and-demand marketplace. The imagination never quite hits second gear. Does the imagination atrophy, from such chronic inactivity? I suspect that it does. 13

All I know is that hunting—beyond being a thing I like to do—helps keep my imagination vital. I would hope never to be so blind as to offer it as prescription; I offer it only as testimony to my love of the landscape where I live—a place that is still, against all odds, its own place, quite un- 14 like any other. I don't think I would be able to sustain myself as a dreamer in this strange landscape if I did not take off three months each year to wander the mountains in search of game, to hunt, stretching and exercising not just my imagination, but my spirit. And to wander the mountains, too, in all the other seasons. And to be nourished by the river of spirit that flows, shifting and winding, between me and the land.

Thinking Critically

1. Go to the website of the Sierra Club at <http://sierraclub.com/>. In what ways might "Why I Hunt" seem at odds with that organization's goals? How does Rick Bass anticipate and respond to possible objections from his main audience for this essay?

2. What is an *apologia?* Could "Why I Hunt" be considered an apologia? Why, or why not?

3. What is it about the Yaak Valley that, according to Bass, makes hunters of people?

Writing Critically

1. Many of the writers in Chapter 5 discuss the moral and spiritual values associated with consumerism. In an essay, discuss how the lifestyle that Rick Bass describes in "Why I Hunt" either supports or refutes another writer's observations about consumerism.

2. What does it mean to be a "steward"? Research the moral and ethical implications of "stewardship." In what ways do Rick Bass, Erik Assadourian (in the preceding selection), David James Duncan (see pp. 360–65), or other writers whom you find appropriate define and advocate for "stewardship"? In what ways might the concept of "stewardship" be problematic for the conservation of public lands and the formulation of a federal environmental policy?

3. Examine your own eating-related ideologies. Do you hunt or fish? Are you strictly vegan? Is your idea of a square meal one that comes in a takeout box? Do you shop at a local co-op, or purchase only organic foods for your children? In an apologia, define and defend the morals and values that affect what you consume.

Strange Bedfellows
or Natural Allies?

SIERRA MAGAZINE

> A *sidebar* is a brief article that appears on the same page as a main article in a newspaper or magazine or on a website. The sidebar usually elaborates on information in the main article. The following text was a sidebar to Rick Bass's essay "Why I Hunt" when it was published in *Sierra* magazine.

The Sierra Club has serious political differences with the National Rifle 1 Association, but the two organizations can agree on one thing: The Katy Prairie in Texas, a winter home for millions of waterfowl that nest in the Midwest and Canada, should be protected. "It's perfectly obvious to anyone with half a brain that if you're going to enjoy the fruits of the outdoors, you're going to have to take care of it," says NRA director Sue King.

Working with Marge Hanselman, former conservation chair for the 2 Houston Group of the Sierra Club, King has lobbied city officials and testified at hearings to oppose construction of an airport that would obliterate the prairie. She even donated the proceeds from a women's target-shooting event to the Sierra Club and the Katy Prairie Conservancy. "Sue King is a strong woman and one of the most avid conservationists I know," Hanselman says.

According to the Theodore Roosevelt Conservation Alliance, most 3 hunters and anglers have strong conservationist leanings. A study the organization completed in January 2000 found that 83 percent of hunters and 86 percent of anglers support keeping the remaining wild areas in national forests free of roads. Both groups place a high value on protecting water quality (98 percent of hunters and 99 percent of anglers); providing habitat for endangered species (93 and 94 percent, respectively); and preserving places for solitude and experiences close to nature (91 and 92 percent).

Given these shared passions, environmentalists have much to gain from 4 banding together with hunting and fishing groups. Sporting enthusiasts are numerous in some states with lots of public land, like Wyoming and Nevada, where environmentalists tend to be on the defensive. National environmental groups have a combined membership of more than 5 million, with millions more in local and state organizations. Add that to the nation's 50 million hunters and anglers, and you have a formidable grassroots force.

The Sierra Club is already working with dozens of sporting groups around 5 the country. Our New York activists held a fish-in on the Hudson River, catching and releasing fish to publicize the need to clean up General Electric's

PCB pollution in the waterway. We are teaming up with hunters in North Dakota who are opposed to oil and gas development in the Little Missouri Grasslands, and with both hunters and anglers in Wisconsin to fight the mining industry. In the broader Great Lakes area, the Sierra Club has joined forces with the National Wildlife Federation and Trout Unlimited to protect wetlands and enhance water quality. "The Clean Water Act has greatly improved our lakes and streams," says hunting and fishing guide Gary Engberg. "But we still need to ensure the fish we catch are safe for all to eat."

Such alliances could be increasingly important. President George   6
W. Bush has suggested that the Arctic National Wildlife Refuge, a nesting ground for hundreds of thousands of migrating waterfowl, is a good place for oil and gas drilling. He is also trying to overturn the plan that put 58 million acres of wild forests off-limits to logging and roadbuilding. "As the Sierra Club works to defend these places, we will continue to reach out to the hunters and anglers who have a stake in them," says Sierra Club legislative director Debbie Sease. "We're natural allies."

Thinking Critically

How does "Strange Bedfellows or Natural Allies?" complement "Why I Hunt" by Rick Bass? Why might the editors of *Sierra* magazine have placed these two articles together?

Writing Critically

Is environmentalism a blue-state or a red-state issue? Support your argument by visiting the websites of at least three of the organizations mentioned in this article.

Lifelike

SUSAN ORLEAN

Susan Orlean's marvelously bizarre book *The Orchid Thief: A True Story of Beauty and Obsession* (1998), describing her adventures with a renegade Florida orchid-gatherer with a gift for finding the rarest of blooms, was the basis of the 2002 movie *Adaptation* (Meryl Streep played Orlean). Orlean wrote for the *Boston Globe* and *Rolling Stone* before joining *The New Yorker* as a staff writer in 1992. Her many essays, collected in *Saturday Night* (1990), *The Bullfighter Checks Her Makeup: My Encounters with Extraordinary People* (2000), and *My Kind of Place:*

Travel Stories from a Woman Who's Been Everywhere (2004), demonstrate what the *New York Times Book Review* defines as the Orlean style: "stylishly written, whimsical yet sophisticated, quirkily detailed and full of empathy for a person you might not have thought about empathetically before . . . yet the whole would feel somehow suffused with her [Orlean's] personality." "Lifelike" first appeared in *The New Yorker* in June 2003 and was reprinted in *The Best American Essays 2004*. In an interview with Powells.com, Orlean described her method of working and, without using the word *ethics,* described the ideal *ethos* for a curious journalist: "Somebody said to me, 'How do you manage to be so empathetic with so many different kinds of people?' I'm lucky because it's really not a conscious thing. I don't think of it as not looking down on someone or not being intimidated. While I'm in someone's world, I have to accept its parameters. What difference does it make how it compares to *my* world? My world isn't the standard by which others are judged. Plus, I love the experience of adopting a different perspective and seeing what it looks like. It's like traveling to another country. And there are people who travel in opposition, constantly, to the places they visit, while others travel close to the place."

As soon as the 2003 World Taxidermy Championships opened, the heads came rolling in the door. There were foxes and moose and freeze-dried wild turkeys; mallards and buffalo and chipmunks and wolves; weasels and buffleheads and bobcats and jackdaws; big fish and little fish and razor-backed boar. The deer came in herds, in carloads, and on pallets: dozens and dozens of whitetail and roe; half deer and whole deer and deer with deformities, sneezing and glowering and nuzzling and yawning; does chewing apples and bucks nibbling leaves. There were millions of eyes, boxes and bowls of them; some as small as a lentil and some as big as a poached egg. There were animal mannequins, blank-faced and brooding, earless and eyeless and utterly bald: ghostly gray duikers and spectral pine martens and black-bellied tree ducks from some other world. An entire exhibit hall was filled with equipment, all the gear required to bring something dead back to life: replacement noses for grizzlies, false teeth for beavers, fish-fin cream, casting clay, upholstery nails.

The championships were held in April at the Springfield, Illinois, 2
Crowne Plaza hotel, the sort of nicely appointed place that seems more
suited to regional sales conferences and rehearsal dinners than to having
wolves in the corridors and people crossing the lobby shouting, "Heads up!
Buffalo coming through!" A thousand taxidermists converged on Springfield to have their best pieces judged and to attend such seminars as
"Mounting Flying Waterfowl," "Whitetail Deer—From a Master!," and
"Using a Fleshing Machine." In the Crowne Plaza lobby, across from the
concierge desk, a grooming area had been set up. The taxidermists were
bent over their animals, holding flashlights to check problem areas like tear
ducts and nostrils, and wielding toothbrushes to tidy flyaway fur. People
milled around, greeting fellow taxidermists they hadn't seen since the last
world championships, held in Springfield two years ago, and talking shop:

"Acetone rubbed on a squirrel tail will fluff it right back up."   3

"My feeling is that it's quite tough to do a good tongue."   4

"The toes on a real competitive piece are very important. I think Bondo   5
works nicely, and so does Super Glue."

"I knew a fellow with cattle, and I told him, 'If you ever have one still-   6
born, I'd really like to have it.' I thought it would make a really nice
mount."

That there is a taxidermy championship at all is something of an as-   7
tonishment, not only to the people in the world who have no use for a
Dan-D-Noser and Soft Touch Duck Degreaser but also to taxidermists
themselves. For a long time, taxidermists kept their own counsel. Taxidermy, the three-dimensional representation of animals for permanent display, has been around since the eighteenth century, but it was first brought
into popular regard by the Victorians, who thrilled to all tokens of exotic
travel and especially to any domesticated representations of wilderness—
the glassed-in miniature rain forest on the tea table, the mounted antelope
by the front door. The original taxidermists were upholsterers who tanned
the hides of hunting trophies and then plumped them up with rags and
cotton, so that they reassumed their original shape and size; those early
poses were stiff and simple, and the expressions fairly expressionless. The
practice grew popular in this country, too: by 1882, there was a Society of
American Taxidermists, which held annual meetings and published scholarly reports, especially on the matter of preparing animals for museum
display. As long as taxidermy served to preserve wild animals and make
them available for study, it was viewed as an honorable trade, but most
people were still discomfited by it. How could you not be? It was the business of dealing with dead things, coupled with the questionable enterprise
of making dead things look like live things. In spite of its scientific value,

it was usually regarded as almost a black art, a wholly owned subsidiary of witchcraft and voodoo. By the early part of the twentieth century, taxidermists such as Carl E. Akeley, William T. Horneday, and Leon Pray had refined techniques and begun emphasizing artistry. But the more the techniques of taxidermy improved, the more it discomfited: instead of the lumpy moose head that was so artless that it looked fake, there were mounts of pouncing bobcats so immaculately and exactly preserved they made you flinch.

For the next several decades, taxidermy existed in the margins—a few 8 practitioners here and there, often self-taught, and usually known only by word of mouth. Then, in the late 1960s, a sort of transformation began: the business started to seem cleaner and less creepy—or maybe, in that messy, morbid time, popular culture started to again appreciate the messy, morbid business of mounting animals for display. An ironic reinterpretation of cluttered, bourgeois Victoriana and its strained juxtapositions of the natural and the man-made was in full revival—what hippie outpost didn't have a stuffed owl or a moose head draped with a silk shawl?—so, once again, taxidermy found a place in the public eye. Supply houses concocted new solvents and better tanning compounds, came out with lightweight mannequins, produced modern formulations of resins and clays. Taxidermy schools opened; previously, any aspiring taxidermist could only hope to learn the trade by apprenticing or by taking one of a few correspondence courses available. In 1971, the National Taxidermy Association was formed (the old society had moldered long before). In 1974, a trade magazine called *Taxidermy Review* began sponsoring national competitions. For the first time, most taxidermists had a chance to meet one another and share advice on how to glue tongues into jaw sets or accurately measure the carcass of a squirrel.

The competitions were also the first time that taxidermists could com- 9 pare their skills and see who in the business could sculpt the best moose septum or could most perfectly capture the look on a prowling coyote's face. Taxidermic skill is a function of how deft you are at skinning an animal and then stretching its hide over a mannequin and sewing it into place. Top-of-the-line taxidermists sculpt their own mannequins; otherwise they will buy a ready-made polyurethane-foam form and tailor the skin to fit. Body parts that can't be preserved (ears, eyes, noses, lips, tongues) can be either store-bought or handmade. How good the mount looks—that is, how alive it looks—is a function of how assiduously the taxidermist has studied reference material (photographs, drawings, and actual live animals) so that he or she knows the particular creature literally and figuratively inside out.

To be good at taxidermy, you have to be good at sewing, sculpting, paint-   10
ing, and hairdressing, and mostly you have to be a little bit of a zoology nerd.
You have to love animals—love looking at them, taking photographs of
them, hunting them, measuring them, casting them in plaster of Paris when
they're dead so that you have a reference when you're, say, attaching ears or
lips and want to get the angle and shape exactly right. Some taxidermists
raise the animals they most often mount, so they can just step out in the back
yard when they're trying to remember exactly how a deer looks when it's
licking its nose, especially because modern taxidermy emphasizes mounts
with interesting expressions, rather than the stunned-looking creations of the
past. Taxidermists seem to make little distinction between loving animals
that are alive and loving ones that are not. "I love deer," one of the champi-
ons in the Whitetail division said to me. "They're my babies."

Taxidermy is now estimated to be a $570-million annual business,   11
made up of small operators around the country who mount animals for
museums, for decorators, and mostly for the thirteen million or so Americans who are recreational hunters and on occasion want to preserve and
display something they killed and who are willing to shell out anywhere
from $200 to mount a pheasant to several thousand for a kudu or a griz-
zly bear. There are state and regional taxidermy competitions throughout
the year and the world championships, which are held every other year;
two trade magazines; a score of taxidermy schools; and three thousand visits to Taxidermy.net every day, where taxidermists can trade information
and goods with as little self-consciousness as you would find on a knitting
Web site:

"I am in need of several pair of frozen goat feet!"   12

"Hi! I have up to 300 sets of goat feet and up to 1000 set of sheep feet   13
per month. Drop me an email at frozencritters.com . . . or give me a call
and we can discuss your needs."

"I have a very nice small raccoon that is frozen whole. I forgot he was   14
in the freezer. Without taking exact measurements I would guess he is about
twelve inches or so—very cute little one. Will make a very nice mount."

"Can I rinse a boar hide good and freeze it?"   15

"Bob, if it's salted, don't worry about it!"   16

"Can someone please tell me the proper way to preserve turkey legs and   17
spurs? Thanks!"

"Brian, I inject the feet with Preservz-It . . . Enjoy!"   18

The word in the grooming area was that the piece to beat was Chris Krueger's   19
happy-looking otters swimming in a perpetual circle around a leopard frog. A
posting on Taxidermy.net earlier in the week declared, "EVERYTHING about

this mount KICKS BUTT!!" Kicking butt, in this era of taxidermy, requires having a mount that is not just lifelike but also artistic. It used to be enough to do what taxidermists call "fish on a stick" displays; now a serious competitor worries about things like flow and negative space and originality. One of this year's contenders, for instance, Ken Walker's giant panda, had artistry and accuracy going for it, along with the element of surprise. The thing looked 100 percent pure panda, but you can't go out and shoot a panda, and you aren't likely to get hold of a panda that has met a natural end, so everyone was dying to know how he had done it. The day the show opened, Walker was in the grooming area, gluing bamboo into place behind the animal's back paws, and a crowd had gathered around him. Walker works as a staff taxidermist for the Smithsonian. He is a breezy, shaggy-haired guy whose hands are always busy. One day, I saw him holding a piece of clay while waiting for a seminar to begin, and within thirty seconds or so, without actually paying much attention to it, he had molded the clay into a little minklike creature.

"The panda was actually pretty easy," he was saying. "I just took two 20
black bears and bleached one of them—I think I used Clairol Basic. Then I sewed the two skins together into a panda pattern." He took out a toothbrush and fluffed the fur on the panda's face. "At the world championship two years ago, a guy came in with an extinct Labrador duck. I was in awe. I thought, What could beat that—an extinct duck? And I came up with this idea." He said he thought that the panda would get points for creativity alone. "You can score a ninety-eight with a squirrel, but it's still a squirrel," he said. "So that means I'm going with a panda."

"What did you do for toenails, Ken?" someone asked. 21

"I left the black bear's toenails in," he said. "They looked pretty good." 22

Another passerby stopped to admire the panda. He was carrying a groom- 23
ing kit, which appeared to contain Elmer's glue, brown and black paint, a small tool set, and a bottle of Suave mousse. "I killed a blond bear once," he said to Ken. "A two-hundred-pound sow. Whew, she made a beautiful mount."

"I'll bet," Ken said. He stepped back to admire the panda. "I like do- 24
ing re-creations of these endangered animals and extinct animals, since that's the only way anyone's going to have one. Two years ago, I did a saber-toothed cat. I got an old lioness from a zoo and bleached her."

The panda was entered in the Re-Creation (Mammal) division, one of the 25
dozens of divisions and subdivisions and sub-subcategories, ranging from the super-specific (Whitetail Deer Long Hair, Open Mouth division) to the sweepingly colossal (Best in World), that would share in $25,000 worth of prizes. (There is even a sub-sub-subspecialty known as "fish carving," which uses no natural fish parts at all; it is resin and wood sculpted into a fish form and then painted.) Nearly all the competitors are professionals, and they

publicize their awards wherever possible. For instance, instead of ordering just any Boar Eye-Setting Reference Head out of a taxidermy catalogue, you can order the Noonkester's #NRB-ERH head sculpted by Bones Johnson, which was, as the catalogue notes, the 2000 National Taxidermy Association Champion Gamehead.

The taxidermists take the competition very seriously. During the time I 26 was in Springfield, I heard conversations analyzing such arcane subjects as exactly how much a javelina's snout wrinkles when it snarls and which molars deer use to chew acorns as opposed to which ones they use to chew leaves. This is important because the ultimate goal of a taxidermist is to make the animal look as if it had never died, as if it were still in the middle of doing ordinary animal things like plucking berries off a bush or taking a nap. When I walked around with the judges one morning, I heard discussions that were practically Talmudic, about whether the eyelids on a bison mount were overdetailed, and whether the nostrils on a springbok were too wide, and whether the placement of whiskers on an otter appeared too deliberate. "You do get compulsive," a taxidermist in the exhibit hall explained to me one afternoon. At the time, he was running a feather duster over his entry—a bobcat hanging off an icicle-covered rock—in the last moments before the judging would begin. "When you're working on a piece, you forget to eat, you forget to drink, you even forget to sleep. You get up in the middle of the night and go into the shop so you can keep working. You get completely caught up in it. You want it to be perfect. You're trying to make something come back to life."

I said that his bobcat was beautiful, and that even the icicles on the 27 piece looked completely real. "I made them myself," he said. "I used clear acrylic toilet-plunger handles. The good Lord sent the idea to me while I was in a hardware store. I just took the handles and put them in the oven at four hundred degrees." He tapped the icicles and then added, "My wife was pretty worried, but I did it on a nonstick cookie sheet."

So who wants to be a taxidermist? "I was a meat cutter for fifteen years," 28 a taxidermist from Kentucky said to me. "That whole time, no one ever said to me, 'Boy, that was a wonderful steak you cut me.' Now I get told all the time what a great job I've done." Steve Faechner, who is the president and chairman of the Academy of Realistic Taxidermy, in Havre, Montana, started mounting animals in 1989, after years spent working on the railroad. "I had gotten hurt, and was looking for something to do," he said. "I was with a friend who did taxidermy and I thought to myself, I have got to get a life. And this was it." Larry Blomquist, who is the owner of the World Taxidermy Championships and of *Breakthrough,* the trade magazine that sponsors the competition, was a schoolteacher for three years before setting up his business. There are a number of women taxidermists (one was teaching this year's seminar on Problem Areas in Mammal Taxidermy), and there are budding junior taxidermists, who had their own competition division, for kids fourteen and younger, at the show.

The night the show opened, I went to dinner with three taxidermists 29 who had driven in from Kentucky, Michigan, and Maryland. They were all married, and all had wives who complained when they found one too many antelope carcasses in the family freezer, and all worked full time mounting animals—mostly deer, for local hunters, but occasional safari work, for people who had shot something in Africa. When I mentioned that I had no idea that a person could make a living as a taxidermist, they burst out laughing, and the guy from Kentucky pointed out that he lived in a little town and there were two other full-time taxidermists in business right down the road.

"What's the big buzz this year?" the man from Michigan asked. 30

"I don't know. Probably something new with eyes," the guy from 31 Maryland answered. "That's where you see the big advances. Remember at the last championship, those Russian eyes?" These were glass animal eyes that had a reflective paint embedded in them, so that if you shone a light they would shine back at you, sort of like the way real animals' eyes do. The men discussed those for a while, then talked about the new fish eyes being introduced this year, which have photographic transfers of actual fish eyes printed on plastic lenses. We happened to be in a restaurant with a sports theme, and there were about a hundred televisions on around the room, broadcasting dozens of different athletic events, but the men never glanced at them, and never stopped talking about their trade. We had all ordered barbecued ribs. When dinner was over, all three of them were fiddling around with the bones before the waitress came to clear our plates.

"Look at these," the man from Kentucky said, holding up a rib. "You 32 could take these home and use them to make a skeleton."

In the seminars, the atmosphere was as sober and exacting as a tax-law col- 33 loquium. "Whiskers," one of the instructors said to the group, giving them a stern look. "I pull them out. I label them. There are left whiskers and there are right whiskers. If you want to get those top awards, you're going to have to think about whiskers." Everyone took notes. In the next room: "Folks, remember, your carcass is your key. The best thing you can do is to keep your carcass in the freezer. Freeze the head, cast it in plaster. It's going to really help if your head is perfect." During the breaks, the group made jokes about a T-shirt that had been seen at one of the regional competitions. The shirt said "PETA" in big letters, but when you got up close you saw that PETA didn't spell out People for the Ethical Treatment of Animals, the bane of all hunters and, by extension, all taxidermists; it spelled out People Eating Tasty Animals. Chuckles all around, then back to the solemn business of Mounting Flying Waterfowl: "People, follow what the bird is telling you. Study it, do your homework. When you've got it ready, fluff the head, shake it, and then get your eyes. There are a lot of good eyes out there on the market today. Do your legwork, and you can have a beautiful mount."

It was brisk and misty outside—the antler venders in the parking lot 34 looked chilled and miserable—and the modest charms of Springfield, with its mall and the Oliver P. Parks Telephone Museum and Abraham Lincoln's tomb, couldn't compete with the strange and wondrous sights inside the hotel. The mere experience of waiting for the elevator—knowing that the doors would peel back to reveal maybe a man and a moose, or a bush pig, or a cougar—was much more exciting than the usual elevator wait in the usual Crowne Plaza hotel. The trade show was a sort of mad tea party of body parts and taxidermy supplies, things for pulling flesh off a carcass, for rinsing blood out of fur—a surreal carnality, but all conveyed with the usual trade-show earnestness and hucksterism, with no irony and no acknowledgment that having buckets of bear noses for sale was anything out of the ordinary. "Come take a look at our beautiful synthetic fur! We're the hair club for lions! If you happen to shoot a lion who is out of season or bald, we can provide you with a gorgeous replacement mane!" "Too many squirrels? Are they driving you nuts? Let us mount them for you!" "Divide and Conquer animal forms—an amazing advance in small-mammal mannequins, patent pending!"

The big winner at the show turned out to be a tiny thing—a mount of two 35 tree sparrows, submitted by a strapping German named Uwe Bauch, who had grown up in the former East Germany dreaming of competing in an American taxidermy show. The piece was precise and lovely, almost haunting, since the more you looked at it the more certain you were that the birds would just stop building their nest, spread their wings, and fly away. Early one morning, before I left Springfield, I took a last walk around the competition hall. It was quiet and uncanny, with hundreds of mounts arranged on long tables throughout the room; the deer heads clustered together, each in a slightly different pose and angle, looked like a kind of animal Roman forum caught in mid-debate. A few of the mounts were a little gory—a deer with a mailbox impaled on an antler, another festooned with barbed wire, and one with an arrow stuck in its brisket—and one display, a coyote whose torso was split open to reveal a miniature scene of the destruction of the World Trade Center, complete with little firemen and rubble piles, was surpassingly weird. Otherwise, the room was biblically tranquil, the lion at last lying down with the

Corsican lamb, the family of jackdaws in everlasting, unrequited pursuit of a big green beetle, and the stillborn Bengal tiger cub magically revived, its face in an eternal snarl, alive-looking although it had never lived.

Thinking Critically

1. What techniques does Susan Orlean use in paragraph 1 to get a reader's attention? How did you respond to the paragraph, and what expectations does it give you about the rest of the essay?

2. Visit the website of *The New Yorker* at <http://www.newyorker.com/>, or browse through past issues at your library. Why would a *New Yorker* reader be interested in taxidermy? How does Orlean make the topic interesting to a *New Yorker* reader?

3. When and why does Orlean use process analysis in "Lifelike"?

Writing Critically

1. Consider Orlean's observation (quoted in the headnote) about empathy and her style of journalism. In what way is this an ethical statement? Does Orlean's *ethos* apply to "Lifelike"? Why, or why not? How do other writers in this book who use field research and interviews—for example, Barbara Ehrenreich (see pp. 266–75), Rebecca Skloot (pp. 39–46), David Brooks (pp. 47–57), and Samantha M. Shapiro (pp. 536–46)—display or contradict this ethical position? In an essay, propose a working ethic for journalists writing about different American cultures.

2. Write an apologia for taxidermy that demonstrates the relationship between taxidermists and the natural world. (Use Rick Bass's "Why I Hunt" as a model, but please don't call your apologia "Why They Stuff.")

3. Many of the writers in Chapter 2 discuss, define, and challenge different ideas about "community." In what ways do the taxidermists Orlean describes constitute a "community"? In an essay that draws on field research, explore a "community" based on some shared passion or skill (fans of *Star Trek,* followers of a sports team, Goths, skaters—something local that you can directly report on). Is there a difference between a community and a subculture? Do communities or subcultures based on hobbies and activities also tend to share values?

Over a Barrel

PAUL ROBERTS | A longtime observer of the tensions between business interests and environmental concerns, Paul Roberts is the author of *The End of Oil* (2004). In the course of his research for that book, he spent time in Saudi Arabia and Azerbaijan and interviewed scores of industry and government experts to find support for his argument that for strategic, economic, and environmental reasons the United States must develop alternatives to petroleum. A frequent contributor to *Harper's Magazine,* Roberts was a finalist for the 1999 National Magazine Award for his reporting on the sugar industry. "Over a Barrel" first appeared in the November/December issue of *Mother Jones* magazine. *Mother Jones* magazine is named for Mary Harris "Mother" Jones, an elderly widowed Irish immigrant who in the early twentieth century transformed herself into a leading activist for working people. For more on Mother Jones—the woman, the magazine, the website—go to <http://motherjones.org/index.html>.

It's eight o'clock on a fresh summer morning in Denver, and I'm at a podium before a hundred executives from regional energy companies. Having spent the last few years closely observing trends in the oil industry, I'm often asked to speak about the decline of global energy supplies, the way oil has corrupted U.S. foreign policy, and why the worldwide energy economy needs a radical transformation if we want to avoid catastrophic climate change. Yet while these themes play well to liberal audiences in Boulder and Berkeley, I worry my reception here will be much cooler. Most of these weather-beaten men (and a few women) spend their days squeezing hydrocarbons from the sand and stone beneath the Rockies; if my past observations of the energy industry are any guide, they voted for Bush, support the Iraq war, think climate change is a leftist hoax, and believe the main cause of America's energy crisis is that overzealous regulation keeps drillers like themselves from tapping the most promising reserves of oil and natural gas.

But as I finish my spiel and take questions, my initial assumptions vanish. When I suggest that the Iraq war might not have been motivated *entirely* by America's thirst for oil, many in the room openly smirk, as if I've just suggested that the world is flat. Likewise, few here seem to share the White House's Panglossian view that the United States is sitting atop some massive, but politically off-limits, reserve of natural gas. In fact, as much as these executives would love to sink their drills anywhere they want—and as much as they detest environmentalists for stopping them—no one here believes the volume of natural gas yet to be discovered in the Rockies, or anywhere else in America, would reverse the nation's decline of gas production or let the United States move to a cleaner, more secure "gas" economy. As one executive tells me, "even if all the off-limits land were opened for drilling, all the new gas we could bring on-line wouldn't be enough to replace all the production we're losing from older fields. We'd barely keep production flat."

For those who wonder where the world will be getting its energy a decade from now, confessions like these only confirm what many have feared for some time: namely, that the cheap, "easy" oil and natural gas that powered industrial growth for a century no longer exist in such easy abundance; and that we may have a lot less time than we thought to replace that system with something cleaner, more sustainable, and far less vulnerable to political upheaval.

The evidence is certainly piling up. Pollution levels from cars and power plants are on the rise. Climate change, another energy-related disaster, has begun impacting crop yields and water supplies and may soon provoke political strife. In fact, according to a Pentagon report last October, global warming could make key resources so scarce, and nations so desperate, that "disruption and conflict will be endemic" and "warfare would define human life."

Yet the most alarming symptoms of an energy system on the verge of collapse are found in the oil markets. Today, even as global demand for oil, led by the economic boom in Asia, is rising far faster than anticipated, our ability to pump more oil is falling. Despite assurances from oil's two biggest players—the House of Bush and the House of Saud—that supplies are plentiful (and, as George W. Bush famously put it, that getting the oil is just a matter of "jawboning" "our friends in OPEC to open the spigots"), it's now clear that even the Saudis lack the physical capacity to bring enough oil to desperate consumers. As a result, oil markets are now so tight that even a minor disturbance—accelerated fighting in Iraq, another bomb in Riyadh, more unrest in Venezuela or Nigeria—could send prices soaring and crash the global economy into a recession. "The world really has run out of production capacity," a veteran oil analyst warned me in late August. "Iraq is producing less than a third of the oil that had been forecast, the Saudis are maxed out, and there is no place else to go. And America is still relying on an energy policy that hasn't changed significantly in 20 years."

Nor is it any longer a matter of simply drilling new wells or laying new pipe. Oil is finite, and eventually, global production must peak, much as happened to domestic supplies in the early 1970s. When it does, oil prices will leap, perhaps as high as $100 per barrel—a disaster if we don't have a cost-effective alternative fuel or technology in place. When the peak is coming is impossible to predict with precision. Estimates range from the ultra-optimistic, which foresee a peak no sooner than 2035, to the pessimistic, which hold that the peak may have already occurred. In any case, the signs are clear that the easy oil is harder to find and what remains is increasingly difficult and expensive to extract. Already, Western oil companies are struggling to discover new supplies fast enough to replace the oil they are selling. (Royal/Dutch Shell was so concerned about how declining discovery rates would devastate its stock price that it inflated its reserves figures by 20 percent.)

Worse, according to a new study in the respected *Petroleum Review,* in   7
the United Kingdom, Indonesia, Gabon, and 15 other oil-rich nations that now supply 30 percent of the world's daily crude, oil production—that is, the number of barrels that are pumped each day—is declining by 5 percent a year. That's double the rate of decline of even a year ago, and it has forced other oil producers to pump extra simply to keep global supplies steady. "Those producers still with expansion potential are having to work harder and harder just to make up for the accelerating losses of the large number that have clearly peaked and are now in continuous decline," writes Chris Skrebowski, editor of *Petroleum Review* and a former analyst with BP and the Saudi national oil company. "Though largely unrecognized, [depletion] may be contributing to the rise in oil prices."

If there is one positive sign, it's that the high prices seem to have finally   8
broken through America's wall of energy denial. In fact, while energy experts like Skrebowski have been fretting about oil dependency and depleting reserves since the 1970s, today's energy anxiety is no longer coming simply from academia or the political margins. In recent months, energy problems have come under intense focus by the mainstream media, filling radio and TV talk shows and newsmagazines. Whereas official U.S. policy still blames OPEC for our oil woes, even right-of-center, pro-business outlets like *Business Week, The Economist,* and *Fortune* have acceded that the biggest risk for U.S. energy security isn't "foreign" producers or even environmentalists, but rather a decades-old domestic energy policy that remains focused almost entirely on finding new supplies while doing nothing to curb demand. "Much as we might like to, we can't blame it on OPEC," noted *Fortune* in August. "After all, Americans have been on a two-decade oil pig-out, gorging like oversized vacationers at a Vegas buffet."

What's more, while a powerful, ideologically driven minority—led,   9
sadly, by the Bush administration—continues to insist that energy security is simply a question of drilling in the Arctic National Wildlife Refuge (ANWR) or browbeating OPEC, outside the White House, and certainly

outside the Beltway, there's a growing push to build a fundamentally new energy system. Thus, while the Bush administration dithered on climate change and the future of energy, individual states, like California and New York, enacted their own alternative energy policies and even sued utilities over carbon dioxide emissions. The corporate world, once a stalwart opponent of any policy reform, has become startlingly progressive. Toyota and Honda are busily rolling out hybrid cars. Agriculture and insurance firms warn of the future costs of oil-price swings and climate change. And energy companies like BP and Shell, eager to profit in the new energy order, are developing new fuels and technologies to help reduce oil use and emissions.

And if most U.S. consumers still share the administration's energy   10
obliviousness (U.S. gasoline consumption continues to rise, despite high oil prices), some in Congress have become downright activist. Last year in the Senate, Republican John McCain and Democrat Joseph Lieberman came close to passing a climate policy far beyond anything the White House has countenanced. In fact, even some traditional oil-and-gas politicians appear to see the writing on the wall. For example, U.S. Senator Lisa Murkowski, a Republican from Alaska and still an ardent supporter of drilling for oil in ANWR, nonetheless concedes "this nation needs to do a far better job of energy conservation and needs to develop alternative energy technologies to wean us from fossil fuels."

Thinking Critically

1. What does it mean to have a "Panglossian view" (paragraph 2)?

2. What preconceived notions did Paul Roberts have about the executives of the regional energy companies he writes about in "Over a Barrel"? What other surprising or "startling" discoveries does he make that challenge traditional ideas about who supports reliance on petroleum and who supports developing alternatives?

3. What do you know about *Mother Jones* magazine? How does Roberts accommodate, educate, or otherwise engage that specific audience? In what ways might his article change if he were writing for a business magazine, a general-interest magazine, or an automotive magazine?

Writing Critically

1. Keep track of all the automobile advertisements you see in a week, paying particular attention to the contexts of those ads. Within what context are you most likely to see an ad promoting a car's safety features? Its fuel economy? Its speed or attractiveness? Which television programs include commercials for luxury cars, and which programs feature ads for minivans?

Within the highly competitive world of automotive sales, then, what conclusions can you draw about the "ideal" consumer of fuel-efficient cars?

2. Rick Bass and *Sierra* magazine (earlier in this chapter) and "Over a Barrel" all blur the standard ideological boundaries between environmental interest groups, finding surprising alliances between otherwise opposing viewpoints. Choose an environmental issue of local importance (such as a recycling campaign on your campus, a move to subsidize public transportation in your neighborhood, or an effort to clean up regional waterway). In an analytical essay, describe the environmental problem and the varying approaches to solving it that different groups are taking. This is not an argument. Your rhetorical task here is not to promote one particular approach or suggest an alternate solution. Rather, do some investigating into *every* interest involved in addressing the issue, and—if you can—describe ways in which seemingly divergent interest groups can find common ground.

Alaska: Oil's Ground Zero

JEFFREY BARTHOLET, ADAM ROGERS, AND MICHAEL HSU

This article, along with many photographs, charts, graphs, and maps, appeared in the August 13, 2001, issue of *Newsweek*. Lead author Jeffrey Bartholet, the foreign editor of *Newsweek*, has been a bureau chief for the magazine in Jerusalem, Tokyo, and Nairobi. Adam Rogers is a Washington-based reporter for *Newsweek*, writing about science, technology, and society. Michael Hsu was a New York–based reporter for the magazine. *Newsweek* magazine, which is owned by the Washington Post Company, is a large-circulation general-interest publication. Its online presence at <http://www.msnbc.msn.com/id/3032542/site/newsweek/> is a joint venture with the television network NBC; the two entities frequently cooperate on news programs and investigations.

If you want somebody to fly you over the towering peaks of the Brooks   1
Range and drop you onto the spongy tundra of the Arctic National Wildlife Refuge, Dirk Nickisch is your man. Dirk is a former rodeo rider and crop-duster, a wiry fellow with sharp eyes and prickly whiskers whom some in his home state of North Dakota have likened to a coyote. He meets clients at a gravel airstrip in a Gwichin Indian village just south of the

range. Dressed in oily pants and a baseball cap, he kicks the tires on his 1952 single-prop de Havilland Beaver, shoulders the rear rudder back and forth to be sure it's still in working order and tells you, if you ask him, that he reckons his Pratt & Whitney engine has been overhauled "a few times." He doesn't have much time for people who stand around asking questions without making themselves useful, however. So he rolls four plastic barrels of fuel under the plane and puts you to work with a hose and a squeaky hand pump.

Nobody would mistake Dirk Nickisch for a tree hugger. But as he takes   2 off and flies over the northern mountains of Alaska—into one of the last unspoiled wilderness areas of America—he explains (if you ask him) why he doesn't want multinational oil companies to explore and drill for oil in any part of the refuge. "I moved up here because it's the last place like this," he says, looking out the windscreen over the southern reaches of the 19 million-acre refuge. Then he nods toward the peeling plastic of the dashboard, where a black-and-white photo of his two kids is stuck among pinwheel gauges measuring altitude and direction. "My little boy was 3 months old when he first saw the caribou come through the coastal plain," he says. "I don't want to leave him and his kids a bunch of old oil wells and some empty promises."

Minutes later, with snow-streaked peaks a few hundred feet below us,   3 the vintage engine starts to cough and sputter. Dirk turns a worn red handle to switch gas tanks, and adjusts the throttle. The engine finds its voice again, and from here on in, the ride is smooth. We cross the range and glide between the Sadlerochit Mountains to our left and the white sluice of a small glacier to our right, cushioning down toward a 1.5 million-acre plain that has, from above, the tawny, matted appearance of buffalo hide. "This is the wildest place left in Alaska," Dirk says after landing on a strip of knee-high willow shrubs near the Jago River, "the wildest place left in the United States." Then he climbs back in his Beaver and flies off, leaving me and three companions (two photographers and environmentalist Dan Ritzman) in a seemingly lonesome land, silent but for the wind and the rushing river—the sort of quintessentially Alaskan place that touristy T-shirts in Anchorage refer to as "the last frontier."

America's founding myths are largely about taming wild places. The   4 frontier shaped the American character even as we shaped it, moving from the Allegheny Mountains to the Mississippi, and onward to the Missouri, the Rocky Mountains and the Pacific. But the frontier is all but gone now, and what remains occupies a unique place in the American psyche. Alaska has the largest area of wilderness lands in the country by far—an area roughly the size of Maine, New Hampshire, Vermont, Massachusetts,

Rhode Island, Connecticut, New Jersey, Delaware and Maryland combined. Yet it also has the nation's two largest oilfields, and is second only to Texas in proven reserves of crude. Alaskans use more energy per capita than any other people in the country, and scientists who study global warming say that no state is more affected by climatic change. As it is, average temperatures in Alaska have spiked close to 5 degrees since the 1960s, and the polar sea ice has thinned by 40 percent over the same period.

A trip to Alaska's Arctic refuge is a confrontation with choices: should   5
we drill or protect wilderness? Which do we value more: greater American oil production or a landscape largely untouched by the hand of man? The Bush administration wants to drill in the ANWR coastal plain, arguing that new oil discoveries are vital to maintain the lifestyles to which we have all become accustomed. And President Bush last week won a big round in that fight, when the House of Representatives voted to allow Arctic refuge drilling. (The key to victory was the muscle of the unions, which expect ANWR oil development to produce hundreds of thousands of new jobs around the country.) Now the issue will move to the Senate, where leading Democrats have vowed to keep the oilmen out of a place that environmentalists call "America's Serengeti."

In this debate, Alaska itself has taken on a symbolic heft beyond its   6
value as a wilderness preserve or as a source of oil. Once again, the way Americans engage their frontier will reflect, in no small measure, the national character. Are we energy gluttons, or hopeless romantics wedded to a utopian vision of the natural world? Are we conservationists or materialists? In a country where most people support government conservation efforts, yet sales of gas-guzzling SUVs are soaring, some might argue that we're simply a people who hope and believe that we can have it all.

Most Americans who want to protect the Arctic refuge will never see it,   7
and there's good reason for that. In February when the sun hardly comes up, temperatures drop to an average of about 4 degrees below zero. And in the endless days of July, visitors can hardly breathe without sucking mosquitoes down their throats. Some Alaskans familiar with the refuge, like oil consultant Ken Boyd, don't understand the attraction of the place. "You can't see the end of the world from there, but you're pretty darn close," says Boyd, a geophysicist who once directed Alaska's Division of Oil and Gas.

Nobody really knows how much petroleum there is under the ANWR   8
coastal plain. Although oil seeps out of the tundra in some places—staining bogs with a bluish-black sheen—some scientists believe the seeps are evidence that a potential reservoir underneath has been crushed and ruined over geologic time. The most recent study by the U.S. Geological Survey, published in 1998, concluded that several oil deposits—what some geolo-

gists call a "string of pearls"—are located mainly in the west of the ANWR coastal zone. The survey gave a wide range of estimates for how plump those pearls might be. Environmentalists often cite the USGS study to argue that the refuge will likely produce 3.2 billion barrels of oil—less than half of what the United States burns in a single year. That assessment is based on a future oil price of about $20 per barrel. At about $15, it could become uneconomical to produce any oil at all. Then again, the USGS estimates for oil that is "technically recoverable"—if oil prices and cost weren't a factor—range from 5.7 billion to 16 billion barrels. "It's got billions of barrels of potential and a lot of unknowns," says Boyd.

Keeping ANWR off limits has undoubtedly increased America's re- 9
liance on oil imports, even if only marginally. Slightly more than half the oil Americans consumed last year was imported, compared with 37 percent in 1980. And the Energy Information Administration projects that dependence on foreign oil will only surge further in the decades ahead.

So if we don't drill in ANWR, where will we drill? Just last month the 10
Bush administration sharply scaled back plans to exploit oil reserves in the eastern Gulf of Mexico after Florida politicians and businessmen—led by Gov. Jeb Bush—balked. California has also rejected offshore-drilling proposals. Yet a majority of Alaskans, including Democratic Gov. Tony Knowles, favor drilling in the Alaska refuge—in part because the state and its citizens largely depend on the oil industry for jobs and revenues. "We can fulfill the image and vision of Alaska as the nation's storehouse of wilderness areas . . . as well as its storehouse of energy," says Knowles. "We can have them both."

Environmentalists have their own win-win argument: Americans could 11
save far more oil by increasing energy efficiency, they say, than could ever be drilled in places like ANWR. And those savings would reduce U.S. dependence on foreign oil, limit U.S. production of greenhouse gases and husband America's resources for another day. As it is, although Americans account for just 4.5 percent of the world's population, they consume nearly a quarter of the world's energy. Europeans pay roughly twice as much at the pump for premium gasoline, and American cars use one third more energy than European cars. The Natural Resources Defense Council, an environmental organization, estimates that increasing fuel-efficiency standards for new cars to 39 miles per gallon over the next decade would save 51 billion barrels of oil over the next 50 years, many times more than even the most optimistic predictions for the Arctic refuge. But the House of Representatives last week, at the same time it approved ANWR drilling, rejected a proposal to substantially boost fuel-efficiency standards for SUVs.

Defenders of the refuge as a wilderness area believe, in any case, that 12
the ecosystem has an intrinsic value beyond oil. They point out that it is

one of the last places in the United States where a visitor can still witness a great migration of animals—in this case, caribou. The 130,000-strong Porcupine Herd, named so because it winters near the Porcupine River in Canada, moves every summer into the coastal plain, where the cows usually give birth. The caribou favor the ANWR coast as a natural maternity ward because predators are more scarce here than in the foothills and mountains. Nutritious grasses also are plentiful, and offshore breezes help fend off summer mosquitoes. (Alaskan officials maintain that drilling would have no significant effect on the caribou; conservationists disagree.)

In three days and nights camping on the plain in June, we saw about 20 caribou—the full herd didn't make it to its traditional calving ground at the usual time this year because of unusual weather conditions. We also spotted an arctic peregrine falcon, plovers and several other species of birds, arctic ground squirrels and, during our flight out, a herd of shaggy musk oxen. Despite plentiful scat around our campsite, we encountered no grizzlies. But we did find the elusive arctic woolly bear caterpillar, which can live for up to 14 very frigid years before blossoming into a moth. 13

Geologists argue that with new technologies, including 3-D seismic mapping and horizontal drilling over long distances, they can exploit ecologically sensitive areas with minimal disruption. Conservationists dispute that, but many also argue that the petroleum geologists miss a larger point: that global warming from the burning of fossil fuel presents an even greater potential danger to arctic ecosystems. Polar bears may or may not be affected by seismic thumping, but they surely will suffer from the rapid melting of their habitat. As it is, several animal species are mysteriously declining in Alaska—including a species of sea lion and harbor seals in the Gulf of Alaska—and some scientists attribute that to warming trends. 14

Arctic drilling will also directly impact local peoples, for good and bad. The 260 Eskimos who live in the village of Kaktovik support onshore oil drilling. And it's not hard to see why. "We don't have any other economy up here," says Kaktovik Mayor Lon Sonsalla, who hails from Wisconsin and married into the local community after coming to the village during a military stint in 1977. "If you take away the oil money, you've got a subsistence way of life. All of a sudden you'd be trying to find food, stay warm, keep out of the wind. That would be your main occupation: staying alive." 15

Yet opponents of oil exploitation in ANWR include a separate group of native Alaskans who live to the south of the refuge. The Gwichin Indians of Arctic Village worry that oil development will harm the Porcupine caribou herd, which they have hunted for generations. That doesn't 16 mean they aren't open to outside influence: the Gwichin live in electrified homes, watch satellite TV and many drive all-terrain vehicles they call "four wheelers." Yet they equate the potential loss of the caribou with the destruction of buffalo herds for the Sioux, a prelude to cultural catastrophe. "If there were no caribou, we wouldn't have lived here for thousands of years," says Trimble Gilbert, 66. "That's who we are and where we came from."

It's clear that a nonnative like Dirk Nickisch, who flies for a living, needs oil as much as the next guy. But he's also made a conscious choice to lead an austere life. "I have a lot of time up here to think about things," he says. "A lot of people want their high ideals as long as it doesn't cost them anything. They want to save the environment, but they also want to drive their SUVs." Last winter Dirk and his wife, Danielle, sold their three-bedroom, 1-bath ranch-style house in Fairbanks in favor of a 16-by-24-foot cabin with a loft and a wood stove. "We have a simpler life and have come to enjoy the simpler things." 17

Many Americans appreciate that sentiment, but would not want to live that life. They may be willing to accept modest changes in their lifestyles, but for how long and to what extent? For an environmentalist out on the coastal plain of the Arctic refuge, in that brief but beautiful season between the harsh winter and the full onslaught of the mosquitoes, the choices seem simple enough. "In 50 or 100 years, would you stand out here and look back and think to yourself, 'Thank God we opened this area for oil'?" says Dan Ritzman. "No, you wouldn't. You'd say, 'Thank God we had the foresight to recognize that there are some places with more value than that.' " Three thousand miles and a world away, in the air-conditioned corridors of Washington, the battle is still on. 18

Thinking Critically

1. Can you identify an ideology, a political agenda, or an argument in "Alaska: Oil's Ground Zero"? Compare what you observe in this article and at *Newsweek*'s website with the reports and essays from more politically aligned publications such as *Mother Jones* (see the previous selection, Paul Roberts's "Over a Barrel"). What should you consider about the source of information you consult for your own research and argument projects?

2. Who is the "we" referred to in paragraph 5?

3. This article originally appeared a month before the terrorist attacks of September 11, 2001. In what ways might 9/11 and its ongoing aftershocks have changed the angle and approach of "Alaska: Oil's Ground Zero"?

Writing Critically

1. As an exercise in critical evaluation of online sources, visit the following websites (all located through Google searches using search terms in "Alaska: Oil's Ground Zero"):

   - <http://anwr.com/>
   - <http://www.anwr.org/>
   - <http://www.savearcticrefuge.org/>
   - <http://arctic.fws.gov/>
   - <http://www.nrdc.org/land/wilderness/anwr/anwr2.asp>
   - <http://www.alaska.net/~gwichin/>
   - <http://www.kaktovik.com/>

   Write a profile of each site, describing its timeliness, its sponsorship, its primary purpose and audience, and other important details. In an essay, discuss how any or none of these sites contribute a full and accurate picture of the ongoing debate over drilling in the Arctic National Wildlife Refuge.

2. In paragraph 4, the authors claim that "America's founding myths are largely about taming wild places." In a research paper, discuss these "founding myths," their origins, and in whose interest they continue to be perpetuated. Your research could include visual, literary, and musical interpretations of these "founding myths."

3. In the last paragraph of this article, environmentalist Dan Ritzman notes that the Arctic National Wildlife Refuge has "more value" than its oil. What does he mean by "value"? In an essay that uses classification, describe the different "values" the ANWR has for each interested party mentioned in "Alaska: Oil's Ground Zero." In each case, what are those "values" based on? Which set of values seems, at the time of your writing, most likely to prevail?

The New Soccer Moms

WILLIAM SCHNEIDER

This article first appeared in *National Journal* and later, on June 13, 2001, in the "D.C. Dispatch" section of *Atlantic Online,* the web-based version of the *Atlantic Monthly.* William Schneider is a resident fellow at the American Enterprise Institute for Public Policy Research. He earned a Ph.D. in political science from Harvard University and has taught at Harvard, Stanford, Boston College, and Brandeis. His research for the American Enterprise Institute focuses on the presidency, politics, and public opinion. Schneider is a contributing editor at *Atlantic Monthly* and *National Journal* and a senior political analyst at CNN. The

Washington Times, a conservative newspaper, has called Schneider "the nation's election-meister." For information about the American Enterprise Institute, go to <http://www.aei.org/>.

The President has just achieved the top item on his agenda—his big tax 1
cut. But the President's job is to address the top problem on the American people's agenda. It's gasoline prices, not taxes. "Energy" topped the list in last month's CNN-*Time* magazine poll, when people were asked to identify the nation's biggest problem. Three times as many named energy as named taxes.

President Bush hasn't really proposed any immediate solution to the energy 2
problem, except for his tax cut. But even if people get a tax rebate check this summer, they're still going to be upset if they have to pay $3 a gallon for gasoline: "You mean the government is giving me money so I can turn it over to the oil companies?"

A President gets in trouble if people think he's paying more attention 3
to his agenda than to their agenda. That holds true for opposition Democrats as well as for the President. By controlling the Senate, Democrats now have a seat at the table. And the energy issue could be their meal ticket.

In Chinese, the word for crisis is the same as the word for opportunity. 4
The Bush Administration certainly sees an opportunity in the California energy crisis—an opportunity to say: "We told you so." Vice President Dick Cheney said on May 25: "If I were to be critical of California, it would be that they didn't address [the energy problem] soon enough, that they knew a year ago they had problems and they postponed taking action because all of the action was potentially unpleasant."

The Administration also sees the energy crisis as an opportunity to 5
score points for free markets and to send a message about the need for new production. "The energy plan I lay out for the nation harnesses the power of modern markets," Bush said in St. Paul, Minn. "The problems in California show that you cannot conserve your way to energy independence," he said in Pennsylvania.

For the Bush Administration, the energy problem is an opportunity to 6
teach the country an economics lesson. Fair enough. But the issue may give Democrats an even greater opportunity, because politics is a short-term business. The crisis is now. People want help now. Giving people immediate help is becoming the Democrats' mantra. House Democratic Leader Richard A. Gephardt of Missouri: "This is a short-term problem. It needs a short-term solution." Rep. Anna G. Eshoo, D-Calif.: "We understand

long-term in California, and we understand short-term. . . . My constituents need price relief."

Does Bush's plan offer any short-term relief from soaring energy prices?   7
The American people don't see it. In a Gallup Poll taken last month, nearly two-thirds of respondents said that Bush's energy plan will help, but only after several years. Only 11 percent anticipated any immediate relief.

What kind of immediate relief do Democrats want? Price controls. "Oh   8
no," says the Bush Administration. "That will just make the problem worse." In the long run, that may be true, but the problem is now. "I am not for price controls over the long haul," California Gov. Gray Davis, a Democrat, said on May 29. "But we had them in place for three months last fall. They were working fine. There were no blackouts until the caps were lifted." Davis added mischievously: "Texas this year adopted price relief until 2003. We're just asking to be treated as well as Texas."

Other than conservatives and Republicans, is there any constituency for   9
Bush's energy plan? Yes, there's a powerful, heavily armored constituency, whose way of life is threatened.

In April, Cheney said that, under the Bush plan, Americans can save en-   10
ergy without sacrificing their standard of living. That was good news for Americans whose standard of living involves driving their families around the suburbs in what look like armored personnel carriers. They are the downtrodden and despised minority who own sport-utility vehicles and who are panicked over the prospect of paying as much as 3 dollars a gallon for gasoline to fuel vehicles that get only slightly better gas mileage than a 747.

According to the CNN-*Time* poll, SUV owners have found their cause.   11
Fifty percent of SUV owners said they favored the Bush energy plan, compared with 35 percent of non-SUV owners. When Bush and Cheney argue that there is no way Americans can conserve their way out of this energy problem, SUV owners say: "We hear you." For them, the answer is more gas. Drill we must.

Twenty percent of Americans have an SUV in their household. That's a   12
big constituency, with big cars. Sure, they're wealthier than other Americans. Almost half of SUV owners have incomes over $50,000 a year, compared with just over a quarter of non-SUV owners.

But it's not just income that drives their politics. High-income SUV   13
owners are crazy about the Bush energy plan—61 percent favor it. But among high-income Americans who don't own an SUV, support for the energy plan is 20 percentage points lower. The same holds true for lower-income Americans: Those who own SUVs are much more likely to support the President's energy plan than those who don't. We'll find more gas for you, the President is saying. You won't have to endure the humiliation—or risk—of driving your kids around in a compact.

SUV owners are the new soccer moms. They're President Bush's ar-   14
mored division in the energy wars. After all, a man's car is his castle.

Thinking Critically

1. Working by yourself or with a team, create a webpage or presentation of the news events that William Schneider refers to. What was the context for each event? What was the response to each event? In retrospect, how accurate, prescient, or misguided are the events and policies discussed in this article?

2. How does Schneider characterize "soccer moms," SUV drivers, and other groups?

Writing Critically

1. In paragraph 13, Schneider reports that in 2001 most SUV owners were "much more likely to support the President's energy plan" (and, by extension, President Bush himself) than were non-SUV drivers. Did that same pattern hold true for the 2004 election?

2. What is a "constituency"? Who defines or creates one? How is a constituency different from a community?

The Struggles of Otter 76

CHARLES MCCOY

Charles McCoy is a staff reporter for the *Wall Street Journal* who frequently writes about environmental issues. This article first appeared in the "middle column" of the front page of the *Wall Street Journal* in April 1989. The *Wall Street Journal* is the most authoritative daily business newspaper in the United States, and its front page (which never includes photographs) is usually a mix of current affairs and business news. The middle column of the front page, however, has historically been the home of more thoughtful or offbeat, frequently first-person, feature reporting. (Another, considerably lighter "middle column" article, by Carrie Dolan, appears on pages 388–92.) The *Exxon Valdez*, a massive oil tanker, split apart in the pristine waters of Prince William Sound, Alaska, on March 24, 1989. The resulting ecological disaster continues to haunt contemporary debates about exploring and drilling for oil in Alaska's Arctic National Wildlife Refuge (see "Alaska: Oil's Ground Zero," earlier in this chapter).

Valdez, Alaska

It is 9:32 last Thursday morning, and Otter 76 is fighting for her life. She   1
is pinned to a makeshift operating table in a clammy elementary school
gym, lungs scored by petroleum poisons. She rattles and gasps, slow
spasms rolling up in waves from her hind flippers to her bewhiskered
snout. She foams at the mouth and she excretes crude oil. It takes four men
to hold her down.

"Come on babes, hang on," exhorts Jeanie Clarke, a volunteer otter at-   2
tendant from England. Veterinarian Riley Wilson, also a volunteer, frantically pumps drugs into the animal. "Live, damn it," he mutters, and
implausibly, Otter 76 does live. The seizure subsides. At 9:43, Otter 76
goes back into her pen, and Mr. Wilson shakes his head and tells a colleague: "I didn't think she'd win that battle."

There will be more battles for her a few hours later. Otter 76 is one of hun-   3
dreds of otters plucked from Prince William Sound since Exxon Corp.'s
tanker, the *Exxon Valdez,* ran aground March 24 and smeared the sound's
emerald waters with ten million gallons of oil. Of those otters, only 134 made
it alive into the improvised otter rescue center set up here in a gym by a patch-
work crew of top marine mammal experts, volunteer animal lovers and hired
hands. Their struggles to keep dying otters alive are desperate, touching, occasionally maybe even heroic. Sixty-eight of their otters have died so far.

The otter slaughter has become the most striking symbol of the nation's   4
worst oil spill; the animal's mortality rate here has shocked even otter experts. It is far above anything ever seen in previous oil spills, even though
otter rescue may be the only post-spill operation in which about everything
that can be done is being done. Otters that make it to the rescue center are
swiftly scrubbed clean, pampered and spoon-fed, given oxygen, antitoxins
and antibiotics and tender love and tears and prayers.

And still, they die. In a pen ten yards away from where Otter 76 lies ex-   5
hausted and trembling, a lactating mother otter, its newborn gone, sprawls
listlessly. A young pup, its mother gone, rests fitfully in another pen nearby.
The pup begins to whimper and cry, the mother answers, and a great keen-
ing chorus of otters swells up. Someone suggests maybe bringing mother
and pup together, but it can't be done: Mother's milk is probably poisoned.
So the motherless child and the childless mother sing their strange song, off
and on, for hours.

A day later, they die within two hours of one another.   6

As of yesterday, there were 46 otters checked in at the otter hospital,   7
just a small piece of an environmental picture that seems to darken daily.
Scientists now say that as many as 4,000 otters—more than a third of the
sound's pre-spill population—are presumed dead.

Some 5,000,000 gallons of oil remain on the water. On many miles of   8
shoreline, oil has seeped through the gravelly beaches into subterranean
cavities. Tides will leach that oil back into the waters where the otters
swim, probably for years.

All of which means they will be busy down at the otter rescue center for   9
a long, long time.

The center was thrown together in the first frantic days following the   10
spill by a ragtag team of animal lovers and volunteer veterinarians under
the loose direction of the Sea World Research Center of San Diego, which
is affiliated with the same Sea World that runs the killer whale and porpoise
shows. Exxon is footing the bill, and Sea World's marine mammal experts
say they have a blank check.

In three sleepless weeks, the center has gone from tiny, suffocating quar-   11
ters in a junior college administration building to the less tiny but still suffocating quarters at the elementary school gym. Six rows of wooden pens,
96 pens in all, stretch from beneath one basketball goal to the other. A mix-
master of copper and plastic pipes snakes underfoot and overhead. The
place is wet and the temperature is 47 degrees and it reeks of marine life.
And marine death.

Early in the disaster, as many as 50 boats were retrieving otters and bring-   12
ing them in for treatment. That's down to five boats now, all manned by professional registered otter rescuers. The U.S. Fish & Wildlife Service last week
ordered amateur otter rescuers to cease and desist because "otters are mean
and they bite," a spokesman explains. Five boats on the vastness of Prince
William Sound are like five ants on a parking lot, and a lot of people here
find this an incomprehensible step that will only mean fewer otters saved.

In any event, capturing the otters and getting them back to land can in-   13
deed be tricky work. Until they become too sick to mount any defense, even
oiled otters will scramble and dive to get away from human hands. Mike
Lewis, a biologist with the state's Department of Environmental Conservation, displays a jagged gash that loops around the whole circumference
of his thumb.

"Tried to catch an otter with bare hands and duct tape," Mr. Lewis   14
says. "For the first and last time."

He opens the cargo hatch of his helicopter; the otter, which was finally   15
captured and stuffed in there, chewed through a six-inch section of steel
sheeting. Helicopter pilots say one chopper came within a split second and a
few feet of crashing into the sound when a 100-pound otter the pilot thought
was dead revived and rampaged through the cockpit before being subdued.

Otter 76 presented no such difficulties. She was snared on April 5 while   16
lying in the snow 30 feet from the water's edge on Knight Island, where

A desperate struggle Volunteers fight to save an otter's life after the Exxon Valdez oil spill in Alaska in March 1989. Oil is highly toxic to otters; after washing the animal's hair and skin clean of the goo, blow dryers help to keep the animals warm. Most rescued otters did not survive; untold numbers of sea creatures, birds, and mammals died.

some of the heaviest concentrations of oil hit. She didn't look too bad then. Her coat, golden brown with veils of silver and gray along her neck and snout, was only lightly oiled.

Once caught, otters are brought to a small scrubbing station in the jun- 17 ior college building. This is stage one of otter triage and it can be wild. One day last week four otters arrived, yowling in cages like the ones people use to take their dogs on airplanes. Jeremy Fitz-Gibbon, a barrel-chested mammal expert from the Vancouver Public Aquarium, inspects the otters as otter nurses load syringes and pass out rain gear. "This guy's got oil on him," Mr. Fitz-Gibbon announces.

Neil Utkov, a vet from Memphis who came here as a volunteer, pumps 18 two shots of anesthetic into the struggling otter. What about an injection of antibiotics, someone asks. "Wait until he's out," the vet replies. "I don't want this guy to feel any more hurt than he has to."

In 15 minutes the animal is unconscious and laid out on webbing sus- 19 pended over a basin. A load of Toxiban, a black slurry of activated charcoal meant to absorb oil poisons and pass through the body, is pumped through a tube down the otter's gullet. Then, using Dawn dishwashing liquid and hoses with garden spraying attachments, otter attendants painstakingly knead the animal's fur. Greasy, gray-black stew bubbles up between their fingers. Oil.

It takes about an hour and a half to scrub and dry each otter—almost 20 too long for this animal. Midway into the process, he pops up as if on a spring and begins snapping at his handlers. "Easy boy," Mr. Utkov coaxes. He injects another blast of Valium into the animal, but the otter continues to fidget and writhe for the remainder of the operation.

The otters brought in on this day wear relatively little oil, an encour- 21 aging sign, but no guarantee of survival. R. V. Chalam, a toxicologist and pathologist from San Diego, says one of the things that has shocked scientists here most is the number of different ways in which oil is killing otters. Otters were always known to be particularly vulnerable to oil because they have no blubber and can't float or stay warm for long once oil mats their fur. Most of the missing and presumed dead otters in the sound just sank.

At the rescue center, however, Mr. Chalam's autopsies show that "these 22 animals have livers that are totally destroyed, that crumble in your hand like dust." Additionally, "their immune systems are completely defused, making them extremely susceptible to secondary infection. There is emphysema not only in the lungs but throughout the body."

Mr. Chalam says this means that otters are being violently poisoned by 23 the benzene, toluene, xylene and numerous other toxins in oil, which apparently can invade their bodies through inhalation, ingestion or simple penetration of the pores. In other words, it means "incredible pain."

A few hours after her seizure on April 13, Otter 76 seems to stabilize 24 somewhat. She even tugs at a towel; otters, it turns out, like towels and like to curl up and hide their heads in them. Henry Iverson, an Athabascan Indian who is tending Otter 76, uses tongs to dangle a shrimp in front of her snout and she takes it, a good sign. "Man, I'd like to see her kicking back on a beach with her shades on and a can of beer in her paw," he says. "This girl's been through too much." Otter 76 spends the rest of that day and night resting, trembling some but eating a bit. "Maybe she'll make it," Mr. Iverson says. "At least she's holding her own."

Other otters are not. Outside the gym, ten mesh-covered pens have 25 been set up. The otter doctors have found that moving outside sometimes perks an otter up; some otter attendants have even taken to calling the dimly lit gym the "Death House." But even outside, Otter 81, nicknamed Otto, lies shuddering in a blue cage. Jake Matulka, a volunteer from

Anchorage, kneels motionless in front of the cage, resting his head against it. He watches silently for several minutes. "I think he's going down," Jake says finally, to no one in particular. "Come on bud, play with your towel. Come on."

Otter 81 lingers for about an hour more. He dies at 5:18 p.m. on April 13. 26

Not all the news at the center is so grim. On Friday, April 14, a hand- 27
written sign near the center's entrance proclaims that six otters treated here and shipped out to Point Defiance Zoo near Tacoma, Wash., earlier in the week are still alive and doing well. YEAH!! the sign reads. It is a moment of accomplishment and of progress. The center shipped six otters out to Sea World two weeks ago, but only one survived.

Eventually, all the otters the center manages to save will have to be sent 28
somewhere—and it probably won't be back into the wild. "They can't go home again," says Mr. Fitz-Gibbon. "They're better off in aquariums than in oil." Scientists say they may try transplanting some otters to other regions, but they fear the otters will swim back to their home waters, no matter how distant.

Those who work with the otters stow away the small victories to help 29
them cope. Many of the otter handlers came as volunteers and stayed on as Exxon shifted to a paid staff. Some have been here for weeks, and they've seen a lot of melancholy things. Jeanie Clarke, the English volunteer, was vacationing in Anchorage when the oil spilled. She hitched the six-hour ride to Valdez to help otters; one day two weeks ago, she spent 17 straight hours nursing a pup. "I was sitting in the cage with it, holding it in my arms when it died," Ms. Clarke says. "Even after the tears, that stays in your gut."

Carolyn McCollum, a writer from Cary, N.C., also came to help the an- 30
imals. "I drive a car, I use oil," says Mrs. McCollum, who is 30 years old and pregnant with her first child. "In a sense, I share in the blame for this. I had to do something." She has lost three otters, the most recent one on Friday night.

"She was moaning and crying, like a little girl on a Ferris wheel," 31
Mrs. McCollum recounts. "It got to where I knew she was brain dead, but she was still breathing. You can't just put her in a bag and forget about her." So Mrs. McCollum cradled the otter in her arms until it stopped breathing, some time around 10 p.m.

At about the time Mrs. McCollum's otter died, one of the veterinarians 32
checks up on Otter 76. She has been showing some signs of improvement, eating four shrimp and three pollack earlier that evening. The vet looks her over and scribbles two notations rapidly on Otter 76's chart.

The first is "Possible eyesight loss." The second is "Pregnant." Otter 33
76, it has been discovered, is fighting not for one life, but for two.

The scientists at the center say they're learning as they go. "We know a 34
lot more than we did about the logistics of trying to save animals," says
Terrie Williams, a research physiologist from Sea World who is running the
day-to-day operations of the center. "We know it's a nightmare."

But no breakthroughs on how to actually save otters from oil—what 35
drugs, if any, might limit the corrosive damage, for example—have been
made. The scientists are talking with Exxon about establishing a permanent research facility here to keep searching for more effective treatments.

"That's the only good that could ever come out of this disaster—some 36
knowledge that might help us save animals when this happens again," Ms.
Williams says.

Ms. Williams stands near the pen where, just a few hours before, Otter 37
76 began heaving for breath again. The otter was given Regalan to reduce
inflammation and more Toxiban, the poison absorber. She was force fed,
too, but soon she fell once more into short, jerky convulsions.

At 3:15 a.m. Saturday morning, Otter 76 shuddered one last time and died. 38

Thinking Critically

1. Can you think critically about "The Struggles of Otter 76"? People who craft
   arguments use a mix of *logos, ethos,* and *pathos* to engage and persuade
   their audience. What does each of these terms mean, and how does
   Charles McCoy employ each strategy in "The Struggles of Otter 76"?

2. How, and to what effect, does McCoy use personification?

3. Are you accustomed to happy endings in news stories? Did you think, or
   hope, that "The Struggles of Otter 76" would have a happy ending? (Have a
   look at some of the websites listed below. Of those that suggest a happy
   ending, or at least a positive outcome, who sponsors them and what is
   their purpose?)

Writing Critically

1. They're only otters, after all. Why do the people profiled in McCoy's article
   spend so much time, money, and emotional and intellectual effort on saving the animals' lives? What value do they attribute to the life of each otter? How are those values defined and put to use by different interest
   groups (above and beyond the *Exxon Valdez* incident)?

2. A 2005 Google search using the terms "Exxon Valdez" turned up these
   websites among the top 20 hits. Visit each site and evaluate its credibility,

bias, and accuracy. (You could combine this work with a similar writing assignment for another selection in this chapter, "Alaska: Oil's Ground Zero?") To what extent does access to the media control the terms of a national debate?

- <http://www.evostc.state.ak.us/>
- <http://response.restoration.noaa.gov/spotlight/spotlight.html>
- <http://www.exxonmobil.com/Corporate/Newsroom/NewsReleases/ Corp_NR_Valdez.asp>
- <http://www.valdezscience.com/>
- <http://www.greenpeace.org/international_en/news/details?item_id =439825>
- <http://www.valdezresearch.com/>

3. Why did Carolyn McCollum (paragraph 30) decide to help with the otter rescue? How do her efforts—how does anything described in this article—exemplify what Erik Assadourian called the "butterfly effect" in the first selection in this chapter?

SUV Supporters Answer Campaign; Association Finds Own "Jesus" to Drive Point Home

ANNA BAKALIS

This article was published in the July 14, 2003, issue of the conservative daily newspaper the *Washington Times*, founded in 1982 by News World Communications, a company owned by the controversial Unification Church. The company purchased news service United Press International in 2000, adding it to a portfolio that includes newspapers and magazines around the globe. For information about the *Washington Times*, go to <http:// washingtontimes.com/>. You can find a copy of the Jesus Rivera ad online at <http://www.suvoa.com/ press/index.cfm?id=16>.

The Sport Utility Vehicle Owners of America is fighting back against a religious campaign with a tongue-in-cheek ad.   1

"Most people think it's a ridiculous question, and that's the approach   2
that we've taken toward our own ads," said Ron Defore, communications director for the association.

The ad shows a middle-age Jesus Rivera standing next to his SUV, with 3
an elbow resting on the passenger-side mirror, as he waves and smiles. On
the right, it reads: "What does Jesus drive? We asked him," followed by a
few sentences about Mr. Rivera's reasons for buying his 1995 SUV.

The first ad in a monthlong campaign will be published today in re- 4
gional editions of *USA Today* and then expand nationwide.

Jesus' son also drives an SUV, but it is midsize, the ad says. The ads do 5
not say what brands of SUVs the Riveras drive.

The nationwide organization represents 24 million SUV owners. The 6
campaign is being started after a slew of anti-SUV ads.

The anti-SUV campaign, started by the Evangelical Environmental Net- 7
work, says that what a person drives reflects his or her moral choices. It
uses biblical references such as "Love your neighbor as yourself" and "Do
unto others as you would have done unto you."

The environmental network was formed to declare the "Lordship of 8
Christ over all creation" and that certain environmental concerns parallel
moral issues.

Spearheaded by the Rev. Jim Ball, a Baptist minister and evangelist, the 9
organization started the anti-SUV campaign in November.

For the past few months, Mr. Ball and his wife have been traveling 10
through the Bible Belt in a Toyota Prius, a hybrid gas-electric automobile,
to preach the benefits of fuel efficiency as part of a higher authority.

"When you boil down environmental arguments, they're moral argu- 11
ments," Mr. Ball says on his Web site (www.whatwouldjesusdrive.org).
"This is part of loving your neighbor."

No one from his campaign was available to comment yesterday. 12

Mr. Defore said most of the respondents in an informal poll of drivers— 13
some SUV owners, some not—said they were offended by the "What Would
Jesus Drive?" ads, as well as other campaigns equating driving SUVs with
supporting terrorism.

The use of religion to push an environmental issue was a strange con- 14
cept for some, he said. "Most people thought that it was a question that
never should have been asked in the first place," Mr. Defore said.

"What Would Jesus Drive?" is derived from "What Would Jesus Do?" 15
The theme has been used in Christian books and accessories such as
bracelets, ID holders and pins.

Activist groups supporting fuel-efficient cars, such as the Sierra Club, 16
say drivers should have options but that the "What Would Jesus Drive?"
campaign should focus on SUV manufacturers instead of owners.

"We think Jesus would like to save money at the gas station," said Allen 17
Mattison, a spokesman for the Sierra Club in Washington. "Everyone is

allowed to drive what they want, but the car consumer should be aware of what his car does to the environment."

The SUV association's campaign kicks off as Mr. Ball finishes his evan- 18 gelical tour of the South. The campaign is set to continue through the month, but the pro-SUV group did not give more details.

"We wanted to get our message out," Mr. Defore said. "I think this ad 19 does it all."

Thinking Critically

1. What kinds of risks might the Sport Utility Vehicle Owners of America be taking with their "What Does Jesus Drive?" ad? Who would be offended by the ad? Who would be amused?

2. Are you what you drive?

Writing Critically

1. Go online and find examples of anti-SUV advocacy—environmental groups, parodies, and other kinds of awareness raising and activism. Create a presentation in which you show where on the political spectrum each of these ads might be placed, based on their sponsorship and their target audience. What common values and interests unite the anti-SUV movement?

2. A press release from the Sport Utility Vehicle Owners of America announcing the "Jesus Rivera" ad quotes Father Robert Sirico, president of the Acton Institute for the Study of Religion and Liberty and an SUV owner: "The first obligation of a Christian is to answer the Gospel's call for personal conversion. . . . Unfortunately, the anti-SUV crowd is much more interested in promoting a 'green' agenda than it is in serious theological reflection." In a research paper, discuss the teachings of a particular religion or faith tradition or philosophical perspective regarding conservation, consumption, and preservation.

Arguing the Cultural Divides

1. How does the concept of "manifest destiny" continue to shape American attitudes toward a particular environmental issue? Choose an issue explored in Chapter 7 or another contemporary environmental controversy.

2. How is the American wilderness depicted in American popular culture? Choose specific, recent examples from film, television, music, or literature. Are any of the conflicts discussed in Chapter 7 reflected in recent American popular culture?

3. Create a PowerPoint presentation or website that traces how a gallon of gasoline gets from a hole in the ground to the tank of your car. Consult both commercial and scientific sources. You'll probably want to consult an accessible scientific source to find out how petroleum is refined into gasoline, but you'll also want to try to find out where the gas from your particular chain of gas stations comes from.

4. Which arguments for environmental conservation and preservation have the most influence on you—economic, strategic, aesthetic, or moral? (Or perhaps some combination of all four?) Which of those four arguments seems to have the most influence on American society as a whole (for example, in consumer behavior or in the casting of votes)?

CHAPTER 8

The Body Politic: Public Health

A Night in the Emergency Room

TAMARA ODISHO

Tamara Odisho graduated from Rutgers University at Newark (New Jersey) in 2002 with a degree in journalism and media studies. She now lives in California and works on the staff of a member of the California state assembly. *The Newark Metro,* where "A Night in the Emergency Room" first appeared in 2002, is a website created and maintained by students in the Journalism and Media Studies Program at Rutgers-Newark. Newark, New Jersey, is a diverse city across the Hudson River from New York City. On their website, the students explained what they hoped to accomplish: "In pursuit of a national audience, big media from New York City too often skip over day-to-day life in North Jersey. And despite the best efforts of New Jersey newspapers and broadcasters, here in the jumbled old towns and cities of North Jersey there are still plenty of stories waiting to be told. We aim to tell them." The website of *The Newark Metro* is at <http://www.newarkmetro .rutgers.edu/index.php>.

Children are chasing one another around the blue chairs. An old   1
man hunches over and vomits into the garbage. A baby cries hys-

It hurts here Many lower-income Americans who lack medical insurance or whose employers do not provide health care plans, rely on hospital emergency rooms for basic medical care.

terically in her mother's arms. This is the emergency room at the University Hospital in Newark, New Jersey.

It's an early evening in spring. There haven't been any disasters in the 2 neighborhood, nor is there an outbreak of disease. Rather, this is the outcome of a poverty-stricken city. Many citizens of Newark who are unemployed and uninsured cannot afford an office visit with a doctor. So they go to the emergency room, where the poor and under-insured among them receive care for free or at a reduced rate under the New Jersey Hospital Care Payment Assistance Program. Many patients call it "charity care."

Under the program, the New Jersey Department of Health and Senior 3 Services requires 80 of its member hospitals to treat any patient in need of health care regardless of his or her ability to pay, explains Tom Calandra, a research scientist at New Jersey's Department of Health and Senior Services. The program, he said, is active in six of Newark's hospitals.

According to the New Jersey State Health Care website (www.state. 4 nj.us/health) in 2002, University Hospital received close to $85 million for charity care subsidies. University Hospital receives the most money of the participating New Jersey hospitals.

Calandra said the program covers or reduces any costs incurred by either 5 an emergency room visit or any medical situation that calls for a doctor. The program pays for hospital costs but does not cover routine office visits, physicians' bills or prescriptions.

According to eligibility standards, an unmarried patient who makes less 6
then $10,000 annually and who has few assets is a good candidate for charity care. Underinsured individuals are also eligible for some benefits under the program. If a patient isn't aware of the service at the time of the visit, he or she has one year from the date of the visit to apply for charity care retroactively.

At the University Hospital emergency room, the emergency units bring 7
in critically injured patients and set them down next to the others with less urgent conditions. The room is crowded and loud. Its smell is unpleasant.

Many patients, some having waited for more than three hours, go to 8
sleep. Others go shopping across the street at Pathmark while family members anxiously hold their place in line. One frustrated patient begins to argue with a nurse and an uproar follows.

Maria Smith, a 45-year-old resident of Newark, praises the program 9
and says it alleviates many of her concerns. She says that if any of her family members are ill, "I don't have to worry about paying bills I can't afford." She also says that as frustrating as it is to wait, "it's worth it." She says, "I know that I can't afford this on my own and the hospital helps me, so I am willing to wait and take my turn."

Janet McMillan, sitting next to her, snaps at Smith's comment. "What 10
kind of service is this when you have to wait for an hour?" McMillan, recently laid off, says she can't wait to find a job with health insurance. "I hate having to wait to be seen by a damn doctor."

A nurse, who wouldn't disclose her name, says: "We try to make every- 11
one's stay pleasant. We know it's hard but we are short staffed." She adds: "Many aren't here because of an emergency per se, but we care for them, and they should understand from our perspective that it is hard to juggle so many people at once."

Many of the patients, she says, qualify for charity care. And although 12
it adds to traffic in the emergency room, she feels it's a "wonderful program" and has great potential in a city like Newark.

Thinking Critically

1. How does Tamara Odisho establish a sense of place?

2. Is "A Night in the Emergency Room" an objective report, a first-person essay, an argument, or some combination of all of these? If you think Odisho is making an argument, what do you think her claim is and how does she support it?

3. How many sources does Odisho consult, and what use does she make of these sources?

Writing Critically

1. Is access to health care a right or a privilege?

2. Borrow Odisho's methodology by arranging to spend the night in a location that encapsulates a larger social, cultural, or political conflict. (Plan carefully in advance to ensure your own safety and to obtain any permissions you need to be on this site. For more information, see the section on field research in the Appendix, "Researching Across the Cultural Divides.") In an essay based on primary sources (information you gather through your own observations and interviews), make a connection between this local site of conflict and the larger issue.

3. Describe a way in which some aspect of medical care is depicted in some medium of American culture. For example, you might argue that contemporary political debates over health care spill over into a particular television drama, or that a particular kind of movie depends on the medical establishment's being portrayed as either "good guys" or "bad guys."

Share the Health

STEPHANIE MENCIMER

Stephanie Mencimer is a contributing editor to *Washington Monthly*, an independent magazine featuring indepth (and occasionally irreverent) reporting and commentary on current American politics. Many reporters and editors for *Washington Monthly* have worked in government, in positions across the political spectrum. The magazine is also well known for its essays and reviews on arts and culture. Mencimer, the recipient of the 2000 Harry Chapin Media Award for her reporting on hunger and poverty, has also worked as an investigative reporter for the *Washington Post* and as a senior writer for the alternative weekly *Washington City Paper*. She is a contributor to the Neiman Watchdog Journalism Project at Harvard University—the Web address is <http://www.niemanwatchdog.org/>—a resource for journalists that "seeks to encourage more informed reporting by putting journalists in contact with authorities who can suggest appropriate, probing questions and who can serve as resources." Mencimer was the recipient of a 2004 Alicia Patterson Foundation grant, a prestigious and competitive program that gives investigative print journalists and photojournalists the resources to spend a year researching a topic of social or public interest; her research subject is "The Myth of the Frivolous

Lawsuit." "Share the Health" appeared in *Washington Monthly* in October 1992. For information about this periodical, go to <http://washingtonmonthly.com/>.

Why hasn't the Washington establishment done anything about the health care crisis? Follow us inside the comfy world of presidential and congressional health care. . . .

Until recently, when you thought of Oregonians you probably envisioned Birkenstock-shod tree huggers earnestly sorting plastic from paper in the nation's recycling capital. But if you've tuned in to the nightly news lately, you may have a slightly different image—one of hospitals and doctors and sick people. Legions of reporters have besieged Oregon in the past few months trying to get a look at one of the country's first broad-based efforts to resuscitate an ailing health care delivery system.

For the past five years, as Congress and the White House noodled around on health care reform, Oregon grappled with all the tough issues—cost, access, quality—and came up with a plan to make primary health care available to all the state's residents, regardless of income. Other state legislatures, from Hawaii to Florida to Minnesota, have made moves as well, providing subsidized and even free health care to the working poor. And with all the heat they're now taking from the Bush administration and health care industry representatives, you'd be excused for forgetting that they're an exceptional breed of politicians: ones getting knocked for actually doing something about health care.

So how is it that a few states have the guts to tackle the issue while the Bush administration ducks and Congress covers? Is it Oregon's bracing air? Minnesota's clear water? Or is it that the politicians who make up those legislatures are still real people—people who don't have to read policy tomes to see that America's health care system is in crisis.

Oregon's legislators, for instance, meet once every two years; they're police officers, farmers, electricians, housewives, union bosses, small business owners, real estate agents, and professors who spend the majority of their time in their own communities working regular jobs with regular people. Unlike Bush and members of Congress, who enjoy an extensive network of low-cost medical benefits and perks, Oregon legislators don't need Pennsylvania Senator Harris Wofford to tell them that people are worried sick about health care. Most of the year, they see it firsthand.

Maybe it's asking too much to wish that every U.S. congressman could experience America's health crisis as directly as the average electrician sees it. But a trek through the cushy health care empire of Washington politicians should chill the average Joe's ticker. Few lines, minimal costs, a galaxy of options, and guaranteed coverage make the federal government and Capitol Hill just about the only places in America where health care isn't in crisis. And it also makes one wonder whether the real explanation behind Washington's failure to act on health care isn't a matter of insurance industry PACs or pleas from small business or the other usual suspects, but a product of plain old insulation. Of course, the point isn't that congressmen and other officials should be denied adequate health care. It's that the rest of America should be afforded it, too.

Executive Privilege

Even the plushest hospital couldn't be mistaken for a Ritz-Carlton with   7
catheters; hospitals can be miserable places. But some are less miserable than others, especially when you're North Carolina Rep. Bill Hefner. Last June, when Hefner arrived at Walter Reed Army Medical Center for bypass surgery, there were no suspicious inspections of his insurance card, no long waits in cold rooms full of screaming kids. Instead, he was greeted by an orderly who helped him check in and then escorted him to the Eisenhower Executive Nursing unit. This is a high-security, extra-private VIP wing that sports a stereo (circa 1956) compliments of John Foster Dulles and is decorated with artwork donated by Jackie Onassis and the Eisenhowers. Hefner spent nearly a week and a half being tended by Walter Reed's elite cadre of cardiologists before going under the knife. After surgery, he was afforded eight days to recuperate.

Had Hefner been a private citizen and undergone the same surgery at   8
George Washington University med center, a private hospital a few miles away, the charges would have mounted fast. The actual surgery would have been $8,000, and he would have been charged $2,789 for each day he spent in intensive care and $1,000 a day for a regular room, for a grand total of about $40,000. But as a member of Congress, Hefner paid nothing for his medical care. The only bill he received for his stay was for the room and food (at a relatively cheap $701 daily rate)—the entire sum of which was promptly picked up by his Blue Cross health insurance, provided through the federal government.

Granted, most people with decent health insurance would probably   9
have their bypasses at least partially covered, too. But then again, they might not. Medical costs have risen so steeply that insurance companies now resort to all sorts of creative ways to pinch pennies, such as delaying claim payments, limiting the amounts they pay for some treatments, and subjecting consumers to long waiting periods before they are eligible for coverage. Excluding preexisting conditions from coverage is almost standard. So it should come as little surprise that, according to a recent study, almost half the patients who were unable to pay their hospital bills actually had insurance but their policies simply wouldn't cover their treatments.

And then, of course, there are the 37 million people who have no health   10
insurance.

Rep. Hefner surely had plenty to worry about while in the hospital, but   11
unlike many other Americans, one worry wasn't potential bankruptcy. Perhaps that's why, when you call Hefner's office to find out his position on
health care reform, you're told that he doesn't have one. "He hasn't settled
on his view of what should be done," explains a staffer.

Not that it's fair to single out Hefner. Every day, thousands of Wash-   12
ington policymakers—members of Congress, the Cabinet, the White
House staff—receive similarly user-friendly medical treatment through the
federal insurance plan that the Office of Personnel Management (OPM) ne-
gotiates for 9 federal employers. Under the plan, employees pay, on average, 28 percent of the premium (which works out to $100 a month); the
government pays the rest. The plan is so good it's often considered a model
for national health care that includes the private insurance industry.

It's grand that federal employees are so well taken care of, but compare   13
their plan with what the rest of us face. The federal government gives employees the option of several private insurance plans, all of which provide
mental health care, substance abuse treatment, and some dental benefits,
while regular folks are often at the mercy of a single insurer, chosen by their
employer. If federal employees are unhappy with the plan they choose, they
can try another one during "open season," once a year, without risking loss
of coverage, because OPM makes sure that none of the plans exclude preexisting conditions. The vast majority of us never have this luxury. When John
McGann, an employee at H&H Music Co. of Houston, developed AIDS, his
company switched insurers and presented him with a policy that capped his
benefits at $5,000. He spent the last few years of his life on Medicaid. A
member of Congress, on the other hand, could develop AIDS and cancer and
become an alcoholic simultaneously and his policy wouldn't flinch.

For congressmen, good insurance is only the beginning. Members also   14
have at their disposal a wide range of supplementary medical services—
from free outpatient use of top-flight military medical facilities to the Capitol clinic and on-site private pharmacy. Got a sore throat, Senator Hatch?
Think you have a fever, Speaker Foley? Just walk down the hall, see the
nurse, and say "ahh." Need a checkup, Rep. Gingrich? Prostate acting up
again, Rep. Bateman? The attending physician will send you over to the
Naval med center pronto. In fact, he'll make the appointment himself, and
an orderly will meet you at the front desk to make sure you don't have to
linger with hoi polloi waiting in line.

No wonder it took until last year, when Wofford won his Senate seat in   15
a Pennsylvania special election by stressing the need for universal health

care, for congressional policymakers to realize, at least momentarily, that the issue is a serious source of anxiety for many Americans. In Wofford's wake, they flooded the Hill with 79 different health care bills. But the flurry of paperwork and fiery speeches has resulted in little more than the public illusion that Congress is addressing the issue. Not one of these 79 bills has a prayer of passing this year.

Of course, members will quickly note that they are not as personally in- 16 sulated from the crisis as they used to be. Since the House bank scandal, a few medical perks have been curtailed. For instance, senators now pay $520 a year to use the office of the attending physician, rather than billing the tax-payer. But on the House side, they're still doing it the old-fashioned way: We pay for it. And when members say that they now shell out for the prescriptions they have received free for years, what they really mean is that they pay 25 percent of the bill for drugs—the cost that their insurance won't cover.

Congressional distance from the health frustrations of ordinary Amer- 17 icans becomes jarringly clear when members start to speechify about it. For example, those who have opposed adopting a single-payer system like the Canadian model by arguing that we would have long lines to see a doctor apparently haven't tried making an appointment in our system lately. At George Washington University's health maintenance organization (HMO), for instance, it takes three weeks for a woman to get an appointment to see a physician's assistant to get a refill of birth control pills. And she'd better bring something thick to read when that day arrives. Even routine appointments can take two hours.

Need to see a full-fledged gynecologist? Take two Midol and see him in 18 two months.

Credit Canard

Of course, it's not just the routine annoyances that our representatives 19 are insured against; it's the extraordinary indignities as well. Consider the case of Helen Sanders, a 74-year-old woman in Largo, Florida, who saw a doctor at her Humana HMO in January 1991, when she started losing control of her facial muscles for hours at a time. Her doctors believed that an artery in her neck was 80 percent blocked—a level of blockage that could prompt a stroke at any time. While a series of crucial yet expensive tests were recommended, Sanders couldn't get Humana to approve payment for them. She camped out in the clinic every day for weeks trying to shame the staff into approving the tests. Four months after Sanders' initial diagnosis, a clerk at the clinic told her that her file had been lost and that her doctor was on vacation, so she couldn't get the tests anyway. Skeptical, Sanders went home and called the clinic

Coverage by Type of Health Insurance:
2002 and 2003
(Percent)

2003
2002

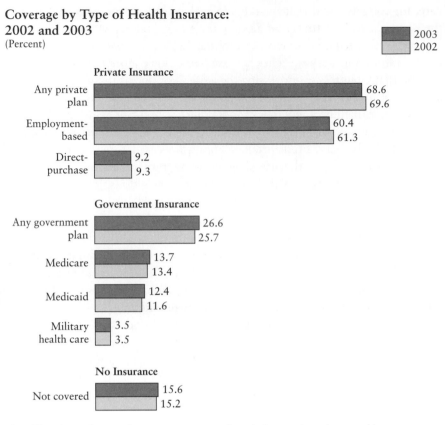

Private Insurance

Any private plan — 68.6 / 69.6

Employment-based — 60.4 / 61.3

Direct-purchase — 9.2 / 9.3

Government Insurance

Any government plan — 26.6 / 25.7

Medicare — 13.7 / 13.4

Medicaid — 12.4 / 11.6

Military health care — 3.5 / 3.5

No Insurance

Not covered — 15.6 / 15.2

Note: The estimates by type of coverage are not mutually exclusive; people can be covered by more than one type of health insurance during the year.
Source: U.S. Census Bureau, Current Population Survey, 2003 and 2004 Annual Social and Economic Supplements.

Take two aspirin More than 15% of Americans have no insurance at all—a larger percentage than are enrolled in health coverage plans for the indigent (Medicaid) or the elderly (Medicare). U. S. Senators' health coverage is under the umbrella category "Any government plan."

that day without using her name and was told her doctor was in the office seeing another patient.

It wasn't until the state insurance commissioner in Tallahassee aggres- 20 sively intervened that Sanders got served by Humana. But by that time, her doctors concluded that she had a 99 percent blockage of the left carotid artery. She could have had a stroke while sitting in the waiting room. Sanders had surgery that day.

Could a Canadian-style system be much worse? 21

George Bush thinks so, and the GOP convention joke about "the ef- 22 ficiency of the House bank and the compassion of the KGB" pretty much sums up the nuances in his argument against nationalized health care. And come to think of it, it's not too surprising that compassion and efficiency are highly prized by the big man: His own health plan— government-provided, of course—offers them in spades. In addition to a private ambulance and a room at Bethesda Naval Medical Center kept ready and waiting just for him, the president has his own personal physician, Dr. Burton Lee III, zealously devoted to monitoring every presidential burp and wheeze. Think Bush was perplexed by those electronic supermarket scanners? Imagine how mystified he'd be by the clerks demanding credit histories from bleeding patients in an inner-city emergency room.

It's not just Bush whose health care comes hermetically sealed. Lee's 23 medical unit cares for all the health emergencies of the White House staff and Cabinet members. While it doesn't offer regular checkups (Bush gets those free at Bethesda), the office does work as a referral service, so if Louis Sullivan (or any of his friends, for that matter) starts having chest pains, Dr. Lee will see to it that he gets proper attention.

"We'll make sure you get into the best location at the best price," Lee 24 says. "I generally make the phone calls myself, call the doctors myself, make the arrangements myself."

That George Bush's doctor makes Marcus Welby seem heartless is 25 good in one respect: It reminds us that there are still compassionate physicians out there. But the White House's enjoyment of such solicitous service may be one reason Bush's solution to the health care crisis, like many other free-marketeers', is a few milquetoasty tax credits, which do little to address some of the basic health-care problems of less pampered patients.

Bush has favored giving tax credits to people too wealthy to qualify 26 for Medicaid but too poor to afford insurance as a way of providing universal coverage without adopting the "socialist" Canadian system. While a tax credit may seem an appealing small government approach, his administration seems to grossly underestimate the size of the credit many uninsured Americans would need to pay for insurance. So you're a diabetic who can find coverage for her preexisting condition only under a plan with a $5,000 deductible—the $1,000 tax credit being bandied around by Republicans isn't exactly a great deal. To cover many of the people who can't afford health insurance, Congress may have to extend tax credits for premiums that are larger than some of the recipients' annual incomes.

Michael Jones, a former loan officer for a real estate finance firm, 27
showed the Senate Labor and Human Resources Committee at a June hearing that paying out more in health care costs than you take in as income is
a real possibility. Jones has been disabled by a rare neuro-muscular disease
and is no longer able to work. Knowing his condition, Jones purchased catastrophic health insurance in 1982 while he was still working, at which
time the premium was about $2,300 a year for unlimited benefits. By 1991,
he was forced to drop the policy because the premiums would have cost
$17,000 a year—substantially more than the Supplemental Social Security
Income he lives on.

A root problem tax credits don't address is the fact that health care 28
costs continue to skyrocket. By the year 2000, the average family will have
seen a greater than 400 percent increase in health care bills since 1980.
Business payments for health insurance will have increased sevenfold in the
same period. But since those figures are as familiar as they are daunting,
one might wonder why the press and other Washington powerbrokers
haven't worked up a full head of steam; why editorials, placards, and banners demanding Storm the barricades! Health care reform now! aren't as
ubiquitous as Mao posters used to be in China. Well, it may be because
those guys aren't exactly waiting in line at Medic-24, either.

While management at the 14th Street McDonald's in downtown Wash- 29
ington, D.C., doesn't even offer medical benefits to most employees, reporters and editors at *The Washington Post* can choose from an array of
policies, none of which exclude preexisting conditions. A paltry $2.50 a
week buys them generous dental, optical, and mental health care benefits
in addition to gold-plated coverage for maternity and hospitalization.

The Washington elite, and increasingly only the elite, tends to have excel- 30
lent and expensive health coverage, paid for by its generous employers. And
that's one reason that, at Georgetown dinner parties, the capital gains tax is
a far hotter topic than health care. Storm the barricades? What's the hurry?

Fixing American health care will demand a full flexing of qualities that
seem lately to be in short supply outside of Oregon: leadership, cooperation, 31
and the courage to fight the health care PACs and to make hard choices
about what we can and cannot afford. It would be nice to think that that
kind of political will can be mustered through intense meditation over Heritage Foundation white papers. Unfortunately, the Washington leadership's
personal investment has always had a way of sharpening political urgency.

But if you're still determined to believe that the D.C. establishment's 32
comfy personal health care system has nothing to do with the dismal health
care prospects the rest of us face, consider one last thing: the force behind
Harris Wofford's decision to seize the health care issue—his wife.

Plagued by chronic health problems, she had received expensive care at   33
the University of Pennsylvania, covered by the sturdy federal insurance he
got when he was appointed to the Senate to replace John Heinz. If Wofford
had lost the election—which for a while looked like a real possibility—he
had more than just his political career to worry about. He had to face the
possibility that he wouldn't be able to get health coverage as a private citizen because of his wife's condition. Sure, PAC money talks, but sick husbands and wives and children tend to talk even louder.

Of course, it's not too genteel to wish that Jesse Helms had to lay awake   34
nights worrying that his heart condition could cost him his house, but one
can't help imagining the result if he did. If Wofford's brush with America's
grim health care reality can put the issue on the table, hundreds of similar
brushes might turn the talk into action. Still, maybe there's a kinder, gen-
tler alternative: Imagine enough Washington politicians suddenly stricken
with embarrassment about how good they have it that they finally summon
up the will to share the health with the rest of us.

Thinking Critically

1. A kind of argument is made by the placement of "Share the Health" and
   the preceding selection, "A Night in the Emergency Room," in this anthology. What do you think that argument might be?

2. What distinction does Stephanie Mencimer make between Oregon's legislators and Washington's elected officials?

3. Which President Bush is Mencimer referring to? Why is it important, when
   doing research for your own essays and reports, to double-check the dates
   of sources?

Writing Critically

1. What does Mencimer suggest about the motivations behind Washington's
   views on health care? Even though this article is in many ways specific to
   the early 1990s, the broader issues she raises remain relevant. Identify
   and define a key moral issue underlying the reasons why some senators
   would either support or work against universal health care, based on
   Mencimer's reporting.

2. Would it be useful to write an essay comparing the standards of medical
   care described by Tamara Odisho in the previous selection and by
   Mencimer? Would it be fair? In an essay, compare and contrast the treatment received by late-night visitors to the Newark emergency room with the
   treatment received by North Carolina representative Bill Hefner at Walter
   Reed Army Medical Center. Can you use this comparison to support a

specific argument about access to health care in the United States? Part
of your essay should examine why this comparison is, or is not, useful for
your argument.

3. If you can afford to live well, should you be embarrassed? Should you feel
guilty if you have access to high-quality health care, education, or housing
because of your income? Why, or why not? (You might want to draw on
some of the readings in Chapter 5 to support your argument.)

Adam and Eve

ERIC SCHLOSSER

> An award-winning journalist in the finest muckraking
> tradition, Eric Schlosser is the author of the bestseller
> *Fast Food Nation: The Dark Side of the All-American
> Meal* (2000) and *Reefer Madness: Sex, Drugs, and
> Cheap Labor in the American Black Market* (2003),
> from which "Adam and Eve" is excerpted. A corre-
> spondent for the *Atlantic Monthly*, Schlosser received a
> National Magazine Award for his in-depth reporting on
> how America's marijuana laws are enforced. A history
> major at Princeton University, Schlosser lived in New
> York City and tried his hand at fiction before his inter-
> ests in social causes turned him to journalism. Describ-
> ing his research for *Reefer Madness* in an interview
> with *Bookpage* magazine, Schlosser said that he begins
> with extensive library research into his topic before
> heading out into the field: "I don't have any researcher
> or anyone helping me. I enjoy the process of discovering
> and all the background reading. It's not miserable work
> at all. And when you then get out in the field, you
> know what you're looking for and the conversations
> are more interesting. . . . It's amazing who you'll meet if
> you just go to Indiana and sit in a bar. A lot of these
> people feel cut off from the media, cut off from the
> mainstream. Once it became clear that I wasn't a narc
> or wasn't going to rat anybody out, it was hard getting
> some of them to stop talking."

Hillsborough, North Carolina, is a charming small town in the coun-   1
tryside near Chapel Hill. Its main street extends for two blocks, lined
with old buildings that the local historical societies have fought to preserve.
There are antiques stores, bookstores, bronze plaques honoring the fallen
heroes of the Civil War, a café, and a hardware store that seems to have
changed little in half a century. The roughly 5,000 residents of the town

have tried hard to maintain its quiet, rural identity, resisting Chapel Hill's more affluent and cosmopolitan pull. Hillsborough is the county seat of Orange County, and the local newspaper is called the *News of Orange*. The town is an odd setting for the headquarters of America's largest mail-order purveyor of condoms, sexual devices, and hard-core videos. PHE Inc., publisher of the Adam & Eve catalogue, is the largest private employer in Hillsborough. The company occupies a modern, three-story office building and warehouse, next to a nursing home and a veterinarian's office. Inside the huge warehouse, shelves thirty feet high hold sexually explicit material, conveyer belts speed merchandise across the building, and automatic sorting machines drop packages into large bins according to the customer's zip code. The day I visited PHE, its mail-order operation seemed high-tech and impressive but surreal. Dainty, white-haired southern women—ladies you could easily imagine singing hymns in a Baptist church—were smiling and chatting and packing brightly colored dildos into boxes.

Philip Harvey, the owner of PHE, could have stepped out of a play by 2 George Bernard Shaw. Harvey is one of the most influential figures in the American sex industry today. The leading producers of hard-core films trek regularly to North Carolina, to visit Harvey and his staff, promote their latest releases, and seek financing for new productions. Harvey is widely respected not only because of his company's huge buying power but also because of his willingness, like Sturman's,* to battle the federal government. Harvey was one of the primary targets of the Justice Department's National Obscenity Enforcement Unit, created after the Meese Commission. His stubbornness helped to derail the war on pornography waged by the Reagan and Bush administrations. Few of his associates in the sex industry are aware, however, that Philip Harvey leads a double life. He spends part of each month in Hillsborough, running PHE, and the rest in Washington, D.C., where he runs a nonprofit corporation devoted to AIDS prevention and family planning.

For more than twenty-five years Harvey has managed family planning 3 programs in developing nations and written dozens of articles on population control for academic journals. He has spent millions of dollars earned in Hillsborough to fund nonprofit programs overseas. Harvey currently supervises projects in India, Ethiopia, Brazil, Vietnam, Malaysia, Indonesia, and the Philippines. This dual life often has its ironies. During the late 1980s, while officials at the Justice Department were doing all they could to put Harvey in prison for obscenity violations, officials at the State

*Reuben Sturman, a wholesale distributor of magazines (some of which were pornographic) who sued FBI director J. Edgar Hoover in the 1960s, is a hero of the free speech movement. See Eric Schlosser's *Reefer Madness: Sex, Drugs, and Cheap Labor in the American Black Market* for more information on Sturman's legal battles.

Department's Agency for International Development were working closely with him to make contraceptives widely available in the Third World.

Harvey has the bearing of a patrician and the slightly rumpled, tweedy   4 appearance of an Ivy League professor, with reading glasses often perched atop his head. He was born in 1942 and raised outside Peoria, Illinois. His father owned a company that manufactured farm equipment. Harvey attended Exeter and then Harvard University, majoring in Slavic languages and literature. After college and a brief stint in the army, he joined the Cooperative for American Relief Everywhere (CARE). Like many idealistic young people in the 1960s, he wanted to experience a different culture and do something useful. CARE sent him to India, where he spent five years distributing American food to schoolchildren throughout the country. Although the amount of food donated by the U.S. government increased each year, the number of Indian schoolchildren in the program increased even faster. Harvey realized that helping India reduce its population growth was ultimately more important than supplying it with surplus grain. After returning from India in 1969 Harvey received a grant from the Ford Foundation to do graduate work in family planning and population control at the University of North Carolina, in Chapel Hill.

As his graduate thesis Harvey submitted a proposal for the mail-order   5 marketing of condoms. His thesis adviser was unaware that what Harvey proposed was a violation of America's obscenity laws. The Comstock Law still prohibited sending contraceptives, or even information about birth control, through the U.S. mail. Undaunted, Philip Harvey and Timothy Black, a British physician and advocate of family planning, set up a mail-order company in 1970 to sell condoms throughout the United States. The firm's questionable legality prevented it from gaining charitable status, and so the two men created a separate nonprofit corporation, Population Services International (PSI), to distribute contraceptives among the poor overseas. Harvey placed ads in college newspapers across the United States, offering condoms through the mail with the pitch: "Sex Is Your Business (Birth Control Is Ours)." Orders started rolling in, and Black soon left for Africa to manage the foreign operation. With the profits from his domestic condom sales, Harvey became a pioneer in the "social marketing" of contraceptives. Instead of relying on overburdened medical and clinical bureaucracies to provide birth control in developing countries, PSI used the same commercial distribution networks that managed to supply even the most remote villages with brand-name consumer goods. High-quality condoms were provided by PSI at low cost to local entrepreneurs, who sold them at a profit. Harvey came to believe that market forces could distribute birth control products more effectively than any government agency.

The ban on selling condoms through the mail was lifted by President   6
Nixon in 1972, and Harvey's business grew. Condoms were still a product
with a bad reputation, kept behind the counter at most drugstores. Even
Playboy refused to run Harvey's condom ads. He came up with all kinds of
promotions to change the condom's tawdry image; once a year he offered a
multicolored Christmas sampler. He was sued by the State of New York,
where condoms could be sold only at pharmacies. The case reached the U.S.
Supreme Court, and Harvey won. Following the advice of Julian Simon's
classic text, *How to Start and Operate a Mail-Order Business,* Harvey tried
to diversify his product line, offering books on birth control, birth control
pills, and pregnancy testing through the mail. None of these products sold
well. He tried selling leisurewear, digital clocks, and model airplanes to his
condom customers, also without success. But every time a book with erotic
pictures appeared in his catalogue, the number of orders soared. Harvey
started the Adam & Eve catalogue in 1975, offering sexually explicit materials, lingerie, and massage oils, in addition to condoms. When hard-core
videos appeared in the catalogue, it became a multi-million-dollar business.

Philip Harvey thought that mail-order was the most socially responsible   7
way to sell sexually explicit material. A mail-order company had few adverse
effects on its community. No customers streamed in and out of its building at
odd hours. There was none of the criminal activity that adult bookstores often attracted. Customers could obtain what they wanted discreetly. And people who were offended by sexually explicit material were not confronted with
public displays of porn or lurid storefront advertising. Hard-core videos could
be shipped throughout the country from North Carolina, unobtrusively, in
plain brown envelopes. But the same factors that made Adam & Eve a great
success also made it a leading target of President Reagan's campaign against
pornography. In the eyes of those who opposed obscenity, there was no proper
way to distribute hard-core videos. As Anthony Comstock had warned more
than a century before, the mail was "the most powerful agent" for disseminating obscene materials, because "it *goes everywhere* and is *secret.*"

By the mid-1980s, Charles H. Keating, Jr., was no longer just a Cincin-   8
nati attorney who crusaded against porn. He'd become one of the leading
fund-raisers for the Republican party, head of the American Continental
Corporation, and owner of the Lincoln Savings & Loan. Keating lobbied
President Reagan for another national commission on pornography, one
that would reach the correct conclusions this time. Both the Meese Commission and the federal legislation that stemmed from it were greatly influenced by attorneys at Keating's antipornography group, now called
Citizens for Decency through Law (CDL). Indeed, the Justice Department's
National Obscenity Enforcement Unit had originally been proposed by

CDL. When it was formed in 1987, CDL attorneys joined the staff. After more than thirty years of campaigning against pornography, Keating had finally gained the power to get something done. His desire to see the nation's porn merchants "rot in prison" now had the full support of the president, the attorney general, and the Justice Department.

The Supreme Court's ruling on obscenity in 1973, which gave local   9
communities the power to enforce their own standards of decency, had originally been intended to protect conservative districts from the looser morality of liberal ones. The National Obscenity Enforcement Unit tried to use the ruling to achieve a very different aim, attempting to impose the morality of conservative towns on the rest of the nation. The unit commissioned studies to discover where juries in the United States were most likely to vote for obscenity convictions—and then it sought the indictment of national distributors, under federal law, in those districts. H. Robert Showers, the head of the unit, was a former assistant U.S. attorney from North Carolina. He thought *Playboy* fit the legal definition of obscenity, hoped to rid the nation of soft-core porn, as well as hard-core material, and often signed his official correspondence "Yours Truly in Christ."

With Project Wormwood, the Reagan Justice Department targeted South-   10
ern California's major producers of hard-core videos. Instead of indicting them in California, where juries were unlikely to convict them, the government sent federal agents from Arkansas, Alabama, Oklahoma, and Florida to a porn industry convention, posing as video store owners. These agents sought out hard-core producers and solicited their products. When hard-core videos arrived by mail at the phony stores in conservative communities—such as Tallahassee, Florida; Tulsa, Oklahoma; and Aberdeen, Mobile, and Birmingham, Alabama—federal prosecutors indicted the California porn companies for interstate transportation of obscene material. Dozens of hard-core producers and distributors were indicted in this way. Wormwood failed, however, to destroy the adult film industry. Through plea bargains and the intervention of sympathetic federal judges, most of the defendants received short sentences and/or large fines. "We always used to worry about being extorted by the mob," one hard-core producer told me, while discussing Wormwood. "Then all of a sudden it was the federal government hitting us up for money."

Project Postporn was aimed at mail-order companies that sold sexually   11
explicit material. The basic strategy was outlined by a CDL attorney in 1983, then described at greater length two years later by Brent Ward, one of Utah's U.S. attorneys, in a memo to Attorney General Meese. Ward argued that mail-order companies should be hit with "multiple prosecutions (either simultaneous or successive) in all levels of government in many locations." He thought that a single company should face as many as thirty-

five different criminal prosecutions at once, all over the United States. The idea, as later adopted by the Justice Department, was not to secure a conviction through an obscenity trial, but to mount so many prosecutions at once that a mail-order company would be forced out of business simply by the cost of mounting a defense. The federal government had almost unlimited resources for such a fight; mail-order companies did not. The U.S. Attorney's Manual permitted such multiple-district prosecutions only in unusual situations, but it discouraged the strategy because of its "unfairness" to the defendant. At the direction of Assistant Attorney General William Weld, the Justice Department later rewrote its manual and "encouraged" multiple prosecutions in obscenity cases.

On May 29, 1986, Philip Harvey's warehouse in North Carolina was   12
raided by approximately thirty federal and state law enforcement agents, including at least one federal agent from Utah. PHE's employees were kept in the building all day for questioning, and their personal belongings were searched. Harvey was caught completely by surprise. Members of the Christian Action League of North Carolina had been ordering Adam & Eve catalogues for years and then complaining to federal officials. But the FBI had investigated Harvey's company in 1984 and had determined that nothing it sold was obscene. Indeed, local FBI agents refused to participate in the raid on Harvey's warehouse. U.S. postal inspectors were recruited instead, some of them joining the investigation with reluctance.

When Harvey's attorneys, John Mintz and Wade Smith (a former FBI ad-   13
ministrator), met with federal prosecutors from Utah and North Carolina to explore a possible plea bargain, they were told that as part of any deal, Harvey would have to stop selling hard-core and soft-core videos. He would have to stop selling books like *The Joy of Sex*. Although financially secure and engaged in meaningful, nonprofit work, Harvey wouldn't accept that sort of deal. He refused to be bullied by the government. "There comes a point in life," Harvey later recalled, "when you simply have to say *enough is enough.*"

Carl Fox, the district attorney in Orange County, North Carolina,   14
thought that prosecuting Philip Harvey for obscenity would be a waste of time and taxpayer money. But George Hunt, the district attorney in neighboring Alamance County, disagreed and indicted Harvey on eight counts of disseminating obscene material under state law. Federal prosecutors assisted Hunt's prosecution. If Hunt could prove that Harvey's merchandise violated the community standards of his own state, obscenity convictions might be easier to obtain elsewhere. In March, 1987, Harvey went on trial in Alamance County. Half of the jurors were born-again Christians, and one was a minister's son. The prosecution showed hard-core videos in the courtroom, including a lengthy orgy scene that featured porn star Vanessa Del

Rio. Harvey's attorney argued that this material appealed to a healthy, not a prurient, interest in sex. He introduced no evidence in Harvey's defense. The jury deliberated for five minutes and then found Harvey not guilty on all counts. "It just seems like the government is trying too hard to regulate what we look at," Robert West, the foreman of the jury, told the *Greensboro News and Record*. Support from the local community gave Harvey a tremendous boost, but his troubles were far from over. "We must regain momentum after the Adam & Eve verdict," one U.S. attorney in North Carolina wrote to his staff, "and come with as many indictments as possible."

The multiple prosecutions of Project Postporn were coordinated by a   15
dozen attorneys at the National Obscenity Enforcement Unit. H. Robert Showers selected the mail-order companies to be targeted, chose the districts in which to prosecute them, set the timetables for prosecution, and demanded approval of all search warrants, indictments, and plea bargains. Postporn was a centrally organized, nationwide effort by the federal government to stop the distribution of all sexually explicit materials through the mail. It achieved a good deal of success. Karl Brussel, his wife, and his son, the operators of a mail-order company called Brussel/Pak Ventures, were indicted in four different districts, with trials set to begin at intervals of two weeks or less. Brussel accepted a plea bargain in which he promised to shut down his business, never sell sexually explicit materials again, and serve a year in federal prison. Avram C. Freedberg, the owner of a Connecticut mail-order company, faced pending indictments in Connecticut, Mississippi, Indiana, and Delaware. When he challenged the Justice Department's tactics, the obscenity unit threatened to indict his wife as well. Freedberg accepted a plea bargain, dissolved his company, and promised never to promote, sell, or distribute predominantly sexual material again. Five other mail-order companies were driven out of business through similar plea bargains—without any judicial ruling that what they sold was obscene.

Aware that federal grand juries in Utah, Kentucky, and North Carolina   16
were investigating Adam & Eve, Philip Harvey struck back. He sued the Justice Department, asserting that its threat of multiple prosecutions abridged his First Amendment rights. In July, 1990, U.S. District Court Judge Joyce Hens Green ruled that the government was indeed trying to suppress "constitutionally protected activities through the use of harassment." Judge Green issued a preliminary injunction that prevented the Justice Department from prosecuting Harvey in more than one district at a time. The Justice Department responded a few weeks later, indicting Harvey on obscenity charges in Utah—even though his company had not sent any catalogues or merchandise to Utah in more than four years. Harvey

challenged the indictment in federal court. On May 26, 1992, the Tenth Circuit Court of Appeals dismissed Harvey's Utah obscenity indictment, declaring that there was "substantial evidence" that the Justice Department had used "repeated criminal prosecutions to chill the exercise of First Amendment rights." Harvey had forced the government to abandon its threats of multiple prosecutions, and he had avoided an obscenity conviction. But his victory was not complete. The Justice Department attacked on a new front, one month before President George H. W. Bush left office, raiding Harvey's warehouse again and seizing a list of his Alabama customers. In a plea bargain with federal prosecutors in Alabama, Harvey later confessed to having violated U.S. postal regulations by using the wrong-sized typeface on his envelopes in 1985, a misdemeanor punished with a $250,000 fine.

Although battling the Reagan and Bush administrations cost Harvey   17
more than $3 million in legal fees, Project Postporn actually helped his company. It wiped out many of his mail-order competitors and dissuaded others from entering the business. About 30 million copies of the Adam & Eve catalogue are now distributed each year in the United States, attracting more than 2 million customers. Most of these customers are white, middle class, married, and suburban. Adam & Eve no longer sends catalogues to the rural areas of some southern states. Customers from those areas have complained, but Harvey isn't seeking another fight with the government. Before including any new product in his catalogue, he now submits it to a group of consultants who belong to the American Association of Sex Educators, Counselors and Therapists. An independent reviewer must conclude that a product is not harmful before Adam & Eve will sell it. Harvey considers the review process valuable not only from a legal point of view but also for his company's morale: three-quarters of PHE's employees are women.

In 1990 Harvey began to produce sex education videos, and his com-   18
pany has become the leader in that field, advertising in mainstream magazines such as *Rolling Stone* and the *Atlantic Monthly.* Harvey feels grateful to have survived an assault by groups who claimed to have "the righteousness of the Lord and the might of the U.S. government" on their side. He still travels regularly to developing nations to meet with the administrators of his family planning projects. One of our conversations was interrupted by a call from Addis Ababa. Harvey now distributes oral rehydration salts in Ethiopia, for children with severe diarrhea, as part of his overseas social marketing program. And he recently added "The Nina Hartley Collection," a line of products endorsed by the star, to his catalogue. The Nina Hartley Love Doll sells for $149.95, batteries not included.

Thinking Critically

1. What rhetorical strategies does Eric Schlosser use in paragraph 1 of "Adam and Eve"? Why does he begin his essay with this information? What underlying significance might he be suggesting by this series of contrasts? What other instances of irony do you note in this article? Does Schlosser make use of irony intentionally, and for what effect? Or is the irony, in at least some cases, purely accidental?

2. What was the federal government's objective in prosecuting Philip Harvey and others through the National Obscenity Enforcement Unit? What arguments were made in Harvey's defense?

Writing Critically

1. As you've seen with other issues discussed in *Many Americas,* occasionally unlikely alliances spring up around provocative social and political issues. In a research paper, describe an unlikely alliance united around one of the issues discussed in "Adam and Eve." How do these otherwise opposing organizations find common ground? How effective is their alliance?

2. The late Supreme Court justice Potter Stewart said, by way of defining pornography, "I know it when I see it." In a research paper, discuss the U.S. Justice Department's working definitions of *obscenity* and *pornography,* and argue how they might apply—or not—to some aspect of popular culture. Begin at the Justice Department's website: <http://www.usdoj.gov/>.

3. How has the marketing of condoms and other "sexual health" merchandise changed in recent years? What are some of the main reasons for these changes? (For example, Schlosser reports that the ban on selling condoms through the mail wasn't lifted until 1972, and for years afterward people were still as embarrassed to purchase them as store owners were to sell them.)

Tex Ed

LYNN HARRIS

Writer, comedian, Yale graduate, and ice-hockey player Lynn Harris is co-creator of the website BreakupGirl.net and author of *Breakup Girl to the Rescue! A Superhero's Guide to Love . . . and Lack Thereof* (2000). She frequently writes about relationships between men and women (especially what goes wrong in those relationships) for magazines including *Glamour* and *GQ.* "Tex Ed" appeared in *Salon.com* in November 2004. Founded in 1995, *Salon.com* is one of the longest-

This article first appeared in Salon.com, at http://www.Salon.com. An online version remains in the Salon archives. Reprinted with permission.

lasting online general-interest publications. The site is
particularly well known for its in-depth and progres-
sively oriented coverage of politics.

Hey, kids! Want to know how to avoid contracting a sexually trans-   1
mitted disease?

"Get plenty of rest."   2

That's one of the eight STD-prevention steps listed in one of the four   3
high-school and middle-school health textbooks approved for state adoption last week by the Texas State Board of Education (SBOE). "When you're
tired, it's hard to think clearly," the text continues. "Don't put yourself in a
situation in which you have to make a tough choice when you're tired." The
other steps include: "Respect yourself" and "Go out as a group" ("You can
also take the pressure off by double-dating"). No mention is made of the
barrier methods of contraception, such as condoms, that help prevent STDs.
One almost expects to see, in its stead, something about "an apple a day."

Since the SBOE's 13–1 vote on Friday, much attention has been paid   4
to a last-minute—and essentially successful—campaign on the part of
one board member, Republican Terri Leo, to change language in the textbooks to define marriage, in accordance with Texas law, as a "lifelong"
union "between a man and a woman" (as opposed to, say, "people,"
"couples" or, God forbid, "partners"). But the focus on what amounts
to a one-sentence edit in one textbook—by the way, you should see the
suggestions of Leo's that didn't make the cut ("Opinions vary on why
homosexuals, lesbians, and bisexuals as a group are more prone to self-
destructive behaviors like depression, illegal drug use, and suicide")—
while plenty alarming, has partially eclipsed the broader sex-education
debate over these books and its implications nationwide. Leo's efforts,
which evidently surprised many of her colleagues, actually came at the
tail end of six months of tumultuous hearings, closed-door committee
meetings, and agitation on all sides over the issue of what to tell the kids
about contraception. And last week it was decided: Don't tell them anything.

"Well, that's Texas," blue-state parents might think. "My kids will still   5
learn to put a condom on a banana." But Texas is, after California, the
second-biggest U.S. textbook buyer—in a market with only four publishing companies. As such, it's uniquely poised to set the standard. "Publishers design their books around what goes on in Sacramento and Austin,"
says Gilbert T. Sewall, director of the American Textbook Council.

Of the four books just approved in Texas, only one of the student edi-   6
tions mentions, in passing, a form of contraception or disease prevention
other than abstinence. Otherwise, it's all abstinence, all the time. If students

want information about condoms, they're going to have to swipe the teachers editions, two of which will include a listing of contraceptives (along with their failure rates). (Teachers editions are annotated versions of the textbooks that include additional information along with teaching guidelines and suggestions.)

"This is sad for Texas teens," said Samantha Smoot, president of the   7
Texas Freedom Network, an advocacy group that calls itself "a mainstream voice to counter the religious right." Smoot estimates that 4 million teenagers will use the books over the 10-year period for which they were approved. Those teens, she says, "will rely on these textbooks for information that is accurate and up-to-date. Instead of doing the responsible thing and providing high school students with lifesaving information about sex and health, the State Board of Education has left them to fend for themselves and get information from each other and sources like the Internet and MTV."

In an odd switcheroo, proponents of abstinence-only sex ed seem to want   8
it that way. "The information is everywhere," says Kyleen Wright, president of the Texans for Life Coalition, who, when asked how kids who choose to have sex should educate themselves about safety, cited the Web sites of archenemies such as the Kaiser Foundation and Planned Parenthood. "It's in libraries," she continued. "These kids aren't living in a bubble."

No, they're not. Texas has the highest birth rate in the nation for teens   9
aged 15–17. Among the nation's 50 largest cities, Austin, Texas, ranks 15th in percentage of births to teens.

Proponents of abstinence-only sex education also suggest that the birds   10
and the bees are best discussed at home with parents. It's a nice thought, says Austin attorney Deena Kalai, who does extensive pro bono work with teens in crisis and who testified against approval of the textbooks. "They're just not sitting around the dinner table having a family chat about sexuality," she says. For many teens, "It's more like, 'Mom's drunk, Dad beats her up.' There's no communication whatsoever."

Currently, only 15 states require that contraception be "covered" (none   11
requires that it be "stressed") in sex education to begin with. But Texas' example helps pave the way for looser interpretations of the notion of "cover." When approving textbooks, the SBOE is charged specifically, and only, with deciding whether the books in question meet the Texas Essential Knowledge and Skills (TEKS) curriculum standards, in this case for health education. TEKS Article 71 requires that students be able to: "Analyze the effectiveness and ineffectiveness of barrier protection and other contraceptive methods including the prevention of Sexually Transmitted Diseases (STDs), keeping in mind the effectiveness of remaining abstinent until marriage." Critics of the textbooks, offering line-by-line analyses of where they fall short, wonder how texts that don't even mention the word "condom" could come

Diapers and diplomas Some communities encourage pregnant teens and teen mothers to complete their high school education through programs such as the New Futures School in Albuquerque, New Mexico, pictured here.

close to satisfying TEKS. Proponents, however, appeared to be satisfied with the mention of contraceptives in the teachers editions. (Leo's efforts to codify heterosexual marriage thus fell far outside the purview of both TEKS and the SBOE. She did not return phone calls requesting comment.)

Even where school districts have some autonomy (and parental input) 12 in terms of setting sex ed curricula above and beyond the state-approved— and therefore covered by state funds—textbooks, their hands are often tied. Any money for supplemental materials must come either from the federal government—which funds only abstinence programs—or from the district itself, which is unlikely to have a slush fund.

Yet according to at least one survey, there are plenty of parents who'd 13 get behind a sex ed bake sale. An August poll commissioned by Protect Our Kids, a coalition founded to oppose the textbooks, found that 90 percent of Texans "favor teaching students age-appropriate, medically accurate information on abstinence, birth control and prevention of sexually transmitted diseases and HIV." That's up from 86 percent in 2001. (A recent Kaiser Family Foundation survey yielded similar results nationally.) "People understand that this is no longer a controversial issue," says Dan Quinn, spokesman for the Texas Freedom Network, a coalition member. "It's astonishing to see that this is still a matter of debate."

Thinking Critically

1. You know from the headnote preceding "Tex Ed" that author Lynn Harris is a comedian and satirist as well as a reporter. Does her work as a comedian, or her style as a satirist, show up in "Tex Ed"? Where, and to what effect?

2. According to Harris, what are the main reasons why parents and educators in other states should be concerned by textbook adoptions in Texas?

3. How balanced is Harris's reporting? (Can you talk about an article in a magazine or newspaper as being balanced or not balanced without disparaging the individual writer or attributing ulterior motives to the publication?) If you were to report on Terri Leo and the Texas State Board of Education's campaign to change language about sexuality in Texas schoolbooks, what additional sources would you consult and why?

Writing Critically

1. Several of the readings in Chapter 9 examine the ways in which schoolyards have become stages for larger social, political, and moral conflicts. Using "Tex Ed" and at least one other reading from *Many Americas,* analyze why it is that the classroom has become a microcosm of a cultural divide.

2. Why is sex education a public health issue? Using Harris's essay as a starting point and conducting additional research as necessary, discuss the impact of sex education on a major public health issue.

3. Compare the websites of major teen-oriented groups that promote sexual health from very different ideological, cultural, and political standpoints. In your essay, describe how you found each website (what keywords did you use? did you get a link from another site?); how clearly each site presents its sponsorship, perspective, and agenda; and the relationship between the site's target audience and the information offered.

Smart and Pretty

VIRGINIA POSTREL

Economic journalist and commentator Virginia Postrel is a columnist for the business section of the *New York Times* and contributes a quarterly column to the business magazine *Forbes.* The author of *The Future and Its Enemies* (1998) and *The Substance of Style* (2003), from which "Smart and Pretty" is excerpted, Postrel examines popular culture and social issues through the lens of economic science. For ten years, she was the editor of *Reason* magazine, a libertarian journal that describes itself as "a refreshing alternative to right-wing and left-wing opinion magazines by making a principled case for liberty and individual choice in all areas of human activity." As editor, she founded the magazine's website, <http://reason.com/>. In an interview about *The Substance of Style* on *Atlantic Unbound,* a web-only publication by the magazine *Atlantic Monthly,* Postrel observed that "I consider it a form of progress that the marketplace gives people not just what they *need* in a subsistence sense, but what they *want.* Because I measure progress as having to do with people's ability to create the kind of lives they want to live. Some happiness comes from big-picture things. But a lot of it also comes from the little daily pleasures of life."

Specialization goes only so far in meeting the aesthetic imperative. No   1
matter how many consultants you hire, personal appearance isn't something you can contract out like gardening or restaurant design. You can pay someone to paint your nails, color your hair, or wax your eyebrows, but they're still *your* nails, *your* hair, and *your* eyebrows. Specialists may do a better, faster job than you could, but you have to be there when they do it. Hence Showalter's* cri de coeur: If technology can make embroidered shoes and typeset résumés cheap and easy, why can't it deliver personal beauty at a lower cost in time and money? *There should be pills for it!*

No form of aesthetics matters more to us than personal appearance, the   2
most inescapable signal of identity. We are not just visual, tactile creatures; we are visible, touchable creatures, inextricably bound to the bodies others see us in. That human consciousness arises from and inhabits physical form is the great mystery and the fundamental reality of our existence. Our bodies are us. Yet our sense of self does not always match our physical form. Our bodies impose definitions and limitations that falsify our identities and frustrate our purposes.

Memoirist Barbara Robinette Moss is a dark-eyed brunette with pale,   3
perfect skin, an oval face, and neat, symmetrical features. Looking out from the pages of a fashion-magazine interview, she seems completely at home. Yet her lovely, tranquil face is not the one nature decreed. "By the time I was thirteen, my face had grown askew," she writes.

> The upper portion of my skull had become so long it forced my lower jaw back, allowing it no room to develop. My puffy, red upper gum

*Elaine Showalter (b. 1941), influential feminist literary critic, professor emerita at Princeton University, and self-described "champion shopper."

line showed, and my upper teeth protruded so much that I couldn't touch my lips together. I could put my baby sister's fist in my mouth without opening it, a game that made her laugh. . . .

I thought of my twisted face as a Halloween mask, hoping to toss it aside. New faces are not easily acquired, though, and if your parents have seven kids and live in poverty, it seems impossible.

In her late twenties, Moss had experimental surgery to change her   4
looks. A teaching hospital covered the cost in exchange for permission to let medical students and a film crew follow the complex operation. Her father warned that Moss wouldn't recognize herself once the doctors finished cutting and moving her bones.

I'll recognize myself, I thought. I've always been right here, underneath, like an underground spring. As I was wheeled into surgery, a few months later, I told the doctor, "Just cut away everything that's not me."

In an interview, Moss says she "always planned on discovering the face I   5
have now. It was like wearing a concrete mask, then just chipping away until I got to the real face underneath. When I finally got my face, I knew it was mine." Some critics see in such dramatic surgical alteration "a thoroughly superficial identity that someone has built with a scalpel." But to the person who inhabits a once-false face, that scalpel-built identity is anything but superficial. It is a surface that finally matches the substance perceived from within.

Advancing biomedical technologies give us control over biological con-   6
ditions our ancestors would have accepted as only natural. Some of these conditions meet the traditional criteria for disease, but many do not, at least not without contortions. Critics of plastic surgery rightly scoff at treating small breasts or big noses as the equivalent of asthma or diabetes. Moss's old face was unusual and ugly, the unwanted product of genetic bad luck, malnutrition, and medical neglect. But it was not, strictly speaking, diseased. Moss had had no accident and suffered no birth defect. By the time of her surgery, her functional limitations had already been repaired with braces and headgear to improve her bite. She could have lived the rest of a normal, healthy life with her old face. But, in some important way, it wouldn't have been the real her. Her inner identity did not match her outer self. High-tech and artificial, aesthetic surgery let her claim her authentic face.

We unnecessarily torture the language when we insist that every undesir-   7
able biological condition must be called a disease in order to justify changing it. It is more accurate to say we are biological creatures whose consciousness defies the limitations of our form. Not all those limitations threaten life or cause physical pain. But that doesn't mean we don't want to alter them—to redesign our bodies for the sake of meaning and pleasure as well as function, to match our outer and inner selves. Indeed, no aesthetic technology is more

welcome, or more potentially meaningful, than one that gives us greater control over our own looks, allowing us to align our bodies with our minds.

As much as we yearn for their powers, however, we often fear the march 8 of beauty technologies. The more our bodies become subject to design—to willful aesthetic control rather than random chance—the more responsibility we face not only for who we are and how we act but for how we appear. That prospect can be exhilarating, but it is also scary. Most of us are not as desperate as Moss. We can live with our old faces, despite their flaws, as long as the rest of the world doesn't expect perfection. But what if standards keep rising? Are we doomed to spend all our time and energy in an impossible quest for beauty?

To understand why that all-consuming quest is an unlikely prospect, we 9 have to separate two aspects of any aesthetic technology: what's possible and what it costs. Many aesthetic results are possible but uncommon, either because they're not desirable or because they're simply too difficult or expensive to justify in most circumstances. With little difficulty, you can have blue hair or, with contact lenses, red eyes. But most people don't want them. And just as not every public rest room has a marble floor, not everyone is up for plastic surgery. The gain is simply not worth the cost. Just because a change is medically possible won't make it pervasive. Cost matters, and so does desire.

It's easy to lose sight of how that balance operates. Both fans and crit- 10 ics tend to hype beauty technologies, treating them as more common than they are. In its annual "Age Issue," *Vogue* informs readers that an "ageless society" is here, courtesy of the plastic surgeon's scalpel:

> Instead of a secret weapon of 50- and 60-year-olds, cosmetic surgery is now a beauty tool seized upon by their daughters. Instead of a painstaking means for serious repair, it is now an often relatively hassle-free method for upkeep, meticulous tweaking, and even age prevention. And instead of a luxury for the wealthy, it is sometimes considered a necessity for anyone with a decent income. . . . With cosmetic-surgery techniques safer, easier, and closer to foolproof—or so women think—the traditional markers of age are fast disappearing from the collective visage of American women.

Vogue paints a misleadingly jolly picture, making surgical "tweaking" 11 sound barely more complicated than manicures. We squeamish readers know better, which is why most of us aren't rushing to make "upkeep" appointments.

The costs that exasperate Showalter also limit our expectations. Most 12 of us don't seriously consider plastic surgery, because it's painful, risky, time-consuming, and expensive. It's gross, and we can't even be sure we'll like the results. We're not going to spend our lives in anesthesia and recovery so surgeons can keep fixing our falling faces. Plastic surgery is more and more common, but it's hardly the norm. The costs—in pain, danger, and time, as well as money—are simply too high.

But suppose cosmetic surgery, or a substitute technology, really were 13 "hassle-free"—as painless, low risk, inexpensive, reliable, and correctable as hair coloring. Our reactions would surely change. When fixing physical flaws is safe and easy, even people who care only a little about their looks will do it, because doing so requires sacrificing very little else. As costs drop, artifice begins to turn aesthetic have-nots into haves. Good teeth and clear skin used to be the unusual markers of exceptional beauty. Now they're the signs only of normal care and attention. Poverty still leaves its marks, as it did on Moss, but even those are often reparable. Technology and commerce bestow beauty more equally than fate. Give us a way to be smart *and* pretty, and we'll take it.

The cheaper and easier aesthetic technologies get, the more we use 14 them. At the same time, however, those falling costs keep look and feel from crowding out all other values. We may be able to have more of everything, especially if incomes are rising. But even in a less optimistic case, we can have a lot more aesthetics in exchange for just a little less of other things. The age of look and feel is a product of those shifting relative costs. As a result, the aesthetic imperative does not consume us. We don't wind up spending all our time and attention on appearances.

Unless, of course, we want to. Just as athletes and intellectuals lead un- 15 balanced lives by the standards of those with other priorities, so some people find enormous meaning and pleasure in personal beauty. A marketing executive and part-time swimsuit model says she happily gave up brainy Washington, D.C., for Miami's high-maintenance South Beach culture of tanning, teeth bleaching, and cosmetic-surgery touchups. "She feels she must be beautiful—svelte, taut, curvaceous, tanned and expensively styled—to belong in this community where striking beauty is common," recounts a reporter. She doesn't mind the effort, or the shallowness of the culture. South Beach suits her. "Like so many other people here, she loves walking into it, competing, posing."

With their single-minded focus on appearance, the denizens of South Beach 16 make a disturbing cultural model. To people with other values and interests, they seem boring and superficial. A society dominated by such people would quickly stagnate. Even the progress of beauty technologies depends on people who care about something more enduring than partying and looking good: surgeons, chemists, computer programmers, dental researchers, and many others. But the beautiful people of South Beach don't represent the future, at least not for most of us. They're just a subculture, a specialized niche made up of those who care about beauty not merely on the margin but first and foremost. These folks aren't waiting for Showalter's time-saving beauty pills.

One of our greatest anxieties about beauty technologies, however, is not   17
that they'll be too dangerous, exclusive, expensive, or time-consuming—
and thus limited to South Beach enthusiasts—but that they'll be too safe,
prevalent, and cheap. Everybody will use them, and we'll all wind up looking the same. To stoke fears of genetic medicine, *World Watch* magazine created a cover montage of naturally brunette people—an Amazonian child, a
sari-clad woman, an African-American boy, and so forth—with bright blue
eyes. The message was clear: If changing eye color becomes too easy, people will alter what nature decrees. The world will get weird and homoge-
neous. Everybody will have blue eyes.

To the disgust of its opponents, genetic medicine promises not only bet-   18
ter health but more aesthetic control, even without the prenatal modifications that are so controversial. Within a decade or two, it's quite possible
we'll be able to build our muscles, cure our baldness, or lighten and darken
our skin with gene therapy. Unlike the genetic engineering that would alter
a person's genetic makeup before birth, gene therapy seeks to change the
cells of an already-living person. People with hemophilia or cystic fibrosis,
for instance, might be cured by inserting genes that change their blood or
lung cells; the genes they pass on to their children would remain unchanged. Although these disease treatments themselves are still in the future, and other sorts of gene therapy may be even further off, a leading
geneticist predicts that cosmetic gene therapy will "spread like wildfire"
once it's affordable and effective.

The more power we achieve over how our bodies look, whether   19
through genetics, surgery, drugs, or other means, the more we will alter our
outer selves to match our inner selves. But as long as those biological decisions are up to individuals themselves, it's foolish to dread a uniformly
blue-eyed world. Plenitude and self-expression are as central to the age of
look and feel as the pleasures of universal forms. We want to look good but
also to look special, to incorporate both the beauty of aesthetic universals
and the markers of unique identity. We don't all dress the same. Why would
we all want the same color eyes?

The age of look and feel works against a single aesthetic standard—   20
whether for persons, places, or things—because the aesthetic imperative itself has emerged from pluralism and the individual pursuit of happiness
and meaning. Most people prefer clear skin, but we like it in many different shades. Some of us even want tattoos. Blond hair is cheap and easy already, and, as a result, has become far more common. But the world is still
full of brunettes, redheads, and the occasional person with green or blue
hair. What is vanishing is not diversity but gray hair, the mark of age, and
even that is unlikely to disappear altogether.

When aesthetic choices are left to individuals, we wind up with variety, 21 because tastes and identities differ. The particular mix itself changes over time, as the desire for novelty keeps any single style from becoming permanent. If cosmetic genetic therapy ever does spread like wildfire, we can expect it to come in a reversible, or changeable, form. Permanent aesthetic modifications are rarely as popular as temporary ones. Reversibility not only lowers risks. It allows for fashion.

Thinking Critically

1. How does Virginia Postrel define aesthetics?

2. How does Postrel use hypothetical situations to advance or support her argument? What qualities must a hypothetical situation have in order to be acceptable in the service of an argument?

Writing Critically

1. In contemporary American culture, what kinds of assumptions about a person's intelligence, ethics, and performance are likely to be made based on that person's looks? On what basis are these assumptions made, and how can they be measured? Are these standards fair? Why or why not? (Your argument should focus on personal aesthetics as defined by Virginia Postrel in "Smart and Pretty.")

2. Is there a difference between having your body physically altered to make it more attractive and using mood- or mind-enhancing drugs to make your personality and behavior more attractive? Are there any circumstances under which people should be required to have cosmetic surgery or take certain medications to enhance their appearance or smooth out their behavior?

3. In paragraph 21, Postrel claims that "When aesthetic choices are left to individuals, we wind up with variety, because tastes and identities differ." Challenge or support her claim as it applies to any aspect of consumer culture (fashion, music, food, automobiles, furniture—anything that meets the general criteria of being desirable but not necessary).

Big Country

RICHARD KLEIN | A professor of French at Cornell University and an unabashed advocate for the exercise of individual choice when it comes to life's pleasures, Richard Klein is the author of *Cigarettes Are Sublime* (1993) and *EAT FAT* (1996). In *Cigarettes Are Sublime,* he explores the seductive image of the cigarette in American and European culture, and he analyzes the seductive allure of

cigarettes in European and American popular culture
and its effect on his own struggle to quit smoking. *EAT
FAT,* which one reviewer called the "first postmodern
diet book," took its own pleasurable toll on Klein; he
revealed to a *Seattle Times* book reviewer that he gained
thirty-five pounds while researching and writing it.
Writing in the *New York Times,* a reviewer praised
Klein's "contrarian originality, his bon vivant's outrage,
his iconoclastic logic as he ranges over the various
aspects of his subject." "Big Country" was the cover
story for the September 19, 1994, issue of the *New
Republic.* Founded in 1914 and based in Washington,
D.C., the *New Republic* covers politics, society, and
culture from a variety of opinions and perspectives. For
more information, go to its website: <http://tnr.com/>.

S tatistics recently released by the Centers for Disease Control confirm what 1
is everywhere visible, the dramatic jump in obesity from 1980 to 1991.
One-third of American adults, up from one-quarter, are overweight. The richest nation in the world is the fattest and growing fatter. Our behinds, seen on
television or on tourists, have become the butt of jokes in every culture but
our own. Weighed down by our guilty burden, more and more obsessed with
fat, we are becoming as a nation increasingly obese. Why now? Why more
than ever do people have fat on their minds, while they add it to their hips?
Perhaps it's the spirit of the times, a heavy moment in some long cycle of fat
years and lean. Or maybe the approaching millennium arouses inordinate
anxieties and a spirit of jubilation, as at New Year's, when we celebrate to
mask the fear of a transitional moment. Perhaps we are entering anew the
banquet years, like those that marked the end of the last century, when every
public and private event was an occasion to be celebrated at great ritual feasts
reflecting confidence, wealth and trepidation. In the next few years banquet-
ing will probably abound. Not just a new century, but a new order dawns,
one hopes—and fears. And in the meantime, what better to do than to eat?

The CDC statistics remind us, too, that the 1980s witnessed the steady 2
impoverishment of the poor and the middle class. You get fatter in this
country as you get poorer, thinner as you get richer. The highest proportion of overweight people are African American women (49.5 percent) and
Mexican American women (47.9 percent). What you weigh, it turns out,
has as much to do with what's in your pocket as what's in your food. Oprah
may be genetically disposed to being fat, but her edifying example reveals
that genetics can be thwarted. In America, money triumphs over the most

resistant fat, which eventually succumbs to the regimes that only the very rich, or the fanatical, can afford.

How can I go on without expressing the rage I feel toward the word and toward the concept of "obesity"? That ugly noun, with its inescapable pejorative implications, this term for unhealthy corpulence, has been mobilized by the medical-health-beauty establishment, and wielded by food packagers, in order to stigmatize people who do not conform to an absurdly restrictive concept of ideal weight. The image of the body beautiful, the ideal of health it promotes, is an ideological construct, a false nature, conceived by a vast industry in order to sell its services and move its products. Removing fat, the latest medical fad (does anyone think it soon won't be something else?), eliminates one more pleasure from our diet. After alcohol and tobacco, now fat has been proscribed. America, under the spur of its persistent Puritanism, cruelly medicalized the pleasures it most permanently indulges—turning every mild narcotic, even art, into a matter of public health and social morality. The health-industrial complex has already deemed food to be medicine, and fat poison.

The constant moralizing about food is becoming feverish. It is nearly impossible to avoid. Why, then, is everybody so fat? And getting fatter? My hypothesis is this: if marketers can create guilt in a population saturated with fat, they can use obesity to sell both health and unhealth. Two messages, simultaneous, contradictory, very effective. The ostensible message is eat no fat; the cynical, maybe unconscious, one is eat.

To wit: Health Valley may make excellent products, but consider the way the company uses statistics provided by the health industry to inform and entice consumers. It tells nothing but the truth, as the truth has been most officially, reliably determined:

> **Why This Fat-Free Chili Is Better for You**
> This chili helps you fulfill the published dietary guidelines of the
> American Heart Association and the National Cancer Society. It is
> fat-free, with no cholesterol. One serving provides 10 percent of the
> U.S. rda of protein, 15 percent of iron and 100 percent of vitamin A
> in the form of beta carotene. Beta carotene is recommended by health
> experts as a key nutrient for maintaining good health. And it contains
> over 50 percent less salt than leading chilis. So you can use this chili
> as part of a healthy diet that may help reduce your risk of heart dis-
> ease and certain forms of cancer.

I rage at this when I see my mother eating Healthy Valley chili filled out with chopped meat, enhanced by cheese, made zesty with salt. It's all right, though, she says to herself. She isn't exactly eating the chili; she's fulfilling dietary guidelines. The more she eats the more she gets of the food medicine it dispenses in the precisely measured, officially approved quantities of the United States Recommended Daily Allowances, especially of beta carotene, recommended by "health experts" (until last month, that is, when it was found not to fend off cancer). She has been lured by the truth on the label into believing she's on the road to getting thinner, while she's actually getting fatter. Her example confirms what a researcher in Philadelphia claims to have discovered scientifically: if people are told food is lower in fat, they tend to eat more of it than they would otherwise.

Go to a supermarket and try to find some fat. From the shelves the boxes 7 and cans scream "no fat." Sometimes you even see New Free, the two words advertisers love most. The more fat-free the better, which means the more it lacks the more it's worth. The supermarket shelves display a whole hierarchy of lack that goes from no fat, to low or lo fat, to less fat, or fewer calories, to the balky litote, "I Can't Believe It's Not Butter," which advertises that it has "50 percent less fat and calories than butter and margarine." It's not exactly good for you, but eat and enjoy; after all, it could be twice as bad.

Observe the dialectical ingenuity it takes to find language to sell what 8 in principle ought not be sellable. Consider the plight of commodities not blessed with no fat. Bacon, for example, has a problem selling itself in the present environment. If not fat-free, but if in fact fat, it can only represent itself as being less than something even more purely more. Swift Premium Sizzlean Breakfast, Lunch and Dinner Strips, to illustrate, have "50 percent less fat than bacon before heating." The advertisers here exploit the ambiguity of the word less, which normally implies that comparative terms are being made explicit, but which in English can stand alone, having only an implied comparison with the Platonic ideal. You don't have to know less than what to be stirred by the appeal of "less fat."

The psychology that motivates the allure of food as medicine is suc- 9 cinctly stated on the package of some Italian biscuits:

> no-no
> "Is a yes-yes"
> New All Natural Biscotti
> Fat-Free Coconut.

No-no is a yes-yes pretty much sums up the rhetorical strategy generating 10 the profusion of figures and forms that sells food in our markets. Like a sexual harasser, the consumer doesn't have to take no for an answer. He can persuade himself that no is yes: a desire that ought to be resisted can be guiltlessly indulged. "Eating fat can make you fat," it says on the chili can. But it neglects to add that eating nothing but fat doesn't necessarily make you obese. It's not eating fat that makes you fat, it's eating. The chili says eat me: no fat in my can, no fat on yours. Of course, there may be circumstances when eating no fat means being thin, but the chili can label creates the illusion that there is some immediate equivalence between this fat and that, between no fat here and no fat there. In fact, eating too much fat-free chili will make you fat.

Ask a Frenchman. It's not the fat we eat. I mean, I have friends from Cal- 11 ifornia who won't go to Paris because they might have to eat there, where everything is fat or prepared in fat. Vegetables are rare. The French hate green. Butter and cheese fill French veins, organ meats and goose fat load their tables; they eat steak and fried potatoes, dessert is ineluctable. And yet they remain as a people less obese than Americans. Ask a French woman who knows America why Americans are obese and she'll say: no discipline of eating. Despite inroads of fast food and progressive industrialization, French eating remains centered around rituals of the meal, with its disciplines. The first rule is no eating between meals. At the beginning of every meal the French wish each other, "Bon appetit." Hunger, the desire to eat, is something to be wished, to be cultivated. Imagine wishing anyone hunger in America. The slightest hint of hunger here instantly provokes a rush to snack. Americans eat all day long, and food is available everywhere. You can eat anything, at any time, in any place. In France, you have to finish your cheese before you get dessert. Pleasure is not immediate; the meal installs an economy of pleasure, which again means manipulating hunger, holding off eating in order to eat later with more pleasure and heightened discrimination.

Fat. A good Anglo-Saxon word. Whereas obese comes from the Latin, 12 *obesus*, "having eaten well," past participle of *obedere*, to eat thoroughly, to devour, to chow down. The noun obesity, rare before the nineteenth century, had a sinister rebirth in popularity under the pen, in the hands of nineteenth-century doctors and health workers seeking to wield power over bodies by policing the language with which one might once have referred, for example, to someone's embonpointment.

By contrast, "fat" is a word that only lately has acquired its unam- 13 biguously negative connotations. If one looks at the many meanings fat has accumulated over its long history in English, one quickly discovers that most of them are positive, flattering, encomiastic, as the Greeks say— bestowing praise. The Teutonic root fat means to hold or contain, like a vessel, particularly a precious one containing baptismal water. Or like a tub. Everything that used to come in a tub or cask was good, like fat, or wine, or beer. Everything tubby is fat. Fat denotes the well supplied: fat purses, fat cheeses. Fat clay is pure; fat wine is fruity, full-bodied; fat land yields abundant returns. A fat position is a desirable one, a fat kitchen is an affluent one and a fat kingdom is where we live.

I think of my mother, who is beautiful, and fat. Who is obese by the 14 doctor's rule. She has lived an excellent life, the last forty years of which she has struggled to be thin, and she did get thin, many times, at vast expense. She lost thousands of pounds, and the more she lost the more she gained, and fat she is to the end. But I know she has never been complacently fat. She has provided herself with the most rigorous check on the pleasure she compulsively seeks. My mother goes to the supermarket to buy some frozen health dinners, grabs a Snickers at the cash register and eats it on the way to the car. First she feels shame for having eaten it all (*obesus*). And then she forgets she ate it at all.

Dieting and overeating is a way of life for my mother; the nature of the quest its rhythm installs is worthy of more respect than it normally receives. It is a kind of yoga, in which you give yourself the pleasure that you simultaneously sacrifice in the name of a higher ideal, making a ritual out of the dialectic of desire and its overcoming. Dieting while growing fatter is an inverted spiritual exercise: every time you break your resolutions you feel such guilt and shame that you eat even more, for consolation and in defiance. More fat motivates more desperate diets, and the yo-yoing builds mountains of it. 15

Other forces speed this cycle along. Statisticians in the bowels of the CDC, actuaries behind gray partitions in Hartford, who (like Wallace Stevens, in their way) divine the heaviness of the republic, recently revised upward, yes upward, the ranges of ideal weight. The U.S. Department of Agriculture has just issued new guidelines defining the "maximum desirable weight" for a man 6' 2½" at 210 pounds, just the amount at which Bill Clinton desirably weighed in at his last presidential checkup. In the race to accommodate more and more fat, one psychologist—Kelly Brownell of Yale—suggests that the best weight for most people is simply the lowest one they've been able to maintain for a year as an adult without struggling. Sound good? 16

At the same time, doctors, as ever faddish, cite new evidence that thin people die young. The clinical director of the National Institute on Aging observes that people middle-aged and older seem to live longer if they're "a bit on the pudgy side." Their fat nourishes them, helps them survive illnesses. That view and the conclusions drawn are contested by the majority of professional people, dietitians and doctors who, viewing the issue dispassionately, insist that it is wrong. They still encourage their patients of all ages to reduce their risk of heart and other ailments that result, they believe, from unhealthy excess weight. In the end, what is one to do? 17

The medicalization of food that accompanies its transformation into a drug has in turn given rise to whole industries of pharmaceutical, medical and nutritional science. Their aim is to find, or at least to sell, a drug that will be an antidote to the drug that makes people fat, namely food. Amphetamines worked for a while by raising metabolisms to way above normal. Though long-term effects of the drugs ended that experiment, we appear poised to be 18 launching a new one. Prozac-like substances, according to *The Wall Street Journal,* are being designed to affect the centers in the brain where happiness resides, turning off depression like a switch. Their aim is not to lift the over-weight to a hypernormal condition, but to drag them out of the depressive state into which their being overweight in this society has thrown them. (Re-minder: one-third of all American adults are overweight.) Given the sur-rounding hysteria, it isn't surprising that being fat makes one blue. Recently, journalist Leslie Lampert disguised herself as obese and, in an article for *The Ladies' Home Journal* titled "Fat like Me," recounted how quickly she be-came depressed. The longer she stayed fat the sadder she became, until in the end she actually got fat from eating to relieve the depression.

Thankfully, the FDA has so far refused to license these chemicals. Nev- 19 ertheless, the very possibility of their deployment shows how far we are pre-pared to go to make the question of weight a medical problem of chemical imbalances. And if the healthy-body-beautiful industry ends by imposing its rhythms on our lives, the marketing possibilities are extraordinary. Compul-sive recreational eating, the restless movement of hand to mouth, will be en-couraged by making food more tasteless, hence more urgently devoured. The obesity it gives rise to will be more and more furiously stigmatized. People will become increasingly depressed at being fat and will spend more and more on food and diets and drugs with the result—if one judges from recent evidence—that we will all be fatter. Fat finds its perfect antidote in pills we pop to shrink the body we are compulsively eating to fatten.

If you think I am exaggerating, consider the logic of the claims found on 20 a bag of Frito-Lays New Baked Tostitos: "Our oven-baked chips let you in-dulge in more snacking fun . . . great taste without guilt. In fact, they have only one gram of fat per serving." For a moment, take that label as an ob-ject of exegesis. It seems unavoidable to note that it is sending a double mes-sage: when you eat me, you eat less, so eat more of me, for the sake of pure recreation. More snacking fun, great taste without guilt. Ordinarily, we know, taste and guilt go together, particularly in this culture. Ordinarily if you push your cart past a bag of Tostitos you think, "No! That's too fat, too good." But these Tostitos are more less, less fat, than ordinary chips. Eat, Eat, I've just made a wonderful decision to eat what I might have passed up—the snacking fun I would have missed. Do marketing strategies like these pro-mote health in our society? Or obesity? The answer, of course, is both, and it works very well, thank you. Except that we keep on getting fatter.

The prejudice that assumes "obese" people are less sexual than normal 21 people ignores the well-known anthropological truth that in many societies women are prized precisely for their great size. Immensely fat they are; "obese" they are not. Were Rubens's women unhealthy, or aren't they the pictures of roseate food health—over-endowed with overlapping folds of delicious fleshiness?

Fat is rococo and beautiful in Boucher, the eighteenth-century court 22 painter. The creamy skin of those large dollops of pink women—ladies, really, with beautiful aristocratic faces, winsome and proud—arouses hunger, quenches thirst. They are at play on billowy couches, and the light suffusing their bodies illuminates the round pillows of downy linen and their satiny flesh, ballooning, effervescent. The most famous Boucher, in the Louvre, features a woman lying on her stomach with her rear in the air looking back in laughter at the painter. The gorgeous display of her colossal adiposis evokes a vastly delicious landscape. O blessed fat!

Face it. Who doesn't dream about fat, spreading its gentle balm over rough 23 surfaces, smoothing hurts and filling up the painful spaces? Fat lends flavor to life, the flavor of everything that smoothly melts in your mouth. Food is the foremost pleasure left to those who despair of having sex. In the age of AIDS, food increasingly permits the displacement of libidinal cathexis—the flow of sexual energy—into substitute gratification. And food, in this country, is everyday becoming more explicitly sexy. Sheila Lukins of *Silver Palate* fame is photographed lying on a table, satirically lowering a bunch of grapes to her deliciously parted lips. There is every reason to expect that the spreading of lo/no fat, with its tasteless blandness, will create in time great national cravings for the pleasure of food, orgies and banquets on a vast scale.

Fat also protects. It is used for defense, like highly developed muscula- 24 tures, concealing the innermost self and putting it at a seemingly greater distance from the world. It makes room and it gives you more room, puts you at a greater distance from others. Not surprisingly, fat is often prized by those in power. It occupies space; it imposes. It lends presence to personality. It serves the interest of what sociologist George Simmel calls the aura of our personality, the signs of physical and social distinction with which we impose our influence on others. From Nero to Henry the VIII, from Winston Churchill to Bill Clinton, fat has always been political.

Helmut Kohl, for example, will probably win a fourth term on a diet 25 that includes pig stomach, saumagen stuffed with potatoes, slab bacon and lard. Annually, he goes to a spa for a month in order to lose twenty pounds; he then proceeds when he returns to his governmental responsibilities to put the weight back on in trump. Every campaign he gets fatter and wins bigger. Kohl's obesity has the virtues of the deutsche mark, whose rough-hewed rotund stability, whose unpretentious but ample solidity, brings peace to the inflation-haunted dreams of the Germans.

Fat also gives dignity to a man whose face does not naturally convey it. 26 William Howard Taft was an enormously fat man—our fattest president.

He was said by his contemporaries to have had a baby face. Bill Clinton's fat has been denigrated by journalists with the same ferocity and cruelty with which it is everywhere stigmatized these days. They see in it the sign of his restless omnivorousness, the compulsive rapidity with which he flits from issue to issue, each one occupying no more of his time than the time it takes to revise his position and pass on to another, just as he goes from burgers to pizza, a piece of cake, diet soda, to filet sandwich, some pot pie: a bite of Bosnia, a taste of Haiti, sushi on crime, munch a bunch of health bill till lunch. In this view of the Clinton presidency, fat is the embodiment of his fatal indecisiveness, his compulsive appetite for policy, his incapacity to stay focused, his constant need for new diversions.

But there is another view, one that does not ridicule this fat, but finds in the 27 presidential girth a sign of what is most impressive and endearing in him. It persists, his fat, despite his exceptional daily athletic feat of running the mile in less than nine minutes. He's corpulent, but he's not unhealthy, obese. And like my mother's, his fat gives me a sense of loving ponderation; what I like most about him is the feeling that this is a man who knows how to sit for a long time and think hard before making fateful decisions. I appreciate that quality, reflected in his fat, in a world in which too many people have instant answers to everything. His fat is quite soothing, if you ask me, just as the rolls on President Taft, at the end of another turbulent century, must have reassured our forebears.

It seems pious to wish that fat were transvalued in this society. It is 28 utopian, no doubt, to imagine another time when being fat would be admired, encouraged and appreciated. But history certainly confirms the suspicion that prejudices against fat obey long historical cycles. Or, at least, that in other ages, fat was beautiful.

Why does fat make people laugh? It is not that fat people are happy; the 29 more laughter they provide, the gloomier they feel. It's that the very appearance of fat, the fact of fat, reveals what ought to be kept hidden, the dirty little secret that the bearer or wearer of fat has a repetitive, compulsive drive to eat. Most of us can hide our vices, if we choose to. Not the fat. Their fat speaks loudly about what is most important in their lives, the minute they walk in a room. That's why fat people spend their lives creating lies about their eating, hiding the moments of bulimia or of repeated sneaking.

Take my mother's fat friend, Jane. For years the two went to spas 30 together. I asked my mother how Jane got so fat. "It wasn't simply genetic," my mother said. "Her father was a 'big' man but her mother wasn't. No, Jane was a sneaky eater."

"What do you mean, Mom?" 31

"She always had candy handy." And as she said that, "candy handy," 32 she made a gesture with her hand like a gambler scooping up the dice, a gesture of urgent appropriation, making yours what no one else at that moment can have. It's mine, this handful of chocolate, and no one is going to interrupt the elegant but powerful gesture with which I take another turn, my turn, my hand at this sure pleasure. This is a pleasure I can enjoy and enjoy being sure in advance of enjoying, since it's always at hand.

"Do you think there are a lot of fat people like Jane who sneak food?" 33 I asked.

"I think most. They want people to think it's genetic." 34

"But why does she have to sneak it? What would happen if anyone saw?" 35

"They'd think she was a pig." 36

"What's a pig?" 37

"A pig is someone who eats when they aren't hungry." 38

"Why do they do that?" 39

"For the pure pleasure of it." 40

"But they're sneaking their pleasure. Maybe they get pleasure from the 41 sneaking?"

"No, I don't think so." 42

"But there has to be a lot of guilt." 43

"Oh! Yes. A lot of guilt." 44

So the pure pleasure of eating without hunger, without need, eating only 45 for taste and well-being, comes accompanied with the cruel inbite of remorse. The pleasure is not pure at all; your conscience is bitten by what you eat. Every time you take that moment out of your day to sink your teeth into the brilliant darkness of a Belgian chocolate, that moment of intense pleasure provokes instantly a pang, a shiver of guilt. Because one cannot live one's life feeling in the eyes of a world like a pig. Poor pig! Little pigs, we know, are like babies, smart silly animals similar to children. Pigs make you laugh because they cannot stop eating. An automatic compulsion, a mechanical repetition, seems to control the pig, and at that moment, for all their resemblance, they are something less than human: little eating machines. We observe them. We observe the distance between their ridiculous shape and our own more or less normal one and we feel superior; at the same time we nervously estimate the not-infinite distance between us and them. Laughter at fat is a compromise between fear that we may be just like those pigs and the fleeting assurance that, at least in our mind's eye, we aren't.

Thinking Critically

1. In what ways does Richard Klein's essay reflect the year it was written? How would his argument change were he to revise this essay in 2005 or 2006?

2. Does "rage" have a place in an argument? How does Klein use his own "rage" to shape his argument in "Big Country"? If you were to write an

argument from a place of personal "rage," what strategies of Klein's would you adapt to use that rage effectively?

3. Klein, a professor of French, is especially interested in the nuances of language. How does he play with the connotative and denotative meanings of different words in "Big Country," and to what effect? Is there a persuasive purpose behind this wordplay?

Writing Critically

1. In his book *Cigarettes Are Sublime,* Klein writes about the temptations of cigarette smoking and the conflicted ways in which smoking is portrayed in popular culture. In "Big Country" he observes that "America . . . cruelly medicalized the pleasures it most permanently indulges—turning every mild narcotic, even art, into a matter of public health and social morality" (paragraph 3). Choose a private pleasure (smoking, drinking, eating, having sex) that has public health implications. Does popular culture play a role in attaching some sort of moral value or stereotype to that behavior? Is there a contradiction between the way that behavior is marketed to consumers and portrayed in popular culture?

2. In recent years, some consumers have sued fast-food restaurants and food manufacturers for contributing to their obesity. Some of these lawsuits were inspired by successful antitobacco litigation. Should corporations that produce and market junk food or fast food be responsible for its effects on their consumers? Use specific recent lawsuits or incidents reported in the media to support your argument. (You might also consult Richard Klein's book *Cigarettes Are Sublime.*)

3. In the previous selection, "Smart and Pretty," Virginia Postrel writes about the chemical, surgical, and genetic lengths to which people will go to achieve a certain standard of aesthetic acceptability. In what ways does Klein challenge a similar "aesthetic"? What is it, according to Postrel and Klein, that really needs to change in America's aesthetic image of the body politic?

Airlines Should Calculate Prices by the Pound

MARC FISHER | *Washington Post* columnist Marc Fisher writes, often provocatively, about daily life, culture, and politics. A selection of his columns is online at <http://www.washingtonpost.com/>. In a 2004 speech to students at Washington and Lee University in Virginia, Fisher reflected on his lifetime as a journalist and his sense of how the media had changed along with American culture: "The past 25 years have brought not only vast changes in the technology and corporate structure of journalism, not only a revolution in the definition of news and the expectations of both news consumers and news providers, but a startling rejiggering of the basic elements of what we do: Truth, fact and information seemed fairly straightforward concepts to most people in the news business a quarter century ago. Today, they're entirely up for grabs." "Airlines Should Calculate Prices by the Pound" appeared in the November 18, 2004, edition of the *Washington Post*.

Two pounds of apples cost more than one. Mailing a big, fat envelope 1 is more expensive than mailing a letter. Smokers pay more for life insurance than do nonsmokers.

So why shouldn't you pay an airline according to how much you weigh 2 and how much space you take up?

A report the other day from the National Center for Environmental 3 Health tells us that our collective national belt-loosening is costing the airlines big money—an extra $275 million in fuel costs in one year to account for the 10-pound average increase in Americans' weight over the past decade.

The airlines are desperately trying to cut fuel costs by cutting the weight 4 they carry—replacing metal utensils with plastic ones, scrapping heavy magazines. But the solution lies directly beneath the floor of the passenger cabin: Charge passengers by the pound, just as freight in the cargo hold is priced.

That would not only help the airlines, but more important, would cre- 5 ate a social and financial disincentive for becoming or staying obese.

As things stand, the one-third of Americans who are not overweight 6 subsidize the two-thirds who are. It's in everyone's interest to shift the balance back toward healthier, slimmer lives.

The last time I took up this quest, a couple of years ago, I had the sad 7 duty to report that L. L. Bean had changed its pricing policy and would charge the same for its clothing no matter the size. It was a big break for the big-boned, and a strike against fairness for everyone else. Traditionally, clothing that's made of more material has, logically enough, cost more than the same item in a smaller size.

But compared with L. L. Bean greedily chasing after the loyalties of its 8 broadening customers, the transportation industry faces a tougher predicament. After all, an airplane seat is only so wide.

Advocates for the obese—yes, they have a Washington lobby, too—re- 9 ject solutions that put the responsibility for obesity squarely on the bellies of the big. The American Obesity Association argues that our commercial and entertainment culture bears a good part of the blame for our becoming a nation of wide loads.

With almost any other malady, we distinguish between people's behav- 10 ior and their affliction. You might behave in ways that make it more likely that you'll get cancer, but when you do get cancer, it's generally perceived as a really bad break that deserves oceans of sympathy. But if you're large, the public reaction is that it's your own darn fault and maybe you should lay off the Mars bars. "We suspend the compassion that we normally feel," as Morgan Downey, director of the obesity group, put it. Instead, we laugh in the general direction of fat people, making a "moral judgment of laziness, lack of self-control, weakness," Downey said.

Fair enough. But accepting the idea that obesity is a community prob- 11 lem actually strengthens the case for creating such disincentives as paying by the pound for air travel.

Yet when Southwest Airlines tried to draw the line against corpulent 12 passengers flowing over onto someone else's seat, the obesity lobby rolled into action. Southwest's policy is simple and fair: If you take up more than one seat, you need to buy the extra seat. The airline refunds the extra charge if there are empty seats on a given flight.

The Obesity Association reacted by asking Southwest to install wider 13 seats for the extra-large. No way, said Southwest, which went ahead with its policy, noting that only six seats per airplane account for their profit margin. Replacing only three rows of seats per plane with extra-wide seats would suck up all their profits, Southwest's president argued.

All that extra weight we're carrying is a burden not only on the airlines' 14 bottom line, but on our very survival. After a commuter plane crashed last year in Charlotte, federal investigators said it might have been overloaded. So the FAA ordered airlines to revise the formula they use to estimate the weights of passengers. The feds tacked an extra 10 pounds on to the assumed average weight of an American adult.

The answer: Public weigh-ins before every flight. Heck, it'll add some 15 entertainment while we wait at the security checkpoints. Shame, a nearly-lost tool of social suasion in this society, is good: Line 'em up, weigh 'em in and watch the pounds come off.

Thinking Critically

1. What genre is "Airlines Should Calculate Prices by the Pound"? How can you tell? What features are unique to this kind of argument, and where are you most likely to find it?

2. What is Marc Fisher's attitude toward obese consumers? How can you tell?

Writing Critically

1. The American Obesity Association is online at <http://www.obesity.org/>. How might a lobbyist from this group argue against Fisher's proposal?

2. Is good health a civic duty? Should it be? Is there a historical precedent for such a view?

Weight Loss Surgery May Soon Be Paid by Medicare

GINA KOLATA

Science writer Gina Kolata, who holds degrees in microbiology and mathematics, is the author of *Ultimate Fitness: The Quest for Truth About Health and Exercise* (2003), *Flu: The Story of the Great Influence Pandemic* (2001), and *Clone: The Road to Dolly and the Path Ahead* (1998). Her reporting on breaking scientific news as well as more in-depth stories on scientific topics have appeared in the *New York Times* since 1987, and she has been unafraid to challenge received wisdom and stir up controversy. Kolata also writes for *Science* magazine, *Smithsonian,* and *Psychology Today,* and she was a Pulitzer Prize finalist for investigative reporting in 2000. She received the 1995 Susan G. Komen Foundation's media award for reporting on women's issues and breast cancer and the annual award given by the American Mathematics Society for reporting on mathematics. Her editor once observed that Kolata "loves to ask the questions everybody is thinking but not asking." "Weight Loss Surgery May Soon Be Paid by Medicare" appeared in the *New York Times* on September 30, 2004.

Carmen J. Pirollo expected his latest attempt to lose weight would take 1
a while. At 5 feet 11 inches, he wanted to weigh 180 pounds, down from 260. A veteran dieter—"I've lost and gained a whole person in my lifetime"—he knew it would not be easy.

But while Mr. Pirollo, a 55-year-old sixth-grade teacher in Haddon 2
Heights, N.J., says he is healthy, he worries that his excess weight might take a toll on his health. And, of course, he wants to look good.

"I'm an American," he says. "We live in a society where people have to 3
be beautiful."

Who should pay for people like Mr. Pirollo to try to lose weight? For 4
decades the answer has almost always been the patients themselves.

That soon may change. 5

At a meeting in November, Medicare's advisers will assess the safety, 6
efficacy and cost of one increasingly popular method of weight loss—
surgery—as a first step in a new policy that could lead to the use of federal money to cover a range of other obesity treatments.

Yet, at a time when coverage by Medicare and other insurers may in- 7
crease, the evidence suggests that few obese people can lose significant
amounts of weight in the long term. And some obesity researchers are also
questioning the fundamental idea that losing weight improves health. Are
weight loss programs, they ask, unnecessary medicine?

"No one wants to hear this," Dr. Jules Hirsch, an obesity researcher at 8
Rockefeller University, said, "but I would ask where the data are."

None of the experts, however, are suggesting that people should aban- 9
don healthy eating habits and exercise, which have clear benefits.

At the moment, Medicare will pay for surgery for obesity when patients 10
suffer other problems associated with the condition, like diabetes. Now,
Medicare says it may decide to cover treatment for those who are simply
obese, meaning their body mass index, a measure of body fat, is at least 30.

The agency said that it would need to determine if obesity treatments 11
help people lose weight and improve their health, adding that as yet it has
no estimate on costs.

The insurance debate, for now, is aimed at the obese, not those who 12
want to lose a few pounds here and there. But that still includes 61 million
Americans, nearly a third of the adult population, and 9 million of
Medicare age, 65 and older.

They include, for example, a woman 5 feet 5 inches tall and weighing more 13
than 180 pounds, or a man 6 feet tall and weighing more than 221 pounds.

The immediate question is whether to cover so-called bariatric surgery, 14
which costs $30,000 to $40,000 if there are no complications, and greatly
reduces how much food can be consumed and the calories that can be absorbed. But commercial diet programs as well as many obesity doctors, including members of the American Obesity Association, whose sponsors
include makers of weight loss drugs as well as companies like Weight
Watchers and Jenny Craig, say they want coverage for other programs, too.

The obesity association said that it planned to use Medicare as a wedge 15
to open the door for broader coverage for the obese and then, possibly, for
overweight Americans.

Obesity, said Morgan Downey, the association's executive director, is a 16
disease, and should be treated. Insurers pay for treating other chronic diseases, he added, although "there are very, very few cures out there."

Doctors, of course, have been telling patients for years that weight loss 17
will greatly improve their health. But, in fact, there is only one long-term

study following obese people who deliberately lost weight—in this case, with weight loss surgery—and comparing their health with that of similar people who did not lose weight. The results were a surprise.

The study of 692 patients by Dr. C. David Sjostrom of Goteborg University in Sweden, found, as expected, that the surgical patients lost weight—68 pounds in the first year and 44 pounds after eight years. 18

Otherwise, the results were mixed. The rate of diabetes among the surgical patients remained steady, at 10 percent, but tripled to 24 percent in the patients who did not have surgery and did not lose weight. 19

Blood pressure, however, was a different story. It fell in the first year after surgery but then crept up again. Eight years later, the blood pressures of the surgical patients were the same as those who did not have surgery. 20

For the minority of obese people who are surgical candidates, the operation can turn their lives around. But they risk serious consequences, like bowel obstructions and malnutrition leading to anemia and bone loss, as well as a 1 percent to 2 percent risk of death. What is not known is whether the surgery's health benefits outweigh its risks over the long term. 21

Dr. Russell Harris, an internist at the University of North Carolina who evaluated weight loss studies for the U.S. Preventive Services Task Force, an independent panel of experts that advises the Agency for Healthcare Research and Quality, said that when it came to surgery, the group decided, "we just don't know" what to recommend. 22

Other studies have focused on populations, trying to determine whether overweight or obese people who voluntarily lost weight were healthier. Some studies found that they were; some found no difference; and some found that they actually died at a greater rate. 23

The reason for the dearth of information on the long-term effects of weight loss, researchers say, is that very few people keep weight off. The National Institute of Diabetes and Digestive and Kidney Disease is now, for the first time, trying to get some concrete answers with an 11-year study of 5,000 overweight and obese diabetes patients. 24

In justifying the new study, its designers state the quandary: "Given the paucity of data on the impact of weight loss on morbidity and mortality, an increasing number of critics in both the lay press and professional literature have questioned whether obesity should be treated at all." 25

Another question raised by obesity researchers is whether a fat person who loses weight is as healthy as a naturally thin person of the same weight. 26

It is true that thinner people tend to be healthier, but studies have found that, biochemically, the formerly fat are like people who are starving: obsessed with food, needing fewer calories to maintain their body weight. Many—again the issue is with the obese, not those who want to lose a few 27 pounds—have slow heart rates after they lose weight and always feel cold; women may stop menstruating, even if they are still relatively fat. Is that better or worse than remaining fat? No one knows for sure.

Another unknown should weight loss turn out to improve health: How   28 much weight must be lost? Most obese people dream of being thin, but researchers say a more realistic goal is losing just 5 percent to 10 percent of their weight. That is the best that can be achieved in clinical trials lasting a year or two, they say, and over the short term, is associated with lower blood sugar and blood pressure.

As for other health benefits, Dr. Hirsch said, "the data get fuzzier and   29 fuzzier."

While scientists ask questions, a robust weight loss industry takes in   30 tens of billions of dollars each year and reaches into all aspects of society. It includes diet foods and beverages, weight loss centers, diet books and prescription medicines, diet supplements, visits to doctors, lab tests, and surgery. The Federal Trade Commission estimates that annual revenue from sales of diet foods and beverages alone reaches $40 billion.

Weight loss surgery alone has begun to hurt insurers. In Pennsylvania,   31 the number of operations went from 674 in 1999 to 6,791 in 2003, and total charges went from $24 million to $242 million. Private insurance paid for 85 percent of the operations. In Florida, Blue Cross Blue Shield announced that it would not pay for the operation after this year, saying its costs nearly doubled in two years, to $17 million a year.

The problem with weight loss, researchers say, is that the advice so of-   32 ten given, eat less and exercise more, has not been much help.

Research studies at academic medical centers, providing intensive diet,   33 exercise and behavioral therapy, result in losses of 8 to 12 percent of body weight in six months. But most people gain the weight back in a few years.

As for commercial weight loss programs, in a two-year study sponsored   34 by Weight Watchers involving 358 people averaging 205 pounds, those assigned to the program lost 6.4 pounds. Participants who were randomly assigned to try to lose weight on their own lost nothing. Neither group showed a change in blood pressure or levels of cholesterol, blood glucose or insulin.

While Weight Watchers did not have much of an effect, "it's as good as   35 most academic centers do," said the study's lead author, Dr. F. Xavier Pi-Sunyer, chief of endocrinology at St. Luke's–Roosevelt Hospital Center in New York.

It is almost impossible to tell the blunt truth about the success rates of   36 treatments, some researchers said. "It is like resisting Mom, apple pie, and the flag," said Dr. Bruce Schneider, associate vice president for clinical research at the Association of American Medical Colleges.

Many said they know the data but encourage patients to continue try- 37
ing to lose some weight, or at least stop gaining, especially those whose
blood sugar level is elevated or who have joint problems that are worsened
by weighing so much. Clearly, doctors have not yet given up on the idea
that weight loss may improve health. Yet, they said, when they urge patients to lower their expectations about how much weight they can lose,
some react with shock.

Dr. Judith Korner, an endocrinologist at Columbia University, tells 38
obese patients that a 5 percent to 10 percent weight loss would be terrific.
"Some of them look at me as though I'm crazy," she said.

Those few who succeed at weight loss may end up on what amounts to 39
a permanent diet. People in a national registry of successful dieters—they
maintained a weight loss of at least 30 pounds for at least a year—report
consuming just 1,400 calories a day and walking, or doing equivalent exercise, for an hour a day.

Still, people who lost weight said they felt better, they looked better, and 40
they found just moving around and going about their daily lives much easier.

That leaves a question, Dr. Hirsch said. "If it's all that good, why don't 41
people maintain their weight loss?"

Mr. Pirollo, who lost 30 pounds since March, said he was confident he 42
would reach his goal and that this time his weight loss would last. He
would like insurers to pay but his latest treatment as a participant in a two-
year clinical trial costs him nothing. Already, Mr. Pirollo reports, his doctor halved his dose of blood pressure medication.

But insurers have to make some tough decisions, said Dr. Madelyn H. 43
Fernstrom, director of the weight management center at the University of
Pittsburgh Medical Center.

"Let's say your weight went down 20 percent, but your blood pressure 44
did not change," she said. "Your self-esteem may be better. But the payer
might say, we're glad you're happy, but the bottom line is, Are you saving
the company money?"

Thinking Critically

1. What are the main challenges of writing about technical or scientific subjects for a general audience? Working with a small group, find articles
   about a specific scientific issue (such as obesity or bariatric surgery) from
   a variety of publications and sources. Remove any identifying information
   from the articles and pass them around. Looking only at the organization
   and content of each article, can you guess its original source or the type of
   publication it first appeared in? What are the key clues?

2. Who qualifies as an authority in this article, and how is their authority established? In your own academic writing, how do you establish your own authority as well as the authority of your sources?

3. What does Dr. Bruce Schneider mean when he says that telling the truth about the dismal long-term effects of popular weight-loss programs "is like resisting Mom, apple pie, and the flag" (paragraph 36)?

Writing Critically

1. How does Gina Kolata's reporting support or refute Virginia Postrel's argument in "Smart and Pretty," earlier in this chapter?

2. In a research paper, briefly discuss the history and purpose of Medicare and the main challenges the program faces in the twenty-first century. What should public health priorities be as the American population ages? What public health issues should be the personal responsibility of individual citizens?

3. Is there an initiative on your campus or in your community to support healthy eating and exercise habits? Who sponsors that initiative? How are people informed about it, and how easy is it to participate? Examine the purpose and effectiveness of such an initiative in an analytical essay. (Or, working alone or with a small group, create a proposal for a specific local initiative to promote healthy eating and exercise habits.)

Arguing the Cultural Divides

1. The issues discussed in Chapter 8 have as much to do with American ideas of morality as they do with American standards of medical care. Choose one of the public health challenges discussed in this chapter, and examine the moral and ethical implications of pursuing one course of action over another. (For example, what are the moral implications of simply eating for pleasure and convenience, of providing school-age children with information about the correct use of condoms, or of enjoying a standard of medical care based on a person's ability to pay?) To what extent do these moral perspectives influence public and political discussion of this issue?

2. Might some Americans be victims of our culture's prosperity and variety? Define a public health problem that seems to be uniquely American. Is it "American" (a) by its very nature, (b) in the population that it most severely afflicts, (c) in the way in which it is depicted in the media, or (d) in the way in which the medical establishment approaches or avoids it?

3. Define a public health issue of immediate importance or interest to you. What resources does your community offer to provide information, support, and care for that issue? Do your local elected officials have any opinion about the issue?

Johnny Can't Read: The Value of an Education

The Equalizers: The Father and Son Who Made a Billion-Dollar Difference for California's Students

DASHKA SLATER

Journalist Dashka Slater was an award-winning reporter and editor for the San Francisco alternative newspaper *East Bay Express* and is a current contributor to *Industry Standard* magazine. Her investigative journalism has won awards from the Media Alliance, the National Council on Crime and Delinquency, and the Hospital Council of Northern and Central California. Slater's first novel, *The Wishing Box,* was published in 2000. "The Equalizers" appeared in the November/December 2004 issue of *Mother Jones* magazine. Founded in 1976, *Mother Jones* magazine is committed to promoting social justice through in-depth investigative journalism. The magazine won the 2001 National Magazine Award in General Excellence and was nominated for National Magazine Awards nine times (winning four times). The magazine is named for Mary Harris

"Mother" Jones, an elderly widowed Irish immigrant who in the early twentieth century transformed herself into a leading activist for working people. For more on Mother Jones—the woman, the magazine, and the website—go to <http:motherjones.org/index.html>.

With six kids ranging in age from 3 to 29, Sweetie Williams has heard 1 a lot of excuses for not doing homework. But four years ago, when his 12-year-old son, Eliezer, told him he didn't have any because there weren't enough books for students to take home, the elder Williams felt it wasn't just another story. A call to Eli's seventh-grade English teacher confirmed the boy's account; books were so scarce at Eli's San Francisco school that assigning homework wasn't an option.

That was hardly the only problem at Eli's school. There were chronically 2 clogged toilets, water fountains with discolored and foul-tasting water, mice-infested classrooms without heat. All in all, it wasn't what Williams had envisioned when he moved his family to California from American Samoa in 1999. "We've been told this is the land of opportunity," he says. "Our children are being deprived of that opportunity. It's not fair."

Williams is a serious man with gentle eyes and a low voice that must 3 serve him well during the Sunday sermons he gives as pastor of the First Samoan Full Gospel Pentecostal Church. He and his wife, Talogasa, work as baggage screeners at the San Francisco airport; she works the swing shift and he works graveyard. He had never been much of an activist, but when Eli's teacher told him about a lawsuit that was being filed by the ACLU over the conditions in California schools, Williams was eager to participate. So was Eli, who didn't see why he shouldn't have the same facilities as kids at schools in richer neighborhoods.

"I was thinking, 'If I'm not going to do it, who is going to do it,'" the elder 4 Williams recalls. "It's a California-wide problem, and it needs to be solved." Indeed, a 2002 poll of California teachers found that nearly a third of the state's 6 million schoolchildren attend schools where there are not enough textbooks to assign homework; 2 million are in classrooms that are uncomfortably hot or cold; and 1.7 million are being educated amid mice, roaches, or rats.

On May 17, 2000, the 46th anniversary of *Brown v. Board of Educa-* 5 *tion,* the ACLU filed a class-action suit that came to represent more than a million California kids, accusing the state of depriving its poor, nonwhite, and immigrant children of the tools they need to obtain the free, common, and equal public education guaranteed by the state constitution. The lead plaintiff was Eli Williams.

Eli did some of the legal legwork, photographing flooded bathrooms and 6 dangling ceiling tiles, and soon found himself getting frosty looks from the

Raise your hand if you know the answer Public school systems around the country struggle to educate a burgeoning population. These students in an overcrowded Miami high school listen to a social skills lecture.

school's principal, who insisted that Eli was exaggerating the situation. Still, Eli had no idea that the suit that bore his name was being carefully watched by educators across the country. "I didn't think it was a big thing," he recalls. "And when I saw it *was* a big thing, I wondered when it was going to end."

Others were wondering the same thing. But then-Governor Gray Davis, 7 a Democrat who claimed education was his top priority, hired a high-priced law firm to fight the suit, dragging it out over four years and ringing up close to $20 million in legal fees. The state's tactics included lining up experts to testify that textbooks and heat were not crucial for learning, and subjecting students, some as young as eight, to days of harsh questioning, often reducing them to tears.

But soon after taking office, California's Republican governor, Arnold 8 Schwarzenegger, called off the dogs. By August, a $1 billion settlement had been reached in *Williams v. California*. The state agreed to immediately spend $188 million to buy books for and make repairs at the lowest-performing schools. The settlement also creates a system for students and teachers to lodge complaints about substandard conditions, and imposes a 30-day deadline for resolving them.

The money comes too late to help Eli. He's a high school senior now, a 9 tall, handsome 17-year-old with his father's eyes and shy smile. "I won't see the fruits of what's going to happen," he says, "but my little sister and cousins and nephews and nieces, they'll see it." Eli's grades could be better—he says he's still struggling to learn material he should have been taught in middle school. Yet he likes his communications class and hopes to go to college next year. Whatever happens, he figures he's learned a valuable lesson, one that can't be found in any textbook. "I learned that anyone can do this," he says. "Anyone can make a change."

Thinking Critically

1. A fundamental irony made Sweetie Williams an activist. What is that irony?

2. What does it mean to work "swing shift" and "graveyard"?

3. What is the ACLU, and why would it be involved in school reform? What is a "class-action suit," and why does the ACLU file one? Why does Slater note that the suit was filed on the anniversary of *Brown v. Board of Education*?

Writing Critically

1. How satisfied were you with your high school education? (If you are a parent, how happy are you with your child's current school?) In an argument that borrows Slater's problem-solving structure, describe an unresolved issue at either your high school or your child's school, and propose a solution.

2. For more information about the *Williams v. California* class-action lawsuit, its settlement, and its ongoing repercussions, go to the California School Boards Association website at <http://www.csba.org/ela/williams_notice.htm> and the activist group Decent Schools for California site at <http://www.decentschools.org/>. Examine the content, accessibility, and visual features of each site. Then, working either by yourself or with a small group, create a proposal for a website to support action regarding a specific issue or controversy on your campus. Your proposal should discuss the kinds of content and resources the site will include; the overall "look" of the site; accessibility and navigation features (including links to other resources); and how people who visit the site could use it to take further action.

Life Way *After Head Start*

DAVID L. KIRP | David L. Kirp is a professor of public policy at the University of California at Berkeley. His writings on public policy issues have appeared in numerous publications, including *The Nation, Harper's Magazine, Commonweal,* and *Tikkun.* Kirp has written, edited, or contributed to numerous books on issues ranging from education to community to the impact of AIDS on American children, including *Almost Home: America's*

> *Love-Hate Relationship with Community* (2000) and
> *Our Town: Race, Housing, and the Soul of Suburbia*
> (1995). His book *Shakespeare, Einstein, and the
> Bottom Line: The Marketing of Higher Education*
> (2003) is a critical examination of changes in American
> university culture. In "What Good Teachers Have to
> Say About Teaching," a statement written for a UC
> Berkeley website, Kirp describes what he hopes students
> in an undergraduate course on AIDS and public policy
> have learned: ". . . at least all this honesty has taught
> them a few things about politics—if only the persistent
> tension between what must be done and what is
> actually doable, if only the lesson that there can be no
> easy reconciliation between personal epiphanies and
> public policies." "Life *Way* After Head Start," appeared
> in the *New York Times* in November 2004.

The power of education to level the playing field has long been an American article of faith. Education is the "balance wheel of the social machinery," argued Horace Mann, the first great advocate of public schooling. "It prevents being poor." But that belief has been undermined by research findings—seized on ever since by skeptics—that federal programs like Head Start, designed to benefit poor children, actually have little long-term impact. 1

Now evidence from an experiment that has lasted nearly four decades may revive Horace Mann's faith. *Lifetime Effects: The HighScope Perry Preschool Study Through Age 40* was released earlier this week. It shows that an innovative early education program can make a marked difference in the lives of poor minority youngsters—not just while they are in school but for decades afterward. The 123 participants in this experiment, says David Ellwood, dean of the Kennedy School of Government at Harvard and an architect of the Clinton administration's original welfare reform plan, "may be the most powerfully influential group in the recent history of social science." 2

The life stories of the Perry students have been tracked since they left preschool in the 1960's. Like so much in education research, the findings have been known mainly in professional circles. But this latest dispatch from the field, confirming the remarkable and enduring impact of a long-ago experience, should alter the way we understand preschool and, maybe, the way society invests in the future. 3

The study began without fanfare in the fall of 1962, several years before Head Start was conceived. In the mostly blue-collar town Ypsilanti, Mich., 21 3- and 4-year-old children started preschool. All of them, as well as 37 4 more youngsters who enrolled over the next three years, were black. They came from poor families, and the South Side neighborhood, with its run-down public housing and high crime rates, was a rough place to grow up.

Based on past experience, it was a near certainty that most of these kids 5 would fail in school. During the previous decade, not a single class in the Perry elementary school had ever scored above the 10th percentile on national achievement tests, while across town, in the school that served the children of well-off professionals, no class had ever scored below the 90th percentile.

The reformers who developed the High/Scope Perry model hoped that 6 exposure at an early age to a program emphasizing cognitive development could rewrite this script. Most children attended Perry for two years, three hours a day, five days a week. The curriculum emphasized problem-solving rather than unstructured play or "repeat after me" drills. The children were viewed as active learners, not sponges; a major part of their daily routine involved planning, carrying out and reviewing what they were learning. Teachers were well trained and decently paid, and there was a teacher for every five youngsters. They made weekly home visits to parents, helping them teach their own children. "The message was, 'Read to your child,'" one woman, whose daughter went to Perry in 1962, remembered. "If you read the newspaper, put your child on your lap, read out loud and ask her, 'What did I just read?' When you take her to the grocery store, have her count the change."

Even though prosperous children had thrived in similar settings for well 7 over a century, 3-year-olds from poverty backgrounds had never had the same chance. Leading developmental psychologists cautioned against the idea. Such an intellectually rigorous regime, they argued, could actually harm such children by asking too much of them.

David Weikart, the moving force behind Perry Preschool, was not 8 convinced. The experts had a theory but no evidence, and Weikart decided to conduct an experiment. From a group of 123 South Side neighborhood children, 58 were randomly assigned to the Perry program, while the rest, identical in virtually all respects, didn't attend preschool. Random assignment is the research gold standard because the "treatment"—in this case, preschool—best explains any subsequent differences between the two groups.

Early results were discouraging. In reading and arithmetic, the preschool-9 ers' achievement scores at 7 and 8 weren't much better than the control group's, and while the preschoolers' IQ scores spiked, that difference soon disappeared. Those results were consistent with the dispiriting conclusion of a 1969 nationwide evaluation of Head Start. That study's key finding—that the boost in test scores recorded by Head Start children faded by second grade—was widely interpreted to mean that Head Start and, by implication, most other early childhood education programs for poor kids, were a waste of time.

But in Ypsilanti the researchers didn't give up. They collected data every 10 year from age 3 through 11, then at ages 14, 15, 19, 27 and now 40—an astonishingly long time span in the research annals. Just as astonishingly, they have kept track of 97 percent of the surviving group. "I've found people on the streets, gone to crack houses where there were AK-47's," said Van Loggins, a gym teacher who coached many of the participants when they were teenagers and who has been interviewing them for 25 years. "I'm bilingual—ghetto and English."

Not only has the Perry study set records for longevity, but it also asks 11 the truly pertinent question: what is the impact of preschool, not on the test scores of 7-year-olds but on their life chances? The answer is positive—a well-designed program really works.

As they progressed through school, the Perry children were less likely 12 to be assigned to a special education class for the mentally retarded. Their attitude toward school was also better, and their parents were more enthusiastic about their youngsters' schooling. Their high-school grade point average was higher. By age 19, two-thirds had graduated from high school, compared with 45 percent of those who didn't attend preschool.

Most remarkably, the impact of those preschool years still persists. By al- 13 most any measure we might care about—education, income, crime, family stability—the contrast with those who didn't attend Perry is striking. When they were 27, the preschool group scored higher on tests of literacy. Now they are in their 40's, many with children and even grandchildren of their own. Nearly twice as many have earned college degrees (one has a Ph.D.). More of them have jobs: 76 percent versus 62 percent. They are more likely to own their home, own a car and have a savings account. They are less likely to have been on welfare. They earn considerably more—$20,800 versus $15,300—and that difference pushes them well above the poverty line.

The crime statistics reveal similarly significant differences. Compared 14 with the control group, fewer preschoolers have gone on to be arrested for violent crimes, drug-related crimes or property crimes. Only about half as many (28 percent versus 52 percent) have been sentenced to prison or jail. Preschool also seems to have affected their decisions about family life. More of the males in the Perry contingent have been married (68 percent versus 51 percent, though they are also more likely than those who didn't attend Perry to have been married more than once) and almost twice as many have raised their own children (57 percent versus 30 percent). These men report fewer serious complaints about their health and are less likely to use drugs.

The newest report attaches a dollar-and-cents figure to this good news.   15
Economists estimate that the return to society is more than $250,000 (cal-
culated in 2000 dollars) on an investment of just $15,166—that's 17 dol-
lars for every dollar invested.

There are no miracles here. Not everyone who attended Perry became   16
a model citizen—the crime figures alone make that plain—and some of
those who didn't attend preschool have fared well. But because their opportunities are so constricted, the odds are stacked against kids who grow
up in neighborhoods like Ypsilanti's South Side. Bluntly put, these are the
children of whom we expect the least—and overall, the life histories of the
control group confirm those expectations.

By contrast, many of those who went to Perry found their way to more   17
stable lives. One graduate, a sales manager, has moved back to the South
Side neighborhood, where he devotes much of his time to his church group,
"giving back" to the community. "I'm still using the discipline of school,"
he said. "The harder you work in school or in life, the more you get out of
it." One Perry alum said that when she was in her mid-20's, living on welfare and "borrowing" from her mother, she "woke up one day to decide
that was just wrong. I apologized to my mother and went to work in the
factory. When I had the money, I bought Mom all new living-room furniture. I stopped dating the wrong kind of guys, and eventually I got married." Now she's a union leader, and when she had children of her own,
there was no doubt they'd go to preschool.

Why did Perry have such an impact? Though the data can't provide a   18
definitive answer, a plausible interpretation is that the experience proved
to be a timely intervention, altering the arc of these children's lives.
Preschool gave them the intellectual tools to do better in school. When they
succeeded academically, they became more committed to education, and so
they stayed on. Then, because a diploma opened up new economic opportunities, crime proved a less appealing alternative.

The strategy first developed at Perry is now packaged as the High/Scope   19
curriculum and is widely used across the nation. Other well-conceived preschool initiatives have also generated impressive long-term results, including the Chicago school district's Child-Parent Center Program, which
brings mothers and relatives into the schools, and the Carolina Abecedar-
ian Project, in which intervention begins during the very first weeks of an
infant's life and carries on until kindergarten.

These successes have given ammunition to those who champion expanded   20
preschool opportunities—not just for poor children but for all children. Oklahoma and Georgia have been leaders in the movement for universal
prekindergarten, and two years ago, Florida became the first state to pass a

constitutional amendment requiring "high quality" preschool for all 4-year-olds. "I testified in Florida," said Evelyn Moore, one of the original teachers at Perry Preschool, who is now president of the National Black Child Development Institute. "The research has been vital in getting people to understand why early childhood education matters." Give us the child to age 7, the Jesuits say, and we'll give you the man. Give us the child at age 3, these findings suggest, and with quality preschool it's possible to work wonders.

Thinking Critically

1. Who was Horace Mann? Why is it important to know who he was, and what he accomplished, in order to better understand David L. Kirp's argument?

2. "Life *Way* After Head Start" originally appeared in the *New York Times.* Is it a straightforward news account, an opinion piece, or some other genre? Which paragraphs of this essay are objective (that is, they report or summarize data), and which are analytical or interpretive? How does the use of both summary and analysis strengthen Kirp's argument?

3. Who is the "we" Kirp refers to in sentences like "By almost any measure we might care about . . ." (paragraph 13) and "Bluntly put, these are the children of whom we expect the least . . ." (paragraph 16)?

Writing Critically

1. Writing summaries of complex data is a key skill in the social sciences, in business, and in many other academic and professional disciplines. Most of "Life *Way* After Head Start" is devoted to a summary of a complex and long-range research study. Visit the website of the High/Scope Educational Research Foundation at <http://www.highscope.org/Research/PerryProject/perrymain.htm>. Draw on the report itself, as well as on the summaries, PowerPoint slides, and other resources found at the site, to write your own summary of the *"Perry Preschool Study Through Age 40."*

2. What factors, according to this article, contributed to the eventual success of the children studied at the Perry preschool? Which of those factors, in your opinion, are the responsibility of individual parents, and which are the responsibility of the larger community or government? Draw from your personal experience (as a student or a parent) as well as from at least two other selections from *Many Americas* to support your argument.

3. What preschool or child-care facilities are available on your campus or in your local community? What factors would be most important to you if you were looking for a good preschool program for your child? Is such a program locally available and affordable? In an opinion piece for your local or campus newspaper, discuss the availability of preschool programs in your community, and argue for a specific change to be made in what such the programs offer, in how they are funded, or in their accessibility and availability.

When Every Child Is Good Enough

JOHN TIERNEY | Reporter and columnist John Tierney joined the *New York Times* in 1990, first as a general assignment reporter on the Metro desk and then as a staff writer for the *New York Times Magazine*. Other journalists (and some detractors) describe Tierney's political leanings as anywhere from libertarian to conservative and certainly to the right of the liberal *New York Times*. Tierney is well known for his contrarian, well-reported, and wittily expressed viewpoints; his 1996 *New York Times Magazine* article "Recycling Is Garbage" received more letters to the editor than any other article the magazine ever published, as well as a book-length rebuke from the environmentalist organization National Resources Defense Council. But it's his column, featured twice weekly since 1994 in the *Times,* that has gained Tierney the most attention. "When Every Child Is Good Enough" appeared in the November 21, 2004, issue. Pranks that Tierney has played in the service of a larger argument include pretending to be a bum outside of Rosie O'Donnell's suburban mansion after O'Donnell lambasted New York mayor Rudy Giuliani's efforts to move homeless people off city streets, hailing taxis outside of banks while dressed as a bank robber, and handing out $20 to New Yorkers who kept their dogs leashed. In an interview with the libertarian magazine the *American Prospect*, Tierney professes that "I've seen people who have turned out to be wrong, older experts who pursued something with the best of intentions. My hope is that that won't happen to me. That if I start seeing stuff where the real world contradicts my theory, then I'll be able to change." Another essay by Tierney, "Republicans Outnumbered in Academia, Studies Find," appears later in this chapter.

The Incredibles is not just an animated adventure for children, at least not to the parents and teachers who have been passionately deconstructing the story of a family of superheroes trapped in suburbia. The movie has reignited one of the oldest debates about child-rearing and society: competition versus coddling, excellence versus egalitarianism.

496

Is Dash, the supersonic third-grader forbidden from racing on the track   2
team, a gifted child held back by the educational philosophy that "everybody is special"? Or is he an overprivileged elitist being forced to take into
account the feelings of others?

Is his father, Mr. Incredible, who complains that the schools "keep in-   3
venting new ways to celebrate mediocrity," a visionary reformer committed to pushing children to excel? Or is he a reactionary in red tights who's
been reading too much Nietzsche and Ayn Rand?

Is Syndrome, the geek villain trying to kill the superheroes, an angry   4
Marxist determined to quash individuality? Or is his plan to give everyone
artificial superpowers an uplifting version of "cooperative learning" in an
"inclusion classroom"?

At one level, the debate is over current controversies in public education: 5
Many parents believe that their children, mostly in elite schools, are being
pushed too hard in a hypercompetitive atmosphere. But other parents are
complaining about a decline in programs for gifted children, leaving students
to languish in "untracked" and unstimulating classrooms. Some critics of
education believe that boys especially are languishing in schools that emphasize cooperation instead of competition. No Child Left Behind, indeed.

But the basic issue is the same one raised four decades ago by Kurt   6
Vonnegut in "Harrison Bergeron," a short story set in the America of
2081, about a 14-year-old genius and star athlete. To keep others from
feeling inferior, the Handicapper General weighs him down with 300-
pound weights and makes him wear earphones that blast noise, so he cannot take "unfair advantage" of his brain.

That's hardly the America of 2004, but today's children do grow up   7
with soccer leagues and spelling bees where everyone gets a prize. On some
playgrounds dodge ball is deemed too traumatic to the dodging-impaired.
Some parents consider musical chairs dangerously exclusionary.

Children are constantly feted for accomplishments that used to be rou-   8
tine. They may not all be honored at a fourth-grade graduation ceremony—the event in the movie that inspires Mr. Incredible's complaint
about mediocrity—but they all hear the mantra recited by Dash's sister in
response to his ambitions.

"Everyone's special, Dash," she says.   9

"Which is another way of saying no one is," he replies.   10

The villain, Syndrome, makes the same point when he envisions em-   11
powering the masses with his inventions.

"Everybody will be super, which means no one will be," he says, glee-   12
ful that he will finally have revenge on Mr. Incredible for snubbing him
during his childhood.

He may be the villain, but you could also see his psychopathology as   13
evidence of the bad effects of status-seeking among children. Even the winners can be victims of competition, said Denise Clark Pope, the author of
*Doing Schools: How We Are Creating a Generation of Stressed Out, Ma-
terialistic and Miseducated Students.*

"When learning becomes about competing with your peers to get ahead,   14
what gets learned is how to compete and not how to learn," said Dr. Pope,
a lecturer at Stanford University's school of education. "Kids learn to cheat,
to raise their hands even when they don't know the answers, to form alliances instead of learning the material we want them to understand."

Her attitude is shared by some parents, especially ones whose children   15
are frantically competing at exclusive private and suburban schools. But
fans of competition complain that it's been de-emphasized for most students. Some schools have dropped honor rolls and class rankings, and the
old practice of routinely segregating smart students in separate tracks has
given way to the heterogeneous "inclusion classroom."

Competition has long been out of fashion at education schools, as in-   16
dicated in a 1997 survey of 900 of their professors by Public Agenda, a
nonprofit public opinion research group. Only a third of the professors
considered rewards like honor rolls to be valuable incentives for learning,
while nearly two-thirds said schools should avoid competition.

To some critics, that cooperative philosophy is one reason that so many   17
boys like Dash are bored at school. "Professors of education think you can
improve society by making people less competitive," said Christina Hoff
Sommers, author of *The War Against Boys* and a resident scholar at the
American Enterprise Institute. "But males are wired for competition, and
if you take it away there's little to interest them in school."

In his new book, *Hard America, Soft America,* Michael Barone puts   18
schools in the soft category and warns that they leave young adults unprepared for the hard world awaiting them in the workplace. "The education
establishment has been too concerned with fostering kids' self-esteem instead of teaching them to learn and compete," he said.

The No Child Left Behind Act was an attempt to put more rigor into   19
the system by punishing schools whose students don't pass standardized
tests, but it has had unintended consequences for high achievers. Administrators have been cutting funds for gifted-student programs and concentrating money and attention on the failing students.

"In practice, No Child Left Behind has meant No Child Gets Ahead for   20
gifted students," said Joyce Clark, a planner in the Pittsburgh public schools'
gifted program. "There's no incentive to worry about them because they can
pass the tests."

The Incredibles might take comfort from a recent report, *A Nation* 21
Deceived: How Schools Hold Back America's Brightest Students, by the
John Templeton Foundation. It summarizes research showing that gifted
children thrive with more advanced material and describes their current
frustration in prose that sounds like Dash: "When they want to fly, they are
told to stay in their seats. Stay in your grade. Know your place. It's a national scandal."

But if they do fly, what happens to the children left on the ground? One 22
of the report's authors, Nicholas Colangelo, a professor at the University
of Iowa who is an expert in gifted education, pointed to research indicating the left-behind do not suffer academically or emotionally.

Other scholars say that these children feel stigmatized and demoralized, 23
and that in practice, a tracking system tends to discriminate against poor
and minority students.

"The public generally seems to have caught on to the social undesir- 24
ability of claiming educational privileges for students who are already relatively privileged," said Jeannie Oakes, a professor of educational equity
at the University of California, Los Angeles. "Superhero kids don't exist in
such abundance that we need to develop special and separate programs for
whole classes of them."

The movie never quite resolves the issue. In the end, Dash is allowed to 25
race but is coached not to get too far ahead of the pack. The writer and director, Brad Bird, offered a less ambiguous answer in an interview. "Wrong-
headed liberalism seeks to give trophies to everyone just for existing," he
said. "It seems to render achievement meaningless. That's a weird goal."

He sounded very much like Professor Colangelo, who says that children 26
want to compete and can cope with defeat a lot better than adults imagine.
"Life hurts your feelings," Mr. Bird said. "I think people whine about stuff
too much. C'mon, man, just get up and do it."

Thinking Critically

1. What kinds of sources does John Tierney draw on to support his argument? Is there anything surprising about his choice of examples or the way
   he uses them?

2. Given the limited resources available for public education, who do you think
   should receive the most attention—"gifted students" or "failing students"?
   Sum up the contrasting arguments offered in "When Every Child Is Good
   Enough."

3. What moral values do you associate with competitiveness? Use sources
   cited by John Tierney as well as your own personal experiences and observations to illustrate these values.

Writing Critically

1. Tierney refers to the 2004 animated film *The Incredibles* and the 1961 Kurt Vonnegut short story "Harrison Bergeron." Using the story or the film (or both), write an essay in which you compare the fictional scenario to a real-world experience or issue.

2. Have you ever participated in any classroom or workplace activity meant to boost your "self-esteem"? Describe that activity and its effect on your self-esteem and on your classroom or workplace environment. Was the activity successful and beneficial, or not?

3. The text of the No Child Left Behind Act is available online at the U.S. Department of Education website: <http://www.ed.gov/nclb/landing.jhtml?src=pb>. Visit the site and evaluate its accessibility and usefulness for different constituencies (parents, teachers, school board members, legislators, and so on). Is there a specifically political or ideological slant to the site? In an analytical essay, discuss the effectiveness of the site and its presentation of the No Child Left Behind Act.

A Nation of Wimps

Hara Estroff Marano

Hara Estroff Marano is the editor at large of *Psychology Today*, a print magazine and website that provides psychological insight, perspectives, advice, and news to a general audience. In her writing for that magazine (including a column, "Unconventional Wisdom") and for other publications and websites, Marano explores issues of family and personal relationships. Her articles have appeared in the *New York Times, Smithsonian, Family Circle,* and *Ladies' Home Journal,* among other national magazines. She is the author of two books, *Style Is Not a Size* (1991), about women, body image, and self-esteem, and *"Why Doesn't Anybody Like Me?": A Guide to Raising Socially Confident Kids* (1998). "A Nation of Wimps" appeared in *Psychology Today* in the November/December 2004 issue.

Maybe it's the cyclist in the park, trim under his sleek metallic blue helmet, cruising along the dirt path . . . at three miles an hour. On his tricycle.

Or perhaps it's today's playground, all-rubber-cushioned surface where kids used to skin their knees. And . . . wait a minute . . . those aren't little kids playing. Their mommies—and especially their daddies—are in there with them, coplaying or play-by-play coaching. Few take it half-easy on the perimeter benches, as parents used to do, letting the kids figure things out for themselves.

Then there are the sanitizing gels, with which over a third of parents now 3 send their kids to school, according to a recent survey. Presumably, parents now worry that school bathrooms are not good enough for their children.

Consider the teacher new to an upscale suburban town. Shuffling through 4 the sheaf of reports certifying the educational "accommodations" he was required to make for many of his history students, he was struck by the exhaustive, well-written—and obviously costly—one on behalf of a girl who was already proving among the most competent of his ninth-graders. "She's somewhat neurotic," he confides, "but she is bright, organized and conscientious—the type who'd get to school to turn in a paper on time, even if she were dying of stomach flu." He finally found the disability he was to make allowances for: difficulty with Gestalt thinking. The 13-year-old "couldn't see the big picture." That cleverly devised defect (what 13-year-old can construct the big picture?) would allow her to take all her tests untimed, especially the big one at the end of the rainbow, the college-worthy SAT.

Behold the wholly sanitized childhood, without skinned knees or the 5 occasional C in history. "Kids need to feel badly sometimes," says child psychologist David Elkind, professor at Tufts University. "We learn through experience and we learn through bad experiences. Through failure we learn how to cope."

Messing up, however, even in the playground, is wildly out of style. Although error and experimentation are the true mothers of success, parents are taking pains to remove failure from the equation.

"Life is planned out for us," says Elise Kramer, a Cornell University 7 junior. "But we don't know what to want." As Elkind puts it, "Parents and schools are no longer geared toward child development, they're geared to academic achievement."

No one doubts that there are significant economic forces pushing parents to invest so heavily in their children's outcome from an early age. But taking all the discomfort, disappointment and even the play out of development, especially while increasing pressure for success, turns out to be misguided by just about 180 degrees. With few challenges all their own, kids are unable to forge their creative adaptations to the normal vicissitudes of life. That not only makes them risk-averse, it makes them psychologically fragile, riddled with anxiety. In the process they're robbed of identity, meaning and a sense of accomplishment, to say nothing of a shot at real happiness. Forget, too, about perseverance, not simply a moral virtue but a necessary life skill. These turn out to be the spreading psychic fault lines of 21st-century youth. Whether we want to or not, we're on our way to creating a nation of wimps.

The Fragility Factor

College, it seems, is where the fragility factor is now making its greatest   9
mark. It's where intellectual and developmental tracks converge as the emotional training wheels come off. By all accounts, psychological distress is rampant on college campuses. It takes a variety of forms, including anxiety and depression—which are increasingly regarded as two faces of the same coin—binge drinking and substance abuse, self-mutilation and other forms of disconnection. The mental state of students is now so precarious for so many that, says Steven Hyman, provost of Harvard University and former director of the National Institute of Mental Health, "it is interfering with the core mission of the university."

The severity of student mental health problems has been rising since 1988,   10
according to an annual survey of counseling center directors. Through 1996, the most common problems raised by students were relationship issues. That is developmentally appropriate, reports Sherry Benton, assistant director of counseling at Kansas State University. But in 1996, anxiety overtook relationship concerns and has remained the major problem. The University of Michigan Depression Center, the nation's first, estimates that 15 percent of college students nationwide are suffering from that disorder alone.

Relationship problems haven't gone away; their nature has dramatically   11
shifted and the severity escalated. Colleges report ever more cases of obsessive pursuit, otherwise known as stalking, leading to violence, even death. Anorexia or bulimia in florid or subclinical form now afflict 40 percent of women at some time in their college career. Eleven weeks into a semester, reports psychologist Russ Federman, head of counseling at the University of Virginia, "all appointment slots are filled. But the students don't stop coming."

Drinking, too, has changed. Once a means of social lubrication, it has   12
acquired a darker, more desperate nature. Campuses nationwide are reporting record increases in binge drinking over the past decade, with students often stuporous in class, if they get there at all. Psychologist Paul E. Joffe, chair of the suicide prevention team at the University of Illinois at Urbana-Champaign, contends that at bottom binge-drinking is a quest for authenticity and intensity of experience. It gives young people something all their own to talk about, and sharing stories about the path to passing out is a primary purpose. It's an inverted world in which drinking to oblivion is the way to feel connected and alive.

"There is a ritual every university administrator has come to fear," re-   13
ports John Portmann, professor of religious studies at the University of Vir-

ginia. "Every fall, parents drop off their well-groomed freshmen and within two or three days many have consumed a dangerous amount of alcohol and placed themselves in harm's way. These kids have been controlled for so long, they just go crazy."

Heavy drinking has also become the quickest and easiest way to gain 14 acceptance, says psychologist Bernardo J. Carducci, professor at Indiana University Southeast and founder of its Shyness Research Institute. "Much of collegiate social activity is centered on alcohol consumption because it's an anxiety reducer and demands no social skills," he says. "Plus it provides an instant identity; it lets people know that you are willing to belong."

Talk to a college president or administrator and you're almost certainly 15 bound to hear tales of the parents who call at 2 A.M. to protest Branden's C in economics because it's going to damage his shot at grad school.

Shortly after psychologist Robert Epstein announced to his university 16 students that he expected them to work hard and would hold them to high standards, he heard from a parent—on official judicial stationery—asking how he could dare mistreat the young. Epstein, former editor in chief of *Psychology Today,* eventually filed a complaint with the California commission on judicial misconduct, and the judge was censured for abusing his office—but not before he created havoc in the psychology department at the University of California San Diego.

Enter: grade inflation. When he took over as president of Harvard in 17 July 2001, Lawrence Summers publicly ridiculed the value of honors after discovering that 94 percent of the college's seniors were graduating with them. Safer to lower the bar than raise the discomfort level. Grade inflation is the institutional response to parental anxiety about school demands on children, contends social historian Peter Stearns of George Mason University. As such, it is a pure index of emotional overinvestment in a child's success. And it rests on a notion of juvenile frailty— "the assumption that children are easily bruised and need explicit uplift," Stearns argues in his book, *Anxious Parenting: A History of Modern Childrearing in America.*

Parental protectionism may reach its most comic excesses in college, 18 but it doesn't begin there. Primary schools and high schools are arguably just as guilty of grade inflation. But if you're searching for someone to blame, consider Dr. Seuss. "Parents have told their kids from day one that there's no end to what they are capable of doing," says Virginia's Portmann. "They read them the Dr. Seuss book *Oh, the Places You'll Go!* and create bumper stickers telling the world their child is an honor student. American parents today expect their children to be perfect—the smartest, fastest, most charming people in the universe. And if they can't get the children to prove it on their own, they'll turn to doctors to make their kids into the people that parents want to believe their kids are."

What they're really doing, he stresses, is "showing kids how to work 19 the system for their own benefit."

And subjecting them to intense scrutiny. "I wish my parents had some 20 hobby other than me," one young patient told David Anderegg, a child psychologist in Lenox, Massachusetts, and professor of psychology at Bennington College. Anderegg finds that anxious parents are hyperattentive to their kids, reactive to every blip of their child's day, eager to solve every problem for their child—and believe that's good parenting. "If you have an infant and the baby has gas, burping the baby is being a good parent. But when you have a 10-year-old who has metaphoric gas, you don't have to burp him. You have to let him sit with it, try to figure out what to do about it. He then learns to tolerate moderate amounts of difficulty, and it's not the end of the world." . . .

From Scrutiny to Anxiety . . . and Beyond

The 1990s witnessed a landmark reversal in the traditional patterns of psy- 21 chopathology. While rates of depression rise with advancing age among people over 40, they're now increasing fastest among children, striking more children at younger and younger ages.

In his now-famous studies of how children's temperaments play out, 22 Harvard psychologist Jerome Kagan has shown unequivocally that what creates anxious children is parents hovering and protecting them from stressful experiences. About 20 percent of babies are born with a high-strung temperament. They can be spotted even in the womb; they have fast heartbeats. Their nervous systems are innately programmed to be overexcitable in response to stimulation, constantly sending out false alarms about what is dangerous.

As infants and children this group experiences stress in situations most 23 kids find unthreatening, and they may go through childhood and even adulthood fearful of unfamiliar people and events, withdrawn and shy. At school age they become cautious, quiet and introverted. Left to their own devices they grow up shrinking from social encounters. They lack confidence around others. They're easily influenced by others. They are sitting ducks for bullies. And they are on the path to depression.

While their innate reactivity seems to destine all these children for later 24 anxiety disorders, things didn't turn out that way. Between a touchy temperament in infancy and persistence of anxiety stand two highly significant things: parents. Kagan found to his surprise that the development of anxiety was scarcely inevitable despite apparent genetic programming. At age 2,

none of the overexcitable infants wound up fearful if their parents backed off from hovering and allowed the children to find some comfortable level of accommodation to the world on their own. Those parents who over-protected their children—directly observed by conducting interviews in the home—brought out the worst in them.

A small percentage of children seem almost invulnerable to anxiety 25 from the start. But the overwhelming majority of kids are somewhere in be-tween. For them, overparenting can program the nervous system to create lifelong vulnerability to anxiety and depression.

There is in these studies a lesson for all parents. Those who allow their 26 kids to find a way to deal with life's day-to-day stresses by themselves are helping them develop resilience and coping strategies. "Children need to be gently encouraged to take risks and learn that nothing terrible happens," says Michael Liebowitz, clinical professor of psychiatry at Columbia Uni-versity and head of the Anxiety Disorders Clinic at New York State Psy-chiatric Institute. "They need gradual exposure to find that the world is not dangerous. Having overprotective parents is a risk factor for anxiety dis-orders because children do not have opportunities to master their innate shyness and become more comfortable in the world." They never learn to dampen the pathways from perception to alarm reaction.

Hothouse parenting undermines children in other ways, too, says An-   27
deregg. Being examined all the time makes children extremely self-conscious.
As a result they get less communicative; scrutiny teaches them to bury their
real feelings deeply. And most of all, self-consciousness removes the safety to
be experimental and playful. "If every drawing is going to end up on your
parents' refrigerator, you're not free to fool around, to goof up or make mistakes," says Anderegg.

Parental hovering is why so many teenagers are so ironic, he notes. It's   28
a kind of detachment, "a way of hiding in plain sight. They just don't want
to be exposed to any more scrutiny."

Parents are always so concerned about children having high self-   29
esteem, he adds. "But when you cheat on their behalf to get them ahead of
other children"—by pursuing accommodations and recommendations—
"you just completely corrode their sense of self. They feel 'I couldn't do this
on my own.' It robs them of their own sense of efficacy." A child comes to
think, "if I need every advantage I can get, then perhaps there is really
something wrong with me." A slam dunk for depression.

Virginia's Portmann feels the effects are even more pernicious; they   30
weaken the whole fabric of society. He sees young people becoming weaker
right before his eyes, more responsive to the herd, too eager to fit in—less
assertive in the classroom, unwilling to disagree with their peers, afraid to
question authority, more willing to conform to the expectations of those on
the next rung of power above them.

The end result of cheating childhood is to extend it forever. Despite all   31
the parental pressure, and probably because of it, kids are pushing back—
in their own way. They're taking longer to grow up.

Adulthood no longer begins when adolescence ends, according to a re-   32
cent report by University of Pennsylvania sociologist Frank F. Furstenberg
and colleagues. There is, instead, a growing no-man's-land of post-
adolescence from 20 to 30, which they dub "early adulthood." Those in it
look like adults but "haven't become fully adult yet—traditionally defined
as finishing school, landing a job with benefits, marrying and parenting—
because they are not ready or perhaps not permitted to do so."

Using the classic benchmarks of adulthood, 65 percent of males had   33
reached adulthood by the age of 30 in 1960. By contrast, in 2000, only 31
percent had. Among women, 77 percent met the benchmarks of adulthood
by age 30 in 1960. By 2000, the number had fallen to 46 percent.

Take away play from the front end of development and it finds a way   34
onto the back end. A steady march of success through regimented childhood arranged and monitored by parents creates young adults who need
time to explore themselves. "They often need a period in college or after-

ward to legitimately experiment—to be children," says historian Stearns.
"There's decent historical evidence to suggest that societies that allow kids
a few years of latitude and even moderate [rebellion] end up with healthier kids than societies that pretend such impulses don't exist."

Marriage is one benchmark of adulthood, but its antecedents extend   35
well into childhood. "The precursor to marriage is dating, and the precursor to dating is playing," says Carducci. The less time children spend
in free play, the less socially competent they'll be as adults. It's in play that
we learn give and take, the fundamental rhythm of all relationships. We
learn how to read the feelings of others and how to negotiate conflicts.
Taking the play out of childhood, he says, is bound to create a developmental lag, and he sees it clearly in the social patterns of today's adolescents and young adults, who hang around in groups that are more typical
of childhood. Not to be forgotten: The backdrop of continued high levels of divorce confuses kids already too fragile to take the huge risk of
commitment. . . .

Children, however, are not the only ones who are harmed by hypercon-   36
cern. Vigilance is enormously taxing—and it's taken all the fun out of parenting. "Parenting has in some measurable ways become less enjoyable than
it used to be," says Stearns. "I find parents less willing to indulge their children's sense of time. So they either force-feed them or do things for them."

Parents need to abandon the idea of perfection and give up some of the   37
invasive control they've maintained over their children. The goal of parenting, Portmann reminds, is to raise an independent human being. Sooner
or later, he says, most kids will be forced to confront their own mediocrity.
Parents may find it easier to give up some control if they recognize they
have exaggerated many of the dangers of childhood—although they have
steadfastly ignored others, namely the removal of recess from schools and
the ubiquity of video games that encourage aggression.

The childhood we've introduced to our children is very different from   38
that in past eras, Epstein stresses. Children no longer work at young ages.
They stay in school for longer periods of time and spend more time exclusively in the company of peers. Children are far less integrated into adult
society than they used to be at every step of the way. We've introduced laws
that give children many rights and protections—although we have allowed
media and marketers to have free access.

In changing the nature of childhood, Stearns argues, we've introduced   39
a tendency to assume that children can't handle difficult situations.
"Middle-class parents especially assume that if kids start getting into difficulty they need to rush in and do it for them, rather than let them flounder
a bit and learn from it. I don't mean we should abandon them," he says,

"but give them more credit for figuring things out." And recognize that parents themselves have created many of the stresses and anxieties children are suffering from, without giving them tools to manage them.

While the adults are at it, they need to remember that one of the goals 40 of higher education is to help young people develop the capacity to think for themselves.

Although we're well on our way to making kids more fragile, no one 41 thinks that kids and young adults are fundamentally more flawed than in previous generations. Maybe many will "recover" from diagnoses too liberally slapped on to them. In his own studies of 14 skills he has identified as essential for adulthood in American culture, from love to leadership, Epstein has found that "although teens don't necessarily behave in a competent way, they have the potential to be every bit as competent and as incompetent as adults."

Parental anxiety has its place. But the way things now stand, it's not being 42 applied wisely. We're paying too much attention to too few kids—and in the end, the wrong kids. As with the girl whose parents bought her the Gestalt-defect diagnosis, resources are being expended for kids who don't need them.

There are kids who are worth worrying about—kids in poverty, stresses 43 Anderegg. "We focus so much on our own children," says Elkind, "It's time to begin caring about all children."

Thinking Critically

1. What claims does Hara Estroff Marano make, and what kinds of evidence does she use to support and illustrate those claims? Does she include opposing perspectives?

2. What is the effect of Marano's opening anecdotes? Identify her use of irony in these first few paragraphs. Does she use irony elsewhere in her argument? To what effect?

3. What connection does Marano make between grade inflation and the lengths to which individual parents will go to protect (or overprotect) their children? What evidence does she offer to support this connection?

Writing Critically

1. How are children depicted in American popular culture? Choose two or three specific films, television programs, animated series, commercials, or other pop culture artifacts that feature children. Analyze these artifacts closely, thinking about their ultimate audience and purpose. What message is being sent to viewers or consumers about the role of children in American society? What values are ascribed, either overtly or covertly, to childhood in America?

2. Compare the precautions taken by the middle- and upper-middle-class parents in Marano's article with the concerns of parents in two other essays in this chapter: Dashka Slater's "The Equalizers" and Whitney Joiner's "One Strike and You're Out of School." Then, in Chapter 11, read the selection from Frank Furedi's *Culture of Fear: Risk-Taking and the Morality of Low Expectations* (see pp. 625–29). How consistent are American values and policies when it comes to raising American children? In an essay that draws on these readings (as well as other sources you find interesting and appropriate), argue for the necessity of recognizing and addressing at least one such inconsistency.

3. How grown-up are you? How grown-up do you need to be? In contemporary society, what does it mean to be an "adult"? Are you in much of a hurry to be one? Or, if you consider yourself an adult, what life experience defined "adulthood" for you?

One Strike and You're Out of School

WHITNEY JOINER

Whitney Joiner is a native of Louisville, Kentucky, who now lives in New York. While she was an undergraduate at Smith College, her writing began appearing in alternative publications such as the New York City weekly *New York Press* (where she later interned). Her investigations of popular culture, social issues, and new media have appeared in *Salon.com, Folio, Inside.com,* and many other online and alternative publications. In 2004, Joiner became the senior associate editor for features at *Seventeen* magazine. "One Strike and You're Out of School" appeared in *Salon.com,* one of the longest-lasting online news and general-interest magazines, in February 2004.

In November 1996, Dustin Seal, then a high school senior, was expelled   1
after authorities at his Knoxville, Tenn., high school found a 3-inch knife in his car. Even though the knife wasn't Dustin's, and even though the friend who'd left the knife in Dustin's car claimed responsibility for it, the administration didn't budge: Under the school's "zero tolerance" policy, every student found with a weapon on campus had to be expelled.

This article first appeared in Salon.com, at http://www.Salon.com. An online version remains in the Salon archives. Reprinted with permission.

Dustin became depressed and withdrawn after his expulsion, says his fa- 2
ther, Dennis, a 58-year-old retired commercial contractor. "He would ask me
constantly: When are they going to let me back in school with my friends?
How can they take everything away from me when I've done nothing wrong?"

The Seals sued the school district and took the case all the way to the 3
Supreme Court, winning at every step. But by the time the court sent the case
back to the local level for Dustin to claim damages, he was too exhausted to
continue fighting. He settled for $30,000 in December of 2001.

Six months later, Dustin spent a June day with his father shooting pool. 4
He went home that night and repeatedly left messages on Dennis' answering machine while Dennis, sick in bed, slept in the next room: "It doesn't
look like we're going to the bike show tomorrow, Dad, but I love you."
"Dad—goodbye."

Then he drew a bath, got in the bathtub, stuck a pistol under his chin 5
and pulled the trigger. He was 22 years old.

Almost two years after his son's suicide, Dennis Seal is suing the Knox 6
County school board for wrongful death, claiming that Dustin's suicide
was a direct result of his expulsion. "It broke his spirit and he never got
over it," says Seal. School district spokesman Russ Oaks wouldn't comment on Seal's case, but, he says, "Zero tolerance has helped to ensure a
safer school environment." The case goes to trial this October.

Clearing his son's name has consumed Dennis Seal's life. "That's all I've 7
done for two years," he says. He's spent well over $30,000 in legal fees,
and is planning to try the case himself, after unsatisfactory experiences
with lawyers spurred him to study for a law degree online through a local
community college. He says he never received a letter of condolence from
the school district.

Dennis Seal's story is perhaps the most harrowing example of a zero 8
tolerance policy gone awry—but it's not the only one. A growing number
of parents across the country are struggling to deal with their children's
expulsions, for what they claim are minor infractions blown out of proportion. According to the National Center for Education Statistics, a zero
tolerance policy is a "school or district policy that mandates predeter-
mined consequences or punishments for specific offenses"—which has all
too often come to mean that whether the drug is cocaine or cold medicine,
whether the weapon is a butter knife or a shotgun, the penalty will be the
same. Like the mandatory sentencing laws of the early '90s, which have
overcrowded prisons with felons convicted of relatively low-level crimes
forced to serve long sentences, zero tolerance is a one-size-fits-all policy,
critics say—and treating every offense the same, regardless of the context,
just doesn't work.

School officials across the country say that after school shootings at Pa- 9
ducah and Jonesboro, Springfield and Columbine, they can't afford to take
chances. And just as no one wants to repeal crime laws for fear of seeming
soft on crime, school districts are reluctant to change zero tolerance policies
for fear of sending the message that discipline in schools is no longer a priority. About 79 percent of public schools have zero tolerance policies for violence and tobacco and 94 percent for firearms, reports NCES.

News stories of children expelled under zero tolerance abound (the girl 10
who was kicked out of school for writing a violent story in her diary; the
boy expelled for lending his asthma inhaler to his asthmatic girlfriend), but

Kids these days All students must pass a metal detector and
security guards at this suburban high school. Gun violence at
high schools in the 1990s caused many school districts to install metal detectors and hire additional security personnel.

what goes unreported is the private suffering endured by families of accused kids: the financial devastation from legal costs and private school tuition; the social isolation, as many must dedicate their time to defending their child; the shame of being seen by the community as a "bad" parent. Worst of all is the emotional toll on the children, who are left with few educational alternatives and deep feelings of anger and betrayal toward a system they've been raised to trust.

Parents affected by zero tolerance are networking through the Web, 11 thanks to sites like EndZeroTolerance.com and e-mail groups like Parents Against Zero Tolerance. Some, like Dennis Seal, have been inspired to take political action—he's running for a school board seat in November—but most depend on the other parents they meet via the Web for legal advice and, especially, emotional support.

"I feel really close to a number of [the parents]," says Mary LeBlanc, a 12 51-year-old Louisiana receptionist whose 17-year-old son Adam was expelled, arrested, chained to the wall of a police station by his ankles and thrown in jail after his younger brother's school bus driver found a drawing in a sketch pad that depicted Adam and his friends attacking the high school with ICBM missiles. "They know exactly where you're coming from and they're very encouraging. It's very difficult to find someone in this community who can sympathize and understand. You find the most comfort from parents who've been through similar things. If I didn't have that, I would've been lost."

The Gun-Free Schools Act, passed by President Clinton in 1994, man- 13 dates a one-year expulsion for any student found with drugs or weapons on campus. The law was designed to protect students from serious dangers, but school boards—the interpreters of the law, since public schools are run at the local level—began to tighten their policies after the mid-'90s spate of school shootings, ushering in the era of zero tolerance. Immediately, suspension and expulsion rates zoomed nationwide. According to the Department of Education's Office of Civil Rights, the total number of suspensions and expulsions for both elementary and secondary schools rose from 1,977,862 in 1990 to 3,150,626 in 2000.

The continuing rapid rise of these numbers prove that zero tolerance 14 doesn't really work, says Russell Skiba, an associate professor in educational psychology at Indiana University and the director of the Safe and Responsive Schools Project, who has just completed two major studies on zero tolerance. "Schools will say, 'We need these policies to keep these schools safe, and if we make any exceptions it'll reduce safety.' The important piece is whether it really *is* making a contribution to our schools. The best data says it isn't."

Even those charged with carrying out the policies don't necessarily 15 agree with them. "I dislike lumping every single case into one category," says Curt Lavarello, executive director of the National Association of School Resource Officers. ("Resource officer" is the official term for school police officers.) "We know the difference between a kid who has a knife because he's a fisherman and a kid who's going to use the knife to stab his classmates. But when you institute a zero tolerance policy, you have no choice: You become more of a robot in your police work."

So why is expulsion no longer a last resort, and how could anyone suspend 16 a child for something as innocuous as bringing Midol to school? "Parents want to be assured that their children will be safe," says Bill Modzeleski, associate deputy undersecretary for the Office of Safe and Drug-Free Schools at the U.S. Department of Education. "I assume that, yes, with 52 million kids and 15,000 school districts there probably are some policies that some individuals call harsh. But there are other parents who say, 'They're not harsh, because those are the same policies that are protecting my son and daughter.'"

School districts and zero tolerance proponents like Modzeleski say that 17 common sense must prevail—that school boards do take extenuating circumstances into account at expulsion hearings and that all children are offered due process. But for parents trying to keep their children in school, common sense seems like the last thing on the minds of the administrators.

Graduate student Howard Hastings, 52, whose 14-year-old son Karel 18 was expelled in 2000 for giving a joint to another child at his Fairfax County, Va., middle school, says that during his son's expulsion hearing, an earlier 10-day absence was seen as suspicious and added to the school's proof of Karel's guilt. It didn't matter that the absence was due to a wrestling injury that left Karel—a local wrestling star—unable to walk for over a week.

Hastings was furious with Karel for his marijuana experimentation, he 19 says, and planned to punish him. He immediately met with the school administration and told Karel to be as honest as possible about the joint he'd given his friend, assuming that if they "played by their rules and did everything the school required," Karel might be readmitted. But the administration was determined to expel Karel, says Hastings, and by the time the school's discipline measures added up—mandating that Karel attend multiple Alcoholics Anonymous meetings and group therapy every week on top of expulsion—Hastings felt that the school's punishment was more than enough. In fact, he now wishes that he hadn't pushed Karel to be completely honest with the school.

"If we had to do it all over again, I might've said, 'Just keep silent,'" says 20 Hastings. "We trusted [the school]. We're used to going in and talking to a teacher about how our kid is doing. But they weren't interested in him at all."

Fairfax County School District coordinator of community relations 21
Paul Regnier notes that Karel pled guilty in court to possession of a controlled substance, and that "the school district felt there was evidence of
distribution"—which factored into its decision to expel.

Mary LeBlanc, the Louisiana mother whose 17-year-old son Adam was ar- 22
rested for a drawing, says that when the school found a box cutter on her son,
they immediately interpreted it as proof of Adam's dangerous nature—even
though she repeatedly told the administration that he needed it at his long-term
after-school job at a family-owned grocery store. "They weren't having any
part of that," she says. "My son was obviously planning something."

Ascension Parish assistant superintendent Donald Sogny, who wouldn't 23
comment specifically on Adam's case, says that the media only gets half the
story. "I'm not going to air a child's dirty laundry," he says. "We can tell
you a lot more that might convince you that maybe it wasn't a small thing."
He also notes that not every child recommended for expulsion ends up expelled: In fact, two cases in his district last month were "modified significantly," he says.

"Zero tolerance looks good on paper," says Diane Rohman, 38, whose 24
son was expelled from high school in the same district where she works as
a middle school art teacher in Stafford County, Va. Rohman estimates that
her middle school has already expelled about three students this year—one
for carrying over-the-counter cold medicine. "It makes it look like we're
doing something to make the schools safe. But I don't think anyone [in the
community] is really aware of what it is."

Rohman's 17-year-old son, Anthony, her only child, was expelled on 25
the first day of his senior year in high school last September after administrators found a marijuana seed in the back seat of his car. Rohman claims
the seed came from a boy who was riding in the back seat of the car. "They
call it due process, but I have never walked into a situation where I felt
that *nothing* I said would've mattered," says Rohman of her son's expulsion hearing. "I knew it was hopeless—appeals never go through. The attorneys said it was a no-win situation with the school." It seemed
especially unjust, she says, "because I'm a colleague of these people. It
made me angrier."

As a single parent on a teacher's salary, Rohman couldn't afford private 26
school tuition, and, like many districts, the other public schools in the
county wouldn't accept an expelled student. So Rohman sent Anthony to
live with her brother in Maryland, four hours away. She visits him every
few weeks, but the separation has been tough. "I knew next year that he'd
be going away to college," she says, "but when it happens within a week—
I just wasn't mentally prepared for it."

The Stafford County Public School District declined to comment on 27
Anthony's case.

Hastings and his wife also sent their son to live with relatives—Karel's 28
grandmother, across the country in Montana—for seven months. As much
as they hated the separation from their son, says Hastings, it was better than
keeping him in the local alternative school, where, ironically, what was designed as rehabilitation for Karel's "drug problem" ended up putting him at
much greater risk. "He was the only little kid there," says Hastings. "Some
of those kids were 18, smoking pot behind the building with no supervision."
Hastings accompanied his son to school every day, worked on his dissertation at a local library, then drove Karel the 45 minutes back home.

Oftentimes, parents' lives are put on hold as they spend months—or 29
years—defending their child. Hastings, a Ph.D. student in cultural studies at
George Mason University, still hasn't finished graduate school. "I hoped I
could get my dissertation wrapped up in that year, and now I still don't have
it," he says. "Almost immediately after Karel's expulsion most of my time was
taken up driving him to various things—to appointments with the school, to
the mandatory AA meetings and therapy." Setting aside his degree has affected his family's finances, he says. "It's cut our earning power. If I don't have
the degree, I can't get the job. And I've had to keep paying tuition."

"At the beginning you think, OK, well, this is going to be an annoy- 30
ance," says D.C. lawyer Paul Brown, 55, whose 17-year-old learning-
disabled son was expelled early in his freshman year. "But it's a two-week
suspension and then expulsion and it just goes *on and on and on*. I thought,
well, I'm sure the school will be reasonable—but by the time you realize
you should've gotten a lawyer, it's too late."

Brown's son brought a toy gun, and real ammunition, to the bus stop 31
to scare the kids who called him a "fag" on a daily basis. "I would have
punished him severely," Brown wrote in an e-mail. But by acting in loco
parentis, the school superseded Brown's parental decisions. "Since the
school came down so hard on him, I had to shift gears to defend my son.
He had no other defenders. I went from feeling that parents and teachers
were united in educating my son to feeling the school system was the enemy." The district allowed his son into a neighboring public school (he'll
graduate this spring), but only after hiring a personal security guard to es-
cort Brown's son everywhere on campus.

Jeanette Hartwell, 47, moved her entire family from Rancho Cuca- 32
monga, Calif., to the neighboring town of Ontario to live with relatives after her son DJ was expelled from Ruth Musser Middle School for joking
with a classmate about opening fire in school with a Glock semiautomatic
handgun. The Hartwells shelled out $15,000 in lawyers' fees to fight DJ's

expulsion. When the board wouldn't allow DJ to return, the family coughed up an additional $13,000 to pay for private school tuition for DJ and his two younger brothers—fees they couldn't afford on Jeanette's husband's salary as a police officer. The Hartwells were forced to sell the home they'd purchased a year earlier.

"It was a nice house, and we'd just begun to think of it as home," says 33 DJ, now 16. He knew the conversation with his friend was inappropriate, says DJ, a self-described loner who loves books and politics. But "I was kind of starved for any sort of friendly interaction," he says. "So if he wanted to start a conversation about it I wasn't going to stop him. I didn't think it was harmful to anybody." That was the last conversation he had with his friend. After his expulsion, DJ says, "I felt very betrayed and very hurt. I was in shock. I felt very alone."

("We're not going to comment on this," said Cathy Preston, adminis- 34 trative assistant to the superintendent of Central School District in Rancho Cucamonga. "That was a private matter and we don't discuss students.")

Besides battling school districts, these parents also struggle to keep their 35 children mentally healthy. As Dustin Seal's case illustrates, expulsion can have a deep effect on a child's emotional state and sense of self. "I see anxiety and depression becoming almost the most powerful things in their lives," says Jerry Wyckoff, a former school psychologist now in private practice in Overland Park, Kan., who has worked with about 15 children embroiled in zero tolerance cases. "The kids just can't understand why this happened to them. They feel completely, totally wronged. Adolescents have trouble trusting adults anyway, and this just confirms that all adults are against me; there's no one in the world who can help me."

For kids who are both expelled *and* arrested, finding a way to move on 36 proves especially hard. Since he had a felony on his record, Dustin Seal wasn't able to find a job after his expulsion. "He wanted to be an attorney," says Dennis Seal, "but he couldn't even work at McDonald's."

And since expulsion means that the student is not only barred from 37 school, but from all school events, activities that might have helped the child—sports or clubs that could raise self-esteem or foster positive relationships with other kids—are now off-limits. Hastings' son, the wrestler, was forced off the team since they trained at the local school.

Rohman's son, Anthony, always loved baseball, she says; playing for the 38 school team was his passion. "After he left," she says, "I found his team jersey in the trash in his room. He was so proud of that before [his expulsion]."

For Brown and his wife, who were active school volunteers and sup- 39 porters, their son's expulsion meant that they ended up ostracized as well. "Once your kid is no longer going to school with other kids, we no longer saw our friends," he says. "We didn't go to the games, we didn't go to the plays. We were totally isolated from people we'd known for years."

"But it's not just the parents who suffer," says Brown. "It's his older 40 brother, too, because you have to focus all your attention on one kid."

Jeanette Hartwell's two younger sons were doing well in the public 41 school when her oldest son, DJ, was expelled. Wary of the public school system, she enrolled them all in private school. "[My middle son] was in the band and played for the school's roller hockey team. He had to leave all that," she says. "It hurt him. He had a lot of friends and was well liked."

While parents like Dennis Seal have thrown themselves into fighting 42 against zero tolerance—Seal says he gets about a call a week from other parents asking for advice—it's been difficult for parents, like Brown, to take any political action toward ending the policies. "It's hard to form a support group of people who hate the school, because you're also ashamed of your status as a parent," he says. "Your kid reflects on you. You go into the school year thinking everything is wonderful and your kid will be educated. Then you find out—oh, my kid is one of *those* kids who shouldn't be in school at all."

Joining Parents Against Zero Tolerance has made Rohman more polit- 43 ically active, she says. She's attended an academic conference about school discipline with other PAZT members, and she presented a lengthy paper to the school board, arguing against her county's zero tolerance policies. The board agreed to start looking at individual cases instead of doling out the same punishments regardless of the details.

After her success with the board, she says, "I do feel like what you say 44 and do can make a difference." But she's not planning to stick around to find out: After the school year is over, she's considering moving closer to her son and finding another teaching position. "I don't feel like I can stay here after this. I love my school; I love my job. I don't want to leave—but I don't want to stay in a county that would do this to my son."

As for Seal, he's determined to make sure that his son did not die in 45 vain. "I have to have closure," he says. "I don't want anything like this to ever happen again."

Thinking Critically

1. What are the origins of the term "zero tolerance"? According to Whitney Joiner's article, what are the main reasons why a school district adopts a zero tolerance policy? What are the main arguments against zero tolerance policies?

2. How does Joiner organize her argument? What does her choice of examples, illustrations, and evidence suggest about her audience?

3. What kinds of stories about zero tolerance policies usually appear in the mainstream media, according to Joiner (and in your own experience)? In what ways is Joiner's "angle" different? What, specifically, is her thesis?

Writing Critically

1. What cultural and moral values are reenforced by zero tolerance policies in the classroom? For further information and resources to support your analysis, visit the websites of the National Center for Education Statistics at <http://nces.ed.gov/>; EndZeroTolerance.com; and the U.S. Department of Education's Office of Safe and Drug-Free Schools at <http://www.ed.gov/about/offices/list/osdfs/index.html?src=oc>.

2. Find out whether the school district for a child in your family has a zero tolerance policy. Create an informational report or website for people in that school district that explains how and why the zero tolerance policy was created, how students, parents, and community members can learn more about the policy, and ways in which the local community has responded to the policy.

3. Although some school districts have zero tolerance policies, the word *tolerance* itself is also used in classrooms, workplaces, the media, and government to discuss something else entirely. Create a taxonomy of the political and cultural meanings of *tolerance.* How does the word's meaning change according to the context in which it is used? What values are ascribed to "tolerance" in contemporary American culture?

Liberal Groupthink Is Anti-Intellectual

MARK BAUERLEIN

This selection and the next one, John Tierney's "Republicans Outnumbered in Academia, Studies Find," appeared in the weeks following the 2004 American presidential election. The authors of both readings cite different polls and studies, ranging from a telephone survey to a scholarly research report, that attempt to quantify "conservative" and "liberal" perspectives and personnel on American college campuses. Mark Bauerlein is a professor of English at Emory University and director of research and analysis at the National Endowment for the Arts. His scholarly interests range from the poetry of Walt Whitman and the works of nineteenth-century American philosophers to the civil rights movement. Bauerlein frequently contributes essays and book reviews to the *Wall Street Journal, Partisan Review,* the *Weekly Standard,* and the London *Times Literary Supplement.* "Liberal Groupthink Is Anti-Intellectual" appeared in the *Chronicle of Higher Education* on November 12, 2004. The print edition of the *Chronicle,* published forty-nine weeks each year, is the leading source of news and job listings for academic communities worldwide. The online version is updated daily and can be viewed at <http://chronicle.com/>.

Conservatives on college campuses scored a tactical hit when the American Enterprise Institute's magazine published a survey of voter registration among humanities and social-science faculty members several years ago. More than nine out of 10 professors belonged to the Democratic or Green party, an imbalance that contradicted many liberal academics' protestations that diversity and pluralism abound in higher education. Further investigations by people like David Horowitz, president of the Center for the Study of Popular Culture, coupled with well-publicized cases of discrimination against conservative professors, reinforced the findings and set "intellectual diversity" on the agenda of state legislators and members of Congress.

The public has now picked up the message that "campuses are havens for left-leaning activists," according to a *Chronicle* poll of 1,000 adult Americans this year. Half of those surveyed—68 percent who call themselves "conservative" and even 30 percent who say they are "liberal"— agreed that colleges improperly introduce a liberal bias into what they teach. The matter, however, is clearly not just one of perception. Indeed, in another recent survey, this one conducted by the Higher Education Research Institute of the University of California at Los Angeles, faculty members themselves chose as their commitment "far left" or "liberal" more than two and a half times as often as "far right" or "conservative." As a *Chronicle* article last month put it: "On left-leaning campuses around the country, professors on the right feel disenfranchised."

Yet while the lack of conservative minds on college campuses is increasingly indisputable, the question remains: Why?

The obvious answer, at least in the humanities and social sciences, is that academics shun conservative values and traditions, so their curricula and hiring practices discourage non-leftists from pursuing academic careers. What allows them to do that, while at the same time they deny it, is that the bias takes a subtle form. Although I've met several conservative intellectuals in the last year who would love an academic post but have given up after years of trying, outright blackballing is rare. The disparate outcome emerges through an indirect filtering process that runs from graduate school to tenure and beyond.

Some fields' very constitutions rest on progressive politics and make it   5
clear from the start that conservative outlooks will not do. Schools of education, for instance, take constructivist theories of learning as definitive, excluding realists (in matters of knowledge) on principle, while the quasi-Marxist outlook of cultural studies rules out those who espouse capitalism. If you disapprove of affirmative action, forget pursuing a degree in African-American studies. If you think that the nuclear family proves the best unit of social well-being, stay away from women's studies.

Other fields allow the possibility of studying conservative authors and   6
ideas, but narrow the avenues of advancement. Mentors are disinclined to support your topic, conference announcements rarely appeal to your work, and few job descriptions match your profile. A fledgling literary scholar who studies anti-communist writing and concludes that its worth surpasses that of counterculture discourse in terms of the cogency of its ideas and morality of its implications won't go far in the application process.

No active or noisy elimination need occur, and no explicit queries about   7
political orientation need be posed. Political orientation has been embedded into the disciplines, and so what is indeed a political judgment may be expressed in disciplinary terms. As an Americanist said in a committee meeting that I attended, "We can't hire anyone who doesn't do race," an assertion that had all the force of a scholastic dictum. Stanley Fish, professor and dean emeritus of the College of Liberal Arts and Sciences at the University of Illinois at Chicago, advises, "The question you should ask professors is whether your work has influence or relevance"—and while he raised it to argue that no liberal conspiracy in higher education exists, the question is bound to keep conservatives off the short list. For while studies of scholars like Michel Foucault, Michael Hardt, and Antonio Negri seem central in the graduate seminar, studies of Friedrich A. von Hayek and Francis Fukuyama, whose names rarely appear on cultural-studies syllabi despite their influence on world affairs, seem irrelevant.

Academics may quibble over the hiring process, but voter registration   8
shows that liberal orthodoxy now has a professional import. Conservatives and liberals square off in public, but on campuses, conservative opinion doesn't qualify as respectable inquiry. You won't often find vouchers discussed in education schools or patriotism argued in American studies. Historically, the boundaries of scholarly fields were created by the objects studied and by norms of research and peer review. Today, a political variable has been added, whereby conservative assumptions expel their hold-

ers from the academic market. A wall insulates the academic left from ideas and writings on the right.

One can see that phenomenon in how insiders, reacting to Horowitz's   9
polls, displayed little evidence that they had ever read conservative texts or met a conservative thinker. Weblogs had entries conjecturing why conservatives avoid academe—while never actually bothering to find one and ask—as if they were some exotic breed whose absence lay rooted in an inscrutable mind-set. Professors offered caricatures of the conservative intelligentsia, selecting Ann H. Coulter and Rush Limbaugh as representatives, not von Hayek, Russell Kirk, Leo Strauss, Thomas Sowell, Robert Nozick, or Gertrude Himmelfarb. One of them wrote that "conservatives of Horowitz's ilk want to unleash the most ignorant forces of the right in hounding liberal academics to death."

Such parochialism and alarm are the outcome of a course of socialization   10
that aligns liberalism with disciplinary standards and collegial mores. Liberal orthodoxy is not just a political outlook; it's a professional one. Rarely is its content discussed. The ordinary evolution of opinion—expounding your beliefs in conversation, testing them in debate, reading books that confirm or refute them—is lacking, and what should remain arguable settles into surety. With so many in harmony, and with those who agree joined also in a guild membership, liberal beliefs become academic manners. It's social life in a professional world, and its patterns are worth describing.

The first protocol of academic society might be called the *Common As-*   11
sumption. The assumption is that all the strangers in the room at professional gatherings are liberals. Liberalism at humanities meetings serves the same purpose that scientific method does at science assemblies. It provides a base of accord. The Assumption proves correct often enough for it to join other forms of trust that enable collegial events. A fellowship is intimated, and members may speak their minds without worrying about justifying basic beliefs or curbing emotions.

The Common Assumption usually pans out and passes unnoticed—except   12
for those who don't share it, to whom it is an overt fact of professional life. Yet usually even they remain quiet in the face of the Common Assumption. There is no joy in breaking up fellow feeling, and the awkward pause that accompanies the moment when someone comes out of the conservative closet marks a quarantine that only the institutionally secure are willing to endure.

Sometimes, however, the Assumption steps over the line into arrogance,   13
as when at a dinner a job candidate volunteered her description of a certain "racist, sexist, and homophobic" organization, and I admitted that I belonged to it. Or when two postdocs from Germany at a nearby university stopped by my office to talk about American literature. As they sat

down and I commented on how quiet things were on the day before Thanksgiving, one muttered, "Yes, we call it American Genocide Day."

Such episodes reveal the argumentative hazards of the Assumption. 14
Apart from the ill-mannered righteousness, academics with too much confidence in their audience utter debatable propositions as received wisdom. An assertion of the genocidal motives of early English settlers is put forward not for discussion but for approval. If the audience shares the belief, all is well and good. But a lone dissenter disrupts the process and, merely by posing a question, can show just how cheap such a pat consensus actually is.

After Nixon crushed McGovern in the 1972 election, the film critic 15
Pauline Kael made a remark that has become a touchstone among conservatives. "I don't know how Richard Nixon could have won," she marveled. "I don't know anybody who voted for him." While the second sentence indicates the sheltered habitat of the Manhattan intellectual, the first signifies what social scientists call the *False Consensus Effect*. That effect occurs when people think that the collective opinion of their own group matches that of the larger population. If the members of a group reach a consensus and rarely encounter those who dispute it, they tend to believe that everybody thinks the same way.

The tendency applies to professors, especially in humanities depart- 16
ments, but with a twist. Although a liberal consensus reigns within, academics have an acute sense of how much their views clash with the majority of Americans. Some take pride in a posture of dissent and find noble precursors in civil rights, Students for a Democratic Society, and other such movements. But dissent from a mainstream has limited charms, especially after 24 years of center-right rule in Washington. Liberal professors want to be adversarial, but are tired of seclusion. Thus, many academics find a solution in a limited version of the False Consensus that says liberal belief reigns among intellectuals everywhere.

Such a consensus applies only to the thinking classes, union supporters, 17
minority-group activists, and environmentalists against corporate powers. Professors cannot conceive that any person trained in critical thinking could listen to George W. Bush speak and still vote Republican. They do acknowledge one setting in which right-wing intellectual work happens— namely, the think tanks—but add that the labor there is patently corrupt. The Heritage Foundation, the American Enterprise Institute, the Manhattan Institute, and the Hoover Institution all have corporate sponsors, they note, and fellows in residence do their bidding. Hence, references to "right-wing think tanks" are always accompanied by the qualifier "well-funded."

The dangers of aligning liberalism with higher thought are obvious. 18
When a Duke University philosophy professor implied last February that

conservatives tend toward stupidity, he confirmed the public opinion of academics as a self-regarding elite—regardless of whether or not he was joking, as he later said that he was. When laymen scan course syllabi or search the shelves of college bookstores and find only a few volumes of traditionalist argument amid the thickets of leftist critique, they wonder whether students ever enjoy a fruitful encounter with conservative thought. When a conference panel is convened or a collection is published on a controversial subject, and all the participants and contributors stand on one side of the issue, the tendentiousness is striking to everyone except those involved. The False Consensus does its work, but has an opposite effect. Instead of uniting academics with a broader public, it isolates them as a ritualized club.

The final social pattern is the *Law of Group Polarization*. That law— as Cass R. Sunstein, a professor of political science and of jurisprudence at the University of Chicago, has described—predicts that when like-minded people deliberate as an organized group, the general opinion shifts toward extreme versions of their common beliefs. In a product-liability trial, for example, if nine jurors believe the manufacturer is somewhat guilty and three believe it is entirely guilty, the latter will draw the former toward a larger award than the nine would allow on their own. If people who object in varying degrees to the war in Iraq convene to debate methods of protest, all will emerge from the discussion more resolved against the war.

Group Polarization happens so smoothly on campuses that those involved lose all sense of the range of legitimate opinion. A librarian at Ohio State University who announces, "White Americans pay too little attention to the benefits their skin color gives them, and opening their eyes to their privileged status is a valid part of a college education" (*The Chronicle*, August 6, 2004) seems to have no idea how extreme his vision sounds to many ears. Deliberations among groups are just as prone to tone deafness. The annual resolutions of the Modern Language Association's Delegate Assembly, for example, ring with indignation over practices that enjoy popular acceptance. Last year, charging that in wartime, governments use language to "misrepresent policies" and "stigmatize dissent," one resolution urged faculty members to conduct "critical analysis of war talk . . . as appropriate, in classrooms." However high-minded the delegates felt as they tallied the vote, which passed 122 to 8 without discussion, to outsiders the resolution seemed merely a license for more proselytizing.

The problem is that the simple trappings of deliberation make academics think that they've reached an opinion through reasoned debate—instead of, in part, through an irrational social dynamic. The opinion takes on the status of a norm. Extreme views appear to be logical extensions of principles that everyone more or less shares, and extremists gain a larger influence than their numbers merit. If participants left the enclave, their beliefs would moderate, and they would be more open to the beliefs of others. But with the conferences, quarterlies, and committee meetings suffused with extreme positions, they're stuck with abiding by the convictions of their most passionate brethren.

As things stand, such behaviors shift in a left direction, but they could 22 just as well move right if conservatives had the extent of control that liberals do now. The phenomenon that I have described is not so much a political matter as a social dynamic; any political position that dominates an institution without dissent deteriorates into smugness, complacency, and blindness. The solution is an intellectual climate in which the worst tendencies of group psychology are neutralized.

That doesn't mean establishing affirmative action for conservative 23 scholars or encouraging greater market forces in education—which violate conservative values as much as they do liberal values. Rather, it calls for academics to recognize that a one-party campus is bad for the intellectual health of everyone. Groupthink is an anti-intellectual condition, ironically seductive in that the more one feels at ease with compatriots, the more one's mind narrows. The great liberal John Stuart Mill identified its insulating effect as a failure of imagination: "They have never thrown themselves into the mental condition of those who think differently from them." With adversaries so few and opposing ideas so disposable, a reverse advantage sets in. The majority expands its power throughout the institution, but its thinking grows routine and parochial. The minority is excluded, but its thinking is tested and toughened. Being the lone dissenter in a colloquy, one learns to acquire sure facts, crisp arguments, and a thick skin.

But we can't open the university to conservative ideas and persons by 24 outside command. That would poison the atmosphere and jeopardize the ideals of free inquiry. Leftist bias evolved within the protocols of academic practice (though not without intimidation), and conservative challenges should evolve in the same way. There are no administrative or professional reasons to bring conservatism into academe, to be sure, but there are good intellectual and social reasons for doing so.

Those reasons are, in brief: One, a wider spectrum of opinion accords 25 with the claims of diversity. Two, facing real antagonists strengthens one's own position. Three, to earn a public role in American society, professors must engage the full range of public opinion.

Finally, to create a livelier climate on the campus, professors must end 26 the routine setups that pass for dialogue. Panels on issues like Iraq, racism, imperialism, and terrorism that stack the dais provide lots of passion, but little excitement. Syllabi that include the same roster of voices make learning ever more desultory. Add a few rightists, and the debate picks up. Perhaps that is the most persuasive internal case for infusing conservatism into academic discourse and activities. Without genuine dissent in the classroom and the committee room, academic life is simply boring.

Thinking Critically

1. Consult each of the sources that Mark Bauerlein cites in his essay. What are the ideological or political affiliations of each of those sources, as best as you can determine? What interest would those organizations that undertook polls or research studies have in their outcomes?

2. What does Bauerlein describe as "conservative values and traditions"? What does he define as "progressive politics"?

3. Does your campus or your classroom have a policy on "diversity"? How is "diversity" defined by that policy?

Writing Critically

1. Bauerlein defines three protocols that define contemporary American academic life: the "Common Assumption"; the "False Consensus Effect"; and the "Law of Group Polarization." Select one of these protocols and, in an essay, either support or refute Bauerlein's definition and illustration of the phenomenon based on your own campus experience. (You might also write about how you've experienced this protocol in other societal realms, such as the workplace or your community.)

2. Under what circumstances are politics and ideology appropriate in the classroom? Is it possible, feasible, or desirable to take a neutral approach to a particular academic subject?

3. Is there a fashionable or desirable political viewpoint on your campus? Create a field guide to the various political and ideological affiliations a visitor to your campus would find. For a conventional example of the field-guide genre, visit the World Wildlife Federation at <http://www.enature.com/guides/select_group.asp>; for a political field guide to the 2004 presidential debate, go to *Slate.com* at <http://slate.msn.com/id/2085967/>.

Republicans Outnumbered in Academia, Studies Find

JOHN TIERNEY

John Tierney is a columnist for the *New York Times;* this article appeared in the "National Desk" section of that paper's news section on November 18, 2004. Other journalists (and some detractors) describe Tierney's political leanings as anywhere from libertarian to conservative and certainly to the right of the liberal *New York Times.* In an interview with the libertarian magazine the *American Prospect,* Tierney professes that "I've seen people who have turned out to be wrong, older experts who pursued something with the best of intentions. My hope is that that won't happen to me. That if I start seeing stuff where the real world contradicts my theory, then I'll be able to change." Another essay by Tierney, "When Every Child Is Good Enough," appears earlier in this chapter.

Berkeley, Calif.

1   At the birthplace of the free speech movement, campus radicals have a new target: the faculty that came of age in the 60's. They say their professors have been preaching multiculturalism and diversity while creating a political monoculture on campus.

2   Conservatism is becoming more visible at the University of California here, where students put out a feisty magazine called *The California Patriot* and have made the Berkeley Republicans one of the largest groups on campus. But here, as at schools nationwide, the professors seem to be moving in the other direction, as evidenced by their campaign contributions and two studies being published on Nov. 18.

3   One of the studies, a national survey of more than 1,000 academics, shows that Democratic professors outnumber Republicans by at least seven to one in the humanities and social sciences. That ratio is more than twice as lopsided as it was three decades ago, and it seems quite likely to keep increasing, because the younger faculty members are more consistently Democratic than the ones nearing retirement, said Daniel Klein, an associate professor of economics at Santa Clara University and a co-author of the study.

4   In a separate study of voter registration records, Professor Klein found a nine-to-one ratio of Democrats to Republicans on the faculties

of Berkeley and Stanford. That study, which included professors from the hard sciences, engineering and professional schools as well as the humanities and social sciences, also found the ratio especially lopsided among the younger professors of assistant or associate rank: 183 Democrats versus 6 Republicans.

The political imbalance on faculties has inspired a campaign to have 5 state legislatures and Congress approve an "academic bill of rights" protecting students and faculty members from discrimination for their political beliefs. The campaign is being led by Students for Academic Freedom, a group with chapters at Berkeley and more than 135 other campuses. It was founded last year by the leftist-turned-conservative David Horowitz, who helped start the 1960's antiwar movement while a graduate student at Berkeley.

"Our goal is not to have the government dictate who's hired but to take 6 politics out of the hiring process and the classroom," said Mr. Horowitz, who called the new studies the most compelling evidence yet of hiring bias. "Right now, conservative students are discouraged from pursuing scholarly careers, because they see very clearly that their professors consider Republicans to be the enemy."

Academic leaders have resisted his group's legislative proposal, saying 7 that discrimination is rare and already forbidden, and they dispute the accusations of faculty bias. Robert J. Birgeneau, the chancellor of Berkeley, said that he was not sure if the new study of his faculty accurately reflected the professors' political leanings, and that these leanings were irrelevant anyway.

"The essence of a great university is developing and sharing new knowl- 8 edge as well as questioning old dogma," Dr. Birgeneau said, "We do this in an environment which prizes academic freedom and freedom of expression. These principles are respected by all of our faculty at U.C. Berkeley, no matter what their personal politics are."

Professors at Berkeley and other universities provided unprecedented fi- 9 nancial support for the Democratic Party this election. For the first time, universities were at the top of the list of organizations ranked by their employees' contributions to a presidential candidate, according to the Center for Responsive Politics, a nonpartisan group.

In first and second place, ahead of Time Warner, Goldman Sachs and 10 Microsoft, were the University of California system and Harvard, whose employees contributed $602,000 and $340,000, respectively, to Senator John Kerry. At both universities, employees gave about $19 to the Kerry campaign for every dollar for the Bush campaign.

One theory for the scarcity of Republican professors is that conserva- 11
tives are simply not that interested in academic careers. A Democrat on the
Berkeley faculty, George P. Lakoff, who teaches linguistics and is the author of *Moral Politics: How Liberals and Conservatives Think,* said that
liberals choose academic fields that fit their world views. "Unlike conservatives," he said, "they believe in working for the public good and social
justice, as well as knowledge and art for their own sake, which are what
the humanities and social sciences are about."

Some non-Democrats prefer to attribute the imbalance to the structure 12
of academia, which allows hiring decisions and research agendas to be determined by small, independent groups of scholars. These fiefs, the critics
say, suffer from a problem described in *The Federalist Papers:* an autonomous "small republic" is prone to be dominated by a cohesive faction
that uses majority voting to "outnumber and oppress the rest," in Madison's words.

"Our colleges have become less marketplaces of ideas than churches in 13
which you have to be a true believer to get a seat in the pews," said Stephen
H. Balch, a Republican and the president of the National Association of
Scholars. "We've drifted to a secular version of 19th-century denomina-
tional colleges, in which the university's mission is to crusade against sin
and make the country a morally better place."

Dr. Balch's organization of what he calls traditional scholars is pub- 14
lishing the two new faculty studies in its journal, *Academic Questions* (online at www.nas.org). In one study, Professor Klein and Charlotta Stern, a
sociologist at the Institute for Social Research in Sweden, asked the members of scholars' professional associations which party's candidates they
had mostly voted for over the previous decade.

The ratio of Democratic to Republican professors ranged from 3 to 1 15
among economists to 30 to 1 among anthropologists. The researchers
found a much higher share of Republicans among the nonacademic members of the scholars' associations, which Professor Klein said belied the notion that nonleftists were uninterested in scholarly careers.

"Screened out, expelled or self-sorted, they tend to land outside of acade- 16
mia because the crucial decisions—awarding tenure and promotions, choosing which papers get published—are made by colleagues hostile to their
political views," said Professor Klein, who classifies himself as a libertarian.

Martin Trow, an emeritus professor of public policy at Berkeley who 17
was chairman of the faculty senate and director of the Center for Studies
in Higher Education, said that professors tried not to discriminate in hiring based on politics, but that their perspective could be warped because
so many colleagues shared their ideology.

"Their view comes to be seen not as a political preference but what de- 18
cent, intelligent human beings believe," said Dr. Trow, who calls himself a
conservative. "Debate is stifled, and conservatives either go in the closet or
get to be seen as slightly kooky. So if a committee is trying to decide between three well-qualified candidates, it may exclude the conservative because he seems like someone who has poor judgment."

The students' magazine, *The California Patriot,* has frequently criti- 19
cized Berkeley for the paucity of conservative views and for cases of what
it has called discrimination against conservative students.

"I'm glad to get the liberal perspective, but it would be nice to get the 20
other side, too," said Kelly Coyne, the editor of the magazine and a senior
majoring in political science. "I'm really having a hard time finding courses
my last year. I don't want to spend another semester listening to lectures
about victims of American oppression."

Thinking Critically

1. Given what you know about John Tierney and about the *New York Times,* is
   there anything interesting about Tierney being the reporter for this story?

2. John Tierney and Mark Bauerlein (author of "Liberal Groupthink Is Anti-
   Intellectual," also in this chapter) write about the same general topic. Describe the similarities and differences in their approaches to that topic,
   paying particular attention to audience, purpose, and genre.

3. The voter registration study cited by Tierney is online at <http://lsb.scu.edu/
   ~dklein/Voter/default.htm>. Is Tierney's discussion of the study complete and accurate? Does he leave anything out? If you were Tierney's editor, what additional sources would you ask him to consult for his report?

Writing Critically

1. Aside from the fact that the *New York Times* (the "paper of record") published this report, are the political inclinations of university professors
   newsworthy? What gives this particular article its newsworthiness?

2. *The California Patriot,* a conservative student magazine at the University of
   California at Berkeley, was founded in 2000 and is online at <http:www
   .calpatriot.org/>. Since 1871, the Berkeley campus's leading student-
   produced newspaper has been *The Daily Californian,* online at <http://www
   .dailycal.org/>. In a comparative essay, objectively evaluate both websites
   (and print editions, if you can get them). You might compare how each site
   covers a particular issue, the explicitness of its ideological perspective, its
   relationship with its readers, or any other areas you think appropriate. How
   unusual are the Berkeley campus and surrounding community in having

multiple media perspectives? How important is having *any* newspaper to a campus community?

3. Have you experienced what you consider to be ideological or political bias in the classroom? Describe the incident and your response to it.

Dorothy, It's Really Oz

STEPHEN JAY GOULD

> Stephen Jay Gould was a professor of geology at Harvard and New York University, the curator of invertebrate paleontology at Harvard's Museum of Comparative Zoology, and a writer with a particular gift for translating the complexities of science into witty, accessible prose enjoyed by scientists and nonscientists alike. Perhaps no other scientist was as associated, at least in the popular mind, with reinvigorating the inquiry into evolutionary processes as Gould. So renowned was Gould's work on evolutionary biology and on bringing scientific rigor to cultural debates that he was even featured on *The Simpsons*. Within the more rarefied precincts of science, however, Gould was (as his obituary notice in the *New York Times* put it) "famed for both brilliance and arrogance . . . both revered and reviled by colleagues." He served as president of the American Association for the Advancement of Science and was a member of the National Academy of Sciences; he was the recipient of a MacArthur "genius" grant and received the National Book Award and the National Book Critics Circle Award for collections of his essays. "Dorothy, It's Really Oz" appeared in the August 23, 1999, issue of *Time* magazine. Stephen Jay Gould died in 2002.

The Kansas Board of Education voted 6 to 4 to remove evolution, and 1 the Big Bang theory as well, from the state's science curriculum. In so doing, the board transported its jurisdiction to a never-never land where a Dorothy of the new millennium might exclaim, "They still call it Kansas, but I don't think we're in the real world anymore." The new standards do not forbid the teaching of evolution, but the subject will no longer be included in statewide tests for evaluating students—a virtual guarantee, given the realities of education, that this central concept of biology will be diluted or eliminated, thus reducing courses to something like chemistry without the periodic table, or American history without Lincoln.

The Kansas skirmish marks the latest episode of a long struggle by religious Fundamentalists and their allies to restrict or eliminate the teaching of evolution in public schools—a misguided effort that our courts have quashed at each stage, and that saddens both scientists and most theologians. No scientific theory, including evolution, can pose any threat to religion—for these two great tools of human understanding operate in complementary (not contrary) fashion in their totally separate realms: science as an inquiry about the factual state of the natural world, religion as a search for spiritual meaning and ethical values.

In the early 1920s, several states simply forbade the teaching of evolution outright, opening an epoch that inspired the infamous 1925 Scopes trial (leading to the conviction of a Tennessee high school teacher) and that ended only in 1968, when the Supreme Court declared such laws unconstitutional on First Amendment grounds. In a second round in the late 1970s, Arkansas and Louisiana required that if evolution be taught, equal time must be given to Genesis literalism, masquerading as oxymoronic "creation science." The Supreme Court likewise rejected those laws in 1987.

The Kansas decision represents creationism's first—and surely temporary— success with a third strategy for subverting a constitutional imperative: that by simply deleting, but not formally banning, evolution, and by not demanding instruction in a biblically literalist "alternative," their narrowly partisan religious motivations might not derail their goals.

Given this protracted struggle, Americans of goodwill might be excused for supposing that some genuine scientific or philosophical dispute motivates this issue: Is evolution speculative and ill founded? Does evolution threaten our ethical values or our sense of life's meaning? As a paleontologist by training, and with abiding respect for religious traditions, I would raise three points to alleviate these worries:

First, no other Western nation has endured any similar movement, with any political clout, against evolution—a subject taught as fundamental, and without dispute, in all other countries that share our major sociocultural traditions.

Second, evolution is as well documented as any phenomenon in science, as strongly as the earth's revolution around the sun rather than vice versa. In this sense, we can call evolution a "fact." (Science does not deal in certainty, so "fact" can only mean a proposition affirmed to such a high degree that it would be perverse to withhold one's provisional assent.)

The major argument advanced by the school board—that large-scale evolution must be dubious because the process has not been directly observed—smacks of absurdity and only reveals ignorance about the nature of science. Good science integrates observation with inference. No process that unfolds over such long stretches of time (mostly, in this case, before humans appeared), or at an infinitude beneath our powers of direct visualization (subatomic particles, for example), can be seen directly. If justification required eyewitness testimony, we would have no sciences of deep time—no geology, no ancient human history either. (Should I believe Julius Caesar ever existed? The hard bony evidence for human evolution . . . surely exceeds our reliable documentation of Caesar's life.)

Third, no factual discovery of science (statements about how nature   9
"is") can, in principle, lead us to ethical conclusions (how we "ought" to behave) or to convictions about intrinsic meaning (the "purpose" of our lives). These last two questions—and what more important inquiries could we make?—lie firmly in the domains of religion, philosophy and humanistic study. Science and religion should be equal, mutually respecting partners, each the master of its own domain, and with each domain vital to human life in a different way.

Why get excited over this latest episode in the long, sad history of   10
American anti-intellectualism? Let me suggest that, as patriotic Americans, we should cringe in embarrassment that, at the dawn of a new, technological millennium, a jurisdiction in our heartland has opted to suppress one of the greatest triumphs of human discovery. Evolution is not a peripheral subject but the central organizing principle of all biological science. No one who has not read the Bible or the Bard can be considered educated in Western traditions; so no one ignorant of evolution can understand science.

Dorothy followed her yellow brick road as it spiraled outward toward   11
redemption and homecoming (to the true Kansas of our dreams and possibilities). The road of the newly adopted Kansas curriculum can only spiral inward toward restriction and ignorance.

Thinking Critically

1. How would you characterize the tone of Stephen Jay Gould's argument? Is it appropriate for his audience and purpose? If this essay were written by someone of lesser stature than Gould, how might you expect it to be different? Be prepared to give specific examples.

2. What, in your own words, are the three points that Gould makes to readers concerned that the debate over evolution in the public schools is related to larger ethical issues?

3. How does Gould define patriotism?

Writing Critically

1. Many of the essays in Chapter 6 of this book explore the tensions between scientists and theologians. How does Gould perceive the relationship between

scientists and theologians when it comes to the teaching of creationism? In an essay of your own, use Gould's essay and at least one selection from Chapter 6 to discuss where scientists and theologians might find common ground.

2. What do you know about the Scopes trial? Prepare a webpage to share with your classmates that provides both visual and textual information about the Scopes trial. Be sure to include your own analytical perspective on why *Tennessee v. John Scopes* still resonates in contemporary American culture.

3. Why has the classroom become the flashpoint of the debate over evolution and creationism?

The Real Message of Creationism

CHARLES KRAUTHAMMER

> *Washington Post* columnist Charles Krauthammer received the 1987 Pulitzer Prize for distinguished commentary for his independent and fiercely well-argued perspectives on national issues. With undergraduate degrees in economics and political science and an M.D. from Harvard University, Krauthammer practiced psychiatry for three years at a Massachusetts hospital before joining the administration of President Jimmy Carter as an adviser on psychiatric research. He joined the staff of the *New Republic* magazine in 1980, moving to the *Washington Post* in 1985. In his biography on the *Washington Post* website, Krauthammer observes that "One of my many missions is putting up a first-line defense against the various enthusiasms of the age—everything from the nuclear freeze to identity politics to the 'recovered memory' movement—which tend to roll over the culture at regular intervals." The following essay appeared in *Time* magazine on November 22, 1999.

When the Kansas Board of Education voted recently to eliminate evolution from the state science curriculum, the sophisticates had quite a yuk. One editorial cartoon had an ape reclining in a tree telling his mate, "We are descended from the Kansas School Board." The decision has been widely derided as a sign of resurgent Middle American obscurantism, a throwback to the Scopes "monkey trial."

Well, to begin with, the Scopes trial is not the great fable the rather fictional *Inherit the Wind* made it out to be. The instigators of the trial were not bluenosed know-nothings wanting to persecute some poor teacher for teaching evolution. They were officials of the American Civil Liberties Union so eager for a test case to overturn a new Tennessee law prohibiting the teaching of evolution that they promised to pay the expenses of the prosecution! The A.C.L.U. advertised for a volunteer and found one John Scopes, football coach and science teacher, willing to take the rap. He later said he was not sure whether he'd ever even taught any evolution.

Son of Scopes is not quite what it seems either. The twist in the modern 3 saga is the injection of creationism as the scientific alternative to evolution. So, let's be plain. Creationism, which presents Genesis as literally and historically true, is not science. It is faith crudely disguised as science.

It is not science because it violates the central scientific canon that a the- 4 ory must, at least in principle, be disprovable. Creationism is not. Any evidence that might be brought—fossil, geological, astronomical—to contradict the idea that the universe is no more than 6,000 years old is simply explained away as false clues deliberately created by God at the very beginning.

Why? To test our faith? To make fools of modern science? This is hardly 5 even good religion. God may be mysterious, but he is certainly not malicious. And who but a malicious deity would have peppered the universe with endless phony artifacts designed to confound human reason?

Creationism has no part in the serious curriculum of any serious coun- 6 try. Still, I see no reason why biblical creation could not to be taught in the schools—not as science, of course, but for its mythic grandeur and moral dimensions. If we can assign the *Iliad* and the *Odyssey*, we certainly ought to be able to assign Genesis.

But can we? There's the rub. It is very risky to assign Genesis today. The 7 A.C.L.U. might sue. Ever since the Supreme Court decision of 1963 barring prayer from the public schools, any attempt to import not just prayer but biblical studies, religious tenets and the like into the schools is liable to end up in court.

That is why the Kansas school board decision on evolution is so significant. 8 Not because Kansas is the beginning of a creationist wave—as science, creationism is too fundamentally frivolous and evolution too intellectually powerful—but because the Kansas decision is an important cultural indicator.

It represents the reaction of people of faith to the fact that all legiti- 9 mate expressions of that faith in their children's public schooling are blocked by the new secular ethos. In a society in which it is unconstitutional to post the Ten Commandments in school, creationism is a back door to religion, brought in under the guise—the absurd yet constitutionally permitted guise—of science.

This pedagogic sleight of hand, by the way, did not originate with reli- 10 gious folk. Secularists have for years been using biology instruction as a back door for inculcating their values. A sex-ed class on the proper placement of a condom is more than instruction in reproductive mechanics. It is a seminar—unacknowledged and tacit but nonetheless powerful—on permissible sexual mores.

Religion—invaluable in America's founding, forming and flowering— 11 deserves a place in the schools. Indeed, it had that place for almost 200 years. A healthy country would teach its children evolution and the Ten Commandments. The reason that Kansas is going to have precisely the opposite—the worst of both worlds—is not because Kansans are primitives, but because a religious people has tried to bring the fruits of faith, the teachings and higher values of religion, into the schools and been stymied.

The result is a kind of perverse Law of Conservation of Faith. Block all 12 teaching of religious ideas? O.K., we'll sneak them in through biology.

This is nutty. It has kids looking for God in all the wrong places. For the 13 purposes of a pluralist society, the Bible is not about fact. It is about values. If we were a bit more tolerant about allowing the teaching of biblical values as ethics, we'd find far less pressure for the teaching of biblical fables as science.

Thinking Critically

1. Compare the first paragraphs of Charles Krauthammer's essay and Stephen Jay Gould's "Dorothy, It's Really Oz" (Gould's essay precedes Krauthammer's in this chapter). In what other *structural* ways are these two essays similar? In what ways are they different? What does this comparison suggest about the *Time* magazine opinion piece as a genre?

2. What, to Krauthammer, is the key significance of the Kansas school board decision? His claim about its significance is different from Gould's conclusions about the decision. How could Krauthammer and Gould support each other's claims?

Writing Critically

1. Krauthammer mentions the great 1960 film *Inherit the Wind,* itself based on the 1950 play of the same name by Jerome Lawrence and Robert E. Lee. Watch the film and read the play. Are the play and film strictly about the Scopes trial, or do the playwrights and the film's director, Stanley Kramer, find in the trial a metaphor for some other aspect of American life? Do Krauthammer and Stephen Jay Gould also find deeper metaphorical significance in the Kansas Board of Education's 1999 decision?

2. Write an update to Krauthammer's and Gould's essays on the 1999 Kansas Board of Education decisions about evolution and creationism.

3. Both Krauthammer and Gould address the role of ethics and values in the school curriculum. Drawing on these two essays (and on any other sources you find appropriate), define what you believe the role of ethics and values in a school curriculum should be.

All God's Children

SAMANTHA M. SHAPIRO

As a senior writer at the Seattle alternative weekly *The Stranger,* Shapiro covered topics in social justice ranging from immigration reform to workers' rights, as well as the intersection of religious faith and public life. Shapiro studied at the Pardes Institute of Jewish Studies in Jerusalem and wrote movingly of the loss of two friends killed in a 2002 bombing at Hebrew University in that city: "We are getting used to the images of a mangled restaurant, bus or street corner; the blood-spattered flesh, the chaotic spray of shoes and book-bags, the neon yellow of the volunteers' vests. We hold our breath during the body count and feel very sorry, but what can we do? It is not possible to remember and mourn even a fraction of the 605 victims. The media knows this. It's hard to imagine that a terrorist attack that killed five Americans anywhere but Israel would be off the TV screen by Friday, but how many times can the same story be reported?" A contributing writer to the *New York Times Magazine,* where "All God's Children" appeared in September 2004, Shapiro has continued to report on the ongoing struggle between Israelis and Palestinians as well as other divisions in the Arab world. Her articles on a wide range of topics have appeared in *Mother Jones* magazine, *Jerusalem Report, Wired, Legal Affairs,* and *The Forward.*

In a cinder-block classroom at the edge of Biola University's manicured 1
campus in a Los Angeles suburb, Craig Detweiler was blasting the music of Nick Cave at his Intro to Mass Media class. Two dozen students were arranged in a horseshoe of swivel chairs, and they were looking blankly at a photo of Cave, a sullen goth-rocker, which Detweiler's laptop was projecting onto a pull-down screen.

Intro to Mass Media is a required class for every mass-communications 2
major at Biola. Each week of the course is devoted to a different type of media. This week, in late March, was music. Lesson 1, on Monday, was the history of music; Lesson 2, today's class, focused on contemporary music.

"Soooo . . . any Nick Cave fans?" Detweiler asked, pacing the room. 3
No one answered.

Detweiler has spiky silver hair and exuberant blue eyes, and he was 4
wearing a Hawaiian shirt and trendy shoes. He brings a kind of affable

sarcasm to a complicated job; he is the chairman of a mass-media department at a university that until 1977 banned all films. "This stuff is pretty hard and dark," he offered, as Cave growled and howled through the speakers of his laptop. "But did you know that Nick Cave wrote an introduction to the Gospel of Mark for a special edition of the Bible published in the U.K.? What do we think of that?" Students spun their chairs and gnawed pen tops.

Like a lot of Christian colleges in the United States, Biola has in recent years made serious efforts to compete academically with secular and more mainstream religiously affiliated colleges. That hasn't meant a reduced emphasis on religious teachings. If anything, the school has intensified its commitment to cultivating devout Christians. But it does mean that the school has expanded its curriculum in areas of study like psychology, bioethics and popular culture, and that it is encouraging a new level of engagement with the secular world. Detweiler, a screenwriter who is something of a maverick on campus and in the evangelical Christian community, is on the front lines of that effort at Biola.

Detweiler fiddled with his laptop, and an image of Bjork appeared on the projection screen. The music switched to a soothing Bjork ballad called "All Is Full of Love." He turned up the volume.

"What do we think of this?" he asked. "Is God in it?"

"To be honest, I have a hard time with that," a student offered tentatively.

Adam Hopkins, a skinny mass-communications major with dark, shaggy hair, said: "I like the music. It's ethereal and beautiful."

"What's that she's singing?" Detweiler asked. "All is full of . . .? All is full of . . .? All is full of what?"

No answer.

"Love!" he shouted triumphantly. "All is full of love! Anybody in this room with that?"

Tracy Woodworth, a polished journalism major in the back of the room, shot up her hand and asked, a little indignantly, "Isn't that just back to the everything-is-love fun, happy relativism?"

Then Christina Young spoke up. She agreed with Tracy. She allowed that the Bjork song reflects "the concept of common grace—that everyone has a taste of God's goodness," but she pointed out that common grace "is not enough for salvation."

Detweiler had an hour's worth of songs and slides stored on his laptop. He clicked through the Klezmer Conservatory Band and "The Best of Tito Puente." He suggested that a recent concert in Los Angeles by Sigur Rós, the Icelandic postrock band, created a "sacred space of beauty" that might be a contemporary "site of general revelation."

The students, all evangelical Christians, were skeptical. "It's hard to 16
think the artist is completely in the right if they don't say the truth—that
Christ is the only way," one remarked.

"This music leads to more music, not to people finding Christ," an- 17
other said.

Detweiler seemed agitated. He kept raising the volume louder and 18
louder. He banged his eraser against the dry-erase board, where he had
written "truth" and "beauty." He told the students that creative people
who start with a message are propagandists, not artists. The teachings of
Jesus, he said, weren't straightfoward moral lessons. "People had a hard
time following Jesus," he said.

At the end of class, Detweiler sighed. "What's the point of today, guys?" 19
No one had an answer. 20

"The spread of indigenous cultural music is pushing hard against ex- 21
clusivism," he said. "Christ is going to be a tough sell in this world, and I
think you're not ready for it. I think you might need to figure out where
God is in this music crossing the globe."

Biola, whose 95-acre campus is in La Mirada, 20 miles southeast of 22
downtown Los Angeles, is part of the fast-expanding movement of
"Christ centered" colleges—schools that are not loosely affiliated with a
church, like Notre Dame or Southern Methodist University, but that integrate Christianity into all aspects of the curriculum and require faculty
members, and sometimes students, to sign a pledge of faith in Jesus Christ.
The 102 American schools in the Council for Christian Colleges and Universities (many of which, like Biola, are nondenominational) represent
just 1.5 percent of the country's total college population, but in the last
decade their enrollment has increased 67 percent, compared with an average increase of just 2 percent for American colleges and universities as a
whole.

Biola's history is entwined with that of evangelical Christianity in the 23
United States. Almost a hundred years ago, the school sponsored a series of
pamphlets called "The Fundamentals," which laid out the principles of the
fundamentalist movement. "The Fundamentals" were a reaction against
Darwinism, modernism and liberal strains in Protestantism, all of which
were seen as challenges to the authority of the Bible as a literal historic account of reality. Biola, then called the Bible Institute of Los Angeles, saw its
mission as training laypeople to preach the Gospel, and later began providing them with tools—like "scientific" arguments that proved the existence
of a creator—to do battle with other faiths and with secular ideas.

When I spoke with Clyde Cook, Biola's genial president, he explained 24
that the university is as committed as ever to the principles articulated in

"The Fundamentals," although, he said, "we've found different and more effective ways to deliver those truths." For one thing, Cook said, while "indoctrination" is "still valuable," the school thinks it is preferable to have students internalize Christian truths through a process of questioning. Cook said he still sees the school's mission as preparing its 5,000 undergraduate and graduate students to spread the Gospel, to argue for Christianity against the tenets of secularism and of other religions. But graduates are no longer necessarily supposed to preach from the pulpit. Instead, Cook said, Biola now aspires "to incarnate those truths in the professions—in business, nursing, movies, government." Students take seminars in which they discuss how to integrate their academic studies with a "Christian worldview." Where Biola once considered certain disciplines, like philosophy, to be irrelevant to Christians, these days it places graduates in top philosophy Ph.D. programs, hoping they will learn to argue in sophisticated secular terms, for example, on behalf of the rights of fetuses.

Over the last 50 years, evangelical Christianity in the United States has 25 moved away from fundamentalism, which is still dedicated to the idea of separation from an ungodly world. Evangelicals believe that the way to change culture is to participate in it, albeit with caution. Particularly in the last decade, as the movement has matured, intellectual institutions—journals, scholarly presses and advanced academic work—have quietly budded within evangelical circles. Biola's evolution from a Bible college to an accredited liberal-arts university offering advanced degrees is just one manifestation of this change.

There are still some schools whose climates remain closer to Biola's 26 fundamentalist origins. Hyles-Anderson College in Crown Point, Ind., forbids male students to have long hair and female students to wear "shorts or slacks." There are also more liberal Christ-centered colleges, like nearby Azusa Pacific University, which (unlike Biola) accepts nonbelievers and allows men and women to mingle more often in the dorms. Older, more elite Christian colleges, like Wheaton in Illinois, whose foundings predated the fundamentalist revolt against the modern world, have always offered a liberal-arts education, though one guided by Christian principles.

Ted Olsen, an editor at the evangelical magazine *Christianity Today,* 27 said that Biola, as an institution, "pretty much falls dead center in the middle of the evangelical movement." Many influential envangelicals have chosen to send their children to Biola. Ryan Dobson, the son of James Dobson, the president of the conservative Christian group Focus on the Family, graduated with the class of 1995, and Amy Warren-Hilliker, the daughter of Rick Warren, the author of the inspirational best seller *The Purpose-Driven Life,* attended a few years ago.

Evangelical Christianity's dance with secular culture has always been a complicated one. Whereas Biola once trained students to use modernism's devices, like the scientific method and rational argument, to undercut modernism, today, in a more postmodern era, it educates its students about the diversity of ideas and cultures and experiences in order to equip them to bring the world a single unchangeable truth. In almost every area of study at Biola, there is some tension between that goal and the academic ideal of free inquiry. But it is in Craig Detweiler's mass-communications department that that tension seems most raw. When the school started a film department 27 years ago, it focused exclusively on making movies for proselytizing purposes. But more recently at the college, and throughout the evangelical movement, there has been a growing interest in the power and influence of Hollywood. And so last year, the school appointed Detweiler, who was born again in college and still keeps a foot planted in the secular world, as the head of the mass-communications department. Detweiler stocked the school's film library with mainstream movies, worked with the administration to draft a policy permitting the viewing of R-rated movies in classrooms and helped recruit Christian executives from Hollywood studios onto a board to finance and advise the department. That board, which includes the producers of the sitcom *Family Matters* and the movie *X-Men,* paid for a TV studio on campus and helps place Biola students in internships at major studios.

In a recent book, *A Matrix of Meanings: Finding God in Pop Culture,* Detweiler argued that God is literally revealing himself in mainstream Hollywood movies like *Magnolia* and *The Matrix.* Detweiler said he thinks Christian films should be able, like those movies, to address dark topics and contain ambiguity, something unresolved or not fully understood. But as he found that day in the classroom, that is a hard quality to combine with the certitudes of evangelical Christianity.

Except for a slightly ominous-looking 60-foot-high photographic-style mural of Jesus painted on the side of a campus building, or the occasional student carrying a large wooden cross from the gymnasium to the student center, the Biola campus appears unremarkable. When I visited last spring, the students looked like typical college kids: there were boys with mod haircuts and girls with eyebrow rings, wearing outfits from Hot Topic and thrift stores. Anywhere that young men and women were allowed to hang out together—dorm lobbies, the local Denny's, parked cars—they did, staying up late flicking pennies at one another, trading laborious massages by the hall microwave.

But the code of conduct each student is required to sign creates a tone 31
on campus that is different from that of most colleges. The code prohibits
drinking, dancing at Biola functions, smoking, premarital sex and visiting
the dorm rooms of the opposite sex outside of designated hours—and even
then, only with open doors. Students take the code seriously. On the whole,
Biola is a preternaturally calm place. The root-beer keg parties can get hy-
per, but never out of control.

The emotion that is most strongly manifested on campus is longing. 32
The worship music at the Thursday night coffeehouse and at chapel often
sounds like an angsty Top 40 guitar ballad. Students sing along to lyrics
like "Lover, love me" with eyes closed, arms raised, shoes off. One student
I met, Nathan Pearsey, who had been exposed to more effusive worship
styles during missionary trips to Mexico and Antigua, liked to prostrate
himself on the floor during chapel and kick his feet like flippers.

Walking across campus at night, I often had the feeling of stumbling upon 33
something too intimate: small groups of students hunched together, arms laid
on one another in prayer, or the occasional pair in a romantic embrace, looking furtively around. Although there are familiar cliques—*Star Wars* dorks,
student-government types, surfers—the typical collegiate social hierarchy
does not apply. There are no cheerleaders or frat boys. Students aren't drawn
from different economic brackets: tuition alone runs more than $20,000 a
year. Campus politics tend to be reflexively conservative.

The sharpest distinction I noticed on campus was the one between 34
the more worldly students and the more sheltered ones. At one end of
this spectrum are the born-agains. Joshua Warren, 22, was a neo-Nazi
when he was a young teenager, and after he recanted those beliefs, he
found his way to Biola through the Christian hard-core scene. He now
plays with a few other Biola students in Phineas, a hard-core band. The
band takes its name from a priest who, in the Book of Numbers, stabs
an Israelite and a Midianite when he sees them having sex in public.
Joshua lives the Biola life: like many students, he has an annual pass to
Disneyland and spends free afternoons strolling Downtown Disney with
a home-schooled friend. But like a lot of Biola students who did not
come from a Christian home—who may have fended for themselves in
the corridors of public schools, who may have used condoms or drunk
margaritas at T.G.I. Friday's before being saved—Joshua has an ease of
social interaction and a kind of restless energy that set him apart from
some of his peers.

At the other end of the spectrum are the kids who were raised in the 35
Christian-school system—at private schools, through home-schooling or
a combination of the two. They are certain of the advantages of their up-

bringings, but a little defensive about them too. The home-schooled kids I met often made a point of telling me that they weren't weird or antisocial, like other home-schooled kids. Ashley Romero, 21, a home-schooled biblical-studies major, broke down the stereotypes for me: "First semester, everyone would make this 'H' hand signal"—she held up the first two fingers of one hand and crossed them with the index finger of the other— "when you did something dorky. The idea is: 'That's so home-school, so nerdy. You can't cut it; you can't integrate.'" On the other hand, Ashley continued, a sure-fire way to land a "godly Christian guy" is to tell him you want to home-school your children. "He'll be smitten," she said confidently.

Defying categorization are students whose parents are missionaries 36 and who grew up overseas, cut off from American culture. They're known as missionary kids, or "third-culture kids." Timothy Carroll, who grew up in Latin America, sometimes wears a colorful Bolivian hat and rarely wears shoes. He says he goes barefoot because that's what he grew up doing and because he wants to remind himself that some people don't have shoes.

One day I was chatting with a communications-studies major named 37 Phil Kilpatrick when a lanky white guy with a crew cut pedaled furiously past us on a dirt bike. "He's from Nigeria," Phil said. "He has killed two possums and a raccoon on campus, with a stick, I think. Some kids saw him doing it once and were traumatized and called campus police. But I think you have to be understanding that some people didn't grow up in America, you know?"

I ate lunch in the cafeteria one afternoon with Laura Walker, a 20- 38 year-old woman with a nose ring, pigtails and a tattoo on the top of her foot that said "God knows" in Greek. Between bites of her meal, she looked both ways and then whispered that she was helping a friend make a movie about "being gay." Later in the week, we met at the off-campus apartment where the film was being shot. "This is the producer's house," Laura explained as we climbed over duffel bags of clothes and studio lights into a room decorated with framed puzzles, scented candles and a Garfield phone. The director, John Huntington LaDue Jr., a gregarious, muscular, blond 22-year-old, bustled around, duct-taping cables and cords to the carpet, hiking his jeans up over the waistband of Calvin Klein underwear.

John is a film major at Biola, and the movie he was shooting, *Becoming* 39 *Peter Pan,* was his senior thesis. It is the story of his struggles with homosexuality. About a year ago, John came out to his friends and a few teachers. Homosexual activity is strictly forbidden at Biola, but John is not the only gay student there. One gay student dropped out last year. Another, deep in the closet, sought out a secret meeting with me at Biola's back gates just to make sure I didn't leave without realizing he existed. Driving across campus, John pointed out a male student he kissed freshman year. The student had decided to be celibate, John said, an option he said he often considered.

Since John came out, his friends told me, he had been "heavily moni- 40 tored" by the school. He was placed in mandatory counseling, which, he said, aimed to teach him that his sexuality is the correctable byproduct of growing up the son of missionaries, a third-culture kid who never knew a real home. John takes his counseling seriously and hopes it will work. "My gay friends are like, 'Oh, you poor thing, you have to get out of that crazy counseling,'" he said. "But I am not so sure they're right. Meanwhile, my Christian friends will tell me: 'Don't go to that gay bar. Don't meet that guy.'"

John is charming and relentlessly enthusiastic on nearly every topic he 41 brings up, from an artsy West Hollywood coffeehouse he recently visited to a six-month-long program he enrolled himself in at a nearby church to cure his gayness. He has made three films during his career at Biola, all of which were considered too outré to be shown at the school film festival. In the first, John personified anorexia as a succubus lesbian demon: a scene in which the succubus licked a girl's ear seductively was deemed inappropriate by the judges. His second film, about a girl who, after a freak car accident, can see people's souls outside their bodies, was too long. *Becoming Peter Pan* would not be shown at the film festival, either, because, John said, "it's too long, and it would offend a lot of people." He was nervous about even showing me the movie in the Biola film department, and when we sat down to watch it, he anxiously fast-forwarded over a scene of two men in bed. "This would make the school die," he whispered. "In Christianity, homosexuality is as bad as murder."

A number of the student films I watched at Biola relied heavily on 42 imagined or dreamlike sequences to fuel the narrative. In one, the plot (girl battles pirate) was driven by a hallucination induced by Dr Pepper and cold medication. In another, a group of students believe they are trapped in a Biola building because a gunman is on campus; in fact, they are deluded because they have consumed too much caffeine. *Becoming Peter Pan* is an especially telling example of the practice: in the movie, homosexuality is portrayed as an alternate universe—literally Never-Never Land. The actor who plays the boyfriend of John's character sometimes appears in a Captain Hook costume, for example.

When I asked John if he planned to look for work as a director after 43 graduation, he grew uncharacteristically wistful: "I used to be really gung-ho about being a director, but over my time at Biola, I feel less that way."

I asked him why, and he looked away. "An artist is supposed to have a 44 voice," he said. "I just don't really think I have a voice."

One morning during my visit, I woke to find that the campus had been 45 transformed into a scene that seemed straight out of a student-film dream sequence. Patches of grass were covered in cardboard and trash. Students wearing torn, dirty clothes pushed shopping carts on loan from the local Albertson's supermarket. There was a pen of goats set up in front of the library, and next to the pen students dressed as Gypsies were selling jewelry.

This was the start of the annual three-day Missions Conference, which 46 brought missionary organizations, recruiters and speakers to Biola. In many ways, the event looked like a multicultural consciousness-raising event on any American campus. One school building was renamed Global Awareness, and students were invited to take off their shoes and walk through rooms covered in dirt, where bamboo curtains blocked the bright California sunshine. Each room was based on a country in need of missionary help; Biola students enacted scenes with Indian untouchables or prisoners in a Yemenite jail. A room based on the United States criticized consumerism and promoted shade-grown "Fair Trade" coffee. At the end of the journey through the Global Awareness building, students were encouraged to pray on Muslim prayer rugs or yoga mats and to wash the dirt off one another's feet in a spare room where New Age music played quietly.

In 1983, Biola changed the name of its missionary-studies department to 47 "intercultural studies." It was more than just a name change; the school's approach to the question of missionary work shifted, too. The goal is still to convert non-Christians around the world, but now the program emphasizes respecting and preserving indigenous cultures, even protecting their land.

These ideas about understanding the value of other cultures coexist a 48 little uneasily with the idea that there is only one truth and that most of those groovy cultures are missing it. One of the breakout sessions at the Missions Conference, led by Prof. Joshua Lingel, was a teaser for Apologetics to Islam, a class that gives students the tools to convert Muslims and also takes them on field trips to halal restaurants in the area to practice. Lingel, a tall, burly, red-haired Biola grad, addressed a packed room, alternating between a friendly cultural lesson and a fire-and-brimstone sermon. "Muslims wear white robes when they go on pilgrimage," he began, carefully explaining Islamic customs. But when a slide showing masses of robe-clad Muslims at Mecca clicked onto the screen, Lingel's measured tone dissolved, and he shouted: "Behold the fields of white! The great seed of the lost! Behold, the time for the harvest is nearing!"

Evangelizing is not an abstract ideal at Biola, or a mission restricted to a 49 few days out of the year. Phineas, the campus hard-core band, sees itself as reaching out to "they that are sick," as described in the Book of Mark, and invites audience members to come up and speak to them about Jesus after the show. Laura Walker told me that she and her friends go to gay dance clubs partly because that's what Jesus would have done. "Jesus spent time with lepers," she said. Many students I met prayed out loud that Jesus Christ would soon "collide" with me and that my reporting would be a vehicle for spreading the Gospel. Students took me to *The Passion of the Christ,* the Mel Gibson movie, and offered to pay for my ticket. In the middle of one interview, a teacher told me that he and his students loved me and explained that that was why they hoped I would realize that my "core beliefs" are wrong.

When I attended church with Biola students, they offered prayers for 50 the salvation of gay neighborhoods in other states, public-school districts near and far, entire Muslim-populated latitudes and longitudes. In church, the students' feelings about the world beyond evangelical Christianity seemed pretty clear-cut; it was going to hell unless it accepted Jesus. But outside church, that relationship seemed more complicated.

In the dorm where I stayed, I lived across the hall from a 19-year- 51 old woman with long blond hair named Brittany Vanderveer. She was shy and serious; her face turned the color of a pomegranate when a friend invited her on a group date. Every Thursday, she and Krista Walthall, 19, a friend from home, went to a coffee shop to meet new people and bring them to Jesus Christ, carrying Bibles in their shoulder bags. They described their trips as daring adventures during which anything could happen, and their faces lighted up as they talked about them. There was the time they met an ex-con sitting in the parking lot and bought him coffee. And there was the evening when Brittany, after praying for boldness for 15 minutes, approached a group of bikers parked outside Starbucks. "My legs were shaking, but I could think perfectly clearly," she said. Although she and Krista have not converted anyone yet, they clearly cherish every encounter.

I went with them one Thursday to the Java Co., a coffee shop a mile 52 from campus where they have made one steady friend: Nicole, a chatty 21-year-old from Brooklyn with an 11-month-old daughter. Nicole works behind the counter. Her tone was breezy and casual, and Brittany and Krista could not quite match it. The women always give great consideration to their interactions with Nicole. They had prayed about the trip to the Java Co. together at breakfast and, separately, the evening before. Frequently, they also pray in the parking lot before entering the coffee shop.

Brittany and Krista hung on Nicole's every word as if they were lucky 53 to be talking to her at all. They interrupted a story about her daughter's birthday party to ask exactly what kind of cake Nicole ordered. Although their purpose in getting to know Nicole was to save her soul, part of their motivation appeared more mundane: Nicole is simply different from any-one they know. The women's interest in her stories, the way they lingered over the details, seemed to express something about the world—the unre-deemed, unsaved, unchurched part—that was not evident in their public prayers in church. Going off campus, even just a mile away, was interest-ing because it was unpredictable. Talking to the Starbucks bikers or Nicole was compelling on its own terms; Brittany and Krista, like many of the Bi-ola students I met, enjoyed not knowing what would happen. On some level, they seemed already to know what Craig Detweiler is trying to teach, and what is evident in the often open-ended, messy tales of the Bible: that the most compelling stories unfold when you don't start out with the answer.

Thinking Critically

1. How does Samantha M. Shapiro establish her persona in "All God's Chil-dren"? How does she get to know the subjects of her article? What are the advantages and disadvantages of this approach to reporting?

2. Shapiro spent a considerable amount of time on the Biola campus and with Biola students and faculty. Why do you think she chose to begin her article with the anecdote about the Intro to Mass Media class?

3. What is Shapiro's thesis, and how does her experience at Biola University support or complicate her thesis?

Writing Critically

1. In what ways is Biola University different from your own campus? How are the Biola students profiled by Shapiro different from you and your peers? Shapiro describes how Biola is "encouraging a new level of engagement with the secular world" (paragraph 5). In an essay, describe how your col-lege encourages (or should encourage) engagement with some aspect of off-campus society. Use Shapiro's information-gathering strategies, includ-ing field research, observation, and personal interviews, to support your claims.

2. Does your campus have a coherent, consistent culture? Does it have a core of values, beliefs, and traditions that are upheld by administrators and faculty and made clear to students? In an essay, describe your cam-pus culture and the values (implicit or explicit) associated with this cul-ture. How does that culture influence the content and context of what you are taught?

3. How is religious faith expressed or demonstrated in your campus community? Are expressions of religious faith encouraged, tolerated, or discouraged? Why or why not? Draw on specific recent events and personal
experiences to illustrate your perspective, and be sure to provide a larger
context as well as opposing or different perspectives.

What Would Jesus Do at Harvard?

Naomi Schaefer Riley

> A 1998 magna cum laude graduate of Harvard, Naomi
> Schaefer Riley is an Adjunct Fellow at the Ethics and
> Public Policy Center, a nonprofit research institute that
> brings together politicians, journalists, social scientists,
> and clergy to examine the links between Judeo-
> Christian-based Western morals and ethics and contem-
> porary social and political issues. Riley is the editor of
> the EPPC's new journal *In Character.* Her first book,
> *God on the Quad: How Religious Colleges Are Chang-
> ing America,* was published in 2005. Riley has con-
> tributed to the *Wall Street Journal, First Things,
> Commentary,* the *New Republic,* and the *Weekly Stan-
> dard,* among other publications. In an interview with
> the *Dallas Morning News* about *God on the Quad,* Ri-
> ley observed that "For people who don't think religion
> has a place in the public square, there's definitely reason
> for concern. Because one thing these college graduates
> all agree on is that their faith has a place out there. It's
> not just something that's private and kept to oneself."
> "What Would Jesus Do at Harvard?" appeared in the
> *Boston Globe* in November 2004.

Walking out of Harvard's Divinity Hall on a recent afternoon, Harvey Cox's mood does not seem affected by the cold, damp weather
or the deafening sounds of nearby construction. All the way back to his
office, he's happily singing the much-covered reggae song "By the Rivers
of Babylon." The lyrics, of course, are not entirely original. They're
adapted from Psalm 137 and Cox, one of the country's most prominent
theologians, has just used them in his graduate seminar on Jerusalem to
demonstrate how the exiling of the Jews from the city in 587 B.C. echoes
today as far as Rastafarian culture. The theme of exile is reiterated as Cox
plays to his class the solemn Latin chants from the Maundy Thursday

1

service, in which Catholics commemorate the Last Supper, and has students read responsively from the book of Lamentations, which Jews chant on the holiday Tisha B'Av to mourn the destruction of the Temple. By the end of two hours, a student could be forgiven for wondering if he's studying religion or practicing it.

Indeed, Cox has spent his four-decade-long academic career negotiating such delicate boundaries: between scholarship and political activism, between the commitments of faith and the norms of a secular university, between the rational study of religion and an experiential understanding of it. On that last question, Cox is adamant. "Frankly," he tells me in his office atop the main divinity school building, "I think to teach religion and the ethical significance of religious traditions and pretend that it doesn't have emotional, spiritual, and symbolic elements, is to falsify it. It's simplifying unduly what religious traditions are about."   2

Of course, conveying a sense of the experience of religion in a graduate divinity school seminar is one thing. Doing it for a mixed group of undergraduates within a secular liberal-arts curriculum is quite another. But through his course "Jesus and the Moral Life," Cox brought his vision of Christianity to students of all faiths and no faith, and some with no interest in faith—and the students it seems, couldn't get enough. For 15 years, Cox attempted to teach students how to use the Bible and texts inspired by it in order to wrestle both intellectually and emotionally with problems ranging from poverty and racial injustice to abortion, the allocation of health care, and the termination of life support.   3

Cox's course—described in his new book *When Jesus Came to Harvard: Making Moral Choices Today* (Houghton Mifflin)—was consistently ranked one of the most popular on campus, often enrolling more than a thousand students a semester. But more than simply helping a generation of Harvard students find a moral path (or fulfill a graduation requirement). "Jesus and the Moral Life" was Cox's attempt to answer some of the most pressing questions facing American society today: How do you talk about religion in a pluralistic society with a strong Christian and a strong secularist tradition? And how can people come together to explore and derive guidance from a religious tradition they might not share?   4

When Cox was approached in 1981 by some of his fellow professors about teaching a class based on Jesus in the newly founded "moral reasoning" section of Harvard's core curriculum, he balked. "I had my doubts about the idea," he writes in his new book. "I wasn't sure that morality was something one could teach in the classroom." Cox worried that the moral reasoning courses—charged with teaching students to "discuss significant and recurrent questions of choice and value that arise in human experi-   5 ence"—might produce students who "could debate moral dilemmas with flair and proficiency but who lacked any moral conviction about them." In the end, though, Cox relented. His became the first Harvard course with the word "Jesus" in the title since George Santayana taught one in the early decades of the 20th century.

Cox was no stranger to the idea that religion could be a powerfully transformative force. Raised in a small Pennsylvania town in the Baptist tradition, which he describes as "very oriented toward the life and teachings of Jesus," Cox graduated from the University of Pennsylvania and then Yale Divinity School. (He was also ordained a Baptist minister in 1956.) In 1962, shortly after receiving his doctorate in the history and philosophy of religion from Harvard, he served for a year as an "ecumenical fraternal worker" in Berlin, traveling almost daily across the divided city to maintain contact between the two sides. Back in the states he was one of the founders of the Boston chapter of the Southern Christian Leadership Conference under Martin Luther King Jr., a relationship he calls "the single most influential" one in his life.

In 1964, Cox published *The Secular City*, which argued that the growing secularization of Western society represented not a threat to religion but an opportunity, freeing divine presence from institutional confines and loosing it on the messy, complex, pluralistic real world. The book became a surprise bestseller—within a few years it had sold almost a million copies around the world and was translated into 14 languages—and provoked heated debate in theological circles and beyond. But perhaps its most fateful ripples were felt in Latin America, where a Spanish translation was debated and built upon by the exponents of the nascent "liberation theology" movement.

Liberation theology, which originated among Catholic theologians in the wake of the Second Vatican Council, held that Christians should take their lead not from church doctrine or hierarchy but from the example of Jesus, especially with respect to his identification with the poor and outcast. God, according to a famous statement issued by the conference of Latin American bishops in 1968, had a "preferential option for the poor," and it was the duty of clergy to work not just for the salvation of the poor but for the betterment of their life on earth through political and economic justice movements. (In practice, this sometimes meant support for Marxist revolutionaries, which in part led Pope John Paul II to later rebuke the advocates of liberation theology.)

Cox does not claim credit for liberation theology or any of the other liberal lay movements that have swept the globe in the past four decades. Yet as he wrote in 1990, "I like to think that *The Secular City* helped create the climate that forced church leaders and theologians to come down from their balconies and out of their studies and talk seriously with the ordinary people who constitute 99 percent of the churches of the world.

The students in "Jesus and the Moral Life" did not read much liberation   10 theology per se, but the syllabus reflected Cox's longtime focus on Jesus as a living force that moves in an ever-changing world. (Not that the course was apolitical: "As a Samaritan, you are asked to join a newly organized Judeo-Samaritan Liberation Front to seek to overthrow . . . Roman rule over Palestine," began one essay question.) Among the central ideas of "Jesus and the Moral Life" are that Jesus was a storyteller, and that the great power of his moral lessons comes at least in part from the way in which they are told.

Cox is hardly the type to wear one of those "WWJD" bracelets that   11 were popular a few years ago. And he worries that people who ask "What Would Jesus Do?" sometimes come up with "downright silly" answers. (He's particularly critical of fundamentalists who try to simply translate the words of the New Testament into literal lessons for modern life.) But he doesn't think the question itself is absurd. To respond today, though, he writes, "requires a huge step beyond the parameters of most biblical scholarship and ethical theory. It requires a leap into situations Jesus never faced: a leap of imagination. . . ."

According to former students contacted through an alumni list-serv,   12 Cox's class served two main purposes beyond a chance to fulfill the moral-reasoning requirement. For believing Christians, the class demanded that they approach their faith in a more critical and intellectual way. And for curious non-Christians, it gave them a way to approach the subject of Jesus and Christianity without having to attend a religious service or a church-sponsored class.

Some enrolled in the course for other than purely educational reasons.   13 Matthew Florence, who grew up in what he describes as a "Christian fundamentalist home" in rural Tennessee, says he was encouraged to enroll his sophomore year by other members of the Harvard Christian Fellowship, an evangelical student group. "It was part of our effort to counteract the course's supposed liberal biases," he explained in a recent interview. (Cox says he was unaware of this campaign and the other students seemed mostly oblivious to their professor's reputation outside the classroom.)

But in Florence's case, the plan backfired. Florence, who graduated   14 in 1989 and is now living in the Bay Area doing nonprofit work with AIDS patients, remembers that before he took the class, "I thought the written word of God was infallible." It was in Cox's lectures that he first learned that the Gospels give varying accounts of the same events, and that some of them were written decades after Jesus lived. Florence eventually broke with the HCF and helped to form the Seymour Society, a discussion and social service group headed by Rev. Eugene Rivers (founder of Boston's Ten Point Coalition), that, according to Florence, "combined a very liberal social-justice theology with conservative moral theology."

Cox emphasizes that he did not want to teach the class "like an expos." If anything, he wanted to give believers a chance to broaden and deepen their faith. "I find it pathetic that a lot of people have sophisticated notions about poetic theory or biology, but when they talk about religion they are still in 7th-grade Sunday school class," he says. But this wasn't an easy task. "How do you help students move beyond an adolescent conception of their own tradition without feeling they have to kick it?" he asks. 15

Will Meyerhofer, who is Jewish, says that he opted for taking "Jesus and the Moral Life" because he thought it would be untaxing compared with the other moral-reasoning course offered that semester, on German philosophy. (More than one student I interviewed cited the course's nickname, "Jesus and the Easy Life.") Meyerhofer, who graduated in 1989 and is now a psychotherapist in New York, also says he was curious about the New Testament. "I wanted to know what the excitement was about," he says. "This class gave me a sneaky excuse to read it." Meyerhofer remembers being particularly struck to learn that the Last Supper was a Passover Seder. "I remember being a little stunned. These were Jews, this was a Jewish thing." 16

To Cox, the Jewishness of Jesus is absolutely central. "Some people interpret Christianity as being a sharp break from the Jewish heritage," says Cox. "This is not the way I approach it. The more we study late Judaism and early Christianity and the more things we discover like the Dead Sea Scrolls and the Gnostic texts, [the more it] underlines the continuity." Indeed, his own household exemplifies that continuity. His wife, who teaches Russian history at Wellesley, is Jewish, and they are raising a Jewish child, something he describes in his 2001 book *Common Prayers*. 17

"Personally," Cox says, "my going to Torah studies at synagogue or participating in Yom Kippur or a Sabbath meal helps me at a deep emotional and spiritual level to appreciate Jesus more." 18

Cox's former students might be surprised by how he's changed since they took the course. He's still got the look of the "kindly priest" that Meyerhofer remembers. But he doesn't seem the firebrand he once was. For one thing, the religious and political landscape around him has changed. The 19 countries where Cox was fighting for political change, he acknowledges, are now democracies in one form or another. And the central message of liberation theology—that God has a preferential option for the poor—Cox says, has become mainstream, even in evangelical circles. Even his liturgical tastes—he's been attending an Episcopal church rather than his usual Baptist one—are also getting more conservative. He acknowledges feeling comfortable with more formal liturgies and even the pronounced presence of a church hierarchy.

While he did take the bullhorn in the recent student-led living-wage 20 campaign at Harvard, Cox no longer thinks students should become activists during college. Over the course of teaching "Jesus and the Moral Life," Cox came to believe that "a lot of the important battles are going on in the battle of ideas," he says. "The fact is that you are going to have other opportunities to join the picket line, but you're not going to have quite the leisure and the stimulation to think systematically about these issues."

But after an election season marked by sharp polarization over "moral 21 values" and the role of religion in politics, Cox's activism may be called for once again. "The evangelical conservatives have a point," he says. "There is something missing in the public discourse about policies and values and moral choices and so on. . . ." But he's wary of any approach that boils morality down to "hot-button issues, like abortion or stem cell research, which obscure the larger issues of war and peace and poverty" that Jesus addressed. Cox worries, though, that progressives "haven't thoughtfully related their position on issues like poverty to a larger moral tradition, possibly a religiously informed moral tradition, in a way that's plausible to people."

Cox says that if he were to offer "Jesus and the Moral Life" today, he 22 would still teach it the same way. But he does think students' reactions would be different. For example, if he were to invite students to join in with a recording of Handel's "Hallelujah Chorus," as he once did, he wouldn't be surprised if some complained. Today, he says, "nobody quite knows where the line of separation between church and state or education and indoctrination is."

Thinking Critically

1. What was Harvey Cox asked to teach at Harvard, and why?

2. In what ways are Cox's views about the teaching of religion similar to Charles Krauthammer's argument about creationism in the public schools (also in this chapter)?

3. Look up the journals and newspapers to which Naomi Schaefer Riley has contributed, as well as the website of the Ethics and Public Policy Center at <http://www.eppc.org/> and the foundations that provided grants to support Riley's work on *God on the Quad:* the Templeton Foundation at <http://www.templeton.org/>; the Randolph Foundation (no website, but you can find plenty of information online); the John M. Olin Foundation at <http://www.jmof.org/>; and the Phillips Foundation at <http://www.thephillipsfoundation.org/>. What do these organizations have in common? What does their support of Riley's work suggest about the ideological basis of her book? (You can always learn a great deal about a researcher's agenda and contexts by looking into who funds and supports her or his work. Include a query into the financial support a researcher or publication receives as part of your critical evaluation of sources for your own academic work.)

Writing Critically

1. Harvey Cox observes that "nobody quite knows where the line of separation between church and state or education and indoctrination is" (paragraph 22). In an essay, define *education* and *indoctrination* within a specific context (such as your own campus, an issue in the news, or some other reading in *Many Americas*). Where do *you* think the "line" between education and indoctrination is, as you have defined those two terms? Must that line be defended at all costs, or is there room for flexibility and negotiation?

2. Harvard, a secular institution, requires students to pass a course in "moral reasoning" (not necessarily based in a faith tradition). Does your campus have a similar requirement? Should it?

Like It or Not: Social Educators Must Keep Up with Popular Culture

JEFFREY PASSE

This article first appeared in the scholarly journal *Social Education*, the flagship journal of the National Council for the Social Studies, in 2002. The journal addresses issues facing social studies classrooms from kindergarten through college. Its website is at <http://www.socialstudies.org/publications/se/>. Jeffrey Passe is a professor of reading and elementary education in the College of Education at the University of North Carolina at Charlotte. In 2003 he received the College's Faculty Award for Sustained Service to Public Schools.

M y friend was indignant. "There is no way that I will watch *Survivor!*" 1
He was firmly opposed to low-brow television that appealed to the
worst instincts of humanity.

I had the same objections to WWF wrestling, Jerry Springer, and the 2
multitude of award programs. But, I argued, we still have to watch them.

As educators, we need to know what our students are watching. If we 3
wish to understand their references, their role models and anti-role models—
indeed, if we want to know what makes our students tick—we have to be in
touch with the popular culture that influences them. We need to understand
why everyone is excited after someone is voted off the island. We need to recognize why tests should not be given the morning after the final episode of
Dawson's Creek.

But we are more than educators. We are social educators. We are his- 4
torians, sociologists, anthropologists, and all the other "ists" of social science. We must use current events, which include popular culture, in our
teaching. Doing so may be the best way to enable students to grasp social
studies concepts.

Take NASCAR as an example. As a transplanted New Yorker in North 5
Carolina, I have come to accept stock car racing as cultural currency
among my students, just as major league baseball was for my circle of
friends in New York.

The death of race-car driver Dale Earnhardt was not just another un- 6
fortunate accident in a sport in which death is an inevitable byproduct. It
was an event. My students wanted to discuss it. They needed to discuss it.
It was a teachable moment!

As a social studies educator, I had several options. We could explore so- 7
ciological implications about the attractions of danger to many Americans.
Or we could consider what anthropologists tell us about how societies
mourn the death of a hero. We may examine the political dimensions of requiring increased safety regulations in auto racing. Or we may consider,
perhaps crassly, the economic windfall that will result because of increased
attention to NASCAR events.

Each of these approaches would be helpful to students who are strug- 8
gling with the abstract nature of social science. They may benefit from the
concrete examples that will dominate media coverage in subsequent weeks.
A skillful teacher can point out similarities between popular culture and required social studies content. Earnhardt's death is hardly comparable in
importance to the death of President Franklin D. Roosevelt, but a discussion of the reaction to the fatal stock car accident may help students understand how people reacted to the loss of FDR. Teachers could make more

suitable connections to the loss of John Lennon, Princess Diana, or Kurt Cobain. Such discussions would help students grasp how those deaths were central elements in the lives of particular generations, thus developing a historical awareness that would have been difficult to achieve through conventional social studies instruction.

The preservice teachers in my elementary social studies methods course   9 had their own unique interest. They saw the Earnhardt tragedy as an opportunity to teach young children about death. They had wrestled with the issue of appropriateness. On one side was the fact that many of the children in the elementary school had never experienced the death of a loved one. My students didn't want to disturb their innocence. On the other hand, some children had already suffered the death of a grandparent, parent, sibling, or even a pet.

Through discussion of Dale Earnhardt's death, these future teachers   10 came to realize that death is so pervasive that it cannot be kept out of their students' consciousness. The only way to avoid it would be to ignore popular culture, which is what my indignant friend would have me do. Ignoring popular culture may be fine for those who do not have to influence children's lives. For teachers, it is a requirement.

Fortunately, teachers at all grade levels have access to a variety of ma-   11 terials on teaching about death. The Association for Death Education and Counseling (www.adec.org) is an excellent resource.

My way of dealing with the demands of popular culture is to view it as   12 an assignment. When I was a child, I always loved it when my teachers assigned me to watch a television show for homework. I would announce to my family at the dinner table that math and spelling would have to wait for one night—I had to watch television!

So, I turn on the tube and try to grasp the popular boy bands on MTV.   13 I check out the teen magazines in the supermarket. I sit through the latest slasher flick at the movie theater. I log on to eBay, Instant Messenger, and the newest video games. I even watch NASCAR.

Every once in a while, I am entertained. But deep down, I know that I   14 am a better teacher and a better social educator as a result of my forays into popular culture. I don't do it for very long, however. After all, I have other things to do. For instance, the Yankee game is on in fifteen minutes.

Thinking Critically

1. Who are the various audiences for Jeffrey Passe's argument? How many different categories of students and teachers is he discussing?

2. What does Jeffrey Passe see as the pedagogical reasons for bringing popular culture into the classroom, or encouraging students to share their pop culture interests in a classroom context?

3. How does Passe define popular culture?

Writing Critically

1. Could the arguments Passe makes about engaging the popular culture interests of students also apply to engaging the religious or faith-based interests students bring to the classroom? Why or why not?

2. Read M. Graham Spann's "NASCAR Racing Fans: Cranking Up an Empirical Approach" (see pp. 591–99) and Selena Roberts's. "Sports Rage Has Yet to Reach the Ovals" (see pp. 600–02). How do those writers apply sociologicalor journalistic perspectives and tools to NASCAR? How effectively do they use NASCAR as an example of a larger American cultural or social phenomenon?

3. Describe a particularly effective or very ineffective use of popular culture in one of your classrooms. What made the teacher's approach either meaningful or misguided? (Approach your description of the lesson and your analysis of its effectiveness objectively, treating both the teacher's aims and the responses of fellow students with interest and respect rather than sarcasm.)

Arguing the Cultural Divides

1. Many of the writers in Chapter 9 seem to imply that American priorities for the education of American children are misplaced. Referring to at least three of the selections in this chapter (and to relevant sources outside of *Many Americas*), write an essay in which you define and contextualize a "value" attached to education and describe how contemporary policies, popular culture, or some other factor have distorted, exploited, or denigrated that value. What *specific* steps would you recommend to restore that value?

2. Select one of the issues raised in Chapter 9, and in a research paper discuss the ways in which social class and personal financial stability influence the way that issue is perceived and addressed.

3. What does "in loco parentis" mean, and how does it relate to what Americans expect from their schools?

4. In "Liberal Groupthink Is Anti-Intellectual" and "Republicans Outnumbered in Academia," Mark Bauerlein and John Tierney draw conclusions about the political and ideological inclinations of higher education faculty. Draw up a

list of no more than ten questions based on these two articles, and ask ten different faculty members at your campus for an interview on the subject. (You might offer to provide them with copies of these two articles.) Follow the guidelines for consulting experts and professionals and conducting interviews in the Appendix, "Researching Across the Cultural Divides" (see pp. 726–47). In an essay, discuss what your interviews reveal about the political views of your campus faculty.

CHAPTER 01

Values, Media, and Entertainment: What's the Frequency?

Has the Mainstream Run Dry?

JAMES PONIEWOZIK

> James Poniewozik joined *Time* magazine as media
> and television critic in 1999 after two years as me-
> dia critic for *Salon.com*. His essays about and re-
> views of popular culture, ranging from television
> coverage of the Iraq war to changes in the way
> families are portrayed in sitcoms, have appeared in
> numerous publications and websites. Poniewozik
> is a frequent commentator on National Public
> Radio. "Has the Mainstream Run Dry?" appeared in
> *Time* in December 2003. For more of Poniewozik's
> writing, go to <http://www.time.com/time/>.

Americans under 50, as the cliché goes, were raised by the mass   1
media. And this fall, as grown children sometimes do, some of
them began to neglect their mother. On the major broadcast TV networks, ratings among viewers 18 to 49 years old (the group most
closely watched by advertisers) were down 8%. The drop-off was
even worse among men under 35, the couch potatoes of the future.
The rejection was almost poignant. You don't call? You don't write?
It would kill you to pick up a remote?

    The networks—which stood to lose hundreds of millions of ad   2
dollars—blamed the Nielsen rating service. Advertisers blamed the

programming. But the real blame belongs to a historical force more powerful than a Nielsen box, more pernicious than a stack of bad *Coupling*
scripts and not limited to TV: the end—or at least the extreme makeover—
of the mass-media audience as we have known it.

For more than two decades the networks have competed with cable.   3
Now they also vie with home video, computer games and the Paris Hilton
sex tape on the Internet. The old three-network system swore by L.O.P.,
least objectionable programming. Now sizable chunks of the audience, especially young viewers, demand most objectionable programming—unusual, gross, risqué. If you don't give it to them, they'll watch *Punk'd* or
play Manhunt instead. If you do, you may lose your other viewers to
HGTV or Lifetime. In the most mass of mass media, it is no longer possible to please most of the people most of the time.

But this is not only TV's curse. (Or blessing? More on that later.) In   4
all of entertainment we are moving from the era of mass culture to the
era of individual culture. Ask the music-biz professionals, if you can talk
them off the ledges outside their offices. Album sales were down more
than 5% from 2002's already dismal results, thanks largely to illegal music downloading. Legitimate online sellers like iTunes threaten to kill the
album, the format that made entertainers into auteurs in the rock era, and
to usher in the era of every man his own mix master. The movie industry
has not been as badly hit by piracy—yet—but it went through a summer
of surefire hits (*Hulk,* the *Tomb Raider* and *Charlie's Angels* sequels) that
weren't. What's saving that business is DVDs—now a greater source of
revenue than the box office—whose appeal is that, by offering special features, extra scenes and alternative camera angles and endings, they allow
everyone to watch the same movie differently and separately. (Cannily,
the apocalyptic chiller *28 Days Later* was released in theaters with two
endings—a made-for-theaters DVD.) The *New York Times Magazine* recently heralded theater for one—mini-plays designed to be seen by one
person at a time.

There are two stories here, a business one and a cultural one. The busi-   5
ness one should not deeply interest you unless you were hoping a Hollywood
mogul would buy you a Hummer for Christmas this year. But the cultural
story is about all of us—the Whitmanian, immigrant America of contradictory multitudes. Americans do not have a shared ethnic past or state religion.
We have Jessica Simpson. Once, when tens of millions of people listened to
the same summer hits, watched the same sitcoms and cried together in movie
houses, the mass media defined what mainstream meant—what ideals we
valued, how much change we would tolerate. If it's harder and harder to define mainstream pop culture, is there a mainstream at all?

Of course, no sooner had the printing press been invented than some   6
pundit was probably bemoaning how people, individually consuming those
newfangled "books," would lose the community spirit engendered by Passion plays and witch burnings. And it's worth remembering that mass culture was a 20th century anomaly. Before film and broadcasting, the idea of
a giant country, much less the world, sharing a common culture was ludicrous. Travel 100 miles or so, and you'd encounter different dialects, values
and folkways. Even religion could spread only so far before being locally
amended by, say, a king needing a quickie divorce. Mass culture flattened
out dialects and provided new Americans with a quick if superficial means
of assimilation. But it developed only because the technology for mass communication was invented before the technology for mass choice. In the late
1940s some 80% of TVs tuned in to *Texaco Star Theater* because, yes, Milton Berle was funny but in part too because not much else was on.

But if mass media was a technological accident, it was also an idea, in   7
synch with other ideas of its time. It was part of the mid-20th century age
of bigness, centralization and consolidation—Big Government, the draft,
central cities, UNIVACs, lifetime employment and evil empires you could
find on a map. And its decline is in synch with a world that is increasingly
decentralized, atomized and à la carte—tax revolts, the volunteer "Army
of One," suburbs, the Web, job hopping and stateless terrorism.

As the war in Iraq showed, social and cultural fragmentation can mir-   8
ror and even abet each other. Normally you can count on war to bring a
country together, as happened for a while after 9/11. But Iraq quickly
found the U.S. divided, both within itself—Michael Moore at the Oscars
and the Dixie Chicks vs. Toby Keith—and against much of the rest of the
globe. There was a corresponding theme of us—or rather U.S.—against the
world in 2003's pop culture. Overseas artists critiqued America for the way
it reacted to 9/11 (in the short-film anthology *11'09"01* and at "The American Effect" at the Whitney) and for its pop-culture excesses (in the London opera Jerry Springer). *Joe Millionaire 2* featured a fresh-scrubbed
cowboy from Texas romancing 14 worldly European bachelorettes under
the pretense that he was a multimillionaire—a devilish if inadvertent satire
of U.S.-Europe relations, playing off each side's worst stereotypes of the
other (the lying cowboy vs. corrupt, chain-smoking Old Worlders). Maybe
the most plangent treatment of American isolation was Sofia Coppola's
Lost in Translation, with Bill Murray and Scarlett Johansson as Americans
in a Tokyo so alien, it might as well have been Neptune.

And in Iraq, unlike Vietnam, there was no Walter Cronkite to speak for   9
the great middle. Ratings for cable news shot up, while big-network news-
casts stayed level or even dropped. Some viewers' media choices became a

kind of political secret handshake. Pro-war, you watched Fox News, learned that the war was a rout and disdained the liberal big media. Anti-war, you watched BBC News—or al-Jazeera on satellite—learned that the war was a quagmire and disdained the jingoistic big media. Pox on both your houses, you watched Jon Stewart.

Or you voted none of the above. What network did the most people   10 watch the night the ground war began? NBC. While ABC and the Fox network went with war news, the Peacock had the sense, bravery and civic responsibility to air . . . *Friends.*

In an overentertained, overmediated society, mainstream culture be-   11 comes more and more a secondhand experience. We are less influenced by books, movies, CDs and plays—who has the time?—than by what we hear about them through the media. *Queer Eye for the Straight Guy,* for instance, helped prompt a national seminar on gay-straight relations—even though only a couple of million of us actually watched any given episode. Only so many people were technologically intrepid enough to track down the Hilton video online—but the so-called scandal (which was what, exactly—that a woman had sex with her boyfriend?) helped draw millions to her reality show, *The Simple Life.* We may not have watched the MTV Video Music Awards—but we all knew about Britney tongue-wrestling Madonna.

Amid all this media-generated controversy, it could be difficult for a creative   12 work itself to stir up the culture. In 1994 Quentin Tarantino's *Pulp Fiction* generated volumes of discussion about movie violence. In 2003 *Kill Bill Vol. 1—* which made *Pulp* look like *Toy Story*—landed nearly as softly as villainess Lucy Liu did when she collapsed bloodily into the snow in its climax. Dan Brown's *The Da Vinci Code,* involving a theory that Mary Magdalene may have been Jesus' wife and the mother of his child, intrigued readers and sold millions of copies, but it was ABC News that really took religious fire when it raised the same question in a prime-time special. In fact, it was easier for a work to provoke discussion if no one saw it. Possibly the most debated works of 2003 were *The Passion of the Christ,* Mel Gibson's unfinished movie about the Crucifixion; *The Reagans,* a TV biopic that no one outside CBS saw before the network canceled it under protest; and Daniel Libeskind's World Trade Center rebuilding design, which spent most of the year on the redrawing board.

This dichotomy—between the buzz culture and the culture we actually   13 consume—also created two kinds of celebrities: those we wanted to see on the screen or hear on the radio and those we just wanted to read about in *Us* or *People.* Occasionally, the categories overlapped, as with Beyoncé, who conquered the news racks and the CD racks. But in other cases—notably Ben and Jen and Gigli—fame and commercial fortune were, if anything, inversely proportional. And whereas 2002 gave us famous has-beens, like Ozzy

Osbourne and Anna Nicole, 2003 was the year of famous never-weres. Ally Hilfiger and Jamie Gleicher of MTV's *Rich Girls,* for instance, seem to have been created out of thin air so we could envy and sneer at them at once.

Notoriety still paid in 2003, to an extent. Rapper 50 Cent parlayed a   14 tabloid-lurid story—he has been shot, he claims, nine times—into the year's top-selling album. And Demi Moore helped her celebrity profile by hooking up with Ashton Kutcher—more, probably, than she helped her summer flick, *Charlie's Angels: Full Throttle.* But whom did we actually want to see in a movie?

We'll have the fish, please.   15

Finding Nemo was the kind of exception that proves that just when   16 you're ready to declare the mainstream dead, it swims up and bites you on the tush. The year's top-grossing movie was also an example of just what it takes—in a culture broken down by tribes and ages and demographics— to make an across-the-board hit. People flocked to *Nemo* because it was a good movie, of course. It was moving, it was beautifully animated. And who doesn't like a good ink-spurting joke? But more important, it was about easy-to-agree-with universals: loving your family, learning to live with risks. (It was the sort of movie that, before the statute of limitations expired, we would have called "post–Sept. 11.") And it had a cast whose appeal was not laser-targeted toward young urban males or moms over 40. Black or white, young or old, liberal or conservative, we all feel pretty much the same about fish, except that some of us don't like tartar sauce.

Other times, though, you don't immediately recognize the voice of the   17 mainstream even when it shows up on your TV and belts out "Mack the Knife." Clay Aiken, the skinny, geeky *American Idol* runner-up who was the year's surprise recording star, was, you might say, so mainstream that he was weird: a straitlaced, smiling, asexual whippet who loved to sing standards. *Idol*'s judges, and record-company execs, doubted that Clay could make it in the pop market of 2003. One multiplatinum CD later— *Measure of a Man,* so pure it floats—he proved them wrong and showed that in some ways the mainstream is now itself a niche.

Aiken's sales, by the way, outstripped those of Ruben Studdard, the   18 moon-faced R.-and-B. crooner who won *Idol.* So who speaks for the mainstream, the TV audience voting with its phones or the music audience voting with its wallets? Is a thing mainstream only to the extent that we're willing to pay money for it?

Well, that doesn't hurt—this is America. Aikenmania also showed how   19 the culture is increasingly in the hands of nontraditional commercial tastemakers like Wal-Mart. *Measure* was sold largely to kids and parents in checkout lines—people who might never set foot inside a record store. With almost 3,000 locations in the U.S., Wal-Mart is more of a broadcaster than

NBC is. And it's using that power culturally—deciding this year, for instance, to exclude racy "lad" magazines like *Maxim* from its news racks. Big discounters also helped popularize conservative-pundit books and the *Veggie Tales* Christian videos. Likewise, *Queer Eye* brought us together through consumerism: gay or straight, it said, we stood united in our need to blow $40 on a bottle of moisturizer. (The show was perhaps the most visible sign of masstige, the fashion world's rather oxymoronic new term for bringing prestige style to the masses—Isaac Mizrahi at Target, for instance.) The Fab Five made gay culture cross over with promises of bourgeois paradise, just as 50 Cent, Jay-Z and many before them brought hip-hop culture over with tales of bling-bling. Big pimpin', meet big primpin'.

But wait a second here. Which one is mainstream? The Fab Five, show- 20 ing up to make over—and showily flirt with—an ex-Marine (who whipped up a lovely soufflé)? Or Aiken, who cut the patriotic single "God Bless the USA" with his *Idol* mates during the war and strenuously purged sex—any kind of sex—from his music and persona? 50 Cent, who sold more than 6 million copies of Get Rich ("I'm high all the time/I smoke that good s_____")? Or Wal-Mart, which carried only the bowdlerized version of his album? The de-religionized spirituality of Mitch Albom's No. 1-selling *The Five People You Meet in Heaven?* Or the literalistic Christianity of the No. 1-selling thriller *Armageddon,* from the Left Behind series? Fox News, which carried the flag (in the corner of its screen) for Bush's war? Or the Fox network, which scandalized cultural conservatives with its reality shows and aired *The O.C., The Simple Life* and *Arrested Development,* three of 2003's strongest pop-culture jabs at the rich?

In American culture, as in American politics, it was possible to assem- 21 ble a case for two entirely different visions of the mainstream: one libertine, irreverent and p.c., the other traditional, devout and PG. It's tempting to borrow the electoral blue-state/red-state template and say there are two mainstreams, equal and opposite—but that beggars the definition of mainstream, no? The year 2003, we've heard, was when the swing voter became irrelevant. It could be that our pop culture too no longer has that swing.

Unless—pardon me, Carson Kressley, for the pun—it swings both ways. 22

The year 2003 introduced a new phrase to the cultural vocabulary: 23 *flash mob,* an instant gathering of people, organized on the Internet, who receive an e-mail or cell-phone message, show up en masse at a designated spot, perform some absurd act (quack like ducks, bang their shoes on the pavement) and then disperse.

Mainstream culture today is like a flash mob. Those who are part of it 24 know they're part of it, even if it doesn't congregate as often as it did back when 30 million people would watch a network show on a typical night.

Every so often, we get the call—we gather for *Joe Millionaire* or buy that Harry Potter book. Then, show over, book read, we scatter: back to VH1 or our *Scarface* DVDs or our scrapbooking chat rooms.

Increasingly, the events that most deeply, if briefly, unite that floating 25 mainstream are deaths: Johnny Cash, Bob Hope, Katharine Hepburn. The intensity of response to the passing of John Ritter, a likable actor from a campy '70s sitcom, seemed to surprise even his fans. In a culture with few common cultural referents, the past is what we share the most. (Perhaps for the same reason, 2003's Broadway shows with broad mass appeal tended to be revivals like *Long Day's Journey into Night* and *Wonderful Town*— and the music business heaved up a slew of standards albums.) When old stars pass, they take with them a piece of a time when we weren't so niched and subdivided by the market and our own choices. To make the metaphor a little homier, the pop-culture mainstream is a family that used to get together for dinner once a week but now does so only at weddings (or dating-show finales, anyway)—and funerals.

But don't mourn those old days. However community-building the old 26 big aggregators were (the three networks, Top 40 radio), they also tended to kill idiosyncrasy (with a few hard-fought exceptions like *Cash*). That cable serves smaller audiences allowed it this year to produce more polarizing—but better—TV: FX's *Nip/Tuck,* ESPN's *Playmakers,* HBO's *Angels in America.* (Though, granted, as the debate over the FCC's media-ownership rules noted, most of the open mouths providing those voices are still connected to the corporate lungs of a few giant media companies.) And if iPod users pick and choose singles rather than pay $18 for filler-loaded albums (which were invented more for business than artistic reasons in the first place), it frees them to sample more genres and artists. The trade-off is a flightier, more mercurial and more tabloid pop culture. Its one unifying trait, perhaps, is simply the desire to check out what all the fuss is about. But at least we're still connected enough to care about one another's fusses now and again.

The monolithic mainstream culture of the 20th century helped define 27 what it meant to be American. But it was un-American at heart. The phrase *E pluribus unum* aside, America was founded on fragmentation—by people fleeing religious, political and cultural "community" in the Old World. Nearly 200 years ago, Alexis de Tocqueville wrote that a strength of the new nation was its abundance of space. Here, unlike in Europe, the citizens could be united when they needed to and be alone when they wanted to. In an older, more crowded America, we find that space virtually—inside a screen, a book, a set of headphones. This is our last frontier, and it goes on forever.

Thinking Critically

1. How does James Poniewozik use process analysis, cause and effect, and comparison/contrast to structure and support his argument? Create different summaries or outlines of the essay that focus on just one of these rhetorical strategies.

2. To what extent is Poniewozik's argument dependent on allusions, references, and illustrations? This essay was first published in late 2003. Since that time, how many of the performers, films, television shows, and so on, that he mentions have become obscure, unpopular, or irrelevant? Does that shift in itself support or refute his argument? What are some of the risks inherent to writing about popular culture or in using examples from popular culture as evidence for an argument?

3. How does Poniewozik define *mainstream,* and why is it critical to his argument that he redefine that word?

Writing Critically

1. How does anyone get to be an "expert" in popular culture and the media? James Poniewozik has a bachelor's degree in English and took graduate courses in fiction-writing at New York University. Choose two or three other media critics and reviewers, from local or national publications, and arrange to interview them (see the Appendix, "Research Across the Cultural Divides" for guidelines on the ethics and etiquette of interviewing). How did they become "experts" on popular culture and the mass media? How do they perceive their role in American media culture? What do they have in common or believe that media writers in general have in common with each other?

2. Poniewozik observes in paragraph 4 that "we are moving from the era of mass culture to the era of individual culture," and he goes on to argue this claim using popular culture as evidence. How might other writers in *Many Americas* support or refute this claim?

3. In paragraph 13, Poniewozick describes a "dichotomy" between two kinds of "celebrity." How does he define those two kinds of celebrity? Whom do you consider to be an example of each kind of celebrity? What kind of need do those celebrities fulfill for their audiences? What does their celebrity say about the values and needs of the larger culture?

Experimental Programming

Douglas Rushkoff

Douglas Rushkoff, a professor of media culture at New York University's Interactive Telecommunications Program, lectures about media, society, and change at conferences and universities around the world. He is a frequent commentator on National Public Radio's news and information program *All Things Considered,* and he has been a guest on network television news programs as well as on the cable television program *Politically Incorrect.* Rushkoff has written and hosted documentaries about media, culture, and change, including the acclaimed PBS documentary *The Merchants of Cool,* which you can watch at <http://www.pbs.org/wgbh/pages/frontline/shows/cool/>. An adviser to the United Nations Commission on World Culture, Rushkoff is also on the board of directors of the Media Ecology Association. He is the author of *Media Virus: Hidden Agendas in Popular Culture* (1994), *Cyberia: Life in the Trenches of Hyperspace* (1994), *Playing the Future: What We Can Learn from Digital Kids* (1996), *Coercion: Why We Listen to What "They" Say* (1999), and *Nothing Sacred: The Truth About Judaism* (2003). "Experimental Programming" was published in the anthology *Killed: Great Journalism Too Hot to Print* (2004). In the prologue to the essay, Rushkoff explains how this essay came about and why it was eventually "killed" (rejected) by *Seed* magazine.

This piece was inspired by an episode of *Joe Millionaire* in which I watched a young woman—who had, most likely, performed oral sex on a man she believed to be a millionaire—finally learn that he was just a low-paid construction worker. I'll admit, her face at that split second—the moment between the horrific revelation and her effort to mask her sense of shame—displayed more genuine pathos than a full season of *ER.* But this reality program, like so many that went before and after, derived its entertainment value from the humiliation of its real life subjects.

It occurred to me that reality TV scenarios are set up in much the same way as now-forbidden psychology experiments. As luck would have it, a brand-new magazine called *Seed* had just asked me to write a regular column about how mainstream media perverts or expresses science. So it seemed like the perfect match. I had a meeting with the editor who loved the idea. He pitched it to his publisher, who approved the topic. A month later, I was on my fifth rewrite.

The editor seemed to think each revision would satisfy his publisher's concerns, but the pieces always came back to me with requests for more science. More Darwin. Something. Ultimately, the piece was canned. The publisher, I later learned, didn't consider psychology to be a science.

In some ways the magazine industry works like a science experiment or a reality TV show, too. It's not that editors hope to humiliate their writers. It's that each assignment is really just the testing of a hypothesis: can this subject/writer combination yield a piece that we'll want to publish months from now?

That's why contracts have clauses about "kill fees," and why magazines assign many more articles than they ever run. Editors might like the piece just fine—but it may not reflect whatever they have told their publisher or what the publisher has told their advertisers about the magazine's "direction." In fact, an increase in killed pieces is a good sign that a magazine has lost its way, or is desperately trying to find one.

Still, the net effect can feel as humiliating as if it were intentional. I like to remind myself at such moments that the editors handing down inconsistent, contradictory orders must feel pretty exposed and humiliated, too. They're the ones whose judgment has been overridden, not me. Plus, I've been paid, at least in part, for a piece I'm now free to place elsewhere. They're stuck at the scene of the crime.

An apparently random sample of average people is divided into two   1
groups: teachers and students. Each student sits on one side of a wall trying to remember a sequence of words, while the teacher sits on the other and is instructed to deliver an electric shock at each wrong answer. The voltage is increased, until the student is writhing around on the floor and screaming in agony. How far will each teacher go? Will he or she deliver a lethal dose? Finally, it will be revealed to the teachers that their "students" are really actors, pretending to be painfully shocked. Won't they be embarrassed when we all see how easily they can be turned into sadists?

No, this isn't one of next season's reality shows but a real psychology   2
experiment carried out at Yale University in 1961 by Dr. Stanley Milgram. Participants were so anguished over their capacity to inflict pain on demand that the much-publicized saga led to new ethical guidelines for psychological experimentation.

No such restrictions appear to apply to reality television programs,   3
where sustained sadism of this sort can be observed somewhere on the TV dial pretty much any night of the week. Just when it seems as though this genre, if we can call it that, has finally peaked, a new crop of shows even more outrageously cruel or dishonest with its participants than the last appears on the horizon. Welcome to the American media-space, where neither a psychology degree nor an ethics certificate is required for us to look in on psychological terrorism, just for the fun of it.

How did television fall to such new lows? The abuse of traditional sto- 4
rytelling techniques certainly had something to do with it. Ever since Aristotle intuited the "arc" of increasing tension and release that serves as the
dramatic spine of any successful play, writers have been honing this formula down to its most crude and utilitarian essence: create characters we
like, put them in danger, and give them an easily digestible solution before
the end. It's led to a predictability in mainstream drama and comedy that's
nauseatingly claustrophobic. Shows that aren't assembled through focus
groups are written by committee, so that anything resembling nuance or
meaning is ironed out before they reach the commercial airwaves.

Any real messages are reserved for the sponsors, who use the very same 5
arc to program product preferences. We don't call the stuff on television
"programming" for nothing. It's not the schedule or television being programmed; it's us. So, for about twenty seconds we are brought up the incline
plane of increasing stakes—A yucky pimple? Fired from work? Carpet
stains? Social anxiety?—and in the last ten seconds all is set right by the sponsor's product: a new cream, an investment, solvent, or pill. In ancient drama,
these quick-fix solutions were called deus ex machina, in which a god would
descend from the heavens to save the hero from an otherwise tragic circumstance. Now, a "miracle" product serves that same function. But relentless
exposure to these mini-dramas has made television audiences cynical and difficult to please. Having seen the machinery of storytelling at its most manip-
ulative, viewers have grown suspicious of narrative in general.

In such an environment, reality television was initially greeted as libera- 6
tion from the captive spell of the programmer. By throwing a dozen real people (or, at worst, wannabe actors) in a house, on an island, or in a chateau,
and forcing them to come up with their own dialogue, these unscripted
shows seemed to release audiences from the predictability of crafted drama
and to replace it with the spontaneity—and the stakes—of real life.

Unlike scripted shows, with their preprogrammed agenda, reality pro- 7
grams project an aura of fair play, not unlike live sporting events. This is a
competition, the format seems to say, in which only the laws of natural selection will determine who is left on the island at the end of *Survivor*, or which
of the handsome men will win the affections of the single Bachelorette.

As hardened media consumers, of course, we may wonder just how 8
much the producers of such shows actually leave to chance. But in a world
where everything from the job market to the stock market to national elections appears to be in some measure fixed, even the illusion of real-life
competition on a level playing field can be appealing.

So instead of Darwin's Galapagos, we get the island of *Survivor*, where 9
only the strongest and most cunning will make it to the end of their battle

against the elements, insects, starvation and each other. And we, the viewing public, get to watch the participants, stripped of the artificial pretenses and conveniences of modern life, duke it out as humans were "meant" to.

On *Temptation Island,* real couples test the bounds of their socially constructed unions by mixing with buff and buxom singles in bathing suits who have no purpose but to seduce. Participants who actually had sexual intercourse with the tempters might be said to represent the triumph of "untamed" animal instincts over social and cultural "programming." On this rawest of narrative levels, reality shows seem to be about restoring what audiences conceive of as the natural order. Even the talent show *American Idol* means to replace—for one lucky winner, anyway—the insiderly, casting-couch-driven culture of the music industry with a fair, democratically chosen pop star. 10

But while such moments may seem to restore a sense of fair play to television, reality shows are anything but natural selection. They may not be scripted, but any connection between shows like *Survivor* or *Joe Millionaire* and real life is purely coincidental. In fact, they are fixed decks, where the preliminary conditions and choice of participants yield a predictable array of possible outcomes. 11

It's not just because the eight MTV veejay hopefuls on the *Real World* wouldn't normally find themselves living together in a fabulous loft in Seattle. Rather, it's because these totally crafted productions are based on premises as far removed from reality as TV's classic situation comedies were. Back in television's so-called "golden years," situation comedies were precisely that: situations. A guy's uncle is a Martian. My horse can talk. Your mother is a car. That's why they were called *situation* comedies—because the situation drove the comedy. Today's sitcoms have no situation to speak of: some friends drink coffee in the same place. An office where, uh, people work. One of our friends is gay. 12

While today's sitcoms more closely resemble real life, at least in their situational components, reality TV has staked its future on the absurdity of its setups. Far from focusing on ordinary human behavior, these shows are coming to resemble laboratory experiments (with poor controls) in which conditions are set up in a very particular way so that the most dramatic (read: painful or humiliating) results can emerge. 13

Like psych experiments, each show has an implicit assumption. What will happen if people are put on an island where they must depend on one another for survival? To forestall the "uninteresting" possibility that they might just learn to get along, what if we require that the group vote one person off every day? That should tip the balance toward down-and-dirty in the "survival of the fittest" maneuvering. What if a group of pretty women compete for the attention of a multimillionaire? Been there. Okay, 14 what if he's not really a millionaire, but only pretending to be? That brings an undercurrent of humiliation to even the most innocent of encounters. Cool. What if we go Big Brother one better by putting a group of formerly famous people in a house together? What could be more pathetic than a houseful of one-time winners desperately trying to prove that they are not losers—and failing miserably.

It is immediately apparent that these shows aren't "reality" programs 15 at all, but precisely constructed exercises in humiliation. We watch them not to enjoy the seemingly natural (but ultimately spurious) unscriptedness of these shows, but because we find the cruelty itself so compelling. Even a reality show as seemingly innocuous as *The Osbournes* finds its core entertainment value in the sad pathos of its drugged, mentally-ill protagonist and his dysfunctional family.

An all-too-human tendency to not only tolerate but even participate in 16 the infliction of pain and suffering on others—especially on those who cannot fight back—was observed in another infamous psychology experiment that was later condemned for unethical treatment of unwitting test subjects. The Stanford Prison Experiment of 1971 split a random group of men into "prisoners" and "guards." Almost immediately, the guards took it upon themselves to develop increasingly humiliating tortures for their prisoners to endure. In fact, they were so successful at concocting demeaning situations that the experiment, planned for two weeks, was cut short after just six days.

Are we, the television audience, aligning ourselves with those "prison 17 guards" when we take delight in the humiliation of reality show participants? What was it, after all, that compelled more Americans to tune in to the final episode of *Joe Millionaire*—a show where women competed desperately for the hand of a fabulously wealthy hunk they had not yet learned was actually a construction worker of limited means—rather than watch Dan Rather's exclusive interview with Saddam Hussein? Wasn't it the chance to see, from a safe distance, the shock and humiliation on the face of a woman who had engaged in a sex act under false pretenses only to be rejected in the end by Joe, our avatar?

It's one thing to admit that the popularity of this kind of show exposes 18 unpleasant truths about human nature. But can such cruel diversions actually turn us into crueler people? A study released recently by two psychologists at the University of Michigan suggests just that. It found that men who had frequently watched violent programs as children were more likely to shove people than those who watched them less.

Other studies have concluded that after being shown violent TV programs, children are more inclined to behave violently toward their peers. 19

And such links aren't limited to just physical behavior. In 2002 researchers at the National Institute on Media and the Family attempted to demonstrate that watching violent TV makes kids not just more physically violent, but "relationally violent"—in other words—meaner.

Such research is famously fraught with difficulties. For example, just because socially and physically violent people watch meaner, more violent programs doesn't mean that such shows *cause* mean and violent behavior. It might just be that people with an especially strong tendency to behave violently gravitate to TV shows that specialize in violence. 20

But even if TV cruelty only panders to existing tendencies in some of us, we engage in tele-sadism at our own risk. This is the real lesson to be learned from those psychological experiments of the past that look so much like today's reality programs. In the Milgram experiment at Yale, it was the "teachers"—the pain *givers*—who, confronted by their own capacity to mete out punishment, became wracked with guilt and shame. These were ordinary folks who discovered they were capable of great cruelty, as long as it was somehow "justified" by the situation. Either the infliction of pain was presented as being "good" for the recipients (the actors who pretended to suffer), or it was seen as a "natural" outcome of the social hierarchy set up in the experiment. So who was *ultimately* responsible for inflicting the real pain in these experiments? The researchers who devised the experiments in the first place! And like the pain givers who were merely "following orders," these researchers had elaborate justifications for their actions, based on the perceived value of their work to science and to society at large. 21

Indisputably, there's a harsh emotional price to be paid by even passive observers of cruelty. The pleasure we take from watching cruelty also requires justification, some internal adjustment of attitude that blames the unwitting victim for being greedy or stupid or self-deluded or in some other sense "deserving" of his or her treatment. 22

In the great uncontrolled social experiment that is network TV, we, with remote controls in our hands, are the test group. The question is, how far will we go? How much cruelty on the part of the producers will we find "enjoyable"? Long ago, the limits of audience appetite were tested in this fashion, bringing us the death matches of the Coliseum in Imperial Rome—and we know what happened to the society that sponsored them. But unlike the Romans, this time we have no emperor to blame. By rewarding reality shows with high ratings we the audience are in fact responsible for their continued success—which means that we are ultimately responsible, in cahoots with the producers and the networks, for the pain and humiliation inflicted. Now *that's* interactive entertainment. 23

Thinking Critically

1. What analogy does Douglas Rushkoff make to explain the effectiveness of certain television advertisements?

2. *Seed* magazine, for which this article was originally written, is online at <http://www.seedmagazine.com/>. How would you characterize the audience for *Seed*? What can you find out about the magazine's purpose and the kinds of articles it is likely to publish? If you were Rushkoff's editor, why would you have "killed" this article? What suggestions for revision might you have given?

3. Study Rushkoff's concluding paragraph, connecting each sentence to a point made earlier in the essay. What is the effect of this conclusion on you as a reader? (For example, who is the "we" referred to in all but the last sentence of this paragraph?)

Writing Critically

1. Research Dr. Stanley Milgram's inquiries into the psychology of obedience. Why does Rushkoff begin his essay with a brief description of one of Milgram's experiments? How fully does he make use of Milgram's work? In an essay, analyze the implications of Milgram's discoveries as applied to a contemporary media phenomenon of your own choosing.

2. In "The Unreal Thing" (see pp. 640–48), Adam Gopnik uses the fictional world of *The Matrix* films to describe a contemporary kind of relationship with the "real" world. Drawing on Gopnik's and Rushkoff's arguments, describe the way a particular genre of popular media convinces its consumers that its version of the world is "real."

3. Why is it interesting, if not entertaining, to watch other people humiliate themselves or be humiliated? What historical precedents are there for such spectacles? What conflicting or mixed messages does American popular culture send about the nature of humiliation?

Daytime TV Gets Judgmental

HARRY STEIN

Harry Stein wrote about ethics for the *Wall Street Journal* and *Esquire* magazine and is a contributing editor at *City Journal*, where "Daytime TV Gets Judgmental" appeared in the Spring 2004 issue. The son of acclaimed dramatist Joe Stein (*Fiddler on the Roof; Your Show of Shows*), Harry Stein grew up with impeccable East Coast liberal credentials. His perspective changed with the birth of his daughter, and he chronicled that change in his memoir *How I Accidentally Joined the Vast Right-Wing*

Conspiracy (and Found Inner Peace) (2000). His most
recent book, *The Girl Watchers Club: Lessons from the
Battlefield of Life* (2004), is an affectionate, candid
portrayal of four World War II veterans, including his own
father-in-law. Asked by an interviewer about the "Girl
Watchers" and their generation's impact, Stein observed
that "I would have to say that their most significant
contribution has been the attitude with which they imbued
the country: a kind of unflagging optimism which I truly
believe is more evident in America than any other place on
the planet. That is something that's hard to quantify, but it
has contributed enormously to our collective well being."
City Journal is a quarterly published by the Manhattan
Institute, a private think tank that analyzes public policy
and cultural issues—especially issues that affect urban
America—from a market-oriented perspective that
emphasizes personal responsibility. Much of *City
Journal's* past and present content is available online at
<http://www.city-journal.org/>.

Forget Janet Jackson's notorious Super Bowl "wardrobe malfunction"; for- 1
get the soul-deadening sexuality constantly displayed on MTV; Exhibit A
in the argument that television is a purveyor of rotten values remains the longtime champ: *The Jerry Springer Show.* Only, here's the weird thing: in its current incarnation, Springer's latter-day freak show also provides evidence of a
growing resurgence in this country of higher standards of decency and morality. It's a trend nowhere more evident than on daytime television.

Not that I mean to credit Springer with anything resembling good taste. 2
For 12 years now, the former Cincinnati mayor and would-be Democratic
Senate candidate has presided from his Chicago studio over a program
whose socially redeeming value registers well into the minus range. Here,
every day—in some markets, twice and thrice a day—family members parade their shared carnal adventures, and morbidly obese, slatternly, foul-
mouthed women battle over useless, slack-jawed men; while the audience
(whose female members get in on the act by exposing their breasts in exchange for bead necklaces), urges them on, chanting "whore, whore,
whore" or, less creatively, "Jer-*ry*, Jer-*ry*, Jer-*ry*."

Here's the description of one recent episode on the show's own website. 3
"Debbie is torn between her current husband and her ex-husband, who happened to be buddies when they were in jail together! She admits she has feelings for them both but in the end says her ex is the jailbird for her! Next . . .
Loretta has been dating April for 6 months but has also been sleeping with

April's sister for 3! She plans to break up the family and leave April for her sister today! Then . . . Lynnette is here to steal her cousin's man, Thaddeus! She has absolutely no remorse for her betrayal but gets a taste of her own medicine when Thaddeus chooses his long time lover, Lynnette's cousin!"

Truly, there is no rational defense for this festival of perversity, and one can only guess at its effects on those who view it day after day after day—many of whom reportedly are college students, who regard it as a goof. Presumably even their more socially progressive instructors, tutored in the doctrines of Derrida and Foucault, hesitate to go quite as far in their libertine enthusiasms as Jerry, who once broadcast a show on bestiality, featuring a young woman who had an affair with her dog and a man describing his five years of wedded bliss with a horse named Pixel. 4

How then could anyone regard Springer's circus as a reason for optimism? Well, for one thing, it used to be even worse. Until 1999, guests would actually brawl on Jerry's stage—indeed, the producers encouraged them to do so—going at each other with fists and bared nails, often inflicting real damage. But after intense pressure from critics, including Chicago religious figures, the show discontinued the mayhem—with great reluctance, since it was a ratings-grabber. "We will produce and distribute a program that we feel is responsible—no violence, physical confrontation or profanity," read the press release issued at the time. Now guests merely *try* to get at each other, held apart as they flail away by a crew of massive guys, whose leader, Steve, has become another star of the program. 5

More to the point, Springer ends every broadcast with a brief segment called "Jerry's Final Thought," in which he pretends to wring some social, even moral, meaning from the insanity just concluded. "The fact is," he intoned on a recent show about cheating—in one guise or another, the subject of almost *every* installment—"if you're willing to screw over a family member or friend for a screw with his or her mate, how can you ever be committed to any relationship—and why would anyone be willing to risk being committed to you?" 6

Never mind that as he reads from the monitor, Springer radiates smarmy insincerity. Given the context, it says quite a bit that vice goes out of its way to pay tribute to virtue. 7

It's easy to make the case that, in the vast wasteland that is broadcast television (as FCC chairman Newton Minnow had it more than 40 years ago), daytime TV has long been the most barren region of all—home not only to the bathetic soaps, with their ludicrous plot twists, but also to creaky sitcoms, retreads of game shows long since departed from prime time, and featherweight talk shows that feature either sob stories or actors energetically plugging their latest projects. 8

Yet there is also daytime's version of reality television. In important re- 9
spects, it is far more real—and certainly more telling about the state of the
culture—than the stuff that goes by that name in the evening.

Springer's show is the nadir of the genre, the television equivalent of 10
maggots churning on rotten meat. Nonetheless, even it, in its disturbing and
often depressing way, is revealing. Talk about the *other* America! Like it or
not, people like Springer's guests really are out there, in apparent profusion,
stealing each other's mates, cursing up a storm, drinking, and beating the
hell out of each other, literally and figuratively. (One can only thank one's
lucky stars that they are surely among the 50 percent of Americans who
never think to vote—and won't, at least until Jerry goes back into politics.)

Generally speaking, though, daytime reality television gets more recogniz- 11
ably real as the day goes along. Considerably more reputable than Springer
(for however much that's worth) is the show that follows him in the New York
market: *Maury*. For while Maury Povich, husband of newscaster Connie
Chung and son of legendary *Washington Post* sportswriter Shirley Povich, also
presides over an exploitation fest—airing shows, for instance, on mothers accused of seducing their daughters' boyfriends—he is clearly far more willing to
cast the proceedings as socially beneficial and even morally instructive.

Trading largely in messy interpersonal relations, Maury likes to present 12
himself as a seeker of truth. Among his staples: using a lie detector to determine if one party in a relationship, usually the guy, is guilty as accused
of cheating (he usually is). But Povich's real specialty, the gimmick around
which almost every other broadcast revolves, is the paternity test. The formula never varies. A woman, usually very young and very often black or
Hispanic, comes onstage and declares, either angrily or tearfully, that she
knows a given man fathered her child. After a couple of minutes of this
drama, the accused male walks out—often, depending on how he's just
been characterized, to audience jeers—and just as vigorously denies that he
is the father. The denial routinely involves the guy pointing toward a large
picture of the kid in question, which is displayed at the back of the set, and
emphasizing how dramatically the child's features differ from his own.
He'll often cast aspersions on the mother's character, too, peppering them
with variations of the words "slut" and "whore."

At this point, Maury says something along the lines of, "Well, let's find 13
out." Ripping open a large manila envelope, he withdraws a sheet of paper and solemnly pronounces, "When it comes to two-year-old Jadiem,
Corey, you *are* the father," or, just as often, "When it comes to ten-month-
old Treasure, Earnell, you are *not* the father."

If the woman finds herself vindicated, she is apt to leap to her feet, exul- 14
tant, and berate the man. One mother I saw spun around, thrust her backside

to the camera and, pointing, screamed at the newly established dad, "Kiss my ass!" When the man is victorious, he is likely to strut, or throw up his hands in triumph like an athlete, while the woman, bursting into tears, runs backstage, Maury trailing—and both followed by a cameraman who records the host consoling her.

This human drama makes, I'm embarrassed to admit, for riveting tele- 15 vision. But there is also enough sociology at play to leave one feeling only slightly unclean. For what we are witnessing here are flesh-and-blood examples of underclass pathology. The supply of accusers and accused seems inexhaustible. On one recent installment, the mother was back for a fifth time, testing two men (the seventh and eighth she'd had tested overall) for paternity of her toddler Mustafa—neither proving a match, as it turned out.

The host's attitude toward all this dysfunction is somewhat ambivalent. 16 Unfailingly, if the DNA establishes a given man as a child's father, Maury forthrightly asks the guy if he now intends to become part of the child's life. The typical response: "Yeah, I'm a man, I'll step up to the plate." Or: "I'm a man, I take care of my business."

Nor, at least occasionally, does Povich try to hide his distress over what 17 is unfolding before his cameras. "Sophia, let me ask you a question, because a lot of people are wondering this," he said gently to one young woman before the results were in. "You say you got pregnant with him [once before], and had a miscarriage, and you say he laughed at you. So why would you sleep with him again?" Of course, she could offer no plausible answer. "You've got two children together," he said to another couple, screaming profanities at each other after the show had established the man's paternity. "Don't you want them to grow up in a home where their mother and father respect each other? Don't you want that?" The thought seemed not to have pierced the consciousness of either.

Yet from Maury there is never any real condemnation. Though the 18 show pays lip service to the resurgent traditionalist virtue of accepting personal responsibility, the host often still seems to embrace the doctrine, so fashionable among post-sixties elites, that no sin is greater than passing judgment. The show typically ends not just without any expression of commonsense outrage—"*You've had six kids by five different women? What is WRONG with you?!*"—but also without any attention paid to the obvious, larger issue: the utter moral chaos of the world these guests inhabit. (The same moral schizophrenia appears in the commercials between segments. Nearly half the ads are pitches for job training—in air-conditioning or automotive repair, say, or hairdressing or secretarial work. The rest seem to be for sleazy ambulance-chasing law firms: "If you've been injured in an accident, tell the insurance company *you* mean business!")

The one word almost never heard on *Maury* is "marriage"—the prac- 19
tice of which offers the best hope of refuge for these desperate women and
their fatherless children. Of course, this neglect of marriage, too, is of a
piece with contemporary elite attitudes, which not only tend to portray
matrimony as confining but, with celebrity unwed mothers like Calista
Flockhart in mind, often celebrate single motherhood as a valid alternative
life-style—as if the decision of an unmarried Hollywood starlet to have a
child is remotely akin to that of a 17-year-old girl in the South Bronx.

Even as I was monitoring the Povich show, the *New York Times* ran a 20
hostile lead editorial on the Bush administration's $1.5 billion initiative in
support of marriage. "The whole idea of encouraging poor people to get
married and stay married through classes and counseling sessions," the
Times complained, "ignores the main reason that stable wedlock is rare in
inner cities: the epidemics of joblessness and incarceration that have stripped
those communities of what social scientists call 'marriageable' men."

The *Times* editorial board might well take a few mornings off to watch 21
Maury. Many of the men who appear on Povich's stage for paternity tests are
neither jobless nor criminally inclined. More than a few, in fact, are bright and
charming. As one explained himself, moments before being nailed as the father (possessed of all the breezy confidence of billionaire producer Steven Bing
before a DNA test established *him* as the father of Elizabeth Hurley's child):
"Any time I wanted a booty call, I'd call her. . . . She's the neighborhood 'ho.' "
And, he added for good measure, "The baby does not look like me at all."

But if Povich tends to avoid passing judgment, daytime television from late 22
morning into the afternoon now offers an array of other personalities whose
job *is* to judge: the TV judges ruling on real cases in their courtroom sets.

In recent years, these judge shows have proliferated at an astonishing 23
rate. In the New York market alone there are now seven on view every weekday—five ruled over by bona fide ex-jurists gone showbiz (the other two
"judges" are lawyers). These shows provide yet another snapshot of latter-
day American culture and mores—and not an especially pretty one, since it
reveals a culture in considerable ethical disarray. Though this ethical breakdown is not exactly news, these shows powerfully demonstrate the degree to
which moral laxity can wreak havoc in individual lives. Here we find parents
ready to explain away even the most egregiously antisocial behavior by their
children; motorists who believe the requirements of registration and insurance need not apply to them; legions of people who readily justify having
trashed others' property; and many, many jerks who borrow money from
friends and lovers and later blithely insist that the loans were gifts.

At the same time, the collective success of such shows signals something 24
more encouraging: the public's yearning for real accountability and rigorously

enforced standards. For though the TV judges vary a good deal in personal style, in the end what they share is of vastly greater importance: each is an unapologetic advocate of old-fashioned, no-excuses, responsible behavior. Indeed, in their judicial robes, dispensing commonsense justice between commercial breaks, they are probably the closest many Americans come to having authority figures in their lives. And though the shows are entertaining, each judge clearly takes his or her educative role extremely seriously.

By far the most familiar of the judges is, of course, the genre's reigning superstar: Judith Sheindlin—Judge Judy. Appointed by then-mayor Ed Koch to New York's family court in 1982 and named four years later the court's supervising judge in Manhattan, Judge Judy, whose syndicated show launched in 1996, is so fierce a proponent of responsible behavior that comedy shows like *Saturday Night Live* have had easy fun parodying her. Anyone who comes before her court who has failed to behave well—whether by ignoring a contract or just fudging the truth—can expect the fourth degree, often followed by a dose of withering sarcasm or outright scorn. "Don't try and pull the wool over my eyes," she has warned hundreds of times, "I'm *smarter* than you!" 25

One particularly satisfying recent case pitted a young motorcycle cop against a young California woman, who'd brought along her parents to testify on her behalf. It seemed that after the cop had stopped the attractive and self-assured woman for speeding, she let it drop that her father was himself an officer, recently retired. Then, as the motorcycle cop wrote out her ticket, she called her dad on her cell phone, got out of the car, and said: "My father wants to speak to you." 26

The officer, annoyed, refused to take the phone and, as the young woman indignantly put it, "stuck his hand in my face" and ordered her back into the car. She got her ticket. On returning home, she fired off a letter to the cop's department complaining about his ostensibly rude behavior. 27

Throughout their daughter's account, the parents stood proudly at her side, confident of vindication. After all, hadn't the officer been needlessly rude? And why hadn't he done them the courtesy of taking the phone, when, as they put it, the father only wished to discuss the car's paperwork? 28

Talk about foolish! Hadn't they ever seen the show? Did they have no idea who they were dealing with? The storm swiftly broke. Judge Judy, her voice dripping contempt, tore into the three of them. What did they think she was, *stupid*?! The girl was "a spoiled brat," the parents enablers. How dare they try to pretend their intent hadn't been to induce the cop to forgo the ticket! And how utterly loathsome that they'd try to wreck this honest cop's career by placing a nasty letter in his file! And, to the parents: "Don't try to tell me you didn't help write it!" By the time she finished, the three of them fairly slunk out of court. 29

Watching such dazzling performances—and, of course, that is what 30 they are—who can doubt the reason for Judge Judy's immense success? In a world too much at ease with debased standards, her willingness to call rotten behavior precisely what it is, without the slightest patience for the excuses and rationalizations so commonly heard, is intensely bracing.

It's not just Judge Judy; impatience with ethical laxity is common to all 31 the TV judges. Take Judge Marilyn Milian, who in the New York market presides over *The People's Court* on WCBS at the same hour that Judge Judy metes out her tough justice on WNBC.

In presentation, the two judges could hardly be more dissimilar. A feisty, 32 attractive Hispanic redhead, Milian is promoted on the network as "the hottest judge on television," and she flashes much saucy good humor. But the former Jeb Bush appointee to the Miami Circuit Court is as hard-nosed as Judge Judy about adherence to the law—and about civil behavior.

One show I saw involved a woman who'd stiffed an appliance store 33 on a refrigerator and then had the gall to sue it for harassment when it tried to collect. Milian's patience with the woman, already thin, evaporated entirely when the woman refused to stop talking out of turn. "Get her out of here," Milian tersely instructed her bailiff. Moments later, after finding for the store owner, Milian addressed the woman's countersuit: "*and you, madam,*" she shouted, loud enough to be heard in the adjacent room, to which the woman had been banished, "*get a big, fat zero.*" Milian cupped her hands above her head, forming a goose egg, to drive the point home.

Significantly, only one of the seven judges plying the New York airwaves— 34 the affable Houston attorney Larry Joe Doherty, presiding over *Texas Justice*—is a white male; four are African-American. And two of those four are women. While "Judge" Mablean Ephriam, the L.A. attorney who runs *Divorce Court,* is limited to handling squabbles between soon-to-be ex-spouses, Judge Glenda Hatchett, formerly chief presiding judge of the Fulton County, Georgia, juvenile court, roams across the vast landscape of contemporary duplicity and malfeasance. But youthful offenders are her specialty.

Her penchant for dramatic "interventions" with such offenders makes 35 her the closest thing daytime TV has to a wild-eyed judicial activist. One broadcast, for example, featured a teenage girl who had turned against her mother and joined a gang, with whom she committed various crimes. But now, in Hatchett's courtroom—her anguished, devoted mother beside her—the girl was persuasively contrite. So, invoking her best creative powers, the judge ruled that mother and daughter do a stint for Habitat for Humanity, working side by side.

In another case, also featuring a desperate mother and a child who'd gone 36
bad, Judge Hatchett lectured the mother to get some spine. Then, in a surprise
twist, Hatchett concluded by addressing her own mother, sitting in her courtroom. "I want you to spend some time [with the woman] after the show,
Mama, 'cause she needs to understand that mothers don't put up with this kind
of carryin' on. You can tell her about that—'cause I was a living witness!"

The prize for Number One hard-ass TV judge, though, could either go 37
to Judge Joe Brown, formerly of the Shelby County criminal courts in
Memphis, or to Judge Greg Mathis, recruited from Michigan's 36th District Court. Both of these black men grew up in rough urban neighborhoods, and for each, his past is central to his worldview. Both talk a lot
about character, responsibility, and the meaning of real success. Both will,
when appropriate, slide from law-school English to street-speak. Hardly
incidentally, and far more than is the case with the other TV judges, both
deal on their shows with drug cases.

Listening one afternoon to garbled testimony from a witness in a case 38
concerning an unpaid loan allegedly spent on methamphetamine, Mathis
looked out over his courtroom set and pronounced, with no hint of a smile:
"Children, *this* is your brain on drugs." "You're telling me that when your
husband was taking his drug-addicted friend to the projects, he had *no idea*
what was goin' on?" he scornfully asked a woman in a later segment,
whose car had been seized in a drug bust. As a viewer from Chicago en-
thused on the program's website, "Judge Mathis recognizes game when it's
in his courtroom, and doesn't go for it!"

Neither does Judge Brown, who, as *Ebony* magazine put it, "is the 39
voice of the community that demands justice, the voice that demands that
people step up and take responsibility for their actions and do the right
thing." (This is a very different community from the one the Jesse Jacksons
and Al Sharptons of the world talk about, and doubtless *Ebony* is correct
to identify it as speaking with the authentic communal voice.)

Indeed, by far the most severe tongue-lashing that I've heard delivered by 40
any TV judge came courtesy of Judge Joe Brown. Its recipient: a tough-talking
middle-aged woman—a reformed junkie—whose daughter had accused her of
taking out credit cards in the daughter's name and racking up thousands of
dollars of purchases. The mother readily admitted to the daughter's charge,
telling Judge Brown it was her *right* to take the money, since the daughter owed
her. When she was a young woman, the ex-junkie opined, "My mother made
me pay $100 every two weeks. . . . That was teaching me responsibility."

Judge Brown's manner is laconic, and usually he hears a fair bit of evi- 41
dence before passing judgment. But this time he couldn't contain himself.
"She didn't do too well, did she?" he countered. "You turned into a junkie."

"But I got back on track," the women retorted. "I don't think I owe her 42 money. I think she owes *me* money," she continued, returning to the case at hand. "I spent thousands of dollars raisin' her, so I opened up a couple of credit cards in her name to reimburse myself." Anyway, she added in yet further self-exoneration, she and her daughter fought quite a bit, and "I was very angry with her when I did this."

This spiel proved the final straw for the judge, who lashed out at the 43 mother like an avenging angel. "Do you know the worst adversity she's had to face in her life?" he asked rhetorically, nodding toward the daughter in the plaintiff's box. "It's *you*! You are one of the reasons the inner cities have gone straight to hell," he thundered. "It's kinda hard to come up with language, lady, to describe your despicable conduct. You are a disgrace and a bloody shame to the human race. You ought to be in jail. . . . You might run into some of your old junkie friends."

Perhaps the most surprising evidence on daytime TV of the growing 44 thirst for moral direction, however, is the phenomenal success of Dr. Phil McGraw—surprising because, as a TV personality, Dr. Phil was the creation of Oprah Winfrey, the medium's icon of touchy-feely nonjudgmentalism. Whereas the telegenic Winfrey is an reluctant to censure as she is generous with hugs and kisses, Dr. Phil is at once folksy and hard as nails, trading in rigorous standards and never timid in laying out the consequences that follow for those who try to slide by in life without meeting them. "You are conning yourself, you are conning your husband, you are conning your family, but you *ain't* conning me," he sternly told a woman whose repeated infidelities threatened her marriage. "You got an excuse for *everything*."

Though McGraw's show covers human folly in many dimensions (lately, 45 compulsive overeaters), the host is at his most compelling when addressing Americans' chronic unseriousness about the meaning and obligations of marriage, especially where children are concerned—in short, doing exactly what the elite media has attacked George W. Bush for doing. "What is *wrong* with you guys?" he demanded of one couple, who regularly battle viciously in front of their kids. "You have no idea how sick they are of listening to you two go back and forth. How sick to death they are of opening that door every time they come home and wondering, 'What is it today?' "

On the same show, hearing the wife concede that, if given the chance, 46 she wouldn't marry her husband again, Dr. Phil looked at her with genuine pity. He himself had been married for 28 years, he told her, and if at that moment he learned that for some reason the marriage wasn't legal, "I'd get right up and find her and marry her again."

The audience greeted this comment with heavy applause. Moments 47 later, at the show's end, McGraw strode down the aisle to greet his wife,

Robin, who sits in the audience, and, as happens every day, they walked out together, arm in arm.

Many who regard themselves as sophisticated surely find this tableau   48 of togetherness both stagy and corny. But who can doubt that, in a world teeming with narcissism and amorality, in which so many in authority refuse to judge or uphold standards, it serves as a model and an inspiration for millions of Americans?

Thinking Critically

1. Harry Stein describes two different kinds or categories of television programs. How does he connect these two categories and use both to support his thesis?

2. How would you describe the audience for *City Journal*? What level of familiarity might those readers have with the kinds of programming that Stein describes? How likely would they be to agree with Stein's conclusions? (Consider the many other publications, think tanks, and media outlets referred to in *Many Americas*. Which of those other publications would be *least* likely to publish "Daytime TV Gets Judgmental," and why?)

3. What does Stein mean by "judgmental"?

Writing Critically

1. In the preceding selection, Douglas Rushkoff argues that the audience for reality television shows takes pleasure in the humiliation of others. Extend his argument to the kind of programming that Harry Stein describes. Why is there such a large and eager audience for this kind of programming?

2. Spend a week watching some of the programs described by Stein. What kind of "normal" or "law-abiding" behavior do these shows promote and uphold? Stein notes that shows like *Maury* highlight "underclass pathology." What do you notice about the social class of most of the guests on *Maury* and *The Jerry Springer Show* and the litigants in courtroom programs like *Judge Judy*? What is the implied link made by this programming between social status and "decent" behavior? Although Stein does not refer to other sources in his own observational essay, you should consult relevant outside sources (sociologists, media critics, legal scholars) to support your own argument.

3. Why would anyone want to share potentially embarrassing and deeply personal troubles on national television?

Jesus Climbs the Charts: The Business of Contemporary Christian Music

MARK ALLAN POWELL

Theologian Mark Allan Powell is New Testament professor at Trinity Lutheran Seminary, an ordained Lutheran minister, and the author of many books and articles. His *Encyclopedia of Contemporary Christian Music* (2003) was named Book of the Year by the Association of Recorded Sound Collections, a group of professional music critics, professors, collectors, and performers. Long before he became a theologian and minister, Powell was a Texas-based rock journalist and critic. In an interview with *Christianity Today* magazine, he described the mixed reactions his work on contemporary music received from his more traditional colleagues: "When I was pitching the book, an editor of a publishing company told me, 'I can't understand why this stuff is important when I don't know anything about it.' When I hear that attitude, it smacks of elitism. The church's intellectuals want to say this music, that is so meaningful to literally millions of people, cannot be important because it doesn't appeal to us." "Jesus Climbs the Charts: The Business of Contemporary Christian Music" was published in the December 18, 2002 issue of *Christian Century* magazine. Defining itself with the slogan "Faithful living, critical thinking," *Christian Century* has since its founding in 1884 promoted a progressive and socially conscious approach to both faith and public life. In 1963, Martin Luther King Jr. sent his "Letter from Birmingham Jail" to *Christian Century*. To find out more about this magazine, go to <http://www.christiancentury.org/>.

"We weren't really sure what to do," Daniel Davison said, after his entire rap-metal band Luti-Kriss got "saved" at an Assemblies of God revival service. "But we figured we should stop cussing so much in our songs. And . . . maybe we can write songs about God!" Inexplicably, the group changed its name to Norma Jean and by this August they were on the cover of *HM* magazine, the Christian music industry's premiere publication covering hard rock artists.

Such bands are a dime a dozen these days, though they cost a bit more   2
than that to book. At one time, the Christian rock scene was a cultural
ghetto, frequently ridiculed and easily avoided. But now Christian rock is
big and loud; it'll shake your windows and rattle your walls.

It comes in all varieties. John Michael Talbot, a Roman Catholic, and   3
Michael Card, a Baptist, write soft, reflective pieces informed by years of
theological and liturgical study. Kirk Franklin revitalizes black gospel music with choir anthems spiked with rap, hip-hop and R&B.

A genre distinction is usually drawn between "contemporary Christian   4
music" (ccm for short) and "modern worship music." The great majority
of ccm artists do not envision their music being used in church (as is Talbot's, Card's and sometimes Franklin's); they expect it to be played in
homes and automobiles just like regular pop music.

One Christian rock star told me, "I'm not trying to change what goes   5
on in church. I think it would be a bad idea to make worship more entertaining. I just want to make entertainment more worshipful."

Typical of that trajectory is the aptly named Memphis blues band Big   6
Tent Revival, which states in one of its songs: "The Bible talks about a
book of names / Souls rescued from the flames / Tell me, brother, when it's
all through / Will you know Jesus, and will He know you?"

Christian rock traces its roots to the Jesus movement of the early 1970s.   7
Now that it's over 30, some of its aging hippie progenitors are beginning to
wonder if it can still be trusted. The scene was once the haunt of radicals—
anti-establishment Jesus freaks whose passionate piety sometimes covered
a multitude of theological and musical sins. In the 1980s, it became an industry, and in the 1990s, an empire. In 2001, music categorized as ccm accounted for more than $1 billion in sales—up 12 percent in a year when
the recording industry as a whole took a downturn. *Newsweek* ran a cover
story on "Jesus Rock" and HBO's *The Sopranos* featured a humorous sub-
plot about the mob family trying to get in on the action.

But is the music any good? More specifically, how does ccm hold up ar-   8
tistically (as music) and theologically (as a reflection of the Christian faith)?

Artists in the Christian rock scene have a tendency to copy the styles of   9
successful mainstream performers in order to provide godly alternatives to
whatever is popular at the time. Artists like Third Day ("the Christian Hootie
and the Blowfish") and Rebecca St. James ("the Christian Alanis Morissette")
have been marketed as though they were low-fat cheese: "almost as tasty as
the real thing—and better for you!" Still, there are numerous artists who don't
fit this stereotype, and even those who do often transcend it. Most of the major players in ccm perform at an artistic level consistent with that of the general market, with enough creativity to avoid being imitative.

It is hard to imagine anyone who likes Billy Joel or Paul Simon not en- 10
joying Steven Curtis Chapman's musical style. Chapman is to pop music
what *The Waltons* was to television: he has a sweet, homey and nostalgic
sound. His songs have strong melodies and catchy hooks, like songs from
the 1960s, and they are sung with warmth and tenderness.

BeBe and CeCe Winans are an African-American duo (brother and sis- 11
ter) who draw on both gospel and R&B roots to craft polished recordings
that showcase their impressive vocal abilities. CeCe is Christian music's
Whitney Houston, and Houston has cited CeCe as "my personal favorite
singer." BeBe recently shook up the Christian music world with allegations
of racism in the industry, accompanied by hints that he might abandon ship
for a career in the general market. He told *CCM* magazine, "It's more difficult to be raped by people who are supposed to be kindred spirits than by
people who don't know who Jesus is."

Jars of Clay has a less commercial sound that appeals to "alternative 12
rock" fans drawn to groups like R.E.M. or Matchbox Twenty. The band
has enjoyed some crossover success in the secular market. Its first album
went double platinum with astonishing sales of over 2 million copies (making it one of the best-selling albums of 1996). The band's third disc was
chosen by *Playboy* as Album of the Month. (Its fourth album, *Eleventh
Hour,* was reviewed in the April 24–May 1 *Century.*)

D.C. Talk is a vibrant, racially integrated group that has been on the 13
cutting edge of the rock industry. Its best song, "Jesus Freak," is now a
standard of modern rock. The first-ever wedding of rap and grunge, it succeeded in winning over many general market broadcasters—even *Rolling
Stone* magazine loved it, though it ridiculed the lyrics. Often loud and
brash, D.C. Talk can also be soulful and sensitive. In "What If I Stumble?"
singer Toby McKeehan reflects upon his celebrity status: "What if I stumble? What if I fall? What if I go and make fools of us all?"

One of the biggest success stories in recent Christian music is the rap- 14
core trio P.O.D. (short for Payable On Death). "Rapcore" is a relatively
new style of music that sets rapped lyrics (usually screamed) to the
sounds of heavy metal; it is not for the faint of heart. P.O.D. is good at
it, though the group has received little support from the Christian music
industry and quite a bit of criticism when it toured each year as part of
the "Ozzfest," a raucous rock festival headlined by one of conservative
Christianity's worst nightmares, Ozzy Osbourne. Over the years, the
blatantly Christian band screamed its way into the hearts of rowdy
crowds, and by 2002 it had sold millions of albums and become one of
the hottest acts in the land. Suddenly P.O.D. was on the cover of *HM*
magazine and was featured in the more cautious *CCM,* where the trio

copped a bit of an attitude: "Oh yeah! Now you down with P.O.D.! Where was you before?"

In 1997, *Rolling Stone* reviewed a sampling of 30 Christian rock songs   15
and rendered this verdict: the Christian songs were no more insipid or derivative than 30 songs "randomly selected from the Billboard Hot 100 in a given week." Such a backhanded compliment pays homage to the newfound professionalism of ccm, as compared to the atrocious production standards that marked the music for its first two decades. Today, the artists have talent, the producers have money and the companies have experience.

Still, talent, money and experience do not necessarily yield good art.   16
The songs may be catchy and they may be performed well, and the music can still have the artistic appeal of advertising jingles. Frank Hart of Houston's hard-rock band Atomic Opera says that he hates most Christian music because it is "not art but propaganda."

Christian music fans often complain that bands like Sixpence None the   17
Richer (named for a C. S. Lewis quote) or The Choir (an especially artistic combo of Episcopalians) don't mention Jesus enough in their songs. A band named All Star United recorded a song called "Smash Hit" in 1997 mocking this Christian music industry obsession ("Join his name to any cause, say his name to get applause"). Ironically, the song became a smash hit on Christian radio on the strength of its chorus ("This Jesus thing—it's a smash hit!").

The good news (artistically) for the Christian music scene is that these   18
sorts of rebels continue to appear. Rock stars are hard to tame, and the ccm industry has seen a steady stream of artists like Larry Norman, The Seventy Sevens and Michael Knott who refuse to toe the line and do what is expected of them. They also tend to bite the hands that feed them, taking on the culture, the church and even the music business itself. I enjoy the irreverent humor (though not the music) of Christian goth band Dead Artist Syndrome: "Jesus I love you, but I don't understand your wife / She wears too much make-up and she always wants to fight / In my world of black and gray, she argues shades of white."

The two biggest rock bands in America right now are groups fronted   19
by Christians who have nothing to do with the Christian music industry. Creed and U2 regularly pack stadiums, win Grammy Awards and fill the airwaves with spiritual songs. Scott Stapp of Creed and Bono of U2 view themselves simply as artists and entertainers. When their art reflects their faith, it does so naturally, in an honest, uncontrived and vulnerable way. Their songs sometimes also express their doubts, their lusts and even their blasphemies. In 2001, U2 had one of the top albums of the year (*All That You Can't Leave Behind*) with an allegorical, 11-song tribute to a lover (or,

more likely, mother figure) identified as "Grace": "She takes the blame, she covers the shame, she travels outside of karma."

What about the theology? Naturally, there are degrees of theological so- 20 phistication in this music, which reflects a wide swath of American religious traditions. Jars of Clay is often cited as an example of a group that manages to be both subtle and profound. *Christianity Today* once dubbed it "the band that Luther and Calvin would have liked," perhaps because of its U2-like obsession with grace. A primary focus of its songs is the fragility of the human condition, rendered only more ambiguous when viewed from a perspective of faith. The group's very name is taken from 2 Corinthians 4:7 ("We have this treasure in clay jars"), and one of its best songs is "Frail."

Still, many ccm artists perform songs that are neither profound nor sub- 21 tle, some of which are dismissed by critics as "happy-in-Jesus songs." Defenders say such music stands in the grand tradition of summer camp songs like "Do Lord" and "Give Me Oil in My Lamp"—pleasurable ditties that are simply expressive of Christian joy without any pretense of addressing life's complexities.

The problem with that argument is that Christian music often occupies 22 a major, even defining role in the lives of its more ardent listeners. The music is not just material for a campfire sing-along; it becomes a soundtrack for people's lives. Individualistic piety and crass sentimentalism can be innocent enough in small doses, but some fans and performers seem to think that faith consists of little else.

In the 1980s, militant triumphalism reigned in the lyrics. Three of 23 Christian music's biggest stars (Petra, DeGarmo & Key and Matthew Ward) recorded three different songs titled "Armed and Dangerous" (based on Ephesians 6). These songs, and many like them, presented Christians as a force that (in the words of Ward's song) "will not stop until all Christ's enemies lay dead at our feet"; one hopes they meant only to slay spiritual enemies, not bodily ones.

The 1990s showed little improvement in the area of social commentary. 24 The topics of choice were harlots in the White House, baby-killers and anyone opposed to prayer in public schools. At least five songs were sung from the perspective of a fetus who, endowed with adult intelligence, knows that he or she is about to be aborted; in one case, the fetus asks Jesus to come into his (already beating) heart so he or she becomes a Christian before being killed.

I'd put about 10 percent of current ccm into the "theologically mature" 25 category exemplified by Jars of Clay, Sixpence None the Richer, The Choir and some lesser-known artists. Another 10 percent can be written off as sensationalist trash marred by the kind of ignorant extremism noted above.

As for the rest, it's not too profound or thought-provoking, but it can generally pass as harmless, sometimes even inspiring entertainment.

A positive assessment of this music's theology depends on recognizing   26
a legitimate role for emotion in faith. Many composers of rock music maintain that the primary intent of their songs is not to convey a message but to engage emotions.

Likewise, Christian music usually succeeds (if at all) by being empa-   27
thetic. D.C. Talk's "Jesus Freak" seeks to express the fear that an adolescent believer harbors about being labeled or ostracized on account of his or her faith: "What will people do if they hear that I'm a 'Jesus freak'?" Apparently a lot of adolescents identified with that song, though the lyrics would win no prizes for poetic art.

With rapcore, subtlety is pretty much ruled out from the start. P.O.D.   28
screams anguished laments about urban blight and broken homes with enough streetwise agitation to appall many listeners. Band members also relate sordid testimonies of growing up in a drug-ridden ghetto in southern California. Printed on a page, their lyrics might seem a tad predictable or simplistic. It is the band's defiant delivery of those lyrics that renders them prophetic, transforming them into postmodern, melodramatic oracles of doom.

On a different note, Christian folksinger Bob Bennett scored a hit with   29
a song he wrote for his children while going through a divorce: "There is no such thing as divorce between a father and his son / No matter what has happened, no matter what will be / There's no such thing as divorce between you and me . . . Sometimes I cry over the things I can't undo / And the words I never should have said in front of you / But I pray the good will somehow overcome the bad / And where I failed as a husband, I'll succeed as your dad." That's about as sentimental as a song can get, but there is emotional power in such heartfelt words.

A critique of ccm must examine not merely the songs but the industry   30
itself. Christian music is now big business, and few critics think its success is entirely a good thing. Even Start Moser, an industry insider who was once the head of Word Records, has said that the acronym ccm might better stand for "commercial Christian music." The problem, Moser continues, is that the Christian music business arose to serve the needs of a revival, but once the revival was over and "the wave of the Spirit went flat," the business was in place and had to keep churning out products. "In many ways," says Moser, "I think we created a monster."

The business interests of the ccm industry are often sustained through ap-   31
peals to a "Christ against culture" paradigm. The industry encourages reports about how Christian artists are persecuted in the general market, and fans are sometimes exhorted to listen exclusively to Christian music. *Campus Life*

magazine features a regular column that suggests Christian music alternatives to fairly innocent secular artists (Christians should listen to Third Day instead of Hootie and the Blowfish). On Reformation Day 1998 Steve Camp (musician-turned-senior-statesman) published "107 Theses," including the claim that believers who sign contracts with secular record companies are "unequally yoked" and guilty of "spiritual adultery," and the contention that "a song written by an unsaved person cannot embody sanctified truth."

It is ironic (but surely no coincidence) that the ccm industry's insistence 32 on segregation from "the world" comes at the very time that Christian artists like D.C. Talk, Jars of Clay and P.O.D. are enjoying unprecedented success in the general market. Not surprisingly, a number of Christian artists are now bothered by what they regard as the "mammon-inspired isolationism" of the Christian music scene, which *Rolling Stone* recently described as "a parallel universe—a world unto itself." A major act named Caedmon's Call (named after the seventh-century monk) scored a 1998 hit with a song that proclaimed, "This world has nothing for me"; later the composer confessed a secret irony: by "this world" he meant "the world of ccm."

As that double entendre suggests, many Christian artists (not to mention 33 fans and critics) have noticed that the more separate from the world the ccm industry seeks to be, the more worldly it seems to become. Several young Christian stars have struggled to reconcile Christ's call to self-denial with their record company's desire to put their names and faces on T-shirts and magazine covers. Strangely, Reunion Records promoted Joy Williams by distributing 2002 calendars that display the 17-year-old singer in a variety of attractive poses. Daniel Smith of the eclectic pop band Danielson dismisses the whole notion of a Christian music market by saying, "I just find it hard to believe that Christ wants to be in a market. Didn't he turn over those tables?"

The Christian music subculture is a microcosm of popular religion in 34 America. It's also a laboratory within which various theological questions are engaged. A couple of decades ago—in the wake of the first scandals in the ccm field—the industry revisited the Donatist controversy: Can the Holy Spirit minister through songs performed by unholy vessels?

Recently, the favorite topic has been vocation: Is there a distinction be- 35 tween the "call to ministry" incumbent on all Christians and the call to professional ministry as a vocation? Might some Christian musicians (like Stapp and Bono) receive only the first but not the latter? And what exactly does ministry mean? Can entertainment count as ministry, or does ministry mean (as one voice in the discussion claims) "winning people to Jesus and discipling them in their walk"? As near as I can tell, no one involved in this argument has read Luther on the subject but quite a few have arrived independently at positions similar to his.

The industry's grappling with theology is fascinating to observe, quite 36 apart from the question of whether the music is any good or not. In 1999, Sixpence None the Richer scored a crossover number-one hit on general market radio with their romantic ballad "Kiss Me." The Gospel Music Association immediately ruled the song ineligible to receive any of its Dove Awards because, though it's a nice song, there is nothing especially Christian about a woman wanting her husband to kiss her. Singer Leigh Nash and her newlywed husband (the composer) attempted to explain that they don't experience faith as some compartmentalized religious aspect of life, but to no avail.

Two years earlier, an album by a Christian country-rock band called 37 Vigilantes of Love included a song that rivaled the Song of Solomon in its celebration of marital sex. Aghast, Family Christian Bookstores (the single largest distributor of Christian music) pulled the product from its shelves, leaving more than one pundit to wonder whether the chain fully appreciates just where children come from.

Joe Bob Briggs once defined contemporary Christian music as "bad songs 38 written about God by white people." There was enough truth in that description to get laughs, but it's not really accurate. The field is diverse—ethnically, stylistically and theologically. One can list problems—triumphalism, commercialism, individualism, and a few we have not touched on here (a virtual dearth of inclusive language and an uncritical approach to scripture)—but such dysfunctions are also endemic to American popular religion.

And there remain the Christian music rebels who acknowledge no 39 parentage in this world save an adoption by grace, who give voice to those who feel estranged from church and society alike. The late Mark Heard wrote their anthem: "We are soot-covered urchins running wild and unshod / We will always be remembered as the orphans of God."

Thinking Critically

1. How does Mark Allan Powell use classification as a strategy for organizing his argument? Why is that strategy a good choice for this kind of subject matter?

2. At what places in this essay is Powell writing as a theologian, and at what points does he rely on his experience as a rock critic? How do these two areas of expertise complement each other? How does Powell make these two seemingly irreconcilable perspectives work together?

3. In your own words, describe each inconsistency and paradox that Powell finds in the "ccm" industry. Does he propose a solution for any or all of these issues?

Writing Critically

1. Explore a contemporary social issue or cultural phenomenon through the lens of faith-based reporting and criticism. (See the website for *Many Americas* for links to publications sponsored by a wide range of faiths, denominations, and belief systems.) What differences are there between the way in which these publications discuss a cultural or social issue and the approaches of more mainstream, general-interest publications? (Have you ever been dissuaded from citing such a publication as a reference in an academic paper? What would you do if you were?)

2. In "Alt.Everything: The Youth Market and the Marketing of Cool" (see pp. 246–57), Naomi Klein describes how subcultures and youth movements become defined and commodified by marketing professionals. How do Klein's observations apply to the groups and audiences that Powell describes? What kinds of moral judgments are made about artists, rebels, and rockers who "sell out," and who makes those judgments?

3. The boundary between church and state is continually argued and tested in American politics. Is there a similar "no man's land" between religion and popular culture? How are faith, religion, or religious practices depicted on prime-time television? Do characters in mainstream movies go to church or take action based on religious principles?

NASCAR Racing Fans: Cranking Up an Empirical Approach

M. Graham Spann

Sociologist M. Graham Spann teaches at Lees-McRae College in North Carolina. This article was published in the *Journal of Popular Culture* in 2002. A publication of the Popular Culture Association, the *Journal* describes its aims on its website: "The popular culture movement was founded on the principle that the perspectives and experiences of common folk offer compelling insights into the social world. The fabric of human social life is not merely the art deemed worthy to hang in museums, the books that have won literary prizes or been named 'classics,' or the religious and social ceremonies carried out by societies' elite. *The Journal of Popular Culture* continues to break down the barriers between so-called 'low' and 'high' culture and focuses on filling in the gaps a neglect of popular culture has left in our understanding of the workings of society."

The death of Dale Earnhardt on the last lap of the 2001 Daytona 500   1
brought unprecedented media attention to NASCAR fans. Media
sources showed fans gathered at racetracks, churches, and other memorial
services where they prayed, cried, and talked to each other about what
Earnhardt meant to them personally, and to the quality of their lives.
Nearly 4,000 people attended a service at the Bristol Motor Speedway in
Tennessee, and the Governor of South Carolina declared the week of
March 13th, 2001, "Dale Earnhardt Memorial Week." These examples illustrate the connection between NASCAR fans and American popular culture. NASCAR racing fans are some of the most loyal sports enthusiasts
and represent a population ready for increased analytical consideration.

Social scientists have paid little attention to fans of automobile racing in   2
the United States. Of particular note is the lack of empirical research on
NASCAR fans. On any given weekend from the middle of February to the beginning of November social scientists can find hundreds of thousands of people gathered at automobile race venues across America. The Memorial Day
Winston Cup race in Charlotte, North Carolina, for example, typically draws
in excess of 180,000 people. NASCAR (National Association of Stock Car
Auto Racing) is an organization that governs a set of rules regarding the technical and engineering components of racing cars; as well as race rules, regulations, logistics, marketing, and general business practices of the sport.
NASCAR, founded in 1947, held many of its races in the southern part of the
United States, but it is no longer constrained by southern consumers or venues (Fielden). In the past five years, construction of racetracks has taken place
in decidedly non-southern places like Chicago, Illinois; Las Vegas, Nevada;
Loudon, New Hampshire; and Fontana, California. Clearly, people from
many different geographic regions now go to the races, making racing one of
the most attended cultural and sporting events in America (Howell; Lord).

The search for patterns among groups of people is a basic task of social   3
scientists and this paper suggests a five-fold approach for discovering patterns among NASCAR fans. All sports are embedded in the general patterns
of social interaction and organization in society, so the premise here is that
NASCAR fans are people participating in collective behaviors that have consequences for individuals (Mills; Nixon & Frey). These consequences may
range from unwittingly perpetuating inequality to the development of identity in a (racing) social context. As such, this paper suggests gathering data
on (1) the demographic composition of NASCAR fans, especially class, race,
and gender; (2) the cultural and sub-cultural phenomena of fans including
the role of heroes in fans' lives; (3) fans' sense of community; (4) how fans
create their identities around racing norms and values; and finally, (5) the organizational structure of fans. The hope is that scholars of popular culture,

sports sociology, and the like will gain some insight into fans of NASCAR racing that will help them set forth a productive research agenda.

Demographic Composition

Fans are enthusiastic admirers of a person, organization, or movement 4 (Volger & Schwartz). One popular myth about NASCAR fans is that they are all white, working-class males. Concomitantly, some assume that racism and sexism also flourish among these males given that the Confederate flag is a widely displayed symbol at race venues. Social scientists need good information about socially sanctioned exclusivity, intentional or otherwise, among NASCAR fans. We need to critically examine the demographic composition of fans. It is not the case that NASCAR fans are only from one social class position. An increasingly large number of dominant group members from higher classes enjoy the sport. Business executives are now using skyboxes at racetracks to entertain clients, just as they do in professional basketball or football. Furthermore, though income is only one proxy measure of class position, it is worth noting that nearly 13% of NASCAR fans have a household income above $75,000 a year (Simmons Market Research Bureau, Inc.; Performance Research).

Most social scientists agree that it is difficult to separate social class descriptions of Americans from their racial composition. That is to say, racial and ethnic minorities disproportionately occupy status positions near the bottom of the class structure. Clearly, an athlete's race is an organizing feature of most professional sports. Some suggest that overt racism exists when whites occupy more leadership positions and blacks occupy more subordinate positions (Myers). The notion of "stacking" comes to mind here. Loy and McElvoge show how racial segregation in professional sports is positively correlated with the centrality of position. Black athletes are often forced to compete among themselves, rather than with members of other racial groups, for team membership and playing time because they do not typically occupy the most powerful positions (Nixon & Frey).

Wendell Scott is one of the few black drivers in NASCAR's history 6 (Howell), but NASCAR teams currently have limited minority representation. This might partially explain the mostly white fan base. Fans of professional sports typically identify with members of their same racial and ethnic background, but NASCAR, as represented by its top series "The Winston Cup," currently has no drivers from underrepresented groups. Crews who work on the racecars are more racially diverse, but crews typically receive less media and promotional attention than drivers do. Ask any NASCAR fan that you know who their favorite "right tire changer" is and you will likely get a blank look of confusion. If, however, we compare racing drivers to football quarterbacks and racing crews to football linemen, then the stacking hypothesis is useful.

Nixon points out that when elite sports organizations use exclusive social and economic membership criteria, they reinforce historical segregation patterns. The appeal, then, of certain sports to dominant group members may be a basis for boundary maintenance (Schwalbe, Godwin, Holden, Schrock, Thompson, Wolkomir). The social class of sports fans may vary over time within a nation or community, as well as across nations and communities (McPherson, Curtis & Voy). Collecting data on the demographic composition of NASCAR fans should provide some interesting cross-cultural data because other race organizations in other countries (i.e., Formula 1) may have a more diverse fan base in terms of class, race, and gender. 7

The gender composition of NASCAR fans could also be included in any demographic investigation. Women drivers have historically been a part of NASCAR racing, but currently only Shawna Robinson is a competitive driver. Messner argues that the propensity for men to be more involved in sports than women is part of our socially constructed cognitive images of what men and women are supposed to be and do. Dominant ideologies of what it means to be a woman or a man typically reflect deeper-seated structural arrangements of society, especially patterns of power, status, and social class. Interestingly, nearly 39% of NASCAR fans over 18 are women (Simmons Market Research Bureau, Inc.; Performance Research). Given generally acknowledged differences in socialization practices between females and males, we might partially explain the rather large proportion of female sports fans to changing gender expectations in society (Risman). 8

About 40% of NASCAR fans have attended college (Simmons Market Research Bureau, Inc.; Performance Research), but investigating how level of education affects NASCAR fan participation, their attitudes and beliefs, or other areas of sociological interest has yet to be empirically tested. The same is true for political affiliation. There are, of course, many other demographic variables available for our theoretical propositions, but discovering basic demographics like class, race, gender, education, and political affiliation is a start to an empirical approach of NASCAR racing fans. 9

Cultural and Subcultural Phenomena

The second empirical approach suggested by this paper is examining NASCAR racing fans from a cultural standpoint. Culture is all human-made products, either material or nonmaterial, associated with a society. Culture is the framework where society's members construct their way of life (Nixon & Frey). Howell chronicles the cultural history of the NASCAR Winston Cup Series and posits that the "regional strength projected by NASCAR rac- 10 ing history—its ties to southern culture and folklore—creates a stereotypical depiction of drivers" (117). These stereotypes are reinforced in movies like *Thunder Road* (1958), *The Last American Hero* (1973), and more recently *Days of Thunder* (1990) starring Tom Cruise. But whether these images help constitute a real world subculture remains to be discovered.

Is it the case that NASCAR fans constitute a subculture? Doob defines 11 subculture as the "culture of a specific segment of people within a society, differing from the dominant culture in some significant respects, such as in certain norms and values" (66). Two major subcultural patterns may be present among race fans. The first pattern is usually mutually exclusive: fans of General Motors racing cars, fans of Ford racing cars, and fans of Dodge racing cars. Currently, NASCAR teams field Chevrolet, Ford, Pontiac,[1] and Dodge[2] racing cars. This phenomena is of particular cultural and symbolic interest because all of the cars, regardless of make or model, are hand-built, track-specific race cars. Major automobile producers manufacture few of the mechanical parts; rather, fabricators create cars that look like the major automotive brands. Some teams switch brands by simply putting a different body and name on the same chassis. As Berger once said, things "aren't what they seem." Fan loyalty to a particular brand of car may be relevant to the study of NASCAR fans, but we also need to discover if different norms and values exist for fans of the different makes. More importantly, we could discover the boundaries that people maintain which perpetuate the division between fans of the various makes.

Beyond automobile make, the second subcultural pattern among fans is 12 loyalty to, and identification with, a particular driver. This loyalty also takes on symbolic meaning. Readers may have noticed small round window stickers with numbers on people's cars. These numbers correspond to NASCAR drivers' car numbers and are symbolic representations of driver support. For example, the number twenty-eight matches up with the Texaco sponsored Ford of Ricky Rudd and the number twenty-four represents the DuPont sponsored Chevrolet of Jeff Gordon. Most of us have seen sports news reports of Jeff Gordon winning a race, but many drivers have active fan clubs and loyal, lifelong fan followings. Fans of Dale Earnhardt, for example, have already catapulted him to a hero to be worshipped in the folk religion of NASCAR (Lord; Mathisen). As a hero, Earnhardt becomes a symbolic representation of the dominant social myths and values of society (Nixon).

Clearly, sport and culture are interdependent (Lüschen). Sport is bound 13 to society and structured by culture. Connecting symbolic patterns is an important part of an empirical approach to NASCAR fans. Social scientists could discover if patterns exist between types of fans and the driver(s) they follow. Are fans willing to support their favorite driver if he/she switches

to a different make of car? By looking at fan automotive brand and driver
loyalty, we can better identify cultural and subcultural patterns and discover if NASCAR fans really are a subculture.

Sense of Community

The third empirical approach includes studying fans as members of friend-   14
ship networks who share a common "sense of community" with other fans
(Adams; McMillan and Chavis). Both Tonnies' work on community ty-
pologies and Durkheim's insight into social integration (conscience collective) stress the importance of community in human life. Similarly, sense of
community ought to be important for NASCAR fans. Sense of community
is where people believe their needs can be and are being met by the collective capabilities of the group; feel that they belong; believe that they can exert some control over the group; and have an emotional bond to the group
(Sarason; McMillan). Sport spectating is a social activity (Danielson) and
if NASCAR fans are a subculture then we should find a higher sense of
community among them. Melnick sees sport spectatorship as enhancing
people's lives by "helping them experience the pure sociability, quasi-
intimate relationships, and sense of belonging that are so indigenous to the
stands" (46). Spreitzer and Snyder found that 75% of women and 84% of
men viewed sport as a good way of socializing with others. We might then
inquire whether sense of community among NASCAR fans exists only at
the track or is it pervasive throughout the fan base.

Identity

Studying identity formation among NASCAR racing fans centers on sub-   15
cultural norms and values. Identity "refers to who or what one is, to the various meanings attached to oneself by self and others" (Cook, Fine, House,
42). Do NASCAR fans build their sense of self around being a "Chevy," or
a "Ford" fan? Fans might reinforce such an identity by cheering for a particular brand, rooting for and belonging to fan clubs associated with a particular driver, and finding themselves in social settings where other people
have similar identity characteristics. We could look at how racing fans construct a sense of self and how that sense of self affects behavior.

Organizational Structures

Finally, social scientists could examine NASCAR auto racing fans from an   16
organizational perspective. We can look at the degree of commitment to
racing as a determinant of placement within a hierarchy (Yinger; Fox). Examining the cultural and subcultural beliefs of fans, their commitment to
particular automotive brands and drivers, their sense of community, and

their identity may give us the social organizational "picture" we need to determine a series of outwardly expanding concentric circles; with the most committed fans occupying the core, inner roles (these will probably be family members and friends who make up the actual teams), and the least involved fans composing the periphery.

Conclusion

As Guttmann notes, sport as a social institution includes a number of qual- 17 ities such as secularism, the ideal of equality of opportunity, specialization of statuses and roles, bureaucracy, quantification of achievement and the keeping of records. By critically examining differences in social class, race, and gender, and by determining cultural and subcultural patterns, we garner insight into the structural foundations of fans' identity, their sense of self, and their sense of community. All of these areas point to the interplay of structural conditions and human action. Why do this? As social science moves into the 21st century, we must study topics people not trained in science can understand. We must continually emphasize the importance of social science and show that the theory and methods of our disciplines can make seemingly ordinary events, like automobile racing, understandable as part of the larger structural and institutional fabric.

Notes

[1]Both Chevrolet and Pontiac are GM brand names.

[2]Dodge recently re-entered NASCAR racing after a 15-year hiatus.

Works Cited

Adams, Rebecca G. "Inciting Sociological Thought by Studying the Dead-head Community: Engaging Publics in Dialogue." *Social Forces* 77(1) (1998): 1–25.

Berger, Peter. *Invitation to Sociology: A Humanistic Perspective.* Garden City, NY: Doubleday, 1963.

Cook, Karen S., Gary Alan Fine and S. House James, eds. *Sociological Perspectives on Social Psychology.* Boston: Allyn and Bacon, 1995.

Danielson, M. N. *Home Team: Professional Sports and the American Metropolis.* Princeton, NJ: Princeton UP, 1997.

Doob, Christopher Bates. *Sociology: An Introduction.* Fifth Edition. New York: The Harcourt Press, 1997.

Durkheim, E. *The Division of Labor in Society.* New York: Free Press of Glencoe, 1893/1964.

Fielden, Greg. *Forty Years of Stock Car Racing.* Revised Edition. Surfside Beach, SC: Galfield Press, 1992.

Fox, Kathryn Joan. "Real Punks and Pretenders: The Social Organization of a Counterculture." *Journal of Contemporary Ethnography* 16(3) (1987): 373–388.

Guttmann, Allen. *From Ritual to Record: The Nature of Modern Sports.* New York: Columbia University Press, 1978.

Howell, Mark D. *From Moonshine to Madison Avenue: A Cultural History of the NASCAR Winston Cup Series.* Bowling Green, OH: Bowling Green State University Popular Press, 1997.

Lord, Lewis. "The Fastest-Growing Sport Loses Its Hero." *U.S. News & World Report* 130(9) (2001): 52.

Loy, John W. and Joseph F. McElvoge. "Racial Segregation in American Sport." *International Review of Sport Sociology* 5 (1970): 5–24.

Lüschen, Gunther. "The Interdependence of Sport and Culture." *International Review of Sport Sociology* 2 (1967): 27–41.

Mathisen, James A. "From Civil Religion to Folk Region: The Case of American Sport." In Shirl J. Hoffman, ed., *Sport and Religion.* Champaign, IL: Human Kinetics, 1992. 17–34.

McMillan, David W. "Sense of Community." *Journal of Community Psychology* 24(4) (1996): 315–325.

McMillan, David W. and David M. Chavis. "Sense of Community: A Definition and Theory." *Journal of Community Psychology* 14 (1986): 6–23.

McPherson, Barry D., James E. Curtis and John W. Voy. *The Social Significance of Sport.* Champaign, IL: Human Kinetics Publishers, 1989.

Melnick, Merrill J. "Searching for Sociability in the Stands: A Theory of Sports Spectating." *Journal of Sport Management* 7 (1993): 44–60.

Messner, Michael A. *Power at Play: Sports and the Problem of Masculinity.* Boston: Beacon Press, 1992.

Mills, Wright C. *The Sociological Imagination.* New York: Oxford UP, 1959.

Myers, Jim. "Racism Is a Serious Problem in Sports." In *Sports in America: Opposing Viewpoints.* San Diego, CA: Greenhaven Press, 1994.

Nixon, Howard L. and James H. Frey. *A Sociology of Sport.* Belmont, CA: Wadsworth, 1996.

Nixon, Howard L. II. *Sport and the American Dream.* Champaign, IL: Human Kinetics/Leisure Press Imprint, 1984.

Performance Research (www.performanceresearch.com).

Risman, Barbara. *Gender Vertigo: American Families in Transition.* New Haven, CT: Yale UP, 1998.

Sarason, Seymour. *The Psychological Sense of Community: Prospects for a Community Psychology.* San Francisco: Jossey-Bass, 1974.

Schwalbe, Michael, Sandra Godwin, Daphne Holden, Douglas Schrock, Shealy Thompson and Michele Wolkomir. "Generic Processes in the Reproduction of Inequality." *Social Forces* 79(2) (2000): 419–452.

Simmons Market Research Bureau, Inc. (www.smrb.com).

Spreitzer, Elmer and Eldon E. Snyder. "The Psychosocial Functions of Sport as Perceived by the General Population." *International Journal of Physical Education* 11(1975): 8–13.

Tonnies, F. *Community and Society.* New York: Harper & Row, 1957.

Volger, Conrad C. and Stephen E. Schwartz. *The Sociology of Sport: An Introduction.* Englewood Cliffs, NJ: Prentice-Hall, 1993.

Yinger, J. Milton. *Countercultures.* New York: Free Press, 1982.

Thinking Critically

1. Who is the audience for this article? What does this audience know, or need to know, about NASCAR racing? How might a NASCAR fan respond to this article?

2. What authorities does M. Graham Spann cite, and how does he cite them? For his audience and purpose, what or who constitutes an "authority" on NASCAR? (For example, in paragraph 6, Spann makes a rather surprising assumption about "any NASCAR fan." On what basis does he make this assumption?)

3. What are the five approaches that Spann suggests for social scientists studying NASCAR fans? How could you use any or all of those approaches to enhance your own academic research?

Writing Critically

1. Both Spann and Selena Roberts (in the next selection), examine the relationship between race and NASCAR. In what ways do their arguments support and refute each other? Why do Spann and Roberts consider the question of race and NASCAR an interesting topic for academic study and editorial commentary?

2. How does Spann describe "subculture," and within what context? Compare his definition of *subculture* with Leslie Savan's discussion of "community" in "Did Somebody Say 'Community'?" (see pp. 77–81), Naomi Klein's examination of the marketing of subcultures in "Alt. Everything: The Youth Market and the Marketing of Cool" (see pp. 246–57), or any other readings in *Many Americas* that define and discuss the nature of community in contemporary American culture.

3. In his conclusion, Spann argues that "As social science moves into the 21st century, we must study topics people not trained in science can understand." Compare this observation to Jeffrey Passe's argument in "Like It or Not: Social Educators Must Keep Up with Popular Culture" (see pp. 553–55). How would you describe the attitude of "the academy" toward nonacademic or popular culture, based on these two articles? You might also consider Mark Bauerlein's argument in "Liberal Groupthink Is Anti-Intellectual" (see pp. 518–25).

Sports Rage Has Yet to Reach the Ovals

SELENA ROBERTS | Sportswriter Selena Roberts is the Knicks beat reporter for the *New York Times* and frequently contributes to the paper's "Sports of The Times" opinion column. An article in *New York* magazine about reporters covering the Knicks referred to Roberts as "the one the players respect," noting the depth of her reporting as well as her style, which an editor at the *Times* called "heart-stopping, incandescent, all-star writing." Roberts covers a range of sports for the *Times,* frequently writing about the ethical scandals that taint pure enjoyment of a game. Her book *A Necessary Spectacle: Billie Jean King, Bobby Riggs, and the Tennis Match That Leveled the Game* was published in 2005. "Sports Rage Has Yet to Reach the Ovals" appeared in the *Times* on November 22, 2004.

HOMESTEAD, Fla.

1   The economics of fan hostility has yet to catch Nascar drivers, who still talk in Tobacco Road speak with their red-state base as a nifty camouflage for their Wall Street wealth as living, breathing commodities.

2   A racial undertone has yet to develop into an unspoken tension between the stars of Nascar and their racing audience because many of the drivers and their fans share a conservative ideology, evangelical roots and white privilege.

3   Nascar does not suffer from the kind of fan derision that is tainting the N.B.A., college sports, pro football or Major League Baseball—not yet, anyhow.

4   For now, the bond between driver and fan still manifests the kind of devotion that leaves Nascar followers in public mourning when tragedy hits a team, as it did when the Hendrick family was devastated by a plane crash last month. Loyalty also prompts members of Lug Nut Nation to change Internet carriers, ink pens and erectile remedies depending on the paint job of their favorite driver's racecar.

5   Imagine how euphoric these devotees were yesterday. In a cleverly conceived, first-ever race to the Nascar championship—giving at least five drivers a shot at the Nextel Cup—Kurt Busch managed to hold off Jimmie Johnson, Mark Martin, Jeff Gordon and Dale Earnhardt Jr. for the title as the final race of the season unfolded inside the Art Deco motif of Homestead-Miami Speedway.

600

Miami, as in the diverse un-South. Art Deco, as in pastel colors of teal 6 and sand.

Apparently, twang is where you make it. At least this is what Nascar is 7 betting on as it has begun dipping into urban markets, from places like Las Vegas to Phoenix, with Staten Island all but lined up with bagels and lox as a potential stop along the lucrative circuit operated by the legendary France family.

The France dynasty has always been innovative, driven to broaden 8 the appeal of a sport that has defied a stagnant landscape. But now they're risking their Carolina roots by exiting charming outposts like Rockingham, N.C. In expanding north and west, capitalizing on big-dollar sites, Nascar has left some of its core crowd dealing with abandonment issues.

"I still love the racing, but we have celebrities in the cars now, for sure," 9 said Scotty Patterson, a fan from Macon, Ga. "It's all big, big, big."

What happens when a sport's identity becomes lost in its excess? What 10 happens when burdened fans feel entitled to mock and taunt players after paying higher ticket prices to witness millionaire moneyball? Or when access to their faves is just a sepia-toned memory? Or when they can no longer relate to the athletes in front of them?

Anger issues happen. It raged to the surface during the disturbing 11 N.B.A. melee that left brazen fans swinging at players, unglued players clocking fans and the habitual hothead Ron Artest rightly suspended for the season by a disgusted N.B.A. Commissioner David Stern.

This is not about the punches at the Palace on Friday night—on many 12 nights fan-player rifts unfold without a fist thrown—but about the fan resentment that is ribboning through sports.

Two weeks ago, hecklers prompted Nebraska Coach Bill Callahan to 13 come dangerously uncorked as he directed a profane outburst at Sooners fans, who were raining oranges on his Huskers. A week ago, outraged football fans phoned ABC to protest the racy skit between Terrell Owens and a desperate housewife, even though N.F.L. games are laden with commercials extolling the virtues of football, beer and busty twins.

Fan interaction has flooded baseball, too. Over the last four years, 14 Dodgers players were punished for brawling in the bleachers, a Royals first-base coach was attacked by two White Sox fans, Rangers outfielder Carl Everett was clunked in the head by a cellphone, and, in September, Texas reliever Frank Francisco bloodied the nose of a woman when he whipped a chair into the stands.

"I can't see Nascar fans turning on the drivers like that," said David 15 Goss, of Jacksonville, Fla.

But is this unconditional love truly without presets? Nascar's niche 16 popularity was founded on the accessibility of Richard Petty, and then the cantankerously lovable Dale Earnhardt.

Earnhardt was known to sit in his $1 million trailer, eating Bumble Bee 17 tuna from the can with a plastic fork, never forgetting his country-grown identity despite his unfathomable wealth. Fans understood him.

This is the trick for Nascar—maintaining its appeal as it grows outside 18 the vacuum of its core. Even now, fans are finding routes to coveted drivers cut off, particularly if the star is Dale Earnhardt Jr.

"You got to put Junior in a separate category when it comes to popu- 19 larity," Gordon said. Junior is the mainstream face of Nascar, the heartthrob of teens, and the son of a grand ghost who drove the black No. 3 car to his death.

"You definitely can't hide from the popularity of the sport," Junior said. 20

And yet, Little E does hide from the dust devil of fame to preserve his 21 sanity for races. Longtime Nascar fans get it, but will a Garbo act play in Portland, Ore.—another potential race site?

It will be intriguing to see how the France monarchy approaches new 22 followers who may not be charmed by Southern accents, who may be more blue than red in their politics, who won't identify with Nascar's roots. As other sports have learned, a fan's love doesn't always grow with the sport.

Thinking Critically

1. How does Selena Roberts characterize NASCAR drivers and their fans? On what does she base this characterization? How might M. Graham Spann reply? (Spann's article precedes Roberts's.)

2. What does Roberts imply about Miami when she describes it as "pastel colors of teal and sand" (paragraph 6)?

3. Do you agree with Roberts that NASCAR is a "red-state" sport? Use an online database or the website of the *New York Times,* at <http://nytimes.com/>, to determine how the *New York Times* uses the term "red state." What kinds of interests and values does the *Times* imply when its writers use "red state" to refer to sports, entertainment, or other cultural events?

Writing Critically

1. How do specific sports, or individual teams, present and market themselves to their audiences? How do advertisements for leagues and franchises appeal to specific demographics? Choose a sport and analyze its advertisements in several media. Roberts's essay provides one model for structuring your essay; and Spann's academic argument suggests five ways of approaching the subject. You might also consider essays in

Chapter 2 about community and in Chapter 5 about marketing and consumer culture to support your own thesis.

2. Read Erskine Caldwell's 1932 novel *Tobacco Road,* which Roberts alludes to in her first paragraph as definitive of the way NASCAR drivers "talk." How do the characters and diction of *Tobacco Road* compare to the way NASCAR drivers and fans are portrayed in contemporary media, and the way they describe themselves? What does Roberts assume about the average *New York Times* reader by evoking *Tobacco Road*?

3. Select a figure from sports, entertainment, or politics who is perceived as accessible to his or her fans. What does it mean to be "accessible" in contemporary American culture?

"Ozzie and Harriet Come Back!": The Primal Scream of Teenage Music

MARY EBERSTADT

A magna cum laude graduate in philosophy from Cornell University, Mary Eberstadt is a research fellow at the Hoover Institution at Stanford University, a public policy think tank founded by former President Herbert Hoover in 1959. According to the Institution's mission statement, "By collecting knowledge, generating ideas, and disseminating both, the Institution seeks to secure and safeguard peace, improve the human condition, and limit government intrusion into the lives of individuals." Eberstadt is a consulting editor at *Policy Review,* (www.policyreview.org), a bimonthly journal published by the Hoover Institution. Her public service career during the Reagan administration included working as a special assistant to Ambassador Jeanne J. Kirkpatrick at the U.S. Mission to the United Nations, as a member of the Policy Planning Staff of the U.S. State Department, and as a speechwriter for Secretary of State George P. Schultz. Her training in philosophy informs her published work on American culture and society. Her articles have appeared in the neo-conservative magazine *Weekly Standard* <http://www.weeklystandard.com> and in the conservative monthly journals *Commentary* <http://www.commentarymagazine.com/> and *American Spectator* <http://www.spectator.org/>. Eberstadt's article "Home-Alone America" in the June–July 2001 issue of *Policy Review* formed the basis of her book *Home-Alone America: The Hidden Toll of Day Care, Behavioral Drugs and Other Parent Substitutes* (2004), from which this selection is excerpted.

If there is one subject on which the parents of America passionately agree, it is that contemporary adolescent popular music, especially the subgenres of heavy metal and hip-hop/rap, is uniquely degraded—and degrading—by the standards of previous generations.[1] 1

At first blush this seems slightly ironic. After all, most of today's baby-boom parents were themselves molded by rock and roll, bumping and grinding their way through adolescence and adulthood with legendary abandon. Even so, the parents are correct: Much of today's music *is* darker and coarser than yesterday's rock. Misogyny, violence, suicide, sexual exploitation, child abuse—these and other themes, formerly rare and illicit, are now as common as the surfboards, drive-ins, and sock hops of yesteryear. So it is little wonder that today's teenage music, more than others before it, is the music parents most love to hate—even parents for whom the likes of Jim Morrison, Janis Joplin and Mick Jagger summon feelings of (relatively) wholesome nostalgia.[2] 2

So overwhelming is the adult consensus about the unique awfulness of this stuff that the c-word, *censorship,* has been raised among people on both sides of the political aisle.[3] And while such efforts have so far scored only limited success, they do demonstrate what most adults feel in their bones: that certain of today's music is egregious by any reasonable standard, as even some executives who profit from it will agree.[4] In yet another expression of adult concern that is without precedent, contemporary rock and rap have lately even caught the attention of several august medical bodies who wonder aloud about its possible malign influence on impressionable minds.[5] 3

In a nutshell, the ongoing adult preoccupation with current music goes something like this: *What is the overall influence of this deafening, foul, and often vicious-sounding stuff on children and teenagers?* This is a genuinely important question, and recent serious studies and articles, some concerned particularly with current music's possible link to violence, have lately been devoted to it. Nonetheless, this is not the focus of this chapter. Instead, I would like to turn that logic about influence upside down and ask this question: *What is it about today's music, violent and disgusting though it may be, that resonates with so many American kids?* 4

As the reader can see, this is a very different way of inquiring about the relationship between today's teenagers and their music. The first question asks what the music *does* to adolescents; the second asks what it *tells* us about them. To answer that second question is necessarily to enter the roil- 5 ing emotional waters in which that music is created and consumed—in other words, actually to read and listen to some of it.

As it turns out, such an exercise yields a fascinating and little-understood 6
fact about today's adolescent scene. If yesterday's rock was the music of abandon, today's is that of abandon*ment*. The odd truth about contemporary teenage music—the characteristic that most separates it from what has gone before—is its compulsive insistence on the damage wrought by broken homes, family dysfunction, checked-out parents, and (especially) absent fathers. Papa Roach, Everclear, Blink-182, Good Charlotte, Eddie Vedder and Pearl Jam, Kurt Cobain and Nirvana, Tupac Shakur, Snoop Doggy Dogg, Eminem—these and other singers and bands, all of them award-winning top-40 performers who either are or were among the most popular icons in America, have their own generational answer to what ails the modern teenager. Surprising though it may be to some, that answer is: dysfunctional childhood. Moreover, and just as interesting, many bands and singers explicitly link the most deplored themes in music today—suicide, misogyny, and drugs—with that lack of a quasi-normal, intact-home personal past.

To put this perhaps unexpected point more broadly, during the same 7
years in which progressive-minded and politically correct adults have been excoriating Ozzie and Harriet as an artifact of 1950s-style oppression, many millions of American teenagers have enshrined a new generation of music idols whose shared generational signature in song after song is to rage about what *not* having had a nuclear family has done to them. This is quite a fascinating puzzle of the times, among the most striking of all the unanticipated fallout in our home-alone world. The self-perceived emotional damage scrawled large across contemporary music may not be statistically quantifiable, but it is nonetheless pathetically, if rudely and sometimes violently, articulated—as many examples demonstrate neatly. . . .

Rappers Ask: Where's Daddy?

Even less recognized than the white music emphasis on broken homes and 8
the rest of the dysfunctional themes is that the popular black-dominated genres, particularly hip-hop/rap, also reflect themes of abandonment, anger, and longing for parents. Interestingly enough, this is true of particular figures whose work is among the most adult deplored.

Once again, when it comes to the deploring part, critics have a point. It 9
is hard to imagine a more unwanted role model (from the parental point of view) than the late Tupac Shakur. A best-selling gangsta rapper who died in a shoot-out in 1996 at age twenty-five (and the object of a 2003 documentary called *Tupac: Resurrection*), Shakur was a kind of polymath of criminality. In the words of a *Denver Post* review of the movie, "In a perfect

circle of life imitating art originally meant to imitate life, Shakur in 1991 began a string of crimes that he alternately denied and reveled in. He claimed Oakland police beat him up in a jaywalking arrest, later shot two off-duty cops, assaulted a limo driver and video directors, and was shot five times in a robbery." Further, "At the time of his drive-by murder in Las Vegas, he was out on bail pending appeal of his conviction for sexual abuse of a woman who charged him with sodomy in New York."

Perhaps not surprising, Shakur's songs are riddled with just about every   10 unwholesome trend that a nervous parent can name; above all they contain incitements to crime and violence (particularly against the police) and a misogyny so pronounced that his own mother, executive producer of the movie, let stand in the film a statement of protesting C. DeLores Tucker that "African-American women are tired of being called ho's, bitches and sluts by our children."

Yet Shakur—who never knew his father and whose mother, a long-time   11 drug addict, was arrested for possession of crack when he was a child—is provocative in another, quite overlooked way: He is the author of some of the saddest lyrics in the hip-hop/gangsta-rap pantheon, which is saying quite a lot. To sophisticated readers familiar with the observations about the breakup of black families recorded several decades ago in the Moynihan Report and elsewhere, the fact that so many young black men grow up without fathers may seem so well established as to defy further comment. But evidently some young black men—Shakur being one—see things differently. In fact, it is hard to find a rapper who does not sooner or later invoke a dead or otherwise long-absent father, typically followed by the hope that he will not become such a man himself. Or there is the flip side of that unintended bow to the nuclear family, which is the hagiography in some rappers' lyrics of their mothers.

In a song called "Papa'z Song Lyrics," Shakur opens with the narrator   12 imagining his father showing up after a long absence, resulting in an expletive-laden tirade. The song then moves to a lacerating description of growing up fatherless that might help to explain why Shakur is an icon not only to many worse-off teenagers from the ghetto, but also to many better-off suburban ones. Here is a boy who *"had to play catch by myself,"* who prays: *"Please send me a pops before puberty."*

The themes woven together in this song—anger, bitterness, longing for   13 family, misogyny as the consequence of a world without fathers—make regular appearances in some other rappers' lyrics, too. One is Snoop Doggy Dogg, perhaps the preeminent rapper of the 1990s. Like Shakur and numerous other rappers, his personal details cause many a parent to shudder; since his childhood he has been arrested for a variety of crimes, including cocaine possession (which resulted in three years of jail service), accomplice to murder (for which he was acquitted), and, most recently, marijuana possession. ("It's not my job to stop kids doing the wrong thing, it's their parents' job," he once explained to a reporter.) In a song called "Mama Raised Me," sung with Soulja Slim, Snoop Doggy Dogg offers this explanation of how troubled pasts come to be: *"It's probably pop's fault how I ended up / Gangbangin', crack slangin', nor given' a f***."*

Another black rapper who returned repeatedly to the theme of father 14 abandonment is Jay-Z, also known as Shawn Carter, whose third and breakthrough album, *Hard Knock Life,* sold more than 500,000 copies. He also has a criminal history (he says he had been a cocaine dealer) and a troubled family history, which is reflected in his music. In an interview with MTV.com about his latest album, the reporter explained: "Jay and his father had been estranged until earlier this year. [His father] left the household and his family's life (Jay has an older brother and two sisters) when Shawn was just 12 years old. The separation had served as a major 'block' for Jay over the years. . . . His most vocal tongue-lashing toward his dad was on the *Dynasty: Roc La Familia* cut 'Where Have You Been,' where he rapped 'F*** you very much / You showed me the worst kind of pain.'"[6]

The fact that child abandonment is also a theme in hip-hop might help 15 explain what otherwise appears as a commercial puzzle—namely, how this particular music moved from the fringes of black entertainment to the very center of the Everyteenager mainstream. There can be no doubt about the current social preeminence of these black- and ghetto-dominated genres in the lives of many better-off adolescents, black *and* white. As Donna Britt wrote in a *Washington Post* column noting hip-hop's ascendancy, "In modern America, where urban-based hip-hop culture dominates music, fashion, dance and, increasingly, movies and TV, these kids are trendsetters. What they feel, think and do could soon play out in a middle school—or a Pottery Barn–decorated bedroom—near you."[7]

Eminem: It's the Parents, Stupid

A final example of the rage in contemporary music against irresponsible 16 adults—perhaps the most interesting—is that of genre-crossing bad-boy rap superstar Marshall Mathers or Eminem (sometime stage persona "Slim Shady"): Of all the names guaranteed to send a shudder down the parental spine, his is probably the most effective. In fact, Eminem has single-handedly, if inadvertently, achieved the otherwise ideologically impossible: He is the object of a vehemently disapproving public consensus shared by the National Organization for Women, the Gay & Lesbian Alliance Against Defamation, William J. Bennett, Lynne Cheney, Bill O'Reilly, and a large number of other social conservatives as well as feminists and gay activists. In sum, this rapper—"as harmful to America as any al Qaeda fanatic," in O'Reilly's opinion—unites adult polar opposites as perhaps no other single popular entertainer has done.

There is small need to wonder why. Like other rappers, Eminem mines the shock value and gutter language of rage, casual sex, and violence. Unlike the rest, however, he appears to be a particularly attractive target of opprobrium for two distinct reasons. One, he is white and therefore politically easier to attack. (It is interesting to note that black rappers have not been targeted by name anything like Eminem has.) Perhaps even more important, Eminem is one of the largest commercially visible targets for parental wrath. Wildly popular among teenagers these last several years, he is also enormously successful in commercial terms. Winner of numerous Grammys and other music awards and a perpetual nominee for many more, he has also been critically (albeit reluctantly) acclaimed for his acting performance in the autobiographical 2003 movie *8 Mile*. For all these reasons, he is probably the preeminent rock/rap star of the last several years, one whose singles, albums, and videos routinely top every chart. His 2002 album, *The Eminem Show,* for example, was easily the most successful of the year, selling more than 7.6 million copies.   17

This remarkable market success, combined with the intense public criticism that his songs have generated, makes the phenomenon of Eminem particularly intriguing. Perhaps more than any other current musical icon, he returns repeatedly to the same themes that fuel other success stories in contemporary music: parental loss, abandonment, abuse, and subsequent child and adolescent anger, dysfunction, and violence (including self-violence). Both in his raunchy lyrics as well as in *8 Mile,* Mathers's own personal story has been parlayed many times over: the absent father, the troubled mother living in a trailer park, the series of unwanted maternal boyfriends, the protective if impotent feelings toward a younger sibling (in the movie, a baby sister; in real life, a younger brother), and the fine line that a poor, ambitious, and unguided young man might walk between catastrophe and success. Mathers plumbs these and related themes with a verbal savagery that leaves most adults aghast.   18

Yet Eminem also repeatedly centers his songs on the crypto-traditional notion that children need parents and that *not* having them has made all hell break loose. In the song "8 Mile" from the movie soundtrack, for example, the narrator studies his little sister as she colors one picture after another of an imagined nuclear family, failing to understand that *"momma's got a new man." "Wish I could be the daddy that neither one of us had,"* he comments. Such wistful lyrics juxtapose oddly and regularly with Eminem's violent other lines. Even in one of his most infamous songs, "Cleaning Out My Closet (Mama, I'm Sorry)," what drives the vulgar nar-   19 rative is the insistence on seeing abandonment from a child's point of view. *"My faggot father must had his panties up in a bunch / 'Cause he split. I wonder if he even kissed me good-bye."*

As with other rappers, the vicious narrative treatment of women in some 20 of Eminem's songs is part of this self-conception as a child victim. Contrary to what critics have intimated, the misogyny in current music does not spring from nowhere; it is often linked to the larger theme of having been abandoned several times—left behind by father, not nurtured by mother, and betrayed again by faithless womankind. One of the most violent and sexually aggressive songs in the last few years is "Kill You" by the popular metal band known as Korn. Its violence is not directed toward just any woman or even toward the narrator's girlfriend; it is instead a song about an abusive stepmother whom the singer imagines going back to rape and murder.

Similarly, Eminem's most shocking lyrics about women are not ran- 21 domly dispersed; they are largely reserved for his mother and ex-wife, and the narrative pose is one of despising them for not being better women— in particular, better mothers. The worst rap directed at his own mother is indeed gut-wrenching: *"But how dare you try to take what you didn't help me to get? / You selfish b****, I hope you f****** burn in hell for this s***!"* It is no defense of the gutter to observe the obvious: This is not the expression of random misogyny but, rather, of primal rage over alleged maternal abdication and abuse.

Another refrain constant in these songs runs like this: Today's teenagers 22 are a mess, and the parents who made them that way refuse to get it. In one of Eminem's early hits, for example, a song called "Who Knew," the rapper pointedly takes on his many middle- and upper-middle-class critics to observe the contradiction between their reviling him and the parental inattention that feeds his commercial success. *"What about the make-up you allow your 12-year-old daughter to wear?"* he taunts.

This same theme of AWOL parenting is rapped at greater length in an- 23 other award-nominated 2003 song called "Sing for the Moment," whose lyrics and video would be recognized in an instant by most teenagers in America. That song spells out Eminem's own idea of what connects him to his millions of fans—a connection that parents, in his view, just don't (or is that *won't?*) understand. It details the case of one more "problem child" created by *"His f****** dad walkin' out."* "Sing for the Moment," like many other songs of Eminem's, is also a popular video. The "visuals" shows clearly what the lyrics depict—hordes of disaffected kids, with flashbacks to bad home lives, screaming for the singer who feels their pain. It concludes by rhetorically turning away from the music itself and toward the emotionally desperate teenagers who turn out for this music by the millions. If the demand of all those empty kids wasn't out there, the narrator says pointedly, then rappers wouldn't be supplying it the way they do.

If some parents still don't get it—even as their teenagers elbow up for   24
every new Eminem CD and memorize his lyrics with psalmist devotion—at least some critics observing the music scene *have* thought to comment on the ironies of all this. In discussing *The Marshall Mathers* LP in 2001 for *Music Box,* a daily online newsletter about music, reviewer John Metzger argued, "Instead of spewing the hate that he is so often criticized of doing, Eminem offers a cautionary tale that speaks to our civilization's growing depravity. Ironically, it's his teenage fans who understand this, and their all-knowing parents that miss the point." Metzger further specified "the utter lack of parenting due to the spendthrift necessity of the two-income family."[8]

That insight raises the overlooked fact that in one important sense Em-   25
inem and most of the other entertainers quoted in this chapter would agree with many of today's adults about one thing: The kids *aren't* all right out there after all. . . . Where parents and entertainers disagree is over who exactly bears responsibility for this moral chaos. Many adults want to blame the people who create and market today's music and videos. Entertainers, Eminem most prominently, blame the absent, absentee, and generally inattentive adults whose deprived and furious children (as they see it) have catapulted today's singers to fame. (As he puts the point in one more in-your-face response to parents: *"Don't blame me when lil' Eric jumps off of the terrace / You shoulda been watchin him—apparently you ain't parents."*)

The spectacle of a foul-mouthed bad-example rock icon instructing the   26
hardworking parents of America in the art of child-rearing is indeed a peculiar one, not to say ridiculous. The single mother who is working frantically because she must and worrying all the while about what her fourteen-year-old is listening to in the headphones is entitled to a certain fury over lyrics like those. In fact, to read through most rap lyrics is to wonder which adults or political constituencies *wouldn't* take offense. Even so, the music idols who point the finger away from themselves and toward the emptied-out homes of America are telling a truth that some adults would rather not hear. In this limited sense at least, Eminem is right.

Notes

[1]By "popular music" I mean the secular commercial, rock and rock-descended songs that dominate FM airwaves, MTV, VH1, and the rest. Christian rock and country music, though also popular genres, are subjects in their own right and not under discussion here.

[2]Special thanks to Rick and Kate Eberstadt whose insights about contemporary music inform this chapter throughout.

[3]In 1985, to take a particularly well-known example, the wives of several congressmen on both sides of the aisle formed a committee led by Tipper Gore known as the Parents Music Resource Center, or PMRC, to educate parents about what is called "alarming trends" in popular music—violence, crime, drug use, suicide, and the rest. In 1995 another coalition led by William J. Bennett and C. DeLores Tucker, head of the National Political Congress of Black Women, put public pressure on media giant Time Warner to modify some of its gangsta rap.

[4]As to the pragmatic success of these efforts, results varied. The PMRC did effect one hoped-for innovation: Some records were marked with a label (known as the "Tipper sticker") that advised parents about what the PMRC called "explicit content," and some record stores agreed to carry those records (though many did not). The Bennett-Tucker effort resulted in a moral victory of sorts: a promise by Time Warner executives that the company would be more assiduous in its own moral policing of the product. Even so, the phenomena of violence and other unwanted themes in current music, which both groups set out to battle, has only grown larger in the years since.

[5]In 2000 the American Academy of Pediatrics, the American Medical Association, the American Psychological Association, and the American Academy of Child & Adolescent Psychiatry all weighed in against contemporary lyrics and other forms of violent entertainment before Congress with a first-ever "Joint Statement on the Impact of Entertainment Violence on Children." As the last-named group explained the collective worry in a subsequent policy statement: "A concern to many interested in the development and growth of teenagers is the negative and destructive themes of some rock and other kinds of music, including best-selling albums promoted by major recording companies."

[6]Shaheem Reid, with reporting by Sway Calloway, "Jay-Z: What More Can I Say," MTV.com, November 12, 2003.

[7]Donna Britt, "Stats on Teens Don't Tell the Whole Story," *Washington Post,* January 23, 2004.

[8]John Metzger, review of "Eminem: the Marshall Mathers LP," *The Music Box* 8, no. 6 (June 2001), available at http://www.musicbox-online.com.

Thinking Critically

1. What is Mary Eberstadt's thesis, and for whom is she writing? What action, if any, does she imply or suggest that her audience should take?

2. Eberstadt draws on a number of rhetorical strategies to advance her argument. Explain how she uses strategies that you would expect to find in a music review, a sociology article, and a literary analysis, among other approaches.

3. Summarize each part of Eberstadt's essay. What logical relationships do you see between and among them? How do these sections progress logically from one stage of her argument to the next?

Writing Critically

1. Elsewhere in *Home-Alone America,* Eberstadt claims that "Baby boomers and their music rebelled against parents *because* they were parents—nurturing, attentive, and overly present (as those teenagers often saw it) authority figures. Today's teenagers and their music rebel against parents because they are *not* parents—not nurturing, not attentive, and often not even there." In an essay, support or refute this thesis, using any of the readings in Chapter 4 as evidence.

2. In "Jesus Climbs the Charts: The Business of Contemporary Christian Music," earlier in this chapter, what key themes does Mark Allan Powell find in contemporary Christian music? In a comparative essay, analyze the lyrics from several of the musically comparable groups Powell describes. What do those lyrics reveal about the artists' and listeners' experiences of family and abandonment? In what ways are those lyrics similar to the ones that Eberstadt describes, and in what ways are they different? What do these similarities and differences suggest about the audiences for both broad categories of music?

3. In an article for *Washington Monthly* magazine about being an African American father in contemporary America, journalist Ta-Nehisi Coates writes: "Much conservative ink has been spilled boiling the problems of black America down to its absent daddies, but no one in the black community needs pundits to lecture him on family values. Deadbeat dads rank about one step below the Klan in popularity among African Americans. Hiphop may be grossly misogynistic, but you will be hard pressed to find a cultural movement that more reveres mothers and reviles fathers. (Indeed, rap's only mother-hater of note is a white guy, Eminem.) The antipaternal sentiment in rap expresses a larger fatigue among African Americans for 'tired-ass' black men who doom kids to fatherless lives. So when Jay-Z says 'Momma loves me, Pop I miss you/God help me forgive 'em, I got some issues,' he isn't simply having a cathartic moment, he is speaking for 70 percent of African American children. He is also speaking for my partner and me." (The full article is online at <http://www.washingtonmonthly.com/features/2001/2003.coates.html>. Another article by Coates appears on pp. 613–19.) Draw from Coates's argument here and from the observations of African American sociologist Elijah Anderson (pp. 194–204) to either support or refute Eberstadt's findings about hip-hop and parental abandonment.

Just Another Quick-Witted, Egg-Roll-Joke-Making, Insult-Hurling Chinese-American Rapper

TA-NEHISI COATES

Ta-Nehisi Coates is a staff writer for the New York City alternative newspaper the *Village Voice* (<http://villagevoice.com/>). His writings on race and culture appear frequently in the *New York Times Magazine,* (where this article was published in November 2004), and in *Washington Monthly* (<http://washingtonmonthly.com/>). Coates has appeared as a commentator on PBS's *The NewsHour with Jim Lehrer* and is a frequent speaker and panelist on issues pertaining to African Americans and the media.

The first time Jin Auyeung heard LL Cool J's "Mama Said Knock You 1 Out," he fell in love. It was the mid-90's, the latter years of hip-hop's golden age. But Jin was about as far from the hip-hop nation as you could get. He was 12 years old, growing up in North Miami Beach, the son of hardworking young immigrants from South China who owned a strip-mall Chinese restaurant. Before discovering LL Cool J, his musical tastes consisted of New Kids on the Block and, he says, "a lot of Michael Jackson."

But "Mama Said" turned Jin into a hip-hop head. In his spare time, he 2 scribbled down and memorized his hero's anthem. Then at parties, whenever the D.J. played "Mama Said," Jin would plant himself in the middle of the dance floor and channel LL verbatim. After he reached high school, Jin expanded his repertory to include the younger artists who dominated hip-hop in the 90's, like Nas, Biggie Smalls and Wu-Tang Clan. At night, instead of doing homework, Jin would sit in his bedroom, transcribing Tupac lyrics and committing them to memory.

North Miami Beach was racially diverse; Jin's family lived on a block 3 with blacks, whites and Latinos. Still, Jin's parents made it clear which side of the racial divide they wanted him to come down on. Their restaurant was in a black neighborhood, a dozen blocks from their house, but they tried to keep Jin off the soul train. Asian merchants and their black customers have often been on uneasy terms. Jin's parents were no exception. As Jin put it to me: "Their view was that some of them"—meaning African-Americans—"are ignorant to us, so we're going to assume that all of them are ignorant to us. I couldn't explain that these were my friends."

No surprise, then, that Jin's love of hip-hop didn't go over so well with   4
his parents. "When I was listening to Michael Jackson, it was like: 'Oh, that's
cool. He's listening to music! It's cute,' " Jin said. "Conflict didn't arrive until I started listening to rap music, and then it was like: 'Yo, what is this? You
really think you're black, Jin? Bottom line—you're not black, Jin.' "

Jin's parents moved to Queens in 2001, and Jin, now 22, still lives with   5
them. They haven't given up on the idea of him marrying a nice Chinese
girl, Jin said, though they have given up on him divorcing hip-hop. They
respect the fact that Jin has gone from imitating LL Cool J to competing
with him. Over the past three years, Jin has earned acclaim in the hip-hop
world for "battling"—a venerable ritual, dating back to the early days of
hip-hop, in which two rappers verbally assail each other. Two years ago
Jin's pugilistic skills earned him a contract with Ruff Ryders, the record label. In its early years, Ruff Ryders enjoyed success with hitmakers like Eve
and DMX, but Eve has left the label, and DMX isn't the platinum-record
machine of past days. The company hopes that Jin's first release, "The Rest
Is History," will improve its prospects.

The record came out last month, and a few weeks before, I had lunch   6
with Jin and his mother, April Auyeung, at Virage, a restaurant in the East
Village. Offstage, Jin has none of the battle rapper's occupational arrogance.
Baby-faced and 5-foot-6, he talks and jokes incessantly. At lunch he ordered
chicken Parmesan and bantered with his mother, reminding her of the family line about Jin's passion for rap lyrics. "We used to joke that we'd brought
home the wrong baby," she said, laughing and gazing over at her son.

Jin's mother's admonition—"You're not black, Jin"—echoed throughout   7
his childhood. But Jin never saw himself as anything but legit. Being Chinese didn't bother him; being confined by it did. So today, Jin accepts his
status as the Great Yellow Hip-Hop Hope, but at the same time, he hates
being called the Asian-American Eminem. It's complicated: he knows he is-
n't black, but he has chosen a medium defined by blackness. Which means
that whether he's rapping about sweatshops, ladies, Tiananmen Square or
partying, Jin is always dancing on the color line.

From the age of 5, Jin helped out in his parents' restaurant. He started   8
by doing small errands and graduated to cleaning toilets, delivering food
and counting money. Rap became Jin's escape. He started reciting his own
lines, and then he took to making crude demo tapes, recording himself rapping over the instrumental B-sides of his favorite singles.

Jin's antics always drew a crowd. His flair for the dramatic made him a nat-   9
ural for battling. At John F. Kennedy Middle School in North Miami Beach,
he liked to challenge other fledgling rappers, usually black kids. An adept battle rapper uses his voice, timing, rhythm and wit to humiliate the opposition

and win over the crowd. But early on, it was Jin who was humiliated, succumbing whenever his opponents hit him with an Asian joke, which they always did. "I used to not know how to handle it, and that's how I'd lose," he said. "I'm battling, kicking my rhymes, and he would come out and say something like: 'I'm hot; you're cold. You should go back home and make me an egg roll.' Something that simple, but he would have the crowd in a frenzy, an absolute frenzy. I would fall victim to it and just wouldn't know what to say."

Battle rappers like to say that there are no rules in the ring, but Jin knew   10
that if he retaliated in kind—if he made any allusions to watermelon or fried chicken, say—it would be a grave transgression. Asian slurs, by contrast, "are absolutely too common for me to get mad at," Jin said. "That's a shame, ain't it?" Ultimately, Jin did what all sharp-witted children of immigrants do—he used humor, disarming his opponents with cracks that recast his ethnicity as a weapon.

"Every person he battled had an Asian remark," said Cedric Reid, a   11
high school classmate of Jin's now at Miami Dade College. "He was ready for stuff like that. He would flip it on them so they knew, 'You got to come at me like a rapper, not like a racist.' And he'd have the crowd on his side."

As Jin raps on his new record, "In every battle, the race card was my   12
downfall / Till I read 'The Art of War' and used it to clown y'all."

In high school, Jin honed his battle skills. He won a local call-in radio   13
contest so many times that the station forced him to retire. He was battling at home too, but in a different way. His parents continued to condemn his burgeoning hip-hop career, and they also banned black and Latino kids from their house. The war on the home front escalated when Jin turned 15 and fell for a black girl at school. When his parents heard the news, they threatened to throw him out of the house.

"There was an ultimatum," Jin said. "The front door was open. It was   14
serious. . . . I left the house for two days and came crawling back. I kept seeing her on the down-low. We eventually parted ways, but not because of my parents."

A year after Jin graduated from high school, his parents closed their   15
restaurant and moved the family to New York City, where Jin's grandparents lived. His father went to work in the family construction business, and his mother focused on bringing up Jin's younger sister. Jin chased battles all over the city, winning small pots of prize money. Two weeks after moving to New York, Jin met Kamel Pratt, who spotted him in an impromptu rhyme session at the corner of Broadway and Eighth Street and not long after became his manager. Pratt introduced him to the local hip-hop scene. He had a lot of time to devote, given that Jin was his first and only client, but he eventually got him his big break, an audition on "Freestyle Friday."

"Freestyle Friday" is a popular televised battle showcase—an *American* 16
Bandstand for the hip-hop set. The broadcast is a segment of *106 & Park*,
a music-video show on Black Entertainment Television. Battle M.C.'s like
Jin see the show as the fastest route to stardom. In February 2002, Jin was
offered a spot on the show in a battle against a rapper named Hassan, the
reigning "Freestyle Friday" champ. Neither Pratt nor Jin was impressed
with Hassan; they figured his main weapon would be the sort of Asian
jokes to which Jin was by now well accustomed—corner stores, Bruce Lee,
fortune cookies, fried won tons and, of course, slanted eyes.

Since the rules of "Freestyle Friday" dictated that Jin go first, he needed 17
to make sure he landed an early crippling shot. He opened with a few standard punch lines about Hassan's name and dress. Then he lowered the boom:
"Yeah, I'm Chinese, now you understand it / I'm the reason your little sister's eyes are slanted. / If you make one joke about rice or karate / N.Y.P.D.
be in Chinatown searching for your body."

The crowd went wild. The show's hosts, Free and A.J., nodded and smiled. 18
DJ Fatman Scoop, a New York radio personality, gave the champion a stern
look and said: "Hassan. Get focused. Immediately." But Hassan was too slow;
he apparently couldn't alter his original strategy. Instead he offered an Asian
joke that landed with a thud, and then with 15 seconds still on the clock, he
stopped in midflow, sighed into the mike, lowered his head and quit. Jin went
on to win "Freestyle Friday" for a record-setting seven straight weeks, and by
the end of his final week, Ruff Ryders had offered him a contract.

The first time I saw Jin, I didn't really see him at all. I was at a friend's 19
house, talking sports, when his wife began frantically gesturing at the TV,
which was tuned to BET. "Have you seen this kid?" she asked. Jin was by then
well into his run on "Freestyle Friday." There was Jin summarily dismantling
some stiff unlucky enough to be attached to the opposing microphone. I
laughed and shrugged the whole thing off. An Asian-American rapper? I
smelled yet another gimmick: the model minority meets the miscreant.

"I think it's a shock for a lot of people to see Jin rap," says Serena Kim, 20
features editor for *Vibe*. And the fact is when you look at Jin, it's hard to
separate what is legitimately interesting about him from the sideshow.
There's something a little shocking about watching him rap, not only because of specific Asian-American stereotypes—the nerd, the overachiever,
the serious kid—but also because of the tension that exists in America between blacks and Asians. When I was a kid, growing up black in Baltimore,
we had a derisive name for the corner store run by Asians. No one debated
it; we didn't think we were being racist. To us, there was only one sort of
racism—the kind that white people perpetrated against blacks.

"As an Asian-American, you're constantly confronted with race," says 21
Hua Hsu, a Chinese-American music writer. "But you don't have that
prominent a role in the discussion. You may feel a spiritual kinship with
blacks and Latinos, but there's no real feeling back the other way."

Making his record, Jin had to confront another sort of obstacle—the in- 22
famous curse of the battle rapper. As flameouts like Craig G and Supernatural have proved, the skills that come with being a great battle rapper—a
quick wit, good stage presence and a combative personality—don't necessarily help make you a successful recording artist. After Jin signed with Ruff
Ryders, the label's co-C.E.O., Darrin (Dee) Dean, tried to impress upon him
that making a record was different than winning a battle. Jin's wit and
charisma would be useful, Dean said, only if Jin could tame them between
16 bars. He would need quality production, musicality, patience and, above
all, style—a persona to set himself apart. Every successful rapper defines
himself in a new way. 50 Cent is the gangsta reborn. OutKast's Big Boi and
Andre 3000 are the kings of eclecticism. It's not enough for Eminem to be
white—he is also hip-hop's dark humorist. So what is Jin?

His first single, "Learn Chinese," was released last year. Like his best 23
battle rhymes, it plays on Asian-American stereotypes while trying to rebut
them. But in emphasizing his ethnicity so blatantly, Jin risked turning himself into an oddity. Ruff Ryders delayed the release of Jin's album several
times before it finally hit the stores. In that pause—and with the release of
"Learn Chinese"—Jin developed a following that sees in him more things
than he ever saw in himself: Jin as Brandon Lee fulfilled. Jin as pan-Asia's
hip-hop ambassador. Jin as avenger of fried-rice jokes.

"I think every Asian-American kid with a passing interest in hip-hop 24
knows who Jin is," says Jeff Chang, author of the forthcoming book *Can't
Stop Won't Stop: A History of the Hip-Hop Generation.* "What little image of Asian-Americans that is out there has been focused on West Coast,
suburban, usually middle-class or upper-middle-class Asian-Americans.
What Jin represents is a completely different kind of thing. He's East Coast
and working class, which speaks to what a lot of Asian-Americans see in
themselves. He's carrying a lot on his shoulders."

Asian-American hip-hop enthusiasts, however, do not make for much 25
of a consumer market. White rappers like Kid Rock and Fred Durst could
sell millions of albums without having a single black fan, but Jin can't make
it big by selling only to the nation's million or so Asian teenagers. "There's
no perception that there is a market out there for a yellow rapper," Chang
said. "Not like there is for white rappers."

In other words, to become a commercial success, Jin has to cast his lot with 26
hip-hop's native constituency—black people. "It's extremely important," says

Serena Kim at *Vibe*. "That's the reason the Black Eyed Peas"—the Grammy-nominated boho-pop rap group—"aren't considered a legitimate group. They're huge, but they don't have a young black fan base. Jin has to develop that audience."

Jin and his producers are still grappling with how to market him. In   27
conversation, they try to play down Jin's ethnicity, and none of the songs on the album are as self-consciously ethnic as "Learn Chinese." But Jin does venture out of conventional rap territory with pleas for cross-cultural tolerance, something that, in the swaggering rap vernacular, runs the risk of unpardonable corniness. Jin told me that he really wants to be known as a workingman's rapper, and the best song on his album, "I Got a Love," a clever tribute to miserliness produced by Kanye West, the Chicago rapper and hip-hop producer, follows in that vein:

> That's why my old chick used to clash with me
> "Jin why you get this fake Louis bag for me?"
> Actually you should be happy I purchased that
> I take this as a sign you don't want the matching hat.

"I can bring to hip-hop that middle-class, hard-working, 9-to-5 average Joe who really doesn't get represented in hip-hop," Jin said. "As much as I love Jay-Z—his lyricism, his charisma, his presence—I can't ever truly relate. I'm not drinking Dom. I'm not cracking 500 Cristal bottles. Flying to St.-Tropez? I never even knew that was a real place."

One night last June, I went with Jin to the Ruff Ryders studio in Yonkers,   28
where he spent four hours recording a track for "The Rest Is History." Randy (Okre Boy) Williams, Jin's session engineer, took Jin's levels and then gave him the green light. The bass-heavy track banged out of several speakers. Jin stood in the booth nodding, half-dancing and rhyming at his cue. The studio grew more crowded as miscellaneous Ruff Ryders—as the company's employees call themselves—filtered in, some to watch Jin, but most to check the score from Game 2 of the N.B.A. finals. Jin finished the track around 1 in the morning, and everyone drifted downstairs to a lounge, to hang out. While the other members of the crew were reading magazines and killing time, Jin opened his laptop on a long boardroom table. He connected wirelessly to the Internet, and he started scrolling through one of his favorite Web sites, a database that archives old hip-hop lyrics.

Jin's eyes were glowing as he focused on the screen, scanning through hip-   29
hop's history and his own. He came upon the lyrics for "Playground," a 1991 hit by Another Bad Creation, a bubblegum kiddie group of the day, and offered up an impromptu version of the song. Everyone cracked up. Jin kept scrolling through the lyrics of hip-hop has-beens, a fraternity he surely hopes not to join.

Jin's album opened at No. 54 on the Billboard chart, selling 19,000 copies 30 in its inaugural week. But in its second week, sales dropped to 10,000 units, and his position dropped to No. 112. "I didn't have any expectations," Jin said when I asked him about the sales. He said he was much more excited about a battle he had just won at the Mixshow Power Summit in Puerto Rico. He took home a $50,000 pot and a Chevrolet Cobalt.

Whether Jin's future lies in battling, making records or both, it was 31 back at that table in the Ruff Ryders studio that he seemed most in his natural element. In the end, Jin's real persona is that of a hip-hop nerd. Even on the verge of potential stardom, or fulfilling his dream, there he was, reciting someone else's lyrics. He was clearly still the same guy who wrote down every word of LL's lyrics, who religiously read *The Source* and who used to walk through shopping malls looking for battles.

It's an identity as real to him as race or class, but not one that will likely 32 make him a platinum artist. As he clicked his way around the site, Jin ran down a few more of his favorites. At first the room was with him, offering responses to his recital—recalling Another Bad Creation's beef with Kris Kross and other assorted trivia from rap history. But by the time Jin made it to the Wu-Tang member U-God's verse in the group's 1997 anthem "Triumph," the others had grown weary.

One of the Ruff Ryders engineers looked up and half-jokingly yelled, 33 "Yo, can somebody shut this kid up?" Jin laughed, scrolled down to another song lyric and kept on rapping.

Thinking Critically

1. What do you expect from the title of this article?

2. How does Ta-Nehisi Coates, an African American writer and hip-hop critic, interweave the history of hip-hop and the subject of race through an essentially biographical article?

3. What role does marketing play in the nurturing of new hip-hop talent? What specific marketing problems are posed by Jin Auyeung?

Writing Critically

1. Being a "hip-hop nerd," observes Coates, is "an identity as real to Jin Auyeung as race or class" (paragraphs 31, 32). Has hip-hop blurred or transcended boundaries of race and class? Is the influence of hip-hop culture on mainstream America similar to the ways in which other forms of art and entertainment have moved, in the past, from the fringe to the mainstream?

2. In the next selection, Diane Cardwell explores another hip-hop-influenced New York subculture. How is cultural diversity expressed in your own community?

Trace the ways in which a form of art or entertainment forms a bond across class, race, or gender in your community.

3. In paragraph 20, Coates candidly reflects on his own experiences with racism growing up in an African American community in Baltimore. As ideas of race become increasingly complex in contemporary American culture, how is the understanding of "racism" changing? In your own community and experience, what kinds of mindsets and behaviors are labeled "racist"? How are those ideas reinforced, and how are they challenged?

Yo! Or Is It Oy? Cultures Blend in Dance Clubs

DIANE CARDWELL

> Diane Cardwell has worked as a writer and editor specializing in popular culture for publications including *Rolling Stone, Entertainment Weekly, Vogue,* and the *Village Voice.* She was a founding editor of the urban music magazine *Vibe.* Cardwell began her career at the *New York Times.* As a story editor for the *New York Times Magazine,* she assigned and edited features on culture and entertainment. She became a reporter on the metro desk in 2000, covering the police, city hall, and Brooklyn beats. This article appeared on the front page of the *New York Times* "Metro" section on December 11, 2004.

Straight out of Crown Heights, Brooklyn, the lanky reggae artist Ma-   1
tisyahu was side-stepping across the stage at the Downtown club in Farmingdale, N.Y., puffing into the microphone like some sort of latter-day Doug E. Fresh.

He had already worked up the crowd with his chanting and crooning,   2
backed by hip-hop-inflected Caribbean rhythms, but at this particular moment Matisyahu was demonstrating his long-honed skills at the beat box. As audience members bobbed their heads, whooped and mimed D.J. scratching motions, Sterling Bailey, a black musician and reggae producer, simply exclaimed "Wow" over and over. Then he leaned in to pronounce, with admiration: "Does he sound like he was raised in the ghetto or what?"

With Ice Cube snarling silently from video screens overhead, Matisyahu   3
began his next number. In Yiddish.

Granted, a bearded, 25-year-old Lubavitcher by way of White Plains   4
wearing a dark suit, brimmed hat and tallit might not seem like the most

obvious candidate for breakout reggae success, but these days mixing Jewish identity with the sounds of hip-hop is far from uncommon.

There is Josh Dolgin, known as So-Called, a performer and producer   5
who blends traditional klezmer music with urban beats, and Hip Hop Hoodios, a Latino Jewish group. From Minneapolis there is Yoni, a socially conscious, culturally Jewish rapper who has been touring with Matisyahu. In Los Angeles a group called Blood of Abraham uses Hebrew names. And in New York, D.J. Hütz of the part-Israeli group Gogol Bordello mixes electronica and a Puerto Rican dance hall form called reggaetón with the Gypsy music of his Ukrainian homeland.

And JDub Records, a nonprofit music label and event producer, is ded-   6
icated to promoting this loosely defined contemporary culture. JDub has released Matisyahu's album, "Shake Off the Dust . . . Arise," and it produces a periodic cross-cultural showcase called the Unity Sessions, which feature Arab, Muslim and Jewish artists performing traditional Middle Eastern music, reggae and hip-hop.

The organization also sponsors events at downtown clubs that are open   7
to all but are intended to help bring together young Jews looking for community outside traditional institutions like the network of Jewish federations or a synagogue.

"Really for us what's Jewish is defined by the artists creating it," Aaron   8
Bisman, 24, founder and executive director of JDub, said during a nouveau burlesque show at the Slipper Room, a club on the Lower East Side he said he was hoping to use for regular parties starting next month. "If someone comes up with something that has lyrics in Yiddish or from ancient Jewish texts, and the melodies are pulled from prayers or whatever, obviously that's Jewish," he continued.

"But if someone is singing in English and it's poetic but it's about their   9
connection to their Judaism or some Jewish aspect of their lives," he added, his voice rising in a verbal shrug, "that's good enough."

At a time when mainstream black rap and the Christian church have   10
been inching ever closer—witness Kanye West's runaway hit "Jesus Walks" and the increasing number of ministries embracing the rhythms and bluntness of hip-hop—so too, it seems, are similar connections surfacing in pop music among Jewish artists.

Perry Farrell (nee Bernstein) of Jane's Addiction explored Jewish mys-   11
ticism through cabala and emerged as DJ Peretz, spinning trance music. The Beastie Boys' latest album. *To the 5 Boroughs,* features the group's most explicit embrace of its Judaism yet, including Adam Horovitz defining himself as a funky Jew and rhyming Piazza with matzoh. For a recent cover story in the irreverent culture magazine *Heeb,* the group posed as

juvenile (or is that Jewvenile?) delinquents in a cash-strewn alley near a bottle of Manischewitz playing with a dreidel instead of shooting craps.

And tonight at Southpaw, a club in Park Slope, a group of artists, in- 12 cluding So-Called, Frank London's Brazilian Brass All Stars and Haale, a Middle Eastern- and rock-influenced singer, are set to perform for JDub's second annual Hanukkah celebration, called Jewltide.

"We founded the label on the belief that there was no one tying all these 13 pieces together," said Mr. Bisman, who studied music business at New York University, has been working as a D.J. since high school and only re- cently sheared off his dreadlocks. ("People asking me to sell them drugs wasn't helping the cause.") "We were looking for innovative, high-quality music that has some sort of, like, proud and authentic Jewish content."

But even as Mr. Bisman and his colleagues approach much of their 14 work with a nudge and a wink—they call their Hanukkah party Jewltide, after all—they shy away from anything that smacks of kitsch.

"We're not interested in something that can also appear at weddings and 15 bar mitzvahs," said Jacob Harris, 24, who attended religious day school with Mr. Bisman as a youth back in Phoenix and now develops artists at JDub. "We're very interested in something that can cross over into the mainstream."

In other words, they are not looking to replicate Adam Sandler singing 16 "The Chanukah Song," as Alexandra Hochster, 22, who organizes the la- bel's New York events, put it, laughing. Still, that provided an odd sort of cultural precedent for what JDub is trying to do.

"That was Adam Sandler standing up and saying, 'Yay, I'm Jewish,'" 17 Mr. Bisman said. "He made a song, he got it on national radio."

The Beastie Boys also serve a symbolic role for young Jews looking to 18 connect to one another and their religion without feeling uncool.

Growing up, Ms. Hochster said, "every Jewish kid thought, 'Well, at 19 some point they were nerdy Jewish kids, too. If they could be cool, there's hope for the rest of us.'"

Indeed, the notion of Jewish artists performing in traditionally black 20 forms is not as incongruous as it might seem. Reggae lyrics, for instance, have often included explicit references to the Old Testament. Matisyahu, who was born Matthew Miller into a non-Orthodox family and converted later, said that upon returning home from Israel as a teenager the closest thing he saw to the authentic Judaism he found overseas was in "Exodus" by Bob Marley.

"It is not Jewish music," he said, "but it is filled with images of Judaism. 21 I created my own internal feelings about what it meant to be Jewish and connected it to reggae music."

In some ways, this culture is simply a natural result of artists raised on 22 punk, hip-hop, reggae and dance music and wanting their Judaism to be a part of their work.

"We now have generations who have grown up with these sounds," 23 said Alan Light, the editor in chief of *Tracks* magazine who wrote his undergraduate thesis at Yale on the Beastie Boys.

"It is essentially impossible to grow up now without hip-hop as part of 24 your musical landscape and your musical experience, even if it's 'I don't like it,'" he added. "At what point do these things cease to be owned by those who initially created them, and they are just set loose on the world for people to play with?"

Apparently, that point has come, and the results are attracting Jews and 25 non-Jews alike.

Eugene Hütz of Gogol Bordello, for instance, is not Jewish but said he 26 feels an affinity for the culture. The music he plays as a D.J. is shot through with elements of dub and electronica and is influenced by his own ethnic mix: Ukrainian, Gypsy, German, Russian. It can sound like Jewish wedding music, even though it is not, he said, but on a recent Saturday night at the Knitting Factory Tap Bar, it was moving an exuberant, sweaty crowd that included young Jews, blacks, whites and a group of puppeteers.

And in Farmingdale, the Downtown club was filled with a similar mix, 27 including a group of modern Orthodox teenagers.

"Normally famous Jewish people are usually, like, people in business and 28 stuff like that," said Dave Stieglitz, 17. "And the fact that this is something that I love and I can listen to him and go to his concerts, it's a lot of fun."

Thinking Critically

1. How does Diane Cardwell use irony to enhance her subject? Irony is often used, in popular culture, to mock. Explain how Cardwell uses it in a positive fashion.

2. How does Aaron Bisman (paragraph 8) define "Jewish"? What does this contemporary and fluid definition suggest about the changing ways in which race, ethnicity, and religion are perceived in contemporary American culture?

3. Why would this article appear as a feature in the news pages of the *New York Times* instead of in the arts section? What is "newsworthy" about it?

Writing Critically

1. Speaking of the Beastie Boys, an old-school hip-hop crew from Brooklyn, a record company publicist says, "every Jewish kid thought, 'Well, at some point they were nerdy Jewish kids, too. If they could be cool, there's hope for the rest of us'" (paragraph 19). Ta-Nehisi Coates, in the preceding selection (paragraph 20), describes the stereotypes faced by Asian kids like rapper Jin

Auyeung: "the nerd, the overachiever, the serious kid." What is it about hip-hop that's "cool"? What does it mean to be a "nerd" in American youth culture, and how does hip-hop disguise or counteract the "nerd" in a kid?

2. Alan Light, the editor in chief of the music magazine *Tracks,* asks in paragraph 24: "At what point do these things cease to be owned by those who initially created them, and they are just set loose on the world for people to play with?" Although he's speaking of hip-hop, adopt his thesis as the basis of an argument about another kind of crossover culture.

Arguing the Cultural Divides

1. Throughout this chapter, writers report on the ways in which popular media are created for and consumed by increasingly specialized or fractured audiences. Sometimes this fracturing seems positive—as when kids from diverse racial and economic backgrounds find a common voice in hip-hop. At other times, this lack of a common culture is perceived as isolating or even elitist. Is there indeed a lack of a "mainstream" in American popular media? Is that a positive development or a cautionary sign?

2. From daytime courtroom "reality" shows to the angry, abandoned voices of some hip-hop and rock stars, American popular media plays an important role in shaping and promulgating values. Select a genre of popular entertainment (it need not be a form discussed in Chapter 10), and demonstrate how it upholds or subverts a particular moral code or set of values. Your essay should also consider the role of marketing and sponsorship in shaping this genre. For example, what kinds of advertisements appear with an "edgy" crime drama? What time of day are videos by a certain artist aired on MTV's networks?

3. Do you and your peers share tastes in music, film, television, and other kinds of popular media? Do you also share similar backgrounds, political inclinations, and moral convictions? Which relationships in your life depend on shared tastes in popular culture, and which relationships are based on mutual values and backgrounds? Is there any common ground? Can—or should—popular culture be used to help establish common ground among otherwise oppositional groups of people?

4. Create an annotated bibliography of recent *scholarly* publications about your favorite sport. (See M. Graham Spann, "NASCAR Racing Fans: Cranking Up an Empirical Approach," for an example of scholarly writing about a sport.) What do these writers contribute toward your understanding and appreciation of this sport? What do they overlook or misconstrue? To whom is a scholarly evaluation of some aspect of this sport most interesting and valuable, and why?

Safe and Secure: What Are We Afraid Of?

11

CHAPTER

from Culture of Fear: Risk-Taking and the Morality of Low Expectation

FRANK FUREDI

Hungarian-born sociologist Frank Furedi has written extensively on the ways in which contemporary Western cultures avoid, suppress, misapprehend, or subvert risk. He is the author of *Where Have All the Intellectuals Gone?: Confronting 21st Century Philistinism* (2004), *Therapy Culture: Cultivating Vulnerability in an Uncertain Age* (2003), and *Paranoid Parenting: Why Ignoring the Experts May Be Best for Your Child* (2002). Furedi's pointed critiques of the privileges enjoyed (and abused) by the elites of America and western Europe transcend easy political labels. "For me," Furedi noted in a recent interview, "real politics today is inseparable from involvement in a battle of ideas. It is only when we begin to take ideas a bit more seriously, that we can move towards a more democratic and genuinely participatory situation." Furedi is a professor of sociology at the University of Kent in England. This selection is the introduction to his book *Culture of Fear: Risk-Taking and the Morality of Low Expectation*, first published in 1995 and revised in 2002 to take into account the impact of the 2001 terrorist attacks.

625

S afety has become the fundamental value of our times. Passions that were 1 once devoted to a struggle to change the world (or to keep it the same) are now invested in trying to ensure that we are safe. The label "safe" gives new meaning to a wide range of human activities, endowing them with unspoken qualities that are meant to merit our automatic approval. "Safe sex" is not just sex practised "healthily"—it implies an entire attitude towards life. The safe-drinking campaigns organized by UK university student unions express a moral statement about campus life. These days, universities actively boast about their commitment to safety in an attempt to attract students.

Personal safety is a growth industry. In a trend which took off in the 2 United States, but has swiftly crossed the Atlantic to the UK, hardly a week now passes without some new risk to the individual being reported, and another safety measure proposed. A wide network of charities and organizations has grown up with a view to offering advice on every aspect of personal safety, and the same concerns are echoed in the programme of every major political party. This development, most clearly expressed through the institutionalization of the phenomenon of the helpline, has made a major impact on social and cultural life.

Every public and private place is now assessed from a safety perspective. 3 Hospital security has emerged as a central concern of health professionals. Concern for protecting newborn babies from potential kidnappers indicates that a preoccupation with safety can never begin too soon. In the USA, a scare about violent babysitters has led to a massive expansion of the nursery security business. Crawford Kindergarten in London was the first nursery in the UK to allow parents to monitor their children from home or the office through closed-circuit television cameras installed in the classroom. In September 1999, Bolton Nursery School in Manchester announced that it had installed a webcam to allow parents to keep an eye on their children via the Internet. A camera fitted into a room at the nursery relays pictures that can only be accessed by parents with individual passwords. In the USA, an Orwellian-sounding Parentwatch, Inc. has set up a website that allows parents to monitor the activities of their toddlers at home or in their nursery. A manual for US parents, entitled *Perfectly Safe*, offers information about how to create "the perfectly safe home." Expectant parents can also rely on a small industry of consultants who are in the business of redesigning homes to make them safe for babies and toddlers.

In UK and US schools, safety is a big issue. The comprehensive range of 4 cameras, swipe cards and other security measures that are now routine make many schools look more like minimum security prisons. Meanwhile, car phones are sold as safety devices to protect women who fear violent attacks on themselves or their vehicles, and the electronics industry speculates that it is only a matter of time before cctvs become a standard household item.

Economic life is clearly oriented towards the avoidance of risk and the promotion of safety. The inexorable rise of health spending in the Western world is conventionally explained as an outcome of the high cost of new medical breakthroughs. However, it is not new medical technology but a concern with minimizing risks that has transformed the health industry into one of the most profitable sectors in the USA and the UK. The growing market for alternative treatments and medicines indicates that it is not just the high-technology variety which is in demand. Products and services that are linked to risk avoidance are doing well. In the UK, bottled water has been the fastest growing sector of the drinks market. Perfectly safe tap water is increasingly regarded as being risky. The growing demand for organic food indicates that the experience of eating is increasingly shaped by concerns about health risks.

Risk avoidance has become an important theme in political debate and social action. The issue of safety has become thoroughly politicized. Governments and officials are routinely accused of covering up a variety of hidden perils and of being complacent in the face of a variety of threats to people's safety. This is the age of consumer activism. . . . [T]he politics of fear has inspired campaigns and protests against the apparent risks inflicted on society by big corporations, scientists and officials. Consequently, it is almost impossible to find a leading politician who will state that something is safe and that the risks involved are well worth taking. From the standpoint of the contemporary political imagination, it makes more sense to take a "precautionary approach" than to reassure. "Better safe than sorry" has become the fundamental principle of political life. This orientation has come to dominate the trade unions. Unions rarely organize industrial action over jobs or pay any more. Instead, the main focus of their energies is lobbying management to improve safety at work and protect their members from a variety of recently discovered work-related diseases. Consequently, work has been recast as a risky experience that threatens employees' health. Trade unions have been in the forefront of constructing the current epidemic of stress.

The politics of fear has all but vanquished the spirit of social activism. This transformation of political life is most strikingly expressed on the university campus. Once upon a time, students used to mobilize around broad political and social issues. Today, this orientation has given way to campaigning around the issue of safety. British student unions have even taken it upon themselves to preach the virtue of sobriety. Whereas in the past, warnings about hitting the bar were confined to coming from grandma and grandpa, today it is the student unions that organize campaigns of "awareness" about the risks of too much boozing. Even drug-taking has become associated with the safety issue. Many now justify their preference for Ecstasy on the grounds that it makes them feel safer. "It's safer than alcohol" is a standard argument used to justify the smoking of cannabis.

Through the media, we are all continually reminded of the risks we face 8
from environmental hazards. When the survival of the human species is said to be at stake, then life itself becomes one big safety issue. And, almost from day to day, the catalogue of new risks confronting us expands further. One day it is thrombosis-inducing contraceptive pills, the next day we are threatened by flesh-consuming super bugs. In the meantime, we cannot trust the food we eat. According to the Food Standards Agency, 14 per cent of UK respondents have had at least one case of food poisoning in 2000. So are we eating worse food than in the past? Not really. Because we are more concerned about the food we eat, we are more likely to complain of suspected food poisoning.

Recent panics about genetically modified (GM) food, the MMR vac- 9
cine and Balkan War Syndrome—none of which were supported by the known facts of the matter—led some observers to ask a few questions about the contemporary obsession with the alleged risks facing society. But even those who react sceptically to a particular panic tend to underestimate the breadth of safety concerns. Public concern about the health risks supposedly linked with mobile phone masts or electricity cables are only the tip of the iceberg. Indeed, such panics often have little to do with the specific issues involved. They are made possible by the way in which a safety consciousness has been institutionalized in every aspect of life today.

Once a preoccupation with safety has been made routine and banal, no 10
area of human endeavour can be immune from its influence. Activities that were hitherto seen as healthy and fun—such as enjoying the sun—are now declared to be major health risks. In the UK, some local councils are worried that children might get injured through conkering—the age-old custom of playing with chestnuts. Consequently, local councils have implemented the policy of "tree management"—cutting down trees—to make horse-chestnut trees less accessible to children. Moreover, even activities that have been pursued precisely because they are risky are now recast from the perspective of safety consciousness. In this spirit, a publication on young people and risk takes comfort from the fact that new safety measures were introduced in mountain-climbing:

> Nobody is going to prevent young men and women from taking risks.
> Even so, it is obvious that the scale of such risks can be influenced for
> the better. During recent years rock-climbers have greatly reduced
> their risks thanks to the introduction of better ropes, boots, helmets
> and other equipment.[1]

1. Plant, M. and Plant, M. (1992). *Risk Takers: Alcohol, Drugs, Sex and Youth* (Routledge: London) pp. 142–3.

The fact that young people who choose to climb mountains might not 11
want to be denied the *frisson* of risk does not enter into the calculations of
the safety-conscious professional, concerned to protect us from ourselves.

The evaluation of everything from the perspective of safety is a defin- 12
ing characteristic of contemporary society. When safety is worshipped and
risks are seen as intrinsically bad, society is making a clear statement
about the values that ought to guide life. Once mountain-climbing is
linked to risk aversion, it is surely only a matter of time before a campaign
is launched to ban it altogether. At the very least, those who suffer from
climbing-related accidents will be told that "they have brought it upon
themselves." For to ignore safety advice is to transgress the new moral
consensus.

Thinking Critically

1. According to Frank Furedi, what is the relationship between "safety" and "risk avoidance"? Does he make a clear distinction between what would seem to be reasonable precautions and what might be exaggerated or inflated attempts to avoid "risk"?

2. How does Furedi support his contention that "the politics of fear has all but vanquished the spirit of social activism" (paragraph 7)?

3. This selection is from the introduction to Furedi's book *Culture of Fear: Risk-Taking and the Morality of Low Expectation.* Based on this introduction, what arguments would you expect to see more fully developed in the book itself? Paraphrase each claim that Furedi makes in this introduction that requires further support.

Writing Critically

1. Furedi offers several brief, general examples of social and political actions that seem to support his contention that "Safety has become the fundamental value of our times" (paragraph 1). Create an annotated bibliography or a blog that provides additional context and evidence for his broader examples.

2. At what point does society's interest in promoting safety impinge on an individual's right to privacy? For example, Furedi notes that many parents now rely on closed-circuit television or webcams to monitor their child-care providers.

3. In what ways is risk-taking an essential part of becoming an independent, thriving adult? Using examples from your own life, discuss how risk-taking and fear have contributed to who you are today.

Rights in an Insecure World

DEBORAH PEARLSTEIN

> Deborah Pearlstein lectures on human rights and national security at Stanford Law School and is director of the U.S. Law and Security Program at Human Rights First. A magna cum laude graduate of Harvard Law School, Pearlstein was a speechwriter for President Bill Clinton. Since the events of 9/11, she has been a vocal advocate for the rights of immigrants and other detainees deemed risks to U.S. security. In 2004, at the invitation of the U.S. Department of Defense, Pearlstein observed the military commission proceedings at the U.S. naval base at Guantánamo Bay, Cuba, where many detainees captured in Afghanistan and Iraq were being held. Her blog on those proceedings is at the Human Rights First website: <http://www.humanrightsfirst.org/ us_law/detainees/military_commission_diary.htm#day1>. "Rights in an Insecure World" was published in the October 2004 issue of the *American Prospect,* a print and online monthly magazine that "strives to beat back the right wing and to build a majority of true patriots who understand what really makes America great."

Almost as soon as the planes crashed into the twin towers, scholars, pundits, and politicians began asserting that our most important challenge as a democracy now is to reassess the balance between liberty and security. As Harvard human-rights scholar Michael Ignatieff wrote in *The Financial Times* on September 12, "As America awakens to the reality of being at war—and permanently so—with an enemy that has as yet no face and no name, it must ask itself what balance it should keep between liberty and security in the battle with terrorism." 1

Long before anyone had a clear idea of what went wrong—much less how to make sure it never happened again—public debate began with the assumption that something about the current "balance" was partially to blame for the attacks' success. As the attorney general testified in December 2001, "al-Qaeda terrorists are told how to use America's freedom as a weapon against us." In embracing the USA PATRIOT Act just weeks after the attacks, congressional member after congressional member stood to explain, as then-Senate Majority Leader Trent Lott put it, "When you're at war, civil liberties are treated differently." Minority Leader Dick Gephardt embraced the assumption as well, saying, "[W]e're not going to have all the openness and freedom we have had." 2

Our open society had made us less secure. The converse was as clear: A 3
less free society would be safer. We had posited a solution before we had
identified the problem. And we had based the solution on the premise that
liberty and security are a zero-sum game.

While the drive to think about September 11 in terms of its implications 4
for personal liberties was understandable, the balance metaphor is badly
flawed. As the commission report itself demonstrates, the fundamental freedoms of our open society were not the primary (or even secondary) reason the
terrorists succeeded on September 11, FBI agents in Minneapolis failed to
search terrorist suspect Zacarias Moussaoui's computer before the attacks, not
because constitutional restrictions against unreasonable searches and seizures
prevented them from doing so but because they misunderstood the tools the
law provided. The vast majority of the September 11 hijackers were able to enter the United States not because equal-protection provisions prevented border
officials from targeting Arab and Muslim men for special scrutiny but because,
according to the commission, "[b]efore 9/11, no agency of the U.S. government systematically analyzed terrorists' travel strategies" to reveal how terrorists had "detectably exploited weaknesses in our border security."

It is also not the case that a society less concerned with human rights is 5
per se better protected from terrorism. On the contrary, some of our most
rights-damaging measures since September 11 have had a neutral or even
negative effect on counterterrorism. Most important, it is not the case that
enhanced security invariably requires a compromise of human rights.

The balance metaphor has made crafting a security policy response to 6
September 11 easy—and often misguided. It has also made policy unduly
prone to undermine human rights. Three years after the fact, both rights
and security are the worse for wear.

Caught in the Balance

The PATRIOT Act became an important first example: It allows the FBI to 7
secretly access Americans' personal information (library, medical, telephone, and financial records, among other things) without needing to
show to an independent authority (like a judge) that the target is particularly suspected of terrorist activity. Yet the September 11 commission's report and other studies done since the attacks suggest that our primary
intelligence failure on September 10 was not having too little information;
our problem was failing to understand, analyze, and disseminate the significant quantity of information we had. For example, Minneapolis FBI
agents did not understand what "probable cause" meant (the level of evidence required to obtain a regular criminal search warrant)—so they did not
understand that they could have secured a run-of-the-mill search warrant on

Moussaoui. This failure is a problem not remedied by the PATRIOT provision that gives the FBI power to trawl secretly through Americans' records. That power is all about gathering more data; it does nothing to address the problem of analysis that we still have. Still, changing the law was fast and easy—far easier than changing culture, competence, or overarching foreign policy. Imposing upon rights could become a policy substitute for enhancing security.

A similar approach was evident in the FBI's "voluntary" interview programs in certain immigrant and minority communities—a process that expended enormous resources and deeply alienated the communities whose cooperation in intelligence gathering may be needed most. After September 11, hundreds of foreign nationals in the United States were wrongly detained, unfairly deported, and subject to mistreatment and abuse under government programs, from special registration requirements to voluntary interviews to the detention of those seeking political asylum from a list of predominantly Arab and Muslim countries. Yet an April 2003 Government Accounting Office report on the effects of these interviews revealed that none of the information gathered from the interviews had yet been analyzed for intelligence, and there were "no specific plans" to do so. Indeed, from a security point of view, information overload can make matters worse. Instead of looking for a needle in a haystack, we must now find a needle in a field full of hay.   8

And just as our security needs for more careful intelligence assessments, thorough analysis, and greater information sharing are at their height, the executive-branch impulse has been to crack down on information shared not only with the public but with Congress itself. In 2003, the executive branch classified 25 percent more information (based on the number of executive-agency determinations that certain information should be classified) than the year before, which itself had seen a large rise. The CIA's numbers went up 41 percent, the Justice Department's 89 percent. At the same time, the amount of information being declassified fell to half what it had been in 2000, and one-fifth of 1997 levels. And this is not just about traditionally classified information. Last December, for example, the Defense Department announced a new policy preventing its own inspector general from posting unclassified information that was, in the Pentagon's estimation, "of questionable value to the general public." At the same time, despite repeated congressional requests over a period of years for complete statistics on how the PATRIOT Act has been used by the Justice Department, information available to Congress remains incomplete.   9

Paradigms Lost

Aggressive or humiliating interrogation is the most pointed example of counterproductive policy. If the most important issue we face in the treat-   10 ment of a suspect who knows the location of a ticking bomb is "what balance" to keep between security and liberty, of course liberty will lose. Saving the lives of 3,000 innocents weighs far heavier in the balance than the rights of any one individual.

But how does aggressive interrogation improve security? Set aside the   11
fact that the certainty of the ticking-bomb scenario never exists in the real world. When John Ashcroft argued that terrorists were trained to "use our freedoms against us," he pointed to an al-Qaeda training-manual instruction that terrorists, if captured, should lie in response to questions from authorities. However, neither the manual nor the attorney general explained how a denial of human rights can overcome the instruction to lie. Are terrorists less likely to lie if we humiliate them in violation of Geneva Convention protections—which we are, after all, bound to obey by law?

To the extent that the United States is able to answer this question—   12
and compared with the counterterrorism expertise in Israel and the United Kingdom, our knowledge is limited at best—published accounts point to the opposite conclusion. As one Army interrogator put it in testimony related to the investigation of Abu Ghraib, "Embarrassment as a technique would be contradictory to achieving results." That is an important reason why the Army field manual has for decades instructed soldiers to avoid such tactics. They of course violate rights. They also do not reliably work. On the other hand, the widespread use and public revelation of such tactics has been powerfully effective in fueling anger and resentment that may feed anti-American terrorism for some time.

Now compare these tactics with security-enhancing measures that require   13
essentially no balancing of security with human rights. For example, a bipartisan array of counterterrorism experts continues to criticize as inadequate inspection regimes for the 7 million cargo containers that arrive in U.S. ports each year—yet all acknowledge the danger of attack through such containers as a significant ongoing threat. The same may be said for the threat of bioterrorist attack, but the largely rights-neutral improvement of international public-health surveillance (which could help identify infectious-disease agents before they enter the United States) has also taken a backseat. And many in Congress have resisted entirely rights-neutral programs that would help the former Soviet Union secure stockpiles of fissile material to prevent it from becoming available on the global black market. And on and on.

This is not to suggest that balancing security interests against liberty   14
interests is never required. It is to emphasize that taking a stone away from the rights side of the scale does not necessarily give the security side an advantage any more than taking a stone away from the security side strengthens rights. It is to underscore that viewing the issue of security

post-September 11 as an exercise where rights and security are opposed is likely to produce both poor security policy and rights-damaging results.

The Moral Equivalent of Law

If escaping the balancing framework is important to making good judg- 15 ments about security policy, it is essential to preserving a regime of human rights under law. The dangers of this have been acutely evident in the new U.S. approach to detention and interrogation. Since early 2002, the White House has insisted that the president has the power to designate American citizens "enemy combatants," and thereby deprive them of the constitutional protections of the U.S. criminal-justice system, of, indeed, any legal rights at all. More or less the same position has applied to the U.S. detention of thousands of foreign nationals held indefinitely in a global system from Iraq to Afghanistan to Guantánamo Bay.

As White House Counsel Alberto Gonzales put it in a speech defending 16 the combatant-detention policy to the American Bar Association's Standing Committee on Law and National Security, at issue in these cases was "the balance struck by this administration between protecting our country and preserving our freedoms." This balance had to be struck by the chief executive as "a matter of prudence and policy"—not one fixed in some more permanent domestic or international framework of rights, or one unduly constrained by law. "You have to realize," the president's lawyer told the Supreme Court, "that in situations where there is a war . . . you have to trust the executive to make the kind of quintessential military judgments that are involved" in interrogating detainees under U.S. control. This was not just about a particular entitlement—to a lawyer, to confidentiality, or to due process. This was about the idea of rights itself.

This argument took center stage this past spring when the Supreme Court 17 heard its first three cases arising in the war on terrorism. In each of these cases—two involving the detention of U.S. citizens as "enemy combatants," one involving the detention of hundreds of foreign nationals beyond U.S. borders—the president argued that we should abandon reliance on law according to standards known to all and fixed in advance (the very definition of the rule of law) and move toward a more "flexible" anti-terrorism system where the rule of the road is not law but (in every case, at any moment) balance. Would an enemy-combatant detainee ever be able to assert his innocence to someone other than his interrogator? one justice asked during oral arguments. "As I understand it," the president's lawyer answered, "the plan on a going-forward basis, reflecting the unique situation of this battle, is to provide individuals like [Yaser Esam] Hamdi, like [Jose] Padilla, with the equivalent" of some review. "We don't know for sure."

By most accounts, the Court's decisions in these cases were a victory 18
for human rights. In the case of U.S. citizen Hamdi, eight of the nine justices rejected the White House assertion that the president alone determined what rights Hamdi was entitled to receive. The federal courts will
also have a role now in checking presidential power to detain foreign nationals at Guantánamo Bay. And while U.S. citizen Padilla may have to
jump through additional procedural hoops, Hamdi's case put the hand-
writing for him on the wall: There would be no such thing as a rights-less
citizen of the United States.

Nonetheless, these cases presented questions about government power 19
and law that were staggeringly fundamental. And judging by the United
States' ongoing detention of individuals in uncertain status around the
world, and its ongoing resistance to allowing Guantánamo Bay detainees
to challenge their detention in federal courts, the administration's basic position remains: Rules can be made "going forward"; on any given day,
those rules may not be available for consideration by a court; and the rights
available in each situation are "unique." In the rush to adjust the balance,
we are abandoning the idea at the core of international human-rights law
that some measures are fixed.

Conceiving our primary post-September 11 challenge as what balance 20
to keep between liberty and security leaves us prone to see links between
liberty and security where they need not exist, and prone to see rights under law as just another weight that can be readily removed from the scale.
In fact, the basic balance between liberty and security in U.S. law was established in some detail centuries ago, at a time when the United States as
an enterprise had never been more vulnerable or less secure. It included a
commitment to the idea that people should be able to know in advance
what the law is, and that if circumstances—like pressing new challenges to
national security—required the laws to be changed, the people would have
a say in how to change them. We have called that commitment the rule of
law. And human rights are meaningless without it.

Thinking Critically

1. Deborah Pearlstein begins this essay by defining, and challenging, two basic warrants (assumptions) that prominent U.S. senators made immediately after the attacks of September 11, 2001. What are those warrants?
   Do you agree with Pearlstein that they are logically deficient?

2. Go to Pearlstein's blog on the trials of detainees at Guantánamo Bay:
   <http://www.humanrightsfirst.org/us_law/detainees/
   military_commission_diary.htm#day1>. She was present at these trials as
   an invited observer and monitor of the proceedings. What are the differences

between her voice in the blog (as a witness) and her voice in this essay? What are the responsibilities of a witness, in contrast with the responsibilities of a news reporter making a broadcast, a trial lawyer presenting closing arguments, or a politician making a speech?

3. How many times does Pearlstein use the word *balance* in this essay? How do the word's connotations change? How does the repetition of *balance,* along with its shifting meaning, shape Pearlstein's argument?

Writing Critically

1. Under what circumstances do "human rights" become negotiable? Select a specific incident *other* than the attacks of September 11, 2001, or the "war on terrorism," and use several different sources to reconstruct the impact of that incident on human rights.

2. Both Deborah Pearlstein and Frank Furedi (in the previous selection) are concerned with security. In what ways do their definitions of *security* complement each other? In what ways do both authors see the emphasis on security as impinging on privacy and civil liberty?

3. What, in Pearlstein's view, is the problem with a "balance metaphor" to describe American security needs after September 11, 2001? Find a metaphor used in contemporary political or cultural rhetoric that does not accurately or logically reflect an actual problem or issue, and write an essay in which you explore the connotative and denotative meanings of the metaphor and the ways in which it is misleading.

When Fear Is a Joint Venture

COREY ROBIN

The author of *Fear: The History of a Political Idea* (2004), Corey Robin is a professor of political science at Brooklyn College and at the Graduate Center of the City University of New York. Robin's academic and research interests include the relationship between fear and freedom, and he has written extensively about contemporary American politics in both academic and mainstream journals. In a 2004 interview with the French newspaper *Le Monde,* Robin noted that "We are, in fact, dependant on what our public and private leaders define as danger or threat. That said, I do not say that Al-Qaeda is not a danger. We all know that it is. However, for me, it's a kind of moral principle: I refuse to let the government dictate to me what I should be afraid of." The following essay was published in the *Washington Post* in October 2004.

Since 9/11, many on the left have accused the Bush administration of ma-   1
nipulating the fear of terrorism for political gain. Democrats denounce
Karl Rove for drawing from a slush fund of popular anxiety to bankroll
the president's reelection. Liberals decry the USA Patriot Act, arguing that
Attorney General John Ashcroft has exploited widespread feelings of vulnerability to reverse decades of progress in the realm of civil liberties. Progressives generally agree that the White House has tried to turn national
security into a mute button, muffling criticism with charges of insufficient
patriotism and warnings about demoralizing the troops.

But fear in the United States is not a government-run monopoly. It's a   2
joint venture between the public and private sector. Sometimes employers
benefit from this collusion, cashing in on the fear of terrorism to restrain
combative unions and dissident employees. Other times the government
benefits, for employers can do what public officials cannot: punish men
and women for their political views. Like so much else in the United States,
fear has been outsourced, and the price is paid in freedom.

While color-coded alerts have little effect on most people's lives, fear can   3
have a real impact when it is leveraged by an employer. In the spring of
2002, for example, shipping companies on the West Coast braced for a bitter showdown with their dockworkers' unions at the negotiating table.
Hoping to blunt labor's ultimate weapon—the strike—the shipping companies joined forces with the Gap, Mattel and Home Depot, which rely on imports from East Asia, and met with officials from the Office of Homeland
Security and the departments of Commerce, Labor and Transportation.

Sympathetic to their concerns, the Bush administration declared the im-   4
pending strike a threat to security and threatened the unions with a declaration of national emergency and the use of federal troops. Though
Defense Secretary Donald Rumsfeld failed to cite any evidence that stopping imports of children's toys from the Philippines would harm the nation's safety—and the dockworkers' unions promised to load and unload
any military shipments even if the ports were closed—the invocation of national security worked. Talk of a strike ceased, and the unions eventually
capitulated.

While in that instance the government mustered the public's fears on   5
behalf of private interests, it has also relied upon private fears—in the
workplaces of even the most high-minded employers—to pursue its goals.
In August, the *New York Times* reported that the American Civil Liberties
Union had signed an agreement promising the government that it would
not employ anyone appearing on official watch lists of suspected supporters of terrorism. Not convicted or even suspected terrorists, but terrorism's
suspected supporters, whose only crime might have been to donate money

to humanitarian groups alleged to support terrorism—or to share a name with someone who had. (Both Teddy Kennedy and Georgia congressman John Lewis found themselves on the list at one point. And in one of those bizarre moments when Kafka becomes comedy, ACLU Executive Director Anthony Romero discovered he was on the list, too.)

Why had the ACLU made this promise? Because it wanted to partici-   6 pate in a government program allowing federal employees to make charitable donations to nonprofit organizations through payroll deductions, and the Bush administration had made refusing to hire anyone on the watch lists a condition of the nonprofits' participation.

As soon as the *Times* exposed the agreement, the ACLU rescinded it.   7 But that didn't end the matter. As Romero said later on National Public Radio, some 2,000 nonprofit organizations—including NPR—receive money through the same contribution program and were expected to sign and comply with the same agreement to police their employees.

Though some might take delight at seeing the nation's premier civil lib-   8 erties organization hoist on its own petard, the ACLU's collusion with the government reveals the dark side of American freedom. For all the legal constraints the Constitution puts on the government, we rarely recognize the ironic by-product of those constraints: the subcontracting of coercion to the private sector. In its search for those who might be conspiring to attack the United States, the government lacked the evidence required by the Bill of Rights to prosecute individuals with suspicious associations and beliefs. So what did the government do? It asked private employers to use their power of hiring and firing—which is not subject to the Bill of Rights—to punish these individuals instead.

It's not just the war on terrorism—with a little help from the Constitu-   9 tion—that drives coercion into the workplace. Employers punish their employees for all sorts of political opinions, even those having nothing to do with national security. Just ask Lynne Gobbell. Last month, *Slate* reported that Gobbell's boss, Phil Geddes, owner of an Alabama company that makes insulation, fired her for driving to work with a Kerry-Edwards bumper sticker on her car.

Gobbell never proselytized on the job, but Geddes was a Bush supporter,   10 who had distributed a flier to his employees explaining why they should reelect the president. Geddes wasn't bothered by his double standard, which allowed him but not Gobbell to campaign. The worksite, after all, was his private property. Nor was he legally in the wrong, although bad publicity apparently led him to offer, through an intermediary, to rehire her. (Gobbell declined.) Strange as it may sound in the land of free speech, employers are generally entitled by law to hire and fire people on the basis of their political views.

At the dawn of American democracy, Alexander Hamilton acknowl- 11
edged that economic sanctions could be a powerful weapon for suppress-
ing unpopular views. "In the general course of human nature," he wrote in
the *Federalist Papers,* "a power over a man's subsistence amounts to a
power over his will." More than two centuries later, Hamilton's insight still
applies; the instruments of the workplace are the favored tools of today's
engineers of opinion. Dissenting individuals are not the only ones who suffer from this intimidation in the workplace. All of us do: When men and
women are not allowed to voice their heterodox beliefs without fear of retribution in the workplace—according to the latest polls, only 22 percent of
Alabama's voters support John Kerry—we are deprived of the information
and diverse views that are critical to democratic deliberation.

There's nothing really new or particularly Republican about this col- 12
laboration between the public and private sector. Back in the 1830s, as
Alexis de Tocqueville traveled around the country, he stopped in Maryland
and asked a distinguished physician why his colleagues publicly professed
their belief in God when they so obviously had "numerous doubts on the
subject of dogma." The man replied that if any doctor admitted he was an
atheist, his "career would almost certainly be broken." Local ministers
would warn parishioners that their doctor was an "unbeliever," and his
practice would soon be finished. While the clergy in Europe used government to defend the faith, their counterparts across the Atlantic enforced belief through the making and breaking of private careers.

In the early years of the Cold War, employers regularly used the fear of 13
communism to stifle unions. Company supervisors kept track of the political beliefs of millions of employees (about 40 percent of the workforce)
and liberal groups swapped political information about their members
with the FBI. So routine—and bipartisan—is this collusion between the
public and private sector that we can give it a name: Fear, American Style.

Fear, American Style is neither part of a nefarious conspiracy nor a di- 14
abolical plot, but the result of people pursuing their interests. It's just business as usual, another day at the office, Adam Smith's Invisible Hand
quietly—and perversely—at work.

Thinking Critically

1. In paragraphs 3 and 4, Corey Robin cites the cooperation between federal agencies and private corporations to stop a labor strike by American dockworkers. Using the Internet, look up information on "Lech
   Walesa" and "Solidarity." Do you notice anything ironic? How does an
   appreciation of this irony change your understanding of Robin's own political viewpoint?

2. What does Robin mean in paragraph 5 when he describes a coincidence as "one of those bizarre moments when Kafka becomes comedy"?

3. What is the ultimate irony that Robin presents in his argument?

Writing Critically

1. Robin, a professor of political science, offers as historical context for his argument the ideas of Alexander Hamilton's *Federalist Papers,* Alexis de Toqueville's *Democracy in America,* and Adam Smith's *Wealth of Nations.* Select one of these texts (all of them are available as online e-text, which makes searching for key phrases such as Smith's "invisible hand" much easier), and in an essay, explain how its author supports (or contradicts) Robin's thesis.

2. Some of the sharpest and most effective political commentary of the past few years has been in the realm of satire—witness Jon Stewart's *The Daily Show* and his best-selling *America: The Book* (2004). Effective satire (like Stewart's) often relies on irony as a rhetorical device; even though Robin's argument is quite serious, he uses irony skillfully to demonstrate certain weaknesses in the logic of the government's position. Select a current controversy and, using irony, write a satirical presentation of both sides of the issue.

The Unreal Thing

ADAM GOPNIK

Adam Gopnik is a staff writer for the weekly magazine *The New Yorker,* to which he has contributed essays and cultural criticism since 1986. From 1995 to 2000 he lived with his family in Paris, writing a series of columns about French life that were later collected in his book *Paris to the Moon* (2000). Gopnik received the National Magazine Award for Essay and Criticism and the George Polk Award for Magazine Reporting. In the following essay, which appeared in *The New Yorker* in May 2003, he explores the phenomenon of the *Matrix* films in the context of post-9/11 American fears. The ways in which "entertainment" culture and political culture reflect each other have long fascinated Gopnik. In a 1996 interview with the French critic Karim Bitar, he noted: "One of the main mistakes we make is to say that there is a cultural ground and a political ground and that they are separate. You have to try and change it not by passing laws but by offering criticism. That's the role of thought. Governments don't exist to change the culture, but that doesn't mean that we don't have to change it as citizens." The full interview is at <http://www.karimbitar.org/gopnik>.

For the past four years, a lot of people have been obsessed with the movie   1
The Matrix. As the sequel, *The Matrix Reloaded,* arrived in theaters
this week, it was obvious that the strange, violent science-fiction film, by
the previously more or less unknown Wachowski brothers, had already inspired both a cult and a craze. (And had made a lot of money into the bargain, enough to fuel two sequels; *Matrix Revolutions* is supposed to be out
in November.) There hasn't been anything quite like it since *2001: A Space
Odyssey,* which had a similar mix of mysticism, solemnity, and mega-
effects. Shortly after its mostly unheralded release, in 1999, *The Matrix* became an egghead *extase.* The Slovenian philosopher Slavoj Zizek's latest
work, *Welcome to the Desert of the Real,* took its title from a bit of dialogue in the film; college courses on epistemology have used *The Matrix* as
a chief point of reference; and there are at least three books devoted to teas-
ing out its meanings. (*Taking the Red Pill: Science, Philosophy and Religion in The Matrix* is a typical title.) If the French philosopher Jean
Baudrillard, whose books—*The Gulf War Did Not Take Place* is one—
popularized the view that reality itself has become a simulation, has not yet
embraced the film, it may be because he is thinking of suing for a screen
credit. (The "desert of the real" line came from him.) The movie, it seemed,
dramatized a host of doubts and fears and fascinations, some half as old as
time, some with a decent claim to be postmodern. To a lot of people, it
looked like a fable: *our* fable.

The first *Matrix*—for anyone who has been living in Antarctica for the past   2
four years—depended on a neatly knotted marriage between a spectacle and a
speculation. The spectacle has by now become part of the common language
of action movies: the amazing "balletic" fight scenes and the slow-motion
aerial display of destruction. The speculation, more peculiar, and even, in its
way, esoteric, is that reality is a fiction, programmed into the heads of sleeping
millions by evil computers. When we meet the hero of the *Matrix* saga, he's a
computer programmer—online name Neo—who works in a generic office
building in a present-day, Chicago-like metropolis. Revelation arrives when
he's recruited by a mysterious guerrilla figure named Morpheus, played by Laurence Fishburne with a baritone aplomb worthy of Orson Welles. Morpheus
offers Neo a choice between two pills, one blue and one red: "You take the
blue pill, the story ends, you wake up in your bed and believe whatever you
want to believe. You take the red pill . . . and I show you how deep the rabbit
hole goes." Neo takes the red pill and wakes up as he really is: a comatose body
in a cocoon, his brain penetrated by a cable that inserts the Matrix, an interactive virtual-reality program, directly into his consciousness. All the people he
has ever known, he realizes, are recumbent in incubators, stacks of identical
clear pods, piled in high towers; the cocooned sleepers have the simulation

piped into their heads by the machines as music is piped into headphones. What they take to be experiences is simply the effect of brain impulses interacting with the virtual-reality program. Guerrilla warriors who have been unplugged from the Matrix survive in an underground city called Zion, and travel in hovercraft to unplug promising humans. Morpheus has chosen to unplug Neo, it turns out, because he believes Neo is the One—the Messiah figure who will see through the Matrix and help free mankind. The first film, which told of Neo's education by Morpheus and his pursuit of the awesomely cute and Matrix-defying Trinity (the rubber-suited Carrie-Anne Moss), ends with Neo seeing the Matrix for what it is: a row of green digits, which he has learned to alter as easily as a skilled player can alter the levels of a video game.

What made the spectacle work was the ingenuity and the attention to detail with which it was rendered. The faintly greenish cast and the curious sterility of life within the Matrix; the reddish grungy reality of Morpheus's ship; the bizarre and convincing interlude with the elderly Oracle; and, of course, those action sequences, the weightless midair battles—few movies have had so much faith in their own mythology. And the actors rose to it, Laurence Fishburne managing to anchor the whole thing in a grandiloquent theatricality. Even Keanu Reeves, bless him, played his part with a stolidity that made him the only possible hero of the film, so slow in his reactions that he seemed perfect for virtual reality, his expressions changing with the finger-drumming time lag of a digital image loading online.   3

If it was the spectacle that made the movie work, though, it was the speculations that made it last in people's heads. It spoke to an old nightmare. The basic conceit of *The Matrix*—the notion that the material world is a malevolent delusion, designed by the forces of evil with the purpose of keeping people in a state of slavery—has a history. It is most famous as the belief for which the medieval Christian sect known as the Cathars fought and died, and in great numbers, too. The Cathars were sure that the material world was a phantasm created by Satan, and that Jesus of Nazareth—their Neo—had shown mankind a way beyond that matrix by standing outside it and seeing through it. The Cathars were fighting a losing battle, but the interesting thing was that they were fighting at all. It is not unusual to take up a sword and die for a belief. It is unusual to take up a sword to die for the belief that swords do not exist.   4

The Cathars, like the heroes of *The Matrix,* had an especially handy rationale for violence: if it ain't real, it can't really bleed. One reason that the violence in *The Matrix*—those floating fistfights, the annihilation of entire squads of soldiers by cartwheeling guerrillas—can fairly be called balletic is that, according to the rules of the movie, what is being destroyed is not real in the first place: the action has the safety of play and the excitement   5 of the apocalyptic. Of course, the destruction of a blank, featureless, mirrored skyscraper by a helicopter, and the massacre of the soldiers who protect it, has a different resonance now than it did in 1999. The notion that some human beings are not really human but, rather, mere slaves, nonhuman ciphers, and therefore expendable, is exactly the vision of the revolutionary hero—and also of the mass terrorist. The Matrix is where all violent fanatics insist that they are living, even when they are not.

It would have been nice if some of that complexity, or any complexity, had made its way into the sequel. But—to get to the bad news—*Matrix Reloaded* is, unlike the first film, a conventional comic-book movie, in places a campy conventional comic-book movie, and in places a ludicrously campy conventional comic-book movie. It feels not so much like *Matrix II* as like *Matrix XIV*—a franchise film made after a decade of increasing grosses and thinning material. The thing that made the Matrix so creepy— the idea of a sleeping human population with a secondary life in a simulated world—is barely referred to in the new movie; in fact, if you hadn't seen the first film, not just the action but the basic premise would be pretty much unintelligible. The first forty-five minutes—set mainly in Zion, that human city buried deep in the earth—are particularly excruciating. Zion seems to be modeled on the parking garage of a giant indoor mall, with nested levels clustered around an atrium. Like every good-guy citadel in every science-fiction movie ever made, Zion is peopled by stern-jawed uniformed men who say things like "And what if you're wrong, God damn it, what then?" and "Are you doubting my command, Captain?" and by short-haired and surprisingly powerful women whose eyes moisten but don't overflow as they watch the men prepare to go off to war. Everybody wears earth tones and burlap and silk, and there are craggy perches from which speeches can be made while the courageous citizens hold torches. (The stuccoed, soft-contour interiors of Zion look like the most interesting fusion restaurant in Santa Fe.)

The only thing setting Zion apart from the good-guy planets in *The Phantom Menace* or *Star Trek* is that it seems to have been redlined at some moment in the mythic past and is heavily populated by people of color. They are all, like Morpheus, grave, orotund, and articulate to the point of prosiness, so that official exchanges in Zion put one in mind of what it must have been like at a meeting at the Afro-American Studies department at Harvard before Larry Summers got to it. (And no sooner has this thought crossed one's mind when—lo! there is Professor Cornel West himself, playing one of the councilors.) Morpheus, winningly laconic in the first film, here tends to speechify, and, in a sequence that passes so far into the mystically absurd that it is almost witty, leads the inhabitants of Zion in a torch-lit orgy, presumably meant to show the machines what humans can do that they can't;

the humans heave and slam well-toned bodies in a giant rave—Plato's Retreat to the last leaping shadow. Neo and Trinity make love while this is going on, and we can see the cable holes up and down Neo's back, like a
fashion-forward appliqué. (Soon, everyone will want them.) No cliché goes
unresisted; there is an annoying street kid who wants Neo's attention, and
a wise councilor with swept-back silver hair (he is played by Anthony
Zerbe, Hal Holbrook presumably having been unavailable) who twinkles
benignly and creases up his eyes as he wanders the city at night by Neo's
side. Smiles gather at the corner of his mouth. He's that kind of wise.

More damagingly, once Zion has been realized and mundanely inhab-   8
ited, most of the magic disappears from the fable; it becomes a cartoon battle between more or less equally opposed forces, and the sense of a
desperately uneven contest between man and machine is gone. The Matrix,
far from being a rigorously imposed program, turns out to be as porous as
good old-fashioned reality, letting in all kinds of James Bond villains. (They
are explained as defunct programs that refused to die, but they seem more
like character ideas that refused to be edited.) Lambert Wilson appears as a
sort of digital Dominique de Villepin—even virtual Frenchmen are now
amoral, the mark of Cain imprinted on their foreheads, so to speak, like a
spot of chocolate mousse. He is called the Merovingian (*Holy Blood, Holy
Grail* having apparently been added to the reading list) and announces that
"choice is an illusion created between zose wis power and zose wisout" as
he constructs a virtual dessert with which he inflames the passion of a virtual
woman. The stunning Monica Bellucci appears as his wife, who sells out his
secrets in exchange for a remarkably chaste kiss from Neo, while Trinity
looks on, smoldering like Betty in an *Archie* comic. (But then Monica is Italian, a member of the coalition of the willing.) Then there are his twin dread-
locked henchmen, dressed entirely in white, who have all the smirking
conviction of Siegfried and Roy. Even the action sequences, which must have
been quite hard to make, remind one of those in the later Bond films; interesting to describe, they are so unbound by any rules except the rule of Now
He'll Jump Off That Fast-Moving Thing Onto the Next Fast-Moving Thing
that they are tedious to watch. A long freeway sequence has the buzzing predictability of the video game it will doubtless become. In the first film, the
rules of reality were bendable, and that was what gave the action its surprises; in the new one there are hardly any rules at all. The idea of a fight between Neo and a hundred identical evil "agents" sounds cool but is
unintentionally comic. Dressed in identical black suits and ties, like the staff
of MCA in the Lew Wasserman era (is that why they're called agents?), they
simultaneously rush Neo and leap on him in a giant scrum; it's like watching
a football team made up of ten-year-olds attempt to tackle Bronko

Nagurski—you know he's going to rise up and shake them off. Neo has become a superhuman power within the Matrix and nothing threatens him. He fights the identical agents for fifteen minutes, practically yawning while he does, and then flies away, and you wonder—why didn't he fly away to start with? As he chops and jabs at his enemies, there isn't the slightest doubt about the outcome, and Keanu Reeves seems merely preoccupied, as though ready to get on his cell phone for a few sage words with Slavoj Zizek. There are a few arresting moments at the conclusion when Neo meets the architect of the Matrix. But by then the spectacle has swept right over the speculation, leaving a lot of vinyl and rubber shreds on the incoming tide.

For anyone who was transfixed by the first movie, watching the new   9 one is a little like being unplugged from the Matrix: What was I experiencing all that time? Could it have been . . . *all a dream?* A reassuring viewing of the old movie suggests that its appeal had less to do with its accessories than with its premise. Could it be that what you took to be your life was merely piped into your brain like experiential Muzak? The question casts a spell even when the spell casters turn out to be more merchandisers than magi.

Long before the first *Matrix* was released, of course, there was a lot of   10 fictional life in the idea that life is a fiction. The finest of American speculators, Philip K. Dick, whose writing has served as the basis of some of the more ambitious science-fiction movies of the past couple of decades (*Blade Runner, Total Recall, Minority Report*), was preoccupied with two questions: How do we know that a robot doesn't have consciousness, and how do we know that we can trust our own memories and perceptions? *Blade Runner* dramatized the first of these two problems, and *The Matrix* was an extremely and probably self-consciously Dickian dramatization of the second. In one of Dick's most famous novels, for instance, *The Three Stigmata of Palmer Erdrich,* a colony of earthmen on Mars, trapped in a miserable life, take an illegal drug that transports them into "Perky Pat Layouts"— miniature Ken and Barbie dollhouses, where they live out their lives in an idealized Southern California. Like Poe, Dick took the science of his time, gave it a paranoid twist, and then became truly paranoid himself. In a long, half-crazy book called *Valis,* he proposed that the world we live in is a weird scramble of information, that a wicked empire has produced thousands of years of fake history, and that the fabric of reality is being ripped by a battle between good and evil. The Dick scholar Erik Davis points out that, in a sequel to *Valis,* Dick even used the term "matrix" in something like a Wachowskian context.

In the academy, too, the age-old topic of radical doubt has acquired re-   11 newed life in recent years. In fact, what's often called the "brain-in-the-vat problem" has practically become its own academic discipline. The philosopher Daniel Dennett invoked it to probe the paradoxes of identity. Robert Nozick, famous as a theorist of the minimal state, used it to ask whether you would agree to plug into an "experience machine" that would give you any experience you desired—writing a great book, making a friend—even though you'd really just be floating in a vat with electrodes attached to your brain. Nozick's perhaps too hasty assumption was that you wouldn't want to plug in. His point was that usually something has to happen in the world, not just in our heads, for our desires to be satisfied. The guerrilla warriors in *The Matrix*, confirming the point, are persuaded that the Matrix is wrong because it isn't "real," and we intuitively side with them. Yet, unlike Nozick, we also recognize that it might be a lot more comfortable to remain within the virtual universe. That's the decision made by a turncoat among the guerrillas, Cypher. (Agents of the "machine world" seal the pact with him over dinner at a posh restaurant: "I know this steak doesn't exist," Cypher tells them, enjoying every calorie-free bite. "I know that when I put it in my mouth the Matrix is telling my brain that it is juicy and delicious. After nine years, you know what I realize? Ignorance is bliss.")

A key feature of *The Matrix* is that all those brains are wired together— that they really can interact with one another. And it was, improbably, the Harvard philosopher and mathematician Hilary Putnam who, a couple of decades back, proposed the essential Matrixian setup: a bunch of brains in a vat hooked up to a machine that was "programmed to give [them] all a *collective* hallucination, rather than a number of separate unrelated hallucinations." Putnam used his Matrix to make a tricky argument about meaning: since words mean what they normally refer to within a community, a member of the vatted-brain community might be telling the truth if it said it was looking at a tree, or, for that matter, at Monica Bellucci. That's because the brains in that vat aren't really speaking our language. What they are speaking, he said, is "vat-English," because by "a tree" they don't mean a tree; they mean, roughly, a tree image. Presumably, by "Monica Bellucci" they mean, "the image of Monica Bellucci in *Malèna*," rather than the image of Monica Bellucci in *Matrix Reloaded*, brains-in-vats having taste and large DVD collections.

Like most thought experiments, the brain-in-the-vat scenario was intended to sharpen our intuitions. But recurrent philosophical examples tend to have a little symbolic halo around them, a touch of their time— those angels dancing on the head of a pin were dancing to a thirteenth-century rhythm. The fact that the brain-in-a-vat literature has grown so abundant, the vat so vast, suggests that it has a grip on our imagination as a story in itself.

And there, in retrospect, might lie the secret of the first *Matrix:* beyond 14
the balletic violence, beyond the cool stunts, the idea that the world we
live in isn't real is one that speaks right now to a general condition. For
the curious thing about the movie was that everybody could grasp the basic setup instantly. Whether it occurs in cult science fiction or academic
philosophy, we seem to be fascinated by the possibility that our world
might not exist. We're not strangers to the feeling that, for much of our
lives, we might just as well *be* brains-in-vats, floating in an amniotic fluid
of simulations. It doesn't just strike us as plausibly weird. It strikes us as
weirdly plausible.

When, in the first film, Neo sees the Matrix for what it is, a stream of 15
green glowing digits, and thus is able to stop bullets by looking at them,
the moment of vision is not simply liberating. It is also spooky and, in a
Dickian way, chilling. This moment is the opposite of the equivalent scene
in *Star Wars,* a quarter century ago, when Luke Skywalker refuses to wear
the helmet that will put him in contact with his targeting machinery, and
decides instead to bliss out and trust the Force, the benevolent vital energy
of the universe. Neo's epiphany is the reverse: the world around him is a
cascade of cold digital algorithms, unfeeling and lifeless. His charge is not
to turn on and tune in but to turn off and tune out.

This moment of discovery—that the world is not merely evil but fake— 16
has become a familiar turn in American entertainment. (*The Truman Show*
does it with stage sets, but the virtual-reality versions are played out in
Dark City and *eXistenZ* and, especially, the fine, frightening film noir *The
Thirteenth Floor,* in which the hero drives to the edge of Los Angeles and
discovers that the landscape beyond is made of the glowing green lines and
honeycombs of a computer graphic—that he has been living his life within
someone else's program.) Even if we don't remotely buy the notion that reality has been drowned by its simulations, we accept it as the melodramatic
expression of a kind of truth. The Grand Guignol is possible only because
the Petit Guignol exists.

There are so many brains in vats around, in fact, that we need to remind 17
ourselves why we don't want to be one. In a long article on the first *Matrix*
film, the Princeton philosopher James Pryor posed the question "What's so
bad about living in the Matrix?," and, after sorting through some possible answers, he concluded that the real problem probably has to do with freedom,
or the lack of it. "If your ambitions in the Matrix are relatively small-scale, like
opening a restaurant or becoming a famous actor, then you may very well be
able to achieve them," Pryor says. "But if your ambitions are larger—e.g., in-
troducing some long-term social change—then whatever progress you make
toward that goal will be wiped out when the simulation gets reset . . . One thing

we place a lot of value on is being in charge of our own lives, not being someone else's slave or plaything. We want to be *politically free.*"

Here's where the first *Matrix* pushed beyond the fun of seeing a richly   18
painted dystopia. Although the movie was made in 1999, its strength as a
metaphor has only increased in the years since. The monopolization of information by vast corporations; the substitution of an agreed-on fiction, imposed from above, for anything that corresponds to our own reality; the
sense that we have lost control not only of our fate but of our small sense of
what's real—all these things can seem part of ordinary life now. ("More Like
The Matrix Every Day" was the title of a recent political column by Farai
Chideya.) In a mood of Dickian paranoia, one can even start to wonder
whether the language we hear constantly on television and talk radio ("the
war on terror," "homeland security," etc.) is a sort of vat-English—a language from which all earthly reference has been bled away. This isn't to say
that any of us yet exist within an entirely fictive universe created by the forces
of evil for the purpose of deluding a benumbed population—not unless you
work for Fox News, anyway. But we know what it's like to be captive to representations of the world that have, well, a faintly greenish cast.

Especially in view of the conventionality of the second film, it's clear   19
that the first film struck so deep not because it showed us a new world but
because it reminded us of this one, and dramatized a simple, memorable
choice between the plugged and the unplugged life. It reminded us that the
idea of free lives is inseparable from the idea of the real thing. Apparently,
we needed the reminder. "Free your mind!," the sixties-ish slogan of the
new film, is too ambitious to be convincing, and betrays the darkness that
made the first film so unusual. "Unplug thy neighbor!," though, still
sounds *just* possible.

Thinking Critically

1. What are the "doubts and fears and fascinations" (paragraph 1) that
   Adam Gopnik argues are represented by the *Matrix* films? To whom do
   those "doubts and fears and fascinations" belong? How does Gopnik use
   those three distinct categories (doubts, fears, fascinations) to structure
   his argument?

2. When writing an essay about a work of art or entertainment a writer must
   be sure to provide enough description of the original work so that a reader
   who might not be familiar with it can follow the essay's argument. How accurate and useful is Gopnik's synopsis of the *Matrix* films? How does he
   make specific connections between moments in the film and other philosophical, political, or cultural circumstances? What is the distinction between a movie review and an essay about a movie?

Writing Critically

1. In paragraph 10, Gopnik says, "Long before the first *Matrix* was released, of course, there was a lot of fictional life in the idea that life is a fiction." Select one or two of the examples (from history, philosophy, or science fiction) of this "idea" that Gopnik cites, and in an essay, explain in greater depth how the example explores the "idea that life is a fiction."

2. Why do you think an essay that explores the "idea that life is a fiction" and the "weirdly plausible" idea that "we might just as well *be* brains-in-vats" (paragraph 13) appears in a chapter about fear and security? Compare Gopnik's conclusions to the "real-world" scenarios described elsewhere in this chapter.

Uncle Sam Is Watching You

DAVID COLE

This review of two recent books about personal privacy and public security appeared in the November 18, 2004, issue of the *New York Review of Books*. This publication was launched in 1963 during a newspaper strike in New York City; its founders envisioned a biweekly magazine that would include not only reviews of books and the arts but extended essays by writers, critics, and intellectuals about politics and current events. (The *New York Review* is where Ralph Nader first published his "manifesto" for consumer justice.) David Cole is a professor at Georgetown University Law Center and is the legal affairs correspondent for the liberal political magazine *The Nation*. In June 2004, Cole appeared on the Fox News talk show *The O'Reilly Factor* to discuss the treatment of detainees at Guantánamo Bay. During the contentious taping, host Bill O'Reilly repeatedly called Cole an "S.O.B."

A Review of *The Intruders: Unreasonable Searches and Seizures from King John to John Ashcroft*, by Samuel Dash, and *The Naked Crowd: Reclaiming Security and Freedom in an Anxious Age*, by Jeffrey Rosen

1.

In October 2003, Congress voted to end Total Information Awareness (TIA), a Pentagon plan designed to analyze vast amounts of computer data about all of us in order to search for patterns of terrorist activity. At the time, the vote in Congress seemed one of the most notable victories for privacy since September 11. Computers record virtually everything we do these days— whom we call or e-mail, what books and magazines we read, what Web sites we search, where we travel, which videos we rent, and everything we buy by credit card or check. The prospect of the military and security agencies constantly trolling through all of this information about innocent citizens in hopes of finding terrorists led Congress to ban spending on the program.

Admittedly, much of the credit for TIA's defeat has to go to the Pentagon's public relations department, which not only gave the program its less than reassuring name, but also came up with a logo consisting of a pyramid topped by a large, digitized eye and the Latin motto *Scientia Est Potentia,* or "Knowledge Is Power." George Orwell and Michel Foucault could hardly have done better. It also helped that the Pentagon's Defense Advanced Research Projects Agency (DARPA), which developed the plan, was headed by John Poindexter, who had been convicted of lying to Congress in the Iran-contra affair, and whose conviction had been overturned on appeal only on a technicality. The vote to kill TIA came shortly after DARPA floated the idea of creating a market for betting on terrorist attacks and other disasters. Still, the fact that Congress rejected TIA seemed to suggest that it was willing to stand up for privacy even in the face of the threat of catastrophic terrorism.   2

But reports of the death of TIA were greatly exaggerated. Federal programs to collect and search vast computer databases for security purposes continue virtually unabated, inside and outside the Pentagon. The congressional ban did not apply to the Pentagon's classified budget, so the military's development of programs to collect and analyze computer data has simply moved behind closed doors. Congress has directed the Department of Homeland Security to develop "data mining and other advanced analytic tools . . . to access, receive and analyze data, detect and identify threats of terrorism against the United States." And with federal funding, several states are cooperating in the Multistate Antiterrorism Regional Information Exchange System, or MATRIX, which links law enforcement records with other government and private databases in order to identify suspected terrorists.   3

The private firm that is running MATRIX, Sesint, based in Florida, previously compiled a "terrorist index" of 120,000 persons using   4

> such factors as age, gender, ethnicity, credit history, "investigational data," information about pilot and driver licenses, and connections to "dirty" addresses known to have been used by other suspects.

Thus, despite the apparent victory for civil libertarians in stopping TIA itself, data mining remains a central instrument in the government's response to the threat of terrorism. As a special committee appointed by Defense Secretary Donald Rumsfeld wrote in its recently released report, "TIA was not the tip of the iceberg, but rather one small specimen in a sea of icebergs."

"Data mining," the computerized analysis of extensive electronic data-   5
bases about private individuals for patterns of suspicious activity, is just
one example of the threats to privacy that Americans have faced following
the terrorist attacks of September 11, 2001. Since then, through the USA
Patriot Act and various executive initiatives, the government has authorized official monitoring of attorney-client conversations, wide-ranging secret searches and wiretaps, the collection of Internet and e-mail addressing
data, spying on religious services and the meetings of political groups, and
the collection of library and other business records. All this can be done
without first showing probable cause that the people being investigated are
engaged in criminal activity, the usual threshold that must be passed before
the government may invade privacy.

Of course, these laws and policies merely authorize such snooping.   6
They do not compel it. The administration's message since September 11
has been "trust us." President Bush and Vice President Dick Cheney say
that critics have cited "no abuses" of the USA Patriot Act, as if to suggest
that absence of visible abuse shows that we can trust them. But the "no
abuses" defense is fundamentally misleading in two respects.

First, there have in fact been abuses of the Patriot Act. In June, a jury   7
in Idaho acquitted Sami Omar al-Hussayen, an Idaho student charged under the Patriot Act for aiding terrorism because he had a Web site that included links to other Web sites that included some speeches endorsing
terrorism. The government never even alleged, much less proved, that al-
Hussayen had intended to further any terrorist activity. Under its theory,
any posting of a link to a Web site advocating terrorism is a violation of
the Patriot Act's ban on providing "expert advice and assistance" to designated "terrorist organizations." If that's true, *The New York Times* could
be prosecuted for including a link to Osama bin Laden's latest recorded
message, and it would be no defense to show that the link was posted solely
for educational purposes.

In another case involving the same Patriot Act provision, the Hu-   8
manitarian Law Project, a human rights group in Los Angeles, faces the
threat of criminal prosecution for advising a Kurdish group in Turkey on
protecting human rights. The project has provided the training precisely
to discourage violence and to encourage the pursuit of lawful means to
advance Kurdish rights in Turkey. Yet the administration claims that it
can prosecute such human rights advocacy as "material support of terrorism," even though it consists solely of speech and is not intended to
promote violence. The courts have thus far ruled that the Patriot Act's
application to such activity is unconstitutional, but the Bush administration is appealing.

Similarly ominous is the case of Khader Hamide and Michel Shehadeh, 9 two longstanding permanent resident aliens from Palestine now in Los Angeles.[1] They have lived in the US for more than twenty-five and thirty years, respectively, and have never been charged with a crime. The administration is trying to deport them under the Patriot Act for having distributed magazines of a PLO faction in Los Angeles during the 1980s. The government does not dispute that it was entirely lawful to distribute the magazines at the time, or that the magazines are themselves legal and available in libraries across the country. Yet it claims that under the Patriot Act, it can retroactively deport the two Palestinians for engaging in activity that would plainly be protected by the First Amendment if engaged in by US citizens.

Still another provision of the Patriot Act allows the government to freeze 10 the assets of any person or entity it chooses, simply by claiming that he or it is under "investigation." It can then defend the action in court with secret evidence, presented to the court in a closed session but not disclosed to the entity or person whose assets have been frozen. The Bush administration has used this authority to close down three of the largest Muslim charities in the United States, without ever having to prove that they actually financed terrorism, and without affording the charities an opportunity to defend themselves.

In July, the administration invoked the Patriot Act to deny entry to Tariq 11 Ramadan, a highly respected Swiss-born Muslim scholar. Ramadan, a moderate hired by Notre Dame to fill a chair in international peace studies, was apparently excluded under a Patriot Act ban on those who "endorse terrorism." The administration has refused to specify his allegedly offending words.

And in September, a federal court in New York ruled that the FBI's en- 12 forcement of still another Patriot Act provision squarely violated the First and Fourth Amendments. The court ruled that the provision, which authorizes the FBI to compel Internet service providers to turn over information about their customers, is invalid because it prohibits the provider from disclosing to anyone—even a lawyer—that the FBI request was made, and effectively precludes any judicial review.

So the first problem with the administration's claim that there have 13 been no abuses under the Patriot Act is that it is simply false. There have been plenty of abuses.

The second problem is more insidious. Many of the Patriot Act's most 14 controversial provisions involve investigative powers that are by definition secret, making it literally impossible for abuses to be uncovered. For example, the act expanded the authority to conduct wiretaps and searches under the Foreign Intelligence Surveillance Act (FISA) without having to show probable cause of criminal activity. We know from a government report that the number of FISA searches has dramatically increased since the

Patriot Act was passed, and for the first time now exceeds the number of conventional wiretaps authorized in criminal cases. Yet that's all we know, because everything else about FISA searches and wiretaps is secret.

The target of a FISA search is never notified, unless evidence from the search is subsequently used in a criminal prosecution, and even then the defendant cannot see the application for the search, and therefore cannot test its legality in court. When the attorney general uses conventional criminal wiretaps, he is required to file an extensive report listing the legal basis for each wiretap, its duration, and whether it resulted in a criminal charge or conviction. But no such information is required under FISA. The annual report detailing use of the criminal wiretap authority exceeds one hundred pages; the report on the use of FISA is a one-page letter.

Another provision of the Patriot Act radically expands the government's ability to obtain personal business records without showing probable cause. Before the Patriot Act was passed, the government had to limit its inquiries to a specific set of financial, phone, and travel records, and these could be obtained only if the target was an "agent of a foreign power." The Patriot Act expanded the definition of records that may be seized, so that it now includes, among other things, library and bookstore records and medical files. And it eliminated the requirement that the person whose records are sought be an "agent of a foreign power." Now the government can get anyone's records. Here, too, the authority is veiled in secrecy. The Patriot Act makes it a crime for the person or organization ordered to produce records to tell anyone about the request. The act does not require the government to notify people whose records have been reviewed, and does not require that any report of its activities be made available to the public.

The Internet service provider that brought the successful challenge to the Patriot Act described above had to violate the law's nondisclosure provision to do so, and the lawsuit itself had to be filed in secret until the court allowed its existence to be acknowledged.

The administration's challenge to critics to come forward with examples of abuse under the Patriot Act is therefore disingenuous. The most controversial provisions contain legal requirements of secrecy that make it literally impossible to provide such examples. Moreover, when the House and Senate Judiciary Committees have requested even the most general information about how the Patriot Act authorities have been used, the administration has refused to supply it.

As Elaine Scarry has written, the government since September 11 has asserted that more and more of the lives of citizens must be open to scrutiny, while simultaneously insisting that more and more of its own operations have to be kept secret.[2] Yet a healthy democracy depends on exactly the opposite—

transparency in government and respect for personal privacy. That is why, following Watergate, Congress in 1974 simultaneously enacted the Privacy Act, which strictly limits federal collection and use of information about its citizens, and expanded the Freedom of Information Act, which gives citizens access to information about their government. Supreme Court Justice Lewis Powell defended the essential role of privacy in a democracy in a landmark 1972 decision invalidating warrantless domestic security wiretaps:

> The price of lawful public dissent must not be a dread of subjection to an unchecked surveillance power. Nor must the fear of unauthorized official eavesdropping deter vigorous citizen dissent and discussion of Government action in private conversation. For private dissent, no less than public discussion, is essential in our free society.

As we all learned on September 11, improved technology has made it eas- 20
ier for terrorists to coordinate their attacks around the world. If improved technology might also help us detect and prevent the next terrorist attack from occurring, we surely must explore those possibilities. But the increased ability to monitor dangerous activity in the digitized age necessarily carries with it the increased ability to monitor political dissent, and history suggests that monitoring the one may quickly lead to monitoring the other. In the interest of identifying terrorists, the Justice Department after World War I created a Radical Alien Division to monitor and track subversive foreigners. When a series of terrorist bombings struck in the summer of 1919, that division responded with the Palmer Raids, in which thousands of foreign nationals were rounded up, denied lawyers, interrogated incommunicado, and issued deportation orders, not for their involvement in the bombings—the bombers were never found—but for their political affiliations.

The fear of communism in the cold war led the FBI to monitor and main- 21
tain files on hundreds of thousands of Americans, including politicians, judges, civil rights activists, and anti-war demonstrators. Before the Republican National Convention in New York, FBI agents confronted peaceful political activists with threats of prosecution if they failed to disclose any information about possible unlawful demonstrations. Such surveillance and harassment has a profoundly chilling effect on people's willingness to engage in the political activity that is essential to a vital democracy. If the threat to privacy seems abstract by comparison to the threat of a terrorist attack, consider what J. Edgar Hoover might have done had he had a program like TIA.

2.

How, then, should the tensions between privacy and security in the war on 22
terrorism be resolved, and who is best situated to strike that balance—the courts, Congress, the executive branch, or the people?

Two books by prominent Washington law professors put forward dif- 23
ferent views about how best to answer these questions. *The Intruders,* by
the late former chief counsel to the Senate's Watergate committee and
Georgetown law professor Sam Dash, who died in May, is a passionate
short history of the Constitution's principal safeguard of privacy, the
Fourth Amendment prohibition on unreasonable searches and seizures.
His book presents a tale of two courts—the Warren Court of the 1950s and
1960s, which aggressively expanded the protection of privacy, and today's
Rehnquist Court, which has just as aggressively decimated those rights.
Like the great lawyer he was, Dash uses his stories to argue persuasively for
the resurrection of meaningful judicial safeguards.

The Naked Crowd, by Jeffrey Rosen, a professor at George Washington 24
University School of Law, considers the political, financial, and psychological
factors that are likely to shape the law of privacy in the decades to come.
Rosen spends less time on the law as such, and more on the social forces at
play in the Internet age; our privacy, he argues, is threatened not only by government programs like TIA but by the public's low estimate of the value of
privacy. Rosen is skeptical about the courts' willingness to protect privacy, but
guardedly optimistic about Congress's ability to do so.

In his book, Dash reminds us that real safeguards against official intru- 25
sion into the lives and affairs of the people took centuries to develop. He
notes, for example, that the Magna Carta did not bar the king from searching private homes whenever he wanted. And until 1961 the US Constitution's protections against unreasonable searches and seizures did not extend
to state and local police, who carry out over 90 percent of law enforcement.
In that year, the Supreme Court first applied the "exclusionary rule" to the
states, meaning that evidence obtained in violation of the Fourth Amendment had to be excluded from the case against a defendant. Similarly, the
Court did not give indigent defendants the right to appointed lawyers until
1963, and did not create Miranda rights in police interrogations until 1966.

There are good reasons why the rights of privacy and liberty flourished 26
in the civil rights era. That period, perhaps more than any other, demonstrated the danger of unconstrained law enforcement, as Southern police
and the FBI alike harassed and prosecuted civil rights activists, using the
criminal law as a means to monitor, regulate, and penalize dissent.

Dash demonstrates, however, that almost as soon as the Fourth Amend- 27
ment was extended to the states, the Supreme Court under Chief Justices
Burger and Rehnquist began whittling away its protections. The Court created many exceptions to the "exclusionary rule" in the 1970s, permitting
illegally obtained evidence to be used, for example, in grand jury, immigration, and civil tax proceedings. In 1978, the Court allowed the government

to use illegally obtained evidence to incriminate anyone other than the person whose privacy rights were violated. In 1984, it ruled that as long as the police obtained a search warrant, the exclusionary rule ought not apply, even if the warrant itself was illegal. These exceptions dramatically weakened Fourth Amendment protections by telling police that they can use illegally obtained evidence for a wide variety of purposes.

The Court under Burger and Rehnquist also directly relaxed the requirements of   28
the Fourth Amendment, allowing a great many kinds of searches without warrants or probable cause at all. Most of these changes were made in the context of the "war on drugs." Because narcotics are easy to conceal and there are often no complaining witnesses to drug crimes, the usual requirement that the police show probable cause that a person possesses an illegal substance before they can search him posed a considerable obstacle to enforcing drug laws. The Court accordingly relaxed the Constitution's requirements. But if the Fourth Amendment could not withstand the pressures of the war on drugs, how is it likely to fare in the war on terrorism?

Both Rosen and Dash express particular concern about data mining,   29
which they compare to the "general warrants" that allowed the British colonial government to search anyone's home, without having any prior ground for suspicion. Like "general warrants," data mining permits officials to search the private computer records of innocent people without any specific basis of suspicion. Objections to "general warrants" inspired the Fourth Amendment; yet the Framers could not have contemplated computerized searches of extensive public and private databases. And therefore, Dash suggests, it is up to the Supreme Court to extend Fourth Amendment principles to modern practices.

Ironically, the Supreme Court decision that is widely credited with   30
adapting the Fourth Amendment to the twentieth century now threatens to render it powerless to regulate data mining and other modern surveillance techniques in the twenty-first. In its 1967 decision *Katz v. United States,* the Supreme Court reversed forty years of precedent and ruled that the Fourth Amendment's prohibition on unreasonable searches and seizures applies to electronic eavesdropping and wiretapping. Federal officials had placed a listening device on a phone booth used by Charles Katz and had overheard him discussing illegal gambling activities. They did not obtain a warrant, because in previous decisions, the Supreme Court had ruled that the Fourth Amendment was not implicated so long as the government's investigatory tactics did not invade a person's property. Since Katz had no "property interest" in the phone booth, the federal government reasoned, there was no need to obtain a warrant to listen in on his phone call.

The Court in the *Katz* case held that the Fourth Amendment "protects   31
people, not places." Under the new approach, the Fourth Amendment is vi-

olated whenever the police invade an individual's "reasonable expectation of privacy," regardless of property rights. Since people reasonably expect their phone conversations to be private, the police cannot listen in without a warrant and probable cause.

The *Katz* decision has long been hailed for recognizing the need to adapt 32 the Fourth Amendment to advances in technology. Once phones could be tapped without going anywhere near a caller's property, the Court's property-based approach no longer made sense. Nothing less than a major shift in Fourth Amendment jurisprudence was required, and *Katz* provided it.

Today, however, a second and equally momentous shift is needed. The de- 33 velopment of computer technologies threatens to radically alter the balance between privacy and security. Computers make it possible to find, store, exchange, retrieve, and analyze vast amounts of information about our private lives in ways that previously were unthinkable. But while the Court's ruling in *Katz* freed Fourth Amendment doctrine from its moorings in antiquated notions of property, its emphasis on "reasonable expectations of privacy" left privacy vulnerable to future advances in technology. As technology makes it increasingly easy to invade spaces that used to be private through the use of enhanced listening, viewing, and other sensing devices, "expectations of privacy" and the protection of the Fourth Amendment may be radically reduced.

The Rehnquist Court's most disturbing application of the *Katz* ap- 34 proach is its determination that people have no "reasonable expectation of privacy" concerning any information they share with others. When we convey information to another person, the Court has reasoned, we assume the risk that the person will share it with the government. On this theory, people have no expectation of privacy when they dial phone numbers, surf the Web, make a credit card purchase, put out their garbage, or talk with people they think are their friends but are in fact informants. As a result, the Fourth Amendment imposes no restriction on the government obtaining such information and subjecting it to searches for suspicious behavior, even when it has no good reason to suspect a person of wrongdoing.

Before the computer, the government's ability to collect and exploit 35 such information was limited. In the future, the possibilities are likely to be unlimited. Computer searches can be used to identify "suspicious" patterns based on peoples' reading habits, travel, Web surfing, and cell phone records, not to mention their age, sex, race, and religion.

The Court's "third-party disclosure" doctrine is as inapt for the com- 36 puter age as its property-based approach was for wiretapping. It is simply wrong to equate sharing information with a private corporation as a prerequisite to having a phone or e-mail line, and sharing that information with the government. It is one thing for AOL to know what Web sites you

We're watching you New technologies, such as this iris scanning kiosk, are being used to confirm identity and allow access to an increasing number of workplaces and airports.

have searched; it is another matter entirely for the federal government to have that information. AOL can't lock you up, and has less reason to harass you for your political views.

As Justice John Marshall Harlan argued in a separate opinion in the 37 *Katz* case, the test of whether the Fourth Amendment is violated should not be merely whether, as a factual matter, society expects a given form of communication to be private, but whether maintaining the privacy of that communication from unwarranted government intrusion is essential to the workings of democracy. On that view, constitutional privacy under the Fourth Amendment is not an objective fact wholly captive to technology, but a social value that we choose to protect despite technological advances.

Jeffrey Rosen suggests that the threats to privacy come not only from 38 technological advances and the courts' failure to confront them, but also from public attitudes. Surveying a wide range of psychological literature, Rosen argues that people are susceptible to powerful irrational fears that compromise their ability to protect their own interests in preserving privacy. Most people, he claims, have "trouble distinguishing improbable events," such as terrorist attacks, "which tend to be the most memorable, from mundane events, which are more likely to repeat themselves." They therefore demand "draconian and symbolic but often poorly designed laws and technologies of surveillance and exposure to eliminate the risks that are, by their nature, difficult to reduce." At the same time, many Americans in the modern age seem to crave exposure more than privacy, as demonstrated, he argues, by the increasing popularity of reality TV, Web logs, and advice books about how to "market" oneself.

The private market only reinforces these tendencies. Rosen shows that 39 the high-tech industry has incentives both to encourage public anxiety about terror threats and to compete for the public dollars that will reward technological "solutions" to the demand for total security. Security is a growth industry; a speaker at a trade electronics forum in Las Vegas estimated that spending on security technologies, including listening devices and databases, will increase by 30 percent a year, reaching $62 billion a year in 2006. Rosen quotes Larry Ellison, Oracle's CEO, who boasts that in the name of advancing national security, his company will create a global database within the next twenty years, "and we're going to track everything."

Rosen agrees with Dash that Fourth Amendment doctrine does not ad- 40 equately protect privacy in today's high-tech world; but he considers it a waste of time to look to the courts for relief. In his view, history shows that Congress is better situated to protect privacy. While the Supreme Court has radically diluted the protection of privacy and allowed government access to financial and other data through its "third-party disclosure" doctrine, Congress has enacted many statutes protecting privacy despite the Court's decisions, including the Privacy Act, the Fair Credit Reporting Act, the Right to Financial Privacy Act, and the Health Insurance Portability and Accountability Act. These laws restrict government access to financial and health-related data, and impose limits on the government's recording of political communications and other First Amendment activities.

Rosen's confidence in the political process is paradoxical, however, since 41 he also believes that the public today is more interested in publicity than in privacy, and that both the public and the commercial markets favor security over privacy. The only sure thing about Congress is that it will respond to public opinion and market forces. If there is no possibility of increasing the public's concern about privacy, there is also little hope for Congress.

This brings us back to Dash's plea that the courts intervene on behalf of privacy. Recognizing the risk that the public and the political process may disregard fundamental rights in times of crisis, the Founders protected those values in a constitution that is difficult to change, and made it enforceable by judges with life tenure. The courts have often failed to live up to their responsibility to protect the Bill of Rights but that is no reason not to hold them to it. If Dash may expect too much from the courts, Rosen asks for too little. 42

The Supreme Court's recent decisions rejecting the Bush administration's sweeping assertion of unchecked authority to lock up human beings indefinitely without trial or hearing illustrate this point. Congress took no steps whatever to confront the President on behalf of the six hundred men held at Guantánamo or the three men held in a brig in South Carolina. Whatever the limitations of its recent decisions, it took the Supreme Court to challenge the President. 43

The ultimate defender of liberty, however, is neither the Court nor Congress, but the people. In 1931 Judge Learned Hand famously warned Yale Law School graduates that 44

> Liberty lies in the hearts of men and women; when it dies there, no constitution, no law, no court can save it. . . . While it lies there it needs no constitution, no law, no court to save it.

Like many memorable quotes, Hand's warning sacrifices nuance for rhetoric. The Constitution, the law, and the courts all serve to remind us of (and therefore to reinforce) our collective commitment to liberty.

But Hand was surely right that we cannot rely *exclusively* on constitutions, courts, or laws. In that light, perhaps the most promising development since September 11 for those who care about principles of liberty and privacy has been the grassroots campaign of the Bill of Rights Defense Committee. The committee was formed immediately after the Patriot Act was passed, by civil rights activists in Amherst, Massachusetts, who had what may have seemed the wildly impractical idea of getting local city and town councils to pass resolutions condemning the civil liberties abuses in the act. The committee began its campaign in the places one might expect—Amherst, Northampton, Santa Monica, Berkeley. But today, more than 340 jurisdictions across the country have adopted such resolutions, including legislatures in four states—Vermont, Alaska, Maine, and Hawaii— and many of the nation's biggest cities, including New York, Los Angeles, Chicago, Dallas, Philadelphia, and Washington, D.C.[3] 45

The resolutions typically condemn not only the surveillance provisions of the Patriot Act—particularly the surveillance of libraries and private records—but also the administration's tactics of mass preventive detention of noncitizens, open-ended imprisonment of "enemy combatants," ethnic pro- 46 filing, and denials of access to lawyers. Although the resolutions don't have much legal effect, they have huge symbolic and organizing value. Each time a resolution is placed on the agenda of a city council, it provides an opportunity to educate the public about the lengths to which the Bush administration has already gone, about the fundamental values that underlie our constitutional commitments, and about the importance of ordinary people standing up and being heard. While the campaign has not had much attention in the national press and has been largely ignored on television, local politicians and active members of both parties have become well aware of it. And the campaign has helped to create a vast network of citizens concerned about liberty and privacy and ready and willing to speak up in their defense.

The quiet success of the Bill of Rights Defense Committee's campaign   47
may well explain the Bush administration's failure thus far to introduce most of what has been dubbed "Patriot II," a draft of which was leaked in February 2003. Among other things, that bill called for presumptively stripping US citizens of their citizenship if they were found to have supported a "terrorist organization." It would also have given the attorney general unreviewable power to deport any nonnationals—presumably including citizens shorn of their citizenship—who, in his opinion, threaten our "national defense, foreign policy, or economic interests."

The campaign of the Bill of Rights Defense Committee may also explain   48
the national tour Ashcroft launched last summer to promote and defend the Patriot Act. When that act was passed six weeks after the September 11 attacks, the vote in the Senate was 98–1.[4] The attorney general doesn't need to waste his time defending a statute with that kind of support. But it has lost much of that support, thanks in large part to the Bill of Rights Defense Committee. Its campaign also likely had an effect in prompting virtually all of the Democratic presidential candidates to condemn the Patriot Act; John Kerry is probably the first presidential candidate from a major party who has run *against* an anti-terrorism law.

Efforts like those of the Bill of Rights Defense Committee underscore the   49
realities of American politics. If there is any hope for Congress, the courts, or even, in another administration, the executive branch, to do something about preserving privacy in the post–September 11 era, ordinary people will have to be mobilized to express their concerns in public. At the same time, the erosion of personal privacy and the erection by the government of walls of secrecy make public debate and resistance all the more difficult and risky. Dash and Rosen argue eloquently for the critical need to protect privacy if we are to preserve democracy. They disagree about the institutions most likely to provide those protections. But they agree that it is up to us to hold our government accountable to the values that gave it birth and justify its very existence.

Notes

[1]I represent both men as well as the Humanitarian Law Project, mentioned above.

[2]Elaine Scarry, "Resolving to Resist," *Boston Review*, February/March 2004.

[3]For details on the campaign, see the Bill of Rights Defense Committee's Web site, www.bordc.org, and the ACLU's report, "Independence Day 2003: Main Street America Fights the Federal Government's Insatiable Appetite for New Powers in the Post 9/11 Era," at www.aclu.org.

[4]Only Wisconsin Senator Russell Feingold voted against it.

Thinking Critically

1. David Cole begins his review of two books about privacy, secrecy, and security by describing different symbols and acronyms used by government and private security agencies. What is the effect of these symbols and acronyms? Is Cole's purpose ironic?

2. "USA Patriot Act" itself an acronym. Go online and find the full text of the USA Patriot Act. What do the letters of the acronym stand for? The full text of the USA Patriot Act is available at the website of the Electronic Privacy Information Center: <http://www.epic.org/privacy/terrorism/hr3162.html>.

3. In what ways does Cole's essay function as a "book review," and in what ways is it an essay that uses the books by Samuel Dash and Jeffrey Rosen to advance Cole's own arguments? What do you expect from a book review?

Writing Critically

1. In an essay, compare Adam Gopnik's observations about the *Matrix* movies and American paranoia with the "real-life" MATRIX that David Cole describes. How does a comparison of these two essays enhance the arguments of each individual author? Are you more inclined, or less inclined, to give credence to either Gopnik (his article precedes Cole's) or Cole after reading these two essays?

2. Describe the rhetoric of the USA Patriot Act. For whom is it written? How would you characterize Cole's critique of it? The full text is available at <http://www.epic.org/privacy/terrorism/hr3162.html>.

3. In paragraph 19, Cole asserts that "a healthy democracy depends on . . . transparency in government and respect for personal privacy." Do you agree or disagree? Be sure to cite at least one additional source in your argument.

Arab and Muslim America: A Snapshot

SHIBLEY TELHAMI

> Previous essays in this chapter deal broadly with issues
> of safety and security in American culture and politics
> after September 11, 2001. In this and following essays,
> the impact of these broader, more abstract practices and
> policies is explored from the perspective of the individu-
> als directly affected. Shibley Telhami is the Anwar Sadat
> Professor for Peace and Development at the University
> of Maryland, a member of the Council on Foreign Rela-
> tions, and a board member of Human Rights Watch.
> Telhami was born in 1951 in a small, remote Arab Is-
> raeli village. His family was Arab Christian; the majority
> of his neighbors were Druse, an independent derivative
> of Islam. Telhami describes the religious diversity of his
> childhood village (Druse, Muslim, Christians, and Jews
> all lived cooperatively, perhaps because of the village's
> remoteness) as one reason why he believes in the possi-
> bility of a peaceful resolution of the Israel-Palestine con-
> flict. Telhami is a Nonresident Visiting Fellow at the
> Brookings Institution, a nonpartisan independent Wash-
> ington, D.C., think tank that provides political and pub-
> lic policy analysis to the government, the public, and the
> press. This essay first appeared in the *Brookings Review*
> in the Winter 2002 issue.

Two Partially Overlapping Communities

There is much that's misunderstood about Arabs and Muslims in Amer-   1
ica. Although the two communities share a great deal, they differ significantly in their make-up. Most Arabs in America are not Muslim, and most
Muslims are not Arabs. Most Arab Americans came from Lebanon and
Syria, in several waves of immigration beginning at the outset of the 20th
century. Most Muslim Americans are African American or from South Asia.
Many of the early Arab immigrants assimilated well in American society.
Arab-American organizations are fond of highlighting prominent Americans
of at least partial Arab descent: Ralph Nader, George Mitchell, John Sununu,
Donna Shalala, Spencer Abraham, Bobby Rahal, Doug Flutie, Jacques
Nasser, Paul Anka, Frank Zappa, Paula Abdul, among many others. Like
other ethnic groups in America, Arabs and Muslims have produced many
successful Americans whose ethnic background is merely an afterthought.

Arab Americans now number more than 3 million, Muslims roughly 6   2
million (though estimates range from 3 million to 10 million). The income
of Arab Americans is among the highest of any American ethnic group—
second only to that of Jewish Americans. Arab Americans have become increasingly politicized over the years. According to a recent survey,
proportionately more Arab Americans contribute to presidential candidates than any other ethnic group—and the groups surveyed included
Asian Americans, Italian Americans. African Americans, Hispanic Americans, and Jewish Americans. Over the past decade especially, Arab-
American political clout has increased. Although Arab Americans were
long shunned by political candidates, President Clinton became the first sitting president to speak at conferences of Arab-American organizations,
and both President Clinton and President Bush have normalized ongoing
consultations with Arab- and Muslim-American leaders. In the fall 2000
election, presidential candidates sought the support of Arab Americans,
not only for campaign contributions, but also as swing voters in key states,
especially Michigan. The September 11 tragedy, coming just as Arab-
American political clout was ascendant, has provided a real test for the
community's role in American society and politics.

Impact of September 11

For Arab and Muslim leaders, the terrorist crisis has been like no other. It   3
has forced them to contemplate profoundly their identity. Are they Arabs
and Muslims living in America, or are they Americans with Arab and Muslim background? The answer came within hours after the terrorist attacks.
Major Arab and Muslim organizations issued statements strongly condemning the attacks, refusing to allow their typical frustrations with issues
of American policy in the Middle East to become linked to their rejection
of the terror. Rarely have Arab and Muslim organizations in the United
States been so assertive.

The enormity of the horror, the Middle Eastern background of the ter-   4
rorists, and the terrorists' attempt to use religion to justify their acts have
inevitably led to episodes of discrimination against Arabs and Muslims, as
well as against those, such as Sikhs, who resemble them. But the support
that both Arabs and Muslims received from thousands of people and organizations far outweighed the negative reaction. Arab and Muslim organizations were flooded with letters and calls of empathy from leaders
and ordinary Americans, including many Jewish Americans, for most understood that at stake were the civil liberties of all Americans.

In large part, the public reaction was a product of quick decisions and   5
statements by President Bush and members of his cabinet, members of

Congress from both parties, and local political leaders. The president in particular acted quickly to make two central points that seem to have resonated with most of the public. The first was that the terrorists did not represent Islam and that Osama bin Laden must not be allowed to turn his terror into a conflict between Islam and the West. The second was that Muslim and Arab Americans are loyal Americans whose rights must be respected. Bush's early appearance at a Washington, D.C., mosque with Muslim-American leaders underlined the message.

The message seems to have gotten through. Despite the fears that many   6
Americans now associate with people of Middle-Eastern background, a survey conducted in late October by Zogby International found that most Americans view the Muslim religion positively and that the vast majority of Arabs and Muslims approve the president's handling of the crisis. (Among Arab Americans, 83 percent give President Bush a positive performance rating.) Moreover, 69 percent of Arab Americans support "an all-out war against countries which harbor or aid terrorists."

Certainly, the events of September 11 will intensify the debate within   7
the Arab and Muslim communities in America about who they are and what their priorities should be. One thing is already clear. Although both communities have asserted their American identity as never before and although 65 percent of Arab Americans feel embarrassed because the attacks were apparently committed by people from Arab countries, their pride in their heritage has not diminished. The October survey found that 88 percent of Arab Americans are extremely proud of their heritage. So far, however, the terrorist attacks have not affected the priorities of the Arab public in America as might be expected, given Arab Americans' deep fear of discrimination.

Typically, Arab-American organizations highlight such domestic issues   8
as secret evidence and racial profiling and such foreign policy issues as Jerusalem, Iraq, and the Palestinian-Israeli conflict. While Arab Americans, like other minorities, are involved in all American issues and are divided as Democrats and Republicans, as groups they inevitably focus on issues about which they tend to agree. The situation is no different from that of American Jews, who are also diverse, but whose organizations largely focus on issues of common interest.

Given the fear of profiling that Arab Americans had even before September, one would expect this issue to have become central for most of   9
them since September 11. And for many it certainly has. Arab-American organizations, especially, have focused on it. But the findings of the Zogby poll among Arab Americans in October were surprising. Although 32 percent of Arab Americans reported having personally experienced

discrimination in the past because of their ethnicity, and although 37 percent said they or their family members had experienced discrimination since September 11, 36 percent nevertheless supported profiling of Arab Americans, while 58 percent did not. Surprisingly, 54 percent of Arab Americans believed that law enforcement officials are justified in engaging in extra questioning and inspections of people with Middle Eastern accents or features.

Though their views on profiling have been mixed since September 11, Arab Americans have been considerably more unanimous on one subject—the need to resolve the Palestinian-Israeli dispute. Seventy-eight percent of those surveyed agreed that "a U.S. commitment to settle the Israeli-Palestinian dispute would help the president's efforts in the war against terrorism." Although most Arab Americans are Christian and mostly from Lebanon and Syria—and only a minority are Palestinians—their collective consciousness has been affected by the Palestinian issue in the same way that Arab consciousness in the Middle East has been affected. In a survey I commissioned in five Arab states (Lebanon, Syria, United Arab Emirates, Saudi Arabia, and Egypt) last spring, majorities in each country consistently ranked the Palestinian issue as "the single most important issue to them personally." The role of this issue in the collective consciousness of many Arabs and Muslims worldwide is akin to the role that Israel has come to play in contemporary Jewish identity.

Like all Americans since September 11, Arab and Muslim Americans are searching for solutions to terrorism. Like all Americans, they are also finding new meaning in aspects of their identity to which they might have given little thought a few short months ago.

Thinking Critically

1. Go to the Brookings Institution website at <http://www.brookings.edu>. Who is the audience for the *Brookings Review,* and what might Shibley Telhami's purpose have been in publishing this article when he did?

2. An extended interview with Telhami is at the website of the Institute of International Studies at the University of California at Berkeley: <http://globetrotter.berkeley.edu/people/Telhami/telhami-con1.html>. How does knowing about Telhami's background influence your reading of this essay? Are you surprised that he does not include more personal background and perspective here?

3. What are Telhami's findings about racial profiling and other "security" measures put into place after September 11, 2001? Are these findings what you would expect after having read earlier essays in this chapter?

Writing Critically

1. Do you identify with any particular religion or ethnicity? How does your affiliation with that group influence your perspective on current events? In an
essay, describe how your personal background influences your perspective
on issues of political and public interest.

2. Do you believe that politicians make any particular effort to reach out to
your economic, religious, or ethnic constituency? What, if any, is the impact
of those efforts on your political engagement? As you draft your essay,
make a conscious decision about whether or not to write from a first-
person perspective.

Fear in the Open City

ANIKA RAHMAN | This essay appeared on the op-ed page of the *New York Times* on September 19, 2001. Rahman graduated from Columbia Law School in 1990 and received a certificate, with honors, in international and foreign law from Columbia's Parker School of Foreign and Comparative Law. An advocate for the rights of immigrants as well as for women's rights internationally, Rahman was founding director of the International Program at the Center for Reproductive Rights. In July 2004, she assumed the office of president of the U.S. Committee for the United Nations Population Fund (UNFPA).

I became a United States citizen four years ago because of my long love af- 1
fair with New York City. After living here for a decade, I felt like a New
Yorker. In this open city, it seems so easy to feel that you can invent yourself and create a unique life. This has been—and undoubtedly will be—the
enduring allure of the city. For me, being a New Yorker has meant a sense
of belonging and of coming home.

Like all New Yorkers, I have been emotional recently. I was paralyzed 2
by fear and horror when I saw the images of jetliners bringing down our
twin towers and threatening our city. I walked through Union Square Park
deeply moved by the pictures of missing persons and the poems. I cried
when I read the farewell messages left by people on hijacked planes for
their loved ones. I shuddered when I walked around eerily quiet Manhattan streeets. And I feared for the future of this city. How will we cope with
the unbearable loss of so many New Yorkers? How long will it take to rebuild the city?

Amid such questions there is an additional nagging fear. I fear being 3 hated and blamed by the very city I love. I am a Bangladeshi woman and my last name is Rahman, a Muslim name. I have read many stories about Sikhs being attacked, mosques being threatened, and Arab-Americans and other Americans from India, Pakistan, Sri Lanka and elsewhere keeping their children at home. I noticed that a Bangladeshi Muslim taxi driver had removed his official papers from the usual place in front of the passenger seat because he feared being identified as a Muslim. My best friend, a turbaned Sikh who is a professor at Princeton University, was harassed as he walked in Chelsea because he was mistakenly viewed as being "Palestinian" and looking somewhat like the men we suspect are the authors of our horror.

I am so used to thinking about myself as a New Yorker that it took me 4 a few days to begin to see myself as a stranger might: a Muslim woman, an outsider, perhaps an enemy of the city. Before last week, I had thought of myself as a lawyer, a feminist, a wife, a sister, a friend, a woman on the street. Now I begin to see myself as a brown woman who bears a vague resemblance to the images of terrorists we see on television and in the newspapers. I can only imagine how much more difficult it is for men who look like Mohamed Atta or Osama bin Laden.

As I become identified as someone outside the New York community, I 5 feel myself losing the power to define myself and losing that wonderful sense of belonging to this city. In a way, the open city becomes closed. If the fear of attack causes America to turn on its people, these terrorists will have been spectacularly successful, more successful, I believe, than they could have expected or even understood.

Thinking Critically

1. Compare Anika Rahman's first-person essay with Shibley Telhami's academic "snapshot" of Arabs and Muslim Americans in the previous selection. Both essays were written in response to the events of 9/11, and both were published soon after those events. In what ways do these essays share a rhetorical purpose? In what other ways might their audiences and purposes overlap? How is your understanding of one of the essays enhanced by the other?

2. Conduct a Lexis-Nexis or other online database search of the *New York Times* for the last two weeks of September 2001. How many first-person accounts are included in the paper? (Pay particular attention to the "Metro" section, which includes many New York–based columnists, and the op-ed pages.) What is the background and perspective of these writers? What do these writers have in common? Are there any unusual or unexpected perspectives or insights?

Gimme! A toddler shops for new wheels at a Toys "R" Us store.

Considering the Image

1. What is your immediate reaction to this photo? Would that reaction change if this was your child (or little brother or nephew)? Why?

2. What does this image suggest about the average American childhood?

3. What might this image imply to writers Paul Roberts and William Schneider about the future of American environmentalism?

Nickel and dimed An increasing number of older workers are taking minimum-wage jobs; many workers also have children and work several such jobs to try to make ends meet. These women work at a Subway store in Arkansas.

Considering the Image

1. This image originally accompanied an article about an increase in the minimum wage. Why would the newspaper's photo editor select this image to accompany such an article?

2. How would this image complement any of the readings in Chapter 5?

Shopping is patriotic Consumer spending buoys the American economy (even as it drives many individual Americans into credit-card debt); many politicians and retailers urged Americans to go shopping to pull the nation out of the post-9/11 economic slump. These shoppers in Los Angeles, CA, played a small part in boosting overall consumer spending in the first quarter of 2004.

Considering the Image

1. What can you infer about the social class of the women in this image and the women in the photograph on the previous page? Do you need the caption for this information, or are there cues in the images themselves?

2. How does this image illustrate any of the arguments made in Chapter 5?

A blessing in the park The Dalai Lama, the globally revered Tibetan Buddhist leader who lives in exile from his homeland, greets a crowd gathered to hear him give a lecture in New York's Central Park in 2003.

Considering the Image

1. According to the *New York Times,* some 65,000 people turned out to hear the Dalai Lama speak on this occasion. In American civic culture, what kinds of events tend to draw very large crowds together?

2. How is this photograph formally composed? What divides the space in this photograph, and what contrasts are suggested by that division?

3. Several writers in Chapter 6 explore the intersections of faith and popular culture. What attracts Americans to the aesthetic or cultural aspects of some religions, even if they have no family heritage connecting them to that religion?

A blessing on the road Pope John Paul II, who survived an assassination attempt in 1981, waves to a crowd from inside the bullet-proof glass vehicle at the 1993 World Youth Day event in Denver, Colorado.

Considering the Image

1. In what ways is this photograph similar to that of the Dalai Lama on the previous page? What does this suggest about the presence of religious leaders in contemporary culture?

2. Compare accounts of the Pope's visit to Denver and the Dalai Lama's 2003 lecture in Central Park. Is there anything particularly American in the ways in which these two men from very different cultures and traditions were greeted by their audiences and the press? How did each man specifically address American issues?

3. What is the place of faith in a secular society?

The butterfly effect In many urban areas, community groups are reclaiming vacant and abandoned lots and transforming them into gardens for local cooperative use. This family is tending their vegetable plot in a communal Los Angeles garden.

Considering the image

1. What does this image imply about the impact of public gardens on local communities? How would that argument change if only one person was pictured here?

2. In "Cultivating the Butterfly Effect" (pp. 393–97) Erik Assadourian describes another community garden in Los Angeles. Although this photograph did not appear with that article when it was published, why might a photo editor select this image as a good illustration of Assadourian's arguments?

Living dolls Victoria's Secret models Heidi Klum, Adriana Lima, Alessandra Ambrosio, Tyra Banks, and Gisele Bundchen pose for photographers during their 'Angels Across America' promotional tour in 2004.

Considering the Image

1. Virginia Postrel (pp. 462–68) argues that as cosmetic surgery becomes less expensivc and less stigmatized, more people (especially women) will undergo procedures to make them more conventionally attractive. What physical features do these five "supermodels" have in common? Is there anything distinctive or unusual about any of these women?

2. Only one of these models is American. Do these women represent an American ideal of beauty, or a more international ideal?

3. How would you describe the way in which these women are dressed? Does beauty have a uniform?

Jesus is my homeboy Christian rock music festivals are increasingly popular, and some evangelists reach out to young people by including Christian rock groups in their crusades. These enthusiastic fans cheer the band DC Talk during the Billy Graham Crusade in 1996.

Considering the image

1. Could this image, or the behavior it captures, be considered ironic? In what way?

2. What might this image suggest about the behavior of young men at any large event—be it a football game, a rock concert, or a religious crusade? (Do women behave any differently?) M. Graham Spann (pp. 591–97) describes ways in which sociologists could study NASCAR fans—how might a sociologist analyze this image?

3. Mark Alan Powell (pp. 583–90) describes the ambivalent responses many music fans and people of faith have towards the mingling of rock music, commercialism, and religion. How does this image illustrate those tensions? Should there be a division between faith and popular culture, as there (technically) is between the church and civic culture?

Writing Critically

1. What is the nature of the fear that Rahman describes, and how does that fear impact the day-to-day lives of New Yorkers? In what ways is this fear similar to that described by other writers in this chapter?

2. Anika Rahman lived in New York City for many years, both as a student and as a professional lawyer, before becoming an American citizen. In paragraph 1, she writes that "I became a United States citizen . . . because of my long love affair with New York." Yet many New Yorkers, especially after the 2004 presidential elections, joked darkly about seceding from the red states of the rest of America. In what ways is New York City especially representative of the United States? In what ways is it completely different, almost its own separate country? (Consider media images of New York City as well as your own personal experiences living in or visiting New York or other major American urban areas.)

Terror in the Skies, Again?

ANNIE JACOBSEN

This article, which first appeared online at *Womens Wall Street.com* in July 2004, provoked a flood of commentary in the media. Some thought Jacobsen was overreacting, allowing her judgment to be clouded by racial stereotypes. Others thought she deserved the citizen's medal of honor. Hundreds of publications picked up on the story, including the *New York Times* and *Time* magazine. Because of her article, Congress (the U.S. House Judiciary Committee) launched an official investigation into flight 327 and the policies of several federal agencies involved. The departments being investigated by Congress include the Federal Air Marshal Service, Immigrations and Customs Enforcement, the Federal Bureau of Investigation, and the Joint Terrorism Task Force. The National Intelligence Reform Act, passed in December 2004, mandates that commercial airline pilots immediately report suspicious in-flight behavior directly to the Transportation Security Administration.

In a recent discussion, Jacobsen noted: "There were extraordinary circumstances that made the article (and the subsequent follow-up articles) unique in the field of journalism—from the reporter becoming the witness, to the influence of web journalism, to the controversial nature of the content. I was aware that this article could bring an immense amount of criticism from readers and the press but I decided to go forward with the story. I wanted to get the truth out despite the possible fallout." For additional reading on the impact of "Terror in the Skies, Again?" and the growing influence of online journalism, see *Foreign Policy Magazine* (November/December 2004) at <http://www.foreignpolicy.com/story/cms.php?story_id=2707>.

Note from the Editors: You are about to read an account of what happened during a domestic flight that one of our writers, Annie Jacobsen, took from Detroit to Los Angeles. The WWS Editorial Team debated long and hard about how to handle this information and ultimately we decided it was something that should be shared. What does it have to do with finances? Nothing, and everything. Here is Annie's story.

On June 29, 2004, at 12:28 p.m., I flew on Northwest Airlines flight #327 from Detroit to Los Angeles with my husband and our young son. Also on our flight were 14 Middle Eastern men between the ages of approximately 20 and 50 years old. What I experienced during that flight has caused me to question whether the United States of America can realistically uphold the civil liberties of every individual, even non-citizens, and protect its citizens from terrorist threats.   1

On that Tuesday, our journey began uneventfully. Starting out that morning in Providence, Rhode Island, we went through security screening, flew to Detroit, and passed the time waiting for our connecting flight to Los Angeles by shopping at the airport stores and eating lunch at an airport diner. With no second security check required in Detroit we headed to our gate and waited for the pre-boarding announcement. Standing near us, also waiting to pre-board, was a group of six Middle Eastern men. They were carrying blue passports with Arabic writing. Two men wore track-suits with Arabic writing across the back. Two carried musical instrument cases—thin, flat, 18″ long. One wore a yellow T-shirt and held a McDonald's bag. And the sixth man had a bad leg—he wore an orthopedic shoe and limped. When the pre-boarding announcement was made, we handed our tickets to the Northwest Airlines agent, and walked down the jetway with the group of men directly behind us.   2

My four-year-old son was determined to wheel his carry-on bag himself, so I turned to the men behind me and said, "You go ahead, this could be awhile." "No, you go ahead," one of the men replied. He smiled pleasantly and extended his arm for me to pass. He was young, maybe late 20's and had a goatee. I thanked him and we boarded the plane.   3

Once on the plane, we took our seats in coach (seats 17A, 17B and 4
17C). The man with the yellow shirt and the McDonald's bag sat across
the aisle from us (in seat 17E). The pleasant man with the goatee sat a few
rows back and across the aisle from us (in seat 21E). The rest of the men
were seated throughout the plane, and several made their way to the back.

As we sat waiting for the plane to finish boarding, we noticed another 5
large group of Middle Eastern men boarding. The first man wore a dark
suit and sunglasses. He sat in first class in seat 1A, the seat second-closest
to the cockpit door. The other seven men walked into the coach cabin. As
"aware" Americans, my husband and I exchanged glances, and then continued to get comfortable. I noticed some of the other passengers paying attention to the situation as well. As boarding continued, we watched as, one
by one, most of the Middle Eastern men made eye contact with each other.
They continued to look at each other and nod, as if they were all in agreement about something. I could tell that my husband was beginning to feel
"anxious."

The take-off was uneventful. But once we were in the air and the seat- 6
belt sign was turned off, the unusual activity began. The man in the yellow
T-shirt got out of his seat and went to the lavatory at the front of coach—
taking his full McDonald's bag with him. When he came out of the lavatory he still had the McDonald's bag, but it was now almost empty. He
walked down the aisle to the back of the plane, still holding the bag. When
he passed two of the men sitting mid-cabin, he gave a thumbs-up sign.
When he returned to his seat, he no longer had the McDonald's bag.

Then another man from the group stood up and took something from 7
his carry-on in the overhead bin. It was about a foot long and was rolled
in cloth. He headed toward the back of the cabin with the object. Five minutes later, several more of the Middle Eastern men began using the forward
lavatory consecutively. In the back, several of the men stood up and used
the back lavatory consecutively as well.

For the next hour, the men congregated in groups of two and three at 8
the back of the plane for varying periods of time. Meanwhile, in the first
class cabin, just a foot or so from the cockpit door, the man with the dark
suit—still wearing sunglasses—was also standing. Not one of the flight
crew members suggested that any of these men take their seats.

Watching all of this, my husband was now beyond "anxious." I decided to 9
try to reassure my husband (and maybe myself) by walking to the back bathroom. I knew the goateed-man I had exchanged friendly words with as we
boarded the plane was seated only a few rows back, so I thought I would say
hello to the man to get some reassurance that everything was fine. As I stood
up and turned around, I glanced in his direction and we made eye contact. I

threw out my friendliest "remember-me-we-had-a-nice-exchange-just-a-short-time-ago" smile. The man did not smile back. His face did not move. In fact, the cold, defiant look he gave me sent shivers down my spine.

When I returned to my seat I was unable to assure my husband that all 10 was well. My husband immediately walked to the first class section to talk with the flight attendant. "I might be overreacting, but I've been watching some really suspicious things . . ." Before he could finish his statement, the flight attendant pulled him into the galley. In a quiet voice she explained that they were all concerned about what was going on. The captain was aware. The flight attendants were passing notes to each other. She said that there were people on board "higher up than you and me watching the men." My husband returned to his seat and relayed this information to me. He was feeling slightly better. I was feeling much worse. We were now two hours into a four-and-a-half hour flight.

Approximately 10 minutes later, that same flight attendant came by 11 with the drinks cart. She leaned over and quietly told my husband there were federal air marshals sitting all around us. She asked him not to tell anyone and explained that she could be in trouble for giving out that information. She then continued serving drinks.

About 20 minutes later the same flight attendant returned. Leaning 12 over and whispering, she asked my husband to write a description of the yellow-shirted man sitting across from us. She explained it would look too suspicious if she wrote the information. She asked my husband to slip the note to her when he was done.

After seeing 14 Middle Eastern men board separately (six together, eight 13 individually) and then act as a group, watching their unusual glances, observing their bizarre bathroom activities, watching them congregate in small groups, knowing that the flight attendants and the pilots were seriously concerned, and now knowing that federal air marshals were on board, I was officially terrified. Before I'm labeled a racial profiler or—worse yet—a racist, let me add this. A month ago I traveled to India to research a magazine article I was writing. My husband and I flew on a jumbo jet carrying more than 300 Hindu and Muslim men and women on board. We traveled throughout the country and stayed in a Muslim village 10 miles outside Pakistan. I never once felt fearful. I never once felt unsafe. I never once had the feeling that anyone wanted to hurt me. This time was different.

Finally, the captain announced that the plane was cleared for landing. 14 It had been four hours since we left Detroit. The fasten seat belt light came on and I could see downtown Los Angeles. The flight attendants made one final sweep of the cabin and strapped themselves in for landing. I began to relax. Home was in sight.

Suddenly, seven of the men stood up—in unison—and walked to the 15 front and back lavatories. One by one, they went into the two lavatories, each spending about four minutes inside. Right in front of us, two men stood up against the emergency exit door, waiting for the lavatory to become available. The men spoke in Arabic among themselves and to the man in the yellow shirt sitting nearby. One of the men took his camera into the lavatory. Another took his cell phone. Again, no one approached the men. Not one of the flight attendants asked them to sit down. I watched as the man in the yellow shirt, still in his seat, reached inside his shirt and pulled out a small red book. He read a few pages, then put the book back inside his shirt. He pulled the book out again, read a page or two more, and put it back. He continued to do this several more times.

I looked around to see if any other passengers were watching. I imme- 16 diately spotted a distraught couple seated two rows back. The woman was crying into the man's shoulder. He was holding her hand. I heard him say to her, "You've got to calm down." Behind them sat the once pleasant-smiling, goatee-wearing man.

I grabbed my son, I held my husband's hand and, despite the fact that 17 I am not a particularly religious person, I prayed. The last man came out of the bathroom, and as he passed the man in the yellow shirt he ran his forefinger across his neck and mouthed the word "No."

The plane landed. My husband and I gathered our bags and quickly, 18 very quickly, walked up the jetway. As we exited the jetway and entered the airport, we saw many, many men in dark suits. A few yards further out into the terminal, LAPD agents ran past us, heading for the gate. I have since learned that the representatives of the Federal Bureau of Investiga-tion (FBI), the Los Angeles Police Department (LAPD), the Federal Air Marshals (FAM), and the Transportation Security Association (TSA) met our plane as it landed. Several men—who I presume were the federal air marshals on board—hurried off the plane and directed the 14 men over to the side.

Knowing what we knew, and seeing what we'd seen, my husband and 19 I decided to talk to the authorities. For several hours my husband and I were interrogated by the FBI. We gave sworn statement after sworn state-ment. We wrote down every detail of our account. The interrogators seemed especially interested in the McDonald's bag, so we repeated in de-tail what we knew about the McDonald's bag. A law enforcement official stood near us, holding 14 Syrian passports in his hand. We answered more questions. And finally we went home.

The next day, I began searching online for news about the incident. There 20 was nothing. I asked a friend who is a local news correspondent if there were any arrests at LAX that day. There weren't. I called Northwest Airlines' customer service. They said write a letter. I wrote a letter, then followed up with a call to their public relations department. They said they were aware of the situation (sorry that happened!) but legally they have 30 days to reply.

I shared my story with a few colleagues. One mentioned she'd been on   21 a flight with a group of foreign men who were acting strangely—they turned out to be diamond traders. Another had heard a story on National Public Radio (NPR) shortly after 9/11 about a group of Arab musicians who were having a hard time traveling on airplanes throughout the U.S. and couldn't get seats together. I took note of these two stories and continued my research. Here are excerpts from an article written by Jason Burke, Chief Reporter, and published in *The Observer* (a British newspaper based in London) on February 8, 2004:

> Islamic militants have conducted dry runs of a devastating new style of bombing on aircraft flying to Europe, intelligence sources believe.
>
> The tactics, which aim to evade aviation security systems by placing only components of explosive devices on passenger jets, allowing militants to assemble them in the air, have been tried out on planes flying between the Middle East, North Africa and Western Europe, security sources say.
>
> . . . The . . . Transportation Security Administration issued an urgent memo detailing new threats to aviation and warning that terrorists in teams of five might be planning suicide missions to hijack commercial airliners, possibly using common items . . . such as cameras, modified as weapons.
>
> . . . Components of IEDs [improvised explosive devices] can be smuggled on to an aircraft, concealed in either clothing or personal carry-on items . . . and assembled on board. In many cases of suspicious passenger activity, incidents have taken place in the aircraft's forward lavatory.

So here's my question: Since the FBI issued a warning to the airline in-   22 dustry to be wary of groups of five men on a plane who might be trying to build bombs in the bathroom, shouldn't a group of 14 Middle Eastern men be screened before boarding a flight?

Apparently not. Due to our rules against discrimination, it can't be   23 done. During the 9/11 hearings last April, 9/11 Commissioner John Lehman stated that ". . . it was the policy (before 9/11) and I believe remains the policy today to fine airlines if they have more than two young Arab males in secondary questioning because that's discriminatory."

So even if Northwest Airlines searched two of the men on board my   24 Northwest flight, they couldn't search the other 12 because they would have already filled a government-imposed quota.

I continued my research by reading an article entitled *Arab Hijackers* 25
Now Eligible for Pre-Boarding from Ann Coulter (www.anncoulter.com):

> On September 21, as the remains of thousands of Americans lay
> smoldering at Ground Zero, [Secretary of Transportation Norman]
> Mineta fired off a letter to all U.S. airlines forbidding them from im-
> plementing the one security measure that could have prevented 9/11:
> subjecting Middle Eastern passengers to an added degree of pre-flight
> scrutiny. He sternly reminded the airlines that it was illegal to discrim-
> inate against passengers based on their race, color, national or ethnic
> origin or religion.

Coulter also writes that a few months later, at Mr. Mineta's behest, the 26
Department of Transportation (DOT) filed complaints against United Airlines and American Airlines (who, combined, had lost 8 pilots, 25 flight
attendants and 213 passengers on 9/11—not counting the 19 Arab hijackers). In November 2003, United Airlines settled their case with the DOT
for $1.5 million. In March 2004, American Airlines settled their case with
the DOT for $1.5 million. The DOT also charged Continental Airlines
with discriminating against passengers who appeared to be Arab, Middle
Eastern, or Muslim. Continental Airlines settled their complaint with the
DOT in April of 2004 for $.5 million.

From what I witnessed, Northwest Airlines doesn't have to worry about 27
Norman Mineta filing a complaint against them for discriminatory, secondary screening of Arab men. No one checked the passports of the Syrian men.
No one inspected the contents of the two instrument cases or the McDonald's bag. And no one checked the limping man's orthopedic shoe. In fact, according to the TSA regulations, passengers wearing an orthopedic shoe
won't be asked to take it off. As their site states, "Advise the screener if you're
wearing orthopedic shoes . . . screeners should not be asking you to remove
your orthopedic shoes at any time during the screening process."

I placed a call to the TSA and talked to Joe Dove, a Customer Service 28
Supervisor. I told him how we'd eaten with metal utensils in an airport
diner moments before boarding the flight and how no one checked our luggage or the instrument cases being carried by the Middle Eastern men.
Dove's response was, "Restaurants in secured areas—that's an ongoing
problem. We get that complaint often. TSA gets that complaint all the time
and they haven't worked that out with the FAA. They're aware of it. You've
got a good question. There may not be a reasonable answer at this time,
I'm not going to BS you."

At the Detroit airport no one checked our IDs. No one checked the 29
folds in my newspaper or the contents of my son's backpack. No one asked
us what we'd done during our layover, if we bought anything, or if anyone

gave us anything while we were in the airport. We were asked all of these questions (and many others) three weeks earlier when we'd traveled in Europe—where passengers with airport layovers are rigorously questioned and screened before boarding any and every flight. In Detroit no one checked who we were or what we carried on board a 757 jetliner bound for America's largest metropolis.

Two days after my experience on Northwest Airlines flight #327 came   30
this notice from SBS TV, The World News, July 1, 2004:

> The U.S. Transportation and Security Administration has issued a new directive which demands pilots make a pre-flight announcement banning passengers from congregating in aisles and outside the plane's toilets. The directive also orders flight attendants to check the toilets every two hours for suspicious packages.

Through a series of events, *The Washington Post* heard about my story. I   31
talked briefly about my experience with a representative from the newspaper. Within a few hours I received a call from Dave Adams, the Federal Air Marshal Services (FAM) Head of Public Affairs. Adams told me what he knew:

There were 14 Syrians on NWA flight #327. They were questioned at   32
length by FAM, the FBI, and the TSA upon landing in Los Angeles. The 14 Syrians had been hired as musicians to play at a casino in the desert. Adams said they were "scrubbed." None had arrest records (in America, I presume), none showed up on the FBI's "no fly" list or the FBI's Most Wanted Terrorists List. The men checked out and they were let go. According to Adams, the 14 men traveled on Northwest Airlines flight #327 using one-way tickets. Two days later they were scheduled to fly back on jetBlue from Long Beach, California to New York—also using one-way tickets.

I asked Adams why, based on the FBI's credible information that terror-   33
ists may try to assemble bombs on planes, the air marshals or the flight attendants didn't do anything about the bizarre behavior and frequent trips to the lavatory. "Our FAM agents have to have an event to arrest somebody. Our agents aren't going to deploy until there is an actual event," Adams explained. He said he could not speak for the policies of Northwest Airlines.

So the question is . . . Do I think these men were musicians? I'll let you   34
decide. But I wonder, if 19 terrorists can learn to fly airplanes into buildings, couldn't 14 terrorists learn to play instruments?

Thinking Critically

1. As you will see in the next essay as well as in numerous online and press responses to Annie Jacobsen's article, many readers found all kinds of

lapses in Jacobsen's logic, rhetoric, and evidence. Review the section on "Analyzing Texts" in Chapter 1, and evaluate Jacobsen's text according to each of the "critical reading" questions. In what ways is Jacobsen's text particularly effective? Can a text have a considerable impact, or even be considered "effective," if readers find its premise to be exaggerated?

2. Jacobsen's article includes a brief "Note" from the editors of *Women's Wall Street.com.* What do you think the purpose of this "Note" could be? Does it have any effect on your reaction to Jacobsen's article?

3. One example of a logical fallacy found in much rhetoric about issues of fear is so-called loaded language. For a definition and description of "loaded language," go to <http://www.fallacyfiles.org/loadword.html>. Review Jacobsen's essay, marking any instances of what you believe to be "loaded language." Discuss your findings with class members, and be prepared to support your perspective.

Writing Critically

1. Rewrite "Terror in the Skies, Again?" from the point of view of one of the Middle Eastern passengers on Jacobsen's flight. Follow her narrative structure, and include as many of the events she describes as you can. Your challenge, however, is to base your revision of the article on what you've learned from writers such as Shibley Telhami and Anika Rahman in this chapter, and from other Arab or Arab American viewpoints that you find through careful research.

2. Drop "Annie Jacobsen" into Google, and select a few of the negative responses to her article that you find there. On what grounds do these other writers disagree with Jacobsen? Which criticisms seem especially relevant and useful, and which seem less well informed? Is it possible to have a level-headed discussion about issues of immediate personal fear?

3. Have you ever been embarrassed or ashamed by your actions in a situation where you were afraid for your personal safety? Describe one such incident in detail, exploring why you made the decisions that you did and why you later felt embarrassed or ashamed. As an alternative, describe a time when you acted from instinct to preserve your personal safety or the safety of someone close to you, even if someone else might find your actions silly or "politically incorrect."

The Hysterical Skies

PATRICK SMITH

Patrick Smith is an airline pilot who writes the "Ask the Pilot" column for the online magazine *Salon.com*. *Ask the Pilot: Everything You Need to Know About Air Travel,* a collection of his columns, was published in 2004. A self-described "pretty liberal guy" who has flown both commercial and cargo planes, he noted in a 2004 interview that "As a general subject, air travel is seemingly apolitical—at least the way others have covered it—but there have been loads of partisan controversies: debates over security, racial profiling of passengers, cockpit guns and so forth." In his column for *Salon,* Smith has tackled everything from the fears fliers have about turbulence, the poor quality of service, and the potential for mile-high romance. In this column, which appeared in *Salon.com* in July 2004, he takes on Annie Jacobsen's "Terror in the Skies, Again?" (the previous selection) from the viewpoint of a pilot and frequent flier.

In this space was supposed to be installment No. 6 of my multiweek dissertation on airports and terminals. The topic is being usurped by one of those nagging, Web-borne issues of the moment, in this case a reactionary scare story making the cyber-rounds during the past week. 1

The piece in question, "Terror in the Skies, Again?" is the work of Annie Jacobsen, a writer for *WomensWallStreet.com.* Jacobsen shares the account of the emotional meltdown she and her fellow passengers experienced when, aboard a Northwest Airlines flight from Detroit to Los Angeles, a group of Middle Eastern passengers proceeded to act "suspiciously." I'll invite you to experience "Terror" yourself, but be warned it's quite long. It needs to be, I suppose, since ultimately it's a story about nothing, puffed and aggrandized to appear important. 2

The editors get the drama cooking with some foreboding music: "You are about to read an account of what happened," counsels a 70-word preamble. "The WWS Editorial Team debated long and hard about how to handle this information and ultimately we decided it was something that should be shared . . . Here is Annie's story" [insert lower-octave piano chord here]. 3

What follows are six pages of the worst grade-school prose, spring-loaded with mindless hysterics and bigoted provocation. 4

Fourteen dark-skinned men from Syria board Northwest's flight 327,   5
seated in two separate groups. Some are carrying oddly shaped bags and
wearing track suits with Arabic script across the back. During the flight the
men socialize, gesture to one another, move about the cabin with pieces of
their luggage, and, most ominous of all, repeatedly make trips to the bathroom. The author links the men's apparently irritable bladders to a report
published in the *Observer* (U.K.) warning of terrorist plots to smuggle
bomb components onto airplanes one piece at a time, to be secretly assembled in lavatories.

"What I experienced during that flight," breathes Jacobsen, "has   6
caused me to question whether the United States of America can realistically uphold the civil liberties of every individual, even non-citizens, and
protect its citizens from terrorist threats."

Intriguing, no? I, for one, fully admit that certain acts of airborne crime   7
and treachery may indeed open the channels to a debate on civil liberties. Pray
tell, what happened? Gunfight at 37,000 feet? Valiant passengers wrestle a
grenade from a suicidal operative? Hero pilots beat back a cockpit takeover?

Well, no. As a matter of fact, nothing happened. Turns out the Syrians   8
are part of a musical ensemble hired to play at a hotel. The men talk to one
another. They glance around. They pee.

That's it?   9

That's it.   10

Now, in fairness to Jacobsen, I'll admit that in-flight jitters over the   11
conspicuous presence of a group of young Arabs is neither unexpected
nor, necessarily, irrational. She speaks of seven of the men standing in
unison, a moment that, if unembellished, would have even the most culturally open-minded of us wide-eyed and grabbing our armrest. As
everybody knows, it was not a gaggle of Canadian potato farmers who
commandeered those jetliners on Sept. 11. See also the legacy of air
crimes over the past several decades, from Pan Am 103 to the UTA
bombing to the failed schemings of Ramzi Yousef, the culprits each time
being young Arab males.

Air crews and passengers alike are thus prone to jumpiness should a cer-   12
tain template of race and behavior be filled. Jacobsen's folly is in not being
able to step back from that jumpiness—neither during the flight itself, at
which point her worry and behavior are at least excusable, nor well after
touching down safely. Speaking as a pilot, air travel columnist, and American, I find Jacobsen's 3,000-word ghost story of Arab boogeymen among the
most overwrought and inflammatory tracts I've encountered in some time.

Most disturbing of all has been the pickup from Internet bloggers and   13
news sources, including ABC, CNN, MSNBC and the *New York Times*.

The writer hops a flight to California on which absolutely nothing of danger occurs, and the following are among the citations:

"Harrowing piece"
"The frightening true story"
"Disturbing account"
"Riveting article"
"An absolute must-read"

"Read all about the breaking Northwest airlines scare," advertises   14
TheLosAngelesNews.com, suggesting perhaps a narrowly averted crash, a bomb defused during flight or a thwarted skyjacking. Click on over to hear instead about the toilet habits of a group of Syrian minstrels and one middle-aged woman's alarmist reaction to them. No matter, over the past week or so Jacobsen has found herself linked and excerpted in every last crevice of the Web. Those of you not convinced of just how paranoid and xenophobic Americans can be, look no further than the following online posts, which, along with thousands like them, have emerged in direct response to this story:

"You will never, ever, catch me on an airplane again!"   15
"My advice would be to de-plane as soon as I counted 14 Arabs   16
as passengers."
"Soon after 9/11 we were in a local McDonald's and a group of   17
Middle Eastern men came in and got carry-out. They sat in their
van for a while then headed North. I felt scared out of my wits. I
wrote down a description of the vehicle and license, but never did
anything with it. Guess next time I won't be so stupid."

Jacobsen spins her experience into a not-so-veiled call for racial profil-   18
ing of airline passengers. Help me out with this one: If only those musicians had been interrogated prior to boarding, it would have been revealed they were, in fact . . . musicians. (They had, of course, endured the same concourse X-ray and metal detector rigmarole as everyone else, and were in possession of valid passports and visas.)

My own feelings on passenger profiling are mixed, and I'm not as liberal   19
on the issue as you might expect. However, I do think singling out a specific ethnicity for extra screening is less a racist idea than a wasteful and ineffective one. Does it not occur to people that Muslim radicals come in all complexions and from many nations—from the heart of black Africa to the archipelagoes of Southeast Asia? (Many Syrians, no less, are fair-haired and light-skinned.) Does it not occur to people that terrorists are clever, resourceful and, in the end, bound to outwit such obvious snares? The notion that 14 saboteurs, replete with silk-screened track suits effectively advertising themselves as such,

would obviously and boisterously proceed in and out of an airplane lavatory, taking turns to construct a bomb, is so over-the-top ludicrous it deserves its own comedy sketch. Indeed, Jacobsen is trying to portray a scene of angst and fear, but she inadvertently scripts out a parody. I half-expected her to tell me that one of the men wore a cardboard sign labeled "TERRORIST."

On Tuesday morning I appeared as a guest on a conservative, drive-time 20 radio show in Philadelphia, and Jacobsen was the hot issue. The host, without much else to go on, proposed the Syrians had choreographed a "dry run" for a future attack. (At one point he referred to the involved carrier, Northwest Airlines, as "Northeastern.") When I dared express doubt, and noted that investigators from the Transportation Security Administration and the FBI had confirmed the men's identities and motives, I was mocked, ridiculed and eventually hung up on. The very suggestion that the men could have been innocent musicians seemed, in the eyes of the host and callers, preposterous. They had to be terrorists. Disagreeing got me called "a frickin' idiot," and a caller demanded to know which airline I worked for so he could be certain never to ride on a plane with a traitor like me at the controls.

Stop the presses: A sequel to "Terror in the Skies, Again?" has now been 21 posted on *Womens WallStreet.com*, in which Jacobsen reinfects the conversation with a fresh dose of mongering. "And I now have another important question," she writes. "Is there a link between my experience . . . and the arrest of Ali Mohamed Almosaleh by Customs agents at the Minneapolis Airport on July 7?" Almosaleh, a Syrian, was allegedly carrying a suicide note and "anti-American material."

Jacobsen's hint at conspiracy, however, is based exclusively on the coinci- 22 dence that Almosaleh and the musicians happen to all be Syrian citizens. I see. That a supposition this groundless and stupid can make it into print and entice the likes of major news networks should outrage any clear-thinking American. How about we seek out all Syrians and put their names on airline blacklists?

Jacobsen's sequel is peppered with incendiary quotes from industry 23 sources. Says an airline pilot: "The terrorists are probing us all the time." Another confides a maddeningly baseless belief that Jacobsen had been "likely on a dry run," while another states, "The incident you wrote about, and incidents like it, occur more than you like to think. It is a 'dirty little secret' that all of us, as crew members, have known about for quite some time."

Which dirty little secret, exactly, are we talking about? That foreigners 24 ride on airplanes?

In a moment of truly ghastly philosophizing, Jacobsen includes a ma- 25 nipulative passage in which she is smitten with anguish as she recollects a photograph taken during the Sept. 11 attacks. She gives us this: "Political correctness has become a major road block for airline safety . . . I think about the meaning of 'dry run.' And then I think about what it means to be politically correct. And I keep coming up blank."

So do I. 26

Aside from matters of politics and general opinion, is Jacobsen playing 27 fast and loose with the facts? There appear to be embellishments in her original tale.

Aboard flight 327, as she, her husband and several passengers and crew 28 are having their nervous breakdowns, comes this instance of B-movie tension: "[The flight attendant] leaned over and quietly told my husband there were federal air marshals sitting all around us. She asked him not to tell anyone and explained that she could be in trouble for giving out that information. She then continued serving drinks."

Are we to believe not only that an airline professional was unwise 29 enough to reveal such a thing, but that a group of marshals—not one, not two, but several—having gotten word that a covey of Arabs were flying to LAX, were on hand to trail and observe them? That's some tight logistical planning. Are we following Middle Easterners through airports now? If so, how does that work at Kennedy International, I wonder, where foreign airliners carrying thousands of passengers arrive daily from Pakistan, Saudi Arabia, Jordan, Egypt, Morocco, the UAE and elsewhere? That's a lot of dry runs, and there's no love lost, after all, between Muslim radicals and the governments who own and operate these airlines—Pakistan International, Saudi Arabian, EgyptAir, Royal Jordanian, etc. Such subtleties are lost on that segment of the public who'd prefer a more digestible cock-and-bull yarn from high above the American heartland. As for those wacky airlines from abroad, why not simply ban them from American airspace?

Clearly I'm in a fit of envy over Jacobsen's cheap grab at notoriety. I've 30 got a book out and could use some publicity. Here, let me give it a try.

Late last summer I boarded a nonstop flight from Dubai, United Arab 31 Emirates, to Newark, N.J. After taking my seat, I noticed that well over a hundred of my fellow passengers looked to be Muslims! Yes, that's the same faith adhered to by those dastardly perpetrators who knocked down our Trade Center and demolished part of the Pentagon. Not only that, but our aircraft, a Malaysia Airlines Boeing 777, was registered and maintained by a company headquartered in a predominantly Muslim nation! What if the cargo holds had been stuffed full of anthrax or TNT by unscrupulous terrorists back in Kuala Lumpur!

Several passengers wore conservative Islamic dress—men in white 32 dishdashas; women concealed in full black burqa. Our plane contained a Muslim prayer enclave (for possible use by terrorists preparing for the throes of martydrom), and the seatback video displayed a graphic of the qibla, showing real-time distance and heading to Mecca. En route to-ward New York, dozens of Muslim passengers were seen socializing and using the lavatories, in some cases blatantly ignoring the illuminated seat-belt sign!

To my relief and utter astonishment, we landed safely (and on time). 33

Jacobsen simmers her own account in gratuitous detail and melodrama. 34 It plays like a Hollywood disaster film—the young child, the would-be vil-lain who smiles innocently in a moment of spooky foreshadowing. We're waiting for the gunshots, the fireball from the lavatory, the marshals jump-ing up to yell, "Hit the floor!"

That her story concludes in such a painfully boring anticlimax ought to 35 be the very point, and in the final few pages she still has time for a con-structive moral, the clear lesson being not the potentials of global terror, but the dangers of our own preconceptions and imagination. Instead, she pulls a vile U-turn and chooses to bait us with racist innuendo and fear-mongering. Nothing happened, but something might have happened, and so it serves us to remain frightened and draconian at all costs, furthering our nation's pathetic embrace of maximum paranoia.

Jacobsen's kicker: "So the question is . . . Do I think these men were 36 musicians? I'll let you decide. But I wonder, if 19 terrorists can learn to fly airplanes into buildings, couldn't 14 terrorists learn to play instruments?"

Excuse me? She concludes, as did the radio host Tuesday morning, by 37 insinuating that the men were terrorists, despite every shred of evidence, not to mention common sense, arguing to the contrary. And with that her article, and her credibility with it, plummets from merely sensationalist to inexcusably offensive.

Thinking Critically

1. How does Patrick Smith organize his critique of Jacobsen's article? Does he focus primarily on her rhetorical fallacies, the flaws in her logic, or something else?

2. How does Smith establish his authority? Does he use his experience and authority in this article to reassure fearful passengers, to specifically ad-dress Jacobsen's circumstances and reactions, or to do something else al-together? (Most likely, all three of these purposes are part of his reason for writing. In your opinion, which purpose is most important?)

3. How does Smith use satire and parody to point out flaws in Jacobsen's ar-gument? Does his use of satire and parody enhance the quality of his argu-ment? What is the line between parody and mockery, and what happens when that line is crossed?

Writing Critically

1. Among the interesting points Smith makes is the almost viral way in which Jacobsen's experience spread through the mainstream media, provoking comments at first like "Riveting article" and "An absolute must-read." Working by yourself or in a small group, construct a timeline that traces the impact of Jacobsen's article. When did it first appear? How soon did other media outlets pick up her story? When did the backlash start? Use your research as the basis for an essay on how the speed of the electronic media can spread fear like a virus. (Another term for an informational virus is *meme.* Look it up online, and use it in your essay if you think it's appropriate.)

2. Would you compromise your own personal safety to make a larger political statement? Have you ever done so? Look up Brent Staples's 1986 essay "Just Walk On By: A Black Man Ponders His Ability to Alter Public Space," available at the time of this writing online at <http://faculty.smu.edu/nschwart/2312/Walkonby.htm>. What are the similarities between Staples's experience and the experiences of the Syrian musicians on Northwest Airlines flight 327?

Homeland Security? Not Yet

HEATHER MAC DONALD

City Journal, in which this essay appeared in Autumn 2004, is a quarterly journal published by the Manhattan Institute, a private think tank that analyzes public policy and cultural issues—especially issues that affect urban America—from a market-oriented perspective that emphasizes personal responsibility. Much of *City Journal's* past and present content is available online at <http://www.city-journal.org/>. Heather Mac Donald is a John M. Olin Fellow at the Manhattan Institute and a contributing editor to *City Journal.* Educated at Yale University and Cambridge University, she received her law degree from Stanford University Law School. She writes extensively on education, racial profiling, and homeland security.

In 1997, government attorneys worried that a proposed anti-terrorism 1
system for airlines might work too well. Although an early prototype of the Computer Assisted Passenger Prescreening System (CAPPS I) assiduously avoided collecting information about a passenger's national origin, religion, race, or sex in assessing the risk that he might be a terrorist, civil rights lawyers in the Justice and Transportation Departments fretted that

the system might *still* be "discriminatory." It still might pull aside "too many" people of Arab descent by looking at, say, frequent travel to the Middle East, among other risk factors.

Given the previous two decades of Islamic terrorism, such an outcome 2 would have been appropriate. But the rights enforcers warned that airlines could face penalties if they selected more than three passengers of the same ethnicity for additional scrutiny on any given flight. So the prototype architects built random hits into their program to ensure that airline screeners would devote as much time searching Lutheran matrons from Minnesota as young men from Saudi Arabia.

Public-policy obsession with avoiding any possible charge of racism 3 was the luxury of an age that believed that the United States faced no greater danger than the bigotry of its own people. Though such thinking should have been cast aside after 9/11, it has not been. The incoherence that existed at the origin of CAPPS I plagues anti-terrorism efforts today. In 1997, the government recognized the reality of Islamic terrorism by building some Islamic-centric features into the program while simultaneously repudiating the consequences of that reality—stricter scrutiny for Muslims. Currently, from immigration enforcement to intelligence gathering, government officials continue to compromise national security in order to avoid accusations of "racial profiling"—and in order to avoid publicly acknowledging what the 9/11 Commission finally said: that the "enemy is not just 'terrorism,' [but] *Islamist* terrorism." This blind anti-discrimination reflex is all the more worrying since radical Islam continues to seek adherents and plan attacks in the United States.

The anti-discrimination hammer has hit the airline industry most se- 4 verely—and with gruesome inappropriateness, given the realities of 9/11 and the Islamists' enduring obsession with airplanes. Department of Transportation lawyers have extracted millions in settlements from four major carriers for alleged discrimination after 9/11, and they have undermined one of the most crucial elements of air safety: a pilot's responsibility for his flight. Because the charges against the airlines were specious but successful, every pilot must worry that his good-faith effort to protect his passengers will trigger federal retaliation.

The DoT action against American Airlines was typical. In the last four 5 months of 2001, American carried 23 million passengers and asked ten of them. (.00004 percent of the total) not to board because they raised security concerns that could not be resolved in time for departure. For those ten interventions (and an 11th in 2002), DoT declared American a civil rights pariah, whose discriminatory conduct would "result in irreparable harm to the public" if not stopped.

On its face, the government's charge that American was engaged in a   6
pattern of discriminatory conduct was absurd, given how few passenger removals occurred. But the racism allegation looks all the more unreasonable
when put in the context of the government's own actions. Three times between 9/11 and the end of 2001, public officials warned of an imminent
terror attack. Transportation officials urged the airlines to be especially
vigilant. In such an environment, pilots would have been derelict not to resolve security questions in favor of caution.

Somehow, DoT lawyers failed to include in their complaint one further   7
passenger whom American asked not to board in 2001. On December 22,
airline personnel in Paris kept Richard Reid off a flight to Miami. The next
day, French authorities insisted that he be cleared to board. During the
flight, Reid tried to set off a bomb in his shoe, but a stewardess and passengers foiled him. Had he been kept from flying on both days, he too
might have ended up on the government's roster of discrimination victims.

Jehad Alshrafi is typical of those who were included in the suit against   8
American. On November 3, 2001, the Jordanian-American Alshrafi was
scheduled to fly out of Boston's Logan Airport (from which two of the hijacked
planes—including American Flight 77—departed on 9/11). A federal air marshal told the pilot that Alshrafi's name resembled one on a terror watch list—
and that he had been acting suspiciously, had created a disturbance at the gate,
and posed unresolved security issues. The pilot denied him boarding. Alshrafi
was later cleared and given first-class passage on another flight.

According to DoT, the only reason American initially denied Alshrafi   9
passage was because of his "race, color, national origin, religion, sex or ancestry." Never mind that there were at least five other passengers of Arab descent on his original flight, none of whom had been given additional
screening or kept from flying. In fact, on virtually every flight on which the
government claims that American acted out of racial animus, other passengers of apparent Middle Eastern or South Asian ancestry flew undisturbed—
not to mention the undoubted thousands of Arab passengers who flew with
American on other flights in the final months of 2001.

If DoT believes that an air marshal's warnings about a passenger's name   10
and suspicious behavior are insufficient grounds for keeping him off a flight,
it is hard to imagine circumstances that *would* justify a security hold in the
department's view—short of someone's declaring his intention to blow up a
plane. Given the information presented to the pilot, the only conceivable
reason to have allowed Alshrafi to board would have been fear of a lawsuit.

And litigation phobia is precisely the mind-set that DoT is hoping to   11
cultivate in flight personnel. Ten days after 9/11, the department started
rolling out "guidance" documents on nondiscrimination. While heavy on

platitudes about protecting civil rights, they are useless in advising airlines how to avoid the government's wrath. The closest the department gets to providing airlines a concrete rule for avoiding litigation is a "but-for" test: "Ask yourself," advise the guidelines, "*But for this person's perceived race, ethnic heritage or religious orientation, would I have subjected this individual to additional safety or security scrutiny?* If the answer is 'no,' then the action may violate civil rights laws."

But security decisions are never that clear. A safety officer will consider 12 many factors in calculating someone's riskiness; any one of them could be pulled out as a "but-for" element. As American's record makes clear, it is almost never the case that someone gets additional screening based on his apparent ethnic heritage or national origin alone; behavior and no-fly-list matching are key in the assessment. (In fact, about half the complainants in the government's action were not even Middle Eastern—many were Hispanic; one was a "Norwegian-Sicilian." DoT simply assumes, without evidence, that American scrutinized the men because of the mistaken belief that they were Arabs, rather than because of their behavior.) A pilot trying to apply the "but-for" test to his own security judgment will inevitably reduce the test to an easier calculus: "Deny passage to someone who is or could claim to look Muslim only under the most extreme circumstances."

In application, the government's "but-for" test reduces to a "never-ever" 13 rule: ethnic heritage, religion, or national origin may play no role in evaluating risk. But when the threat at issue is Islamic terrorism, it is reckless to ask officials to disregard the sole ironclad prerequisite for being an Islamic terrorist: Muslim identity. American officials may still be terrified about naming the threat, but a few Arab commentators are willing to say what the Bush administration will not: "It is a certain fact that not all Muslims are terrorists, but it is equally certain, and exceptionally painful, that almost all terrorists are Muslims," wrote Abdel Rahman al-Rashed, the general manager of the influential Al Arabiya television station, after the school massacre in Beslan, Russia.

Any discussion about how the government should identify Muslim ter- 14 ror suspects has been couched as a referendum on "racial profiling." But "racial profiling" is irrelevant. What is at issue is religious profiling. By definition—by Usama bin Ladin's own definition when he called on all Muslims to kill Americans wherever they can find them—Muslim terrorists must be Muslim. Because religious identity is not always apparent, however, national origin or ethnic heritage should be available as surrogates. Needless to say, Muslim identity should be at most only *one* factor in assessing someone's security risk. Unfortunately, the much-heralded 9/11 Commission report, while correctly naming the nation's primary threat as "*Islamist* terrorism," contains not one word about what the proper role of Muslim identity should be in locating such terrorists, a topic evidently too hot to touch.

Years of government lawsuits over specious employment-discrimination 15 claims have made the airlines gun-shy over "bias" issues. But American Airlines did contest DoT's discrimination action because so much was at stake. Federal law vests final responsibility for flight safety with the pilot. For a passel of discrimination lawyers, months after the fact, to question a pilot's good-faith judgment—made with incomplete information under great time pressure—violates a crucial principle of secure aviation.

American's defense pointed out the behavioral warning signs that had led 16 to the 11 removals. But fighting the government civil rights complex is futile; in February 2004, the airline, while vehemently denying guilt, settled the action for $1.5 million, to be spent on yet more "sensitivity training" for its employees. American's pilots were outraged. "Pilots felt: 'How dare they second-guess our decision?' " says Denis Breslin, a pilots' union official. "We just shake our heads in shame: 'How could the government be so wrong?' "

Not satisfied with just one scalp, the Transportation Department lawyers 17 brought identical suits against United, Delta, and Continental Airlines. While maintaining their innocence, those carriers also settled, pledging more millions for "sensitivity training"—money much better spent on security training than on indoctrinating pilots to distrust their own security judgments.

A former security officer for United Airlines describes the chilling effect 18 that bias investigations have on a pilot's safety decisions. Let's say the government has just raised the terror alert level. Just before takeoff, a flight attendant tells her pilot: "I'm scared of these five guys in back; they're talking intensely, but they get quiet when I pass." The pilot responds: "Tell me more." "I saw them before boarding, and they pretended not to know one another." The pilot observes them and sees the same thing. He decides to take them off that flight for a further security check.

Transportation Department lawyers soon contact the flight manager 19 about a discrimination complaint; the manager interviews the pilot and asks him to write a report. The pilot comes back to work, but week after week he hears nothing about the investigation. DoT is in no hurry. The pilot's anxiety level goes through the roof—maybe he'll be sued or fired.

The next time a security question arises, will he make the same decision? 20 wonders the ex-United official. Not if DoT can help it. "DoT is hoping he changes his behavior and looks for the positive: 'These guys are nicely dressed; I probably intimidate them. Heck, maybe they're talking about women!' "

In addition to individual discrimination suits, the government has con- 21 tinued to sic "disparate impact" analysis on anti-terror measures. One of the most destructive innovations of the rights lobby, such analysis—which assigns bigotry to neutral policies if they affect different demographic groups differently—is suicidal in a war-fighting situation. It rules out every security procedure that might actually be useful in combating Muslim terrorists, since a screening device for Muslim terrorists cannot by definition have the same effect on non-Muslims.

Transportation Department secretary Norman Mineta bears much of 22 the responsibility for the government's irrationality regarding airline security. He infamously maintained in an interview that a grandmother from Vero Beach, Florida, should receive the same scrutiny at the airport as a young Saudi male, and he constantly warns that domestic internment—as in World War II—may be just around the corner. And behind Mineta stands a permanent civil rights bureaucracy fixated on American racism. The same Transportation Department lawyer, for example, who complained in 1997 that the early prototype of CAPPS I might pull out "too many" people of the same ethnicity—Sam Podberesky—led the recent discrimination actions against the airlines. Without strong intervention from Mineta, DoT's anti-discrimination machine, like most of those in the government, would run on autopilot, even though its priorities have been proved disastrously wrong.

In the government's wake, the private civil rights bar, led by the ACLU, 23 has brought its own airline discrimination suits. An action against Northwest Airlines is seeking government terror watch lists, Northwest's boarding procedures, and its cabin training manual. If these materials got loose, they would be gold to terrorists trying to figure out airline security procedures.

Even more dangerous to our domestic defense against Islamic terrorism 24 than the airline absurdity is our failure to control who enters the country. Here, too, fear of offending the race and rights lobbies trumps security. The alien-smuggling trade is the "sea in which terrorists swim," explains David Cohen, Deputy Commissioner for Intelligence at the New York Police Department and a former CIA al-Qaida expert. Most of the 9/11 hijackers, as well as the other Muslim terrorists who planned or committed attacks on U.S. soil before 9/11, knew that when they broke visa and other immigration laws in order to carry out their plans, nothing would happen to them. As an al-Qaida website noted in 2002, only 5 percent of the flood of people and goods that cross the Mexican border each year are inspected. "These are figures that really call for contemplation," al-Qaida added.

As long as illegal aliens continue to defy U.S. entry laws, we will remain 25 as vulnerable as before 9/11. Yet this spring, Asa Hutchinson, the Department of Homeland Security's undersecretary for Border and Transportation Security, shut down a successful border-patrol initiative to catch illegal aliens. A specially trained team had apprehended about 450 border trespassers in several southern California cities. The *Los Angeles Times*, La Raza, and every other advocacy group for illegal aliens protested that the arrests were racially motivated and that they were "scaring" illegal aliens. All too predictably, the White House promptly called the team off, and Hutchinson appeased the race hustlers by denouncing the initiative as "racial profiling."

This July, Hutchinson followed up with a memo to every immigration, 26 border patrol, and customs agent in the country declaring that "preventing racial profiling is a priority mission of this department." One would have thought that guarding public safety would be the Department of Homeland Security's sole "priority mission." But Hutchinson notified the agents that they would all soon be retrained in the "prevention of racial and ethnic profiling."

President George W. Bush declared in 2001: "Racial profiling is wrong, 27 and we will end it in America." It would help if he followed up with a parallel pronouncement: "Illegal entry is wrong, and we will end it in America"— especially since illegal entry is proven to exist, unlike police racial profiling, and it threatens national safety. But any real effort to enforce the country's immigration laws would draw down charges of racism. So although the government has introduced flashy new technologies such as biometric scanning of visa holders at ports of entry, it still fails to devote even remotely adequate resources to core immigration policing.

A glance at a tiny section of the northern border, separating Vermont and 28 a small part of New York from Canada, makes clear how lackluster the government's response to illegal entry remains. Every week, agents in the border patrol's Swanton sector catch Middle Easterners and North Africans sneaking into Vermont. And every week, they immediately release those trespassers with a polite request to return for a deportation hearing, since the Department of Homeland Security failed to budget enough funding for sufficient detention space for lawbreakers. In May, Swanton agents released illegal aliens from Malaysia, Pakistan, Morocco, Uganda, and India without bond. In July, they gave illegals from 11 terror-sponsoring countries a free pass. Since all these aliens chose to evade the visa process, none has had a background check by a consular official that might have uncovered terrorist connections. All are now at large in the country, outside the reach of law enforcement.

The failure to interdict northern trespassers is particularly worrisome, 29 since Canada is a proven springboard for terrorists. Ahmed Ressam, the Algerian caught at the Canadian border with 100 pounds of explosives destined for the Los Angeles airport in December 1999, ran an al-Qaida cell in Montreal, despite having previously been ordered deported by the Canadian government. Two of the seven most wanted al-Qaida members, announced by Attorney General John Ashcroft in May, are naturalized Canadians. One, a Tunisian who has received flight training, has videotaped a "last will" in preparation for "martyrdom"; the other, an Egyptian who allegedly trained in Afghan terror camps, may already have slipped into the U.S. And Mohammed Naeem Noor Khan, arrested in July in Pakistan with detailed computer plans for attacks on financial buildings in New York, Newark, and Washington, visited Canada in 2000 and had recently applied for a return visa.

In response to the detention-space crisis, the Swanton bureau chief admonished his agents in May that before they released an illegal from a terrorist-producing country into the woods, they should write up a Significant Incident Report, listing all "suspicious facts and issues." A typical report: on May 31, agents stopped an illegal Bangladeshi whose visas the State Department had revoked in 2003 and whose driver's-license records contained a notice that he was a member of a terrorist organization. After the FBI told the border agents that it was not interested in the Bangladeshi, the agents released him.

This "catch and release" policy is in force all across the country for the same reason: no detention space. On June 8, agents in the Las Cruces, New Mexico, station apprehended three illegal Pakistanis and promptly let them go. The same day, guards at the Texas Uvalde station released a Bosnian wanted on an Interpol warrant for aggravated rape. The number of people caught at the southern border from "countries of interest"—terror dens— is on the rise; this year's list includes people from Afghanistan, Egypt, Kazakhstan, Kuwait, Indonesia, Iran, Iraq, Lebanon, Saudi Arabia, Somalia, Sudan, Syria, Yemen, and—in greatest numbers—Pakistan. If previous years are any guide, the number of illegals apprehended from "countries of interest" will far exceed 4,000 in 2004. Among them may well be terrorists like Adnan El Shukrijumah, one of the FBI's most wanted al-Qaida operatives, who was spotted just this May in an Internet café in Tegucigalpa, Honduras, but eluded capture. Shukrijumah has met with leaders of the violent El Salvadoran gang Mara Salvatrucha (see "The Illegal Alien Crime Wave," Winter 2004), for help in sneaking into the U.S., according to the *Washington Times*. Law enforcement authorities told the *Times* that al-Qaida is well aware of the border patrol's detention-space crisis and resulting "catch-and-release" policy, which it hopes to exploit to loose its agents into the country.

If the government were serious about ending illegal entry and its threat to national security, it would fund adequate detention space. Instead, it plans to add only 117 new detention beds in 2005 (while probably losing another 1,400 beds for failure to reimburse county and local jails for the space it rents from them). The administration would also enforce the law against hiring illegal aliens, rather than continuing the Clinton administration's disregard for that law. As long as the supply of jobs retains its gravitational pull, the deluge of illegal entrants will flow unabated, bringing terrorists in its wake.

But the administration seems determined to maintain the schizophrenic   33
status quo: we try to catch trespassers at the border, but once they slip
across, they're home free. That was Asa Hutchinson's message to the go-
getter California border agents this spring, and it's also the message of the
executive branch's continued silence on local "sanctuary policies" that forbid police from cooperating with immigration authorities. These bans
mean that the only branch of law enforcement with any hope of actually
apprehending border lawbreakers—local cops—are prevented from arresting immigration felons or notifying immigration officers of their where-
abouts. A bill to encourage cooperation between police and federal
authorities is languishing in Congress, ignored by the White House and
loudly denounced by illegal-alien advocates as an eruption of bigotry. Administration officials have also shied away from the issue of secure identification documents, even though, according to the 9/11 Commission and
every counter-terrorism agent working today, the easy availability of counterfeit identity cards greases the terror machine.

Finally, putting national security ahead of political correctness would   34
mean ending the special status granted Mexican illegals. None of the recent
measures to strengthen border oversight—inadequate in themselves—applies
to Mexicans. Mexicans are exempt from the biometric screening requirements for visa holders, for example, and an August initiative allowing border-
patrol agents to expedite deportation of illegals (a vain change without an
increase in detention space) exempts Mexicans. Meanwhile, the Mexican
government is busily providing cover for its illegal emigrants by furnishing
them with identity documents—"matricula consular" cards—intended to allow them to open U.S. bank accounts or get U.S. driver's licenses. Though the
FBI has denounced the matricula consular card as a security nightmare, since
its background check is so superficial and it is so easily forged, federal authorities are allowing its use to spread across the country.

These authorities seem to believe that they can give a pass to the hun-   35
dreds of thousands of Mexicans who cross illegally every year—thus pla-
cating the race advocates—and still strengthen the border against terrorists.
But since the government forswears consideration of national origin, race,
religion, or ethnicity in its law-enforcement activities, and won't even name
the enemy as Islamism, strict immigration policing across the board becomes
even more crucial for catching terrorists.

Without such enforcement, Muslim terrorists will make use of the in-   36
frastructure of illegality no less successfully than Mexican grape-pickers
and gangbangers. Middle Easterners have already discovered the useful
corruption of Mexican law-enforcement officials. In 2003, authorities
busted Mexico's consul in Lebanon for selling fake visas for up to $4,500.

Her ring had smuggled about 300 Lebanese into the U.S. from Tijuana from 1999 to November 2002. In the last two years, more than 50 other Mexican immigration officers have been indicted for corruption.

President Bush should announce that henceforth, illegal entry will be treated 37 like the crime that it is. To be against alien lawbreakers is not to be against immigrants, he should explain. Border laws protect the country for those immigrants who respect America's laws. Our inability to control who comes into the country is our biggest security threat, he should explain, and we must empower every branch of law enforcement to apprehend the lawbreakers. Washington should allocate the resources to detain and deport illegals, and should start enforcing long-standing laws against employing alien lawbreakers. A deafening roar of "racism" will result; but with the country at war, pandering to the race advocates must give way to protecting American lives.

Even were the government to start enforcing immigration rules, it would 38 still need to find the terror supporters already in the country. Al-Qaida members have roamed the United States for years, recruiting jihadists among citizens and non-citizens. But before 9/11, domestic counter-terrorist intelligence gathering was almost nonexistent, eroded by decades of civil-libertarian grandstanding. The threshold for investigating religious and political groups—above all, radical mosques—was very high; intelligence agents had to wait until a crime had been committed—or was just about to be—before opening an inquiry. Two years before 9/11, the head of the FBI's National Security Division was asked what the bureau was doing about terrorism. He replied: "We aren't violating anybody's civil liberties," reports Richard Gid Powers in his new history of the bureau. In other words: we're not doing much, but at least we won't be sued by the ACLU.

Has the FBI thrown off this deadly inhibition? Answering the question 39 is difficult, since covert operations are by definition secret. A high-ranking official in the FBI's National Security Law Unit, which oversees requests to wiretap foreign agents, claims that the bureau no longer shrinks from opening investigations into Muslim extremists.

Still, other security agencies continue to shy away from any allegation 40 of "profiling." The Department of Homeland Security recently requested that the Census Bureau pull together publicly available information on residential patterns of various "Arab ethnicities." Such information could be key in future terror investigations or outreach programs. Anyone with good computer skills could have produced the identical analysis from data on the Census Bureau's website; none of the information was private. Both the request and the Census Bureau's response were legal. Nevertheless, when the analysis became public this July, an outcry from Arab organizations, privacy advocates, and civil libertarians forced the Department of

Homeland Security to erect safeguards against any similar request in the future. The Census Bureau announced that it will no longer provide law enforcement or intelligence agencies with data on ethnic groups and other "sensitive populations" without reams of red-tape review. So much for information sharing in the war on terror.

The need for intelligence gathering remains urgent, however, since 41 according to many observers, suspicious behavior continues in mosques on the East and West Coasts—and in between. A group of newcomers will separate from the congregation and set up private conversations. "They do disruptive things, trying to pray by themselves in the middle of the ranks," according to Umar Abdul Jalil, a black imam in Harlem and the head of Muslim chaplains at New York City's sprawling Rikers Island jail. "They talk to this person and that person in secret, going into corners." Both blacks and Arabs have tried to infiltrate Jalil's Harlem mosque. What was their agenda? I asked. "I don't know," he said. "We threw them out immediately." Jalil, who is master of the double negative, does admit, however: "I would not say that individuals are not trying to make connections to radical groups, but in my experience, that would be an extreme minority."

In a more radical mosque, the leadership may sanction such breakaway 42 behavior. Prayer groups recruit the hardcore America-haters, who meet in the evenings, according to police observers.

During the 1980s and early 1990s, radical mosques along Brooklyn's At- 43 lantic Avenue, such as Al-Farooq, provided jihadists for the fight against the Russians in Afghanistan and served as a hub for the conspirators of the first World Trade Center bombing in 1993. Several officials, who would only speak on background, believe that similar activity is ongoing, particularly among Brooklyn's Pakistanis. And while some Muslim leaders and worshipers say that there's been a rethinking of anti-American rhetoric after 9/11, others maintain that it has only grown more vituperative in the wake of the Iraq war.

Yet even if the FBI is now fearless about using its surveillance authority, 44 the strategic challenge is daunting. "The dilemma," says a big-city police counter-terrorism official, is that "you can't put a bug in every mosque. And where are you going to put it? In the imam's office? In the corner where they gather? But should it be the same corner? And who's the 'they?'" The only solution, he says, is to develop sources and have them watch.

So far, however, federal and local efforts to penetrate the byzantine world 45 of mosque politics have had limited success. After an FBI outreach to a New York mosque, the imam and his deputies reportedly broke out laughing at their successful snow job: "This is great! They're coming to *us?*" the imam chortled. The situation is the same in southern California. "We'll come back from a Kumbayah meeting with a local mosque," says a police leader, "and realize that these guys who just agreed to help us are in our terror files!" Then there's the inevitable phone call from the imam three weeks later:

"'You need to check this guy out,'" and it turns out that the "suspect" 46 has been opposing the imam in local power plays.

The domestic barriers to tracking down potential terrorists explain why 47 so much of the post-9/11 intelligence in the war on Islamic terror has come from the interrogation of prisoners abroad. Yet that source is about to dry up, in the overreaction to the Abu Ghraib prisoner-abuse scandal. Military and CIA officials have shut down almost all interrogation techniques that were working, such as keeping someone awake over 12 hours a day, because of charges that they constituted "torture."

Domestic intelligence-gathering therefore will become all the more 48 crucial in the coming year. Unfortunately, most Muslim-American organizations—above all, the Council on American-Islamic Relations (CAIR)— send out a nonstop message of victimology, telling Muslims that the United States is their enemy and is stripping them of their civil rights. This summer, CAIR distributed postcards at mosques across the country with the infamous photograph from Abu Ghraib of a hooded prisoner standing on a box with wires hanging from his hands. Juxtaposed with the picture was a 2003 quotation from President Bush saying that the United States was leading the fight against torture. The postcards were supposed to be sent to Congress to demand an end to U.S. government torture. Such propaganda lessens the likelihood that Muslims will volunteer information about possible terror sympathizers in their midst.

All the more imperative, then, that no security officer, whether public 49 or private, should fear that if he acts on reasonable suspicion regarding a possible violation of the law or threat to public safety, his government will accuse him of racism.

The skittishness of an airline executive about the possibility of behav- 50 ioral profiling at American airports should be a thing of the past. Edmond Soliday, former United Airlines Vice President of Safety, lauds Israel's intense scrutiny of passengers. Soliday says he was "profiled" in Israel. "I was a single man alone, with no checked baggage, in that airport for the first time, wandering aimlessly looking for a pay phone. Security hit me." He was intensively questioned, and not just with "seven canned questions preapproved by the Department of Justice, as here." That kind of intervention found two suicide bombers in the Tel Aviv airport, who were walking on the concourse with identical gym bags but pretending not to know each other. Security sweated them and found explosives in their bags. Why don't we do what the Israelis do? I asked Soliday. "I'd be in jail in a week," he replied.

Tiny terror A three-year-old child is screened for weapons at Denver International Airport.

The Transportation Security Administration says it intends to test be- 51 havioral profiling in two airports. Whether it will have the fortitude to stand up against the inevitable charges of discrimination remains to be seen.

For now, officials trying to protect the public risk punishment and oppro- 52 brium, while terrorists trying to invade and destroy the country enjoy politically motivated protection. That's a formula for disaster, and it must change.

Thinking Critically

1. How would you describe Heather Mac Donald's perspective on homeland security? How might Mac Donald respond to Patrick Smith or Annie Jacobsen (their essays precede hers in this chapter)?

2. In your own words, describe the "but-for" test and the "never-ever" rule. Is it possible to apply logical solutions to seemingly subjective, emotion-based problems?

3. How does Mac Donald define *profiling?* In what ways does her definition differ from that of other writers in this chapter?

Writing Critically

1. Mac Donald describes how the infamous images of the torture of prisoners at Abu Ghraib have affected the prosecution and interrogation of terror suspects worldwide. Compare her observations with Deborah Pearlstein's arguments in "Rights in an Insecure World" (earlier in this chapter). In your opinion, what limits on personal liberty may be justified by national security considerations?

2. How does behavioral profiling differ from racial profiling? Is any kind of profiling ever legitimate? Under what circumstances?

3. Have you ever undergone any kind of sensitivity training, perhaps as an incoming college freshman or in the workplace? What did you learn from the training? What was the purpose of the training? If, as Mac Donald argues, one of the key factors motivating the Department of Transportation and other entities that provide sensitivity training is "litigation phobia"—that is, the fear of getting sued—is the sensitivity training really based on humane principles?

Arguing the Cultural Divides

1. In an essay, compare the experiences of Annie Jacobsen (pp. 669–76) with the responses and perspectives of Patrick Smith (pp. 678–83) and Heather Mac Donald (pp. 684–96). Assume that, whatever her interpretation of the experience might have been, Jacobsen is describing an actual series of events that occurred on a specific airplane flight. Do Patrick Smith and Heather Mac Donald propose any solutions that would have both resolved Jacobsen's fears and protected the civil rights of the Syrian musicians?

2. Would you rather be a brain in a vat, comfortable and "safe," or a perpetually hunted and fearful free agent? If we're all being monitored for our own safety, what should the penalties be for "unplugging" our neighbors and breaking free of the "MATRIX"? Draw upon and cite from Frank Furedi, Adam Gopnik, Corey Robin, or David Cole (all in this chapter) in your response.

3 Keep a log for one week, recording every time you make a phone call, use a credit or debit card, send an email, show an identification card, or otherwise have your activity tracked and logged. Choose a few transactions from your log and follow them through, from the point of contact to their eventual destination. (For example, see if you can arrange an interview with a customer service specialist at your bank or your cell phone company, and ask specifically how your personal information is recorded and if anyone else has access to it.) In an essay, describe your findings. What would it take for you to "unplug" yourself? Could you receive a paycheck? Pick up a doctor's prescription? Attend a friend's wedding across the country?

12

CHAPTER

From Outside In: America in the World

America Is Not a Hamburger: America's Attempt to "Re-Brand" Itself Abroad Could Be a Worse Flop than New Coke

NAOMI KLEIN

Canadian-born journalist and activist Naomi Klein writes extensively on consumer culture, with a particular interest in the burgeoning worldwide antiglobalization movement. She contributes a regular column to the *Globe and Mail* in Canada and the *Guardian* in Britain. Her 2000 book chronicling the antiglobalization movement, *No Logo: Taking Aim at the Brand Bullies,* has been translated into twenty-five languages. "America Is Not a Hamburger" appeared in *Fences and Windows: Dispatches from the Front Line of the Globalization Debate* (2002). In a 2004 interview with the PBS program *Frontline*, Klein described the influence of corporate "branding" and of advertising: "Branding, this process of selling an idea as opposed to a product, is not the same as advertising. It's actually in many ways the end of advertising, because it ramps up to the point where you're actually building these fully enclosed

branded [lives], fully synergized branded lives, which is a
lot more expensive than just taking out an ad and saying,
'Hey, guys, we've got a new product coming out.'" As
you read "America Is Not a Hamburger," keep this
distinction between branding and advertising in mind.

When the White House decided it was time to address the rising tides 1
of anti-Americanism around the world, it didn't look to a career
diplomat for help. Instead, in keeping with the Bush administration's philosophy that anything the public sector can do, the private sector can do
better, it hired one of Madison Avenue's top brand managers.

As Under Secretary of State for Public Diplomacy and Public Affairs, 2
Charlotte Beers had the assignment not to improve relations with other
countries but rather to perform an overhaul of the U.S. image abroad.
Beers had no previous State Department experience, but she had held the
top job at both the J. Walter Thompson and Ogilvy & Mather ad agencies,
and she's built brands for everything from dog food to power drills.

Now she was being asked to work her magic on the greatest branding 3
challenge of all: to sell the United States and its "war on terrorism" to an
increasingly hostile world. The appointment of an ad woman to this post
understandably raised some criticism, but Secretary of State Colin L. Powell
shrugged it off. "There is nothing wrong with getting somebody who knows
how to sell something. We are selling a product. We need someone who can
re-brand American foreign policy, re-brand diplomacy." Besides, he said,
"She got me to buy Uncle Ben's rice." So why, only five months in, does the
campaign for a new and improved Brand U.S.A. seem in disarray? Several of
its public service announcements have been exposed for playing fast and
loose with the facts. And when Beers went on a mission to Egypt in January
to improve the image of the U.S. among Arab "opinion makers," it didn't go
well. Muhammad Abdel Hadi, an editor at the newspaper *Al Ahram*, left his
meeting with Beers frustrated that she seemed more interested in talking
about vague American values than about specific U.S. policies. "No matter
how hard you try to make them understand," he said, "they don't."

The misunderstanding likely stemmed from the fact that Beers views the 4
United States' tattered international image as little more than a communi-
cations problem. Somehow, despite all the global culture pouring out of
New York, Los Angeles and Atlanta, despite the fact that you can watch
CNN in Cairo and *Black Hawk Down* in Mogadishu, America still hasn't
managed, in Beers's words, to "get out there and tell our story."

In fact, the problem is just the opposite: America's marketing of itself 5
has been *too* effective. Schoolchildren can recite its claims to democracy,

liberty and equal opportunity as readily as they can associate McDonald's with family fun and Nike with athletic prowess. And they expect the U.S. to live up to its promises.

If they are angry, as millions clearly are, it's because they have seen the   6
promises betrayed by U.S. policy. Despite President Bush's insistence that America's enemies resent its liberties, most critics of the U.S. don't actually object to America's stated values. Instead, they point to U.S. unilateralism in the face of international laws, widening wealth disparities, crackdowns on immigrants and human rights violations—most recently in the prison camps at Guantánamo Bay. The anger comes not only from the facts of each case but also from a clear perception of false advertising. In other words, America's problem is not with its brand—which could scarcely be stronger—but with its product.

There is another, more profound obstacle facing the relaunch of Brand   7
U.S.A., and it has to do with the nature of branding itself. Successful brand-ing, Allen Rosenshine, chairman and CEO of BBDO Worldwide, recently wrote in *Advertising Age*, "requires a carefully crafted message delivered with consistency and discipline." Quite true. But the values Beers is charged with selling are democracy and diversity, values that are pro-foundly incompatible with this "consistency and discipline." Add to this the fact that many of America's staunchest critics already feel bullied into conformity by the U.S. government (bristling at phrases like "rogue state"), and America's branding campaign could well backfire, and backfire badly.

In the corporate world, once a "brand identity" is settled on by head   8
office, it is enforced with military precision throughout a company's oper-ations. The brand identity may be tailored to accommodate local language and cultural preferences (like McDonald's offering hot sauce in Mexico), but its core features—aesthetic, message, logo—remain unchanged.

This consistency is what brand managers like to call "the promise" of   9
a brand: it's a pledge that wherever you go in the world, your experience at Wal-Mart, Holiday Inn or a Disney theme park will be comfortable and familiar. Anything that threatens this homogeneity dilutes a company's overall strength. That's why the flip side of enthusiastically flogging a brand is aggressively prosecuting anyone who tries to mess with it, whether by pirating its trademarks or by spreading unwanted information about the brand on the Internet.

At its core, branding is about rigorously controlled one-way messages,   10
sent out in their glossiest form, then hermetically sealed off from those who would turn that corporate monologue into a social dialogue. The most important tools in launching a strong brand may be research, creativity and design, but after that, libel and copyright laws are a brand's best friends.

When brand managers transfer their skills from the corporate to the 11
political world, they invariably bring this fanaticism for homogeneity with
them. For instance, when Wally Olins, co-founder of the Wolff Olins brand
consultancy, was asked for his take on America's image problem, he complained that people don't have a single clear idea about what the country
stands for but rather have dozens if not hundreds of ideas that "are mixed
up in people's heads in a most extraordinary way. So you will often find
people both admiring and abusing America, even in the same sentence."

From a branding perspective, it would certainly be tiresome if we found 12
ourselves simultaneously admiring and abusing our laundry detergent. But
when it comes to our relationship with governments, particularly the government of the most powerful and richest nation in the world, surely some
complexity is in order. Having conflicting views about the U.S.—admiring
its creativity, for instance, but resenting its double standards—doesn't
mean you are "mixed up," to use Olins's phrase, it means you are paying
attention.

Besides, much of the anger directed at the U.S. stems from a belief— 13
voiced as readily in Argentina as in France, in India as in Saudi Arabia—
that the U.S. already demands far too much "consistency and discipline"
from other nations; that beneath its stated commitment to democracy and
sovereignty, it is deeply intolerant of deviations from the economic model
known as "the Washington Consensus." Whether these policies, so beneficial to foreign investors, are enforced by the Washington-based International Monetary Fund or through international trade agreements, the
U.S.'s critics generally feel that the world is already far too influenced by
America's brand of governance (not to mention America's brands).

There is another reason to be wary of mixing the logic of branding with 14
the practice of governance. When companies try to implement global image
consistency, they look like generic franchises. But when governments do
the same, they can look distinctly authoritarian. It's no coincidence that
historically, the political leaders most preoccupied with branding themselves and their parties were also allergic to democracy and diversity. Think
Mao Tse-tung's giant murals and Red Books, and yes, think Adolf Hitler,
a man utterly obsessed with purity of image: within his party, his country,
his race. This has been the ugly flip side of dictators striving for consistency
of brand: centralized information, state-controlled media, re-education
camps, purging of dissidents and much worse.

Democracy, thankfully, has other ideas. Unlike strong brands, which 15
are predictable and disciplined, true democracy is messy and fractious, if
not outright rebellious. Beers and her colleagues may have convinced Colin
Powell to buy Uncle Ben's by creating a comforting brand image, but the

United States is not made up of identical grains of rice, assembly-line hamburgers or Gap khakis.

Its strongest "brand attribute," to use a term from Beers's world, is its 16
embrace of diversity, a value Beers is now attempting to stamp with cookie-cutter uniformity around the world, unfazed by the irony. The task is not only futile but dangerous: brand consistency and true human diversity are antithetical—one seeks sameness, the other celebrates difference; one fears all unscripted messages, the other embraces debate and dissent.

No wonder we're so "mixed up." Making his pitch for Brand U.S.A. in 17
Beijing recently, President Bush argued that "in a free society, diversity is not disorder. Debate is not strife." The audience applauded politely. The message might have proved more persuasive if those values were better reflected in the Bush administration's communications with the outside world, both in its image and, more important, in its policies.

Because as President Bush rightly points out, diversity and debate are 18
the lifeblood of liberty. But they are enemies of branding.

Thinking Critically

1. What are the ways in which the communities to which you belong (your campus, your town, your place of worship) "brand" themselves? Is the purpose of that brand to include or to exclude? For example, if you wear a sweatshirt with your school's logo on it, do you feel that you're more a part of your campus community?

2. What is the implicit value judgment in Naomi Klein's phrase (in paragraph 1) "in keeping with the Bush administration's philosophy that anything the public sector can do, the private sector can do better"?

3. The PBS program *Online News Hour* posts an interview with Charlotte Beers, the U.S. Under Secretary of State for Public Diplomacy and Public Affairs, at <http://www.pbs.org/newshour/media/public_diplomacy/beers_1-03.html>. After reading this interview, return to Klein's article. Do you think that Klein presents Beers's experience and ideas fairly? Give reasons for your opinion.

Writing Critically

1. What are the inconsistencies that Klein points out between the international policies of the United States and the "brand" campaign piloted by Charlotte Beers? For example, Klein observes that, in some ways, America has been overwhelmingly successful in marketing certain aspects of itself. Create a presentation in which you "pitch" an idea for a marketing campaign to the office of the U.S. secretary of state, taking into account the inconsistencies that Klein describes. You might wish to include visuals or audio in your presentation.

2. Select an advertising campaign that markets an *idea* rather than a product. For example, many advertisers and media outlets produce public service campaigns that encourage kids to stay in school or stay off drugs. How effective are those campaigns, in your opinion? Extend the scope of your research to include any data that supports or refutes your opinion of the campaign's effectiveness.

Innocents Abroad?

Michael Gorra

An English professor at Smith College, Michael Gorra has written on the history of the novel, and his book reviews appear in the *New York Times Book Review,* the *Atlantic Monthly,* and other publications in the United States and Great Britain. His travel memoir, *The Bells in Their Silence: Travels Through Germany,* was published in 2004. "Innocents Abroad?" appeared in the May 2003 issue of *Travel + Leisure,* an upscale monthly magazine about travel, especially to exotic or luxurious destinations. Essays and travelogues by writers and artists are frequently featured in the magazine; its website is <http://www.travelandleisure.com/.

One day in the summer of 2001 I found myself in the old ecclesiastical city of Würzburg, not far from Germany's geographical center, walking up the great staircase of the Residenz, which was begun in 1720 by Balthasar Neumann for the town's ruler, Prince-Bishop Johann Philipp von Schönborn. Built of warm golden sandstone, with an interior of marble and gilt, it was an extravagant place even by the standards of eighteenth-century absolutism. The philosopher David Hume, on a visit in 1748, described it as "more complete and finished" than Versailles—and that was before the paint job. In 1752, Gianbattista Tiepolo was hired to work a fresco over the entirety of the ceiling toward which I was now climbing, and in the process transformed the already majestic flight of stairs into one of the grandest spaces in Europe: the Continent's largest fresco, all the guidebooks say, so large that it's impossible to see the whole thing at once. There's always something behind you or hidden by the turn of the stairs, and each step, each twist of the head, reveals something new, as though the picture were moving around you.

Certainly the vault's subject enforces that sense of cinematic motion, for Tiepolo's project was to paint an allegory of the four continents. As I ascended the first steps, America began to rise before me, a vision dominated by an enormous alligator and a bare-breasted, feather-headdressed maiden. There were palm trees and bows and arrows, Indians and the banners of the conquistadores, high mountains and a cannibal feast, all of it on a dim north wall where the colors seemed misty and low. Then I reached the landing and turned, and on the opposite wall saw bright Europe. Far fewer people here were naked. Instead, there were musicians and painters, crosses and crosiers, Europa with her flower-horned bull, a greyhound, some fragments of architecture, and, away in the corner, Tiepolo himself, looking rather tired.

In making the turn toward Europe, in walking up those stairs, I began, 3 in that summer that now seems so distant, to spin a theory about the whole business of being an American. It was a theory forged during a time of peace and goodwill, when for a few brief moments we Americans seemed as welcome in Europe as at any time since World War II. And it comes back to me today when the newspapers and broadcasts on both sides of the Atlantic are so full of mutual accusations and suspicion. Now that many of us are experiencing a new and alienating wave of European distrust, when we may fear being reviled for our nationality on a continent whose culture we share, it seems necessary to think hard about just what our relation to Europe has been. What has it meant, as a destination rather than a place of origin? What has it said to us, as Americans?

In that June of brilliant, peaceful sunshine, surrounded by Tiepolo's splen- 4 did world, I could not help but see myself as having stepped for a moment into one of Henry James's stories about the American encounter with old Europe. "A Passionate Pilgrim," the title story of his first book, tells the tale of an American who believes he has an ancestral claim to an English manor. The piece is sentimental and far from James's best, but it does supply a necessary phrase, as does a letter he wrote not long after to Charles Eliot Norton: "It's a complex fate, being an American, and one of the responsibilities it entails is fighting against a superstitious valuation of Europe." In fact, the main character in "A Passionate Pilgrim" dies of that superstition, broken by his discovery that England cannot provide a home for him. I had some of that superstition, too, and like James I had a sense that as an American I was both a latecomer to and the inheritor of the world that lay painted on the wall above me. (Though for me that world had been in no way fatal, and the passion part had taken the substantive form of my own marriage to a Swiss art historian.)

Americans used to go to Europe—"old Europe"—in search of a larger life. 5 We went because living abroad expanded our sense of what an American could be; offered, paradoxically, a different and richer and grander way of being an American than we could find at home. In James's day we came to grasp at an antique culture, to talk with a history that stretched back beyond our grandparents; in the 1920s, Ernest Hemingway and F. Scott and Zelda Fitzgerald joined Gertrude Stein in Paris, escaping the insular prohibitions of Main Street. Later, black writers and musicians (James Baldwin, Louis Armstrong, Miles Davis) traveled to Europe, because there they could be American in a way that they couldn't in America itself. But in a sense this was true for all Americans, James included: Europe allowed us to see ourselves in purely national terms, to shuck the more local affiliations of race or region or even family. And the fiction of expatriation, from *Portrait of a Lady* to the early work of Hemingway and on to James Baldwin's *Giovanni's Room* and even Patricia Highsmith's *Talented Mr. Ripley,* has used Europe as a kind of litmus paper against which to test an abstract American identity.

Or at least that's what such fiction used to do. A decade after "A Passionate Pilgrim," and back in Boston for the first time since he had made his own choice of London, James observed that the American writer "*must* deal, more or less, even if only by implication, with Europe; whereas no European is obliged to deal in the least with America." *Not true,* I couldn't help thinking, as I looked up at the camel caravans of Tiepolo's rather Arab-dominated Africa, *not now, not anymore.* We Americans were still nearly all of us superstitious about Europe, we bought its food and cars and cosmetics, its furniture and clothing; it still set the fashions, or some of them. But often it no longer seemed necessary, no longer something with which we were "obliged to deal," and our own country stood in its place, as even James had suspected it someday might. The complexities of our fate might still be worked out in relation to Europe, but not to it alone.   6

    Standing beneath Tiepolo's Asia, with its ruins and elephants and cavalry, it struck me that the books that today use a foreign land to probe our peculiar fate tend to choose a different setting and to belong to a different genre. When he'd settled in Europe, James wrote home: "I take possession of the old world—I inhale it—I appropriate it." Even then, such words no longer seemed a figure of speech. Not America's aspirations but its power, not its innocence but its culpability: those are the terms that today would shape James's "international theme." And now that theme belongs not to the novel of manners but to the thriller, to fiction that in chronicling the American imperium finds its most congenial settings in such places as the Southeast Asia or Central America of Robert Stone's *Dog Soldiers* and *A Flag for Sunrise,* or in the unnamed Middle Eastern kingdom of Henry Bromell's recent *Little America.*   7

Perhaps Patricia Highsmith's Ripley books marked the moment of 8 change. For Highsmith's Tom Ripley the New World is not fresh and promising; instead he finds in France and Italy a chance for the self-invention denied him at home—an ironic inversion of what America itself had offered to so many of the Continent's tired and hungry and poor. Yet Europe is also for him a place free of consequences, a playground where he can literally get away with murder, and in the post-Highsmith novel of expatriation Europe becomes an entirely conventional setting. The Americans in Paris whom one finds in such expertly made novels as Diane Johnson's *Le Divorce* and *Le Mariage* are awkward and ingenuous and perhaps even criminally naïve. The Europeans aren't and lean toward duplicity instead. The terms are all known and settled in advance, the rules firmly and predictably established. In a way, they're the fictional equivalent of the act my wife and I have developed over the years, a practiced routine in which *la différence* can be endlessly discussed and each other's cultural limitations deplored. But neither those books nor that routine itself offers much in the way of surprise. Europe might still provide a sense of individual liberation, I thought, but the cultural stakes in such an awakening were low, a matter of lifestyle.

Yet I felt uneasy with the thrust of that argument even as I carried it 9 down the stairs and across the square in front of the Residenz. It seemed odd to think of Europe as irrelevant in Germany of all places, especially while walking across a square on which the brownshirts had mustered and books had been burned. Here, more than anywhere, was where our hunch-backed era had been determined and deformed. Europe wasn't irrelevant. But it was no longer the inescapable term of comparison.

Or was it? The months since I stood beneath Tiepolo's ceiling seemed 10 at first to confirm Europe's diminished role in shaping our condition, and yet later to give it a renewed importance, the sense that it remains our necessary cultural counterweight. It hasn't always been comfortable to see the debate I had with myself in Würzburg become the material of op-eds and headlines, to find the terms of what had seemed a long-settled relation tossed and turned and argued over. The familiar faults that Diane Johnson describes no longer seem just a question of manners, are no longer the stuff of comedy. They have consequences once more, and have left each side with grave doubts about the other, with the fear that our interests—or maybe just our governments' interests—now diverge, in a way that they haven't for a half century and more. Yet those debates—those doubts—have also revealed the degree to which we remain each other's interlocutors, and in the end our disagreements recall nothing so much as the doubts of marriage itself; a bad patch in something that will nevertheless be patched up. My own marriage has made Europe into a place with which I am indeed obliged to deal and from which I continue to learn, even as our alliance ensures that my wife, too, will have to keep on coming to terms with America. And so it is for our two continents: linked as in any marriage by time, by what's been shared and squabbled over, by what amounts in the end to history. However disagreeably America and Europe may now strike each other, a divorce remains unthinkable.

Thinking Critically

1. Even without visiting the website of *Travel and Leisure,* what can you infer from Michael Gorra's essay about the magazine's target audience? How do you think such an audience would respond to Gorra's essay?

2. With other members of your class, prepare an annotated and illustrated webpage to accompany Gorra's essay. For example, you might want to include information about David Hume; images of Versailles and the Residenz in Würzburg; examples of Gianbattista Tiepolo's art; reviews of the films *Le Divorce* and *The Talented Mr. Ripley* and of Henry James's story "A Passionate Pilgrim," as well as other works that Gorra alludes to. How does familiarity with these cultural touchstones enhance your understanding of Gorra's argument?

3. This essay was published in 2003 and begins with "One day in the summer of 2001" (paragraph 1), "that summer that now seems so distant" (paragraph 3). To what is Gorra alluding? What is the cause of this sense of distance?

Writing Critically

1. What, in Gorra's argument, does it mean to be an "expatriate" American? If you are a U.S. citizen and you have traveled abroad, has that experience either clarified or confused your understanding of what it means to be an American? You might choose to structure your essay around an encounter with a particular landmark or work of art, as Gorra does.

2. Much is made of the fact that so few American students become competent in a foreign language, yet few other societies in the world are as effortlessly polyglot as the United States. If you are multilingual (whether or not you are a U.S. citizen), describe how having several languages has shaped your experience of living in America. If you are a native English-speaker and do not comfortably speak another language, describe a time (either in a particular community or in another country) when you did not understand the language. How did the experience of not understanding, and not being understood, shape your experience of being an American?

The View From Out There

FRANCES FITZGERALD

> This review of Dana Lindaman and Kyle Ward's book
> *History Lessons: How Textbooks from Around the
> World Portray U.S. History* appeared in the *Washing-
> ton Post* in August 2004. Frances FitzGerald's book
> *Fire in the Lake: The Vietnamese and the Americans in
> Vietnam* won a Pulitzer Prize and a National Book
> Award in 1973. A respected historian and muckraking
> journalist, FitzGerald is also the author of *America
> Revised: History Schoolbooks in the Twentieth Century*
> (1979). Her work has appeared in publications ranging
> from *Architectural Digest* and *Rolling Stone* to *The
> Nation* and *Foreign Policy.*

Here are a few things students in this country will not find in their his-   1
tory books but that students from certain other countries may know
for a fact:

   a. Our revolution was inspired by the work of the French Enlighten-
      ment philosophers (not the essays of John Locke).
   b. We won that war largely because the British commanders were slow
      and blundering (not because of the wisdom and determination of
      George Washington).
   c. What we thought of as a revolution was for many inhabitants of
      British North America an extended civil war, in which many were
      forced into exile.
   d. After Gen. Cornwallis surrendered at Yorktown in 1781, the Spanish
      and French fleets opened full-scale war with the British in the
      Caribbean.

As might perhaps be imagined, the facts betray points of view: (a) comes
from a French history text; (b) from a British one; (c) from a Canadian school
history; and (d) from a text published for the English-speaking West Indies.

    Dana Lindaman, a graduate student at Harvard, and Kyle Ward, an assis-   2
tant professor at Vincennes University in Indiana, have compiled this collection of excerpts from other national history textbooks out of concern for the
insularity—or what they call the "isolationist tendency"—of the American
educational system. In fact, U.S. history texts are not as insular as they once
were; nor are they any more insular than most national histories of other
countries. Still, much in this collection would startle not only American high
school students but many of their teachers as well. In addition, while this is

not its purpose, the book, taken as a whole, explains rather better than the punditry mills why many countries, particularly those once known as "the Allies," take such a dim view of the United States.

Reading a book composed entirely of excerpts from textbooks may seem 3 an unpromising activity, but history texts reveal much about national perspectives and prejudices: They are more expressive than government pronouncements; they get into matters diplomats avoid; and yet, as the authors note, they are in varying degrees state-sanctioned and thus official, or semiofficial, stories about the national past. Most reflect public attitudes; all help to create those attitudes because they are the most widely read histories in each country, and because kids read them during the formative adolescent years. What students remember from their reading is not, of course, so clear. (It's certainly not clear in the United States, where history texts run to 1,200 pages and weigh about four pounds.) Still the texts have an authority that books by individual historians lack, for, even in the best school systems, teachers, in their desperate attempt to drum in a few names and dates, rarely question their points of view, and students hazily come to regard what they read as the truth.

History Lessons includes excerpts from a wide range of countries: Rus- 4 sia, Japan, Zimbabwe, Iran, North Korea—but not, for some reason, China. Best represented, however, are the schoolbooks of our continental neighbors and of those European countries long involved with North America. Some of the commentary on U.S. policy is unsurprising. An attentive American high school student could probably guess what a British text would say about D-Day, or what a Mexican text would say about the annexation of Texas, or how a Filipino text would describe the Spanish-American war and its aftermath. But how many Americans know—as Filipino students do—that in 1937 the Philippines sought to join the British Commonwealth out of a well-placed fear that the United States would not protect it from an invasion by Japan? And how many Americans could characterize the Canadian schoolbook view of U.S. history?

According to Canadian texts (six are cited), the United States planned to 5 conquer and annex Canada during the Revolution, the War of 1812, the Civil War and at various points in between. During the Cold War, the United States repeatedly bullied Canada into supporting its aggressive military policies. Canadian officials hoped that NATO would evolve into a North Atlantic community that would act as a counterweight to U.S. influence in Canada, but in vain: Canadian governments had to toe the U.S. line or suffer humiliation. During the Cuban Missile Crisis, Prime Minister John G. Diefenbaker, concerned that Kennedy's belligerence might lead to a nuclear war, waited three days before announcing that Canadian forces had gone on the alert. In the next election, the Americans used their influence to topple the truculent prime minister. Diefenbaker's successor, Lester Pearson, aligned Canada more closely with the United States, but in 1965 he annoyed Lyndon Johnson by calling for a bombing pause and a negotiated settlement to the Vietnam War. In a meeting after the speech, Johnson grabbed Pearson by the lapels and shouted, "You pissed on my rug."

Thus have Canadian texts immortalized the Johnson vernacular.   6

In few countries are the texts so consistently critical of the United States   7
as they are in Canada, but in a couple of cases the rhetoric is alarming. For national security purposes, we should have read Saudi textbooks years ago, for even while Saudi diplomats were cooing to American officials, Saudi students were reading rants about "Crusader" and "Neo-imperialist" attacks on Islam.

Most national school histories take a fairly parochial view of world   8
events: That is their nature. Some, like the French text that gives the French resistance the entire credit for the liberation of Paris in 1945, reveal more about their own countries than about the United States. Others serve to reveal our degree of insularity and self-preoccupation. For example, U.S. texts describe the French and Indian War as a purely American conflict, but British and French texts show the war to be a mere incident in the ongoing struggle between the two European empires. Too, the thoughtful and nationally self-critical Nigerian account of the Atlantic slave trade paints American slavery against a much larger canvas.

On a few issues, the texts of our neighbors and of European countries   9
(at least those that are cited by Lindaman and Ward) directly contradict the received wisdom in U.S. schoolbooks. The purpose of the Monroe Doctrine, they agree, was to assert U.S. economic hegemony in the Americas; Truman's purpose in dropping atomic bombs on Hiroshima and Nagasaki was to frighten the Soviets and prevent them from entering the war against Japan; later the United States overplayed fears of Soviet expansionism. In contrast to American schoolbooks, these texts stress the U.S. pursuit of its economic interests during the Cold War, but then they are in general far franker about economic interests and political power than American texts. Notably, too, European schoolbooks give extensive coverage to 20th-century Middle Eastern conflicts, while American histories hardly mention them.

History Lessons is sloppily edited. (There were 2.5 million, not 25 mil-   10
lion settlers in the American colonies in 1776.) And it could have been better introduced and annotated. For example, the authors suggest that the Cuban account of the Spanish-American war reflects a 20th-century per-

spective. But all textbooks reflect contemporary perspectives; and, if publishers in other countries re-edit and republish their texts every few years, as they do in the United States, then the texts may represent far less stable national attitudes than they appear to. The authors also tell us that most modern French texts are not narratives but collections of primary source materials with short historical summaries. But what are the formats of the other texts they cite? What grades are they designed for? (And, by the bye, how much do they weigh?) Still, the authors deserve a Stakhanovite Hero of Labor award just for reading all of these texts. And they have put together a provocative, timely and surprisingly readable book.

Thinking Critically

1. This essay is a book review. To what extent is Frances FitzGerald's essay what you might expect from a review, and in what ways is it an essay that makes a larger argument, using Lindaman and Ward's *History Lessons* as evidence for a larger argument? Is this essay more effective as a review or as an argument? (Of course, in your opinion, it might be equally effective as both.)

2. FitzGerald begins with four examples from history textbooks from other countries. Do you know enough about any of the events or people named to agree or disagree with these examples?

Writing Critically

1. What subjects in U.S. history were especially emphasized in your high school curriculum? Since then, what have you learned about U.S. history that has surprised you or challenged what you previously learned? In an essay, describe both the subject or subjects emphasized in your high school history class and the surprising or challenging new knowledge you gained later. What, in your opinion, was responsible for your being surprised or challenged by the later information? What does this evolution of your thinking reveal about the way U.S. history was taught at your high school?

2. If you studied U.S. history in another country, describe aspects of the subject about which, in your opinion, Americans are biased or insufficiently informed.

3. If you were required to take a class in world history in high school or in college, describe the curriculum and the political/ideological approach of the teacher and the required textbook. Do you think it is ever possible to study history in a way that is free of bias?

What Is an American Movie Now?

LYNN HIRSCHBERG

> Lynn Hirschberg is editor at large of the *New York Times Magazine;* this essay appeared in the November 24, 2004, issue. Hirschberg's writing about popular culture and the media has also been published in *Vanity Fair, Rolling Stone, Esquire,* and *Harper's Bazaar.*

I. Is the Face of America That of a Green Ogre?

This year's Cannes International Film Festival epitomized the extraordinary global reach of American films—sometimes to the point of absurdity. There were thrilling movies at Cannes—movies that told original, compelling stories about life in Senegal and upper-middle-class Paris and the jungles of Thailand. But those movies (and many others) contrasted sharply with the American films spotlighted at the festival, whose chief purpose, it seemed, was to please the widest possible audience.

Along with weapons, movies are among our most lucrative exports to a waiting world, and in the last seven years or so, it has become clear that the expected audience for nearly all American-made studio movies, the audience they are designed and created for, has shifted from the 50 states to the global marketplace. This change in perspective has, naturally, resulted in a change in content: nuances of language or the subtleties of comedy do not translate easily between cultures, but action or fantasy or animation is immediately comprehensible, even if you live in, say, Japan, which is the country that most big studios long to reach. Films like this year's *Troy* (which was shown at Cannes), *The Day After Tomorrow* and *Van Helsing,* which are not dependent on dialogue, did not play as well as expected in America but became huge hits in many other countries, making several times what they made in the U.S. box office. Thankfully, the so-called specialty divisions of the big studios still try to depict the prevailing mood of the country. But consider a specialty film like *Sideways,* which is the best American movie I have seen this year: it has no international stars and no action, and because the film shifts in tone from comedy to drama in nearly every scene, it is not likely to be easily comprehended by a worldwide audience. As far as the big studios go, *Sideways* is essentially a foreign film made in America.

But *Shrek 2* is not. An American entry in this year's Cannes competition, *Shrek 2* continues the animated saga of the lovable, irascible green creature (whose voice is that of the international star Mike Myers doing a Scottish brogue); his bride, the princess; and his faithful donkey (voice by the very funny Eddie Murphy). *Shrek 2* has the added bonus of Antonio

Banderas, who gives the growing Latin market a chance to cheer for his Puss in Boots. As charming as *Shrek 2* is, I found it an unsettling example of how big studios represent the United States to the world. While other countries have interpreted globalism as a chance to reveal their national psyches and circumstances through film, America is more interested in attracting the biggest possible international audience. At Cannes, war-torn Croatia was shown through the eye of the director Emir Kusturica, the French elite was exposed in *Look at Me,* the fear of female genital mutilation was depicted in Senegal's *Moolaade.* And so on. America had a green fantasy creature and Michael Moore, who went on to win the festival's top prize with his documentary *Fahrenheit 9/11.*

Wandering through Cannes and fighting my way into screenings, I felt a 4 growing frustration that what I loved about American movies (and, by extension, about America) was in short supply, and when I mentioned this to Walter F. Parkes, head of motion pictures at Dream Works SKG, he said: "I know what you're talking about." Parkes, like most of the big studio heads, is in a bind: corporate finances dictate that they cast the widest net possible. That has become the mandate of the studio president. Dream Works, for instance, made *Shrek 2* and is trying to parlay the $436 million success of the film (it is currently the third-highest-grossing movie of all time) into a profitable I.P.O. for its animation division. "Films are the one product that we have that's the first choice around the world," Parkes continued. "So, then, the questions to ask are: Is this the one place that people's fears about globalization are coming to fruition? Is America dominating world culture through the movies it produces? And if so, does that come with certain responsibilities beyond economic ones? These are questions that we have to ask ourselves. And they are different questions than we asked even five years ago."

The day before *Shrek 2* was set to have its premiere at Cannes, Dream 5 Works's representatives placed large plastic bags full of green Shrek ears along the Croisette, the bustling beachfront walkway that dominates the action in Cannes. Even before the festival began, it was feared that protesting French workers would shut it down over a labor dispute. On this day, a group of hundreds gathered outside the Carlton Hotel to denounce the war in Iraq. They were chanting in French for about 45 minutes, until the police broke up the demonstration. Then, as the protesters dissipated into the throng on the Croisette, I watched them, one by one, put on the free Shrek ears. They were attracted, it seemed, by the ears' goofiness and sheer recognizability. Immediately, the crowd, once filled with political fervor, was transformed into a sea of cartoon characters.

I felt embarrassed: America seemed, at best, an absurd, vaguely comic 6 place.

When you look at the big international hits of the year, it is easy to   7
understand why the world views America with a certain disgust. Shrek may
be a lovable (and Scottish) ogre, but nearly every other global hero in
American movies is bellicose, intellectually limited, stuck in ancient times
or locked in a sci-fi fantasy. American films used to be an advertisement for
life in the states—there was sophistication, depth, the allure of a cool, complex manner. Now most big studio films aren't interested in America, preferring to depict an invented, imagined world, or one filled with easily
recognizable plot devices. "Our movies no longer reflect our culture," said
a top studio executive who did not wish to be identified. "They have
become gross, distorted exaggerations. And I think America is growing
into those exaggerated images.

My fear is that it's the tail wagging the dog—we write the part, and then   8
we play the part."

II. Sorry, We Don't Film Here Anymore

Several months after I returned from Cannes, I phoned nearly every big stu-   9
dio chief and queried them about the wages of globalization. Not surprisingly, they all maintained that they chose movies on the basis of whether a
script or story grabbed them, and not according to the dictates of a global
audience. And yet they also acknowledged that they typically build their
slate around the so-called event films, like another *Harry Potter* or *Star
Wars* or *Matrix* installment. Event films are big and expensive and conceived for the largest audience imaginable. To keep costs down, most of
them are shot in other countries. "It used to be Canada," said Jeff Robinov,
president of production at Warner Brothers Pictures, the industry leader in
the global film business. "But the Canadian tax-incentive laws were redefined. London has instituted rebates that have lured production there."

Between mid-October and the end of the year, Robinov will travel to   10
Australia and Rome and twice visit London, Paris and Canada. He's checking on all of his films. He's accustomed to this: the *Matrix* movies were shot
completely in Australia (except for a freeway scene shot outside San Francisco). Shooting overseas saves money and adds to the universal appeal of
the films—the films are set in a movie world with no distinct sense of place;
they could happen anywhere.

Sherry Lansing, Paramount's chairwoman, who just announced her   11
plans to step down, noted that the world marketplace has only recently
become an important factor. "I think CNN brought the world together,"
she told me. "When I worked as a producer and we made *Fatal Attraction*
in the mid-80's, we never even thought of the global audience. Back then,
we thought, If it does well in America, it will do well over there."

But the international success of *Titanic* in 1997 helped to change every- 12
thing. "When *Titanic* opened at only $28 million in the U.S.," recalled
Nina Jacobson, president of the Buena Vista Motion Picture Group at Disney, "everyone called 20th Century Fox and offered their condolences. But
Titanic turned out to be the ultimate international movie. It played very
well in America, but in Japan they loved it, loved it, loved it. It eventually
made $900 million in rentals worldwide. That movie is so big internation-
ally that no one can touch it, but everyone tries."

Titanic was a rarity: a special-effects marvel that helped create two stars 13
(Leonardo Di Caprio and Kate Winslet) and won a hoard of Oscars. (The
success of *Titanic* is daunting even for its creator—James Cameron has not
made a film since.) In 2003, another global milestone was established by
the second *Matrix* film: at the suggestion of its producer, Joel Silver, the
movie was released simultaneously all over the world. "Day and date"
releases are increasingly necessary to capitalize on audience interest and,
more important, to limit piracy. "If you don't release your movie at roughly
the same time all over the world, the video of your movie will be sold on
the streets of Singapore within days of its first release," Jacobson
explained. "I don't want to be the one to say this, but the song is correct:
it's a small world, after all. The audience has merged."

Like other studio heads, she said this matter-of-factly, a statement of 14
fact. But clearly her decision-making has been affected by her observations.
Of course, it's not all blockbusters at the big studios these days. Warner
Brothers, for example, is currently making *Syriana* with George Clooney.
Described by many as one of the best scripts in Hollywood, it is a dark tale
about the global oil business that intertwines Middle Eastern politics and
a story line involving the C.I.A. Meanwhile, Sony, more than most studios,
is diversified, green-lighting *Spider-Man* and *Closer,* a $30 million drama,
directed by Mike Nichols, about two couples who are undone by an affair.
Perhaps wisely, the studio is hedging its bet by stocking *Closer* with the
international stars Julia Roberts and Jude Law. "It's always a decision,"
Jacobson told me. "You might make a choice, for instance, to put John Tra-
volta in *Ladder 49,* as we did, to heighten the national and international
profile of a film. And you have to realize that if you put a sports movie into
production, it will do disastrously internationally. It won't travel no matter how good it is, so you adjust the budget accordingly. The world just
doesn't care about other people's sports."

III. Who Is the Bad Guy Now?

Part of the reason I find the globalization of American movies unsettling is 15
that I can't remember a time when the dialogue at cocktail parties or

between friends or in office meetings has been so lively and political. The shift in the national conversation is missing in our global film identity. For the most part, present-day politics may be too complicated a subject for Hollywood to handle—at least in ambitious feature films.

"You have to make different decisions now," said Lansing, whose com- 16 pany, Paramount, made *Team America,* the puppet comedy in which Kim Jong Il is the archenemy. "It's hard, for instance, to pick a villain with a global audience in mind. If we're in a global market, it's going to be a challenge to find credible villains." The movie *Pearl Harbor* played well in Japan, but generally the studio heads agreed: countries (with the possible exception of North Korea, which is not a big movie market) can no longer be demonized.

Strangely, politics, especially anti-American politics, just might have 17 global appeal. Insiders predict that *The Manchurian Candidate,* with its vague Halliburton-esque conspiracy plot line, will play better to an anti-American international audience than it did here. Warner Brothers has high hopes for the ambiguous villain in *Syriana.* "The enemy is a combination of global business and politics," Jeff Robinov said. "We think that will play well to international markets."

For the most part, however, studios are more comfortable with plots 18 and characters from a parallel universe that does not mirror ours or, really, anyone's. If you want to find anything like the voice of America, you have to see a documentary or a smaller film from one of the specialty divisions of a studio. Jacobson told me: "The chitchat that precedes every pitch meeting has changed. But the pitches haven't. In the movie business, it's hard to be in the moment or of the moment—the economics are too great. That's why there are smaller divisions. They have a different audience."

IV. Why Small American Movies Don't Travel

Unfortunately, the much-admired mini-majors are not always content with 19 a small domestic audience. While I have an enormous weakness for Harvey Weinstein's passion for films, the truth is that he has radically departed from the original idea behind his company, Miramax. Initially, Miramax embraced challenging movies like *My Left Foot, The Crying Game* and *Pulp Fiction.* Weinstein was brilliant at marketing these films, and he developed a brand: a Miramax movie was aimed at certain members of the audience (me, for instance) who wanted an alternative to what the major studios were producing.

After *Pulp Fiction,* which was rejected by major studios, Weinstein him- 20 self started thinking big. Suddenly, small films about fascinating characters were not as appealing as large-scale epics like *Cold Mountain* or *The Aviator,* directed by Martin Scorsese and coming soon from Miramax. "Selling a small movie takes an amazing amount of work," explained one longtime Hollywood observer. "And then you make 8 or 10 million dollars. Harvey saw what the big studios had always seen: if you go big, your presence is larger and your profit is larger. A mediocre film released in thousands of theaters will usually be more successful than a small movie, without stars, that requires clever marketing. Harvey got tired of working that hard. It's easier to put in a big star."

At the moment, the old Miramax model has been adopted by Fox 21 Searchlight, headed by Peter Rice. Searchlight largely concentrates on reaching a small North American audience, and this mandate allowed a director like Alexander Payne to cast four relative unknowns in *Sideways*. Because of its casting, Universal rejected the movie. Actually, George Clooney had sought a part in the film, but Payne said that because of his superstar status he was wrong for the role. "To ask the audience to believe one of the world's most handsome and successful movie stars is now playing one of the world's biggest loser actors is too much," Payne has said. (Clooney agreed: "Alexander was right. I am too famous for what he had in mind. But isn't that part of the problem? As an actor, you don't want to be locked in to big action films. Alexander found the two best actors for the job, but we're all attracted to interesting stories, even so-called stars.")

Other studios are paying attention to Fox Searchlight. Tom Freston, co- 22 president of Viacom, has plans to reinvigorate his own specialty division, Paramount Classics. Still, the specialty division is not a panacea. Payne's stubborn (and correct) belief in his casting choices is unusual enough to be noted in virtually every mention of *Sideways*. In America, most directors have begun to think strategically, like businessmen, and their films have suffered. The studios long for stars, global stars, and the filmmakers, who want to get their movies made, comply.

V. Why Small American Movies Don't Play Well at Home Either

In 1980, Pauline Kael wrote an essay in *The New Yorker* titled "Why Are 23 Movies So Bad? Or, the Numbers." After taking a sabbatical from film criticism and working in Hollywood for about a year, she came to believe that television was ruining the movies. She said that TV watching reduced the attention span of viewers and that the need to sell films to reach these TV-saturated viewers had led to truncated plot lines and worse. Kael longed for the days of the moguls, who, she said, had courage and a respect for quality. She was also a believer in the filmmakers of the 70's. Among her favorites were Hal Ashby, Francis Ford Coppola, Robert Altman, Bernardo Bertolucci and Warren Beatty, who lured her out to Hollywood to work in the business. "In the 70's, audiences were willing to be surprised," Beatty told me recently. "Now people want to know what they're going to get. The studios want to make whatever successful movie is in their rear-view mirror. Now there are two ways of trying to make money on a movie.

You either need to have a brand or you need a sound bite on TV to get   24 audiences into the theater. If those are the rules, then the movies have to conform. And the hallmark of the 70's, the hallmark of any artistic endeavor, was nonconformity."

Oddly, television itself—or cable television, anyway—may have become   25 a refuge of nonconformity. HBO's film division, which is run by Colin Callender, has the luxury of a built-in sophisticated audience. Last year at Cannes, it won the Palme d'Or for *Elephant,* Gus Van Sant's personal meditation on the Columbine massacre. And this year, it presented *The Holy Girl,* a moody story about a teenage girl's emerging sexuality. "In the U.K., where I am from, they believe that you can travel easily between TV and films," Callender explained over lunch in Cannes. "And when you're thinking of HBO, the old paradigms do not apply. We feel we have to offer our subscribers something they can't find anywhere else, not even in movie theaters." HBO Films flexibly adapts its projects to both the big and the small screens. The award-winning film *Maria Full of Grace* plays in the multiplex, and the award-winning *Angels in America* spilled over two nights on TV and is sold on DVD. "Our audience is, first and foremost, the domestic audience," Callender continued. "That helps dictate the focus of the work."

VI. The End of American Movie Influence (or Where Are the Men?)

Today's global audience, it seems, has little interest in the next generation   26 of American leading men. As a rule, international stars, a field dominated by men (only Julia Roberts is truly an international female star), are not American if they are newly emerging. Sure, Tobey Maguire was a great Spider-Man, but he doesn't have a global reach without the red hood. Tom Cruise or Brad Pitt may still draw crowds, but the world's newest stars come from other English-language-speaking countries, like Ireland (Colin Farrell), England (Jude Law, Clive Owen), Scotland (Ewan McGregor) or Australia (Russell Crowe). "What is that?" said Amy Pascal, chairwoman of Sony Pictures Entertainment Motion Picture Group, who just cast Heath Ledger (Australia) as a Los Angeles skateboarder in *Lords of Dogtown.* "I guess all the American men became comedians. They all wanted to be funny. The next generation of stars seem to be a more international bunch, which is great: your access, as a studio, is not limited to the boy or girl next door."

Actually, American movies used to concern themselves with the boy or   27
girl next door. I liked that—those characters had real complications and
possibilities, and still do. But the arrival of globalization is not complicating the American stories being told; it is simplifying them. And that has
consequences. If you think about your life, you may find that films have
been extraordinarily influential. The way you dress, act, talk or walk often
follows what you saw in the movies. And now, instead of being known for
our sense of conversation or style, we are known for our blood and gore.
"I noticed a few years ago," Walter Parkes said, "that gangstas in urban
movies all carried their guns sideways, and wondered if this created a style
for the real world as opposed to being a reflection of the real world."

But what else? I am back to *Shrek.* In that movie, the dialogue is inten-   28
tionally spoofish. The movie is a long riff on pop culture. It is funny, but it
does not inspire, or stir up any large emotions. In the end, it has no resonance, nor does it aspire to any.

In the past, cultures would influence one another through film. The sen-   29
sibility of the French New Wave and the Hong Kong action picture affected
countless young Americans. But that sort of broad foreign influence seems
to be waning. As I write, the biggest hit in America is *The Grudge,* which
is a remake of a Tokyo horror film directed by Takashi Shimizu. He has
already directed the original and three sequels in Japanese. Although it
received poor reviews, *The Grudge* made nearly $40 million on its first
weekend and will probably become a global sensation. In the late 60's and
70's, horror films had the scope of *Rosemary's Baby,* which raised the genre
to a meditation on urban anxiety and rampant ambition. It is doubtful that
anyone harbors similar hopes for *The Grudge.* If this is the new global cin-
ema, it could give the term "horror film" new meaning.

Thinking Critically

1. Why does Lynn Hirschberg use the first person to describe not only her
   opinions but her information-gathering and her thought processes as she
   mulls over her thesis and searches for corroborating evidence and additional opinions? Is using the first person an option for you when you write
   research or analytical essays? Why, or why not? How might your own analytical writing change if you wrote in the first person?

2. In what ways does Hirschberg establish her authority in this essay? What
   kinds of knowledge does she assume her readers share?

3. Hirschberg interviews many studio executives in the course of her
   research. Why does she focus on the perspectives of that group of people? If you were her editor, what other perspectives might you suggest she
   include, and why?

Writing Critically

1. In an essay, discuss how Hirschberg's analysis of the way American films are viewed overseas complements, supports, or refutes Naomi Klein's observations about the "branding" of America (in the first selection in this chapter).

2. Select an American film available on DVD, and watch it at least twice (even if you've already seen it). Before you watch the film for the first time, jot down a preliminary thesis statement about how this movie represents (or misrepresents) some fundamental idea about America. After the first screening, revisit your preliminary thesis. If it's still relevant, watch the film again with particular attention to the images, dialogue, music, or other elements that support your thesis. Finally, write a review of the film that explains its portrayal of some aspect of American culture.

3. According to Hirschberg, a view of American culture based solely on blockbuster American movies would suggest that America "seemed, at best, an absurd, vaguely comic place" (paragraph 6). What kind of a place *is* America?

Terror in America

EDWARD SAID

Edward Said was born in Jerusalem and raised in Egypt. He moved to the United States with his family in 1951, when he was a teenager. Educated at Princeton University (B.A., 1957) and Harvard University (Ph.D., 1964), Said was an influential literary and cultural critic and a noted supporter of the Palestinian cause. University Professor of English and Comparative Literature at Columbia University, Said was best known to the general public as a commentator on Middle Eastern affairs. Perceived as a public intellectual, he for decades advocated Palestinian rights even as he criticized Palestinian policies and leadership. Said was also a distinguished literary critic, the author of the groundbreaking study *Orientalism* (1978), *Culture and Imperialism* (1993), and other books and collections of essays. After a long fight with leukemia, which prompted him to write the hauntingly honest autobiography *Out of Place: A Memoir* (1999), Edward Said died in 2003. The following essay appeared in the British weekly publication the *Observer*, a Sunday newspaper founded in 1791. Unlike readers in most cities in the United States, London readers have a wide range of choices across the political spectrum for both the daily and the Sunday newspapers; the *Observer* and its sister daily newspaper the *Guardian* are considered to be politically liberal and journalistically independent. Said's essay was published on September 16, 2001, when the world was still reeling from the terrorist attacks of a few days before.

Spectacular horror of the sort that struck New York (and to a lesser 1 degree Washington) has ushered in a new world of unseen, unknown assailants, terror missions without political message, senseless destruction. For the residents of this wounded city, the consternation, fear, and sustained sense of outrage and shock will certainly continue for a long time, as will the genuine sorrow and affliction that so much carnage has so cruelly imposed on so many.

New Yorkers have been fortunate that Mayor Rudy Giuliani, a nor- 2 mally rebarbative and unpleasantly combative, even retrograde figure, has rapidly attained Churchillian status. Calmly, unsentimentally, and with extraordinary compassion, he has marshalled the city's heroic police, fire and emergency services to admirable effect and, alas, with huge loss of life. Giuliani's was the first voice of caution against panic and jingoistic attacks on the city's large Arab and Muslim communities, the first to express the commonsense of anguish, the first to press everyone to try to resume life after the shattering blows.

Would that that were all. The national television reporting has of 3 course brought the horror of those dreadful winged juggernauts into every household, unremittingly, insistently, not always edifyingly. Most commentary has stressed, indeed magnified, the expected and the predictable in what most Americans feel: terrible loss, anger, outrage, a sense of violated vulnerability, a desire for vengeance and un-restrained retribution. Beyond formulaic expressions of grief and patriotism, every politician and accredited pundit or expert has dutifully repeated how we shall not be defeated, not be deterred, not stop until terrorism is exterminated. This is a war against terrorism, everyone says, but where, on what fronts, for what concrete ends? No answers are provided, except the vague suggestion that the Middle East and Islam are what "we" are up against, and that terrorism must be destroyed.

What is most depressing, however, is how little time is spent trying 4 to understand America's role in the world, and its direct involvement in the complex reality beyond the two coasts that have for so long kept the rest of the world extremely distant and virtually out of the average American's mind. You'd think that "America" was a sleeping giant rather than a superpower almost constantly at war, or in some sort of conflict, all over the Islamic domains. Osama bin Laden's name and face have become so numbingly familiar to Americans as in effect to obliterate any history he and his shadowy followers might have had before they became stock symbols of everything loathsome and hateful to the collective imagination. Inevitably, then, collective passions are being funnelled into a drive for war that uncannily resembles Captain Ahab in pursuit of Moby Dick, rather than what is going on, an imperial power injured at home for the first time, pursuing its interests systematically in what has become a suddenly reconfigured geography of conflict, without clear borders, or visible actors. Manichaean symbols and apocalyptic scenarios are bandied about with future consequences and rhetorical restraint thrown to the winds.

Rational understanding of the situation is what is needed now, not   5
more drum-beating. George Bush and his team clearly want the latter, not the former. Yet to most people in the Islamic and Arab worlds the official US is synonymous with arrogant power, known for its sanctimoniously munificent support not only of Israel but of numerous repressive Arab regimes, and its inattentiveness even to the possibility of dialogue with secular movements and people who have real grievances. Anti-Americanism in this context is not based on a hatred of modernity or technology-envy: it is based on a narrative of concrete interventions, specific depredations and, in the cases of the Iraqi people's suffering under US-imposed sanctions and US support for the 34-year-old Israeli occupation of Palestinian territories. Israel is now cynically exploiting the American catastrophe by intensifying its military occupation and oppression of the Palestinians. Political rhetoric in the US has overridden these things by flinging about words like "terrorism" and "freedom" whereas, of course, such large abstractions have mostly hidden sordid material interests, the influence of the oil, defense and Zionist lobbies now consolidating their hold on the entire Middle East, and an age-old religious hostility to (and ignorance of) "Islam" that takes new forms every day.

Intellectual responsibility, however, requires a still more critical sense of   6
the actuality. There has been terror of course, and nearly every struggling modern movement at some stage has relied on terror. This was as true of Mandela's ANC as it was of all the others, Zionism included. And yet bombing defenceless civilians with F-16s and helicopter gunships has the same structure and effect as more conventional nationalist terror.

What is bad about all terror is when it is attached to religious and   7
political abstractions and reductive myths that keep veering away from history and sense. This is where the secular consciousness has to try to make itself felt, whether in the US or in the Middle East. No cause, no

God, no abstract idea can justify the mass slaughter of innocents, most particularly when only a small group of people are in charge of such actions and feel themselves to represent the cause without having a real mandate to do so.

Besides, much as it has been quarrelled over by Muslims, there isn't a 8 single Islam: there are Islams, just as there are Americas. This diversity is true of all traditions, religions or nations even though some of their adherents have futilely tried to draw boundaries around themselves and pin their creeds down neatly. Yet history is far more complex and contradictory than to be represented by demagogues who are much less representative than either their followers or opponents claim. The trouble with religious or moral fundamentalists is that today their primitive ideas of revolution and resistance, including a willingness to kill and be killed, seem all too easily attached to technological sophistication and what appear to be gratifying acts of horrifying retaliation. The New York and Washington suicide bombers seem to have been middle-class, educated men, not poor refugees. Instead of getting a wise leadership that stresses education, mass mobilisation and patient organisation in the service of a cause, the poor and the desperate are often conned into the magical thinking and quick bloody solutions that such appalling models provide, wrapped in lying religious claptrap.

On the other hand, immense military and economic power are no guar- 9 antee of wisdom or moral vision. Sceptical and humane voices have been largely unheard in the present crisis, as "America" girds itself for a long war to be fought somewhere out there, along with allies who have been pressed into service on very uncertain grounds and for imprecise ends. We need to step back from the imaginary thresholds that separate people from each other and re-examine the labels, reconsider the limited resources available, decide to share our fates with each other as cultures mostly have done, despite the bellicose cries and creeds.

"Islam" and "the West" are simply inadequate as banners to follow 10 blindly. Some will run behind them, but for future generations to condemn themselves to prolonged war and suffering without so much as a critical pause, without looking at interdependent histories of injustice and oppression, without trying for common emancipation and mutual enlightenment seems far more wilful than necessary. Demonisation of the Other is not a sufficient basis for any kind of decent politics, certainly not now when the roots of terror in injustice can be addressed, and the terrorists isolated, deterred or put out of business. It takes patience and education, but is more worth the investment than still greater levels of large-scale violence and suffering.

Thinking Critically

1. Edward Said lived and taught in New York City at the time of the September 11, 2001, attacks. In what ways does he signal that he is writing for an international audience? How would you describe his voice and perspective in this essay?

2. How does Said describe the impact of the attacks on the self-image of America? How does he describe the images of America that other countries, cultures, and peoples hold? In what ways does Said believe these views can be dangerously inaccurate?

3. Which rhetorical modes does Said use to structure his argument? Annotate the essay, briefly describing Said's strategies in each paragraph.

Writing Critically

1. In paragraph 4, Said argues that "What is most depressing, however, is how little time is spent trying to understand America's role in the world." Is he speaking about individual Americans, about certain American politicians, about the American media? Select a specific group of Americans, or even an individual American, and in an essay analyze your selection's understanding of "America's role in the world."

2. What does Said propose as a resolution to the immediate problems discussed in his essay? In the years since the September 11 attacks, has his solution proved possible, prescient, or naïve?

3. In what other ways is "demonization of the other" an inescapable part of American popular culture, political and civic dialogue, or community life?

Arguing the Cultural Divides

1. Naomi Klein and Lynn Hirschberg analyze the ways in which America's media and political culture presents itself (either knowingly or cluelessly) to the larger world, and Edward Said argues for a more considered and thoughtful understanding of how the rest of the world (especially the Muslim world) perceives the United States. In a research paper, explore the ways in which America has officially used the mass media to promote its culture and image overseas. For example, you might discuss the role of the Voice of America, a radio broadcasting network formed in 1942 and operated by the United States Information Agency. At what point does information or entertainment become propaganda? Can propaganda ever serve a useful and positive function?

2. As a consumer of American popular culture and a participant (even if you're not a citizen) in American political and civic life, do you have any obligations or responsibilities towards ensuring an accurate and fair portrayal of "America" overseas, and an understanding and appreciation of "other" countries and cultures? Write an argument that describes and defends your position.

3. Visit the English-language websites of major international news organizations and evaluate their coverage of an American cultural, social, or political issue. In what ways does this coverage differ from its presentation in American mainstream media? How would you characterize the tone and approach of the international media's coverage? What can you learn from an international perspective on American culture, society, and politics?

English-language international media sites to visit:

British Broadcasting Service <http://news.bbc.co.uk/>.
Canadian Broadcasting Corporation <http://www.cbc.ca/>.
Kyodo News Service, Japan <http://home.kyodo.co.jp/>.
All Africa <http://allafrica.com/>.
Al-Jazeera <http://english.aljazeera.net/HomePage>.
Persian Journal <http://www.Iranian.ws/iran_news>.
The Jerusalem Post <http://www.jpost.com/>.
The Jordan Times <http://www.jordantimes.com>.
China Daily <http://www.chinadaily.com.cn>.
The Times of India <http://timesofindia.indiatimes.com/>.
Daryl Cagle's Professional Cartoonist's Index <http://cagle.slate.msn.com/>.
Nettizen <http://www.nettizen.com/newspaper/>.
Globe of Blogs <http://www.globeofblogs.com/>.

APPENDIX

Researching Across the Cultural Divides

Introduction

The *doing* of research is as important as the *writing* of a research paper. When scholars, professors, scientists, journalists, and students *do* research, they ask questions, solve problems, follow leads, and track down sources. The process of research as well as the writing of the research paper has changed radically over the last ten years. The Internet now makes a whole world of resources instantly available. Skillfully navigating your way through this wealth of resources, evaluating and synthesizing information as you solve problems and answer questions, enhances your critical thinking and writing abilities and develops the tools you will need for professional success.

A research paper incorporates the ideas, discoveries, and observations of other writers. The information provided by these scholars, thinkers, and observers helps to support your own original thesis or claim about a topic. Learning how to evaluate, adapt, synthesize, and correctly acknowledge these sources in your research protects you from charges of plagiarism (discussed later in this appendix). More important, it demonstrates to you how knowledge is expanded and created. Research, and research writing, are the cornerstone not only of the university but of our information-based society.

The research paper is the final product of a process of inquiry and discovery. The topics and readings in this book bring together voices from across cultural, political, and spiritual divides, discussing and debating issues of critical importance to American citizens and observers alike. As you develop a topic, work toward a thesis, and discover sources and evidence, you will use the Internet to bring diverse perspectives to your writing. Your teacher will probably ask you to work in a peer group as you refine your topic, suggest resources to other class members, and evaluate preliminary drafts of your research paper. Although the primary—and ultimate—audience for your research paper is your teacher, thinking of your work as a process of discovery and a contribution to a larger cultural conversation will keep your perspective fresh and your interest engaged.

726

The Research Process

A research paper is the final result of a series of tasks, some small and others quite time-consuming. Be sure to allow yourself plenty of time for each stage of the research process, working with your teacher or with a peer group to develop a schedule that breaks down specific tasks. The four broad stages of the research process are

1. Choosing a topic
2. Establishing a thesis
3. Finding, evaluating, and organizing evidence
4. Writing your paper

Stage One: Choosing a Topic

Reading and discussing the often provocative issues addressed in this book may have already given you an idea about a topic you would like to explore further. A television news report, a website that presented an unexpected viewpoint, or a speaker who visited your campus may also have engaged your attention. Even if your teacher assigns a specific topic area, finding—and nurturing—genuine curiosity and concern about that topic will make the research process much more involving and satisfying than it otherwise would be. Some topics are too broad, too controversial (or not controversial enough), too current, or too obscure for an effective research paper.

Determining an Appropriate Research Topic

Ask yourself the following questions about possible topics for your research paper:

- Am I genuinely curious about this topic? Will I want to live with it for the next few weeks?

- What do I already know about this topic? What more do I want to find out?

- Does the topic fit the general guidelines my teacher has suggested?

- Can I readily locate the sources I will need for further research on this topic?

Exercise: Freewriting

Review your work for this class so far, taking note of any readings in the textbook that particularly appealed to you or any writing assignments that you especially enjoyed. Open a new folder on your computer, labeling it "Research Paper." Open a new document, and title it "Freewriting." Then write, without stopping, everything that intrigued you originally about that reading or that assignment. Use the questions, above, to prompt your thinking.

Browsing

After identifying a general topic area of interest, begin exploring that area by browsing. When you browse, you make a broad and casual survey of the existing information and resources about your topic. There are many resources to consult as you begin to delve into your topic; nearly all of them can be found at your campus library. Begin at the reference desk by asking for a guide to the library's reference collection.

- *General Reference Texts.* These include encyclopedias, almanacs, specialized dictionaries, and statistical information.

- *Periodical Index.* Both in-print and online versions of periodical indexes now exist (the electronic versions are often subscription-only and available only through academic and some public libraries). A periodical index lists subjects, authors, and titles of articles in newspapers, journals, and magazines. Some electronic versions include both abstracts (brief summaries) and full-text versions of the articles.

- *Library Catalog.* Your library's catalog probably exists both online and as a "card catalog"—an alphabetized record organized by author, title, and subject—in which each book has its own paper card in a file. Begin your catalog browsing with a subject or keyword search. Identify the *call number* that appears most frequently for the books you are most likely to use. That number will point you to the library shelves where you'll find the most useful books for your topic.

- *Search Engines.* For the most current and broadest overview of a research topic, a search engine such as Google, AltaVista, or Yahoo! can provide you with an ever-changing—and dauntingly vast—range of perspectives. At the browsing stage, spending time online can both stimulate your interest and help you to focus your topic. Because websites change so quickly, however, be sure to print out a page from any site you think might be useful in the later stages of your research. That way, you'll have hard copy of the site's URL (uniform resource locator, or Web address). (If you're working on your own computer, under "favorites" or "bookmarks" create a new folder entitled "Research Project," and file bookmarks for interesting sites there.)

Stage Two: Establishing a Thesis

Moving from a general area of interest to a specific *thesis*—a claim you wish to make, an area of information you wish to explore, a question you intend to answer, or a solution to a problem you want to propose—requires thinking critically about your topic. You have already begun to focus on what *specifically* interests you about this topic in the freewriting exercise. The next step in refining your topic and establishing a thesis is to determine your audience and purpose for writing.

Determining Your Audience and Purpose

- Where have you found, through your browsing, the most interesting or compelling information about your topic? Who was the audience for that information? Do you consider yourself to be part of that audience? Define the characteristics of that audience—for example, concerned about the environment, interested in global economics, experienced at traveling abroad.

- *Why* are you most interested in this topic? Do you want to encourage someone (a friend, a community leader) to take a specific course of action? Do you want to shed some light on an issue or event that not many people are familiar with?

- Try a little imaginative role-playing. Imagine yourself researching this topic as a professional in a specific field. For example, if your topic is environmental preservation, imagine yourself as a geologist. What would your compelling interest in the topic be? What if you were an adventure traveler seeking new destinations? How would your approach to the topic of environmental preservation change? How about your perspective if you were charged with developing new, more energy-efficient engines for a domestic automobile company?

- If you could have the undivided attention of anyone (other than your teacher) with whom you could share your knowledge about this topic, who would that person be and why?

Moving from a Topic to a Thesis Statement

Although choosing a topic is the beginning of the research *process,* it is not the beginning of your research *paper.* The course that your research will take, and the shape that your final paper will assume, are based on your *thesis statement.* A thesis statement is the answer to whatever question originally prompted your research. To narrow your topic and arrive at a thesis statement, ask yourself specific questions about the topic. For some examples of how to do this, see the "Using Questions" table.

Using Questions to Create a Thesis Statement: Four Examples

General Topic	More Specific Topic	Question	Thesis Statement
Drilling for oil in the Arctic National Wildlife Refuge.	Impact of oil drilling on wildlife in the Arctic National Wildlife Refuge.	How can the migration paths of caribou through the Arctic National Wildlife Refuge be preserved, even if drilling for oil proceeds?	Caribou herds in the Arctic National Wildlife Refuge can be protected if oil companies work constructively with wildlife behavior experts.
Economic security for small rural communities.	Creating economic opportunities for families in small rural communities.	What incentives should be offered to business and industry in order to bring economic opportunity to small rural communities?	Small business loans and tax breaks encourage light manufacturing to relocate to rural areas, providing steady jobs and economic support to struggling communities.
Balancing the right to privacy with "homeland security" policies.	Screening airline passengers for possible security risks.	How can commercial airlines promote safety and security without violating the privacy and civil rights of passengers?	The advertised presence of armed, anonymous "air marshals" on commercial flights may deter potential terrorists as well as reassure travelers prone to suspicion and prejudice.
Public or civic displays of religion.	Recognition of religious celebrations or symbols in public schools.	Should all public schools be forbidden to recognize any religious holiday?	Local school boards and parent-teacher associations, not federal courts, should have the right to make decisions that are appropriate and sensitive to members of the school community.

Stage Three: Finding, Evaluating, and Organizing Evidence

Developing a Working Bibliography

Your working bibliography is a record of *every* source you consult as you conduct your research. Although you might not cite every source in your paper, having an organized record of *everything* you looked at will make drafting the paper as well as preparing the Works Cited page much easier. Some people use their computers for keeping a Works Cited list (especially if they use online databases, which automatically create citations, for much of their research). But most people—even if many of their sources are online—find 4-by-6-inch index cards much more portable and efficient. Index cards allow you to easily rearrange the order of your sources (according to priority, for example, or sources that you need to double-check); they let you jot down notes or summaries; and they slip into your bookbag for a quick trip to the library.

Whether your working bibliography is on a computer or on index cards, always record the same information for each source you consult.

Checklists for Working Bibliographies

Information for a book:

- Author name(s), first and last

- Book title

- Place of publication

- Publisher's name

- Date of publication

- Library call number

- Page numbers (for specific information or quotes that you'll want to consult later)

Information for an article in a journal or magazine:

- Author name(s), first and last

- Article title

- Magazine or journal title

- Volume and/or issue number

- Date of publication

- Page numbers

- Library call number

Information for online sources:

• Author (if there is one)

• Web page title, or title of an article or graphic on the Web page

• URL (website address)

• Date of your online access

Some sites include information on how they prefer to be cited. You'll notice this information at the bottom of a main or "splash" page of a cite, or you'll see a link to a "citation" page.

Sample working bibliography note: Article

Sullivan, Andrew. "A Call to Arms." <u>The Advocate</u> 11 Nov. 2003: 72.

Sample working bibliography note: Online source

Center for Investigative Reporting. "No Place to Hide." <http://www.noplacetohide.net/>.

Consulting Experts and Professionals

In the course of your research you may discover someone whose work is so timely, or whose opinions are so relevant, that a personal interview would provide even more (and unique) information for your paper. Look beyond the university faculty for such experts. For example, if your topic is how your hometown has been affected by Wal-Mart and other "big box" retailers, you might want to interview older town residents and shopkeepers. If your topic is second-generation teenagers balancing conservative backgrounds with American popular culture, hanging out with a group of such kids and talking with them about their lives will give you the kind of first-person anecdote that makes research writing genuinely fresh and original. Think of "expertise" as being about *experience*—not just a title or a degree.

Checklist for Arranging and Conducting Interviews

• Be certain that the person you wish to speak to will offer a completely unique, even undocumented, perspective on your topic. Interviewing some-one who has already published widely on your topic is not the best use of your research time, for you can just as easily consult that person's pub-lished work.

• E-mail, telephone (at a business number, if possible), or write to your sub-ject well in advance of your paper deadline. Explain clearly that you are a student writing a research paper, the topic of your paper, and the specific subject or subjects you wish to discuss.

- An interview can be conducted via e-mail or over the telephone as well as in person. Instant messaging, because it can't be easily documented and doesn't lend itself to longer responses, is not a good choice.

- Write out your questions in advance!

Conducting Field Research

Field research involves traveling to a specific place to observe and document a specific occurrence or phenomenon. For example, if you were writing about the challenges and opportunities of a highly diverse immigrant community, you might arrange to spend a day at a church service, park, or coffee shop. Bring a notebook, a digital camera, a tape recorder—anything that will help you capture and record observations. Although your task as a field researcher is to be *unbiased*—to objectively observe what is happening, keeping an open mind as well as open eyes—you'll want to always keep your working thesis in mind, too. For example, if your thesis is

> Allowing students in highly diverse American communities to create events that celebrate and respect their own cultural traditions within the general American popular culture helps to create understanding between teenagers and their immigrant parents

your field research might take you to a high school in an immigrant community to observe the interactions among teenagers. You'll want to record everything—both positive and negative, both expected and surprising—that you observe and overhear, but you won't want to get distracted by a teacher's mentioning the difficulties of coping with many different languages in the classroom. That's fascinating, but it's another topic altogether.

Checklist for Arranging and Conducting Field Research

- If your field research involves crossing a private boundary or property line—a school, church, hospital, restaurant, and so on—be sure to contact the institution first to confirm that it's appropriate for you to visit. As with the guidelines for conducting a personal interview, inform the person with whom you arrange the visit that you are a student conducting field research and that your research is for a classroom paper.

- Respect personal boundaries. Some people might not want to be photographed, and others might be uneasy if they think you are taking notes on their conversation or behavior. If you sense that your presence is making someone uncomfortable, apologize and explain what you are doing. If they are still uncomfortable, back off.

- When you use examples and observations from your field research in your research paper, do not use the first person as part of the citation. Simply describe what you observed and under what circumstances.

Not recommended: When I visited the dog park to see how the personalities of dogs reflect those of their owners, I was especially attracted to the owner of a bulldog named Max. When I introduced myself to Max's owner, George T., and explained my project to him, George agreed with my thesis and pointed out that the owners of large, athletic dogs like Rottweilers tended to be young men, and the owners of more sedentary dogs (like Max) seemed to be a little mellower.

Recommended: A visit to a local dog park revealed the ways in which the personalities of dogs reflect those of their owners. George T., the owner of a bulldog named Max, pointed out that the younger men at the park were accompanied by large, athletic dogs like Rottweilers, while more sedentary people (like George) tended to have mellower breeds such as bulldogs.

- Be sure that you spell names correctly, that you understand job titles and affiliations correctly, and that you have contact information for any follow-up questions.

- *Always* follow up your field research with a written thank-you note to anyone who helped you gain access, answered your questions, or suggested further resources. If you don't have a mailing address, an e-mail or even a phone call is acceptable. You should also, out of courtesy, offer to share the final results of your research with anyone you spoke to.

Assessing the Credibility of Sources

After browsing, searching, observing, and conversing, you will have collected a mass of sources and data. The next step is to evaluate those sources critically, using your working bibliography as a road map back to all the sources you have consulted to date. This critical evaluation will help you to determine which sources have the relevance, credibility, and authority expected of academic research.

Checklist for Assessing Source Credibility

- Do the table of contents and index of a book include keywords and subjects relevant to your topic? Does the abstract of a journal article include keywords relevant to your topic and thesis? Does a website indicate through a menu (or from your using the "search" command) that it contains content relevant to your topic and thesis?

- How current is the source? Check the date of the magazine or journal and the copyright date of the book (the original copyright date, not the dates of reprints). Has the website been updated recently, and are its links current and functioning?

- How authoritative is the source? Is the author credentialed in his or her field? Do other authors refer to this writer (or website) in their work?

- Who sponsors a website? Is it the site of a major media group, a government agency, a political think tank, or a special-interest group? If you are unsure, print out the home page of the site and ask your teacher or a reference librarian.

Taking Notes

After determining which sources are most relevant and useful, you can begin to read those sources with greater attention to detail. This is *active reading*—annotating, responding to, and taking notes on what you are reading. Taking careful notes will help you to build the structure of your paper and will ensure accurate documentation later. As with the working bibliography, you can take notes either on your computer or on 4-by-6-inch cards. For online sources, you can cut and paste blocks of text into a separate word processing document on your computer. Be sure to include the original URL and to indicate that what you have cut and pasted is a *direct quote* (which you might later paraphrase or summarize). Some researchers cut and paste material in a font or color that is completely different from their own writing, to remind themselves where specific words and concepts came from (and as protection against inadvertent plagiarism).

As you explore your resources, you will take three kinds of notes:

- *Summaries* give you the broad overview of a source's perspective or information and serve as reminders of a source's content should you wish to revisit the source later for more specific information or direct quotes.

- *Paraphrases* express a source's ideas and information in your own language.

- *Direct quotations* are best when an author or subject expresses a thought or concept in language that is so striking, important, or original that to paraphrase it would be to lose some of its importance. Direct quotations are *exact* copies of an author's own words and are always enclosed in quotation marks.

Checklist for Taking Notes

- Take just one note (summary, paraphrase, or direct quotation) on each index card. Be sure to note the complete source information for a quote on the card. "Checklists for Working Bibliographies" on page 731 indicates what information is required.

- Cross-check your note-taking cards against your working bibliography. Be sure that every source on which you take notes has a corresponding entry in the working bibliography.

- Write a subtopic at the top of each card, preferably in a brightly colored ink. Keep a running list of all of your subtopics. This will enable you to group together related pieces of information and determine the structure of your outline.

Sample Note: Summary

Subtopic	commercializing hip-hop
Author/title	Klein, "No Logo"
Page numbers	75
Summary	Corporations that want to reach the lucrative demographic of young people who want to be seen as "cool" create a brand that seems to be part of "cool" or alternative culture.

Sample Note: Paraphrase

Subtopic	commercializing hip-hop
Author/title	Klein, "No Logo"
Page numbers	75
Paraphrase	Apparel companies, especially Nike and Adidas, recognized that the adoption of their products by hip-hop stars could create a huge new market among urban youth and kids who wanted to appear to be as cool as their favorite hip-hop performers.

Sample Note: Direct quotation

Subtopic	commercializing hip-hop
Author/title	Klein, "No Logo"
Page numbers	75
Direct quotation	"So focused is Nike on borrowing style, attitude and imagery from black urban youth that the company has its own word for the practice: *bro-ing*. That's when Nike marketers and designers bring their prototypes to inner-city neighborhoods in New York, Philadelphia, or Chicago and say, 'Hey, bro, check out the shoes,' to gauge the reaction to new styles and to build up a buzz."

Understanding Plagiarism, Intellectual Property, and Academic Ethics

- *Plagiarism.* Plagiarism is presenting someone else's words, ideas, images, or concepts as though they were your own. Plagiarism can be accidental, such as when you forget to add an in-text citation, or it can be deliberate, such as when you decide to "borrow" a friend's paper or hand in something from a website with your own name on it. Most schools and colleges have explicit, detailed policies about what constitutes plagiarism, and the consequences of being caught are not pretty—you may risk anything from failure on a particular assignment to expulsion from the institution. There are two basic ways to avoid plagiarism: (1) Don't wait until the last minute to write your paper. If you wait too long, you may be tempted to take shortcuts. (2) Give an in-text citation (see p. 741) for absolutely everything you include in your research paper that didn't come out of your own head. It's better to be safe and over-cite than to be accused of plagiarism. For a straightforward discussion of plagiarism, go to <http://www.georgetown.edu/honor/plagiarism.html>.

- *Intellectual Property.* If you've ever considered wiping your hard disk clean of free downloaded music files out of the fear of being arrested, then you've wrestled with the issue of intellectual property. Intellectual property includes works of art, music, animation, and literature—as well as research concepts, computer programs, even fashion. *Copyright law* protects intellectual property rights for visual, musical, and verbal works. When you download, for free, a music track from the Internet, you are violating copyright law: the artist who created that work receives no credit or royalties in exchange for your enjoyment and use of his or her work. When you cut and paste blocks of a website into your own research paper without giving credit, you are also violating copyright law. To respect the intellectual property rights of anyone (or anything) you cite in your research paper, you carefully *cite* the source of the information. Using quotes from another writer, or images from another artist, in your own academic paper is legally defined as "fair use" *if* you make it clear where the original material comes from.

- *Ethics and the Academic Researcher.* As you enter an academic conversation about your research topic, your audience—even if it's only your teacher—expects you to conduct yourself in an ethical fashion. *Ethos* literally means "where you stand"—what you believe, how you express those beliefs, and how thoughtfully and considerately you relate to the "stances" of others in your academic community. In the professional academy, researchers in fields ranging from medieval poetry to cell biology are expected to adhere to a code of ethics about their research. Working with the ideas and discoveries of others in their academic communities, they are careful to always acknowledge the work of their peers and the contributions that work has made to their own research. You should do the same. When you leave school, these basic ethical tenets remain the same. You wouldn't hand in another rep's marketing report as your own; you wouldn't claim credit for the successful recovery of another doctor's patient; and you wouldn't put your name on top of another reporter's story. To violate professional ethics is to break the trust that holds an academic or professional community together.

Stage Four: Writing Your Paper

After you gather and evaluate a mass of information, the next step is to begin giving some shape and order to what you have discovered. Writing an outline will help you to think through and organize your evidence, determine the strengths and weaknesses of your argument, and visualize the shape of your final paper. Some instructors will require you to hand in an outline along with your research paper. Even if an outline isn't formally required, it is such a useful tool to help you convert a pile of index cards into a logical, coherent draft that you should plan to create one.

Checklist for Organizing Your Information

- Gather up all of your note cards and print out any notes you have taken on your computer. Double-check all of your notes to make sure that they include accurate citation information.

- Using your list of subtopics, group your notes according to those subtopics. Are some piles of cards enormous, while other topics have only a card or two? See if subtopics can be combined—or if any subtopics could be further refined and made more specific.

- Set aside any note cards that don't seem to "fit" in any particular pile.

- Find your thesis statement and copy it out on a blank index card. Go through the cards for each subtopic. Can you immediately see a connection between each note card and your thesis statement? (If not, set that note card aside for now.)

- Do not throw away any of the note cards, even if they don't seem to "fit" into your current research plan. You probably won't use every single note card in your paper, but it's good to have a continuing record of your work.

Basic Outlining

Many word processing programs include an "outline" function, and your instructor may ask you to follow a specific format for your outline. An outline is a kind of road map for your thought processes, a list of the pieces of information you are going to discuss in your paper and how you are going to connect those pieces of information to each other as well as back to your original thesis. You can begin the outlining process by using the note cards you have divided into subtopics:

    I. Most compelling, important subtopic
      A. Supporting fact, quote, or illustration
      B. Another interesting piece of evidence that supports or illustrates the subtopic
        1. A direct quotation that further illustrates point B
        2. Another supporting point
          a. Minor but still relevant points

Another useful outlining strategy is to assign each subtopic a working "topic sentence" or "main idea." As you move into the drafting process, you can return to those topic sentences/main ideas to begin each paragraph.

The Writing Process

A research paper is more than a collection of strung-together facts. No matter how interesting and relevant each individual piece of information may be, your reader is not responsible for figuring out how the parts make up a whole. Connecting the evidence, demonstrating the relationships between concepts and ideas, and proving how all of it supports your thesis is entirely up to you.

Drafting

The shape of your outline and your subdivided piles of index cards provide the framework for your rough draft. As you begin to write your essay, think about "connecting the dots" between each piece of evidence, gradually filling in the shape of your argument. Expect your arrangement of individual note cards or whole subtopics to change as you draft.

Remember that you are not drafting a final paper, and certainly not a perfect paper. The goal of drafting is to *organize* your evidence, to get a sense of your argument's strengths and weaknesses, to test the accuracy of your thesis and revise it if necessary. Drafting is as much a thinking process as it is a writing process.

If you get stuck as you draft, abandon whatever subtopic you are working on and begin with another. Working at the paragraph level first—using the evidence on a subtopic's note cards to support and illustrate the topic sentence or main idea of the subtopic—is a much less intimidating way to approach drafting a research paper.

Finally, as you draft, be sure that you include either an in-text citation (see p. 741) or some other indication of *precisely* where each piece of information came from. This will save you time when you begin revising and preparing the final draft as well as the Works Cited list.

Incorporating Sources

As you draft, you will build connections between different pieces of evidence, different perspectives, and different authors. Learning how to smoothly integrate all those different sources into your own work, without breaking the flow of your own argument and voice, takes some practice. The most important thing to remember is to accurately indicate the source of every piece of information as soon as you cite it.

This system of indicating where exactly an idea, quote, or paraphrase comes from is called *parenthetical citation*. In MLA and APA style, which are required by most academic disciplines, in-text citations take the place of footnotes or endnotes.

Using Transition Verbs Between Your Writing and a Source

Using conversation verbs as transitions between your own writing and a direct quote can enliven the style of your paper. Other useful transitions include:

> Whitney Joiner argues that . . .
> Jedediah Purdy mourns that . . .
> Joe Miceli remembers that . . .
> Rebecca Skloot compares . . .
> Dan Savage admits that . . .
> Barbara Ehrenreich insists that . . .
> David Brooks vividly describes . . .

Revising and Polishing

The drafting process clarified your ideas and gave structure to your argument. In the revision process, you rewrite and rethink your paper, strengthening the connections between your main points, your evidence, and your thesis. Sharing your essay draft with a classmate, with your instructor, or with a tutor at your campus writing center will give you an invaluable objective perspective on your paper's strengths and weaknesses.

Checklist for Your Final Draft

- Have I provided parenthetical citations for every source I used?

- Do all of those parenthetical citations correspond to an item on my Works Cited list?

- Does my essay's title clearly and specifically state my topic?

- Is my thesis statement identifiable, clear, and interesting?

- Does each body paragraph include a topic sentence that clearly connects to my thesis?

- Do I make graceful transitions between my own writing and the sources I incorporate?

- When I shared my paper with another reader, was I able to answer any questions about my evidence or my argument using sources already at hand? Or do I need to go back to the library or online to fill in any questionable areas in my research?

- Does my conclusion clearly echo and support my thesis statement and concisely sum up how all of my evidence supports that thesis?

- Have I proofread for clarity, grammar, accuracy, and style?

- Is my paper formatted according to my instructor's guidelines? Do I have a backup copy on disk, and more than one printed copy?

Documentation

From the beginning of your research, when you were browsing in the library and online, you have been documenting your sources. To document a source simply means to make a clear, accurate record of where exactly a piece of information, a quote, an idea, or a concept comes from, so that future readers of your paper can go back to that original source and learn more. Careful attention to documentation is the best way to protect yourself against inadvertent plagiarism. There are two ways to document your sources in your paper: within the text itself (*in-text* or *parenthetical* citation), and in the Works Cited list at the end of your paper.

What Do I Need to Document?

- Anything I didn't know before I began my research
- Direct quotations
- Paraphrases
- Summaries
- Specific numerical data, such as charts and graphs
- Any image, text, or animation from a website
- Any audio or video
- Any information gathered during a personal interview

Parenthetical (in-text) Citation

The Modern Language Association (MLA) style for documentation is most commonly used in the humanities and is the format discussed here. Keep in mind that different academic disciplines have their own documentation guidelines and styles, as do some organizations (many newspapers, for example, have their own "style guides"). An in-text citation identifies the source of a piece of information as part of your own sentence or within parentheses. In MLA style, the parenthetical information includes the author's name and the page number (if appropriate) on which the information can be found in the original source. If your readers want to know more, they can then turn to your Works Cited page to find the author's name and the full bibliographic information for that source. Always place the in-text or parenthetical citation as close to the incorporated source material as possible—preferably within the same sentence.

Guidelines for Parenthetical (in-text) Citation

Page Numbers for a Book

The end of the Second World War began Samuel Beckett's greatest period of creativity, which he referred to as "the siege in the room" (Bair 346).
Bair describes the period immediately after the Second World War as a time of great creativity for Samuel Beckett (346).

In the first parenthetical citation, the author is not named within the student writer's text, so the parentheses include both the source author's name and the page number on which the information can be found. In the second example, the source author (Bair) is mentioned by name, so there is no need to repeat that name within the parentheses—only the page number is needed.

Page Numbers for an Article in a Magazine or Journal

Wheatley argues that "America has embraced values that cannot create a sustainable society and world" (25).

Page Numbers for a Newspaper Article

Cite both the section letter (or description of the section) and the page.

A spokesperson for the National Institutes of Health has described obesity as the greatest potential danger to the average American's health (Watts B3).

Website

Arts and Letters Daily includes links to opinions, essays, and reviews of cultural, political, and social affairs.

Article 2 of the proposed Global Code of Ethics for Tourism describes tourism "as a vehicle for individual and collective fulfillment" (world-tourism).

When an online source does not give specific "page," screen, or paragraph numbers, your parenthetical citation must include the name of the site.

The Works Cited List

Gather your working bibliography cards, and be sure that every source you cite in your paper has a corresponding card. To construct the Works Cited list, you simply arrange these cards in alphabetical order, by author. The Works Cited page is a separate, double-spaced page at the end of your paper.

Formatting Your Works Cited List

- Center the title, "Works Cited," at the top of a new page. Do not underline it, italicize it, or place it in quotation marks there.

- Alphabetize according to the author's name, or according to the title (for works, such as websites, that do not have an author). Ignore words such as *the, and,* and *a* when alphabetizing.

- Begin each entry at the left margin. After the first line, indent all other lines of the entry by five spaces (one stroke of the "tab" key).

- Double-space every line.

- Place a period after the author, the title, and the publishing information.

- Underline book and Web page titles. Titles of articles, stories, poems, and parts of entire works in other media are placed in quotation marks.

Guidelines for the Works Cited List

Book by One Author

Bair, Deirdre. <u>Samuel Beckett: A Biography</u>. New York: Simon and Schuster, 1978.

Multiple Books by the Same Author

List the author's name for the first entry. For each entry that follows, replace the author's name with three hyphens.

Thomas, Lewis. <u>The Medusa and the Snail: More Notes of a Biology Watcher</u>. New York: Viking Press, 1979.

———. <u>Late Night Thoughts on Listening to Mahler's Ninth Symphony</u>. New York: Viking Press, 1983.

Book with Two or Three Authors/Editors

Moore-Gilbert, Bart, Gareth Stanton, and Willy Maley, eds. <u>Postcolonial Criticism</u>. London and New York: Addison Wesley Longman, 1997.

Book with More than Three Authors/Editors

Nordhus, Inger, Gary R. VandenBos, Stig Berg, and Pia Fromholt, eds. <u>Clinical Geropsychology</u>. Washington: APA, 1998.

Book or Publication with Group or Organization as Author

National PTA. <u>National Standards for Parent/Family Involvement Programs</u>. Chicago: National PTA, 1997.

Book or Publication Without an Author

<u>The New York Public Library Desk Reference</u>. New York: Prentice Hall, 1989.

Work in an Anthology of Pieces All by the Same Author

Thomas, Lewis. "The Youngest and Brightest Thing Around." <u>The Medusa and the Snail: More Notes of a Biology Watcher</u>. New York: Viking Press, 1979.

Work in an Anthology of Different Authors

Graver, Elizabeth. "The Body Shop." <u>The Best American Short Stories 1991</u>. Boston: Houghton Mifflin, 1991.

Work Translated from Another Language

Cocteau, Jean. The Difficulty of Being. Trans. Elizabeth Sprigge. New York: Da Capo Press, 1995.

Entry from a Reference Volume

For dictionaries and encyclopedias, simply note the edition and its date. No page numbers are necessary for references organized alphabetically, such as encyclopedias (and, obviously, dictionaries).

"Turner, Nat." Encyclopedia Americana: International Edition. 1996 ed.

"Carriera, Rosalba." The Oxford Companion to Western Art. Ed. Hugh Brigstoke. Oxford: Oxford University Press, 2001.

Article from a Journal with Pagination Continued Through Each Volume

Enoch, Jessica. "Resisting the Script of Indian Education: Zitkala Sa and the Carlisle Indian School." College English 65 (2002): 117–141.

Do not include the issue number for journals paginated continuously.

Article from a Journal Paginated for Each Issue

Follow the same procedure for a journal with continued pagination, placing a period and the issue number after the volume number.

Article from a Weekly or Biweekly Periodical

Baum, Dan. "Jake Leg." New Yorker 15 Sept. 2003: 50–57.

Article from a Monthly or Bimonthly Periodical

Perlin, John. "Solar Power: The Slow Revolution." Invention and Technology Summer 2002: 20–25.

Article from a Daily Newspaper

Brody, Jane E. "A Pregame Ritual: Doctors Averting Disasters." New York Times 14 Oct. 2003: F7.

If the newspaper article goes on for more than one page, add a plus sign (+) to the first page number.

Newspaper or Periodical Article with No Author

"Groups Lose Sole Authority on Chaplains for Muslims." New York Times 14 Oct. 2003: A15.

Unsigned Editorial in a Newspaper or Periodical

"The Iraqi Weapons Puzzle." Editorial. New York Times 12 Oct. 2003, 4.10.

Letter to the Editor of a Newspaper or Periodical

Capasso, Chris. Letter. "Mountain Madness." Outside May 2003: 20.

Film, Video, DVD

If you are writing about a specific actor's performance or a specific director, use that person's name as the beginning of the citation.

Otherwise, begin with the title of the work. Specify the medium of the recording (film, video, DVD, etc.).

<u>Princess Mononoke</u>. Dir. Hayao Miyazaki. Prod. Studio Ghibli, 1999. Videocassette. Miramax Films, 2001.

Eames, Charles and Ray. <u>The Films of Charles and Ray Eames, Volume 1: Powers of Ten</u>. 1978. Videocassette. Pyramid Home Video, 1984.

Television or Radio Broadcast

"Alone on the Ice." <u>The American Experience</u>. PBS. KRMA, Denver. 8 Feb. 1999.

Arnold, Elizabeth. "The Birds of the Boreal." <u>National Geographic Radio Expeditions</u>. NPR. WNYC, New York. 14 Oct. 2003.

CD or Other Recording

Identify the format if the recording is not on a compact disc.

Bukkene Bruse. "Wedding March from Osterdalen." <u>Nordic Roots 2</u>. Northside, 2000.

Personal Interview

Give the name of the person you interviewed, how the interview was conducted (phone, e-mail, etc.), and the date of the interview.

Reed, Lou. Telephone interview. 12 Sept. 1998.

Dean, Howard. E-mail interview. 8 Aug. 2003.

Online Sources

Because websites are constantly changing, and "publication" information about a site varies so widely, think about documenting your site accurately enough so that a curious reader of your paper could find the website. When a URL is very long, give just enough information for readers to find their way to the site and then navigate to the specific page or image from there. Provide a date-of-access as well.

Web Page/Internet Site

Give the site title, the name of the site's editor (if there is one), electronic publication information, your own date of access, and the site's URL. (If some of this information is not available, just cite what you can.)

<u>Arts & Letters Daily</u>. Ed. Denis Dutton. 2003. 2 Sept. 2003 <http://aldaily.com/>.

Document or Article from an Internet Site

Include the author's name, document title, information about a print version (if applicable), information about the electronic version, access information, and URL.

Brooks, David. "The Organization Kid." <u>The Atlantic Monthly</u> April 2001: 40–54. 25 Aug. 2003 <http://www.theatlantic.com/issues/2001/04/brooks-pl.htm>.

Book Available Online

The citation is similar to the format for a print book, but include as much information as you can about the website as well as the date of your access to it.

Einstein, Albert. <u>Relativity: The Special and General Theory</u>. Trans. Robert W. Lawson. New York: Henry Holt, 1920. <u>Bartleby.Com: Great Books Online</u>. Ed. Steven van Leeuwen. 2003. 6 Sept. 2003 <http://bartelby.com/173/>.

Wheatley, Phillis. <u>Poems on Various Subjects, Religious and Moral</u>. <u>Project Gutenberg</u>. Ed. Michael S. Hart. 2003. 6 Sept. 2003 <http://ibiblio.org/pub/docs/books/gutenberg/etext96/whtly10.txt>.

Database Available Online

<u>Bartleby Library</u>. Ed. Steven van Leeuwen. 2003. 28 Sept. 2003 <http://bartleby.com>.

Source from a Library Subscription Database

Academic and most public libraries offer to their members access to subscription-only databases that provide electronic access to publications not otherwise available on free-access websites. When you cite a book, article, or other source that you have retrieved from such a database, add to your citation the name of the service and the institution that provided the access.

Mastny, Lisa. "Ecotourist Trap." <u>Foreign Policy</u> Nov.–Dec. 2002: 94+. <u>Questia</u>. 10 Oct. 2003 <http://www.questia.com/>.

Rossant, John. "The Real War Is France vs. France." <u>BusinessWeek</u> 6 Oct. 2003: 68. <u>MasterFile Premier</u>. EBSCO. Maplewood Memorial Library, Maplewood, NJ. 13 Oct. 2003 <http://0-web24.epnet.com.catalog.maplewoodlibrary.org/>.

Newspaper Article Online

Zernike, Kate. "Fight Against Fat Shifts to the Workplace." <u>New York Times</u> 12 Oct. 2003. 12 Oct. 2003 <http://nytimes.com/2003/10/12/national/12OBES.html>.

Journal Article Online

Salkeld, Duncan. "Making Sense of Differences: Postmodern History, Philosophy and Shakespeare's Prostitutes." <u>Chronicon: An Electronic History Journal</u> 3 (1999). 5 Apr. 2003 <http://www.ucc.ie/chronicon/salkfra.htm>.

E-mail

Give the writer's name, the subject line (if any) enclosed in quotation marks, and the date of the message.

Stanford, Myles. "Johnson manuscripts online." E-mail to the author. 12 July 2003.

Electronic Posting to an Online Forum

Many online media sources conduct forums in which readers can respond to breaking news or ongoing issues. Citing from such forums is difficult because many people prefer to post anonymously. If the author's username is too silly or inappropriate, use the title of the post or the title of the forum to begin your citation and determine its place in the alphabetical order of your Works Cited list.

> Berman, Piotr. Online posting. 6 Oct. 2003. Is Middle East Peace Impossible? 13 Oct. 2003 <http://tabletalk.salon.com/webx?13@@.596c5554>.

Credits

Text Credits

Chapter 1

P. 3 Immigration: Making Americans—'Our collective cultural task is to remember what we were and what we still are.' Bennett, William J. *The Washington Post,* December 4, 1994. Reprinted by permission of the author. **P. 6** Andrew Sullivan, "A Call to Arms." *The Advocate,* November 11, 2003, pg. 72. © 2003 by Andrew Sullivan, reprinted with the permission of Wylie Agency Inc. **P. 11** "What's the Matter with America" from *What's the Matter with Kansas* by Thomas Frank, © 2004 by Thomas Frank. Reprinted by permission of Henry Holt and Company, LLC. **P. 14** Excerpt from pp. 70–73 from *Culture War? The Myth of a Polarized America* by Morris P. Fiorina. Copyright © 2005 by Pearson Education, Inc. Reprinted by Permission. **P. 20** Reprinted with permission from the November 29, 2004 issue of *The Nation.* For subscription information, call 1-800-333-8536. Portions of each week's Nation magazine can be accessed at http://www.thenation.com

Chapter 2

P. 39 Rebecca Skloot, "Two Americas, Two Restaurants, One Town" *The New York Times Magazine,* October 17, 2004. Reprinted by permission of the author. "A Writer at Work" and "Reporting the Cultural Divides" by Rebecca Skloot are reprinted by permission of the au. **P. 47** David Brooks, "One Nation, Slightly Divisible." *The Atlantic Monthly,* December 2001. Reprinted by permission of the author. **P. 58** Blake Hurst, "The Plains vs. The Atlantic: is Middle America a Backwater, or a Reservoir?" *The American Enterprise,* March 2002. Copyright 2002 American Enterprise Institute for Public Policy Research. Reprinted by permission <www.TAEmag.com>. **P. 66** Reprinted with permission from Jedediah Purdy, "The New Culture of Rural America," *The American Prospect,* Volume 11, Number 3: December 20, 1999. The American Prospect, 11 Beacon Steet, Suite 1120, Boston, MA 02108. All rights reserved. **P. 77** Leslie Savan, "Did Somebody Say 'Community?' " *Stay Free! Magazine,* Fall 1998. Reprinted by permission of Don Congdon Associates, Inc. Copyright © 1998 by Leslie Savan. **P. 82** Bill McKibben, "Small World: Why One Town Stays Unplugged." Copyright © 2003 by *Harper's Magazine.* All rights reserved. Reproduced from the December issue by special permission.

Chapter 3

P. 93 Reprinted with permission from *The New York Review of Books.* Copyright © 2005 NYREV, Inc. **P. 113** Gary Wills, "The Day the Enlightenment Went Out." *The New York Times,* November 4, 2004. © 2004, The New York Times. Reprinted by permission. **P. 116** Andrea Elliot, "The Political Conversion of New York's Evangelicals," *New York Times,* November 14, 2004, with contributing reporting by Marjorie

Connelly and Jennifer Medina. Copyright © 2004 by The New York Times Co. Reprinted with permission. **P. 121** Deborah Caldwell, "Dispatches from Lancaster: Getting Out the Vote in a Conservative Christian County." This article appeared originally on www.beliefnet.com, the multifaith website for religion, spirituality, inspiration & more. Used with permission. **P. 127** "Right from the Beginning: The Roots of American Exceptionalism," from *The Right Nation: Conservative Power in America* by John Micklethwait and Adrian Wooldridge. Used by permission of The Penguin Press, a division of Penguin Group (USA) Inc. **P. 137** Wendy Kaminer, "The Real Danger Behind the Christian Right: Beware of Conservative Ecumenism." *Free Inquiry,* October-November 2003. Copyright © 2003 by Wendy Kaminer. Reprinted by permission of the author. **P. 145** Alan Wolfe, "Scholars Infuse Religion With Cultural Light." *The Chronicle of Higher Education,* October 22, 2004. Reprinted by permission of the author. **P. 151** Jon Meacham, "What the Religious Right Can Teach the New Democrats: Extremists Aside, America's Evangelicals Have A Message We All Need To Hear." Washington Monthly, April 1993. Reprinted with permission from *The Washington Monthly.* Copyright by Washington Monthly Publishing, LLC, 733 15th St. NW, Suite 520, Washington, DC 20005. (202) 393-5155. Web site: www.washingtonmonthly.com. **P. 160** Hua Hsu, "Vote or Lie: Americans Love to Vote – for Pop Singers, Soft Drinks, or World Series Predictions." *The Village Voice,* October 25, 2004. Reprinted by permission of the author.

Chapter 4

P. 165 Ted Rall, "Money Changes Everything: Coming to Terms with Father's Day." From *Killed: Great Journalism Too Hot to Print.* Copyright (c) 2004 by Ted Rall. Reprinted by permission of the author. **P. 170** © 2004 TIME Inc. reprinted by permission. **P. 173** Tzivia Gover, "Jill and Jill Live on the Hill, but One Must Boil the Water" *The New York Times,* November 28, 2004. Copyright © 2004 by The New York Times Co. Reprinted with permission. **P. 177** "Grieving Our Fertility," from *The Kid* by Dan Savage, copyright © 1999 by Dan Savage. Used by permission of Dutton, a division of Penguin Group (USA) Inc. **P. 184** Cathy Young, "Opening Marriage: Do Same-Sex Unions Pave the Way for Polygamy?" *Reason Magazine,* March 2004. Copyright Reason Magazine. www.reason.com **P. 188** Joe Miceli, "Taking Leave." From *I Thought My Father Was God* by Paul Auster. Copyright (c) 2001 by Paul Auster. Picador USA, 175 Fifth Avenue, New York, NY 10010. Reprinted by permission of Carol Mann Agency. **P. 194** "The Black Inner-City Grandmother in Transition" from *Code On The Street: Decency, Violence, And The Moral Life Of The Inner City* by Elijah Anderson. Copyright © 1999 by Elijah Anderson. Used by permission of W.W. Norton & Company, Inc. **P. 205** Francis Fukuyama, "How to Re-Moralize America." *The Wilson Quarterly,* Summer 1999. Reprinted by permission of the author. **P. 219** "First Comes Love, Then Comes Marriage, then Comes Mary with a Baby Carriage: Marriage, Sex, and Reproduction"

York, NY 10010. Reprinted by permission of Carol Mann Agency.
P. 360 David James Duncan, "Earth Music." *Portland Magazine* Fall 2003.
Reprinted by permission of the author. **P.** 366 Mano Singham, "The Science
and Religion Wars." *Phi Delta Kappan,* v. 81 issue 6, 2000. Coypright
© 2000 by Mano Singham. Reprinted by permission of the author.
P. 382 © 2004 The Economist Newspaper Ltd. All rights reserved. Reprinted
with permission. Further reproduction prohibited. www.economist.com
P. 388 Reprinted with the permission of The Free Press, a Division of Simon
& Schuster Adult Publishing Group, from *Floating Off The Page: The Best
Stories from The Wall Street Journal's 'Middle Column,'* Ken Wells, Editor.
Copyright © 2003 by Dow Jones & Company, Inc. All rights reserved.

Chapter 7
P. 393 Source: Worldwatch Institute, *Worldwatch Magazine,* Jan/Feb 2003.
Reprinted by permission. **P.** 398 Rick Bass, "Why I Hunt" from *Sierra,*
July/August 2001, pp. 58-61. Reprinted by permission of the author.
P. 404 Susan Orlean, "Lifelike." *The New Yorker,* June 9, 2003. Reprinted
by permission of the author. **P.** 414 Paul Roberts, "Over a Barrel." *Mother
Jones,* November/December 2004. Mother Jones Magazine. © 2004,
Foundation for National Progress. **P.** 418 Jeffrey Bartholet, Adam Rogers,
Michael Hsu. "Alaska: Oil's Ground Zero." From *Newsweek,* 8/13/2001,
© 2001 Newsweek, Inc. All rights reserved. Reprinted by permission.
P. 424 William Schneider, "The New Soccer Moms." *The Atlantic* Online,
June 13, 2001. Reprinted by permission of the author. **P.** 427 Reprinted with
the permission of The Free Press, a Division of Simon & Schuster Adult
Publishing Group, from *Floating off the Page: The Best Stories from The
Wall Street Journal's 'Middle Column,'* Ken Wells, Editor. Copyright © 2003
by Dow Jones & Comp **P.** 434 Anna Bakalis, "What Would Jesus Drive?
Apparently a large SUV." *The Washington Times,* July 14, 2003, **P.** C15.
Reprinted by permission of Valeo IP, St. Paul, MN.

Chapter 8
P. 438 Tamara Odisho, "A Night in the Emergency Room." *The Newark Metro,*
November 22, 2004. Reprinted by permission of the author who wishes to
thank Professor Robert Snyder for all his guidance & courage. **P.** 441 Stephanie
Mencimer, "Share the Health." Washington Monthly, October 1992. Reprinted
with permission from *The Washington Monthly.* Copyright by Washington
Monthly Publishing, LLC, 733 15th St. NW, Suite 520, Washington, DC 20005.
(202) 393-5155. Web site: www.washingtonmonthly.com **P.** 450 "Adam and
Eve," from *Reefer Madness* by Eric Schlosser. Copyright © 2003 by Eric
Schlosser. Reprinted by permission of Houghton Mifflin Company. All rights
reserved. **P.** 458 This article first appeared in Salon.com, at http://www.Salon.com
An online version remains in the Salon archives. Reprinted with permission.
P. 462 "Smart and Pretty" [pp. 182–88] from *The Substance of Style* by
Virginia Postrel. Copyright © 2003 by Virginia Postrel. Reprinted by

of Contemporary Christian Music." Copyright 2002 Christian Century. Reprinted with permission from the Dec. 18–31, 2002, issue of *The Christian Century.* **P. 591** M. Graham Spann, "NASCAR Racing Fans: Cranking Up An Empirical Approach." *Journal of Popular Culture* v. 36 issue 2, 2002. Reprinted by permission of Blackwell Publishing. **P. 600** Selena Roberts, "Sports Rage Has Yet to Reach the Ovals." *The New York Times,* November 22, 2004. Copyright © 2004 by The New York Times Co. Reprinted with permission. **P. 603** "Ozzie and Harriet, Come Back: The Primal Scream of Teenage Music," from *Home-Alone America* by Mary Eberstadt, copyright © 2004 by Mary Eberstadt. Used by permission of Sentinel, an imprint of Penguin Group (USA) Inc. **P. 613** Ta-Nehisi Coates, "Just Another Quick-Witted, Egg-Roll-Joke-Making, Insult-Hurling Chinese-American Rapper," *The New York Times,* November 21, 2004. © 2004 Ta-Nehisi Coates. Reprinted by permission. **P. 620** Diane Cardwell, "Yo! Or Is It Oy! Cultures Blend in Dance Clubs," *The New York Times,* December 11, 2004. Copyright © 2004 by The New York Times Co. Reprinted with permission.

Chapter 11

P. 625 Frank Furedi, from *Culture of Fear: Risk-Taking and the Morality of Low Expectation.* (Revised edition.) Continuum, 1997 & 2002, pp. 1–4. Reprinted by permission of The Continuum International Publishing Company. **P. 630** Reprinted with permission from Deborah Pearlstein, "Rights in an Insecure World," *The American Prospect,* Volume 15, Number 10: October 01, 2004. The American Prospect, 11 Beacon Street, Suite 1120, Boston, MA 02108. All rights reserved. **P. 636** Corey Robin, "When Fear is a Joint Venture." *The Washington Post,* October 24, 2004, p. B01. Reprinted by permission of the author. **P. 640** Adam Gopnik, "The Unreal Thing." *The New Yorker,* May 19, 2003. Copyright © 2003 by Adam Gopnik. Reprinted by permission of the author. **P. 649** Reprinted with permission from *The New York Review of Books.* Copyright © 2004 NYREV, Inc. **P. 663** Shibley Telhami, "Arab and Muslim America: A Snapshot." *Brookings Review,* vol. 20, no. 1 (Winter 2002). Copyright 2002 The Brookings Institution. Reprinted by permission of Brookings Institution Press. **P. 667** Anika Rahman, "Fear in the Open City." *The New York Times,* September 19, 2001. © 2001, The New York Times. Reprinted by permission. **P. 669** Annie Jacobsen, "Terror in the Skies, Again?" Women's Wall Street.Com, July 13, 2004. Reprinted by permission of Women's Wall Street.Com and Annie Jacobsen. **P. 678** Heather Mac Donald, author of *Are Cops Racist?* is a contributing editor at the Manhattan Institute's *City Journal* (www.city-journal.org), from whose Autumn 2004 issue this article is reprinted. **P. 684** This article first appeared in Salon.com, at http://www.Salon.com An online version remains in the Salon archives. Reprinted with permission.

Index